Tiny House Photobook:
B/W Pix - Cottage, Bungalow, Beach & Boathouse, Log Cabin, Mud Hut, Cave & Rock Dwelling, Yurt, & the Privy

SHARON BUYDENS

ISBN: 1717579655
ISBN-13: 978-1717579652

DEDICATION

For Tyler. I hope this provides inspiration for your own tiny home.

ABOUT THIS BOOK

This book is low-text, high amount of photographs, for your easy reading pleasure. Photos attributed to the Creative Commons and Pixabay, and many thanks to Raymond Orenda of Organic Food Kenya.

CONTENTS

This page is intentionally left blank

1 STYLES

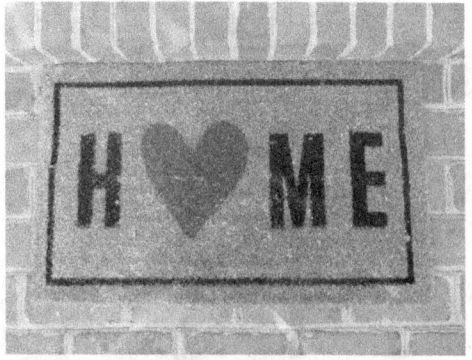

Whether small, quaint, modern, within-city, or in the country, they are all good

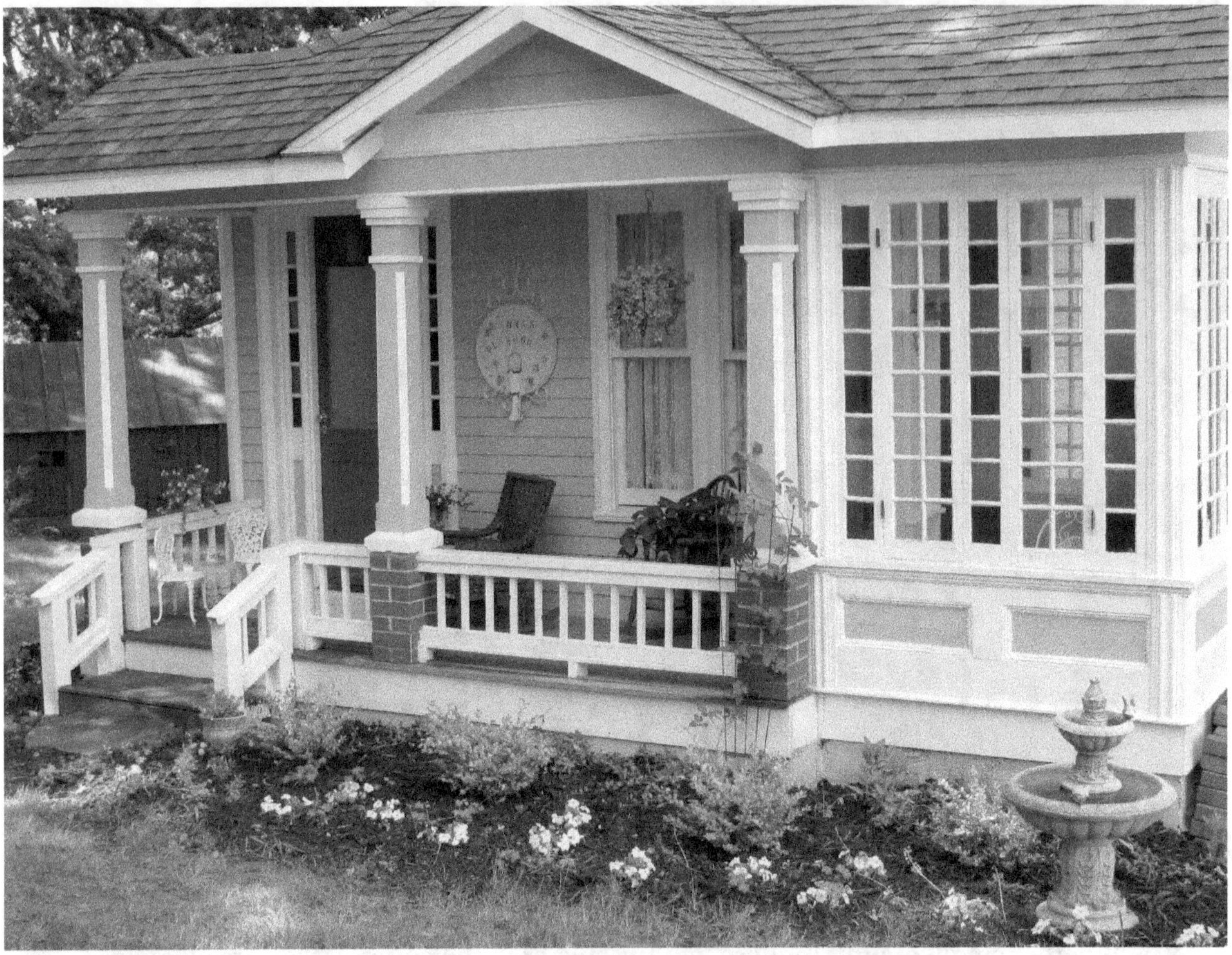

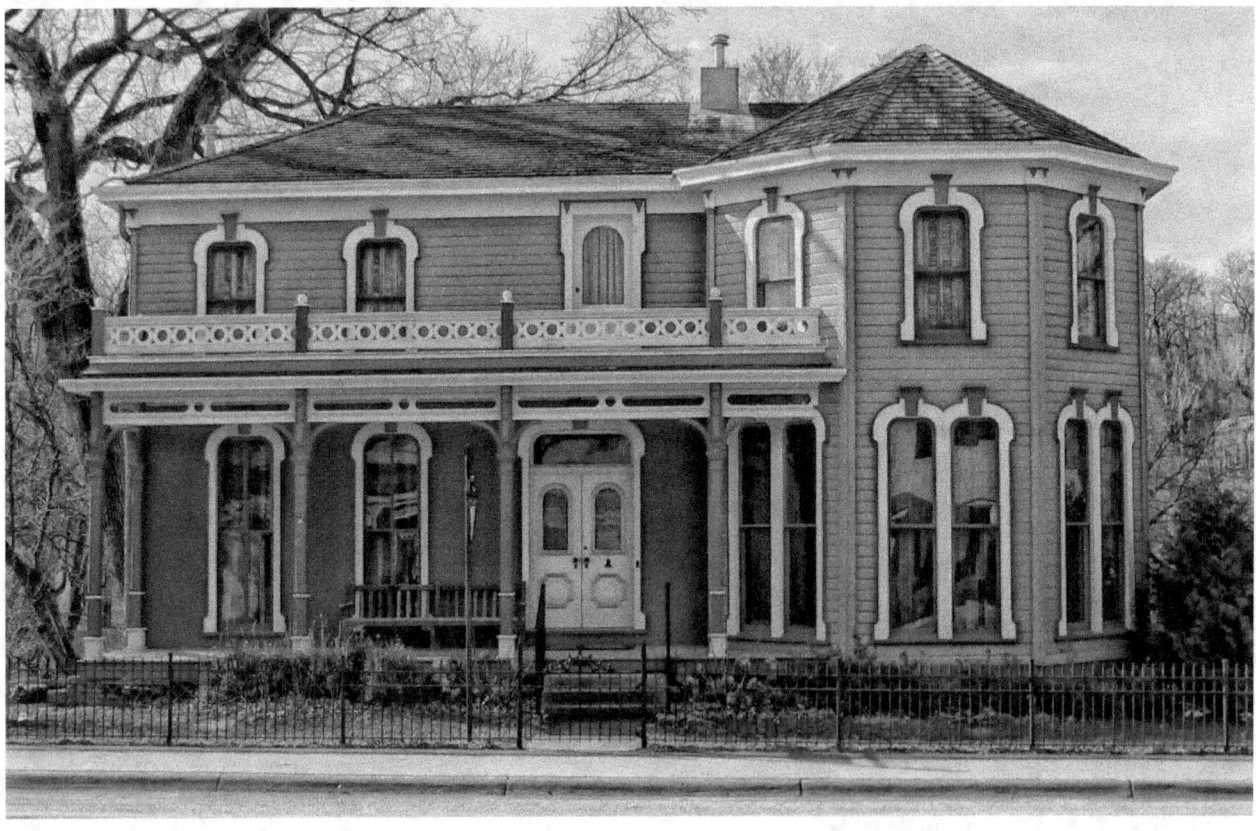

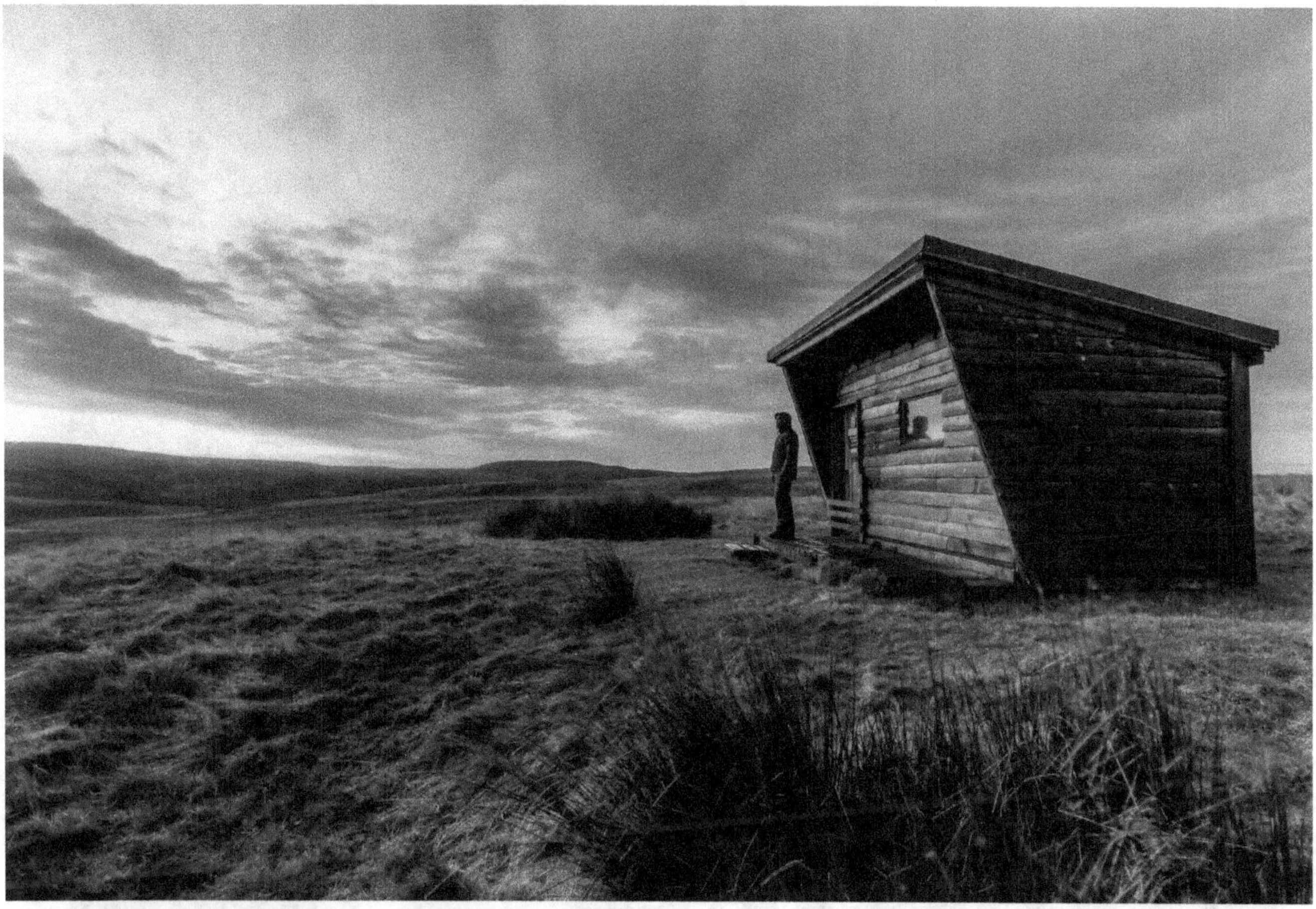

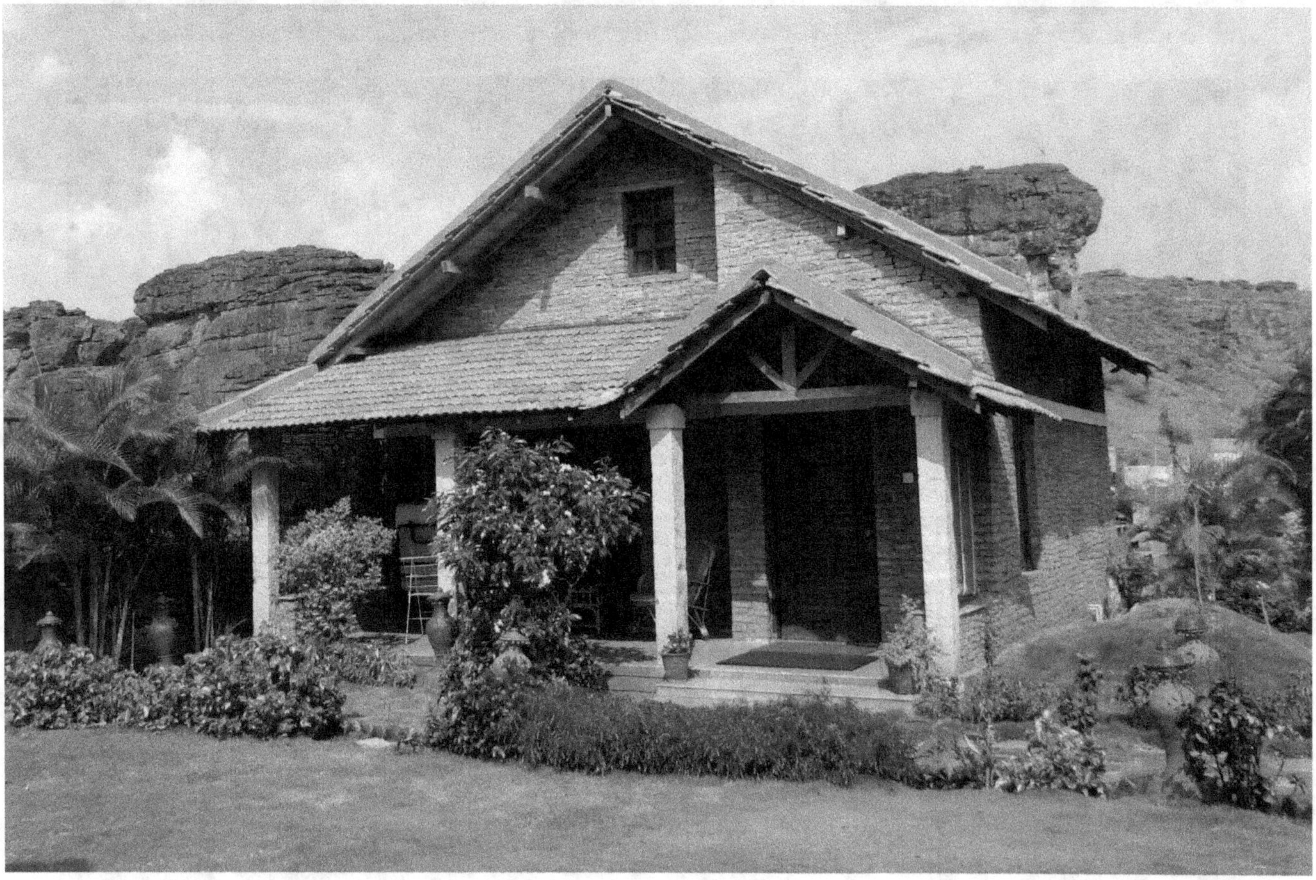

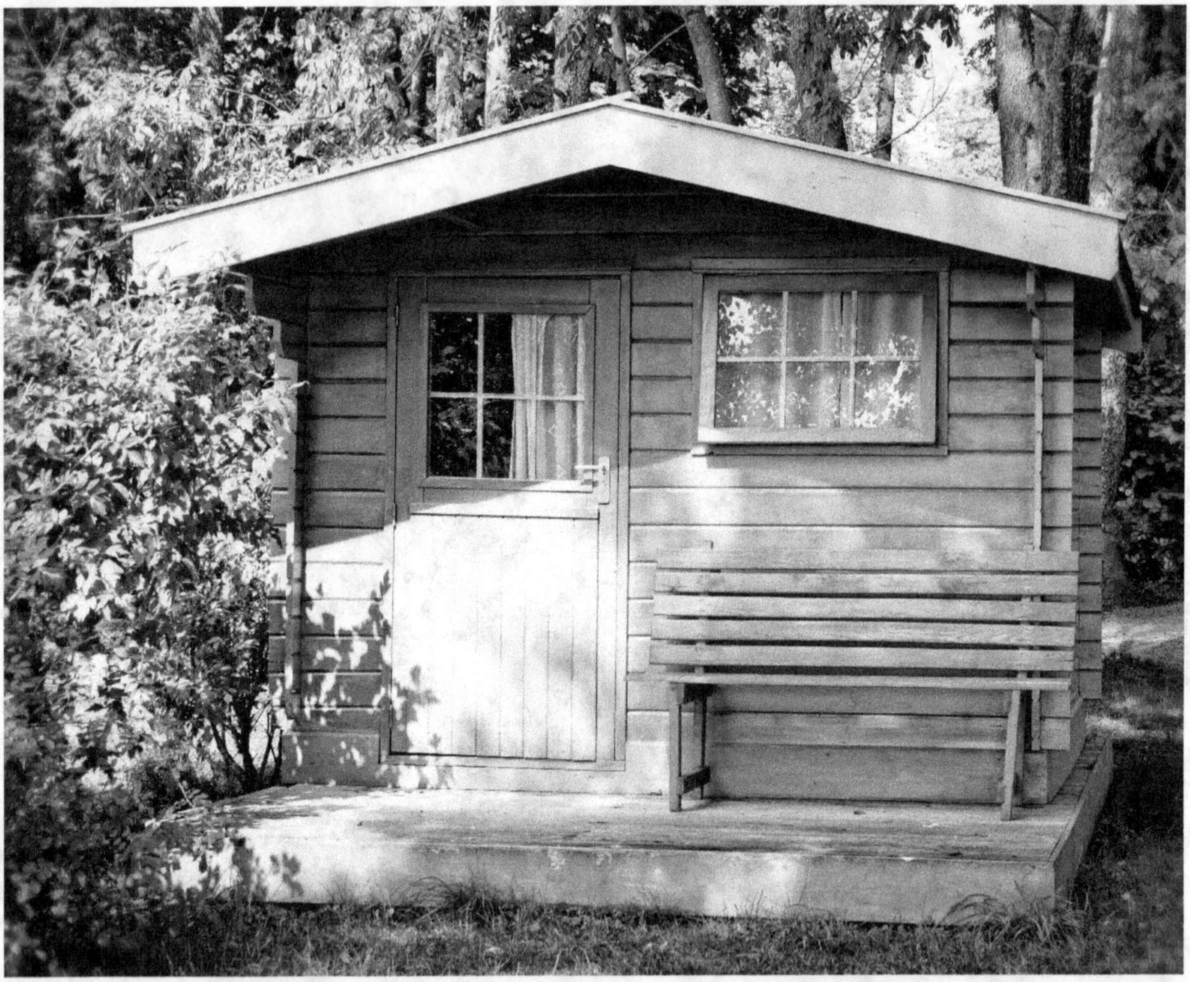

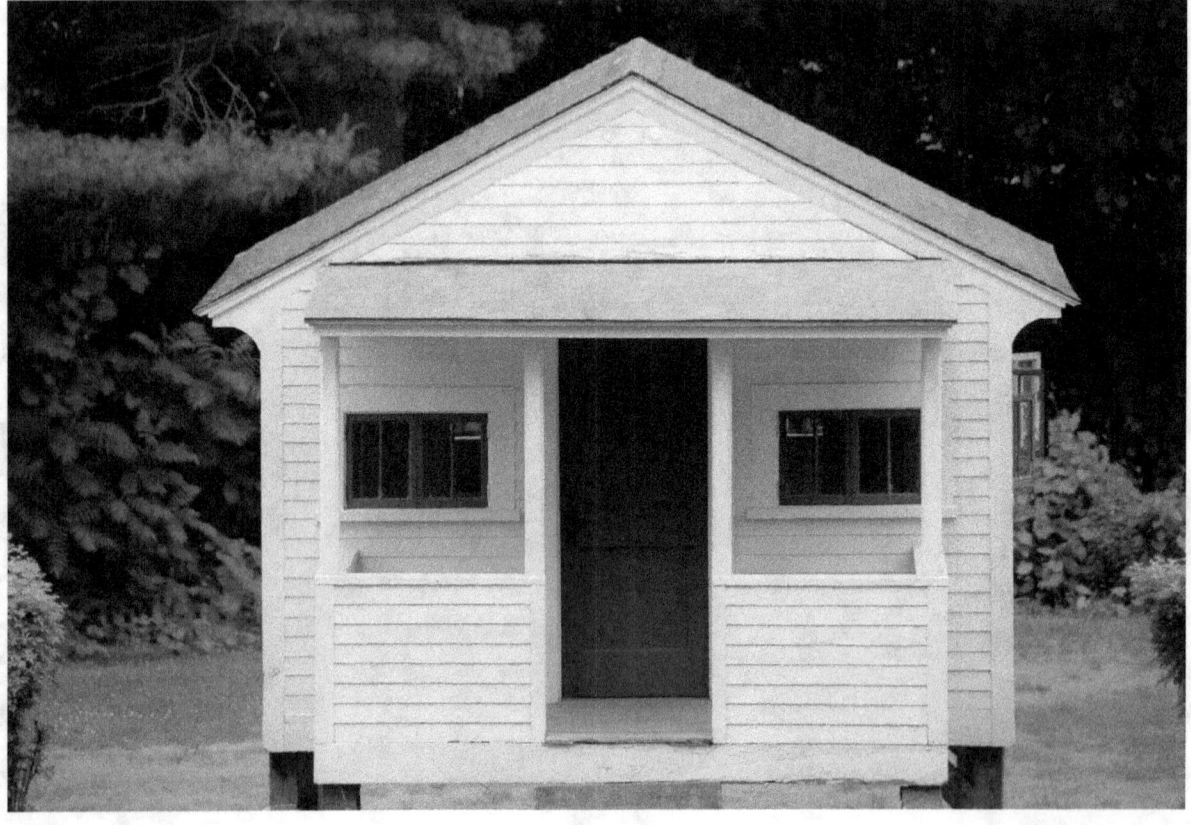

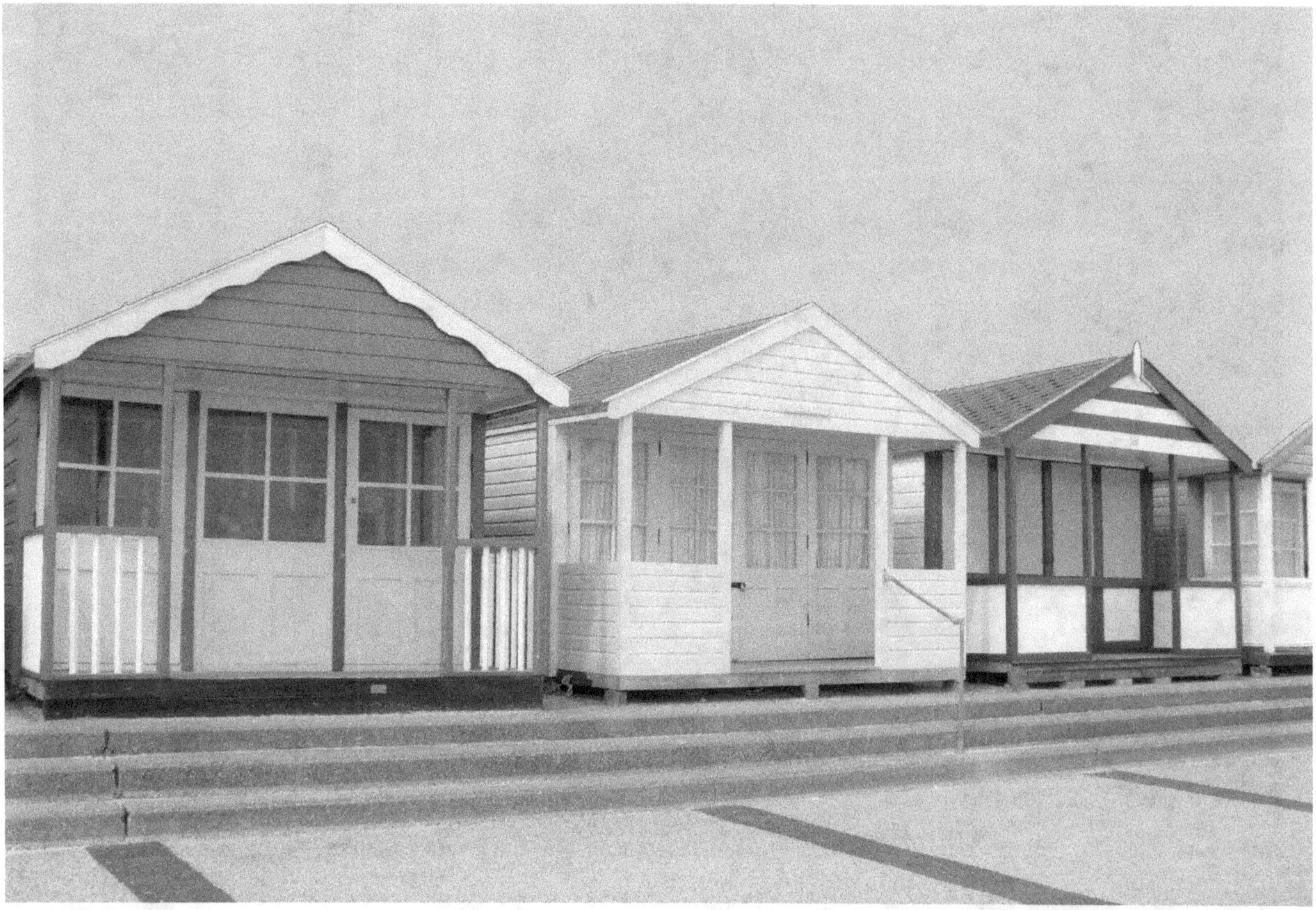

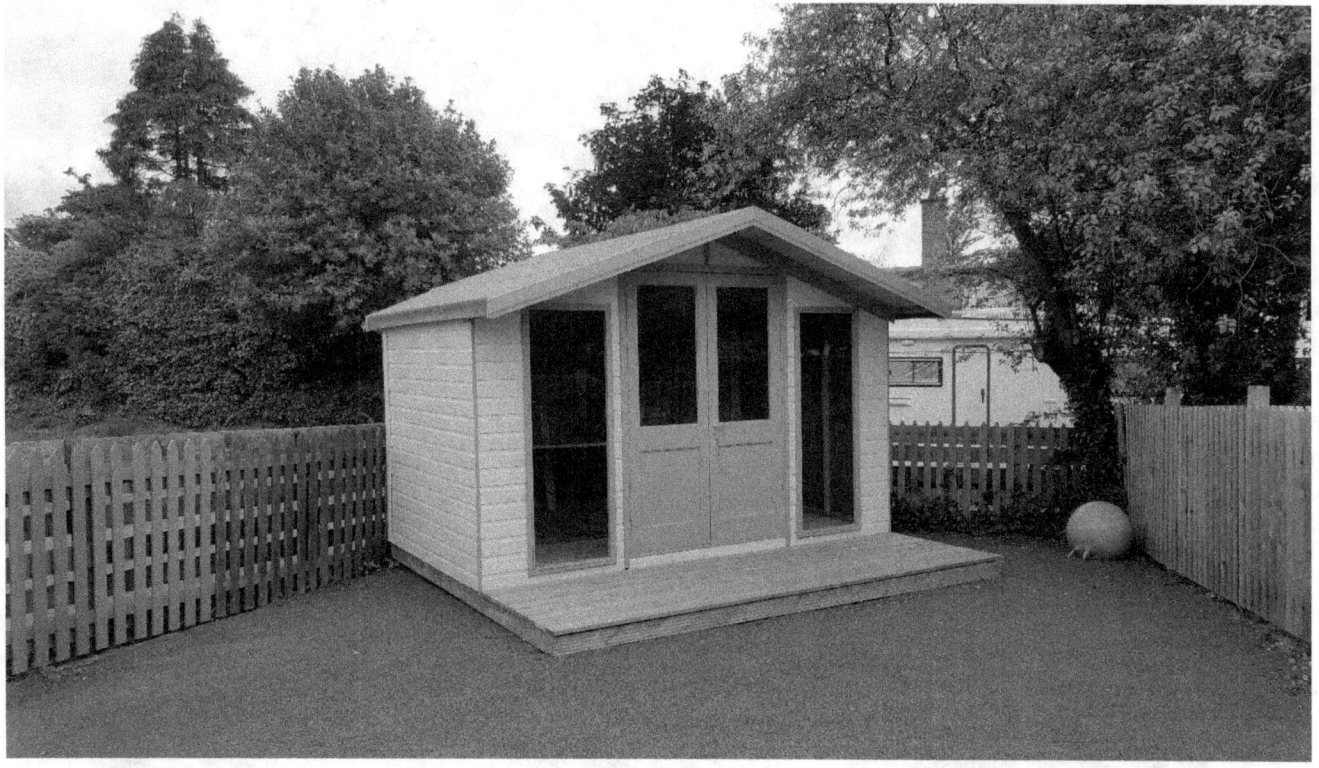

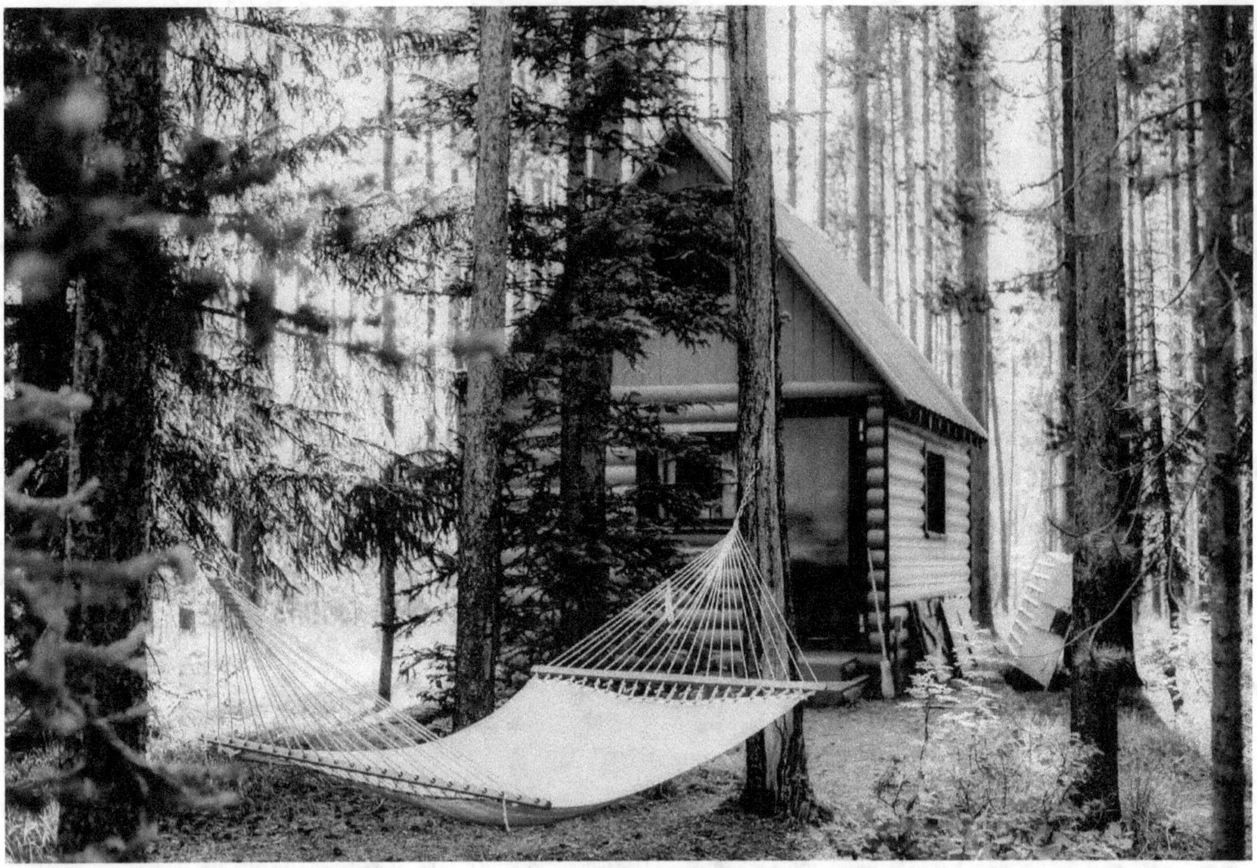

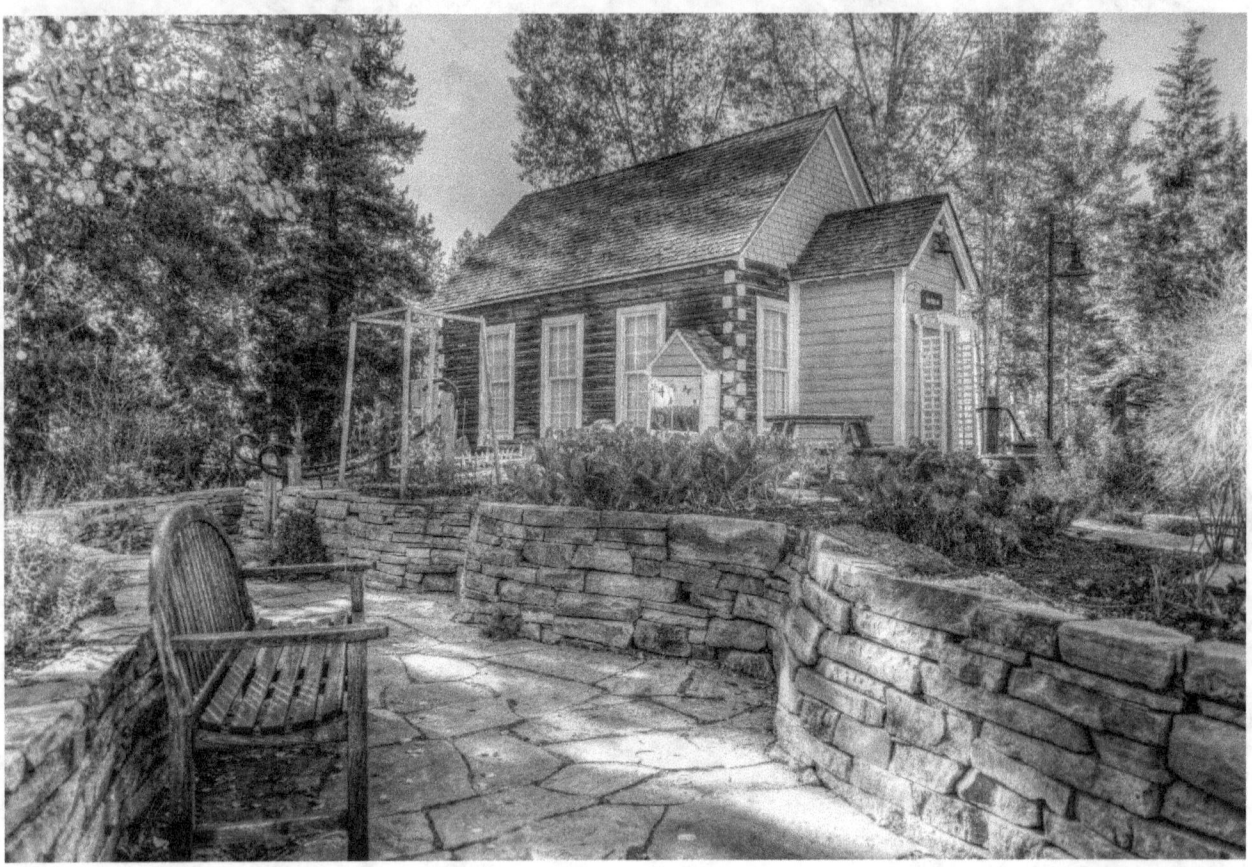

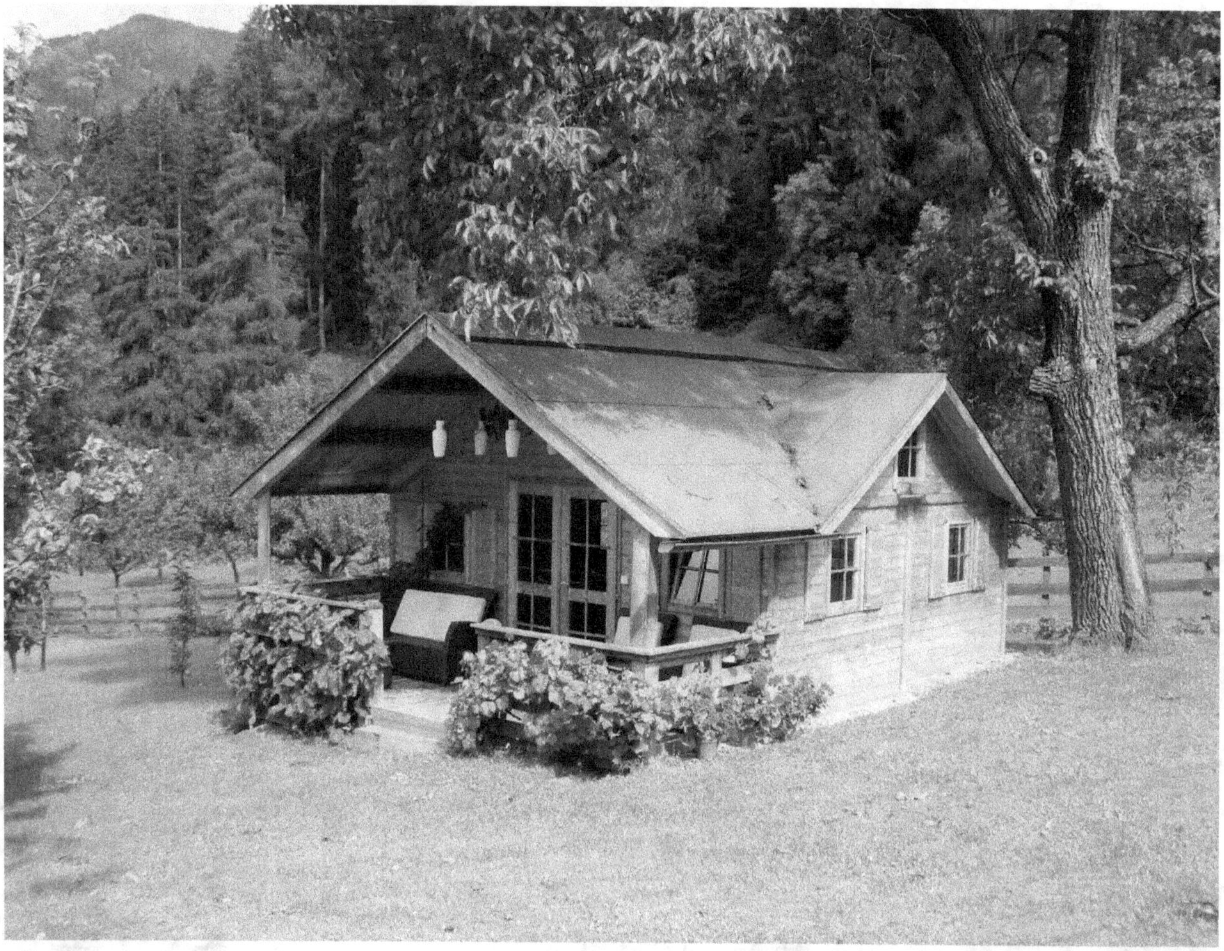

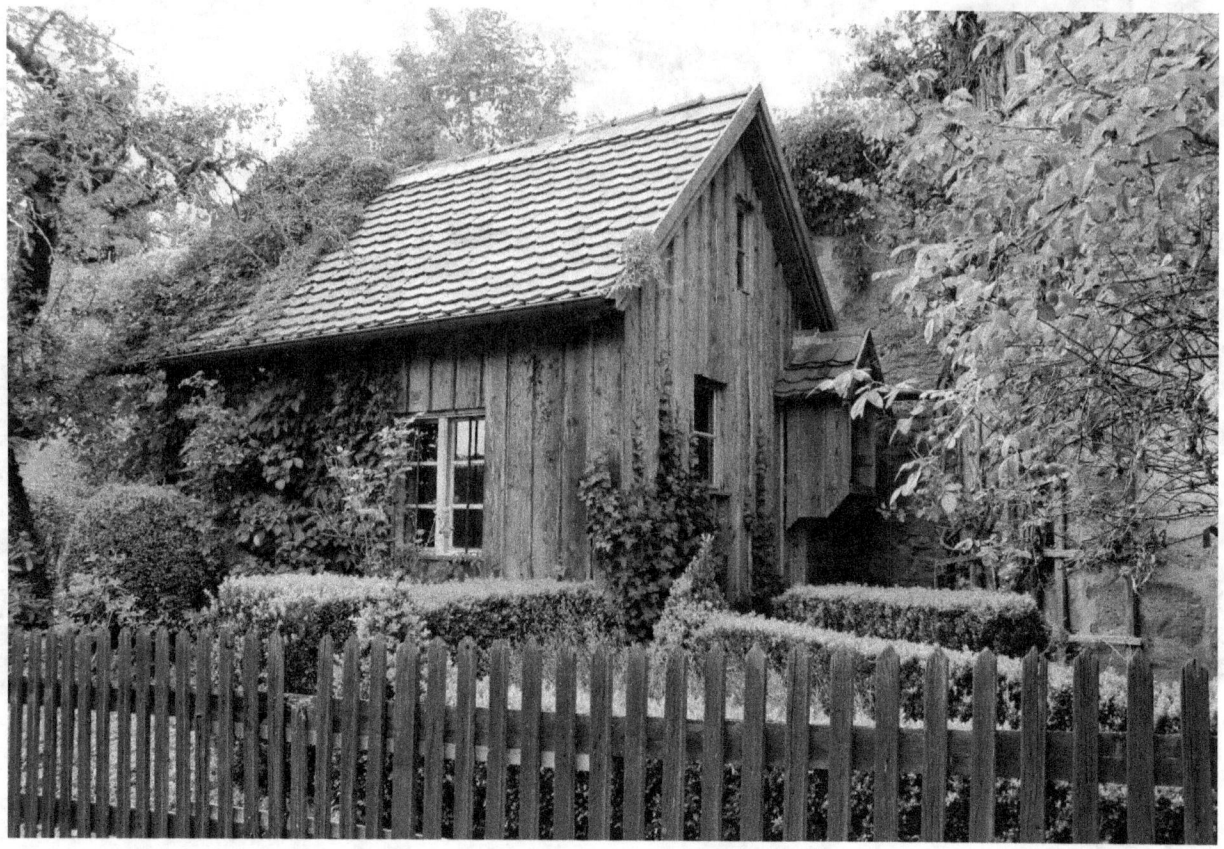

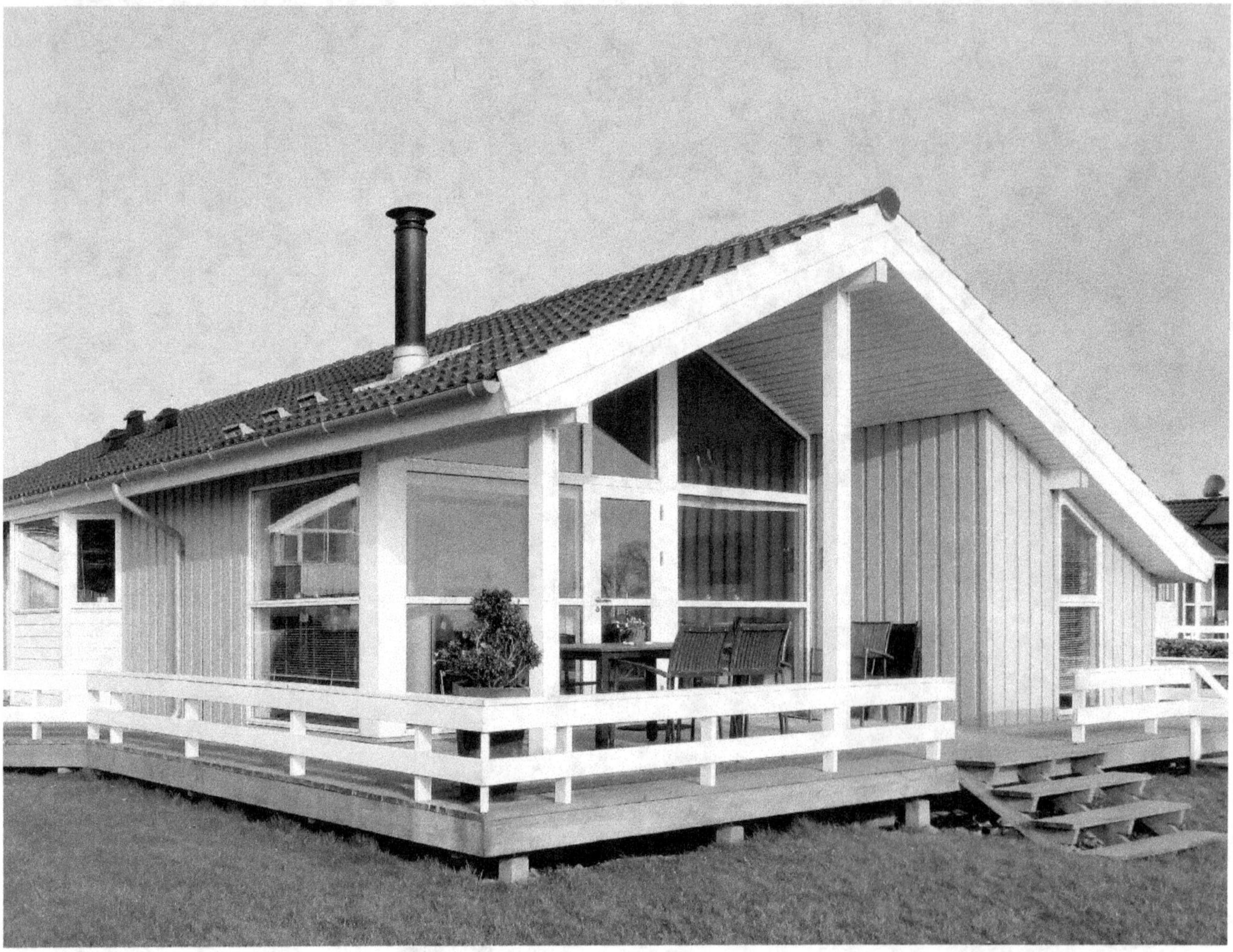

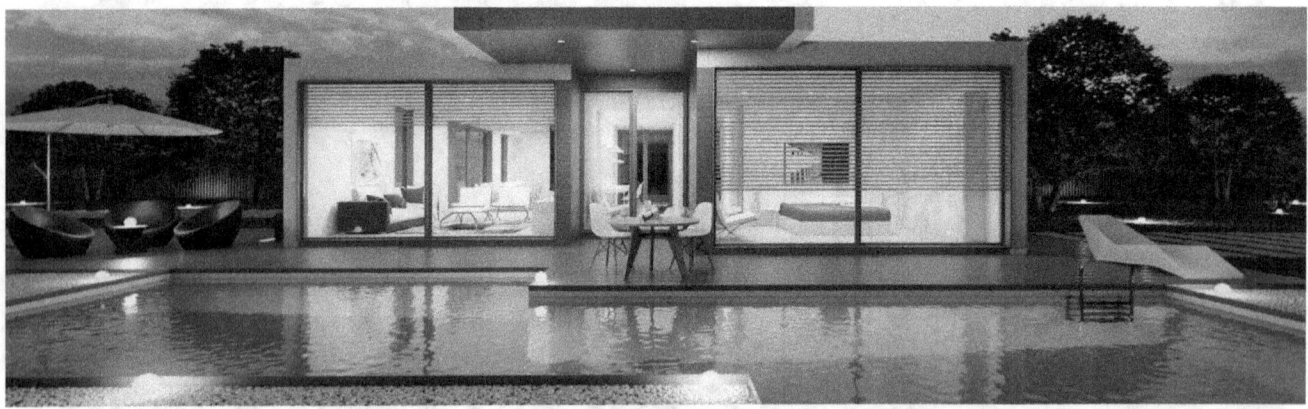

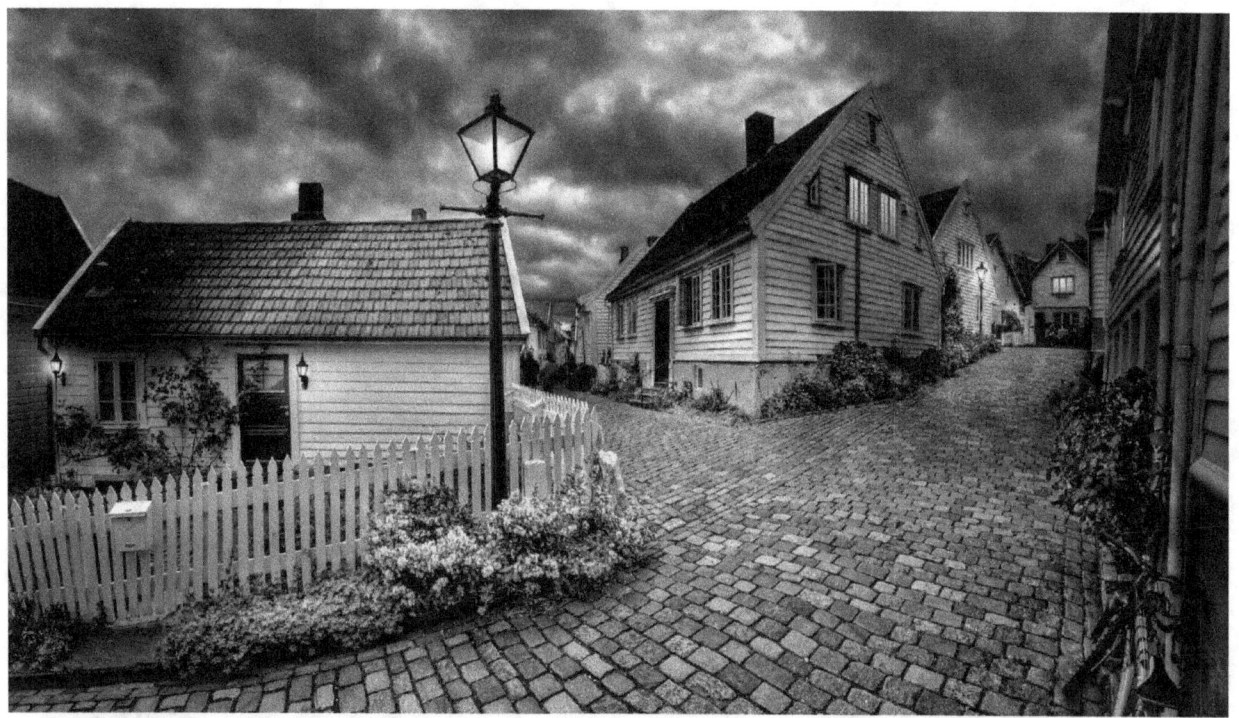

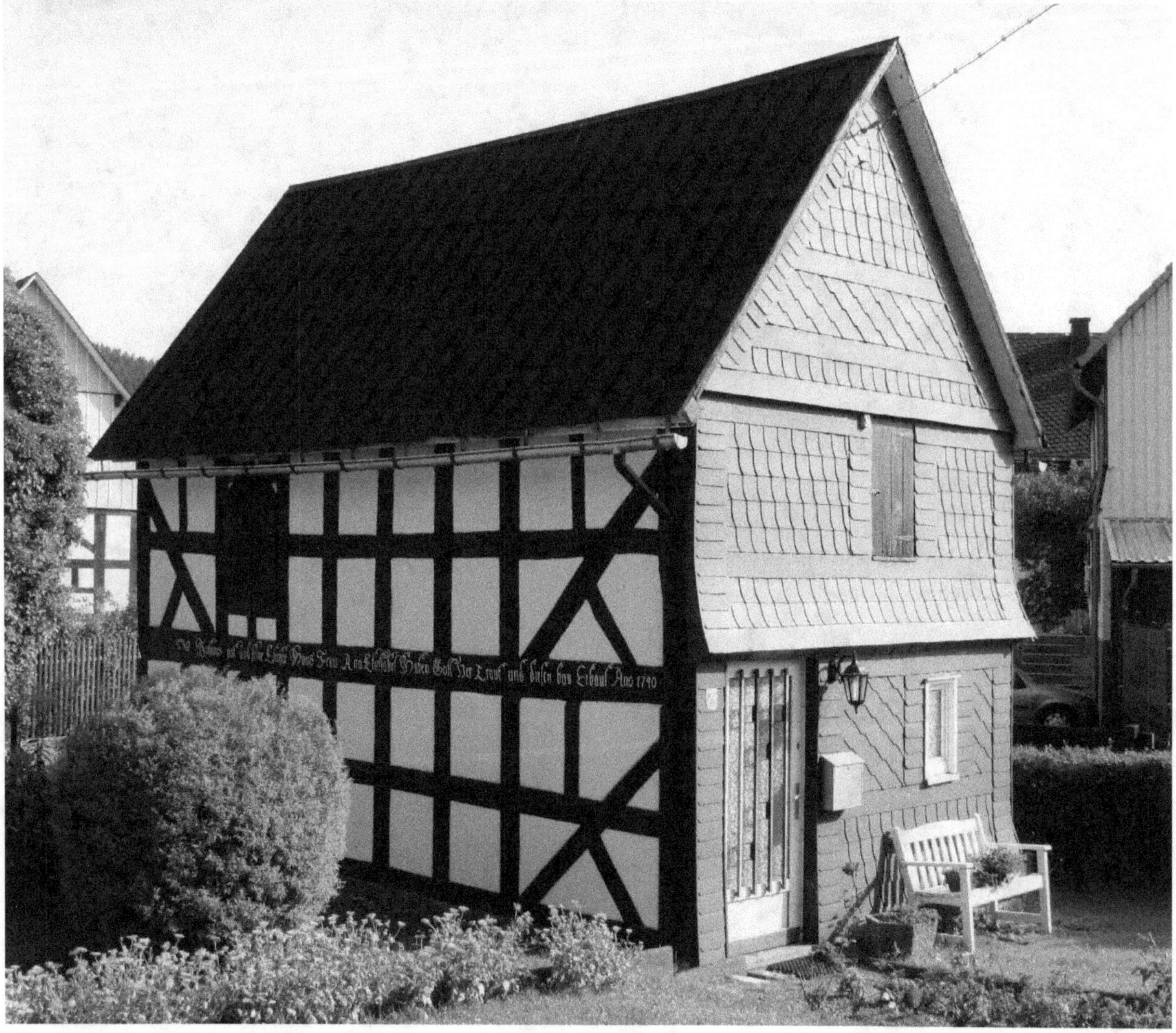

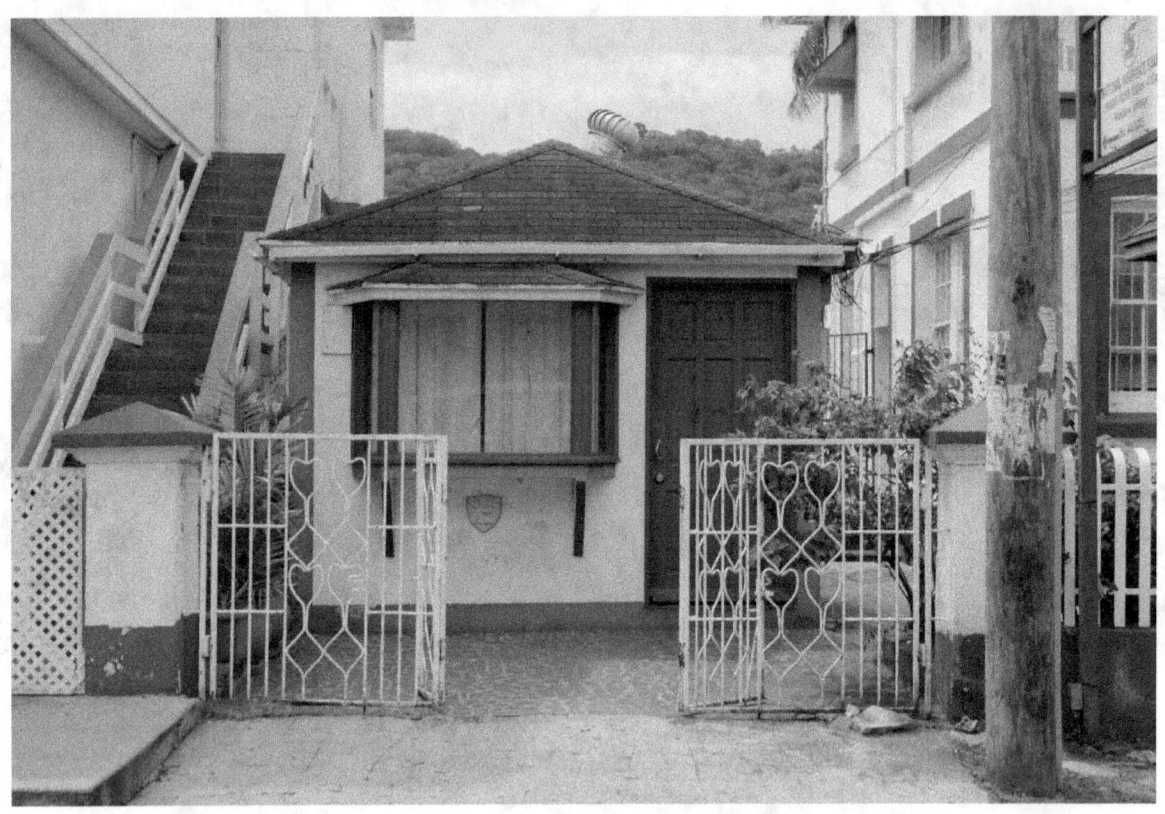

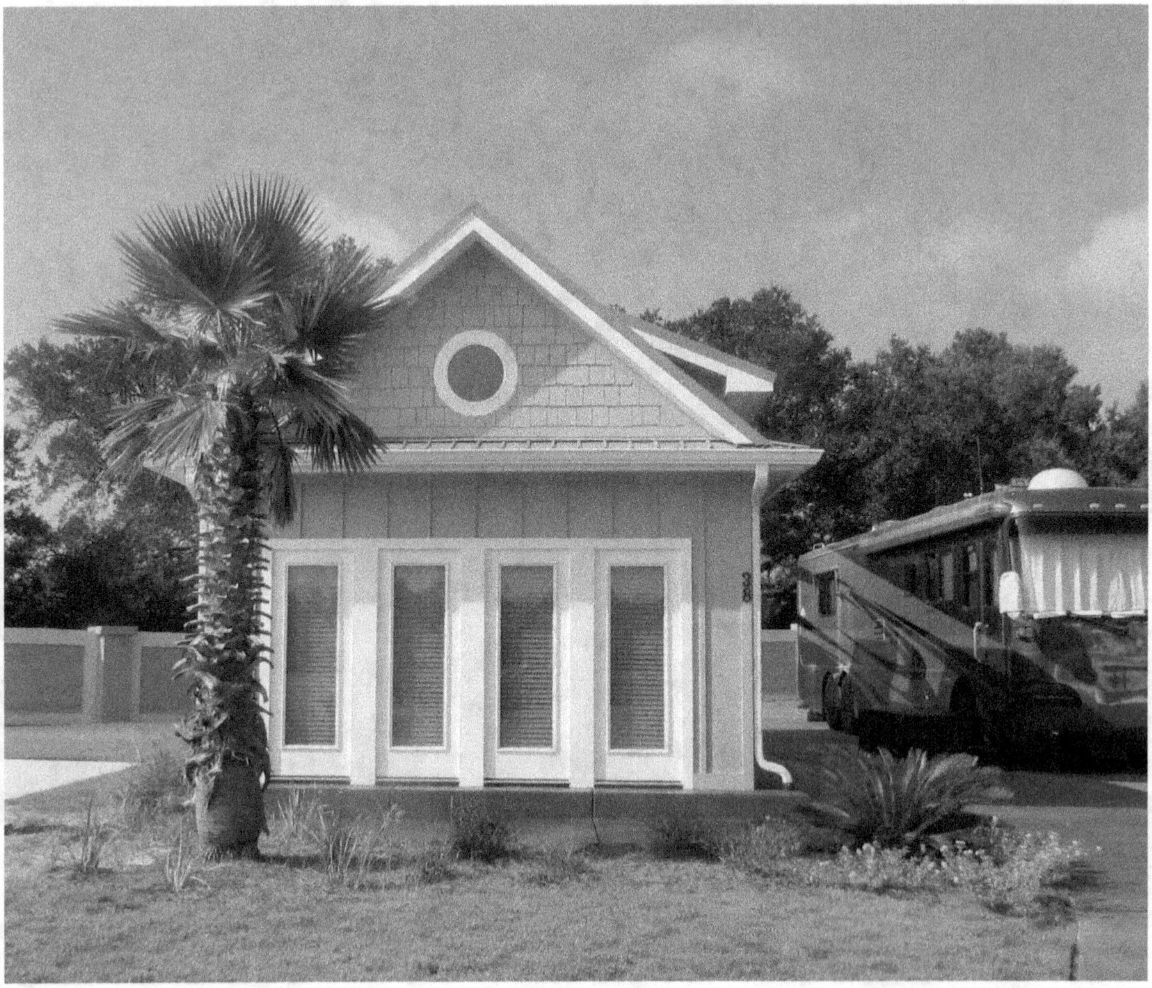

This page is intentionally left blank

2 EARTH

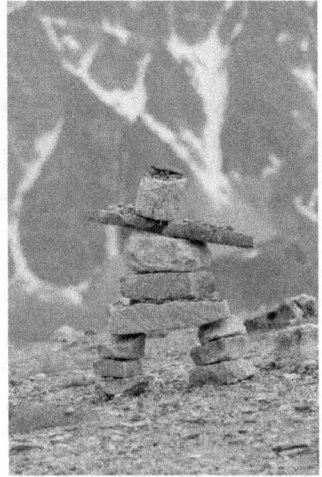

Rock or stone, brick, mountain cottages, sod, farms, and mud huts

Rock / Stone

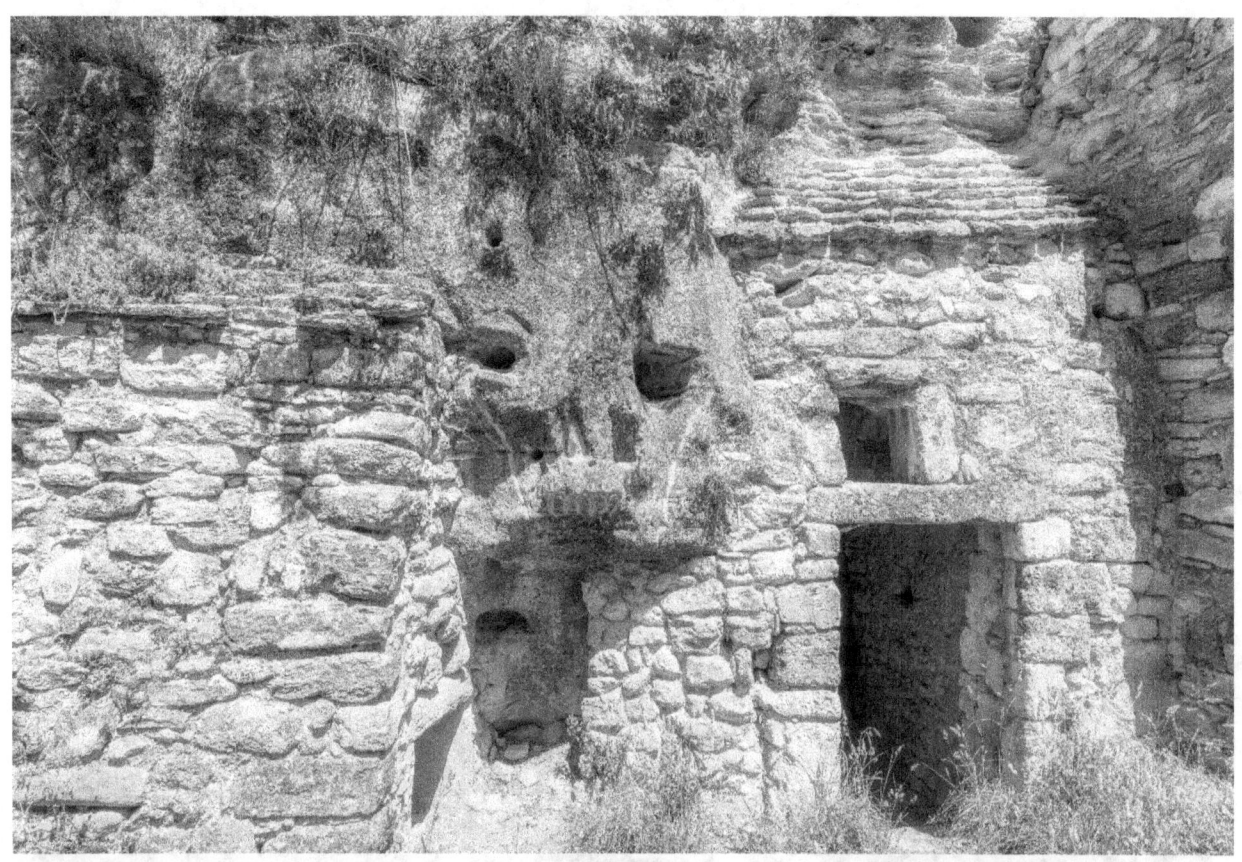

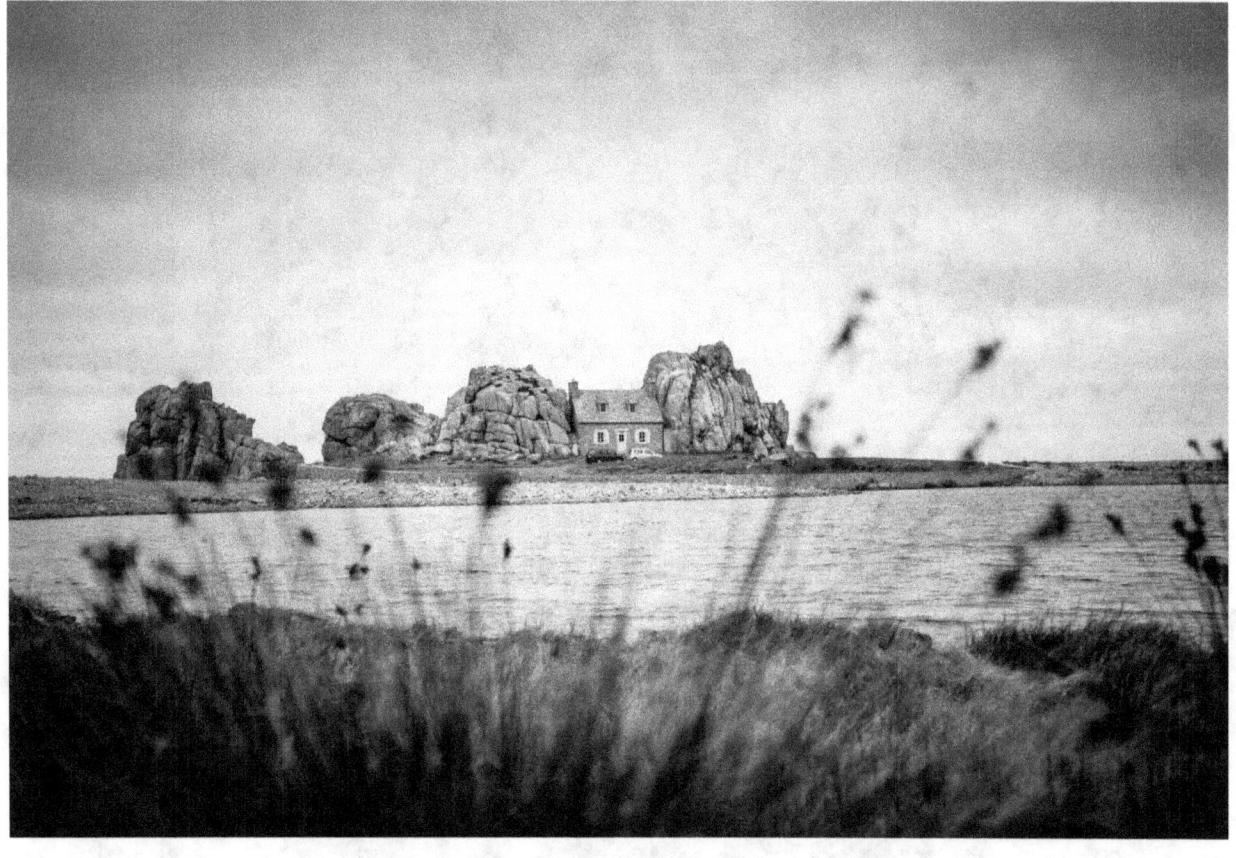

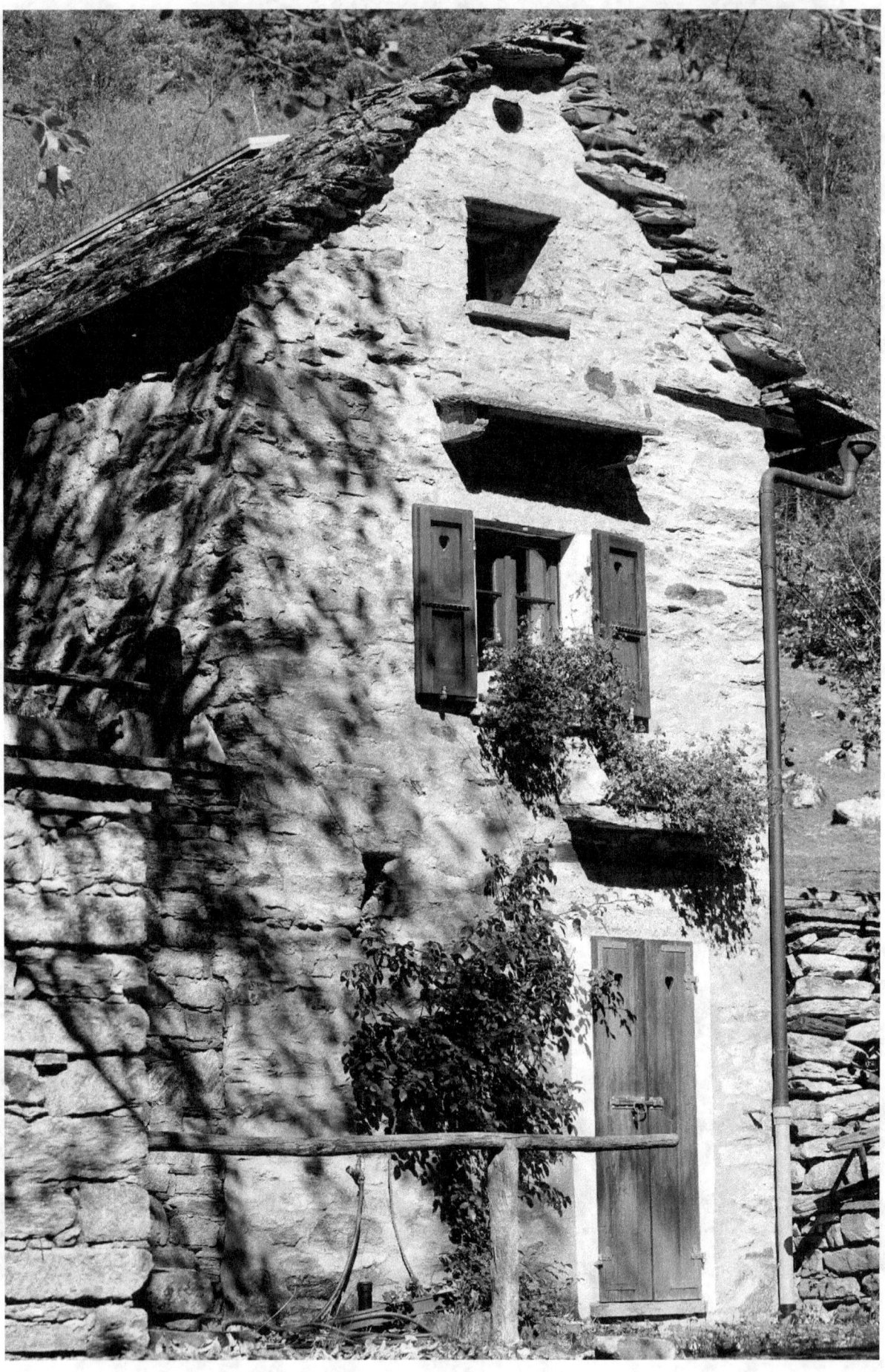

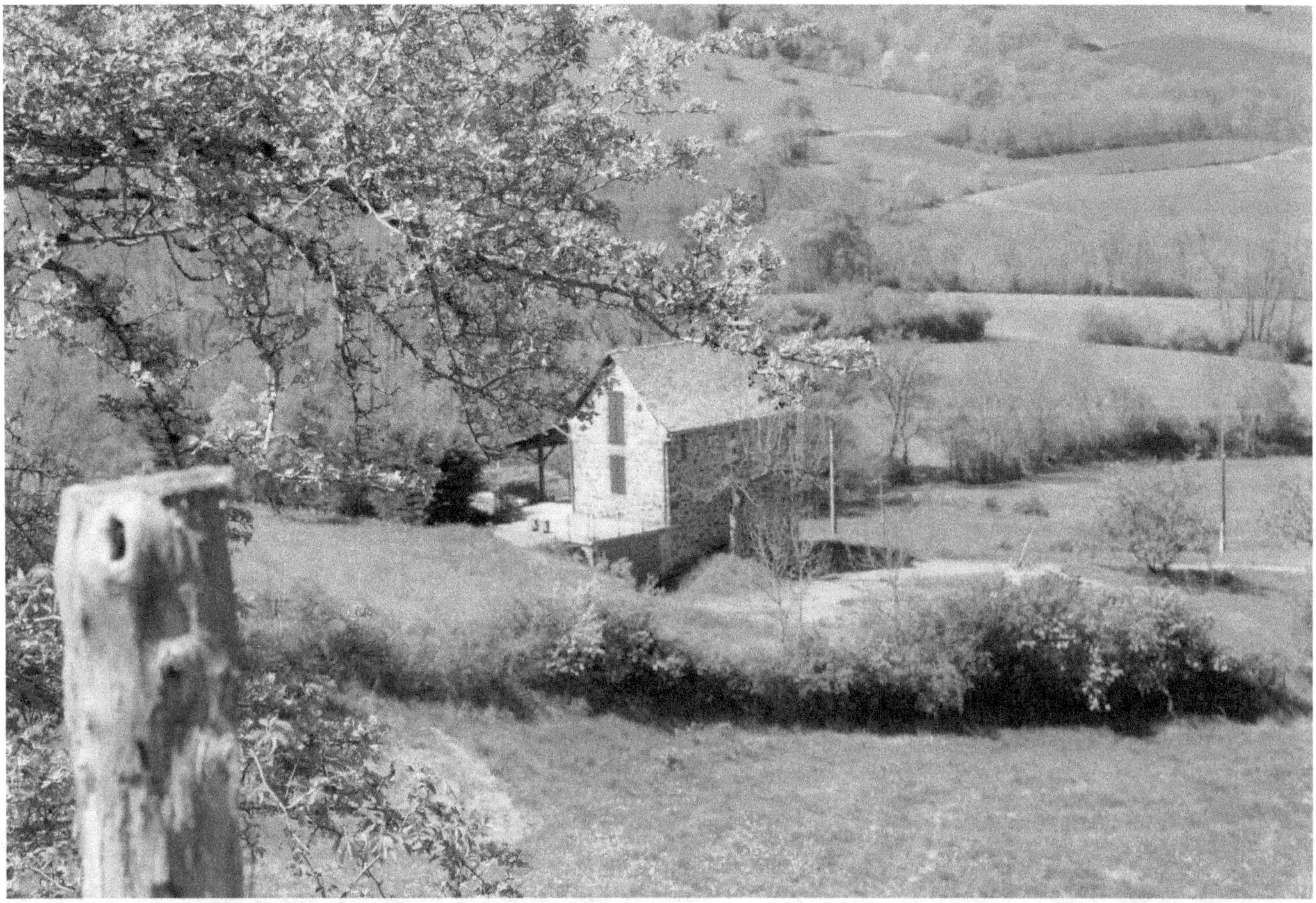

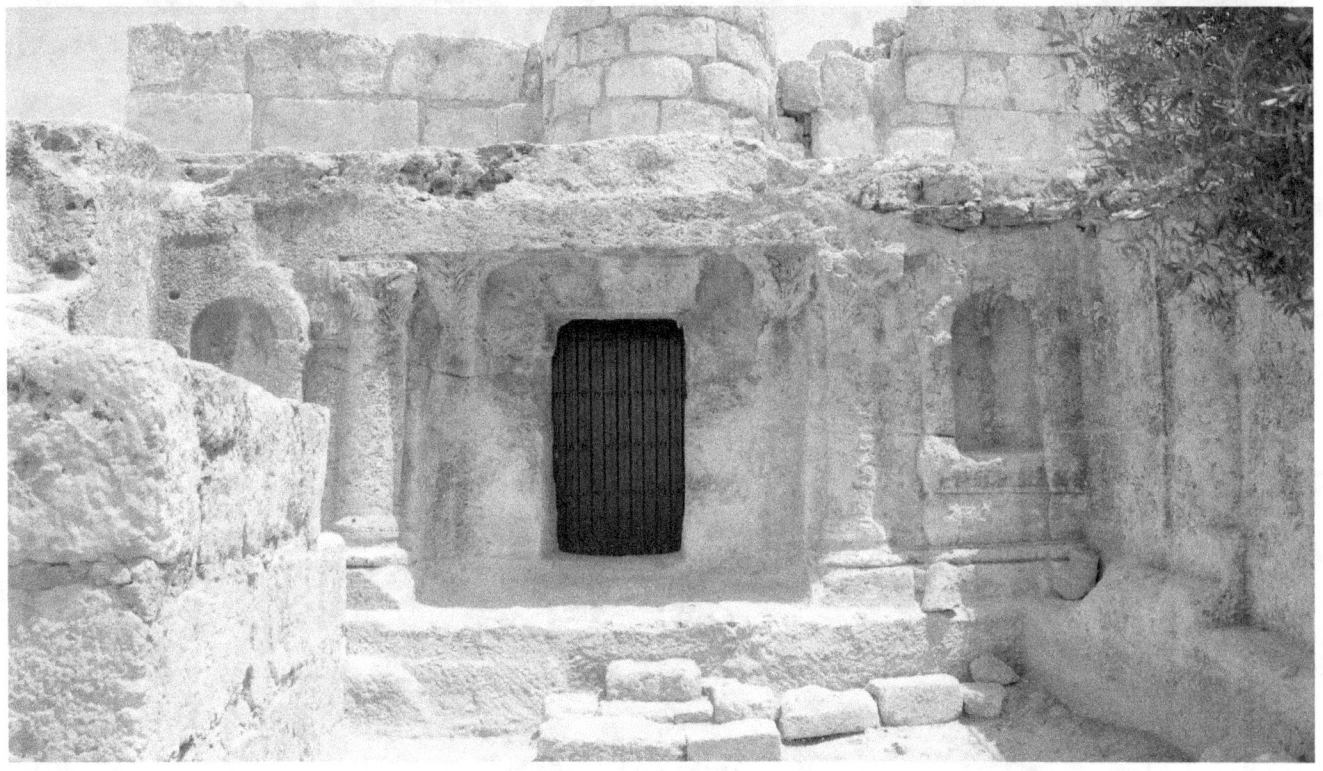

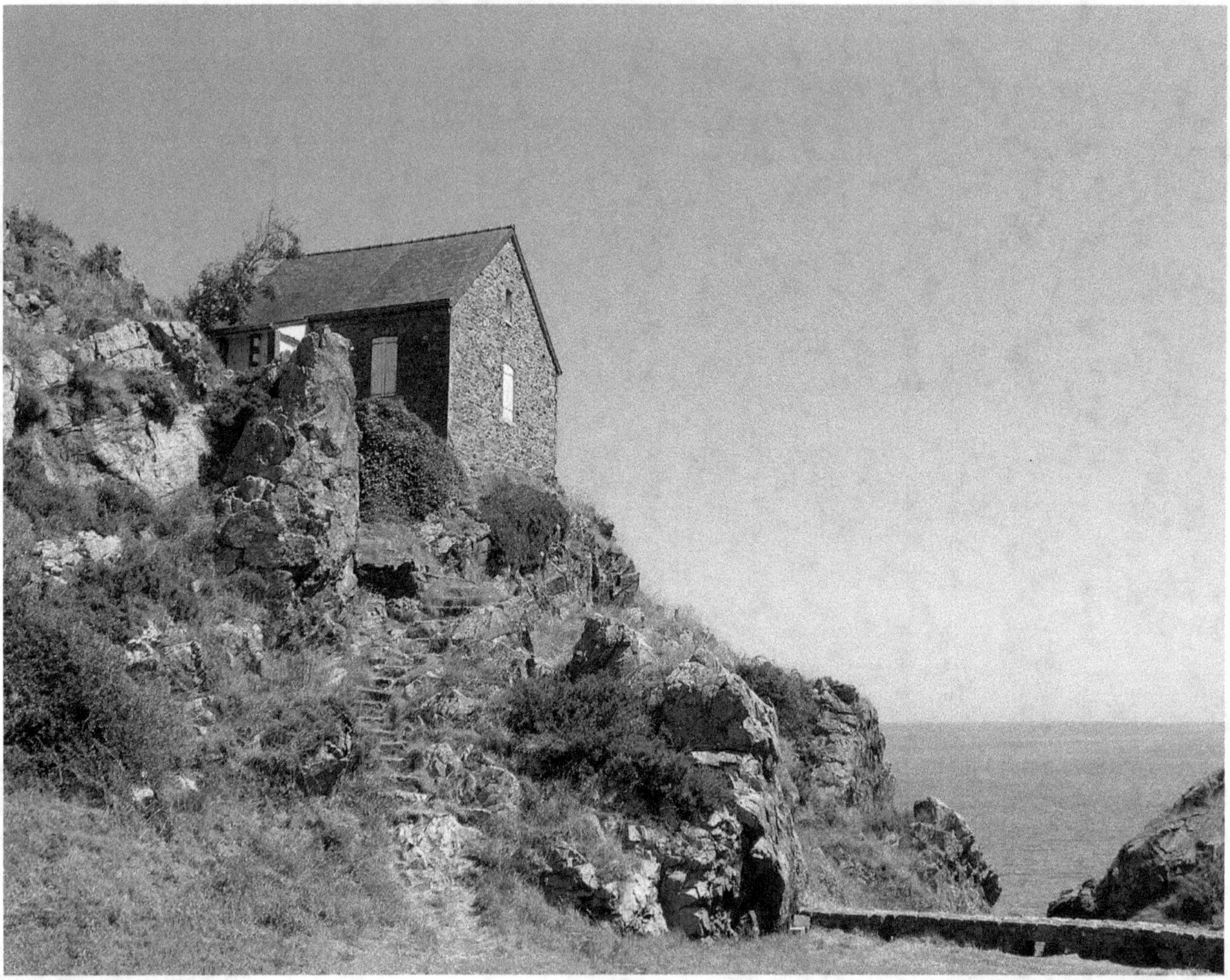

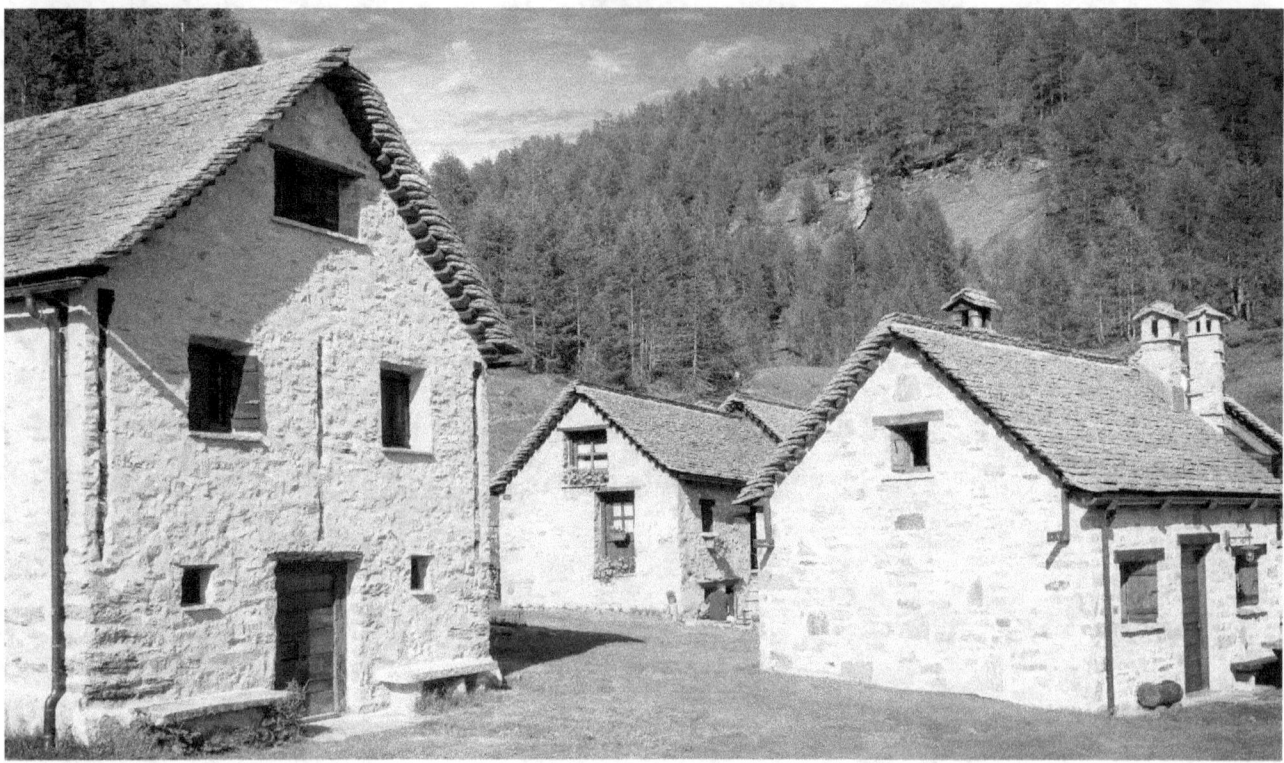

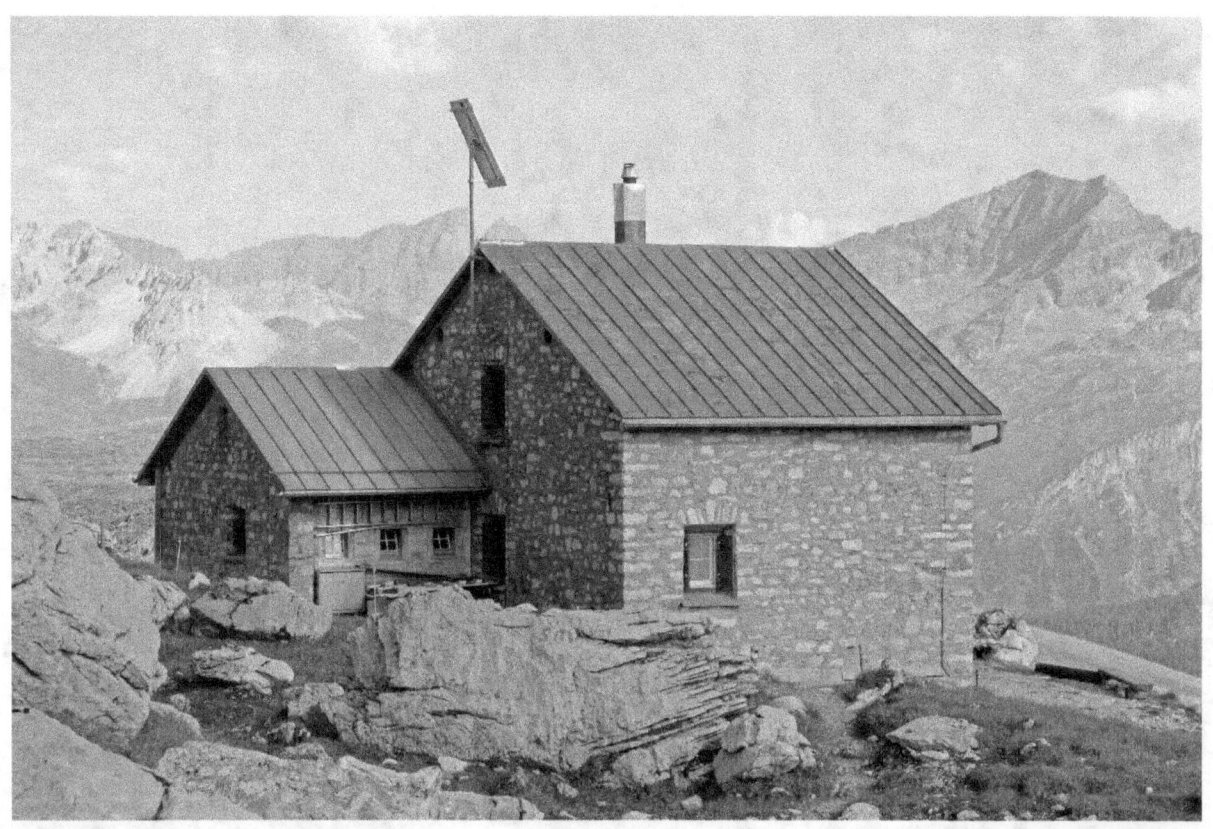

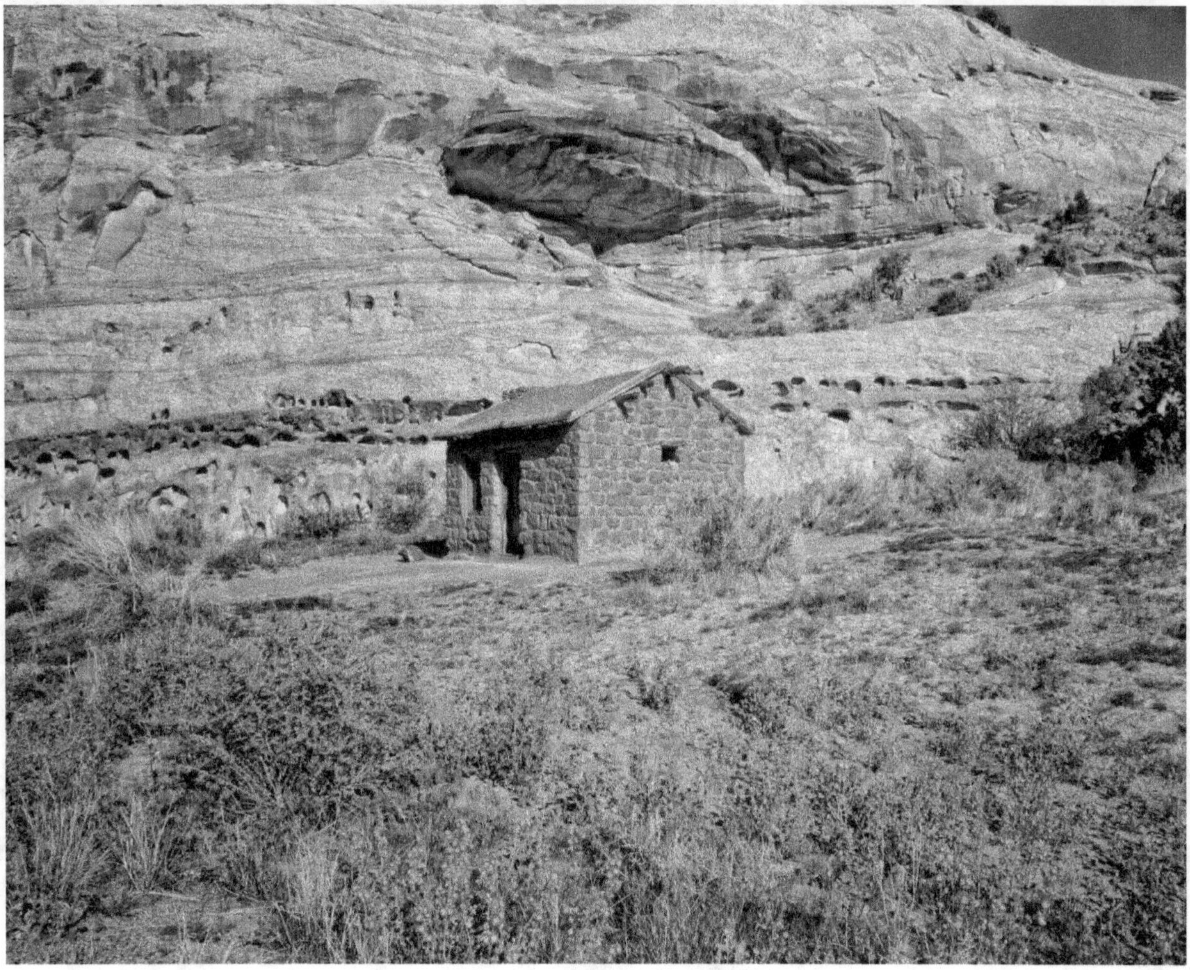

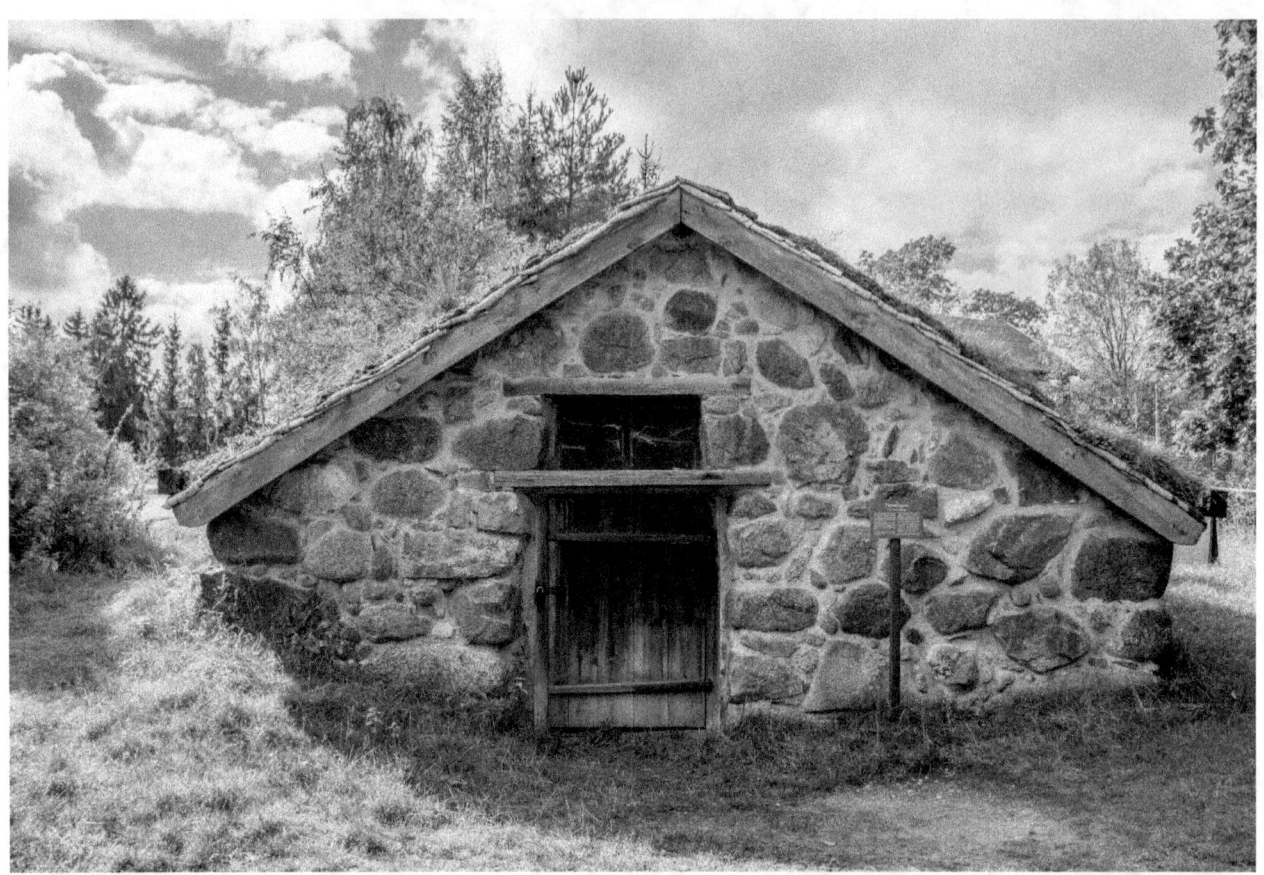

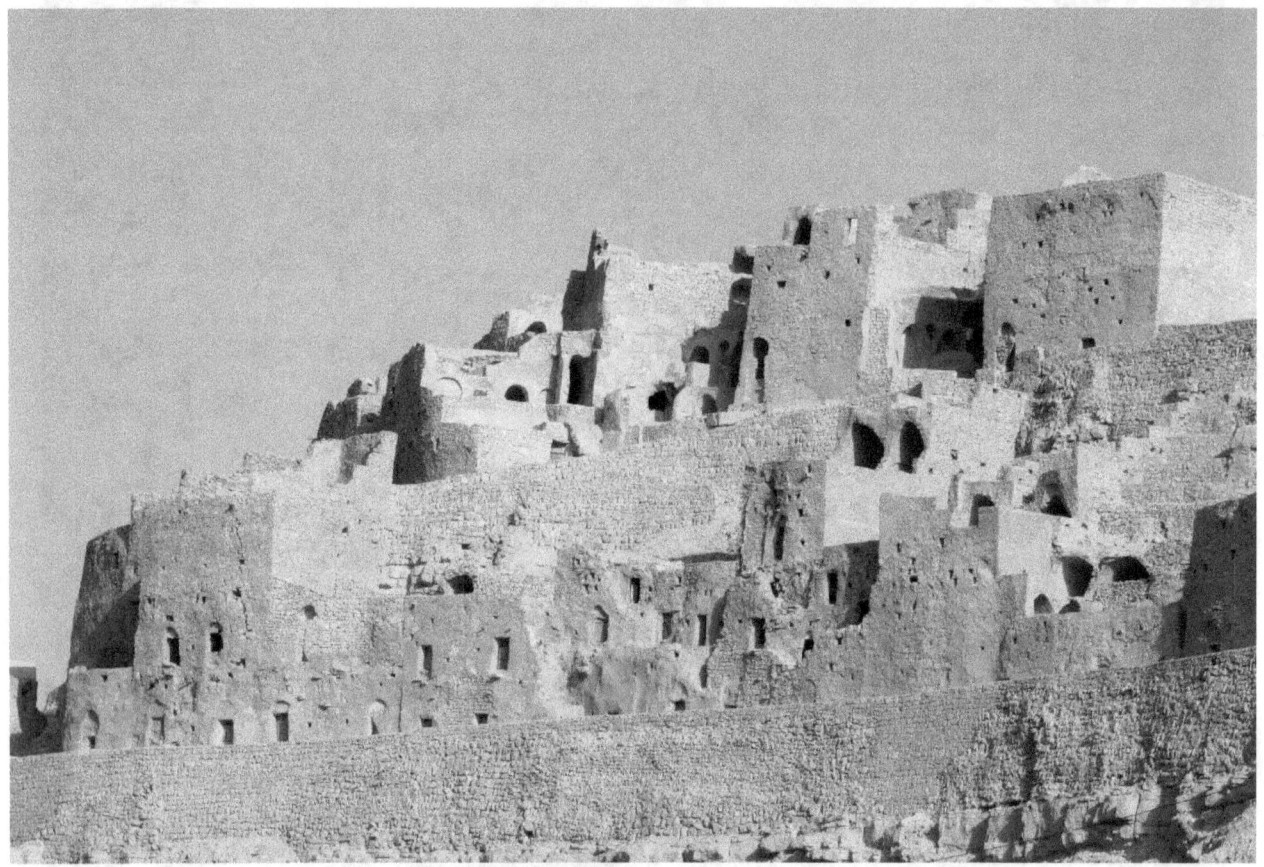

Multiple clumped buildings built with rock in Tunisia

Brick

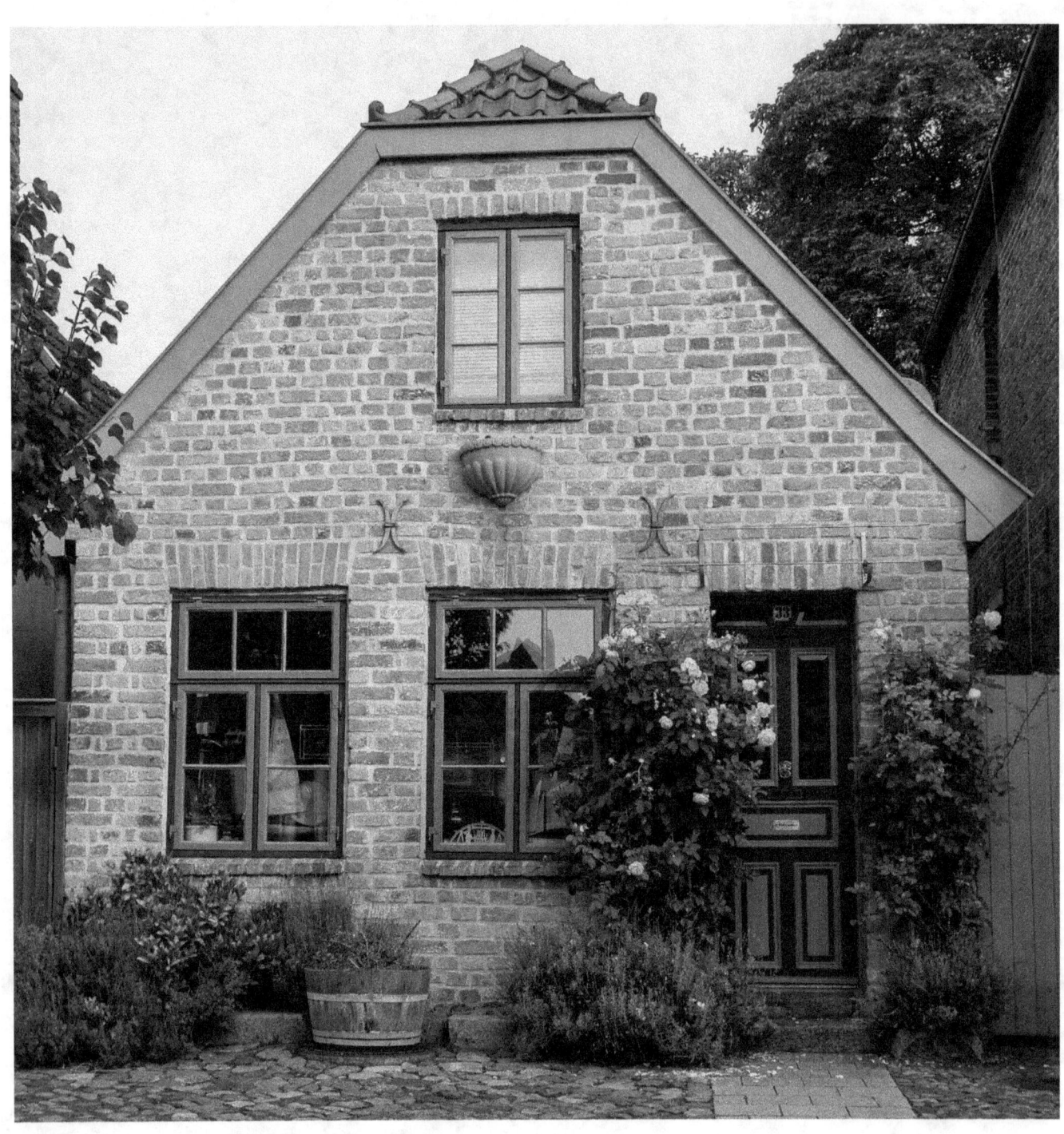

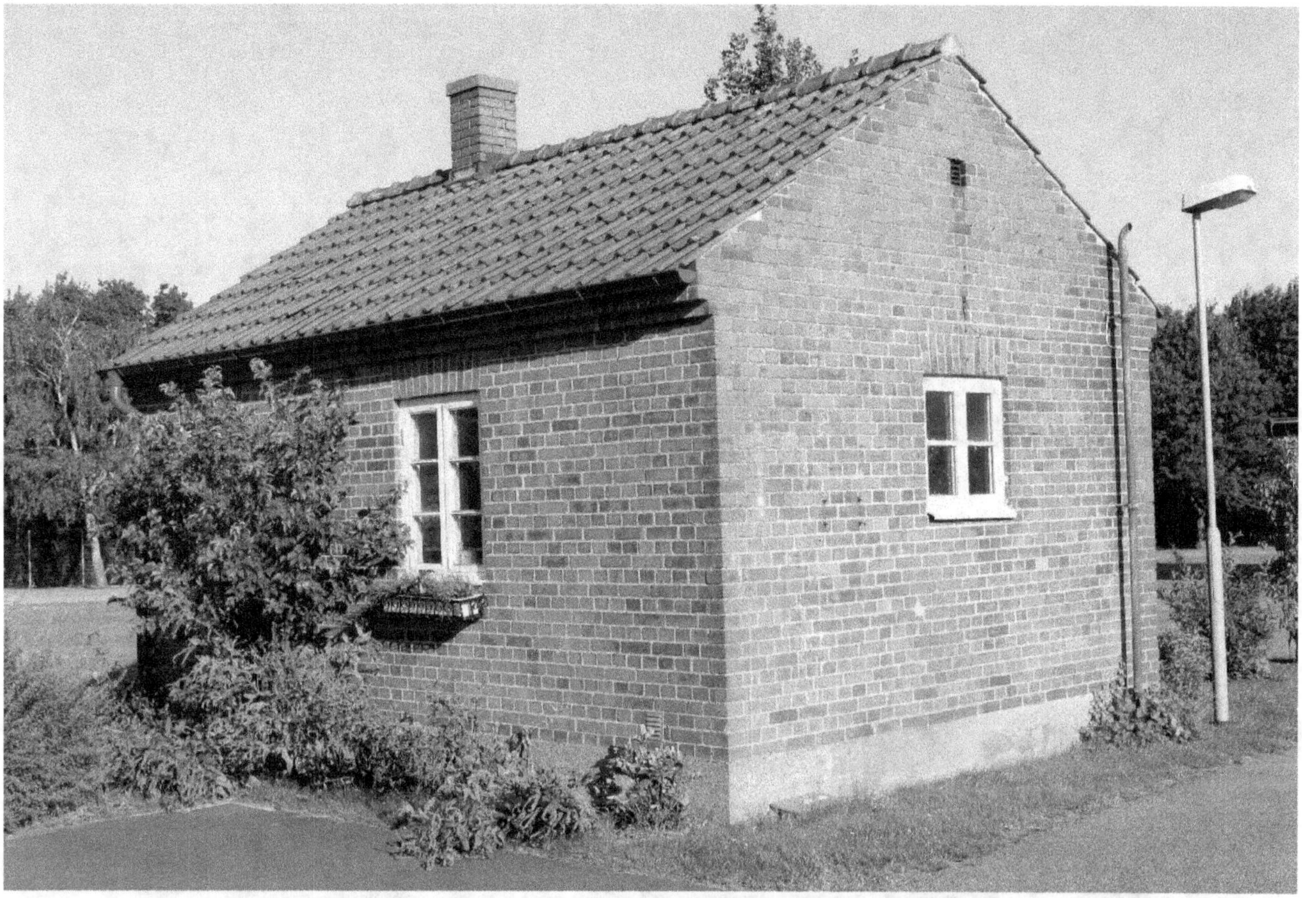

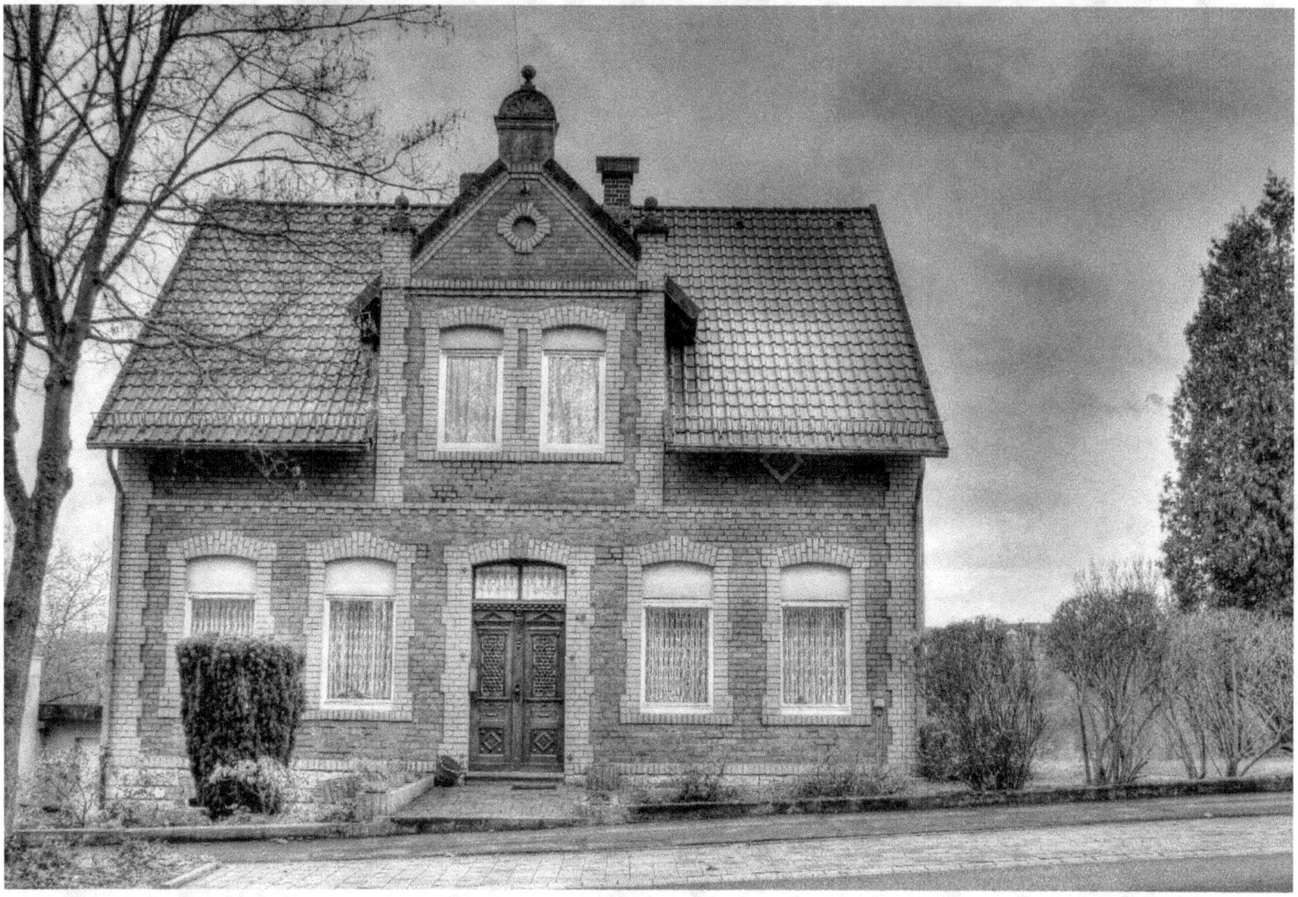

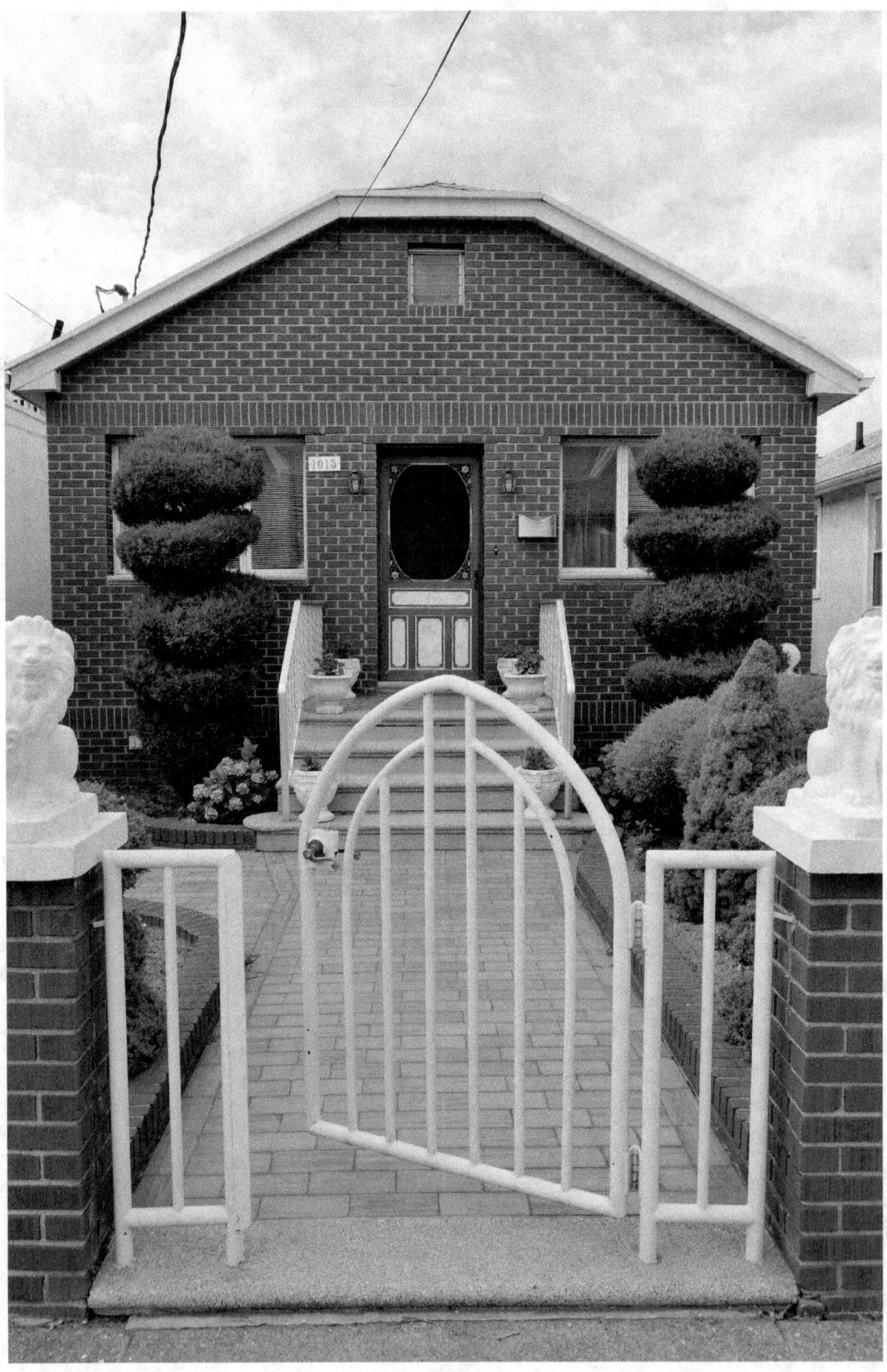

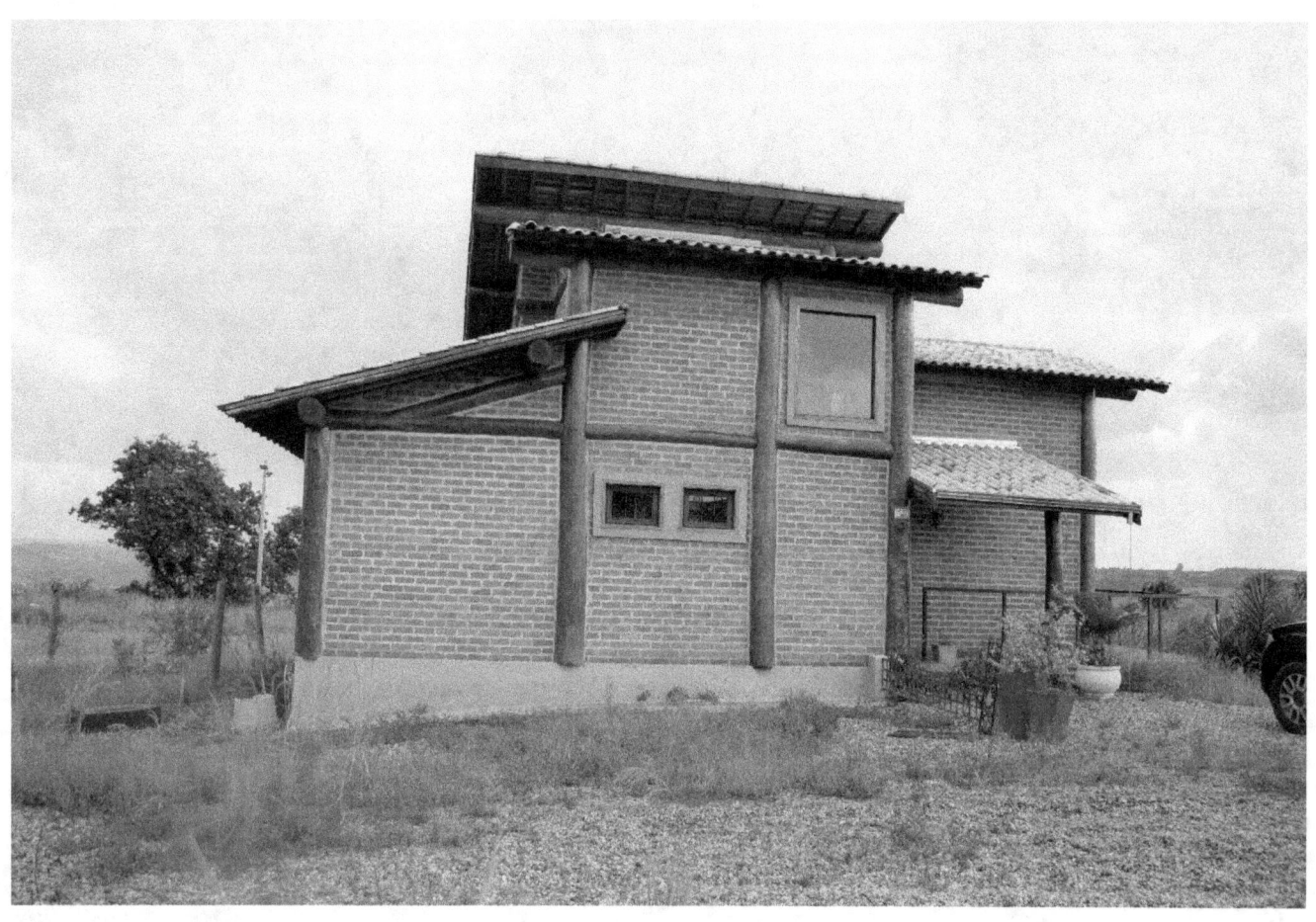

Mountain Cottages

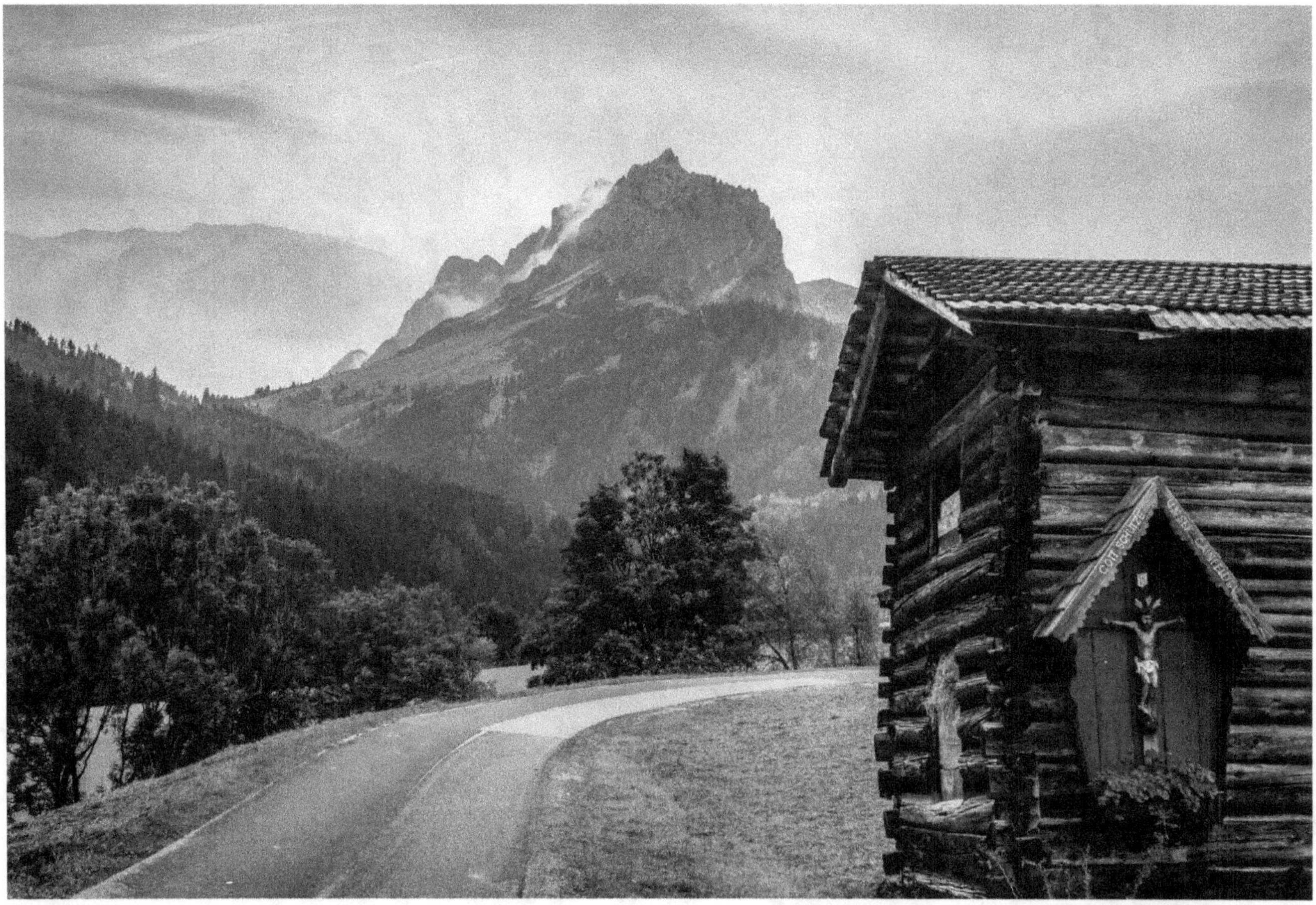

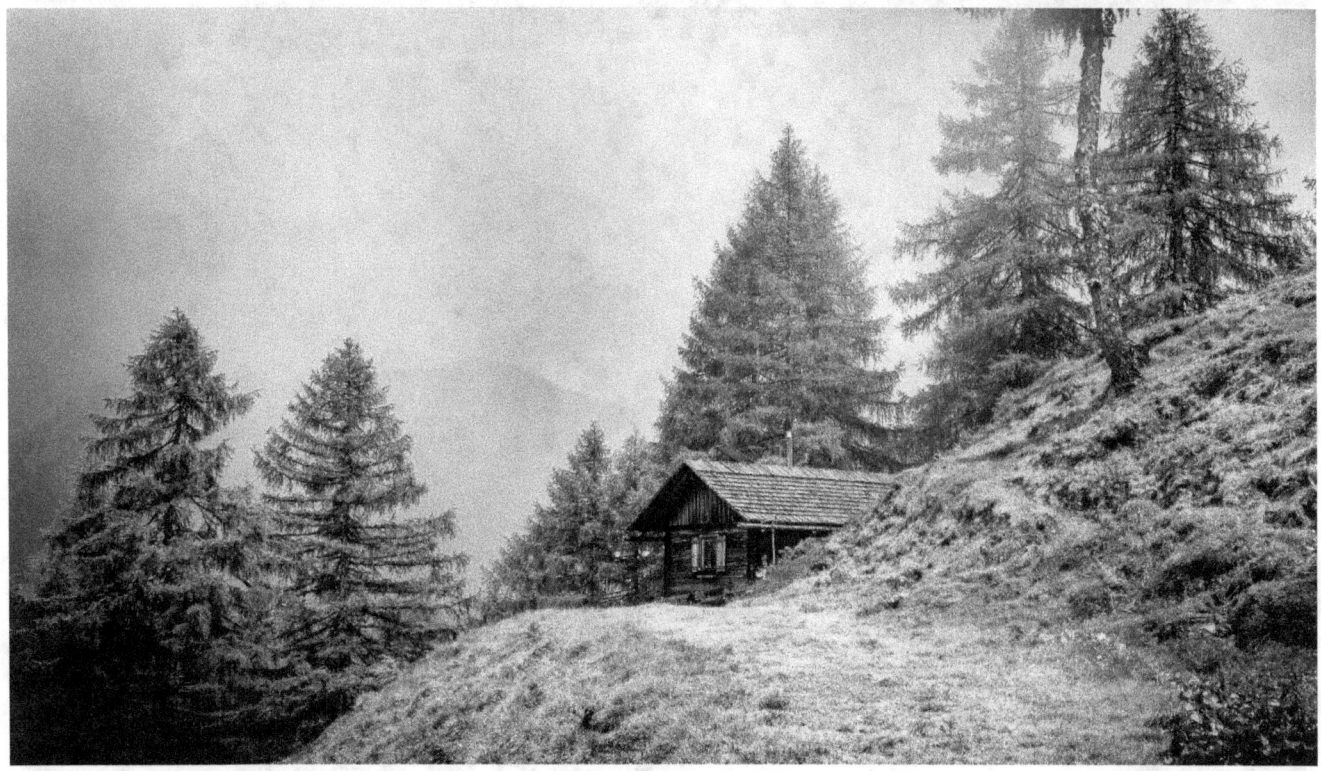

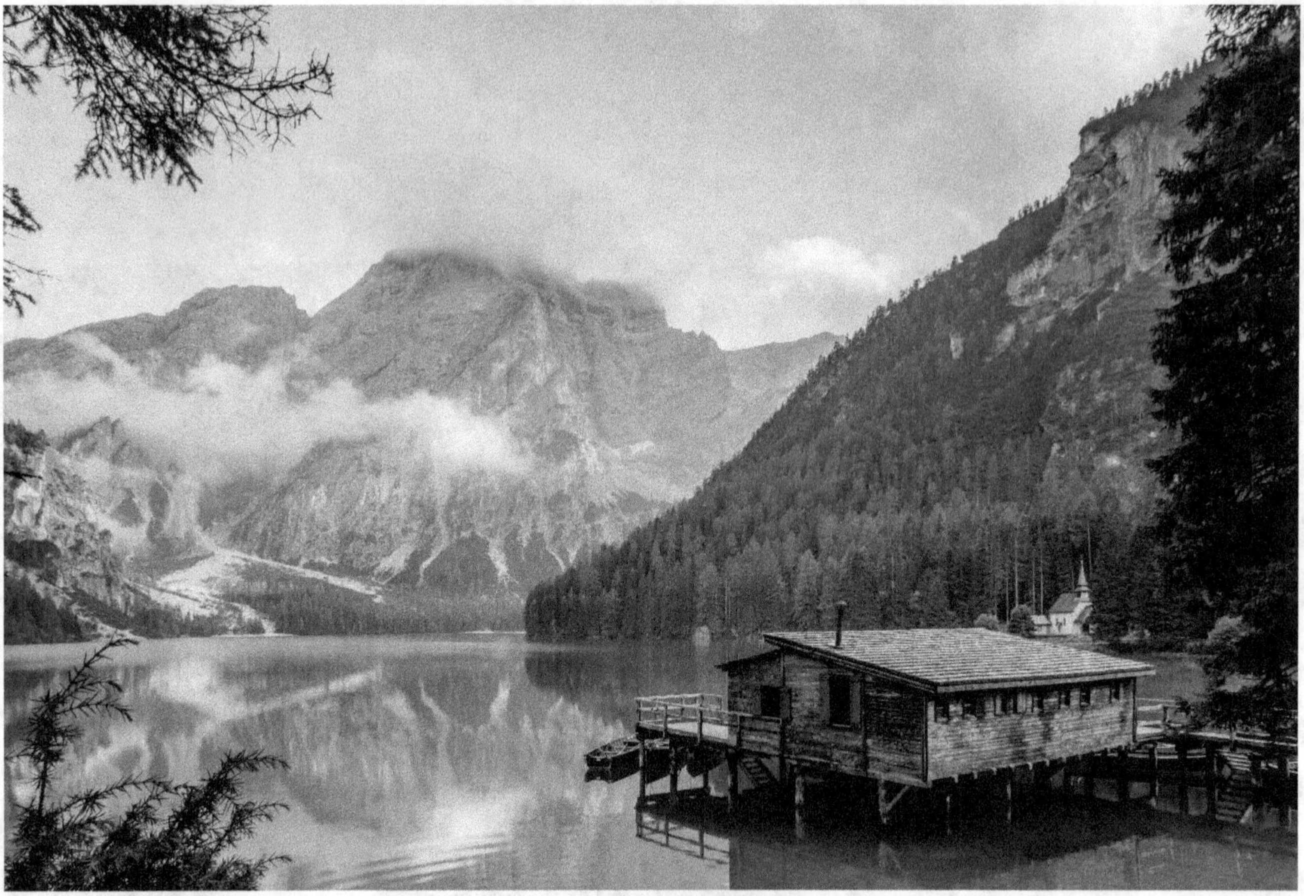

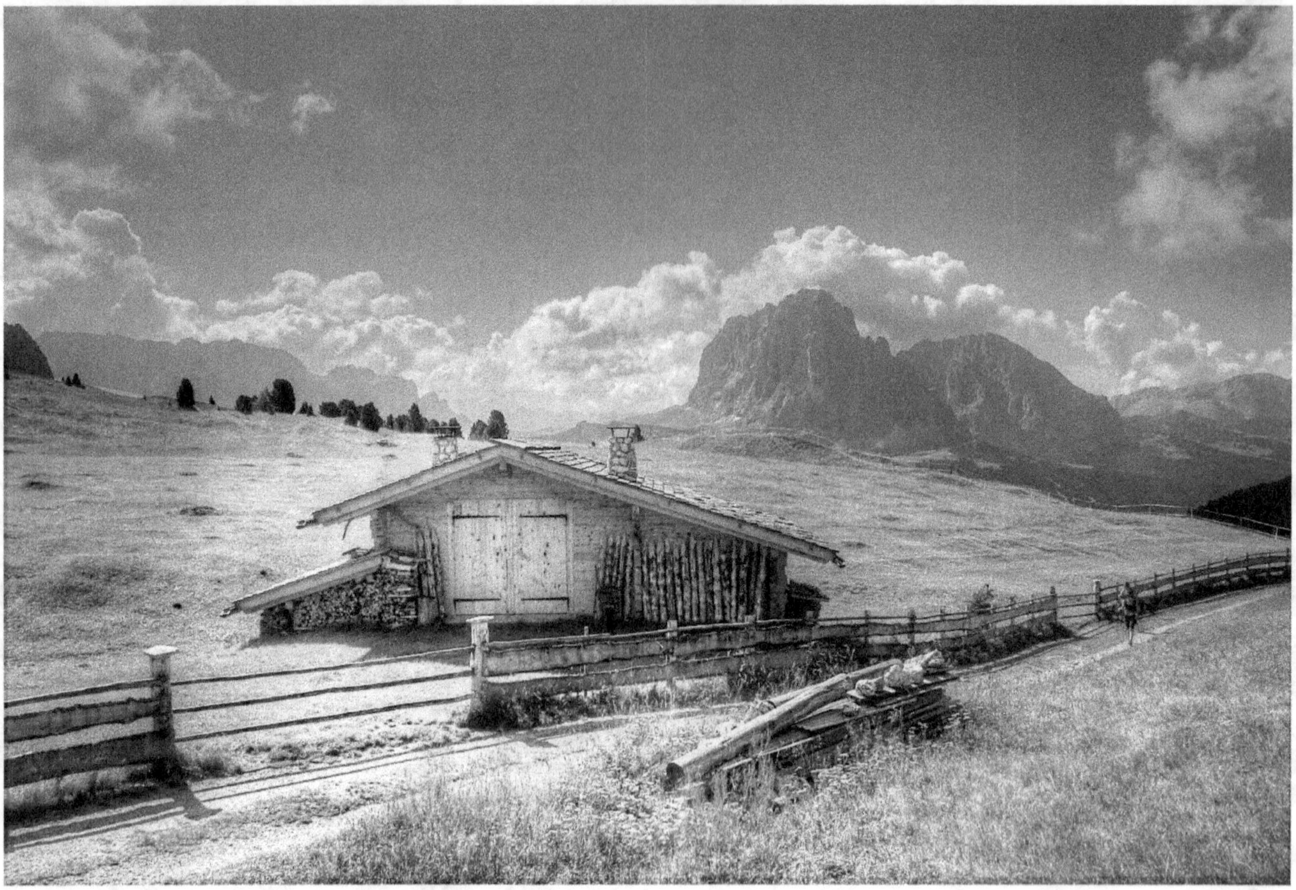

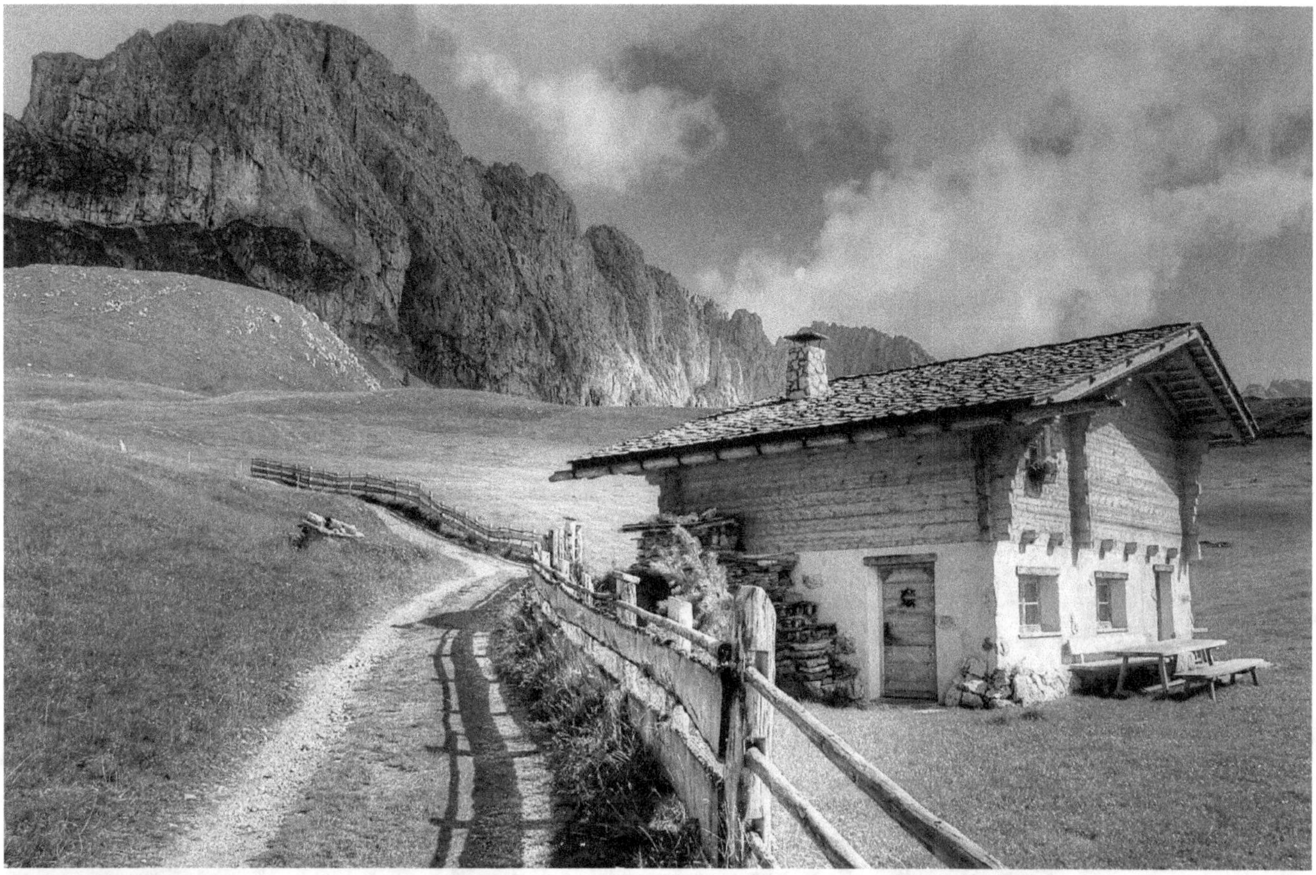

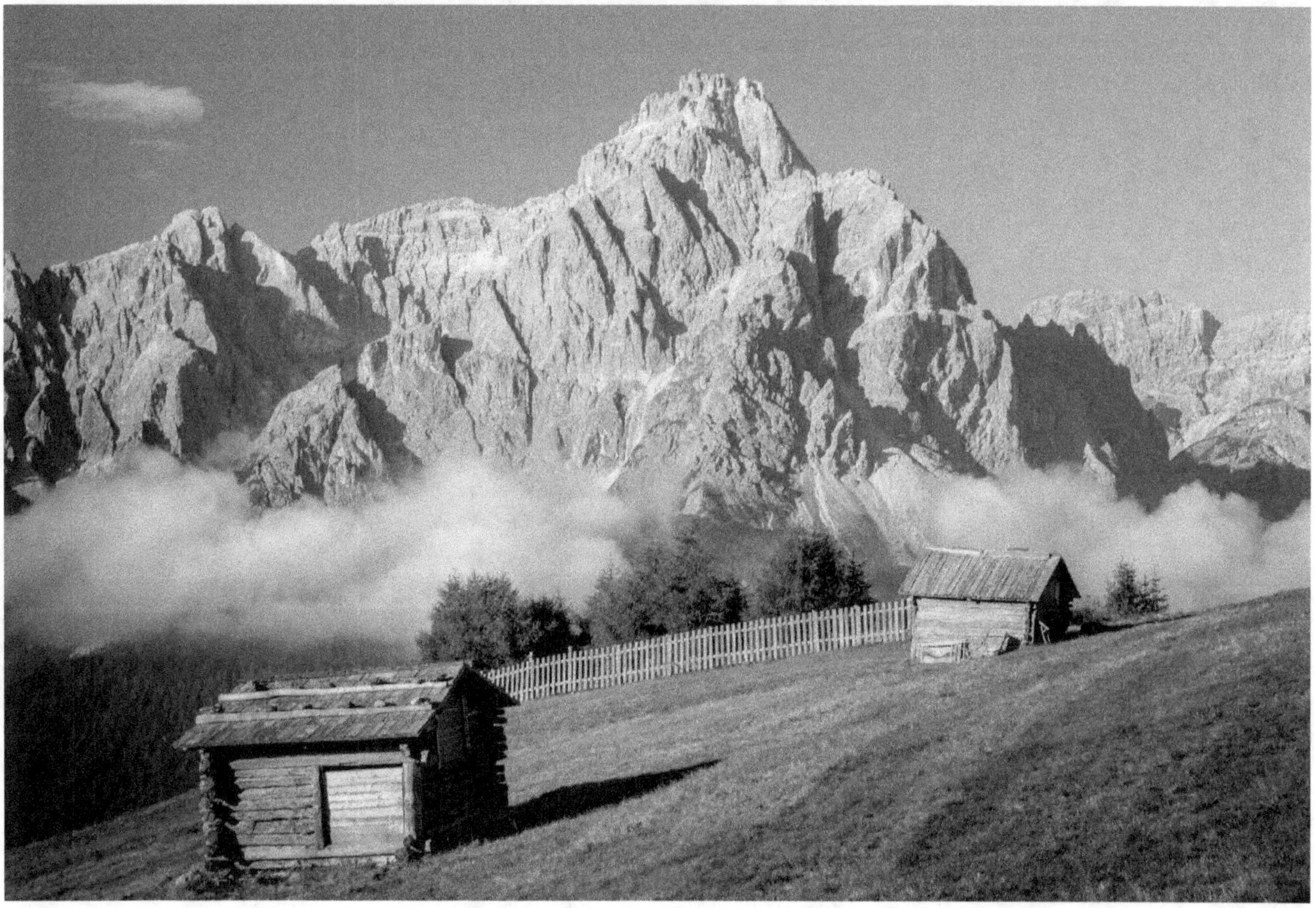

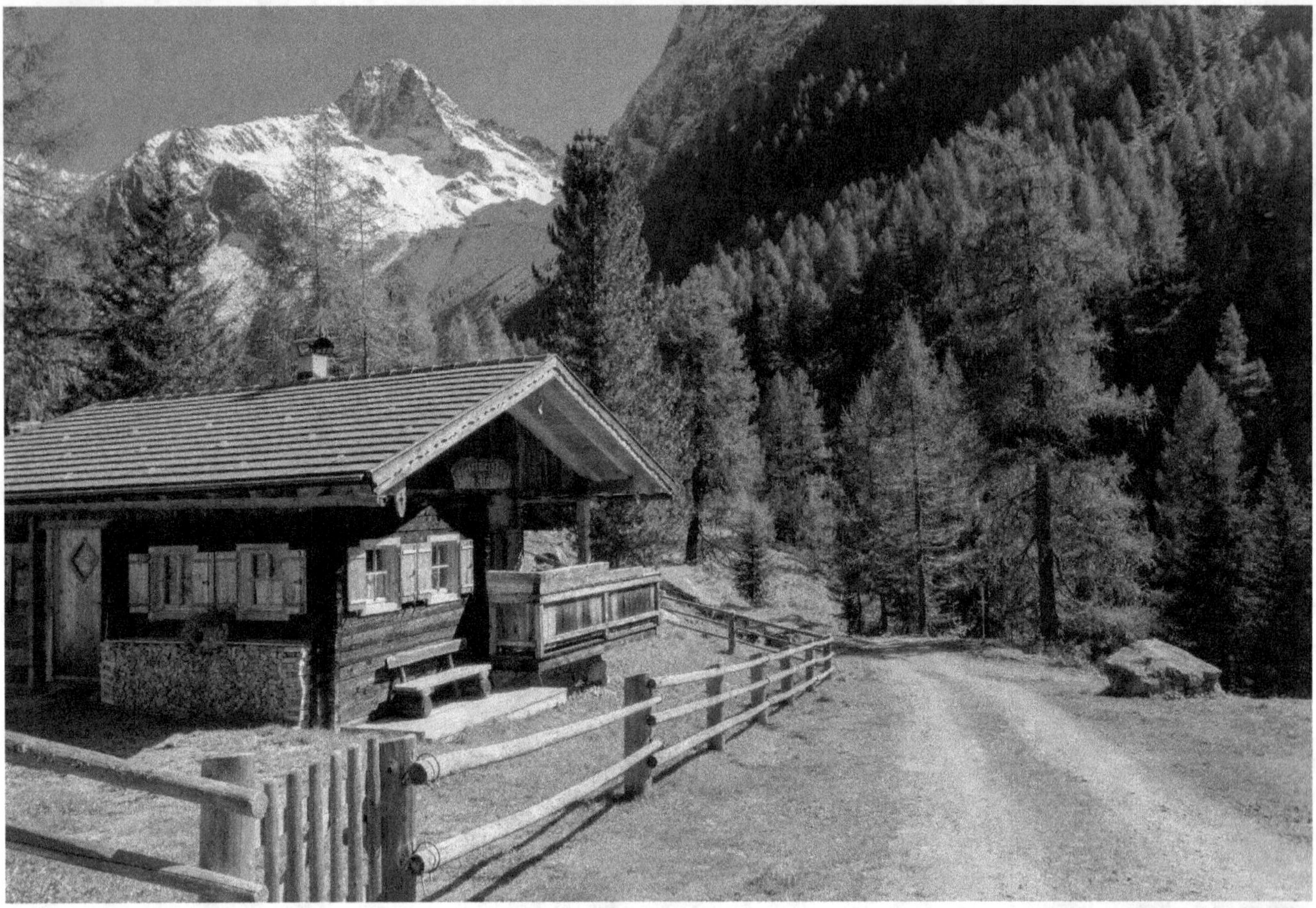

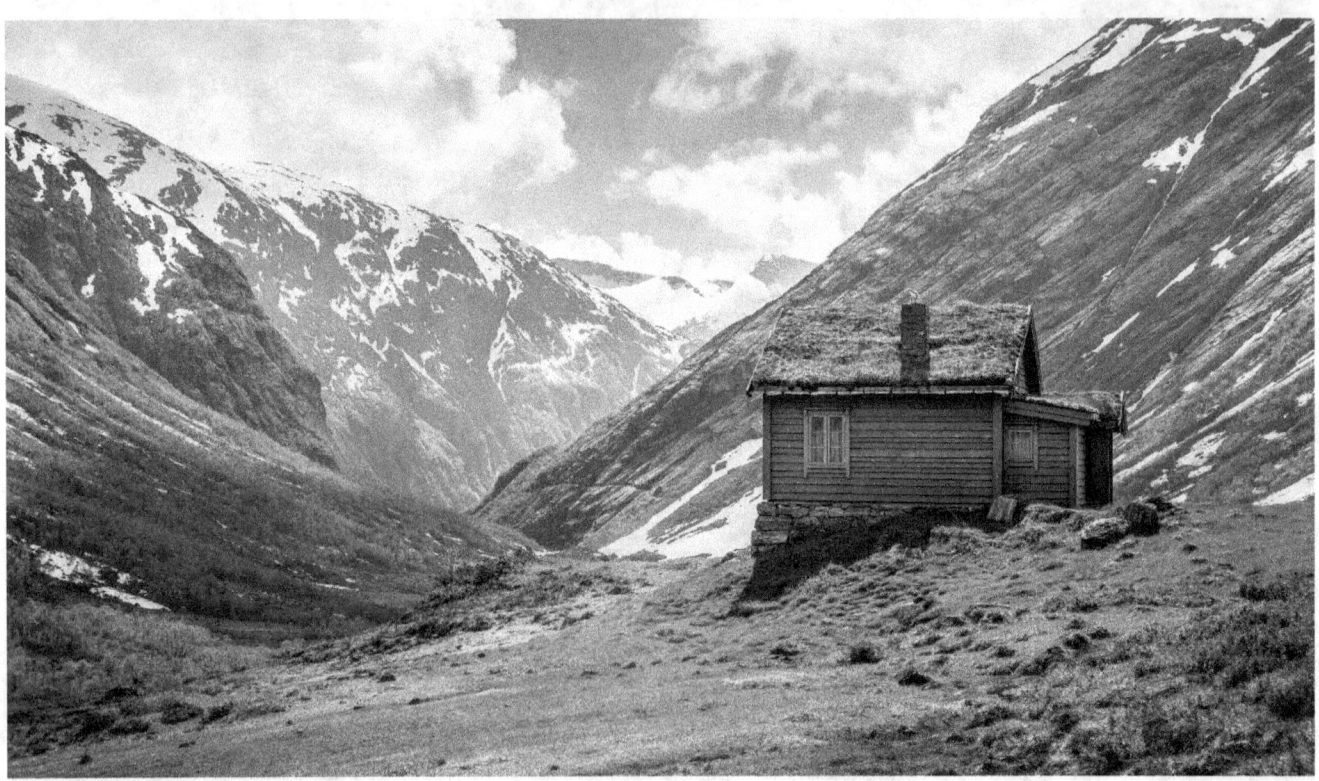

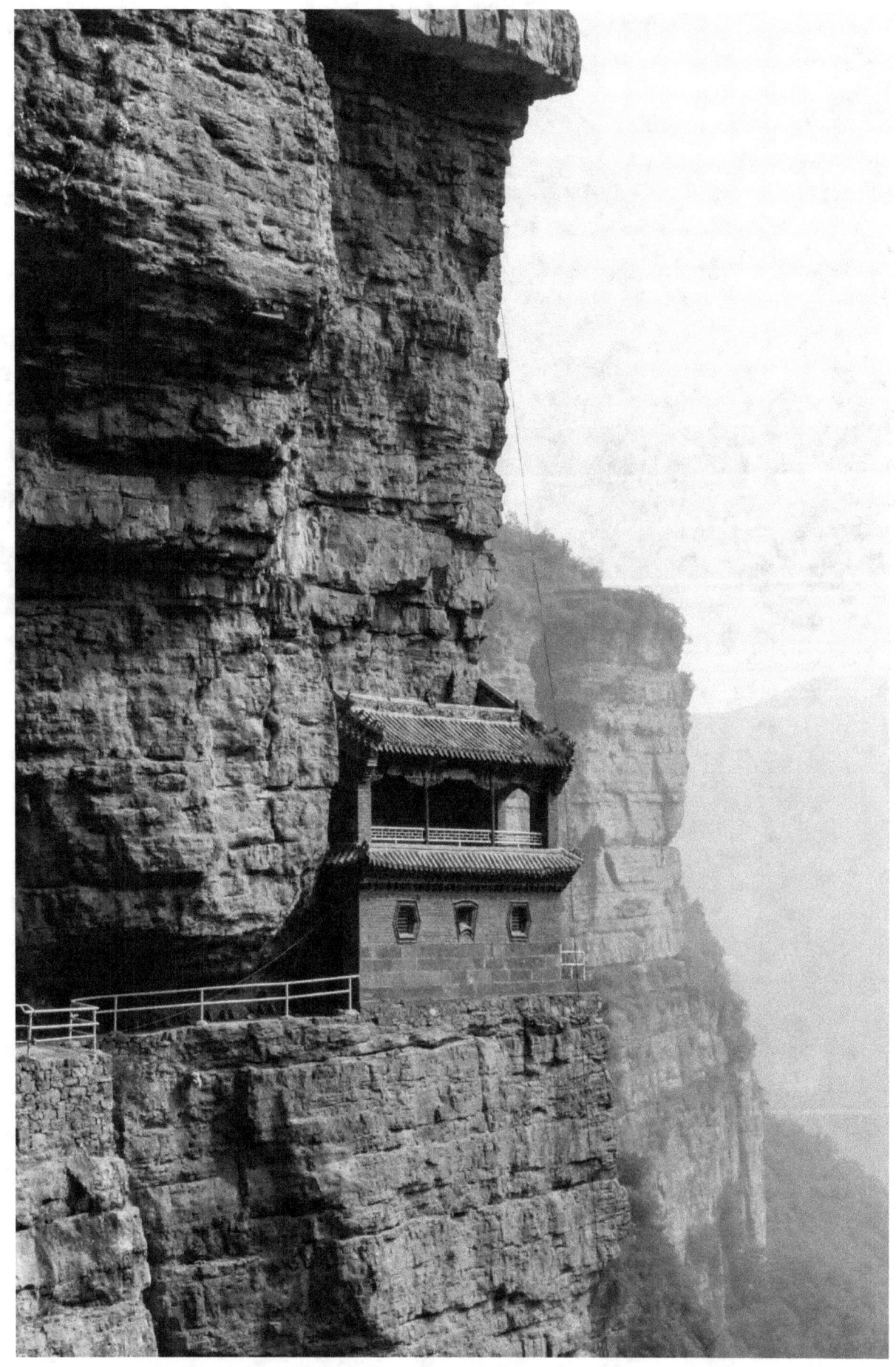

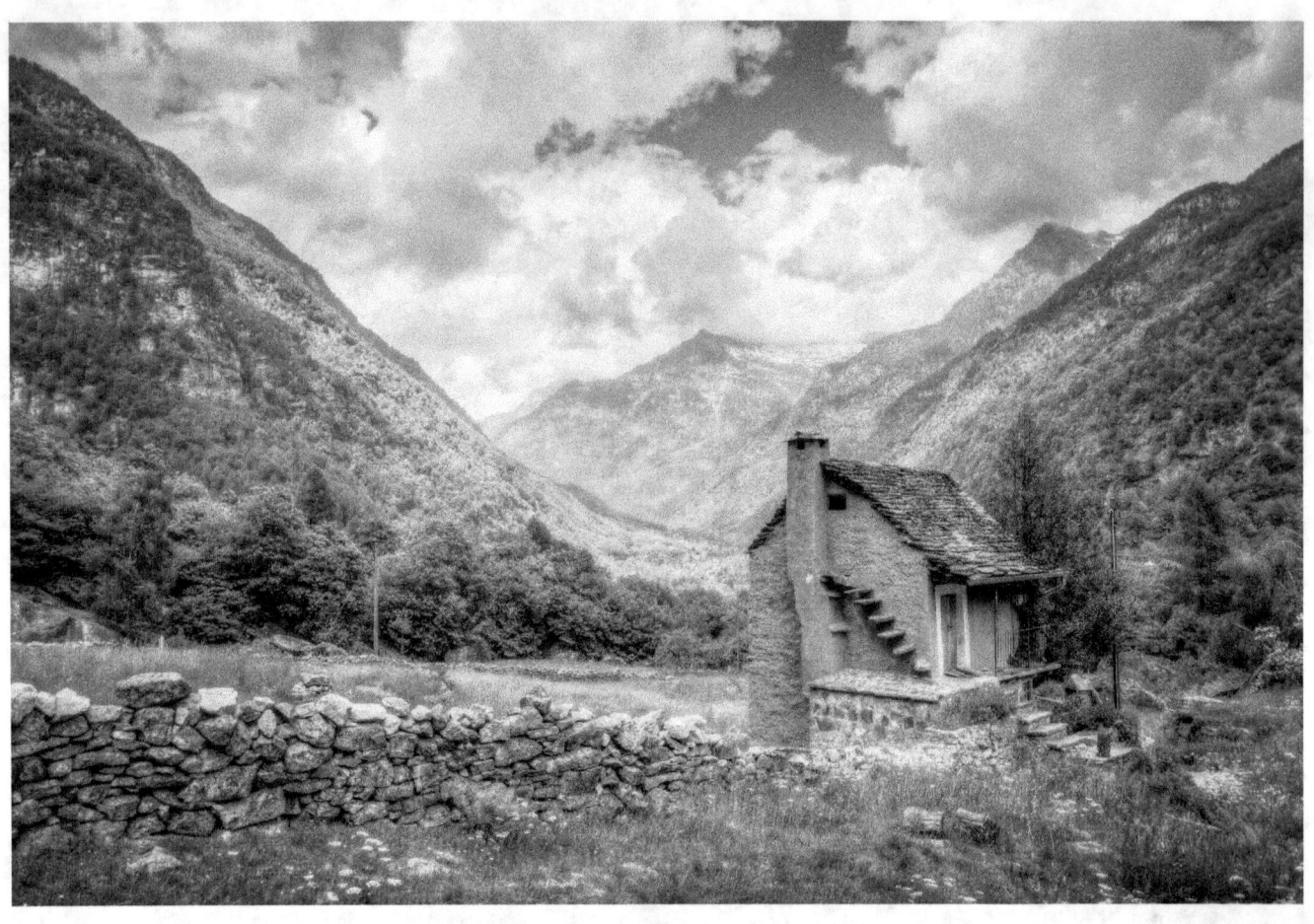

Sod Homes

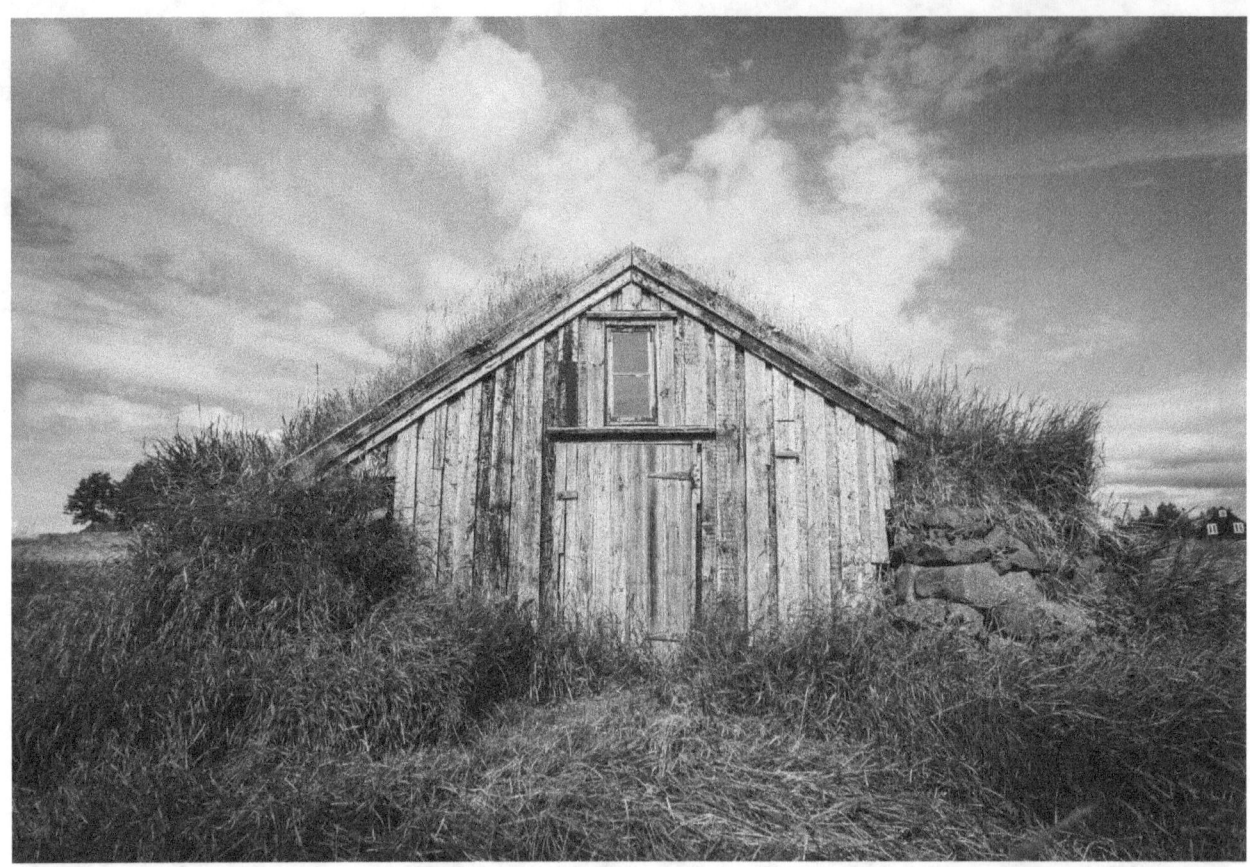

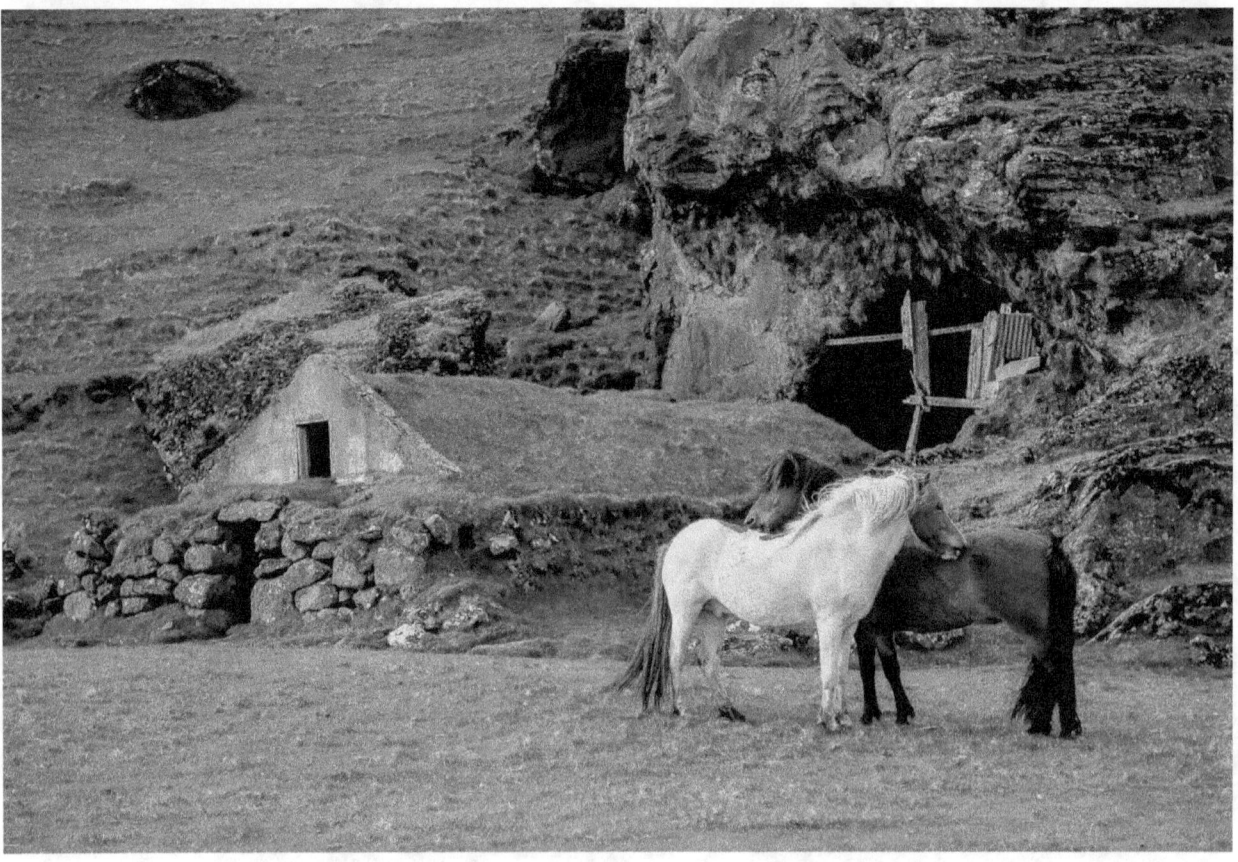

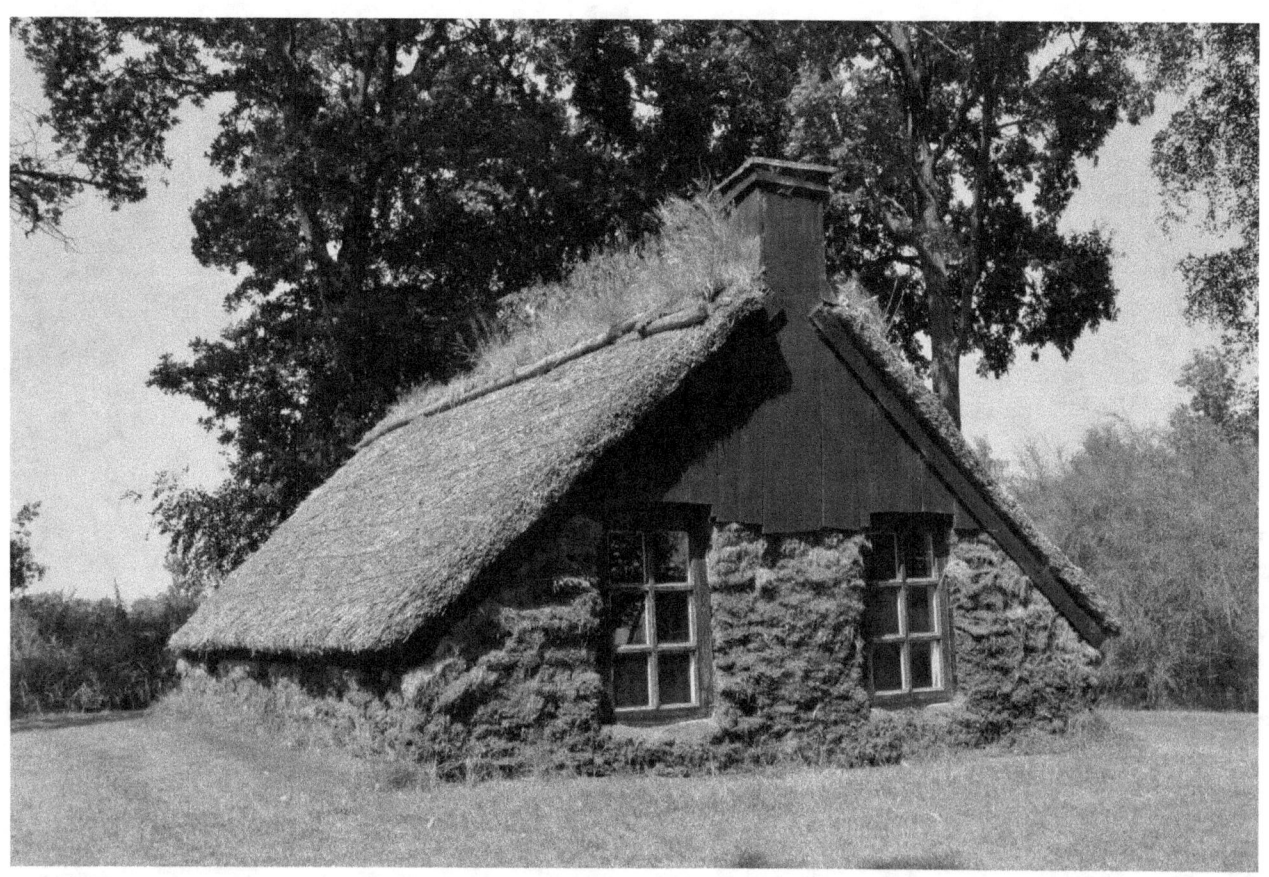

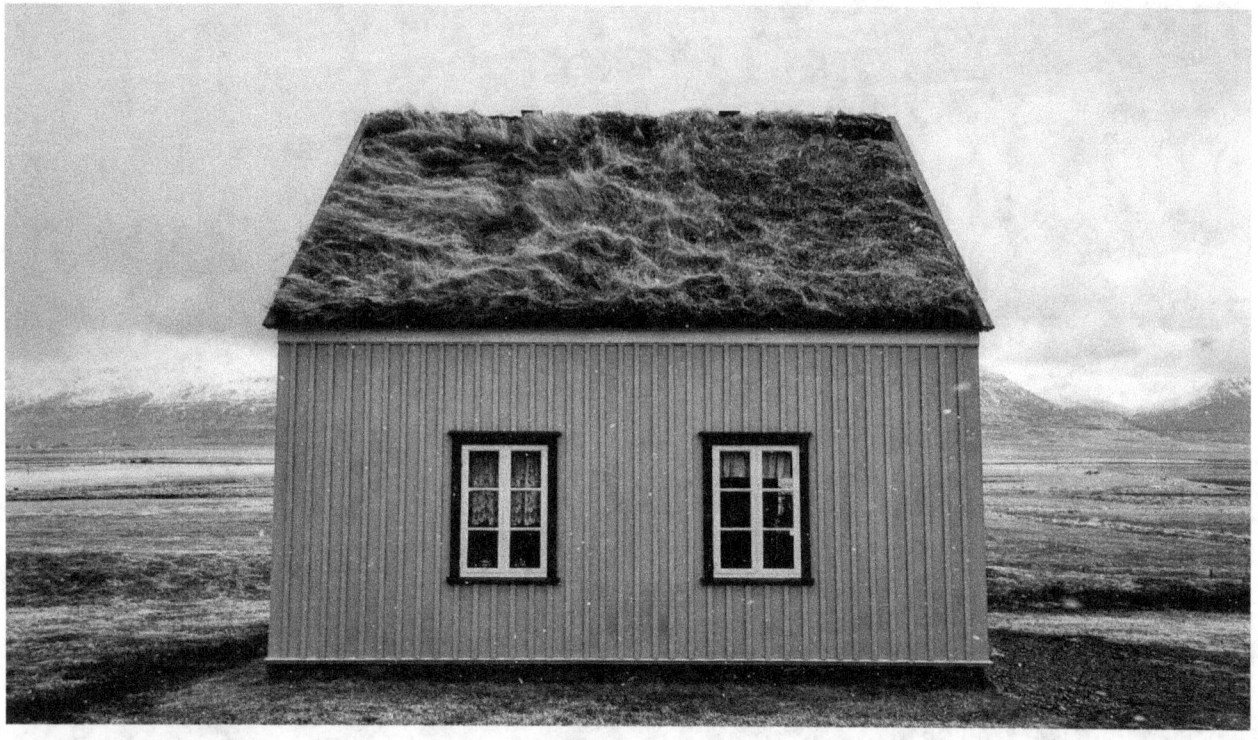

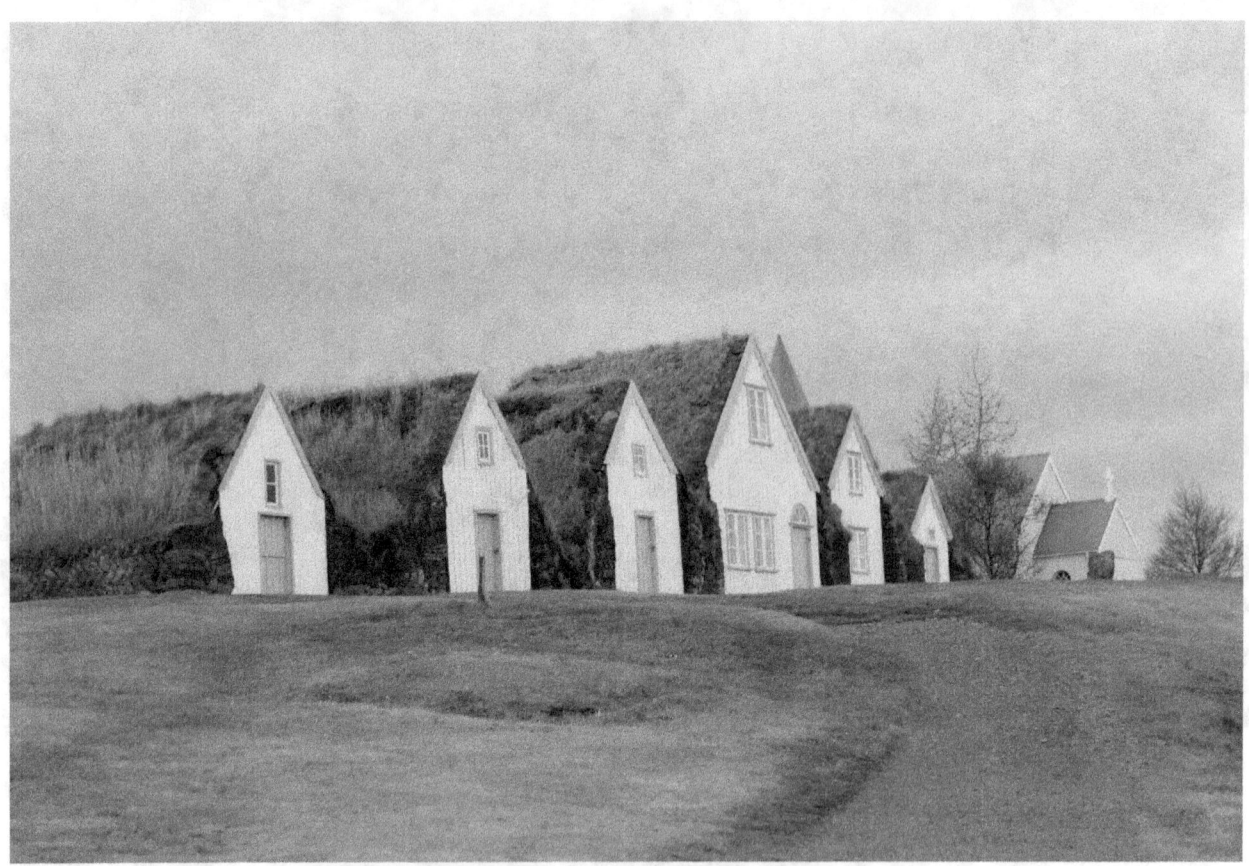

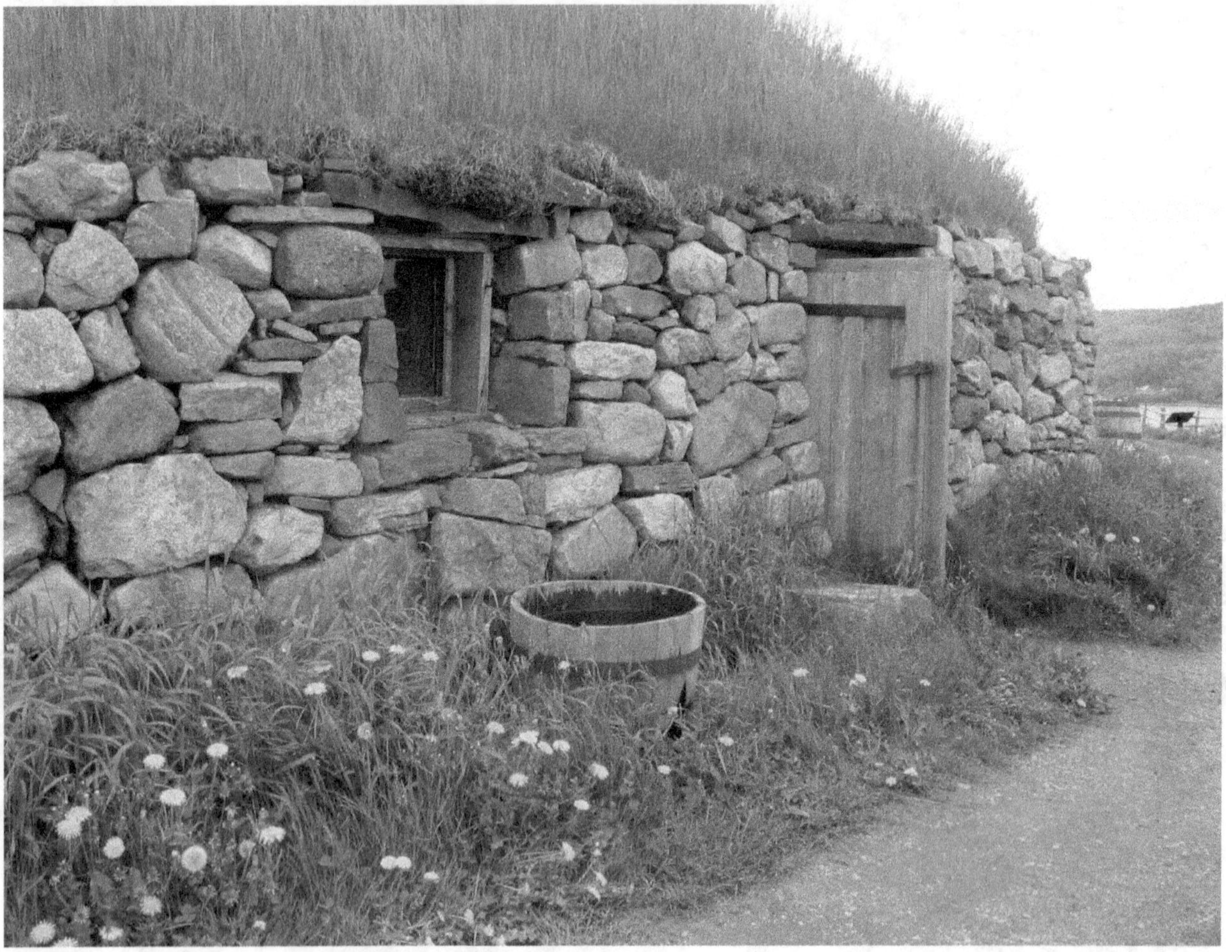

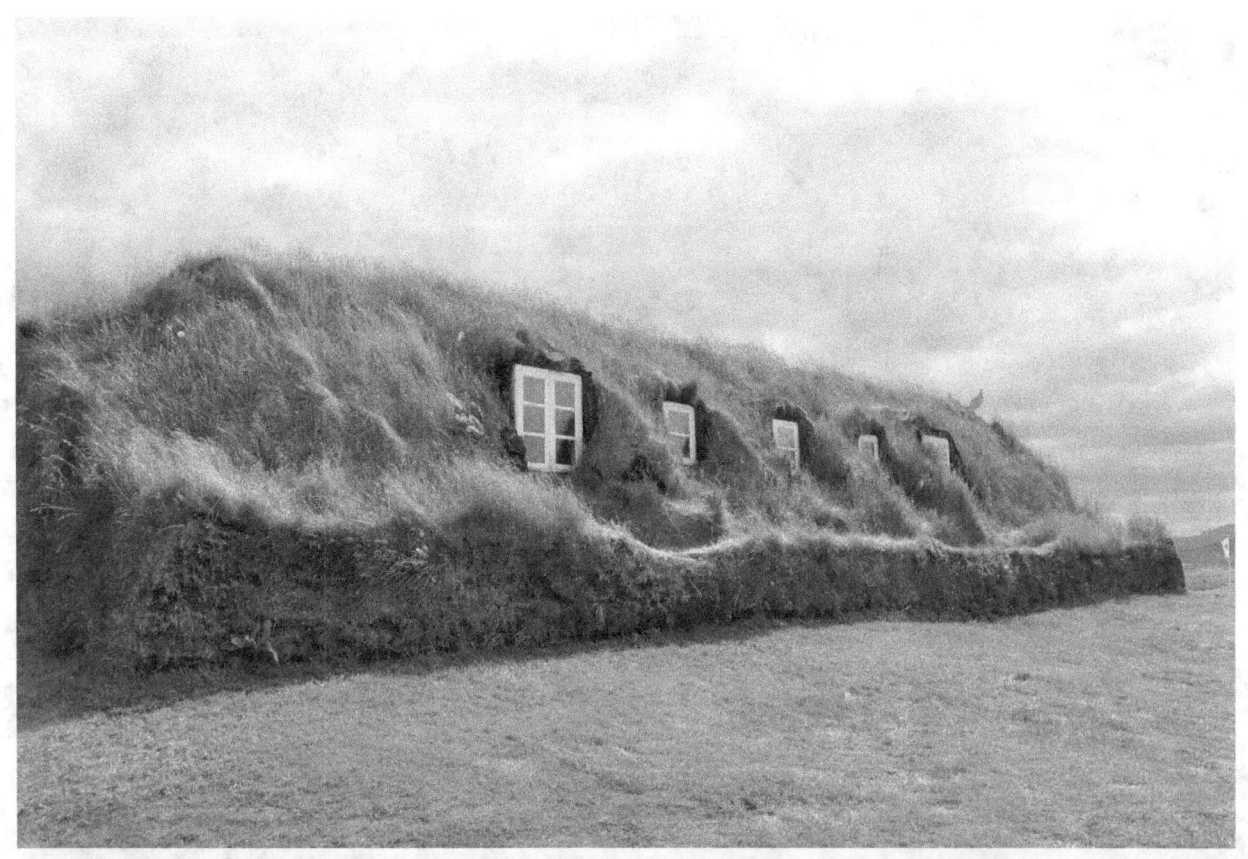

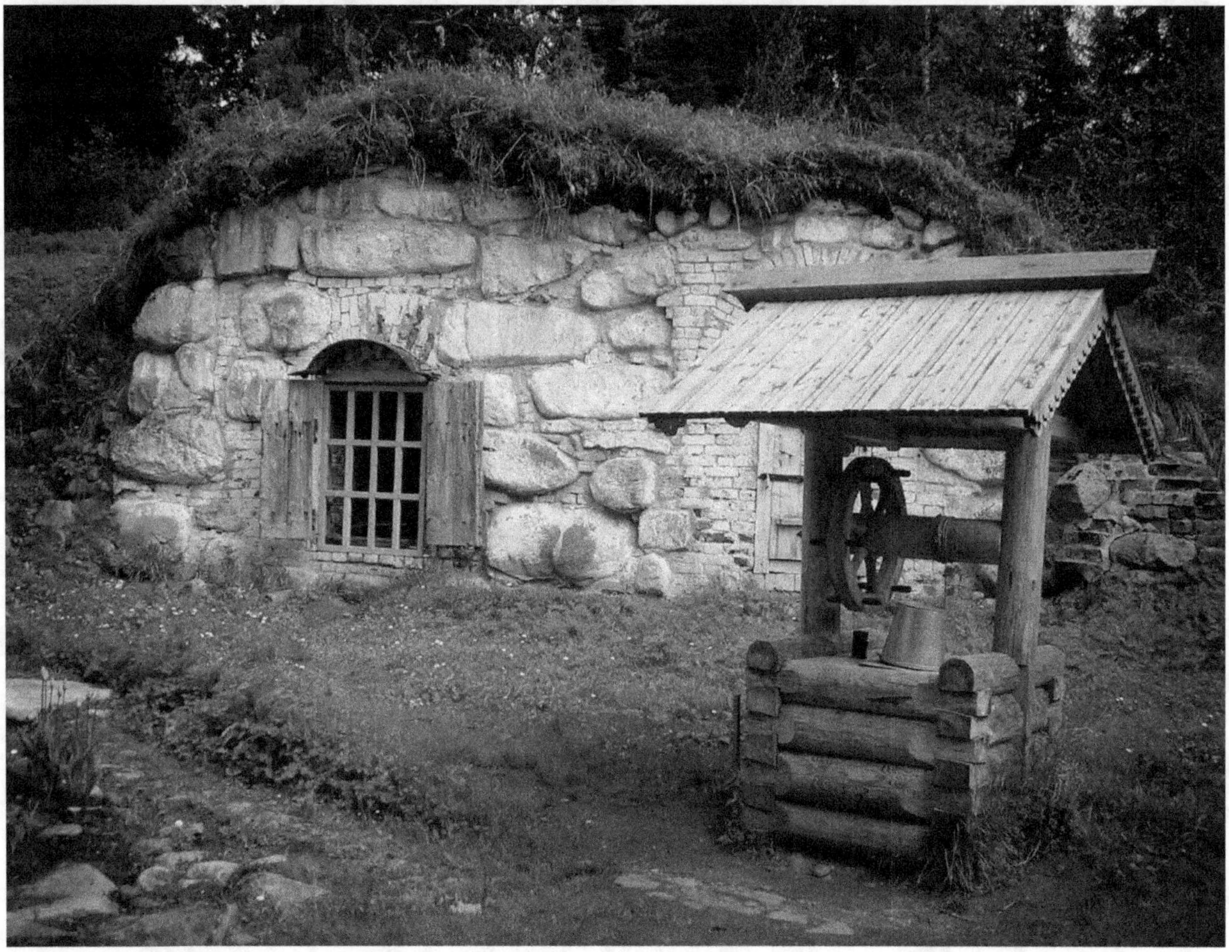

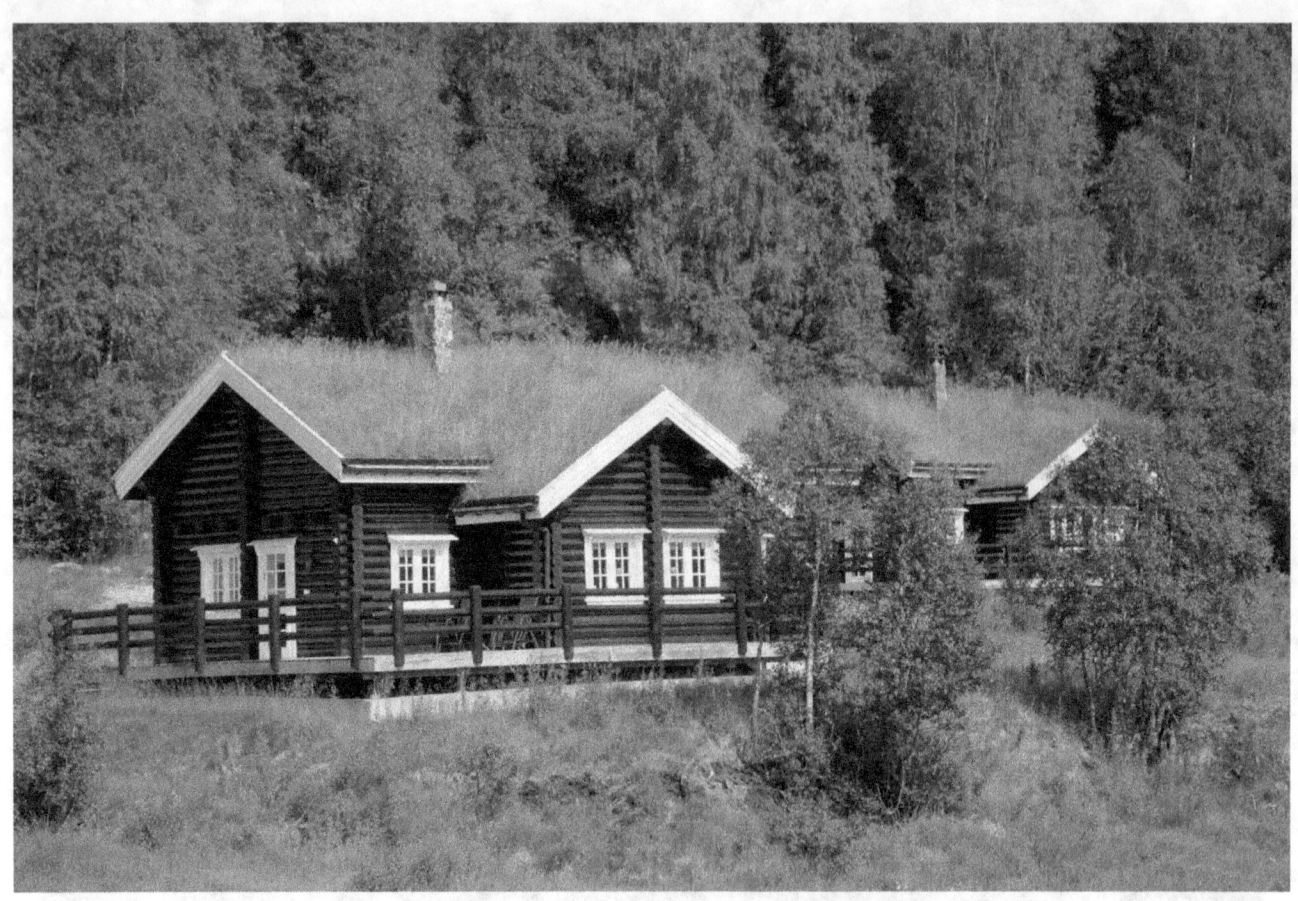

Farm Houses

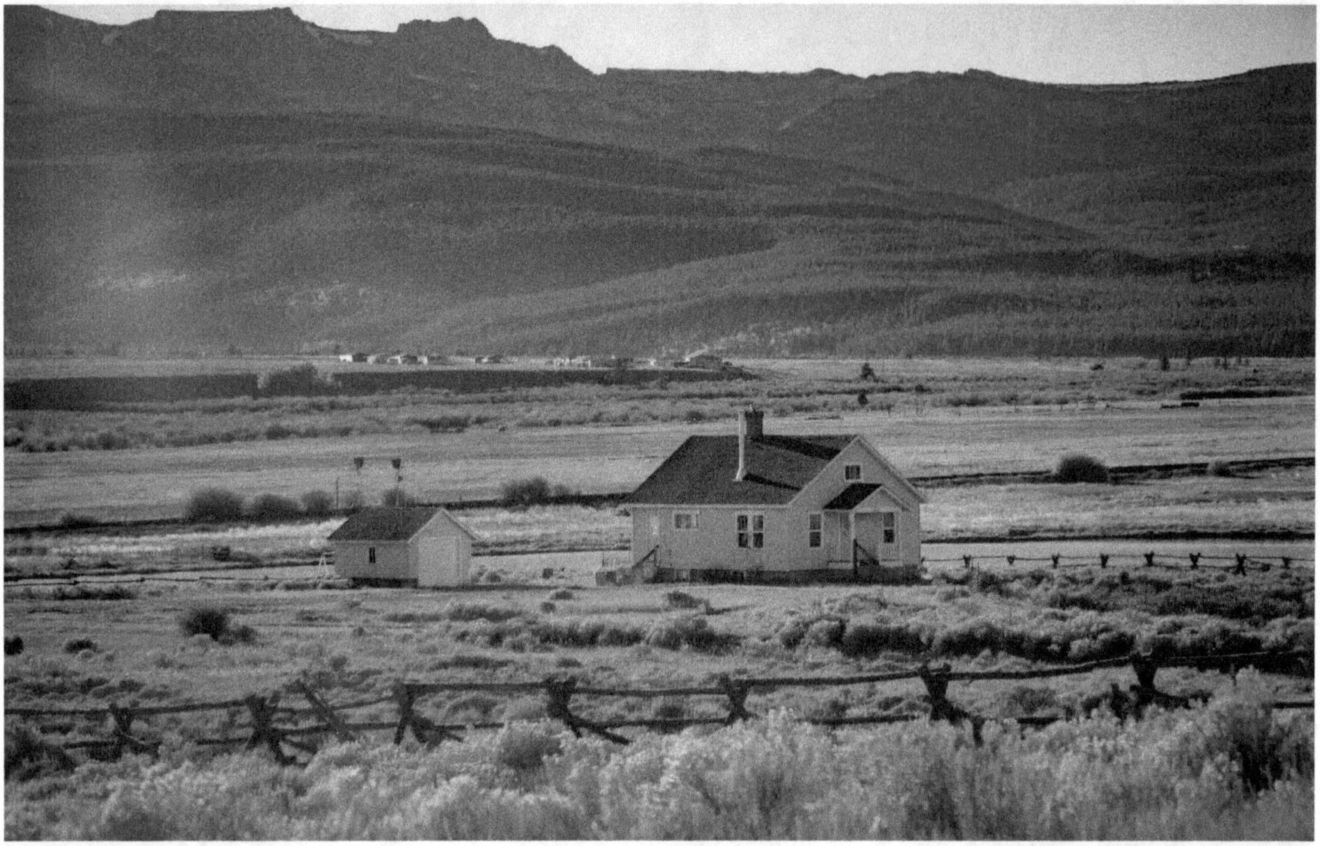

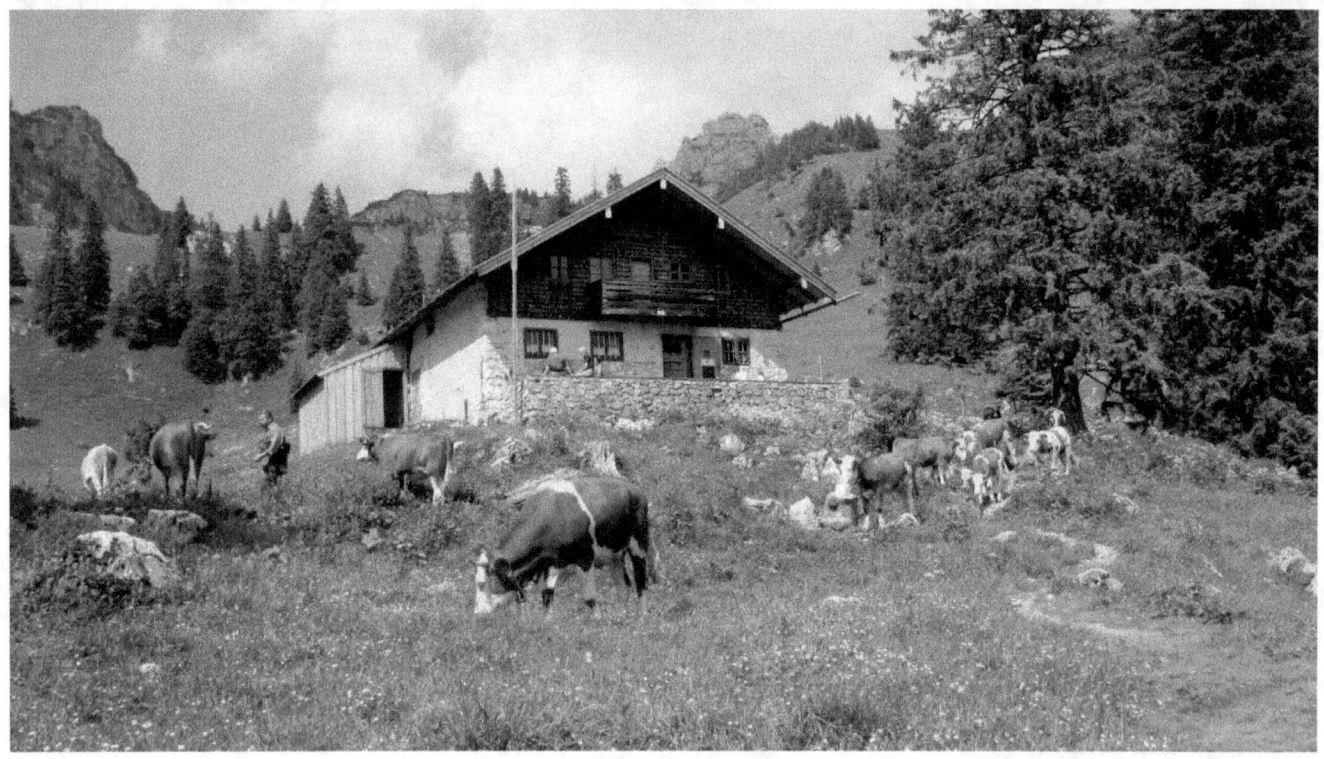

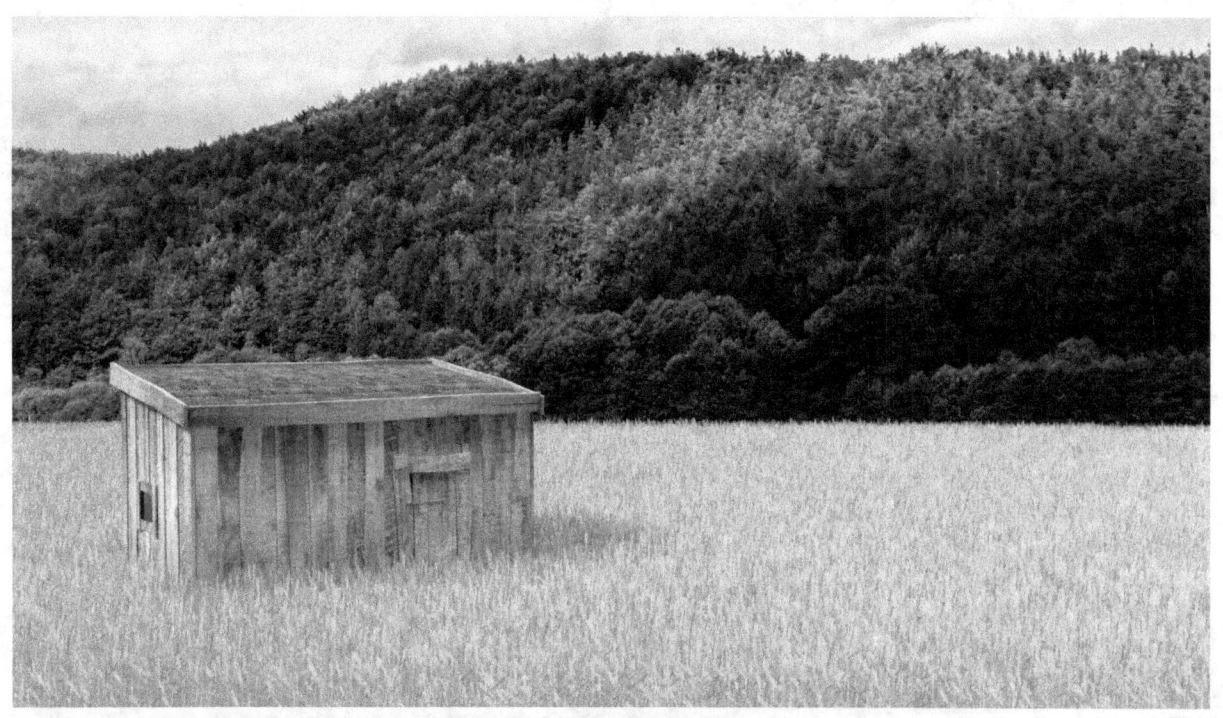

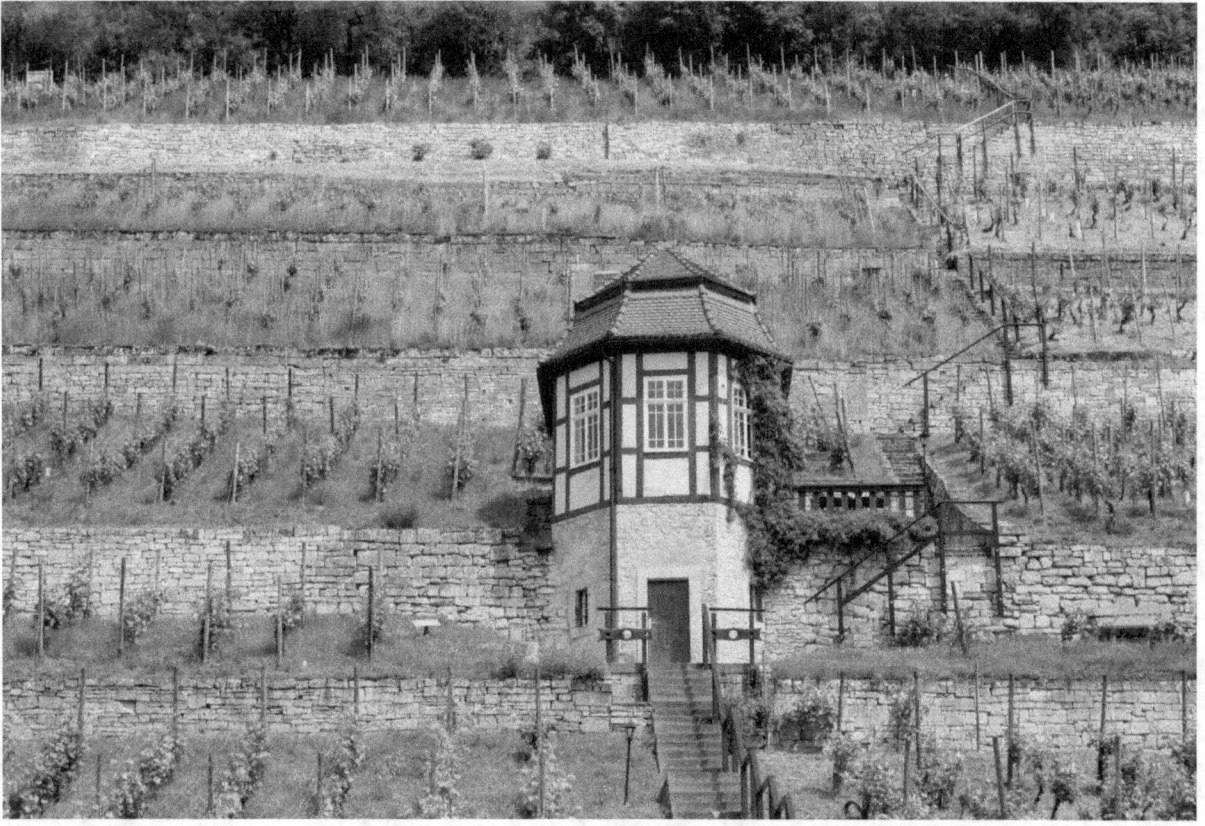

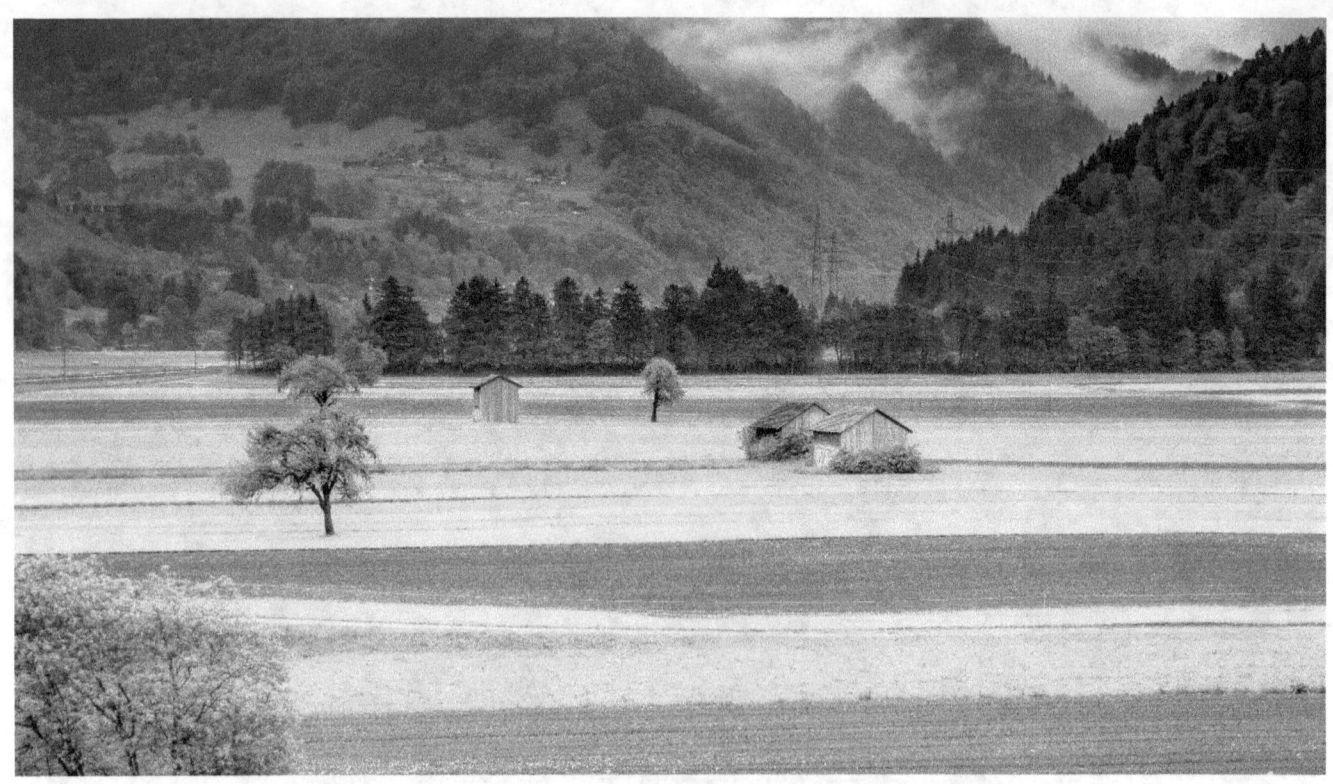

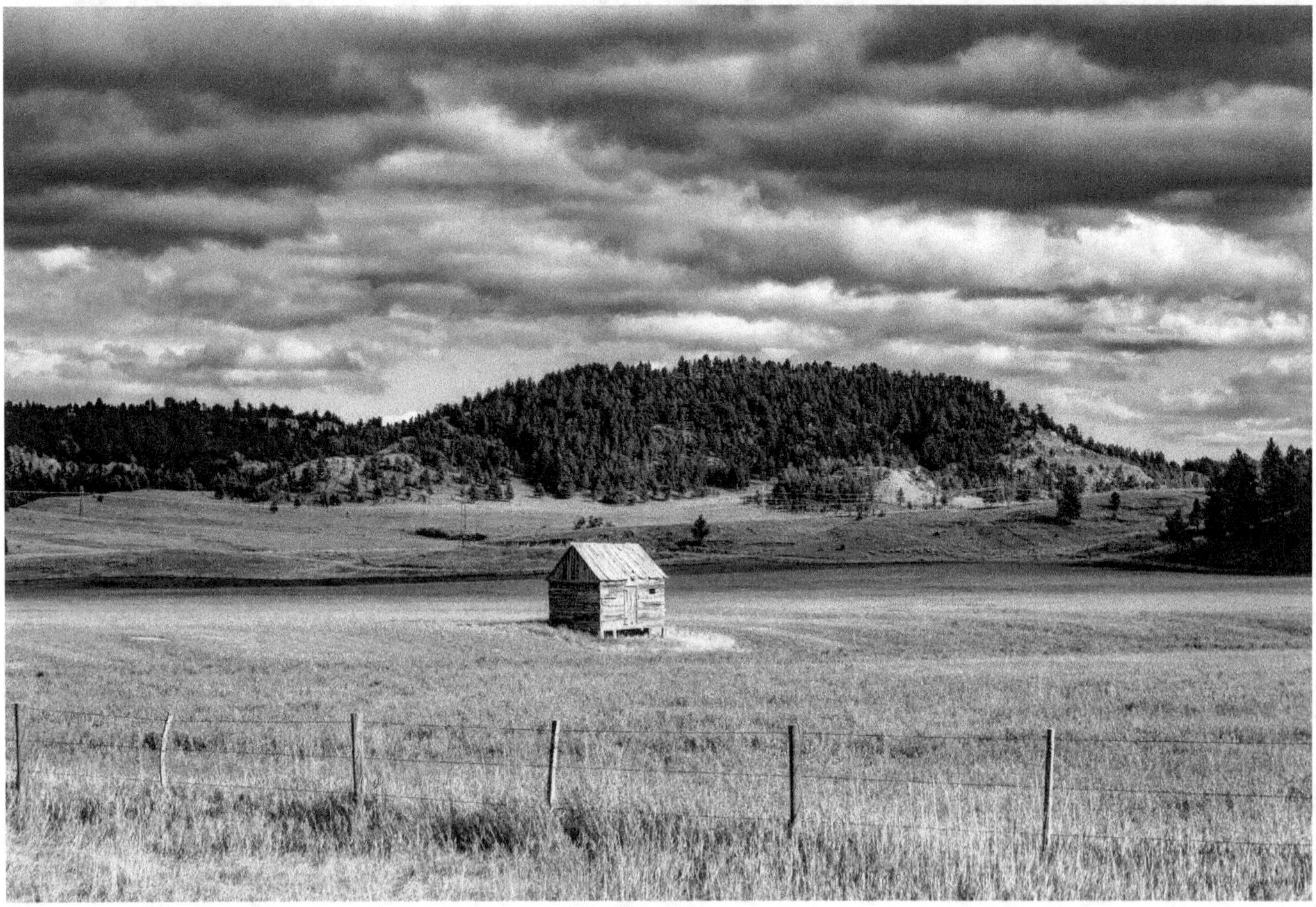

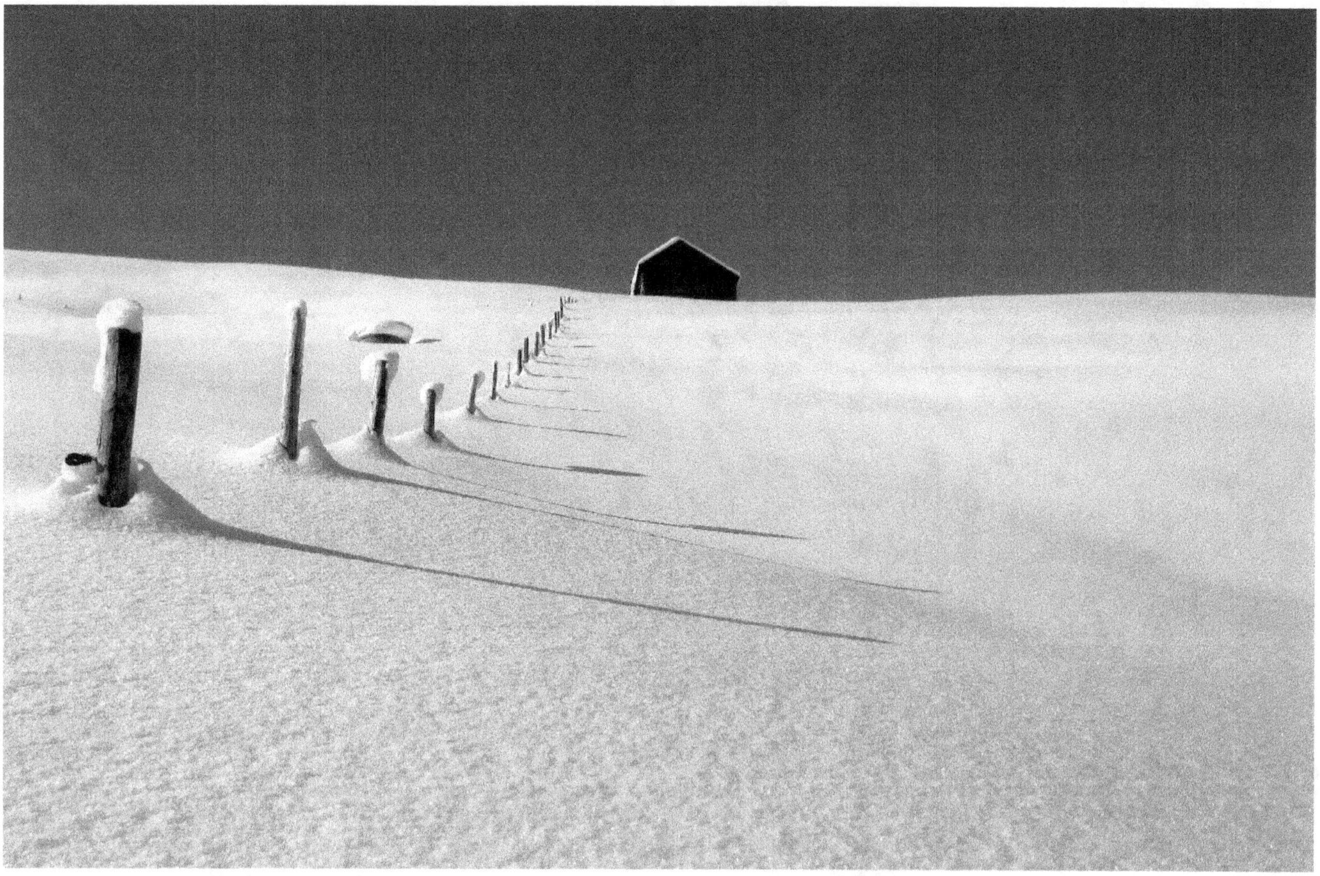

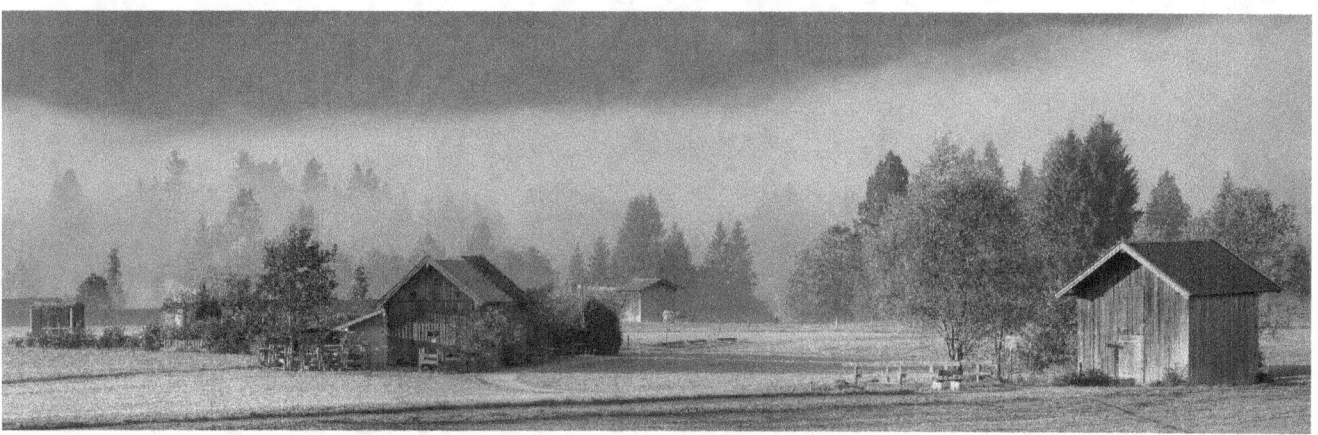

Mud Huts & Adobe

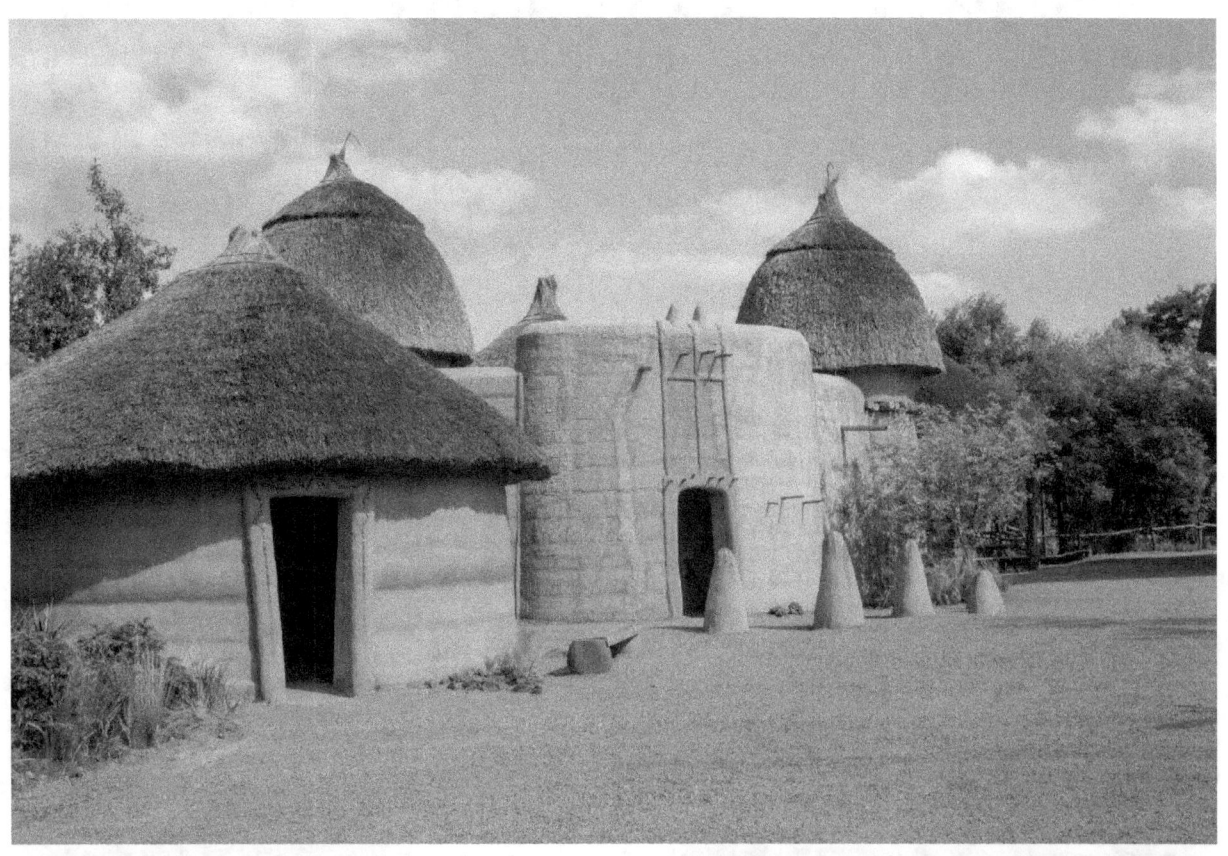

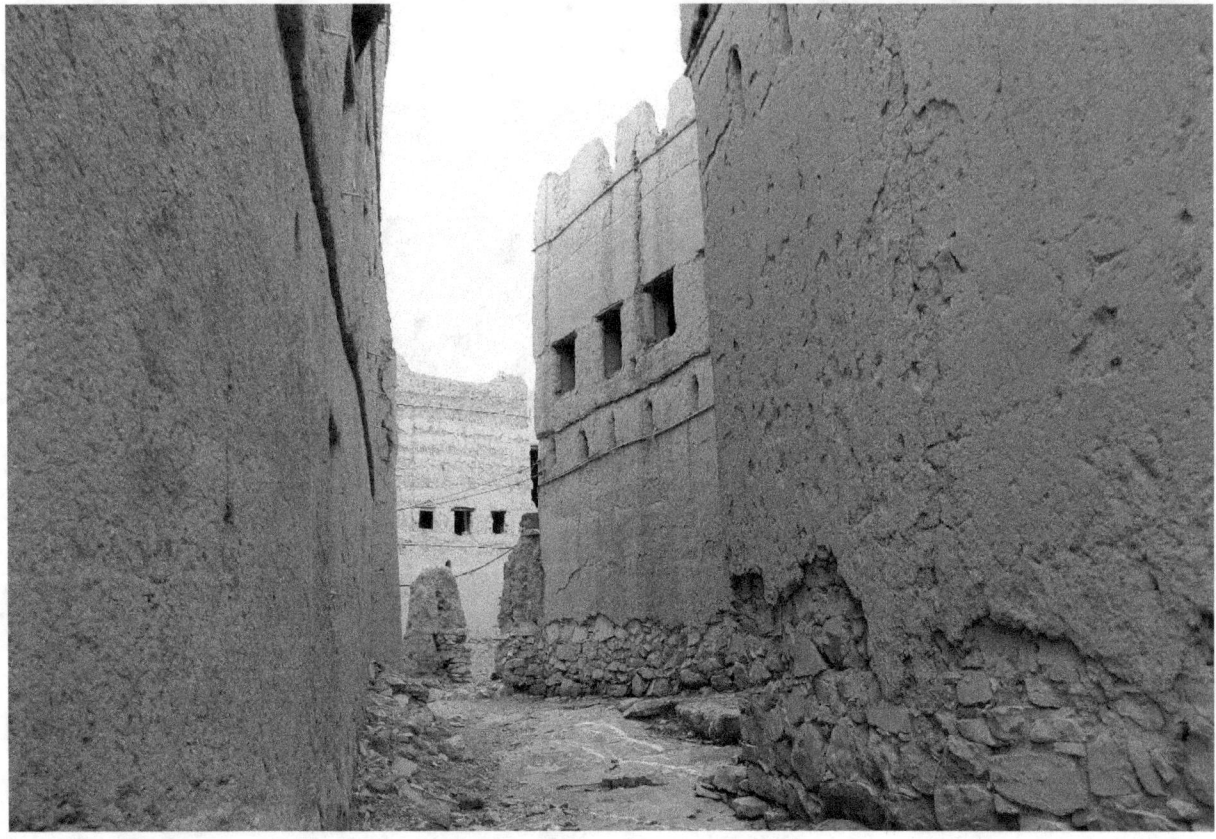

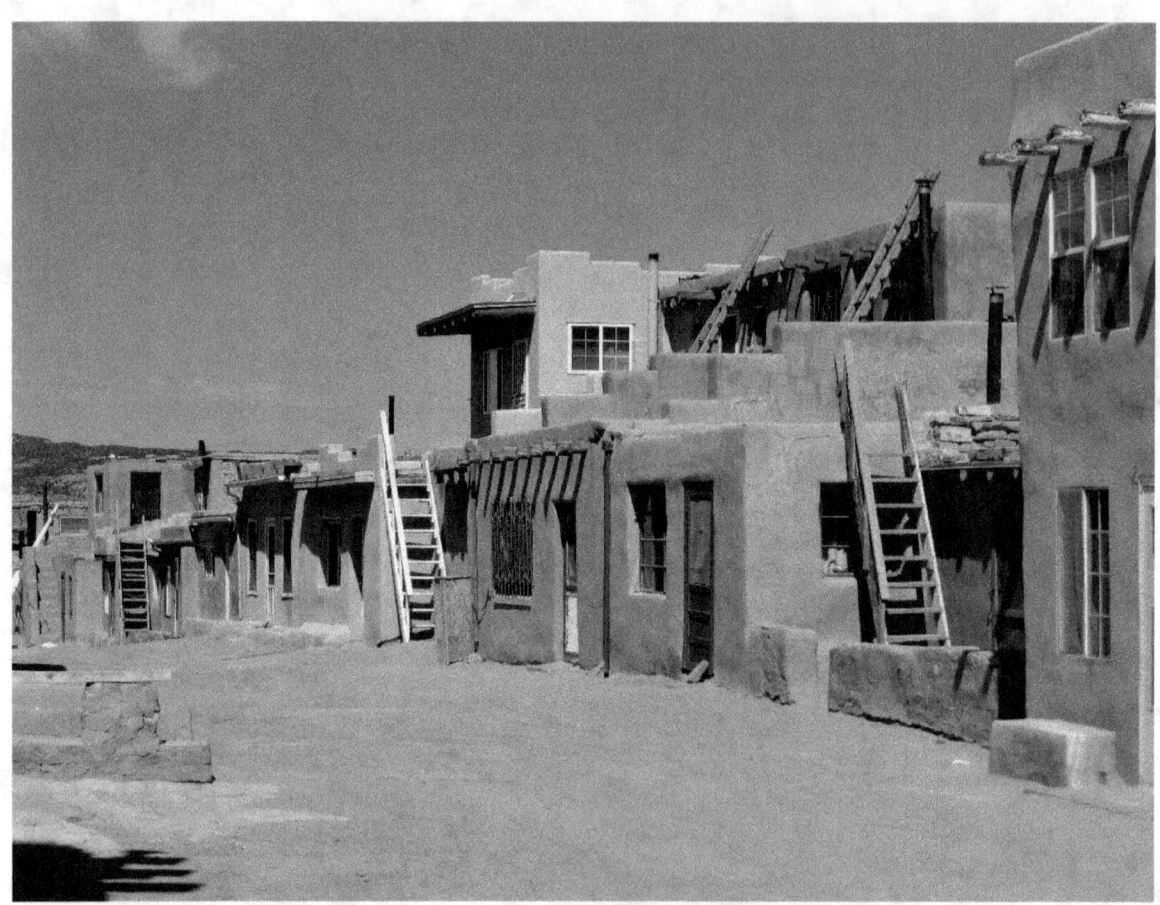

Pueblo (many tiny connected mud block homes)

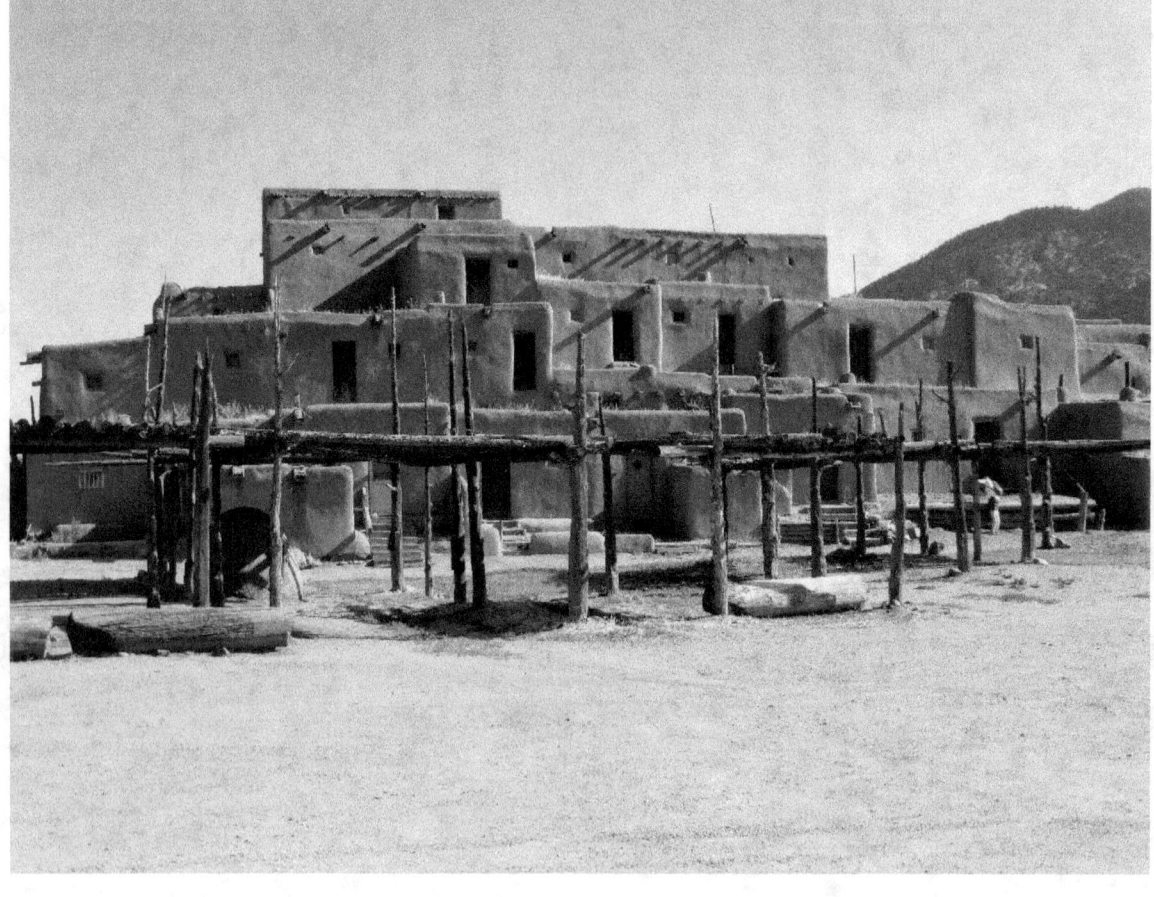

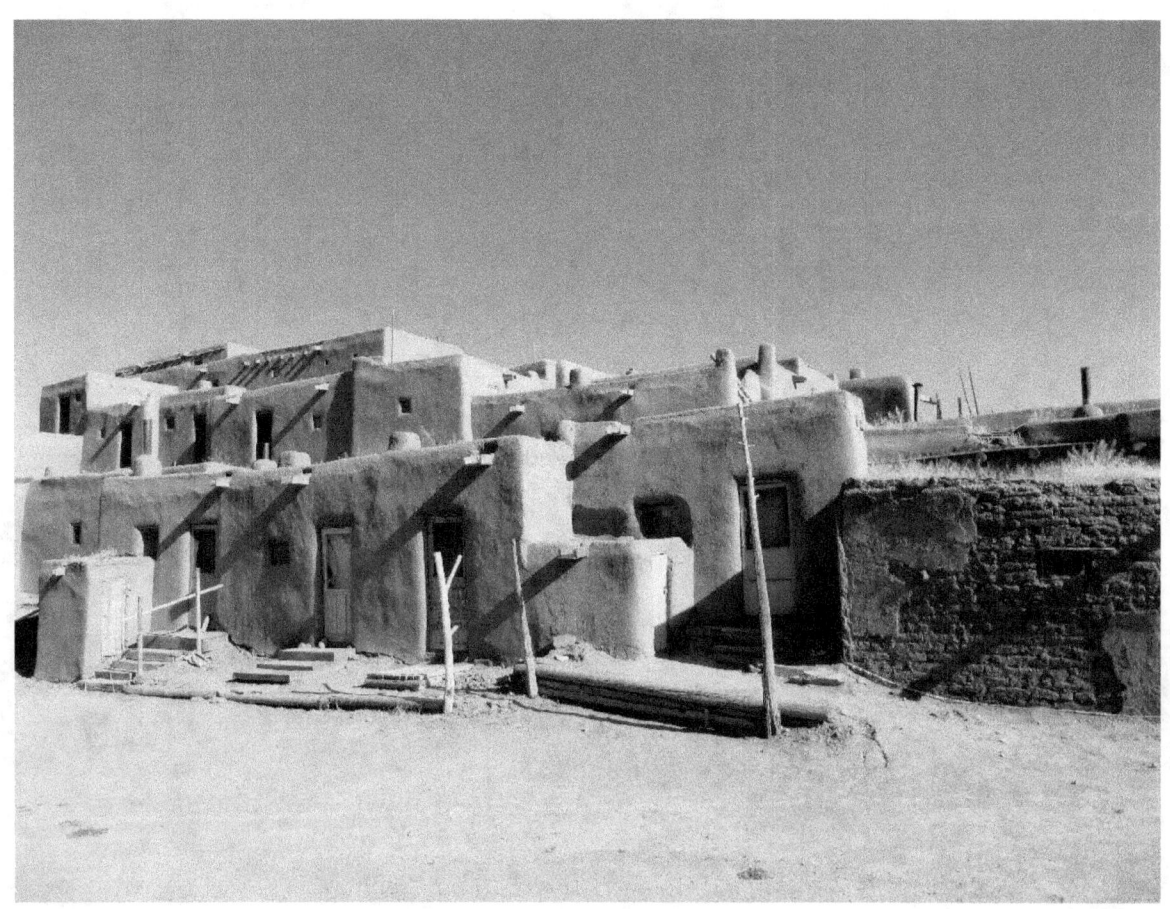

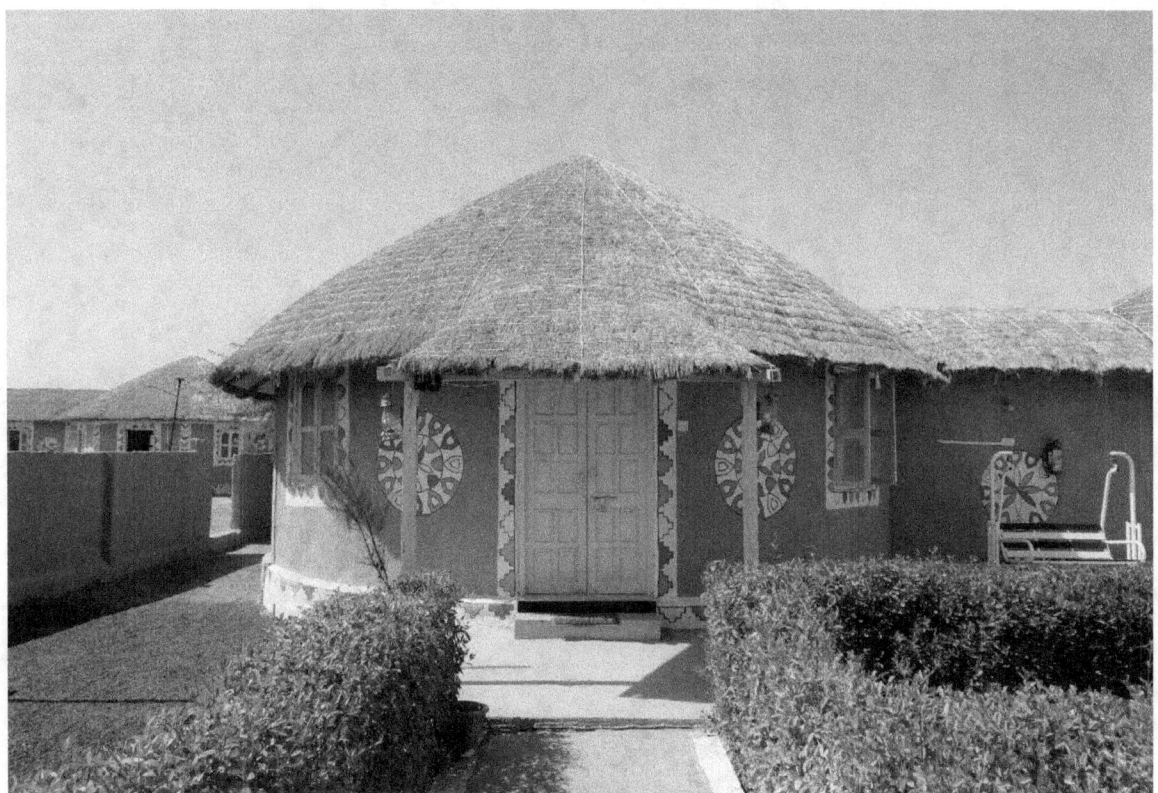

Bhunga

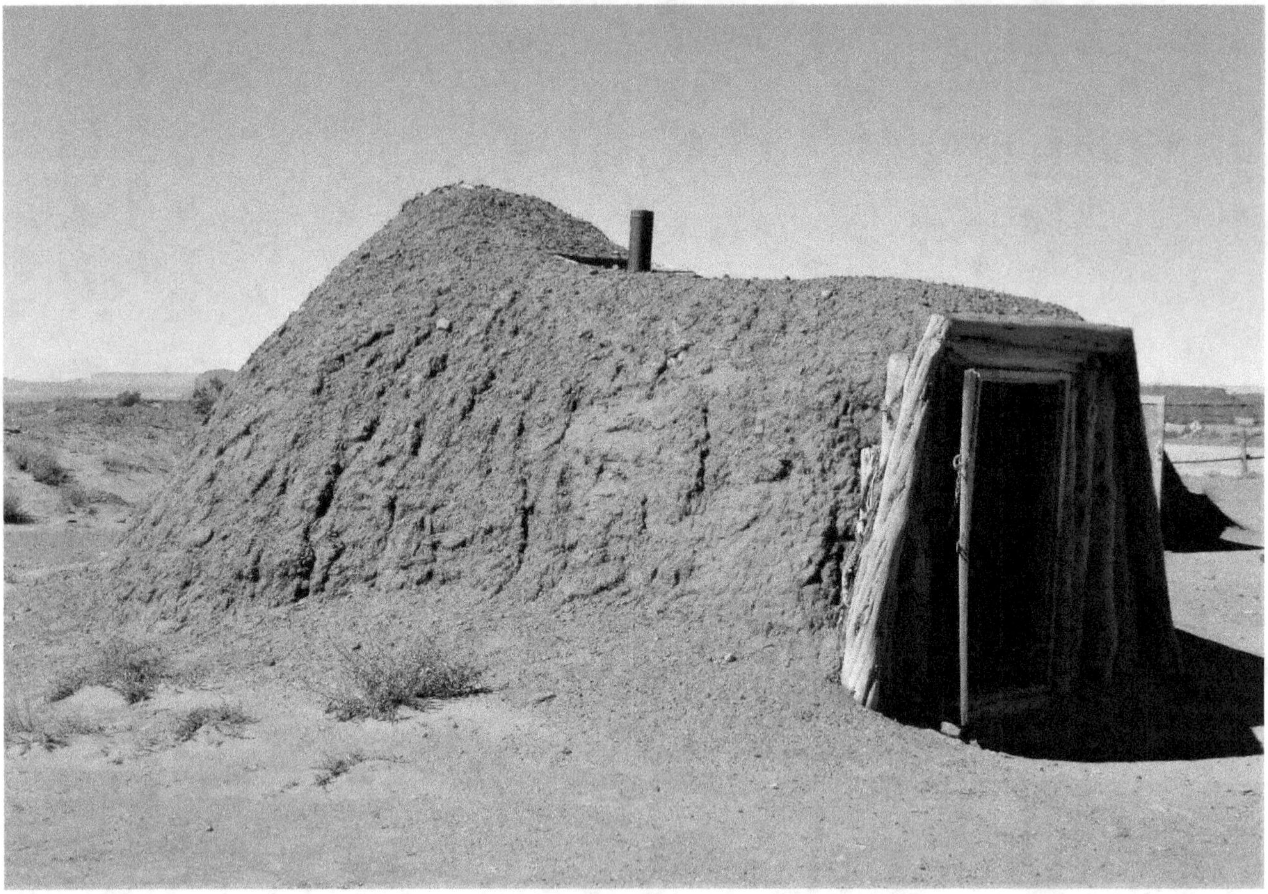

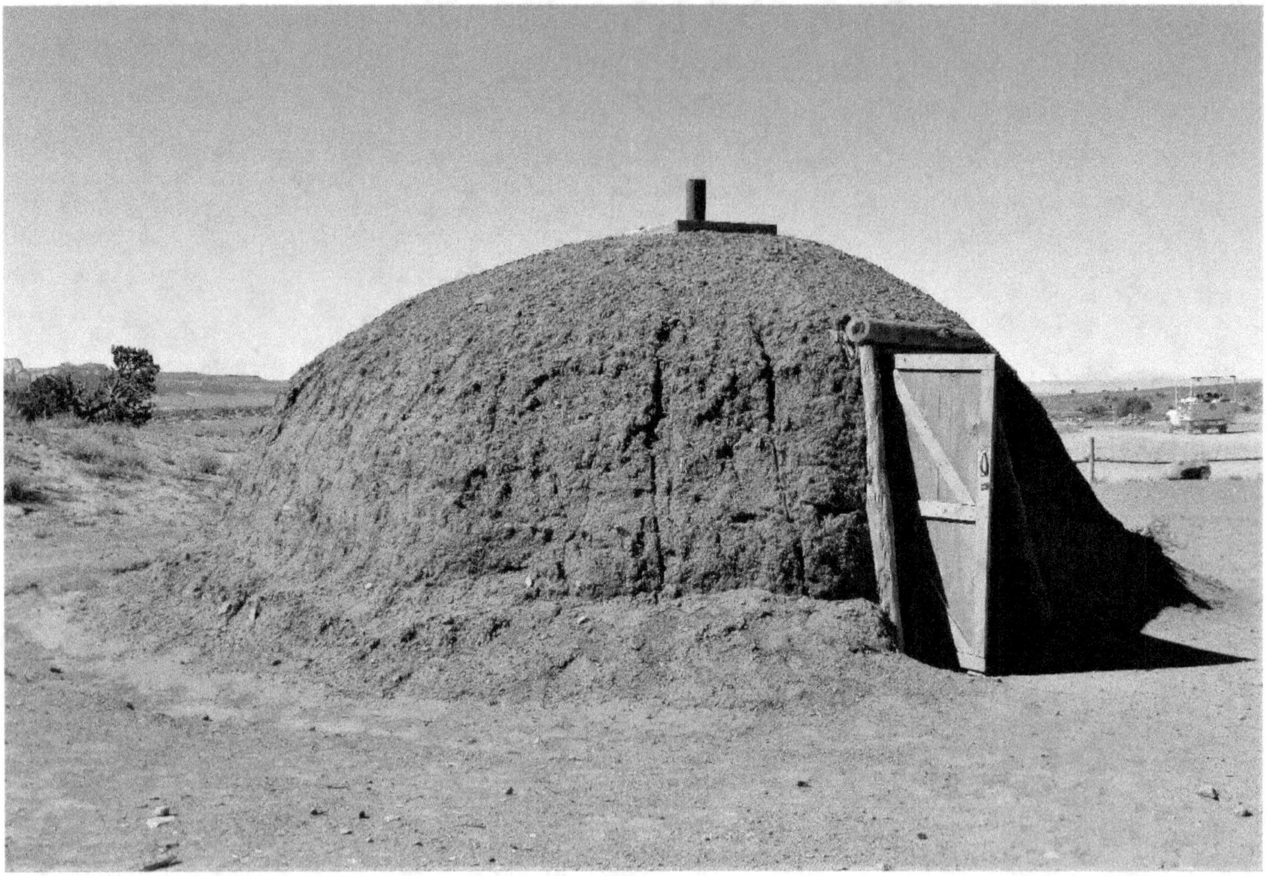

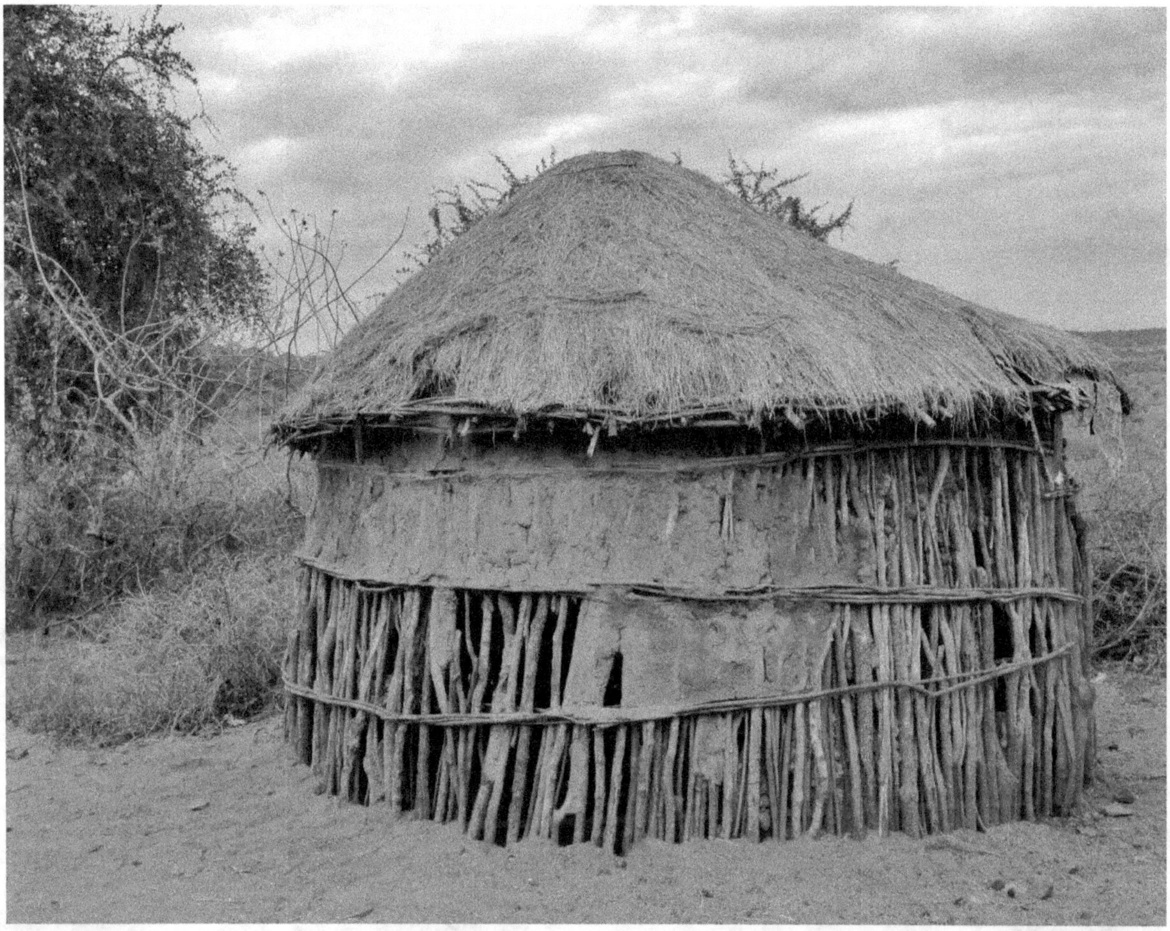

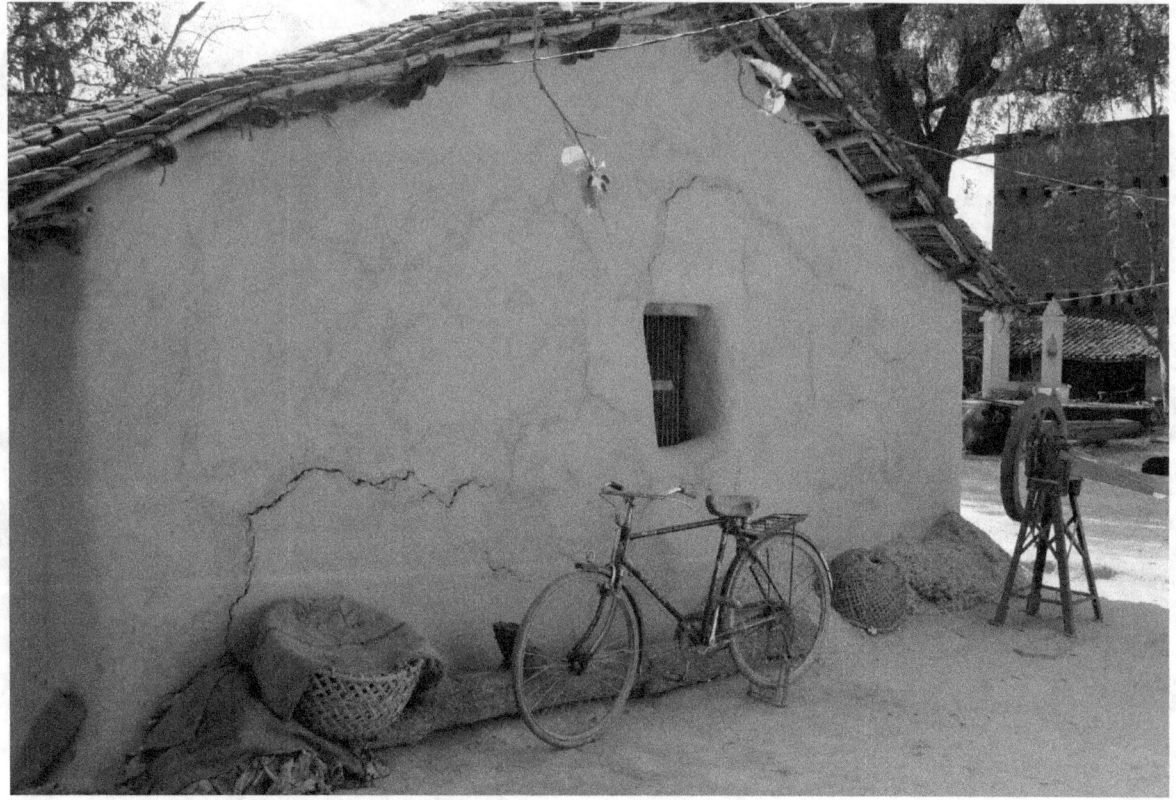

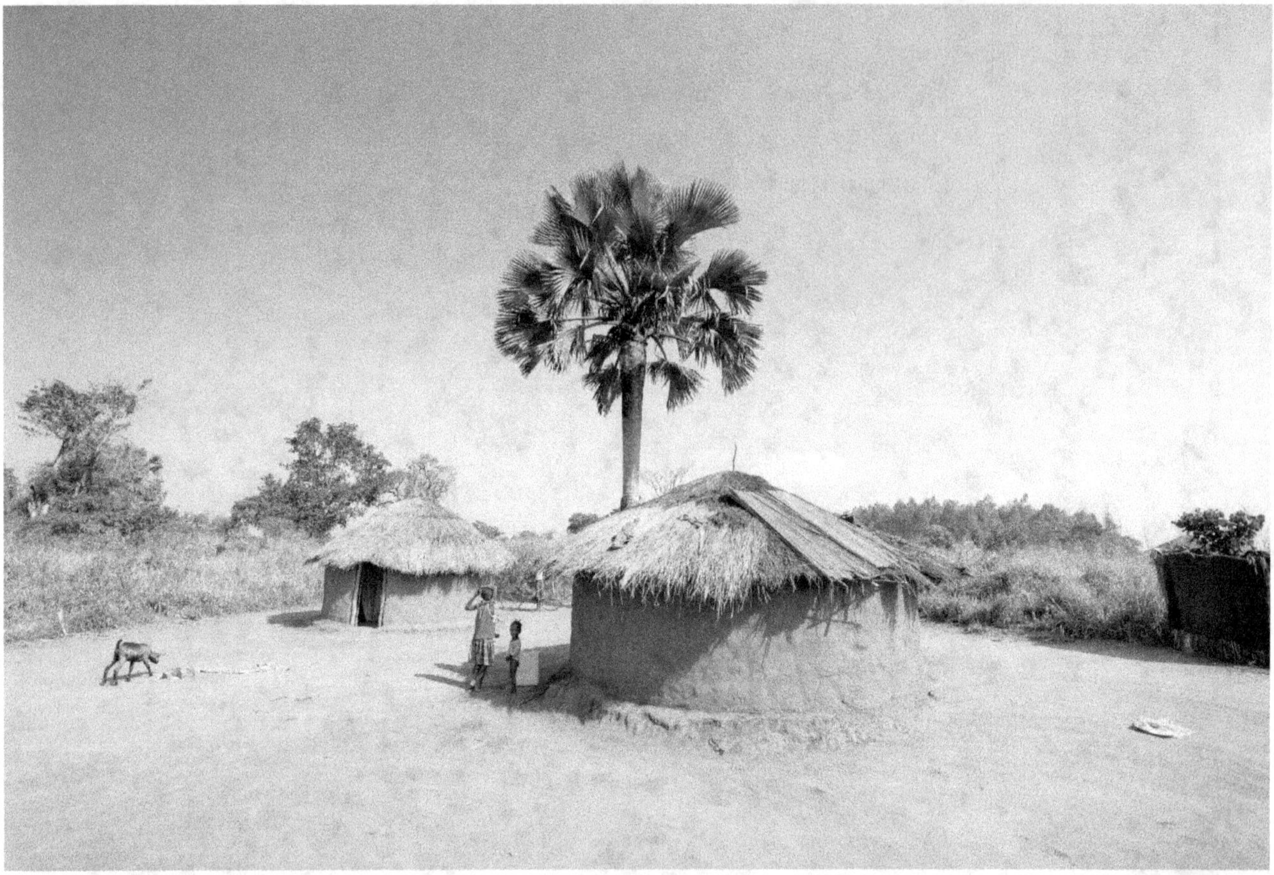

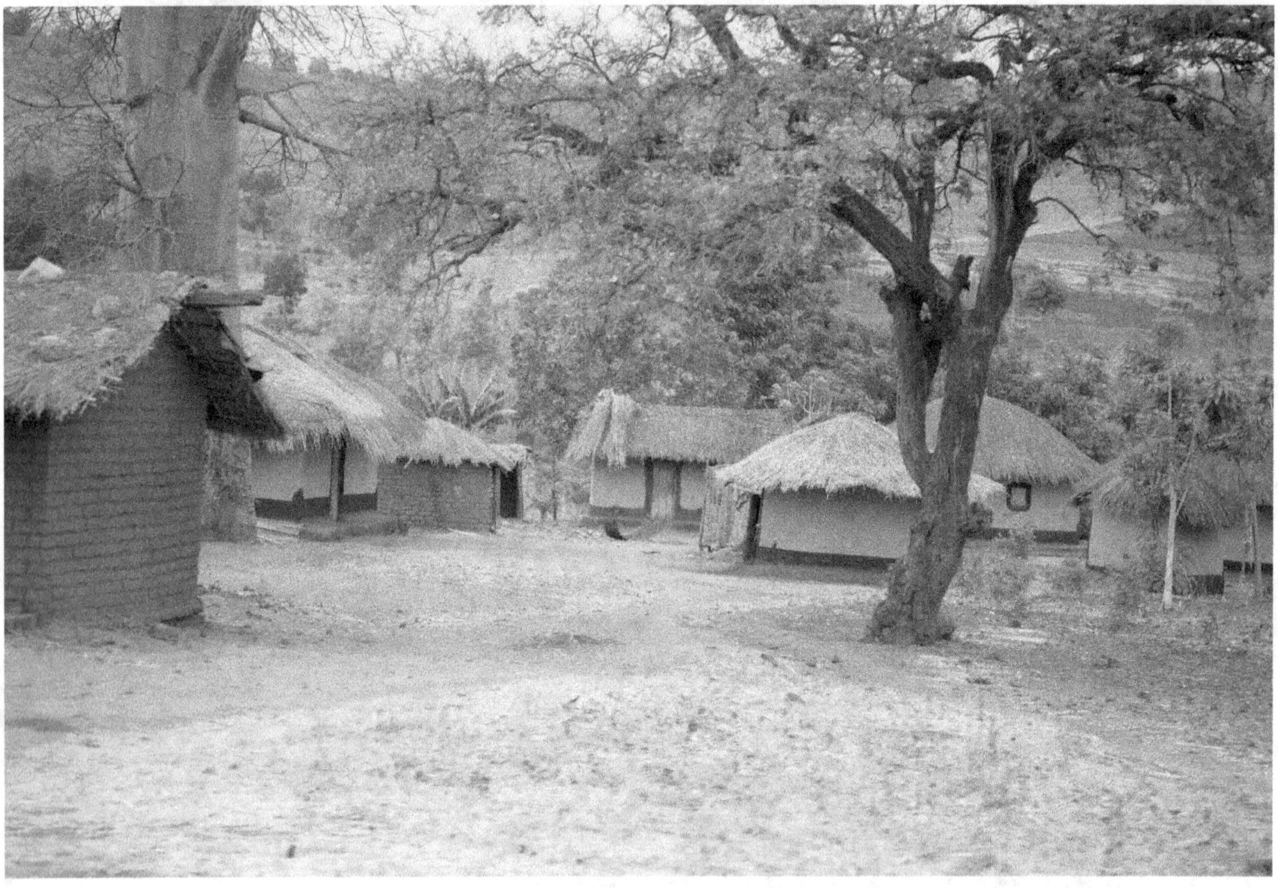

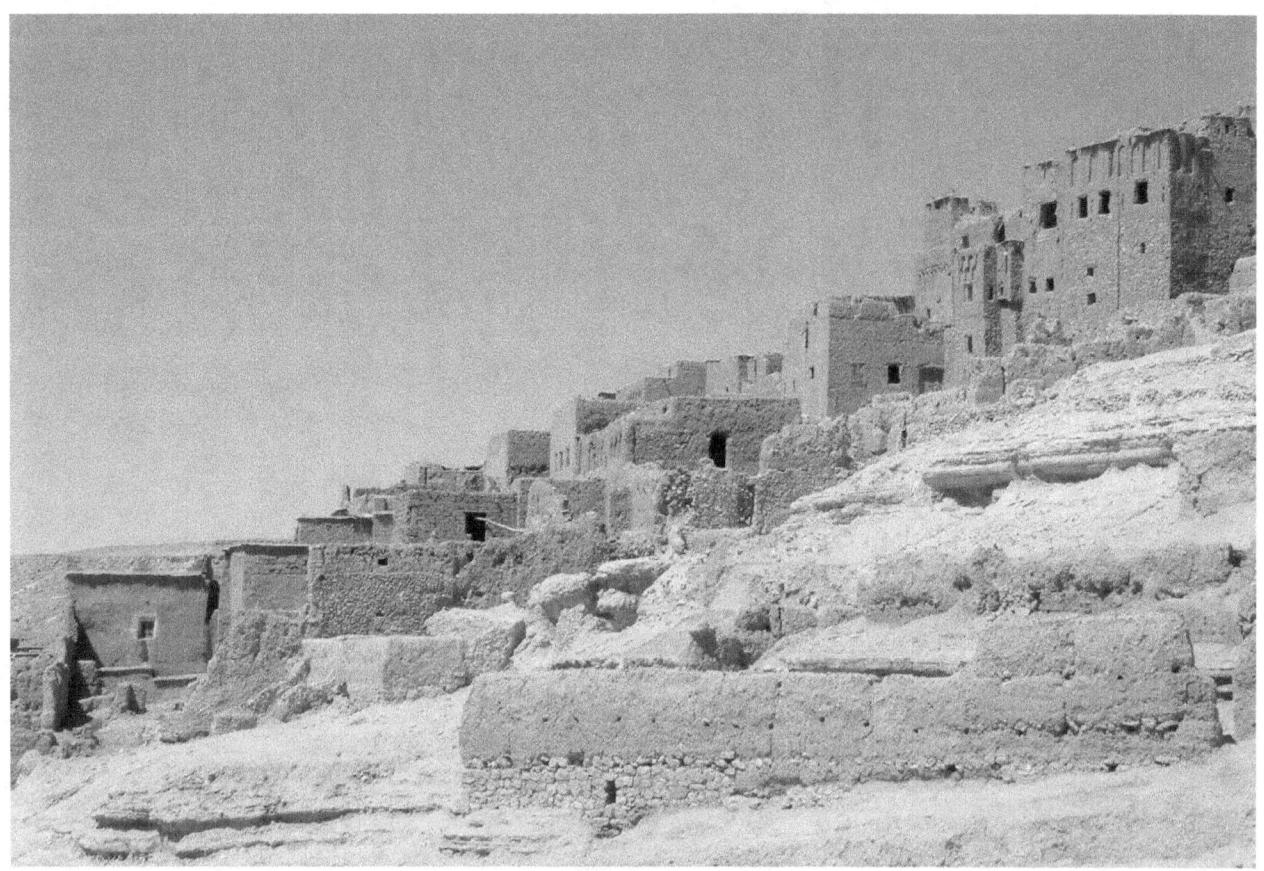

Morocco

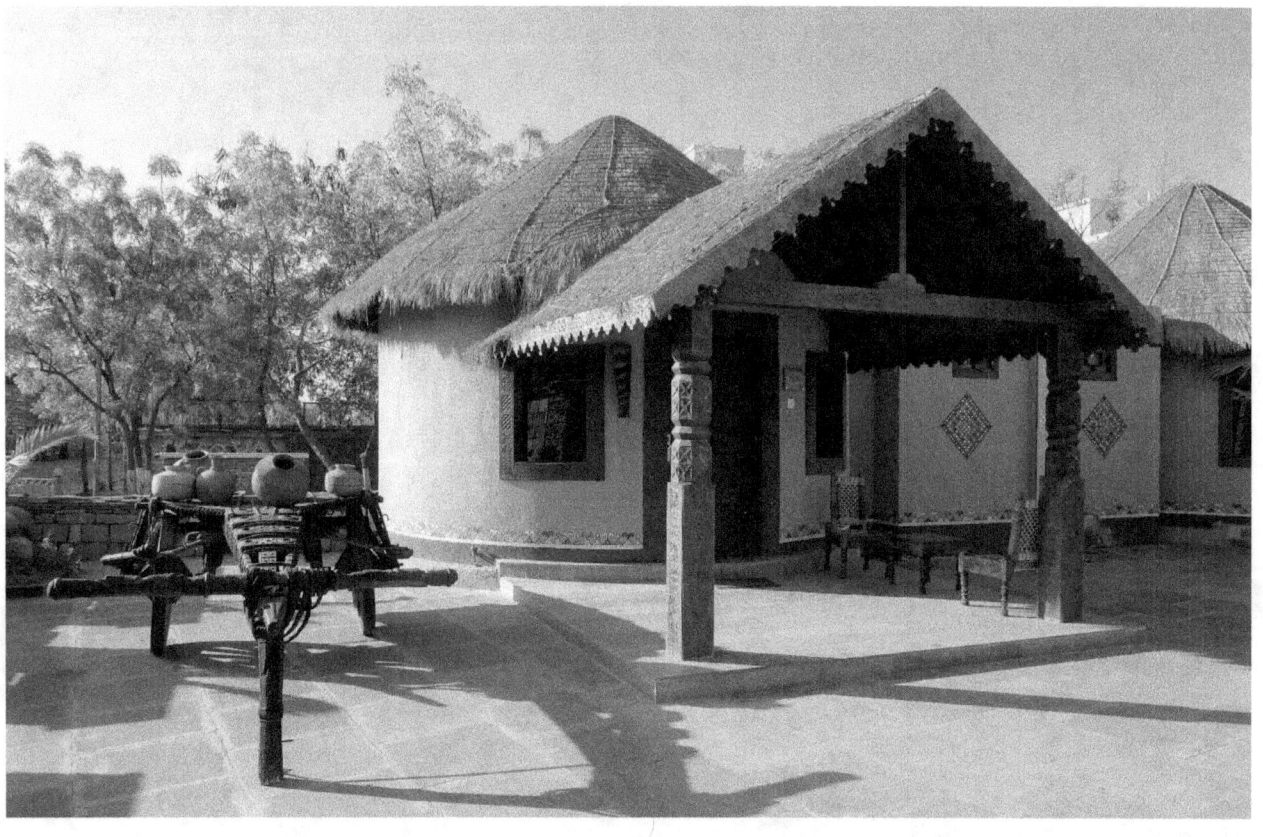

Cave Houses

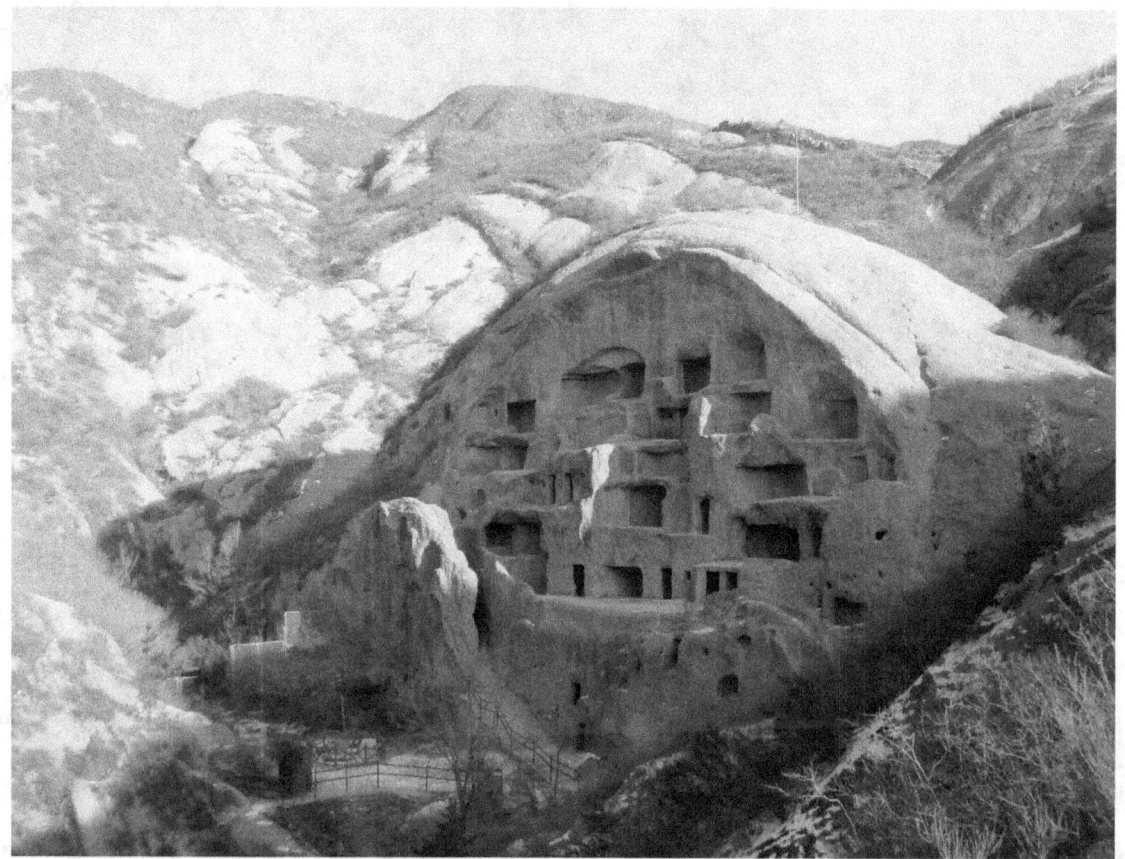

Multiple individual cave dwellings in Guyaju, China

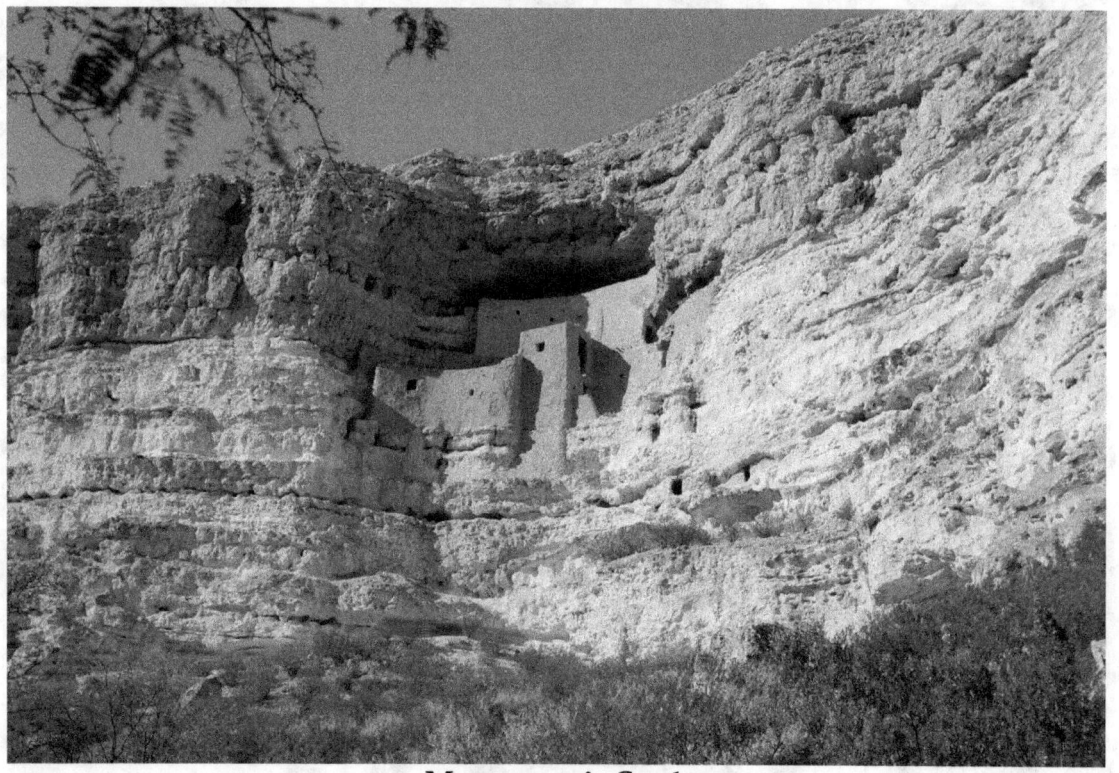

Montezuma's Castle

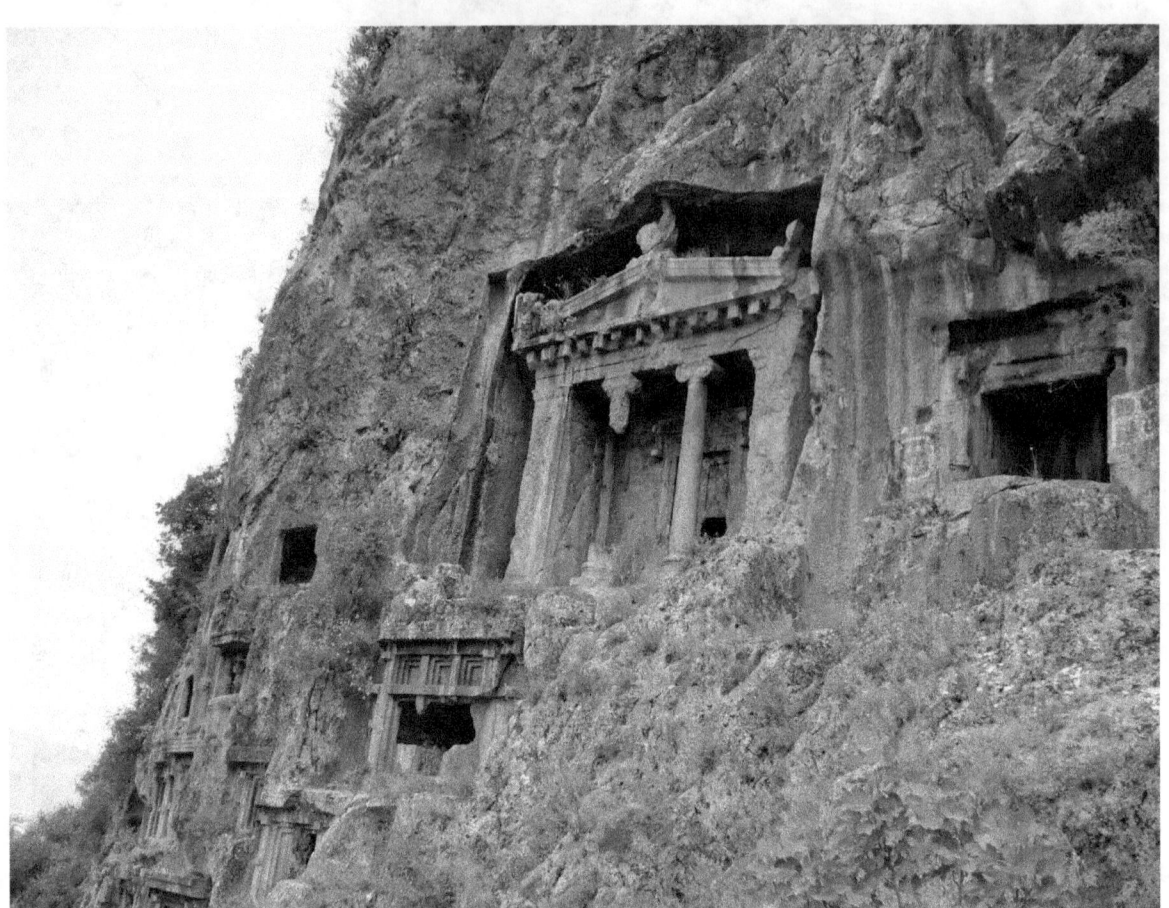

Carved out of stone

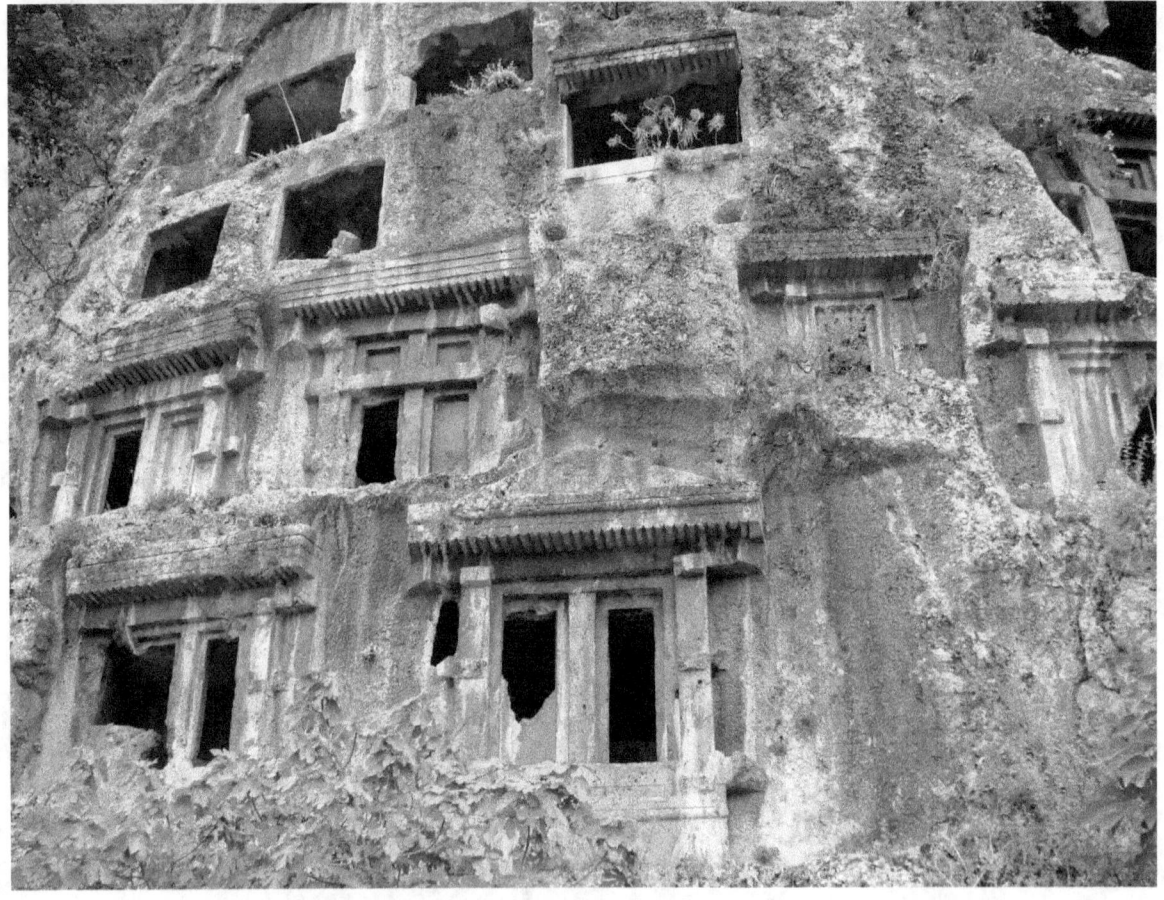

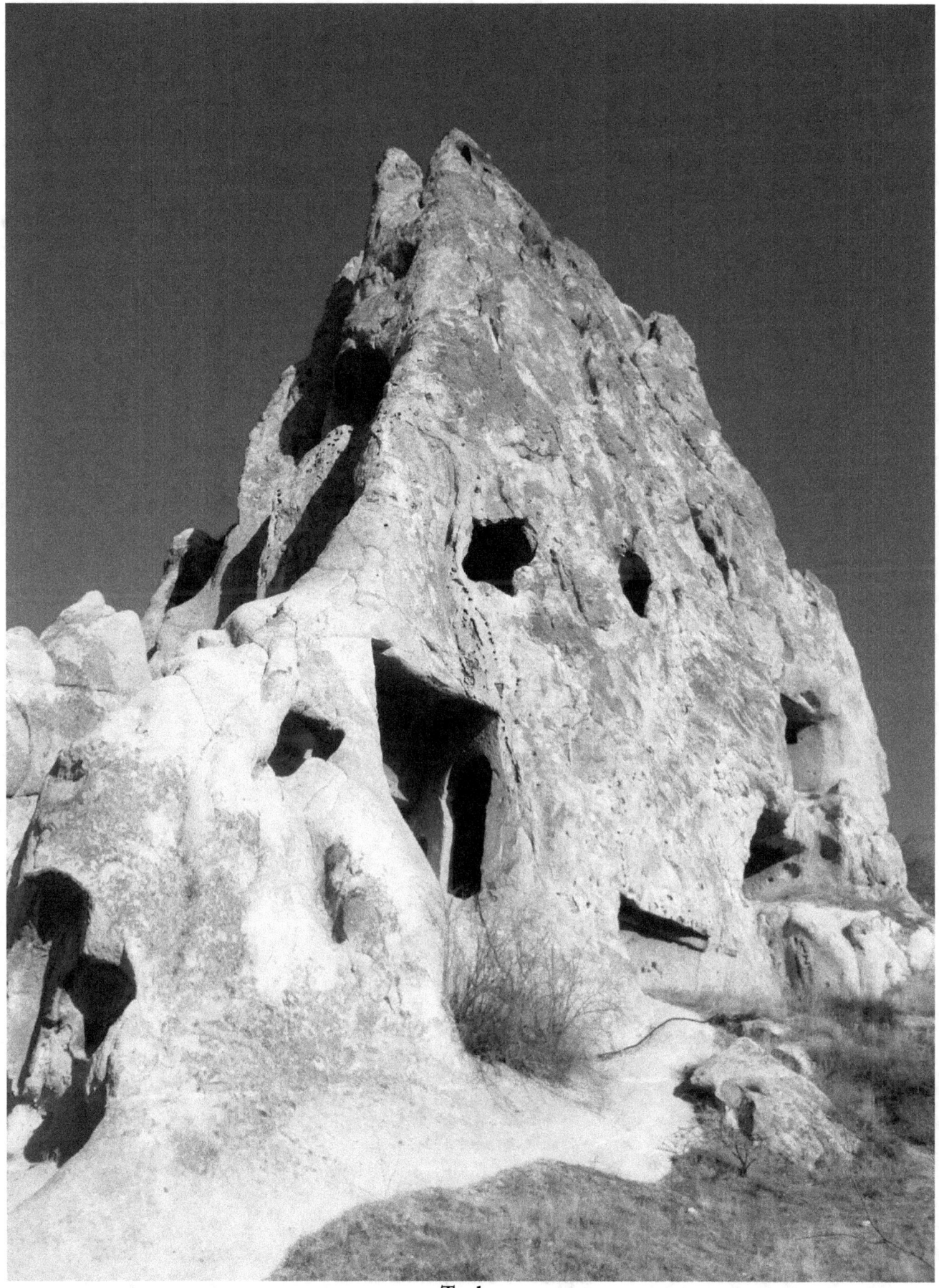

Turkey

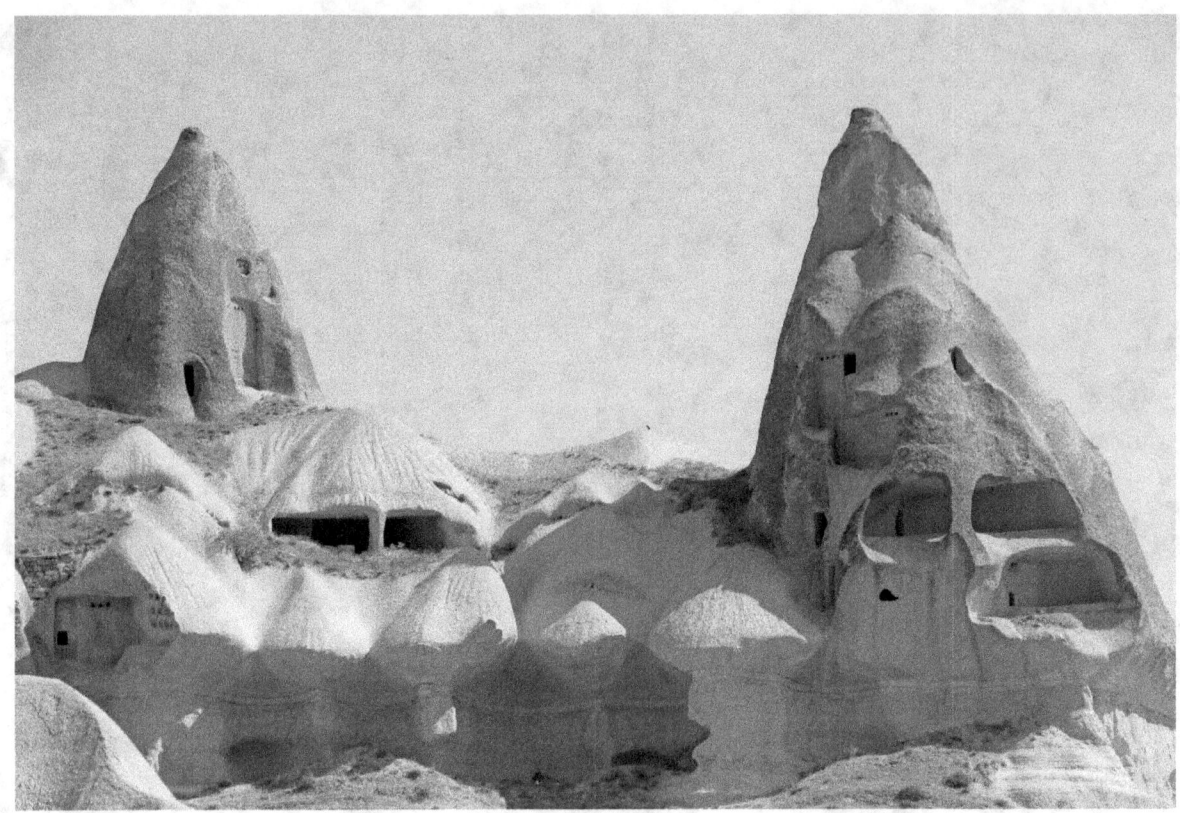

Cappadocia, Turkey

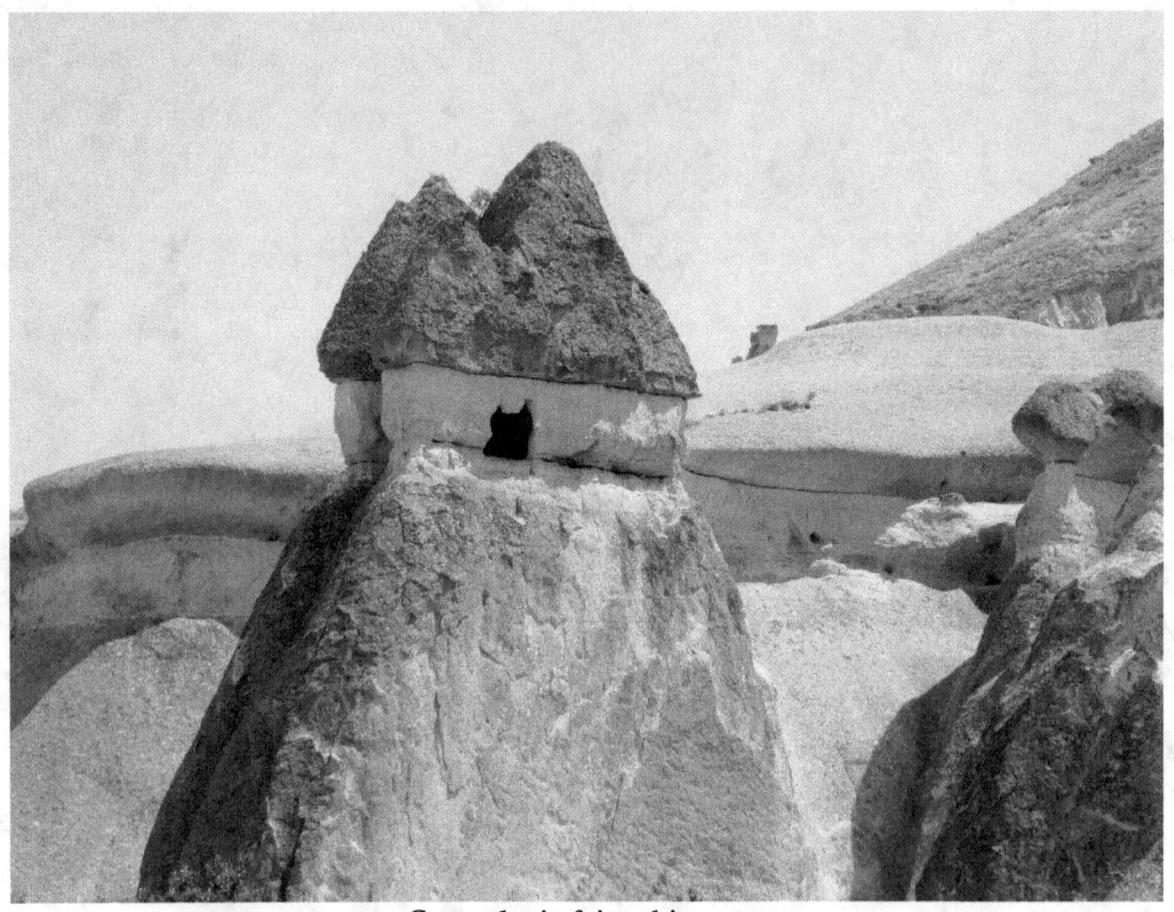

Cappadocia fairy chimneys

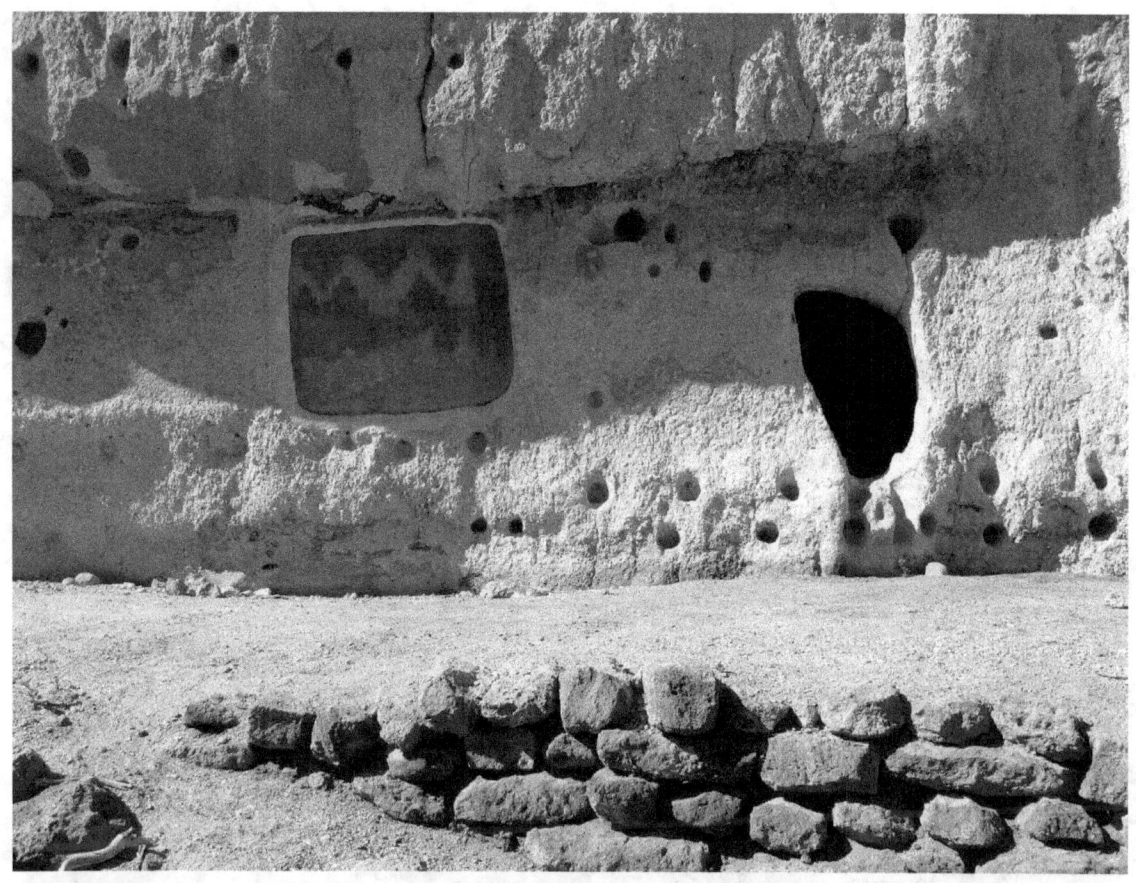

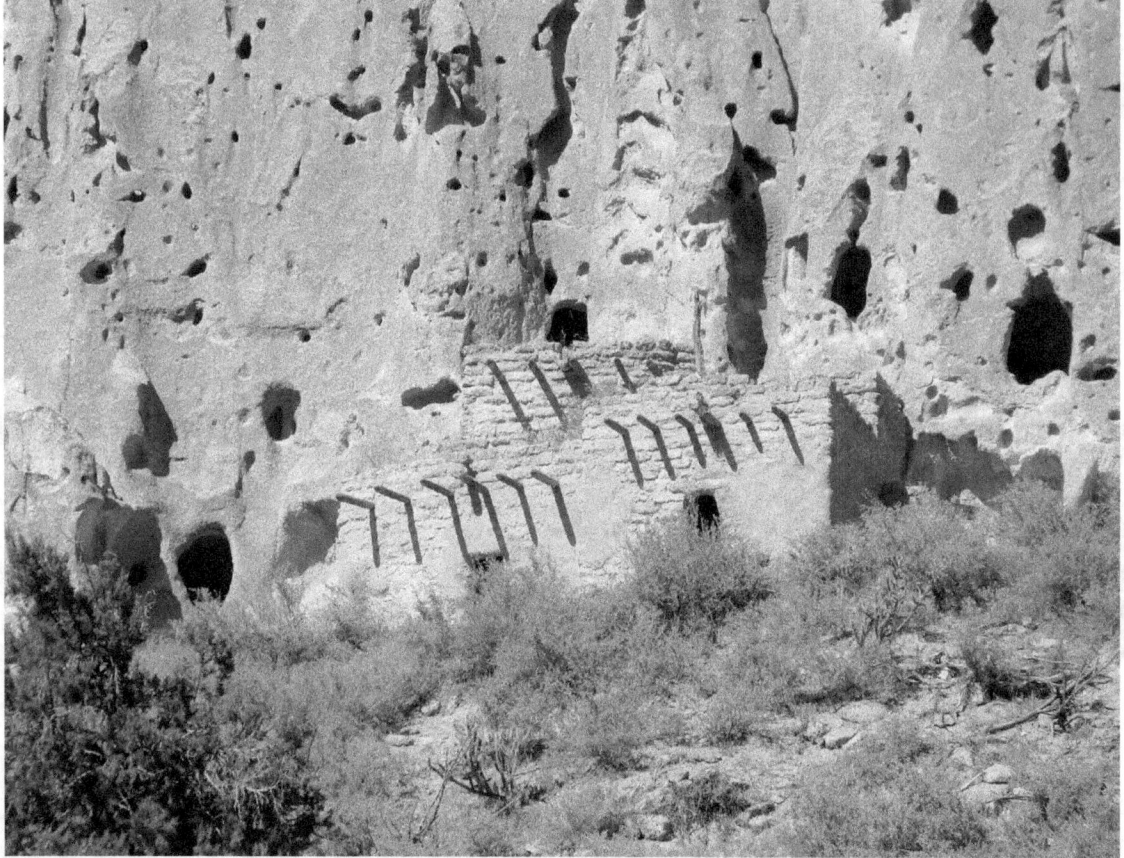

Bandalier National Monument, NM

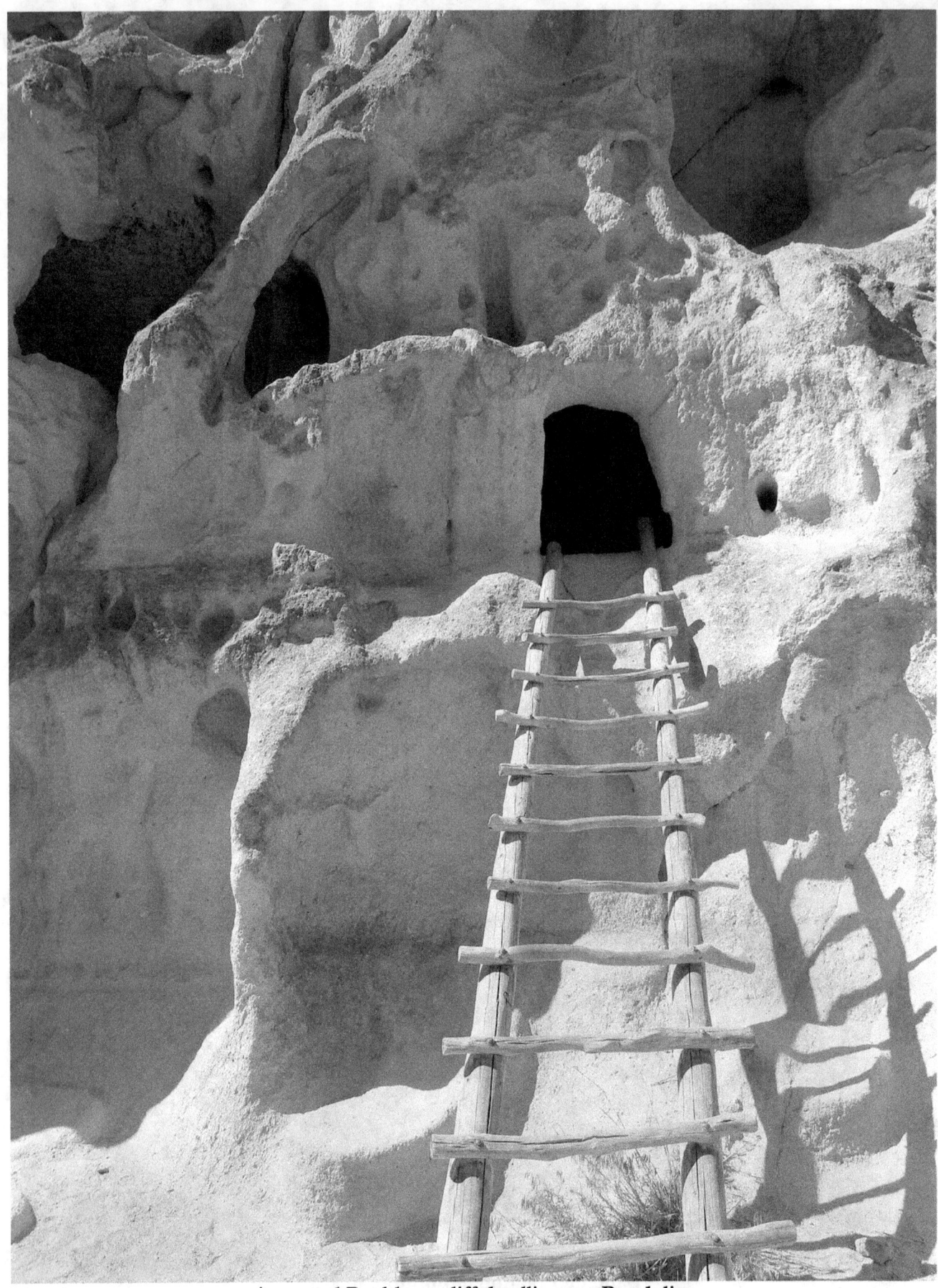

Ancestral Puebloan cliff dwellings at Bandalier

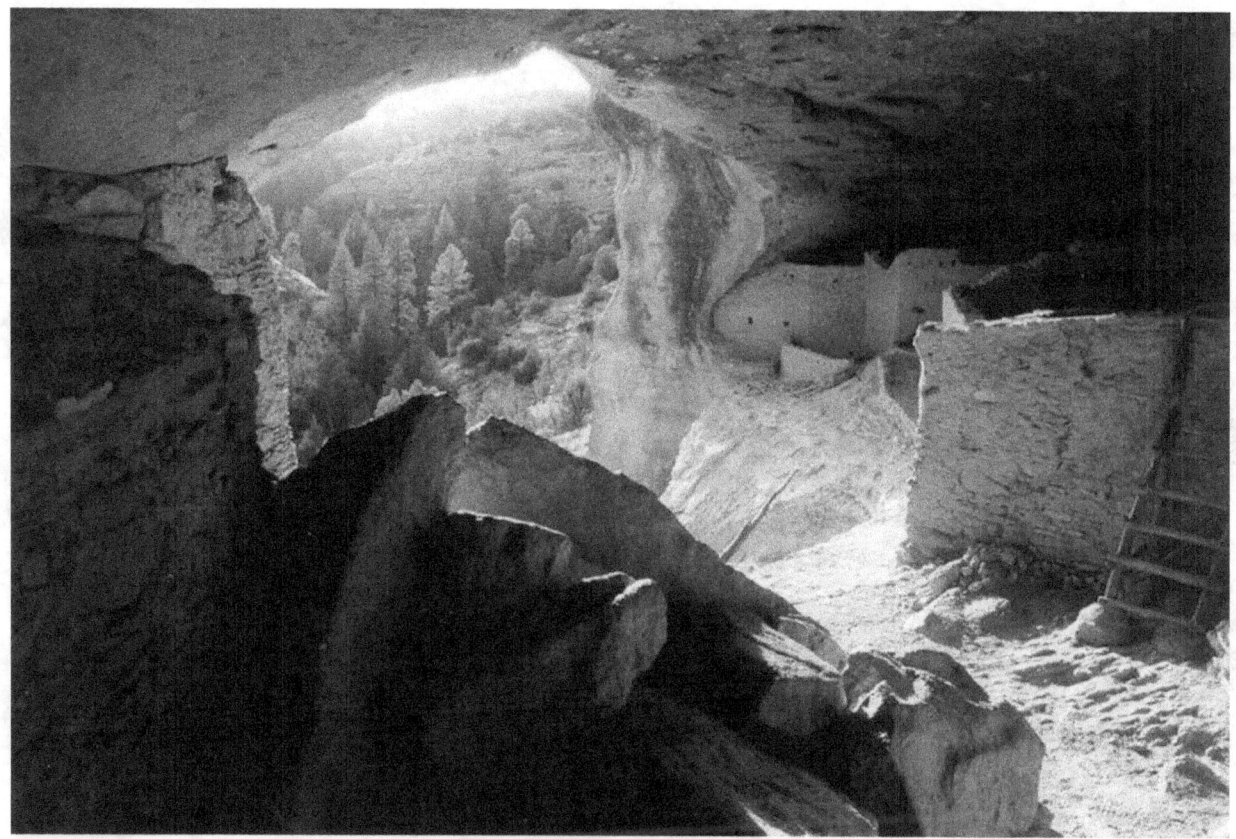

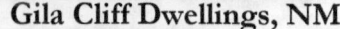
Gila Cliff Dwellings, NM

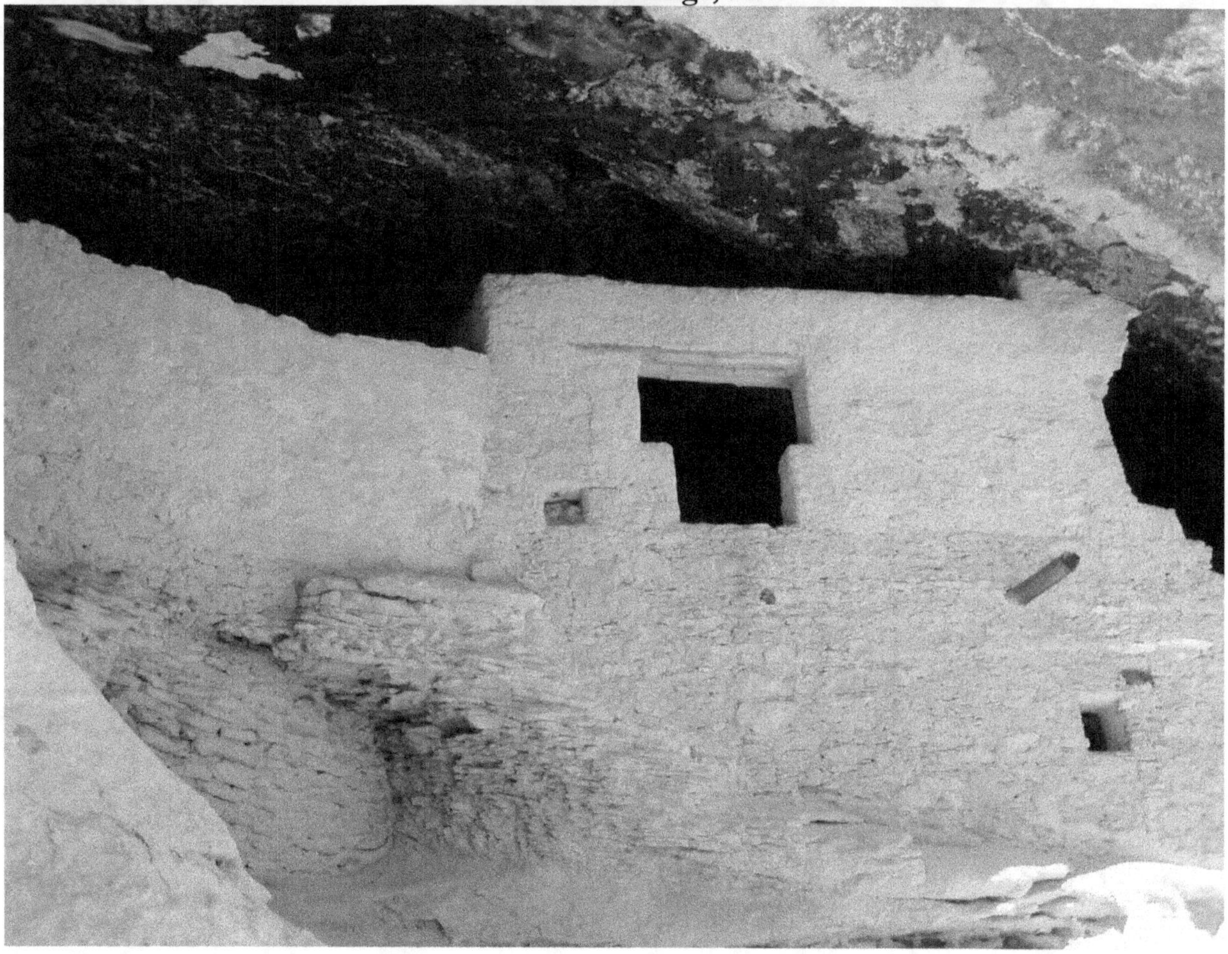

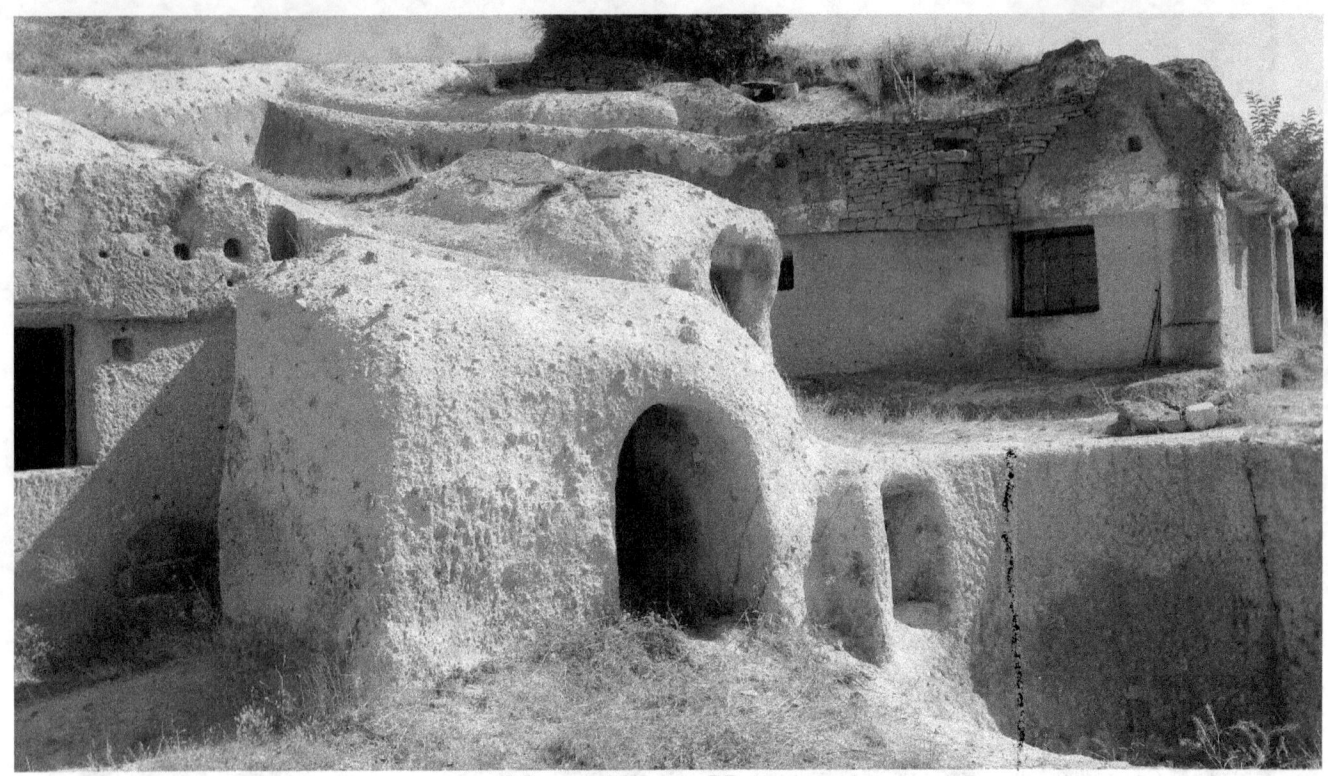

Noszvaj caves, Hungary

This page is intentionally left blank

3 WATER

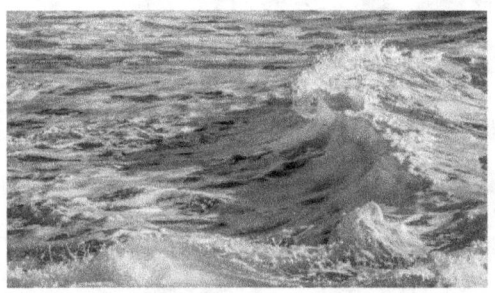

Beach houses, boathouses, fancy and simple, and multiples

Beach Houses

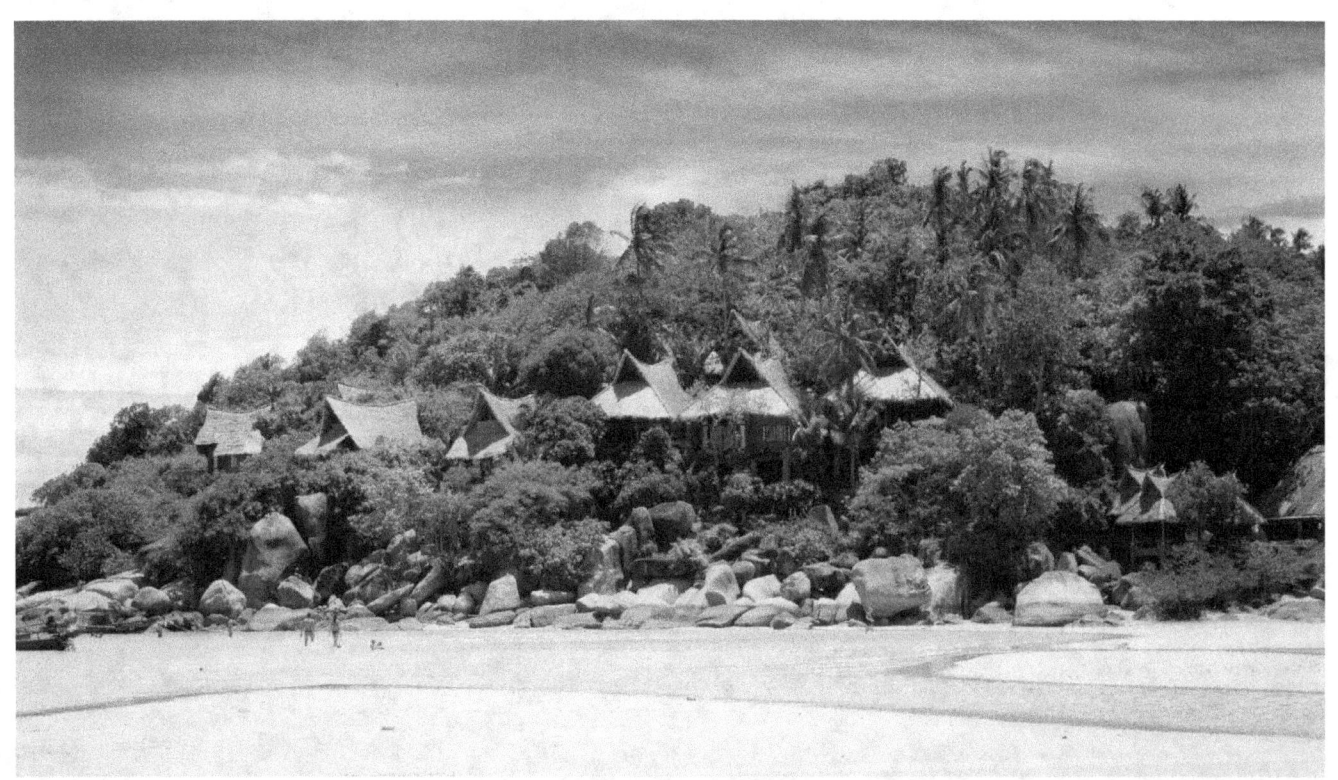

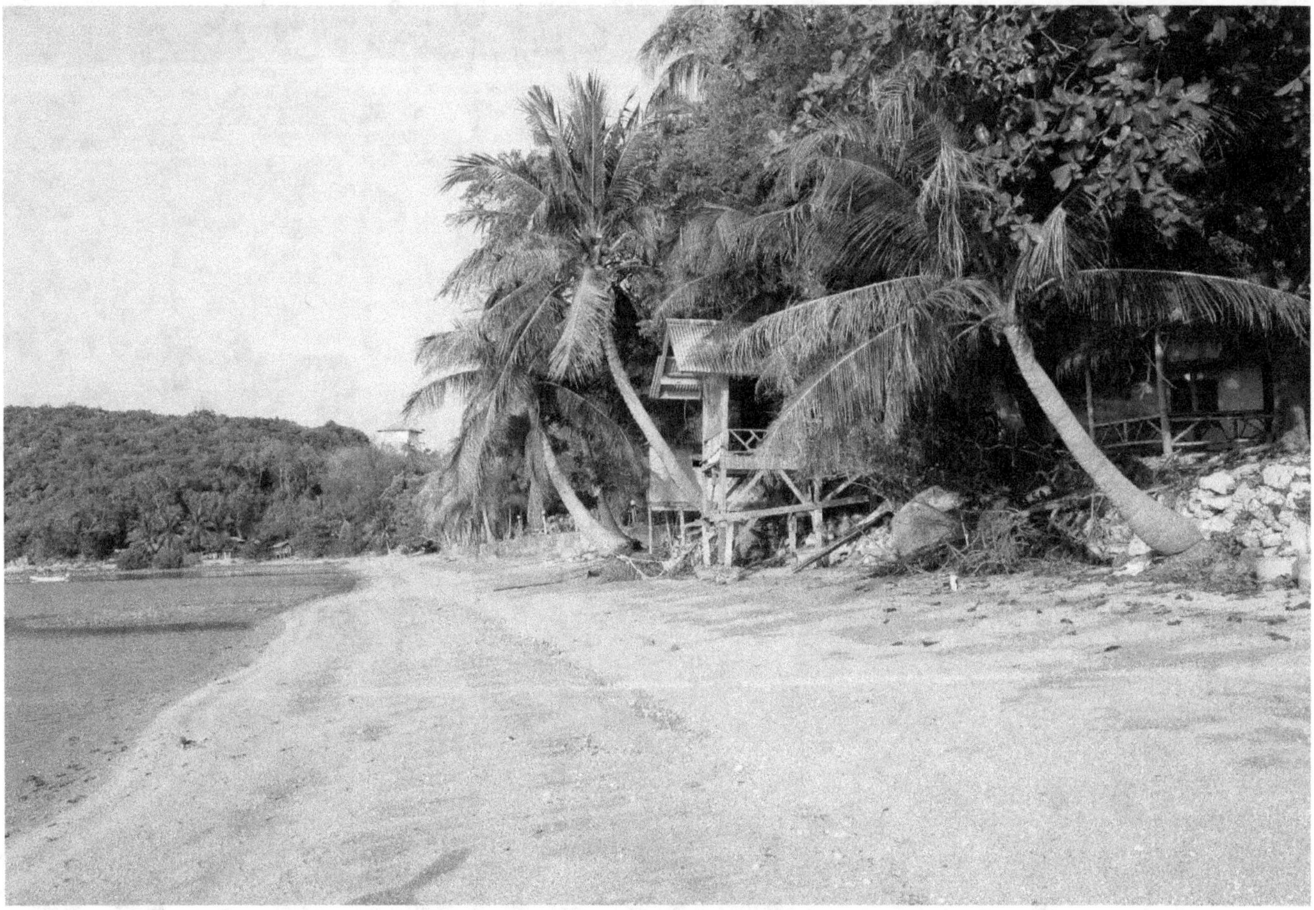

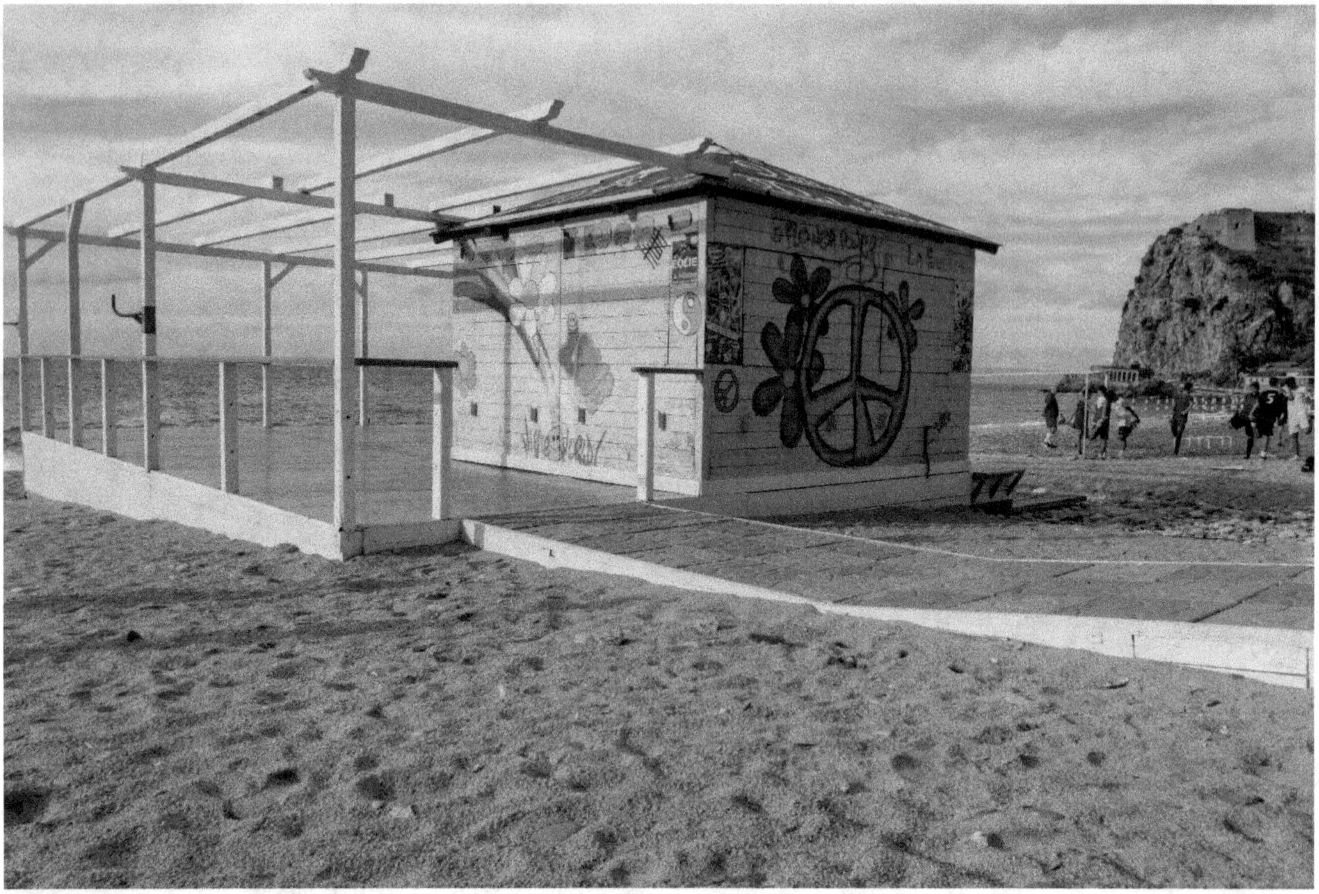

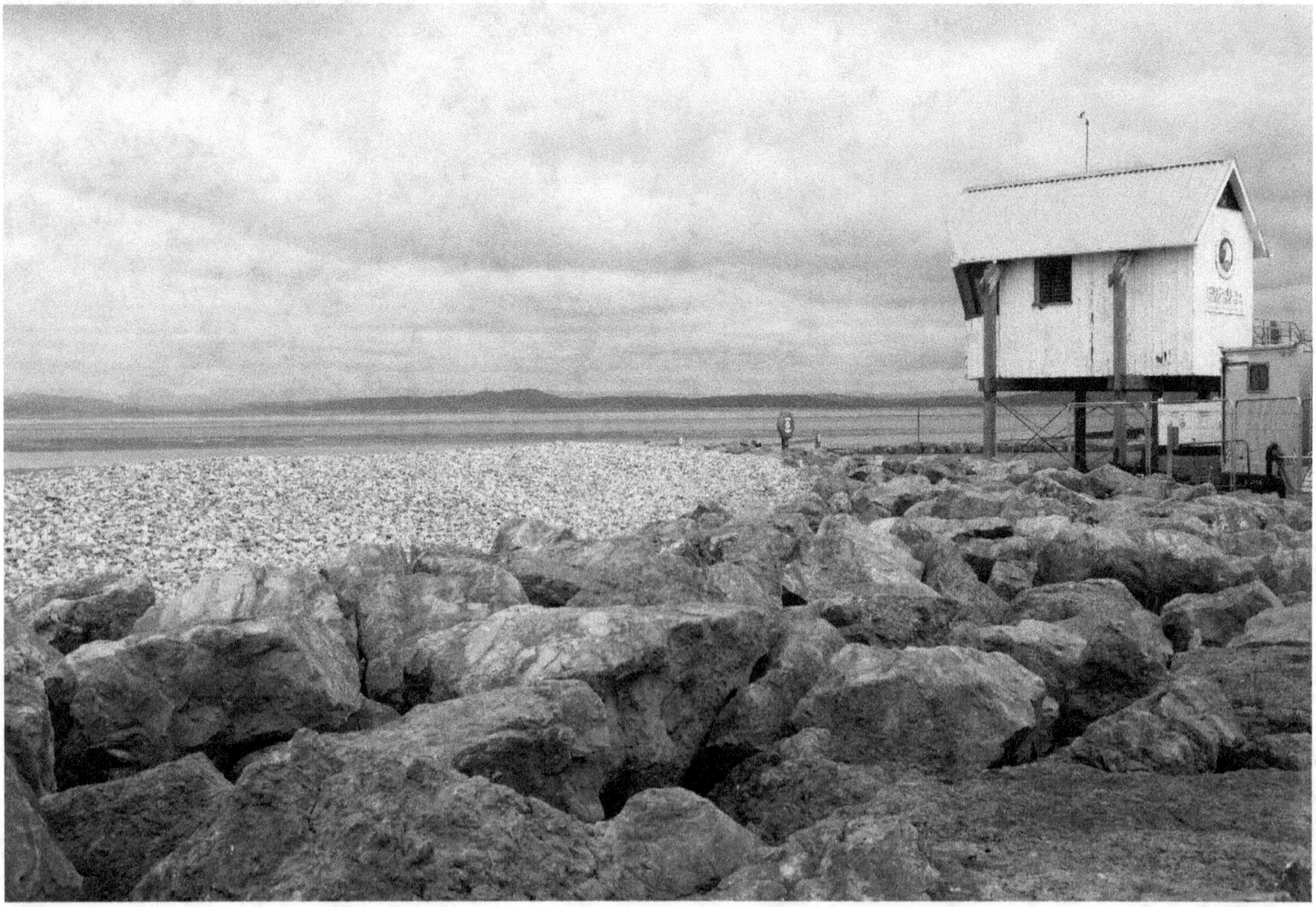

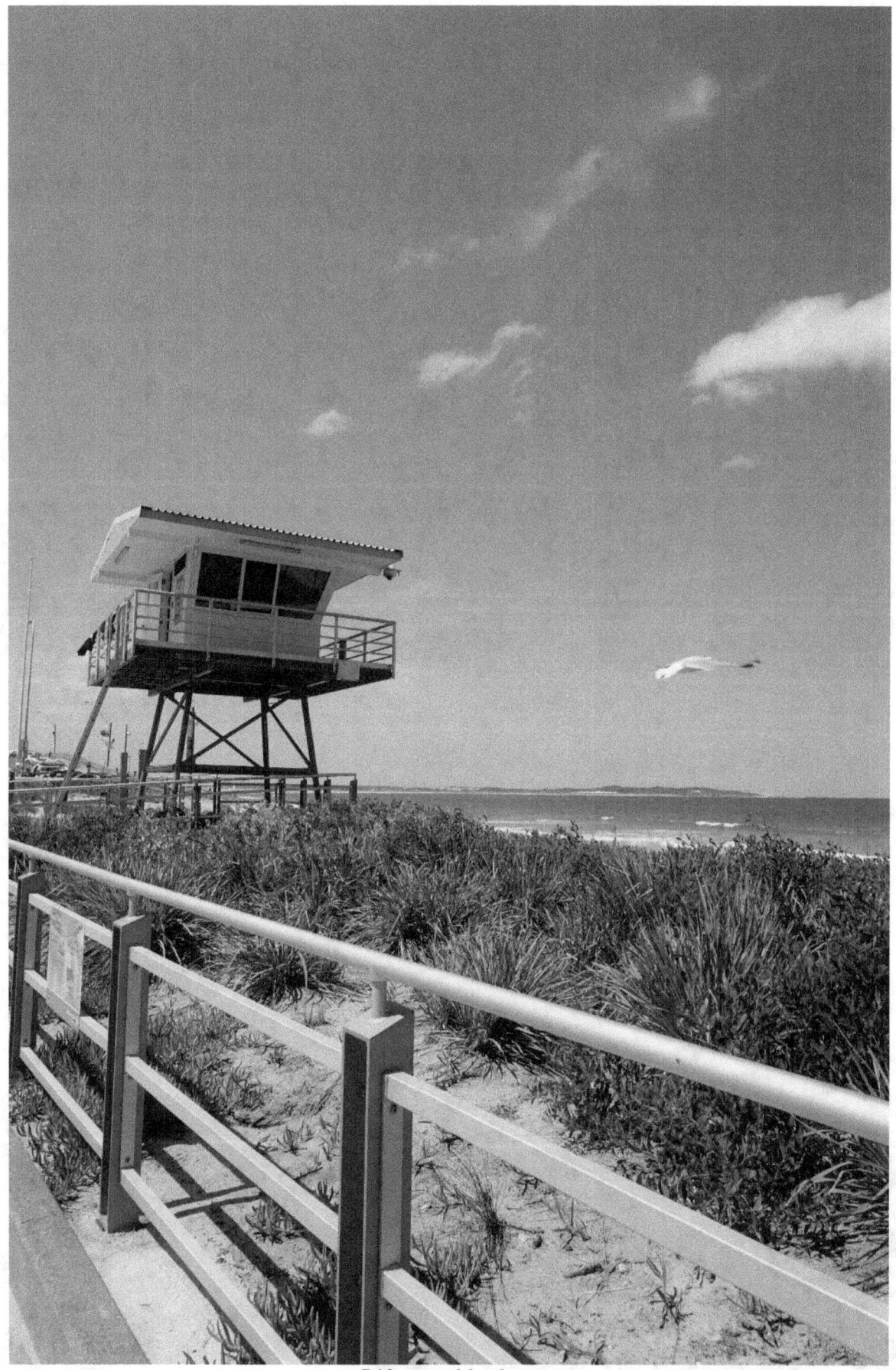

Lifeguard lookout

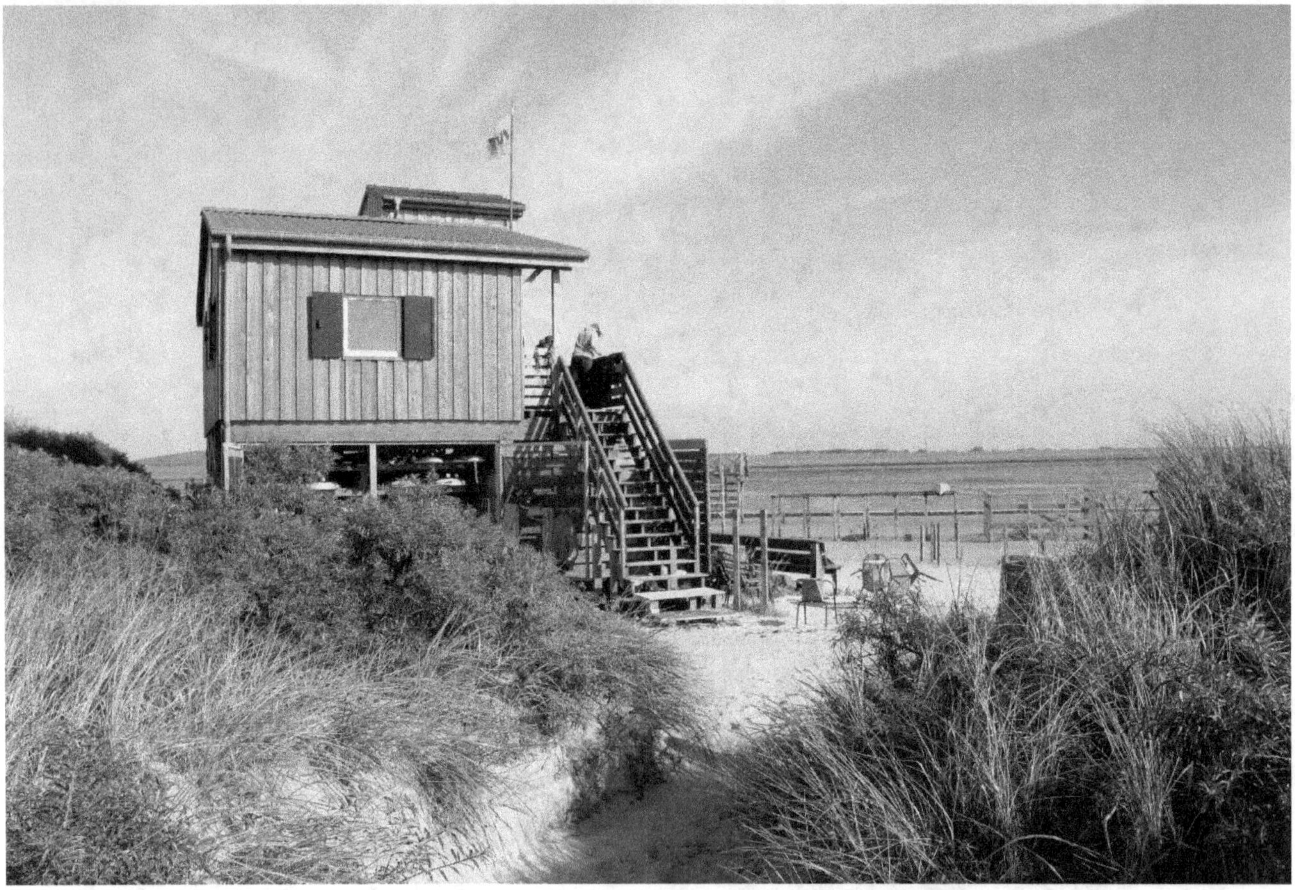

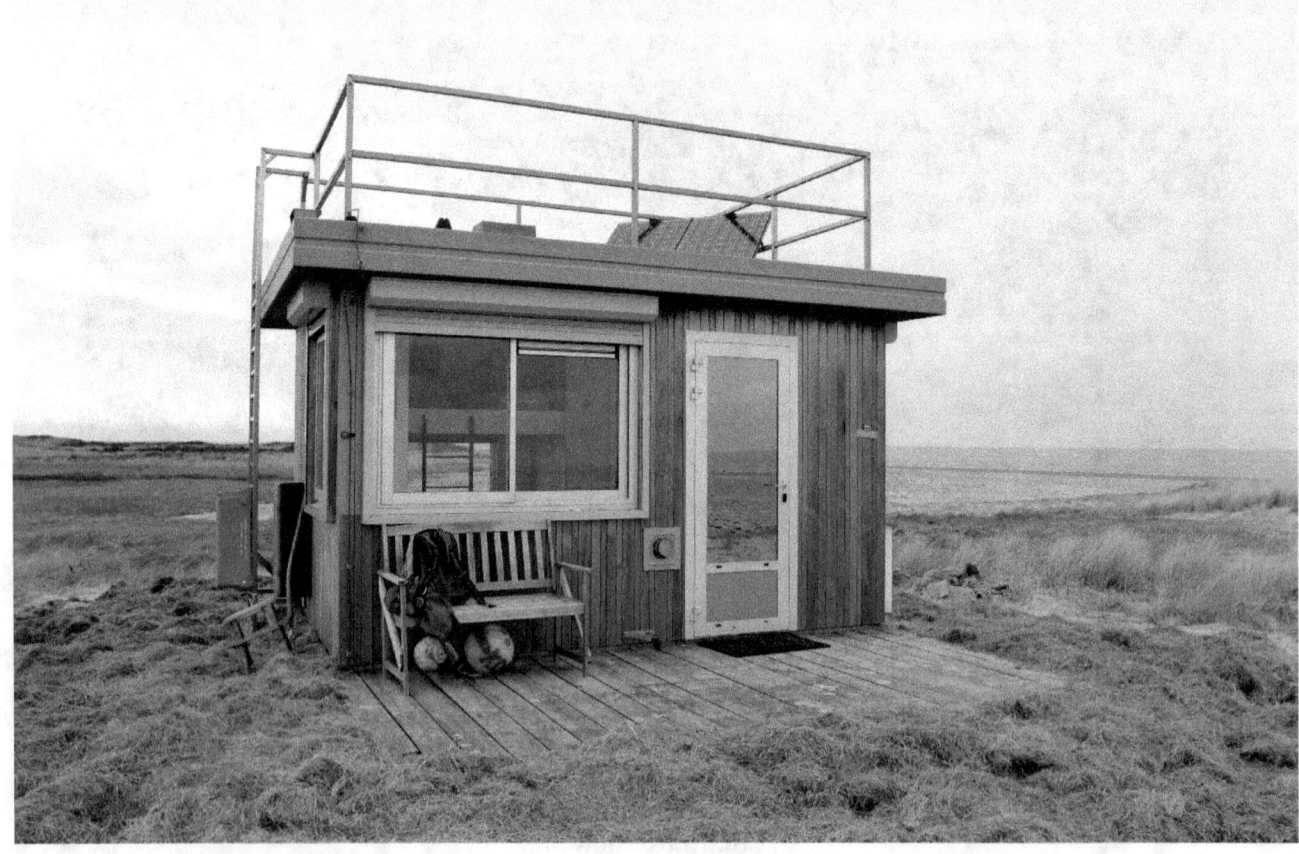

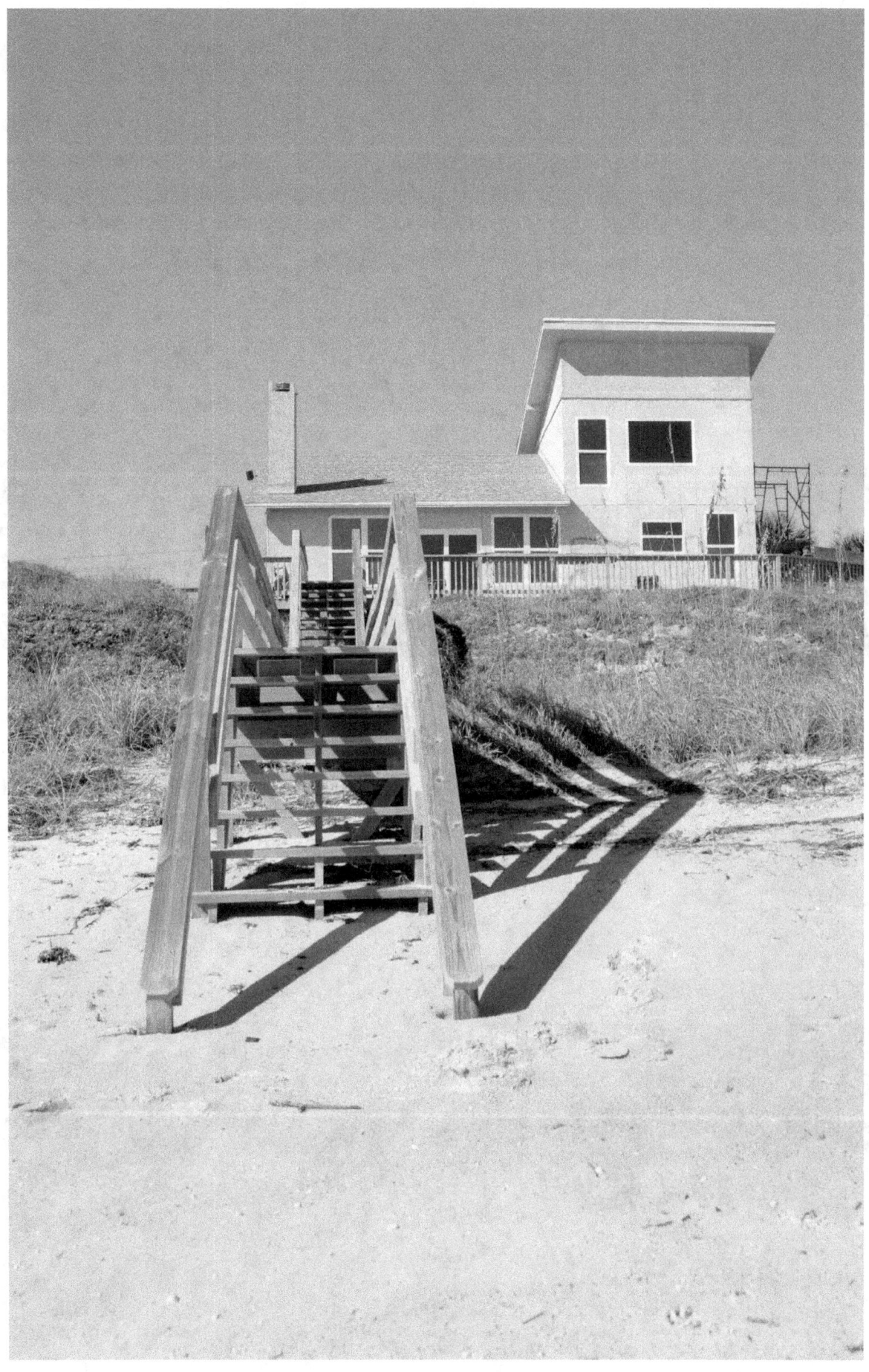

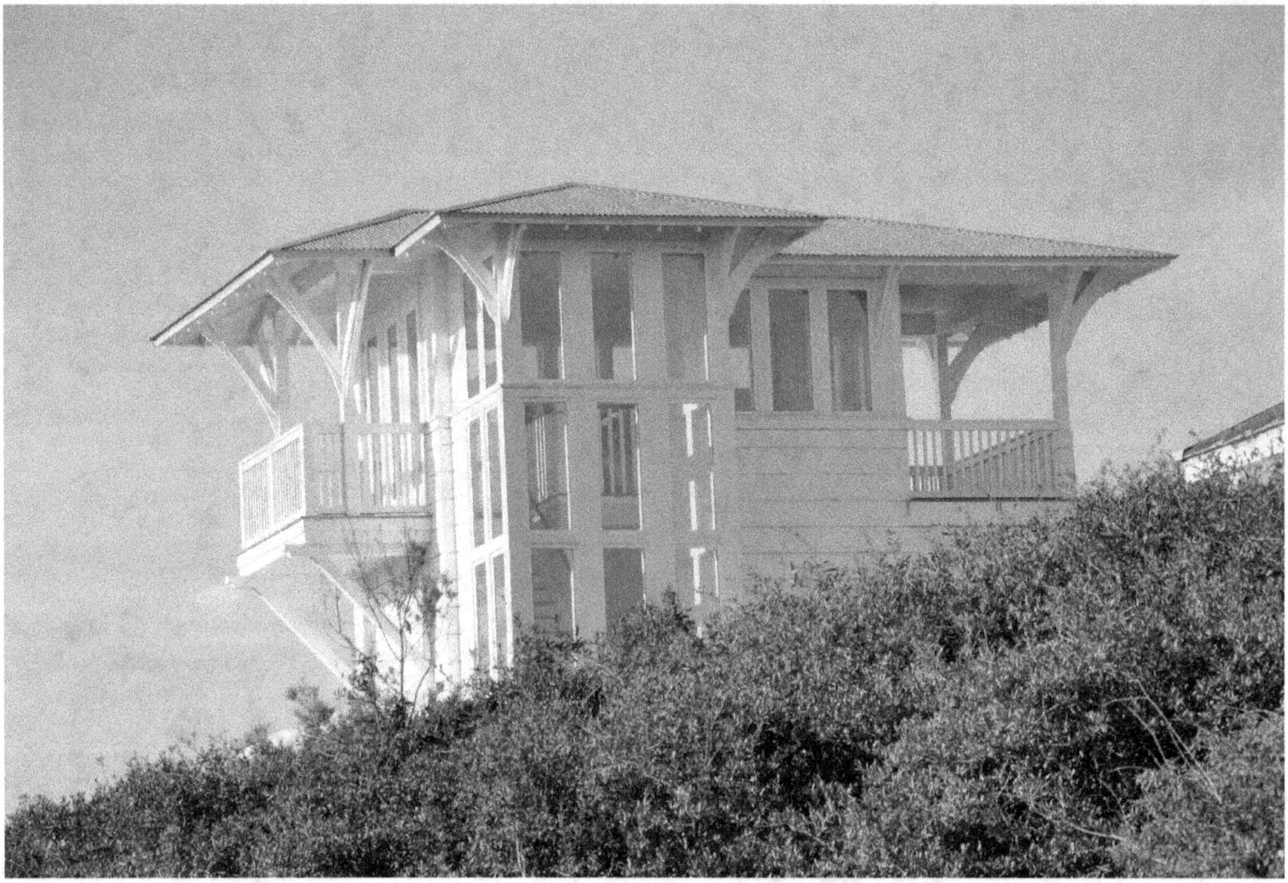

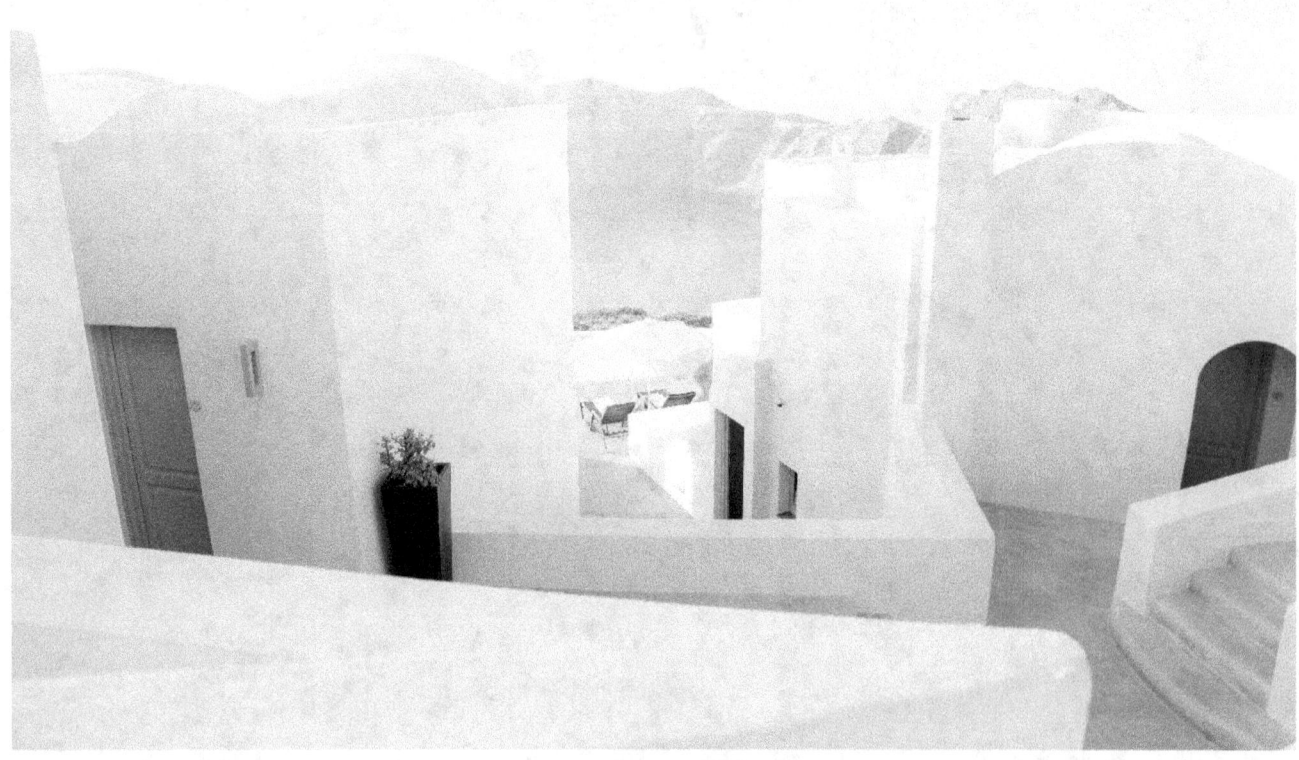

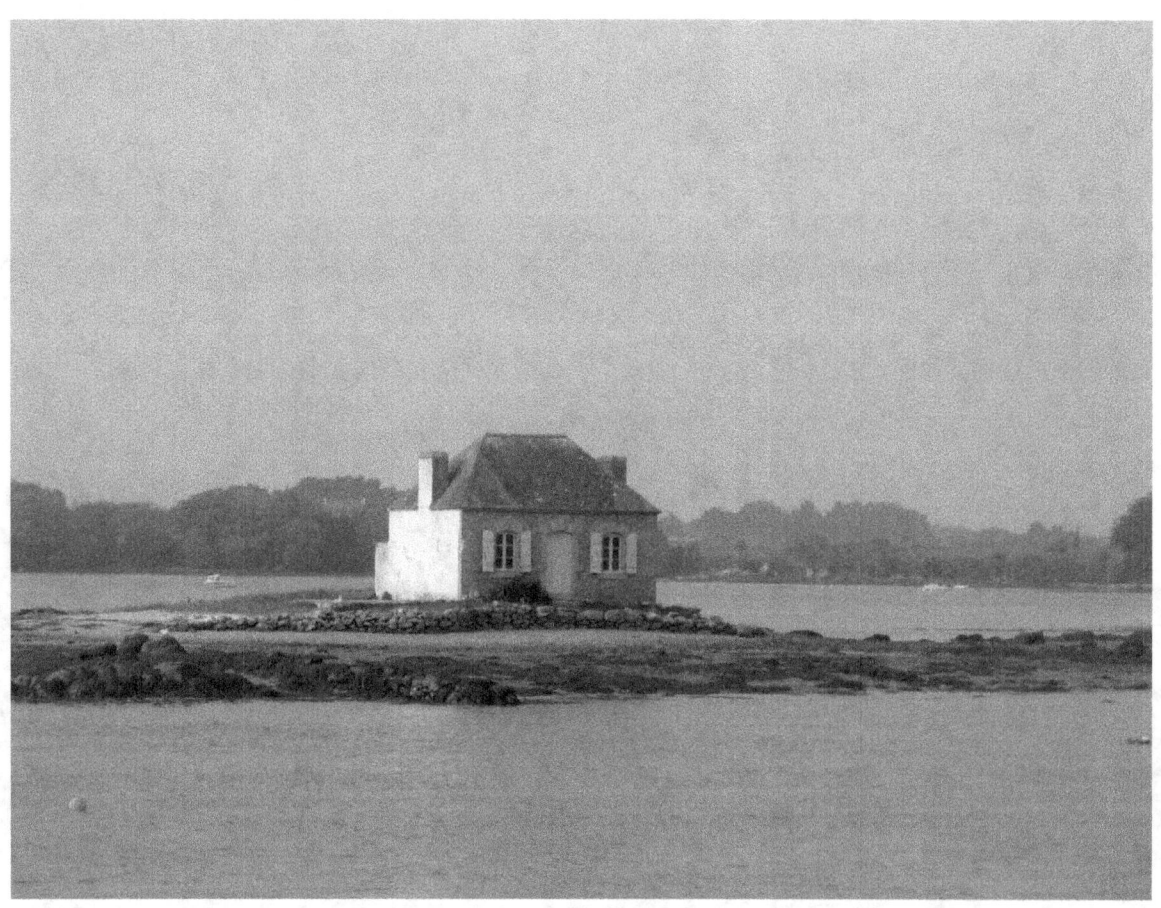

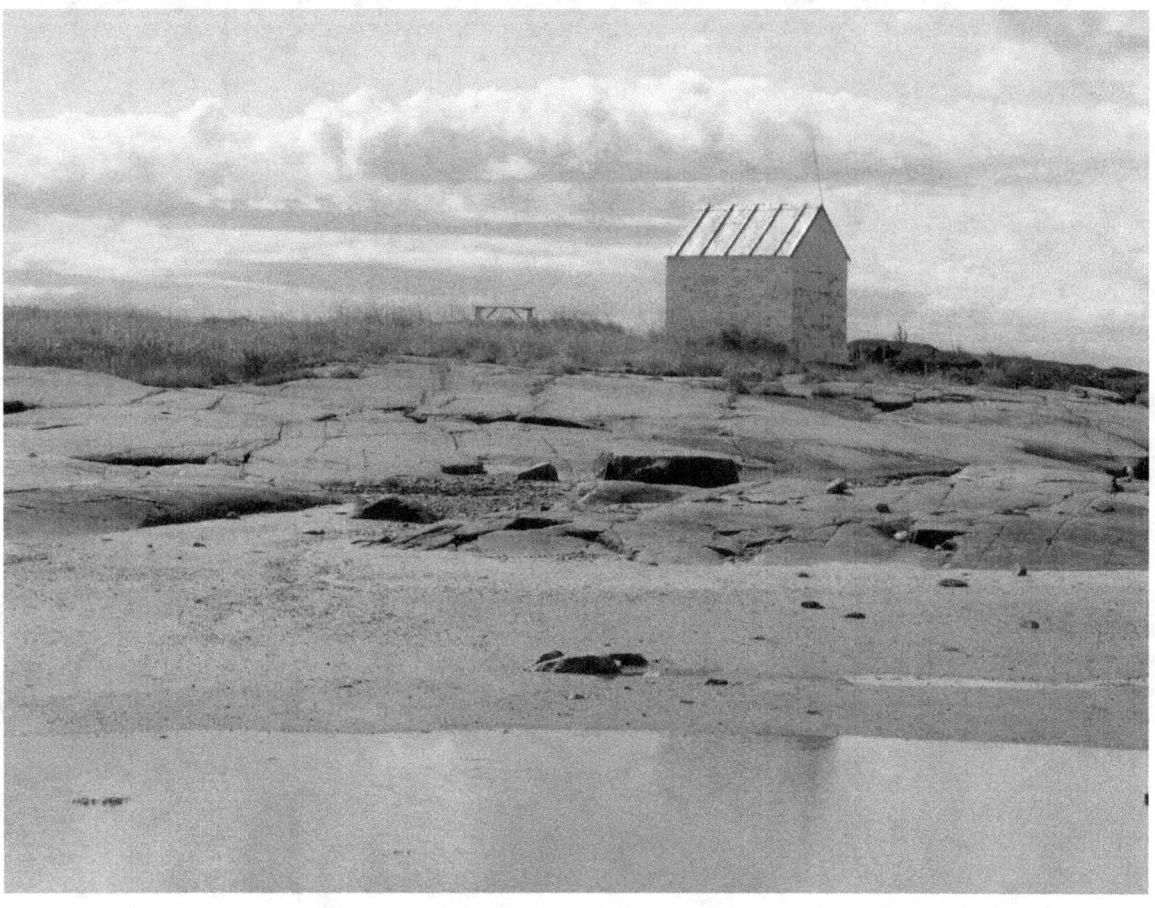

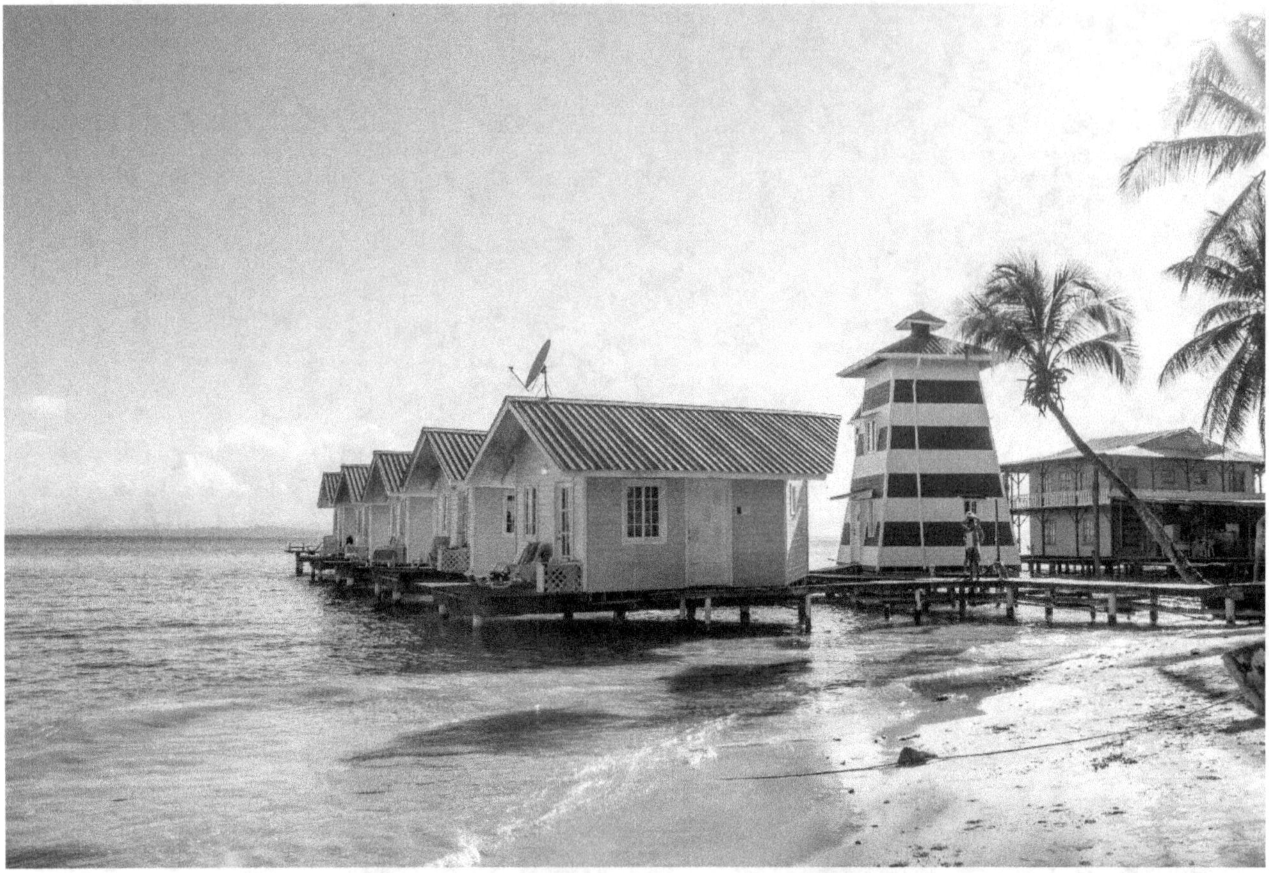

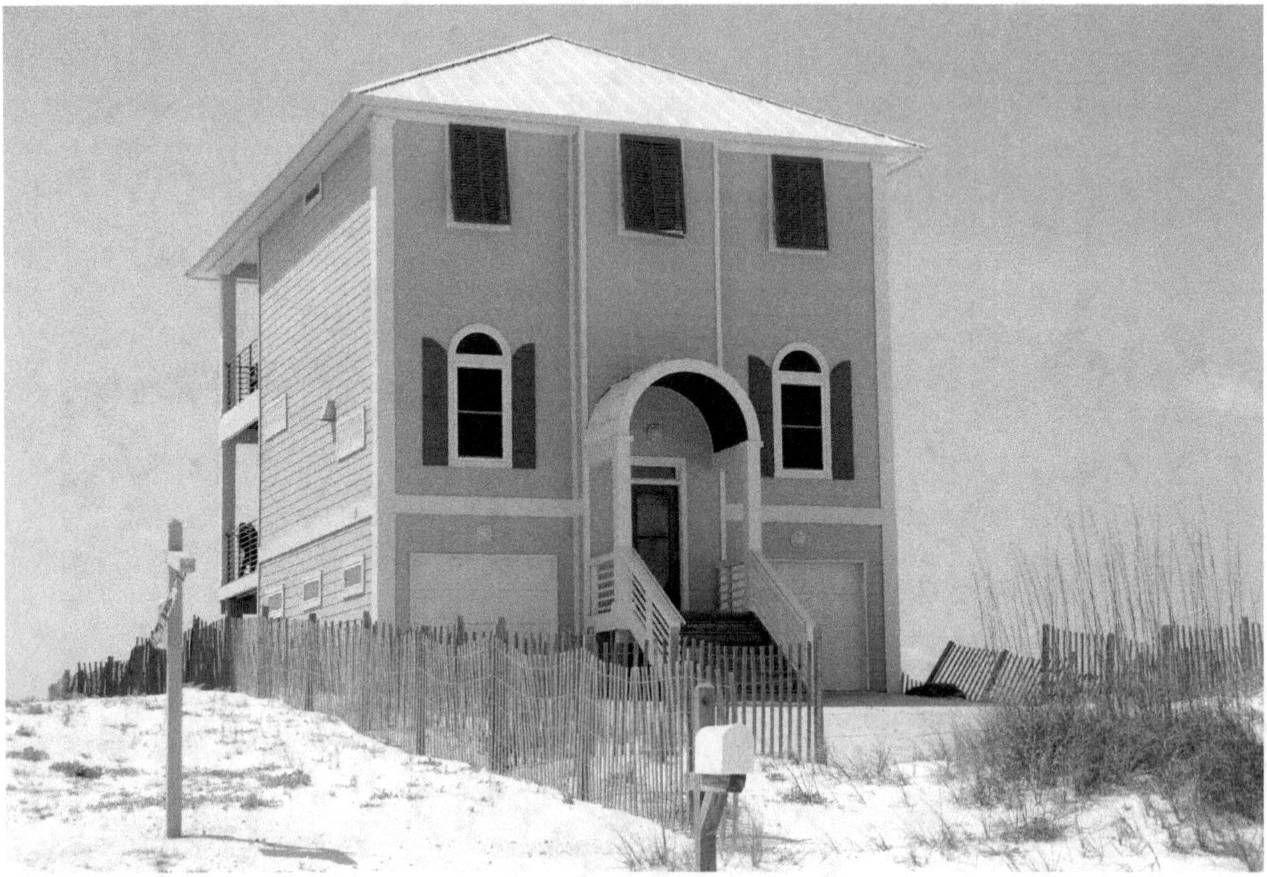

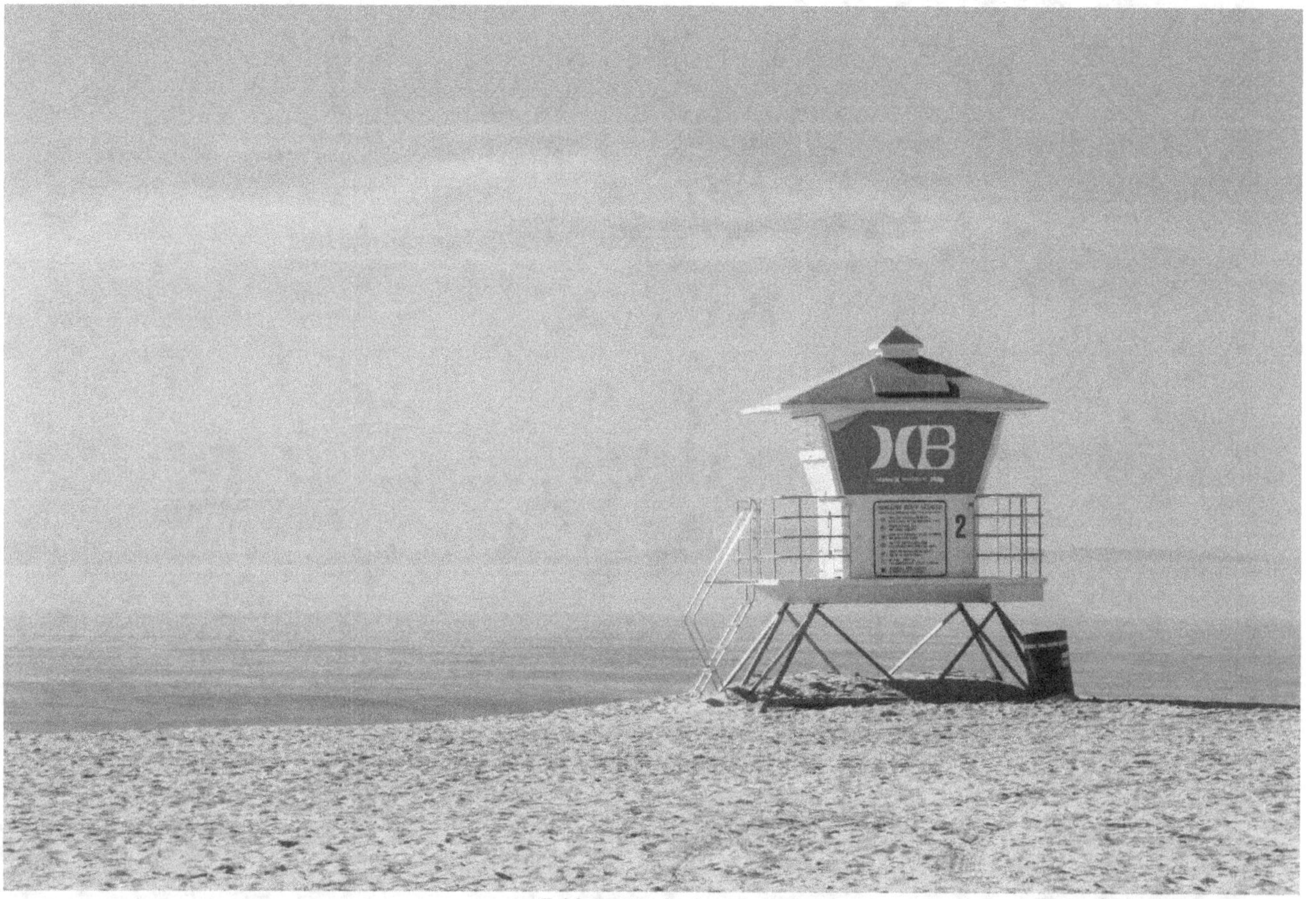

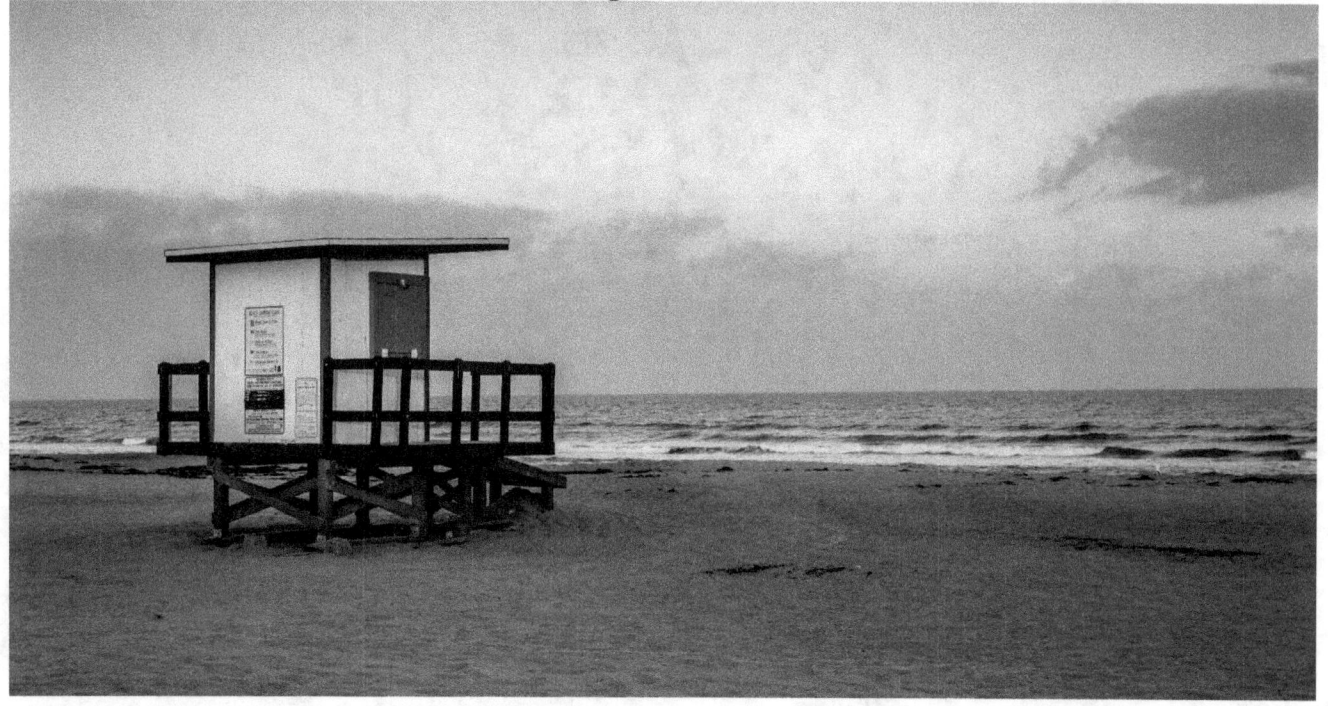

Lifeguard shacks

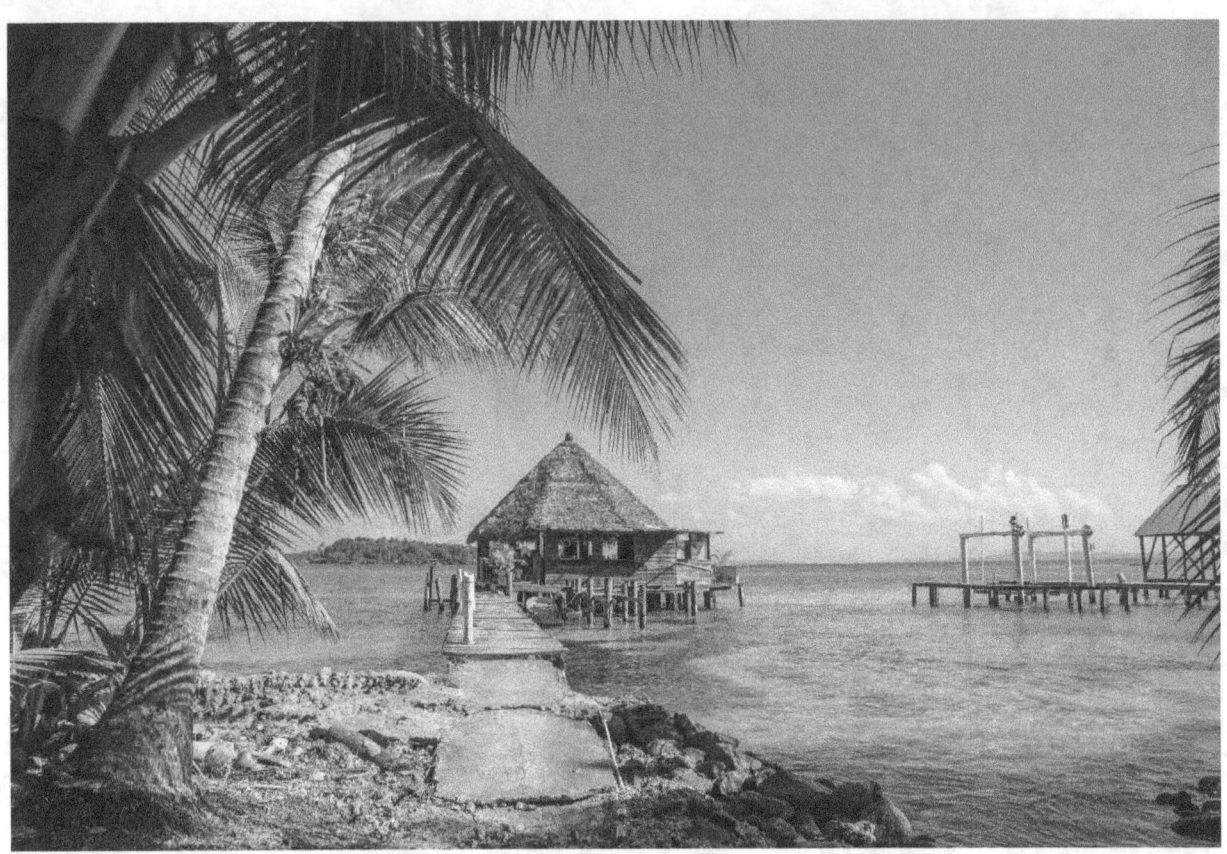

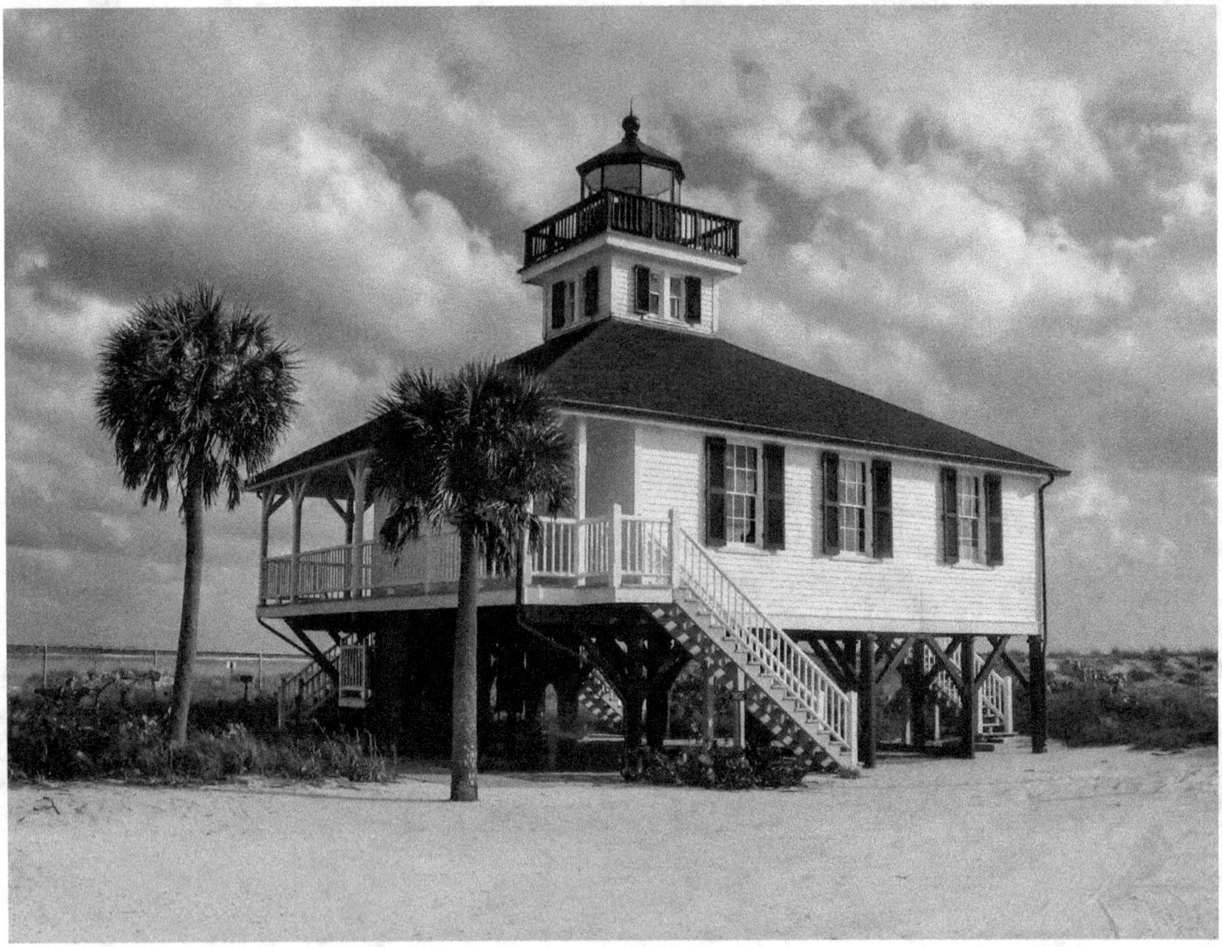

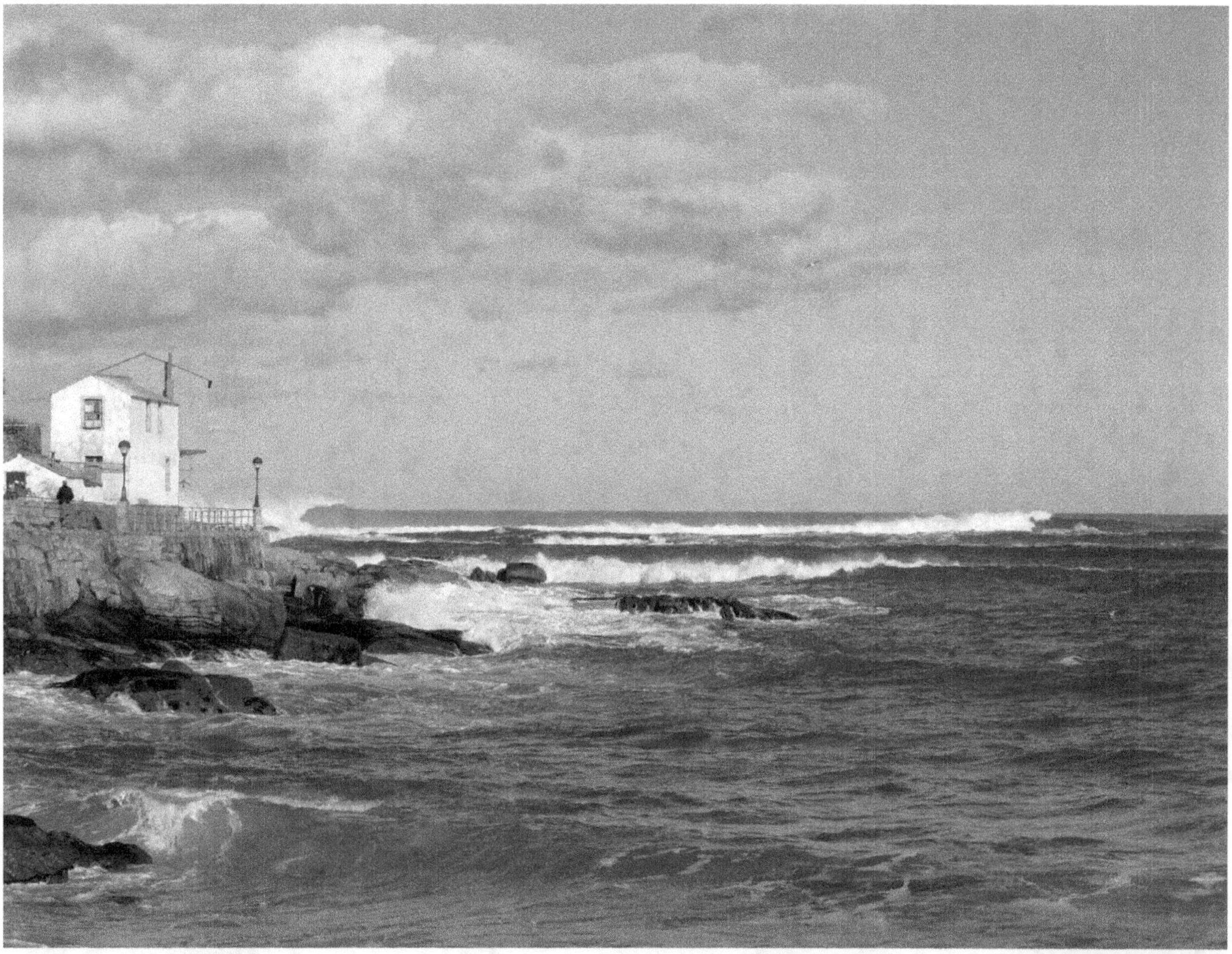

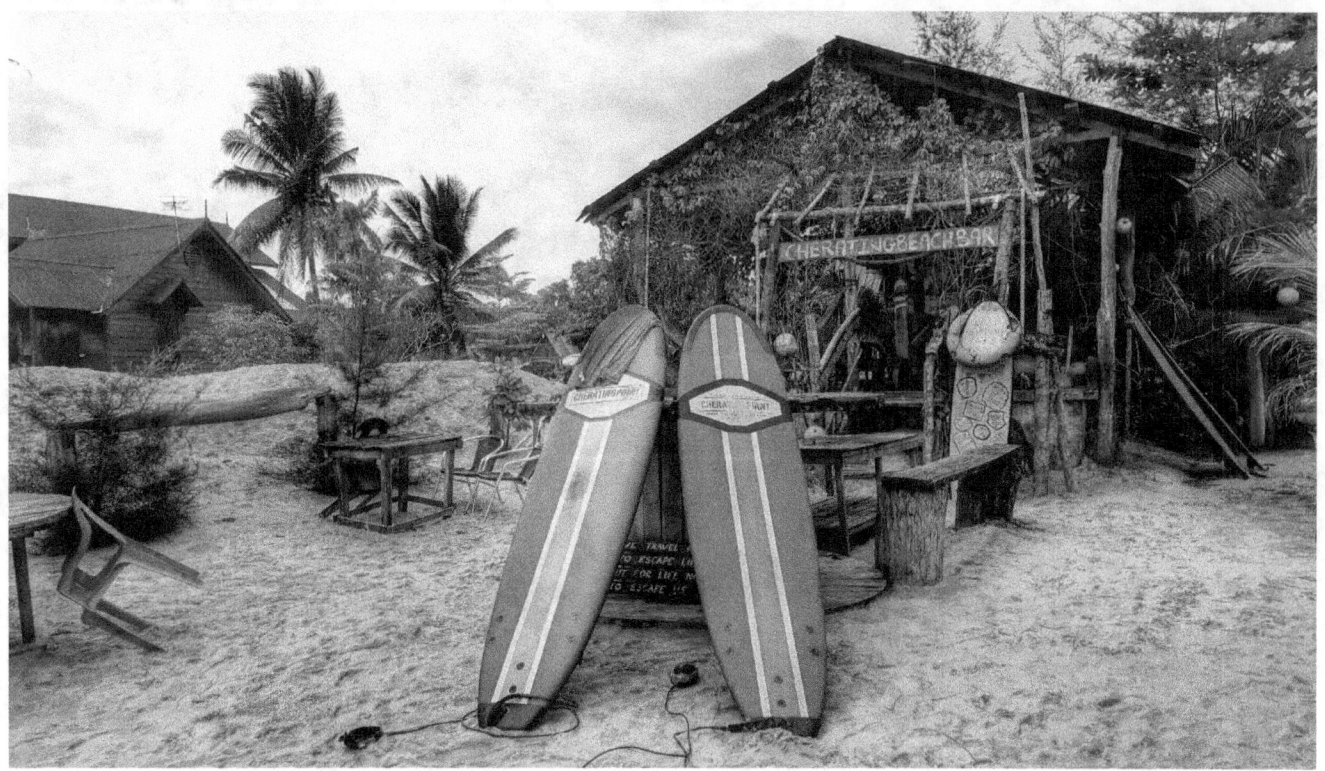

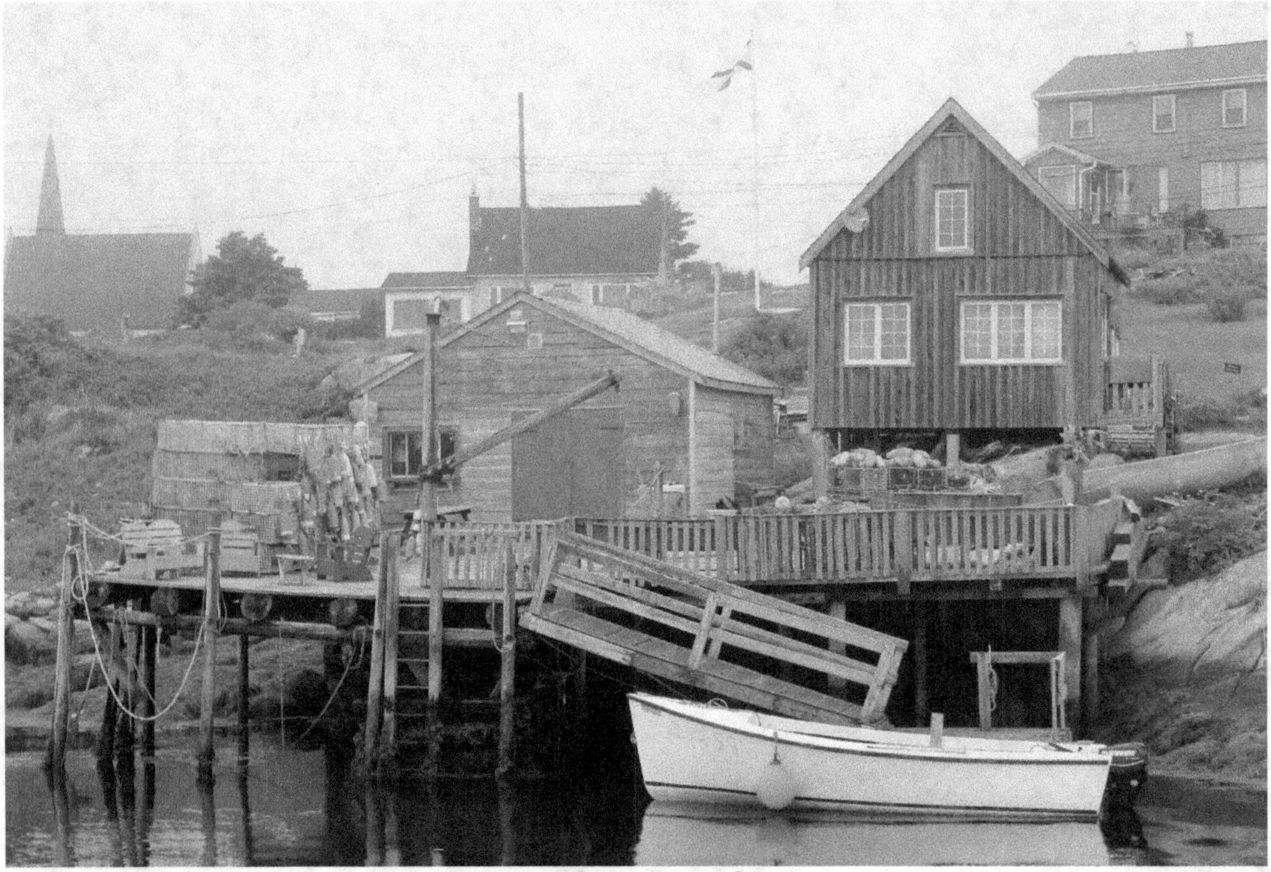

Peggy's Cove, Nova Scotia

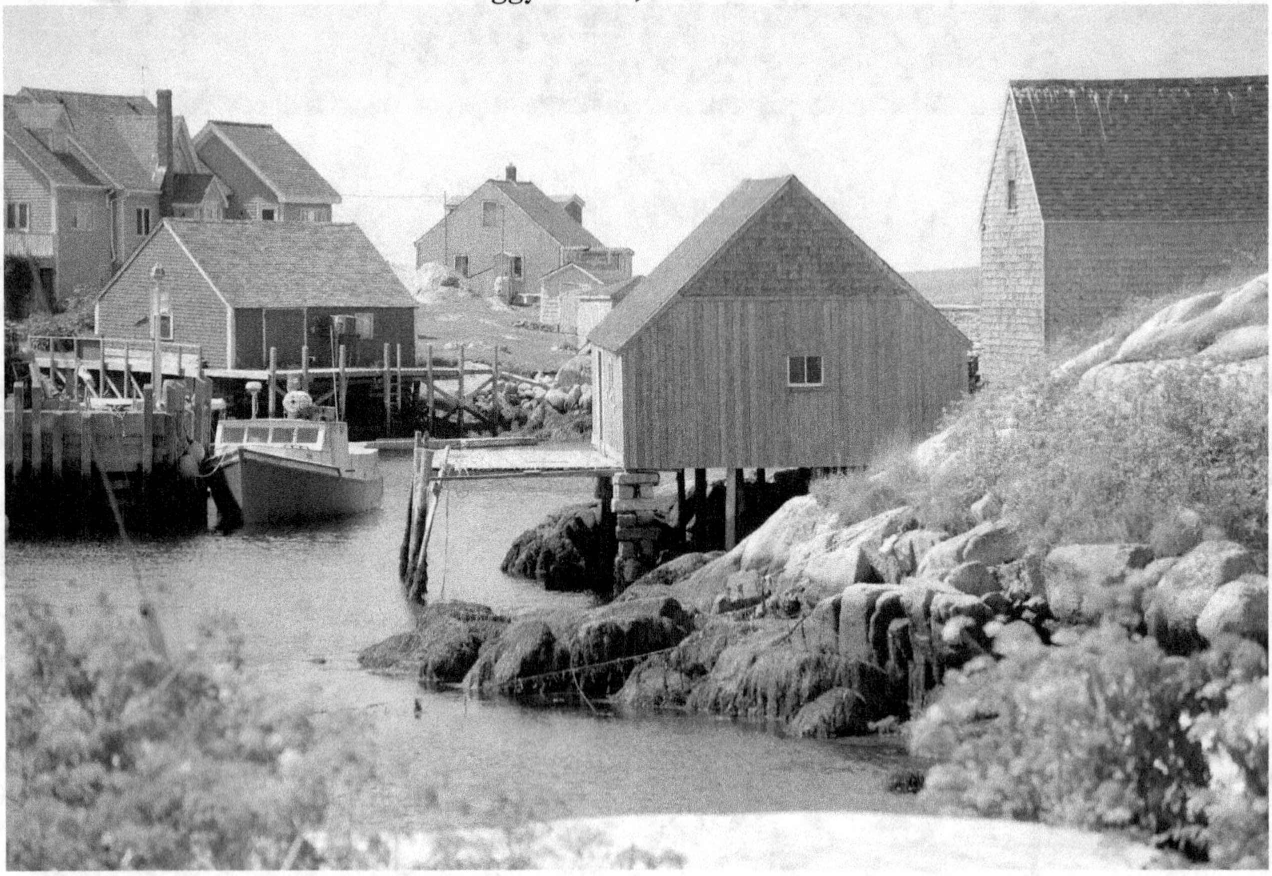

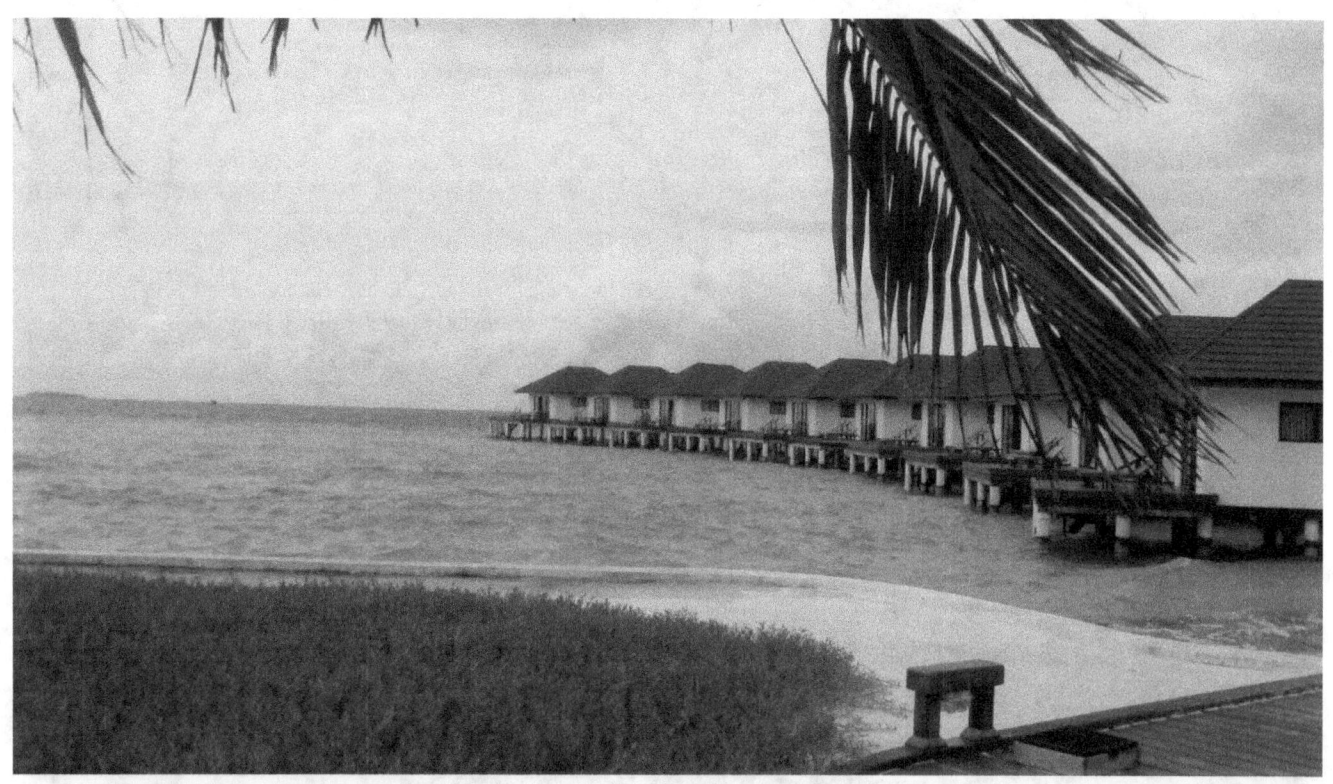

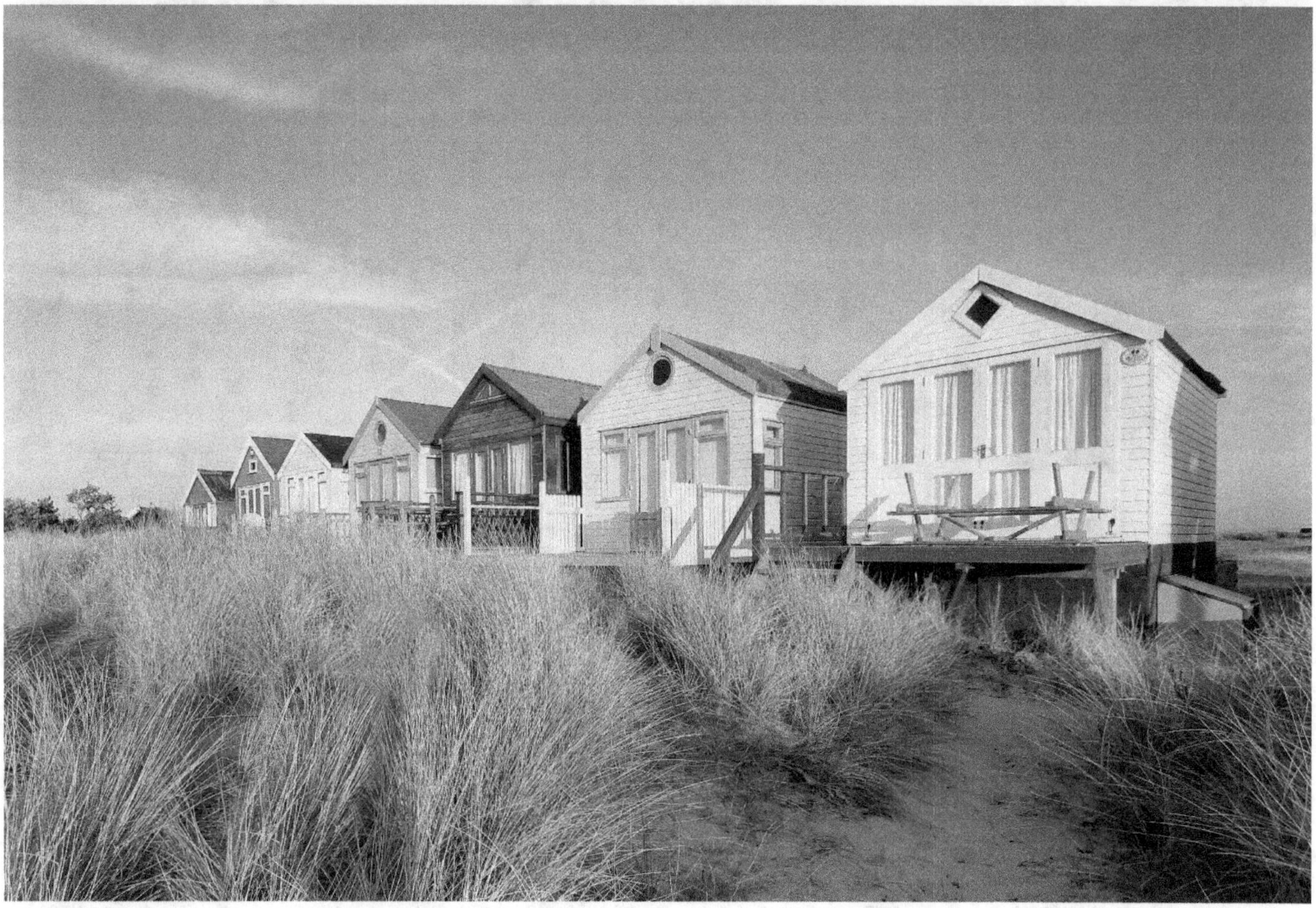

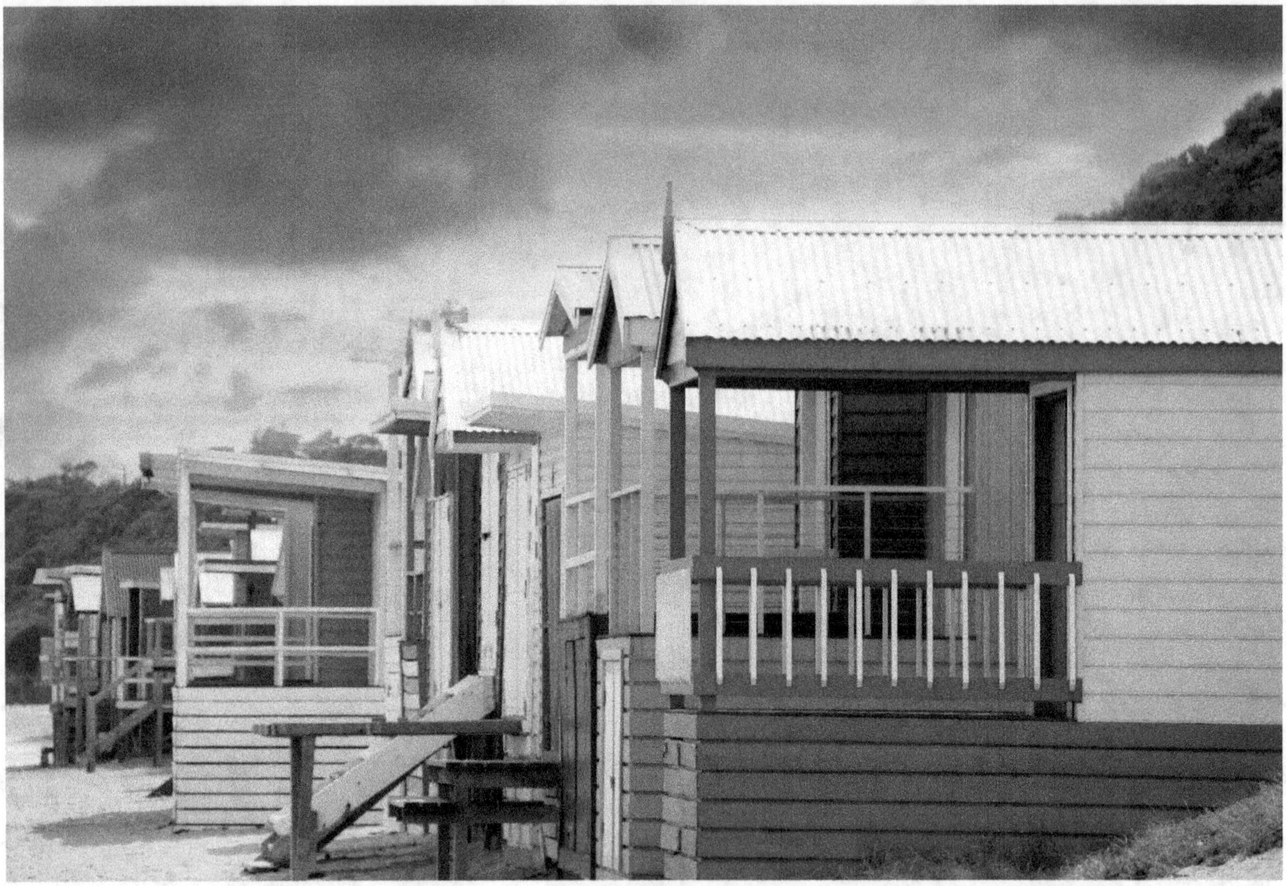

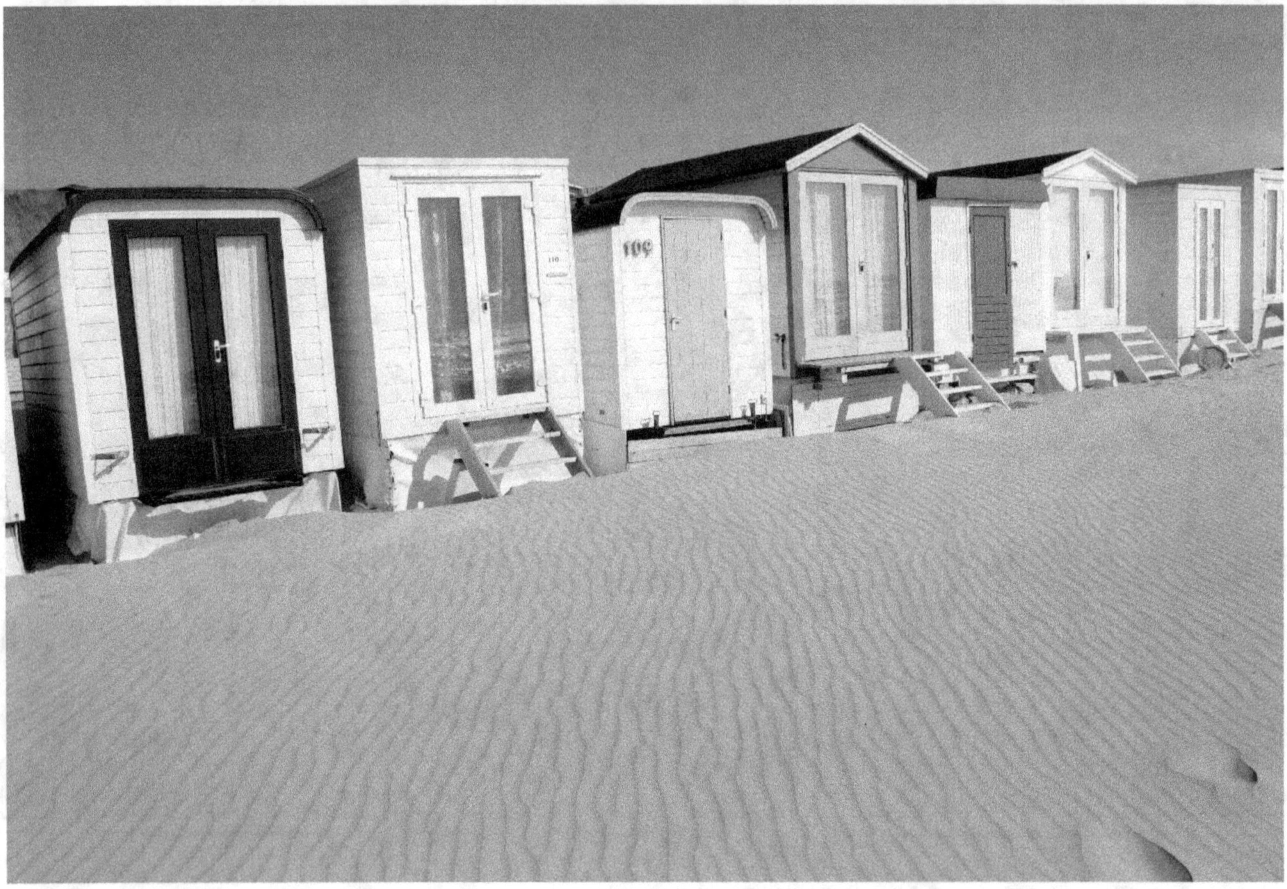
109

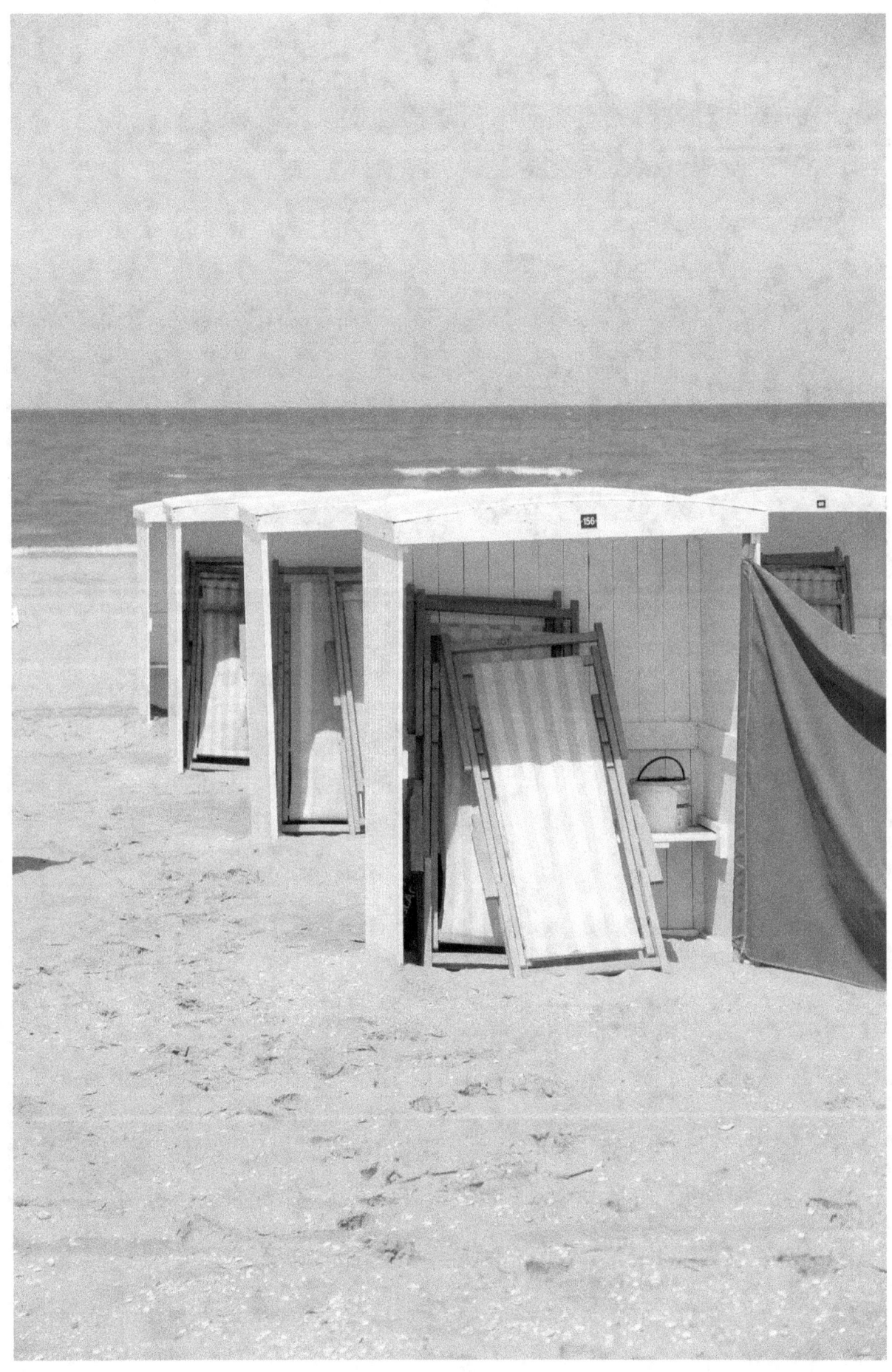

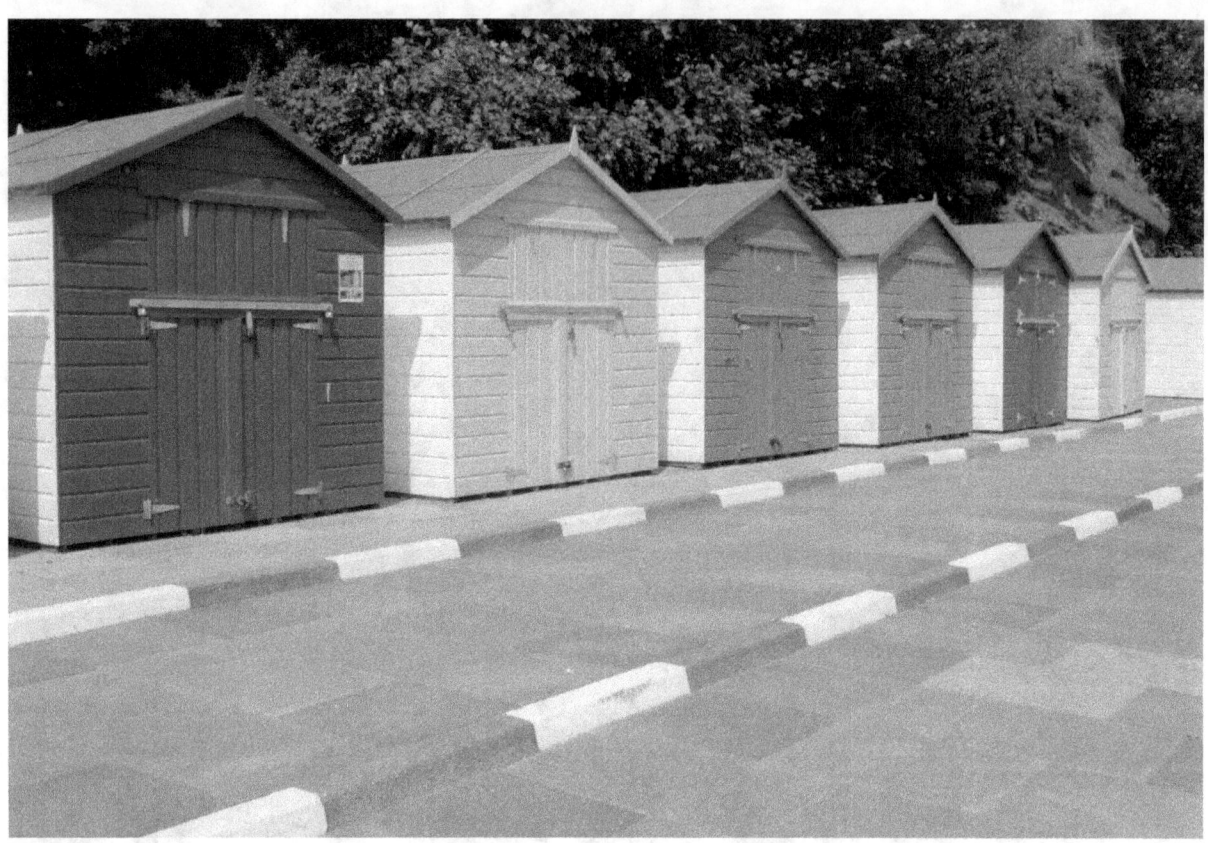

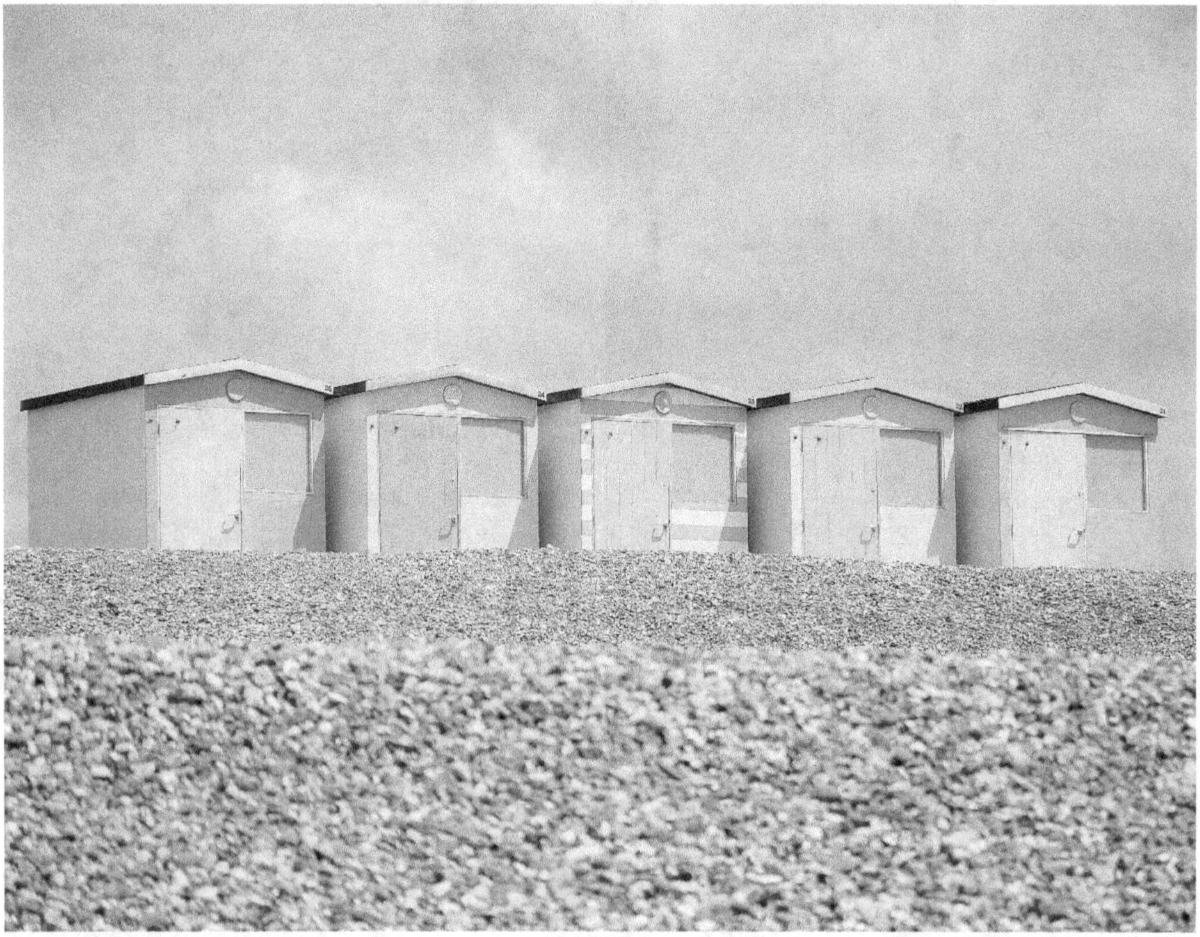

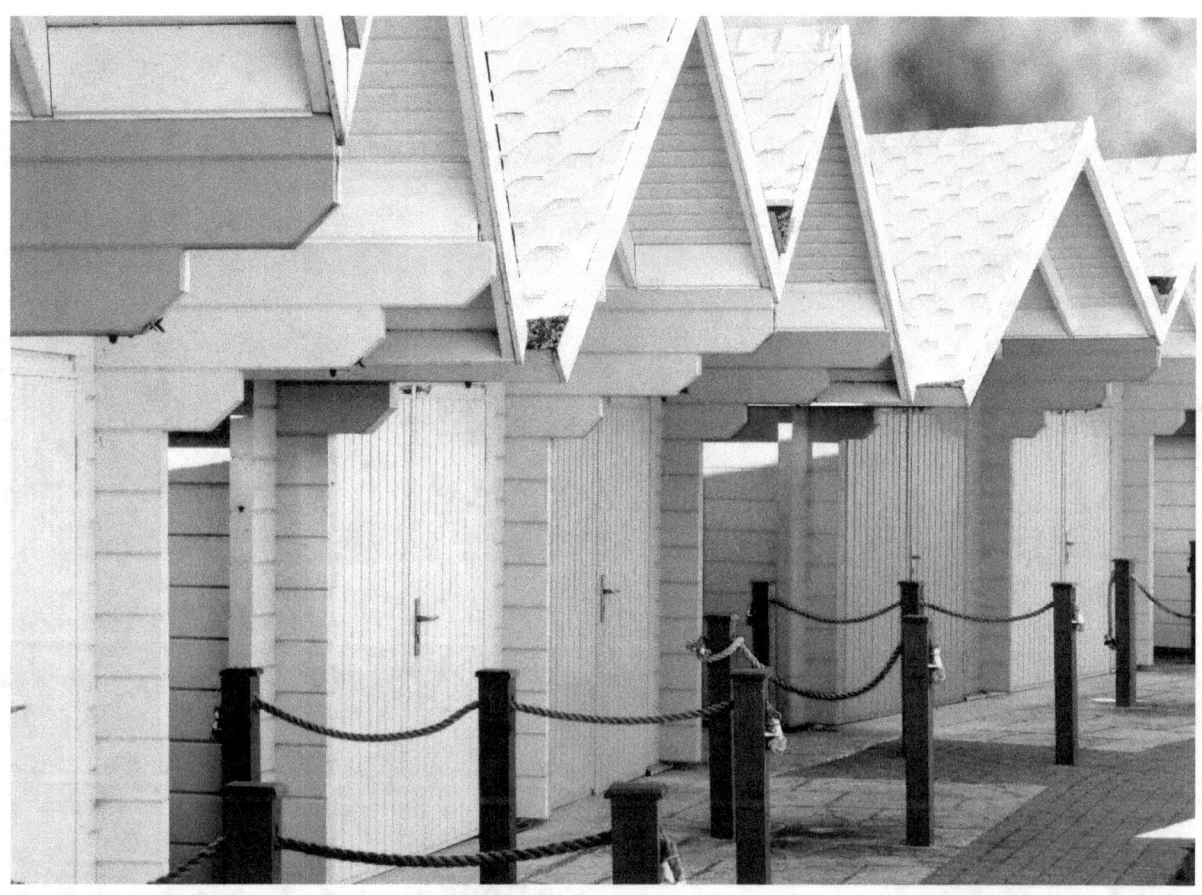

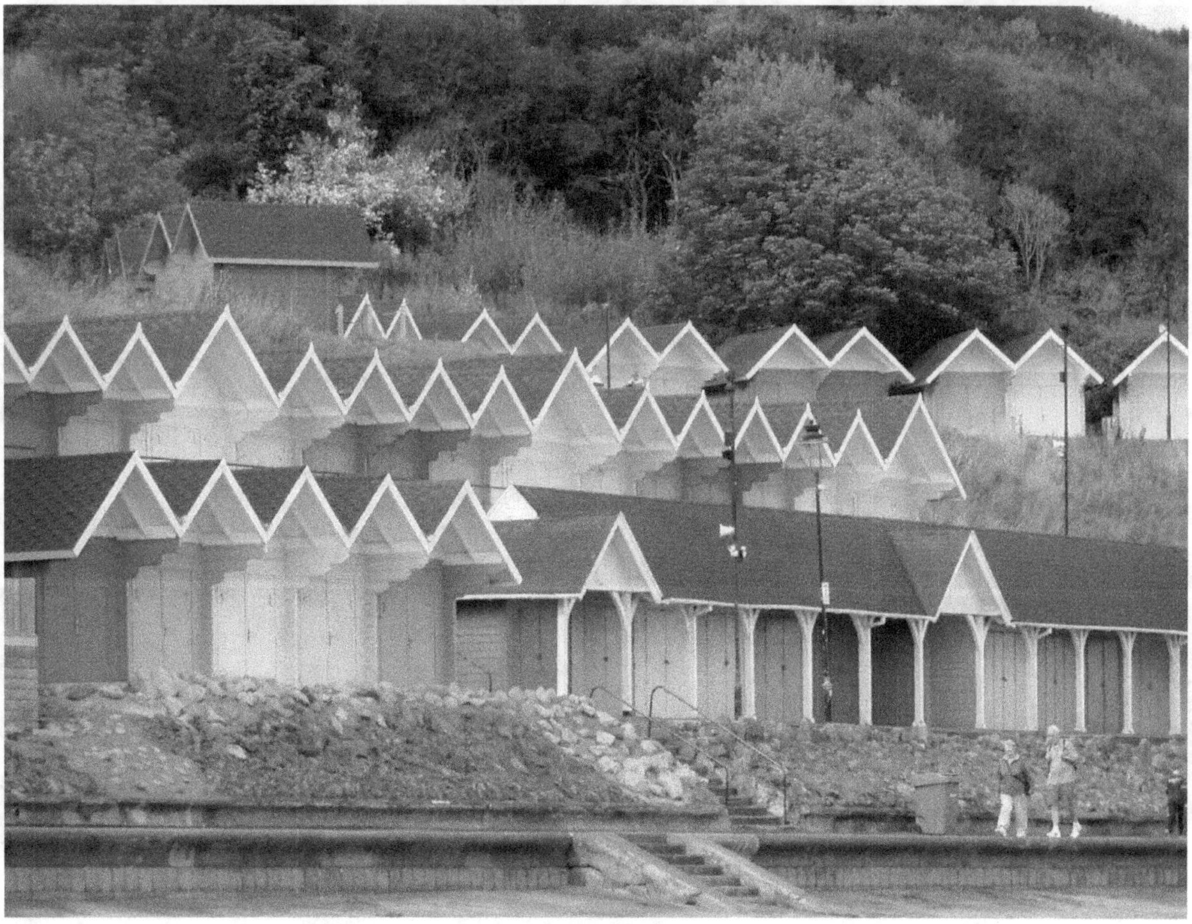

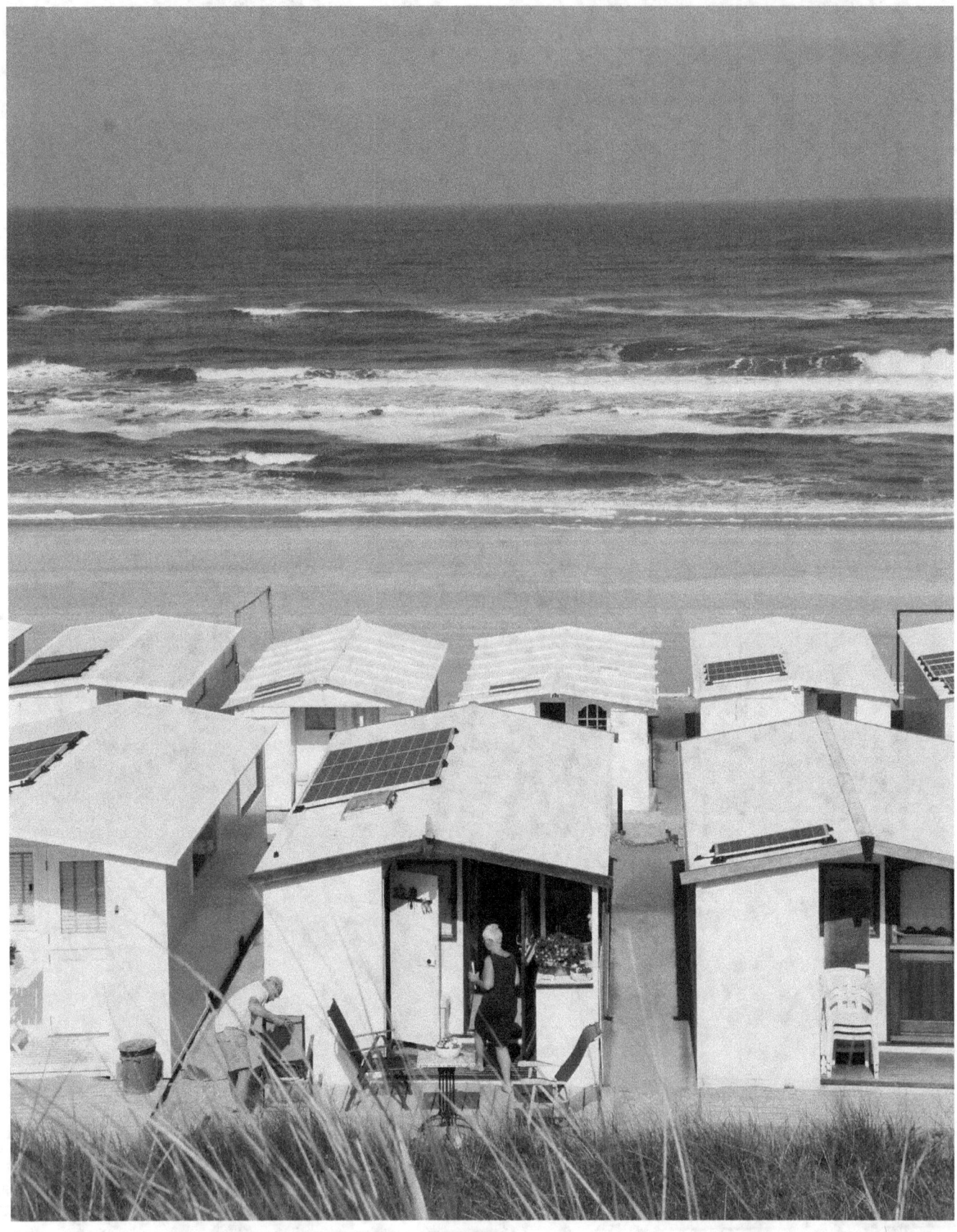

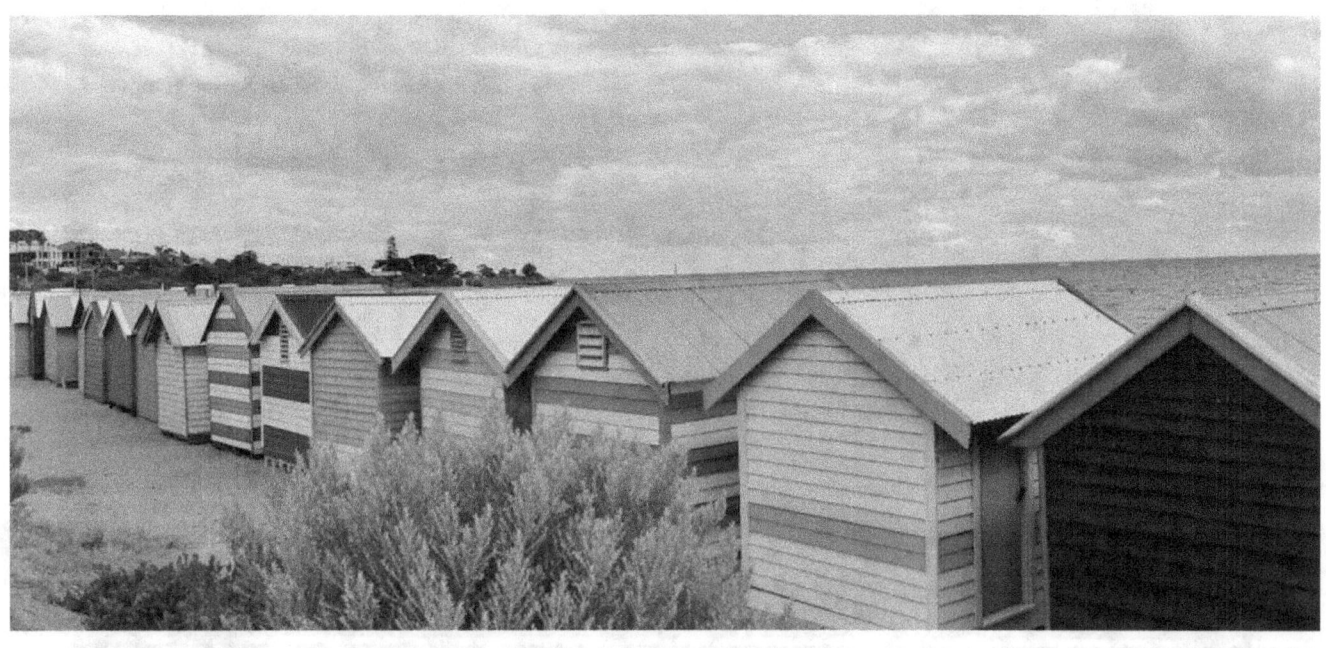

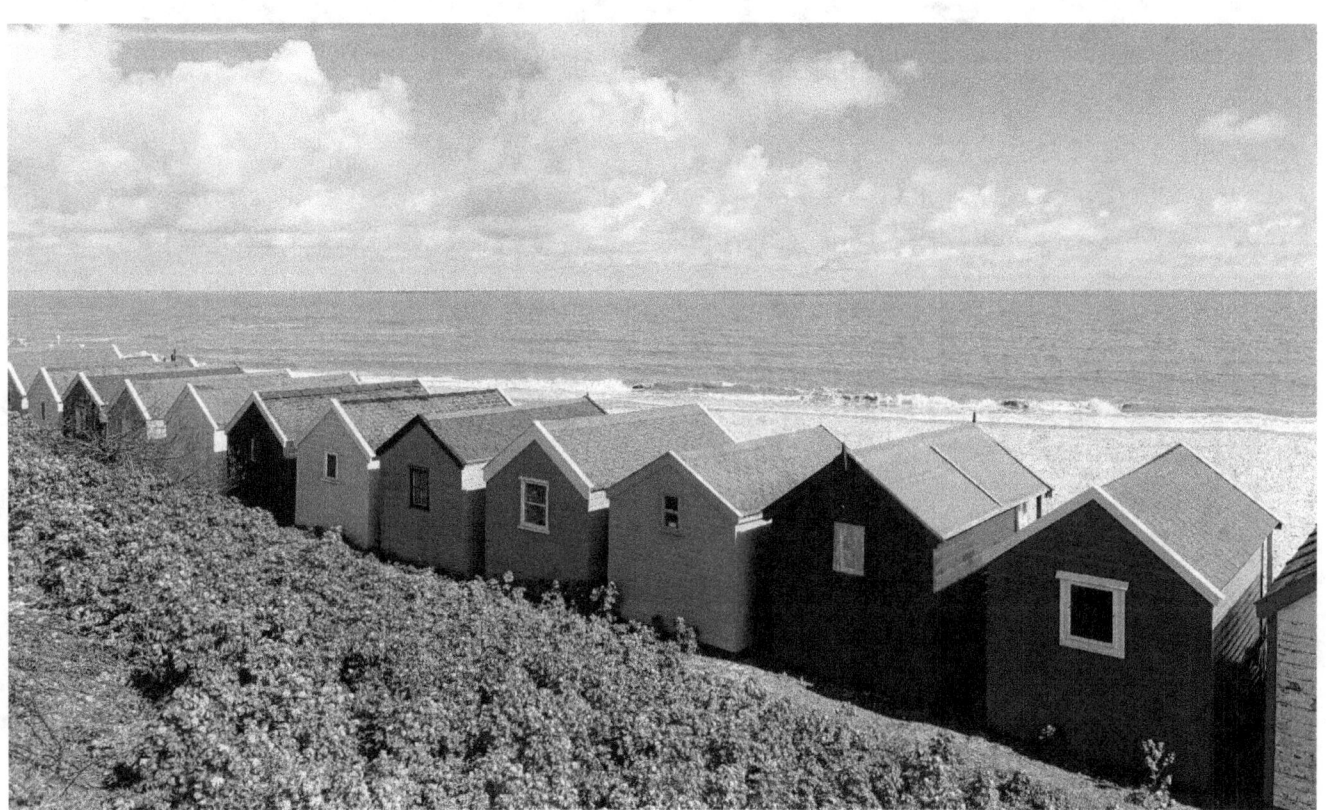

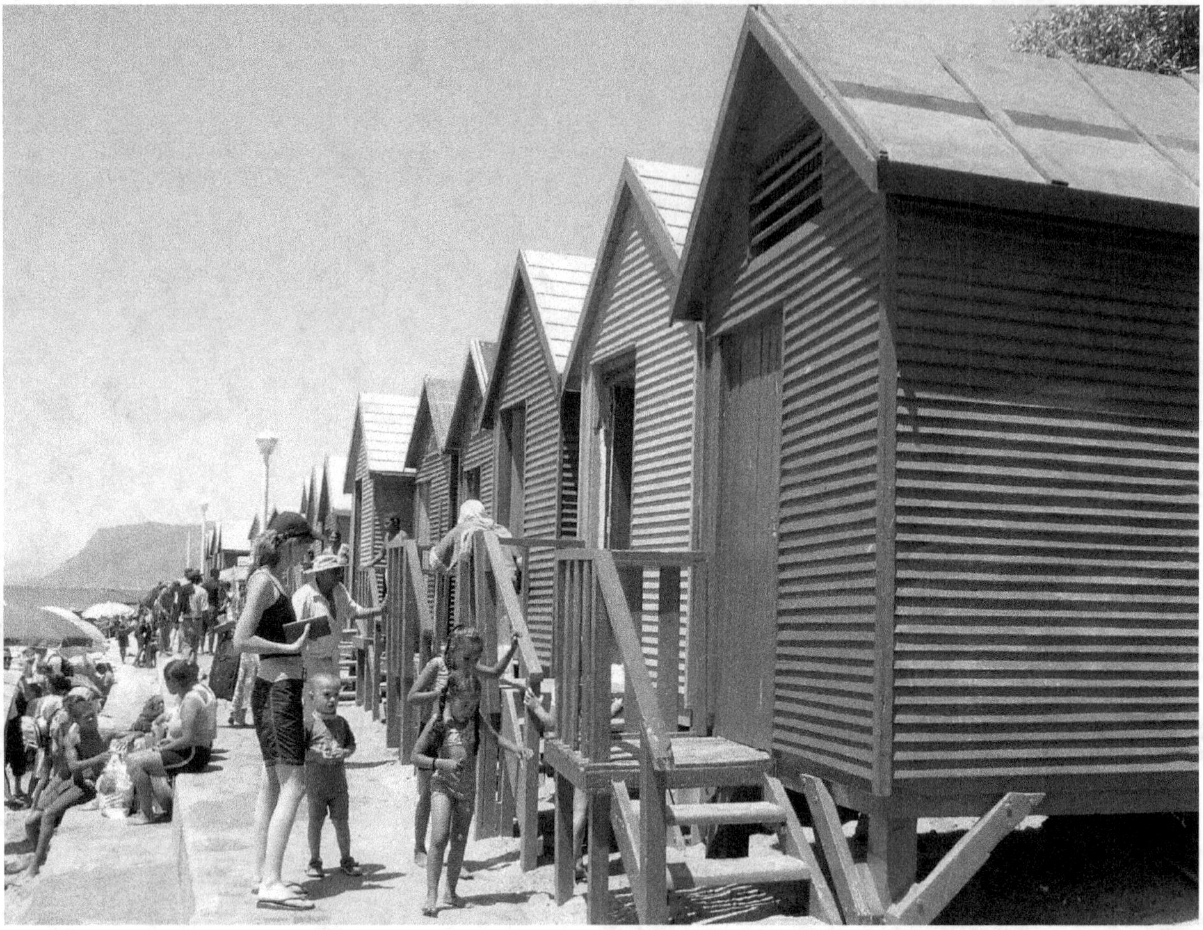

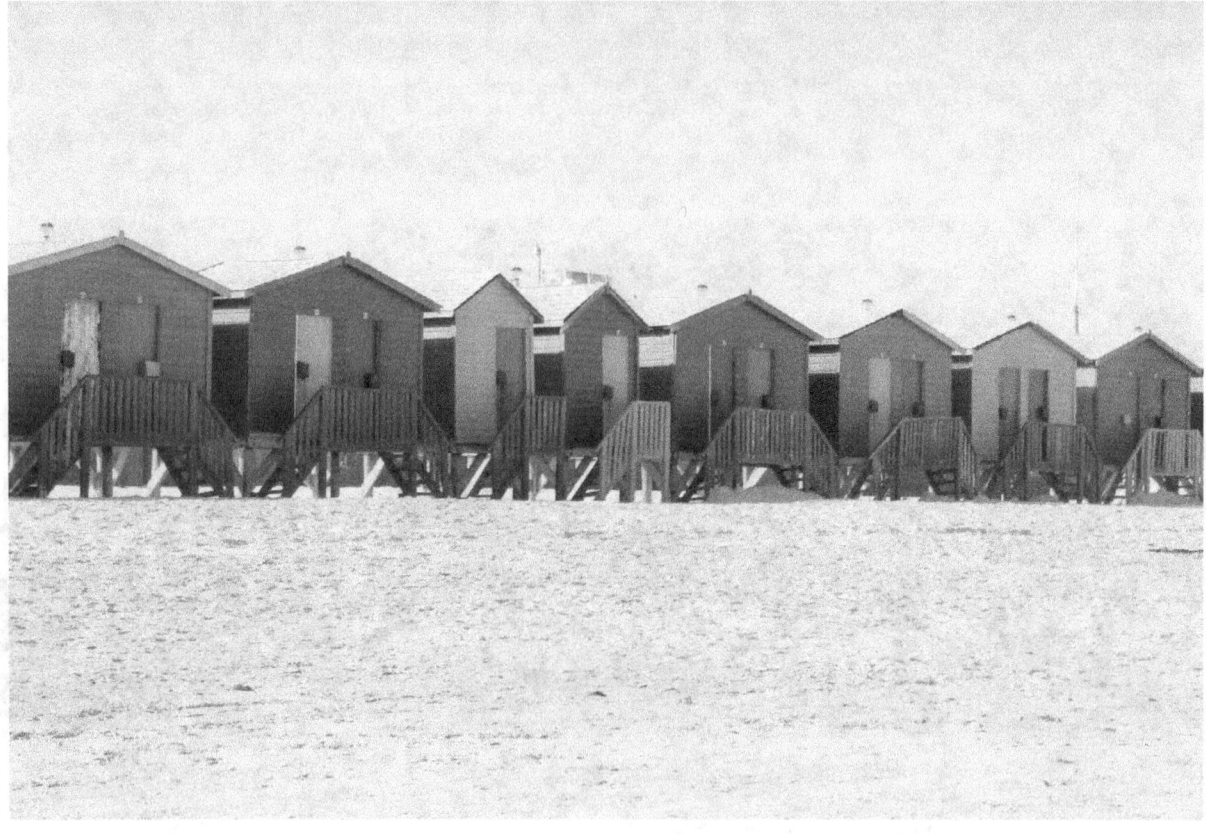

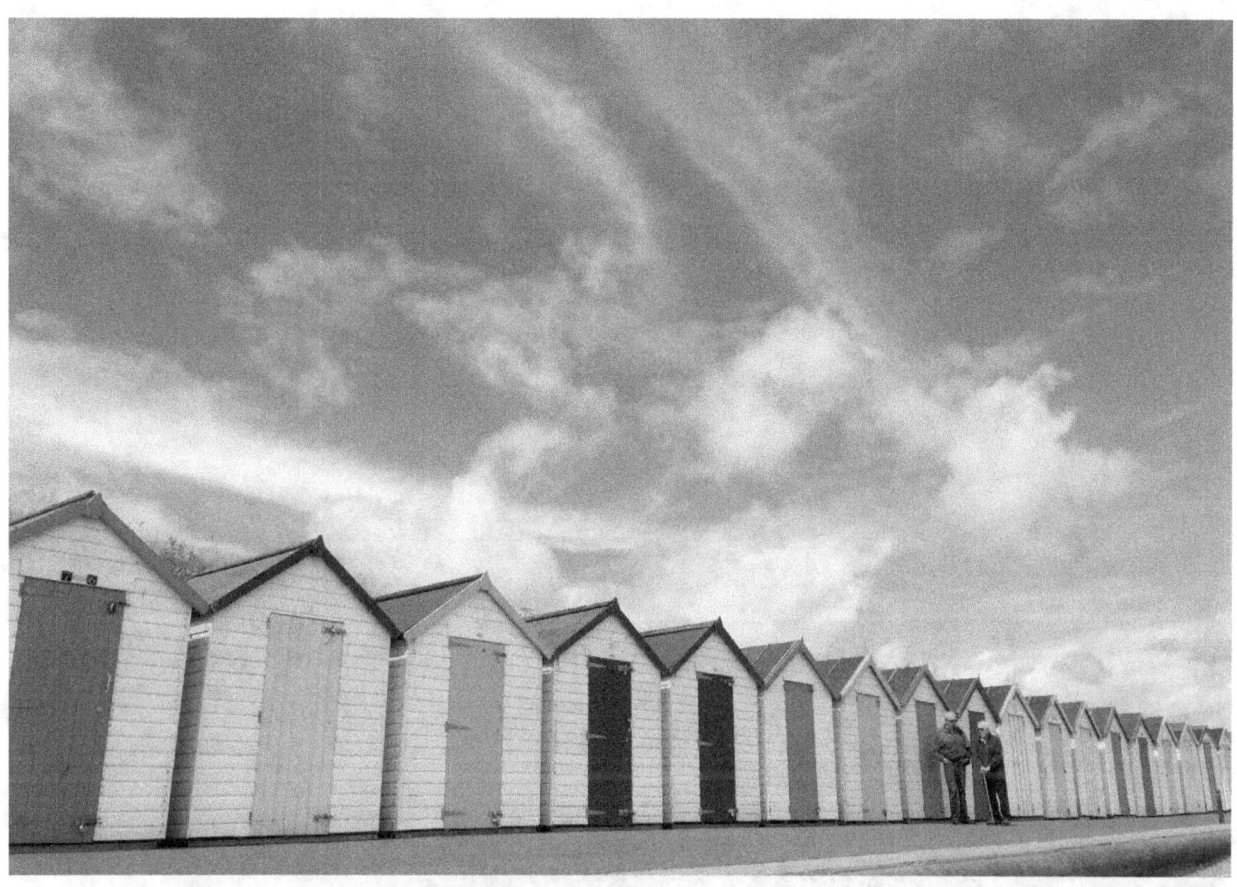

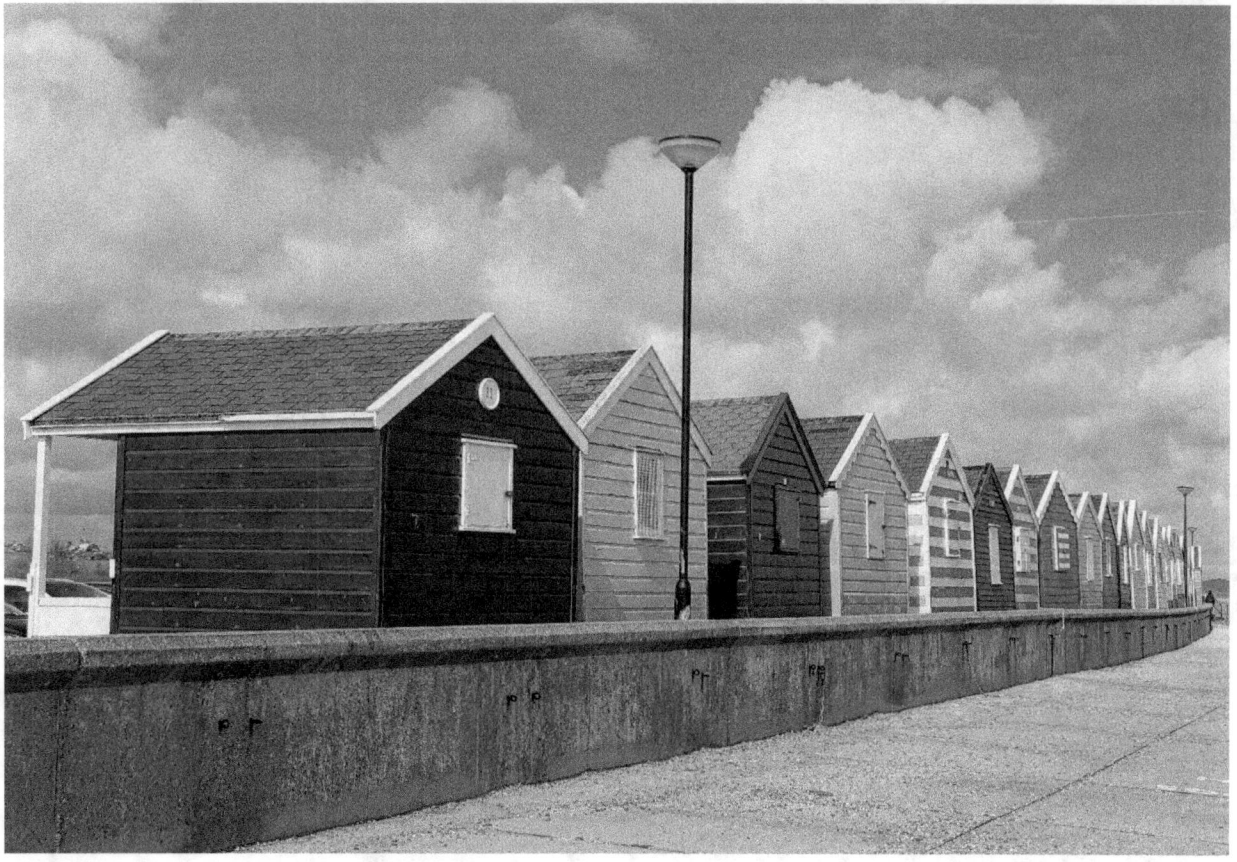

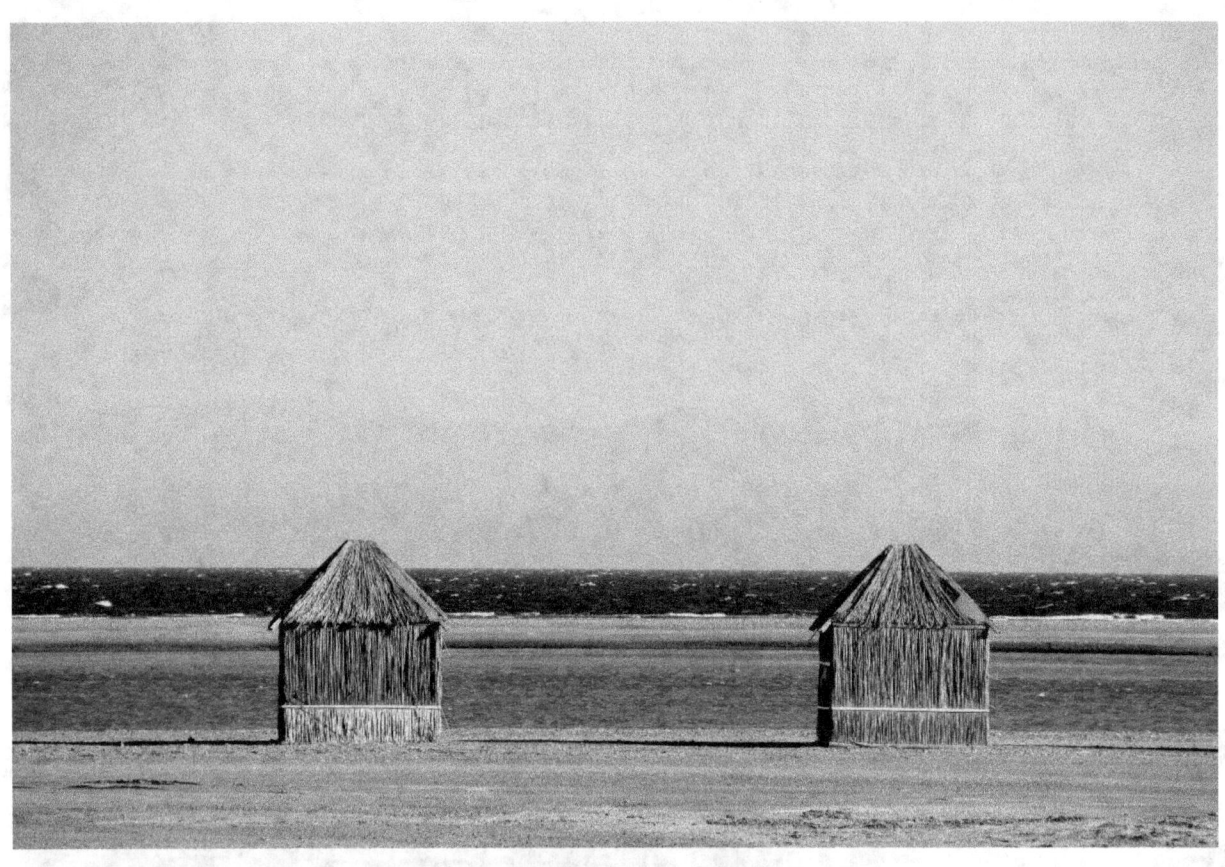

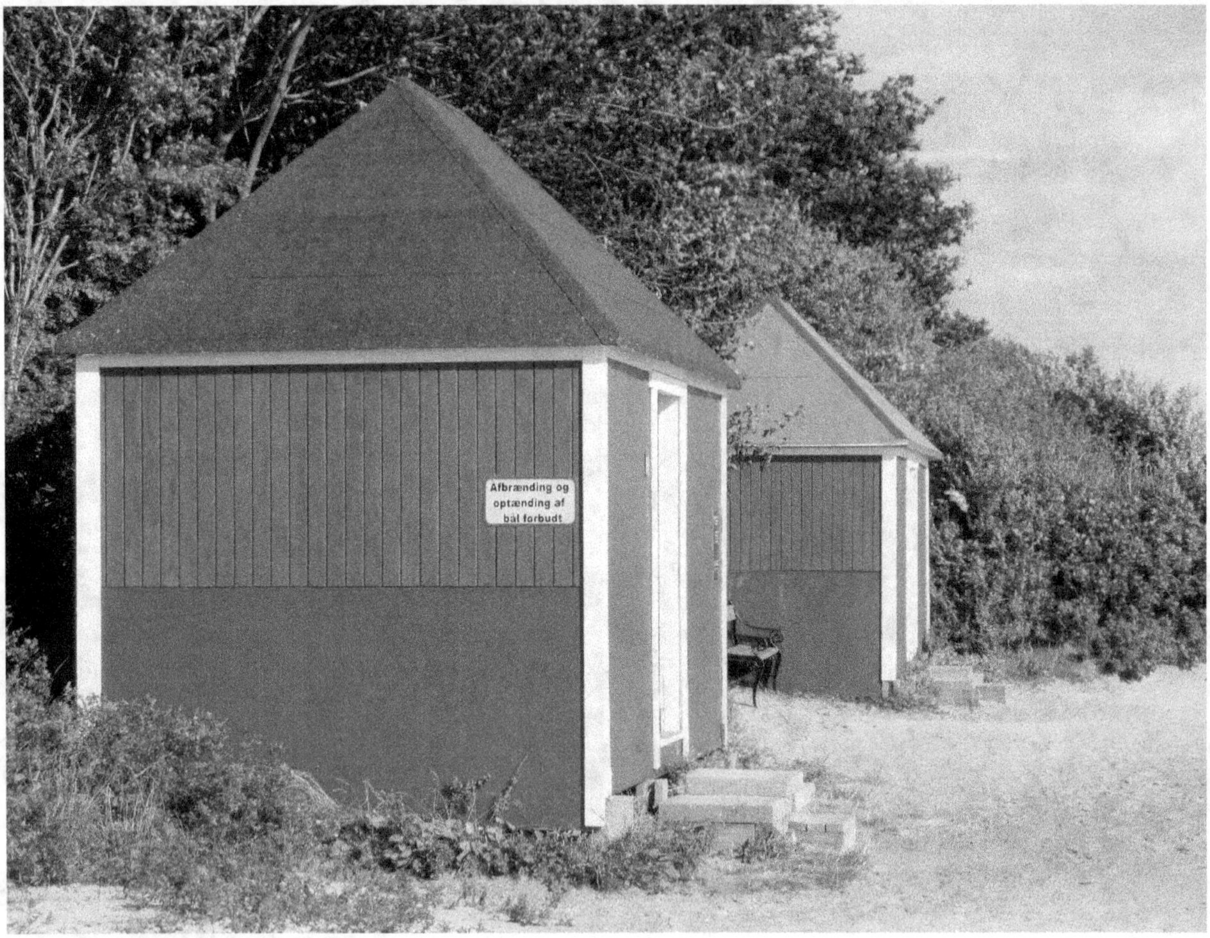

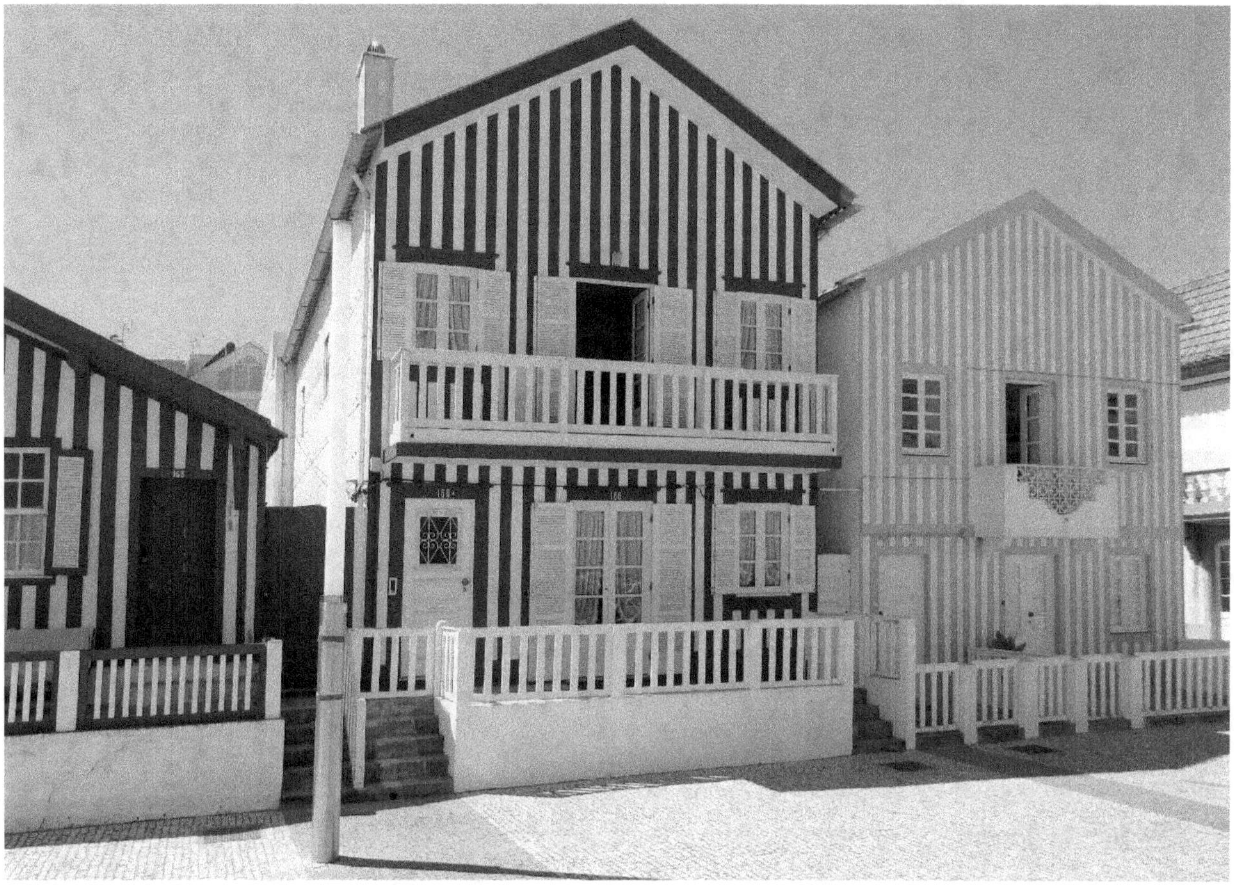

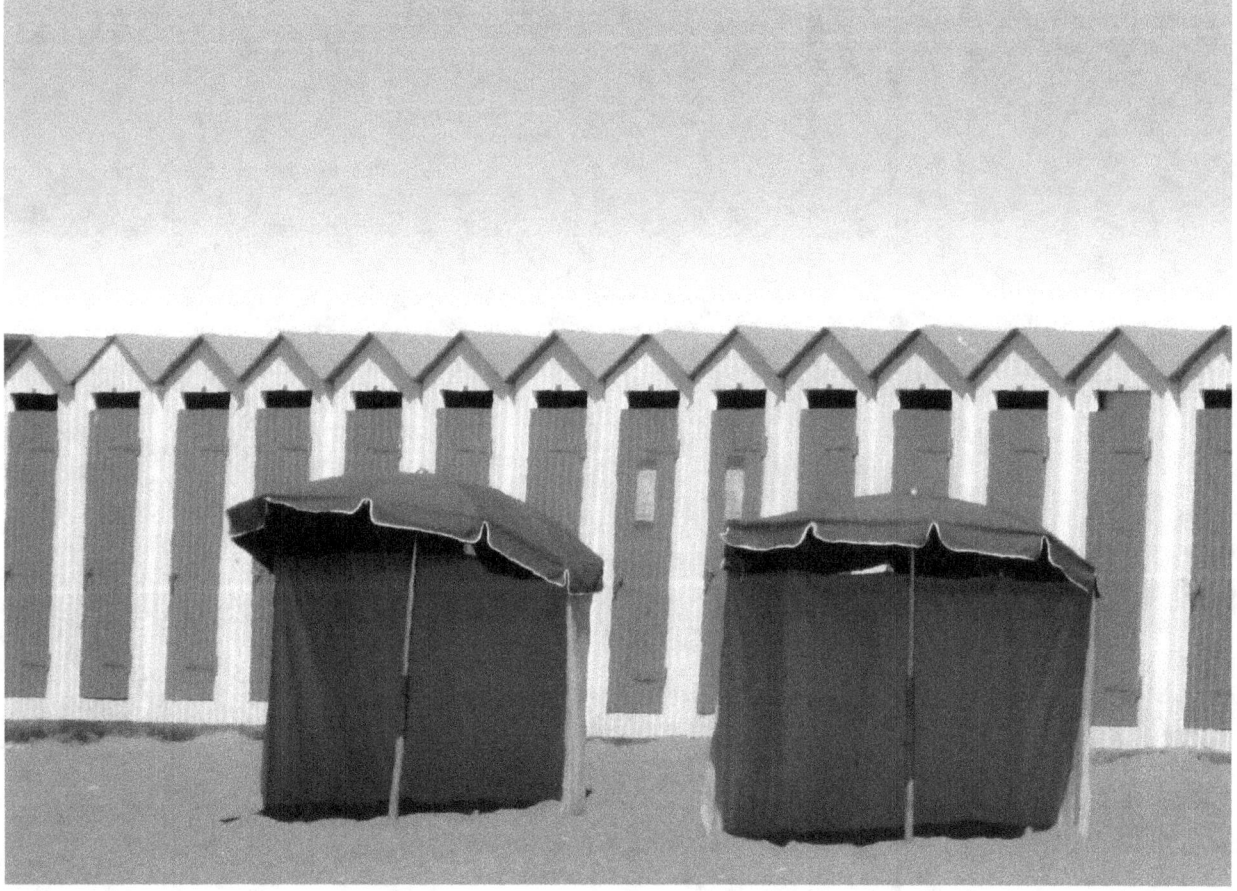

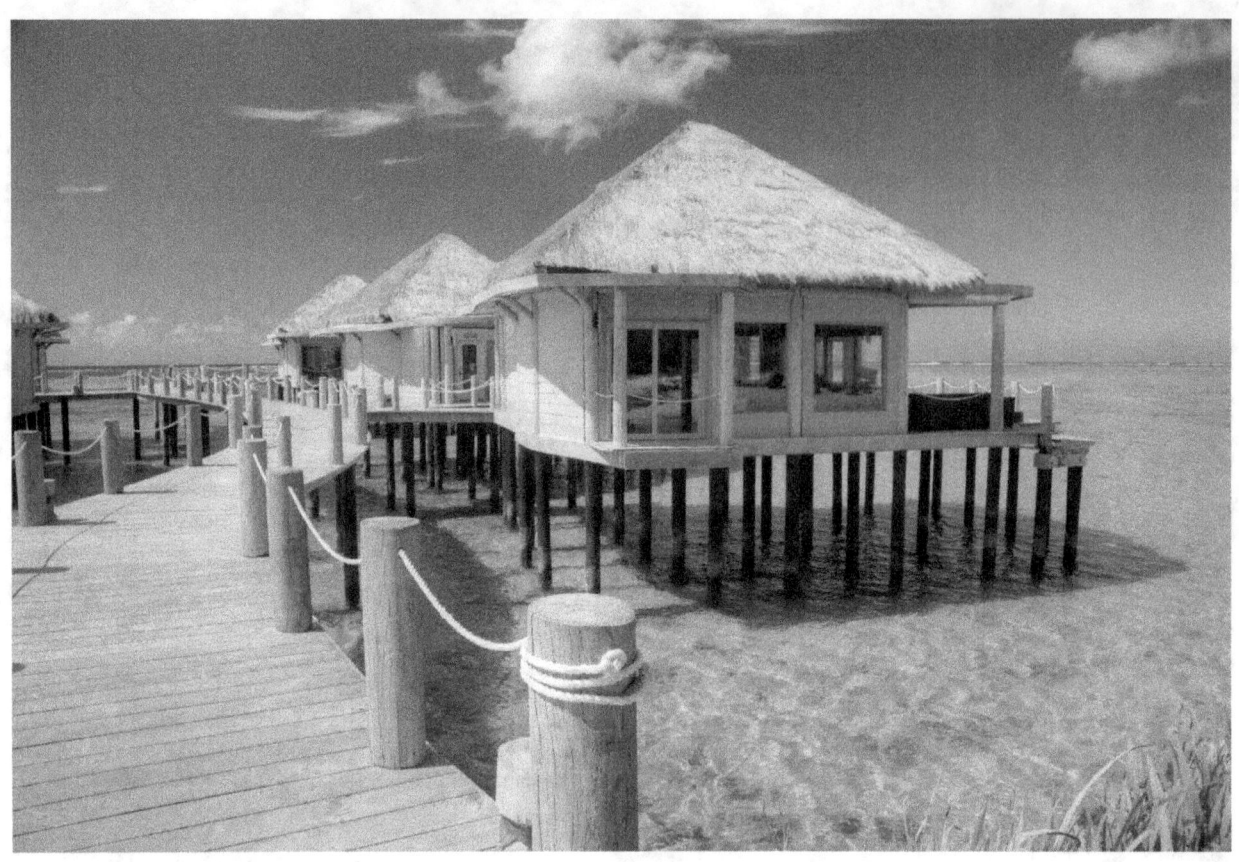

Boathouses

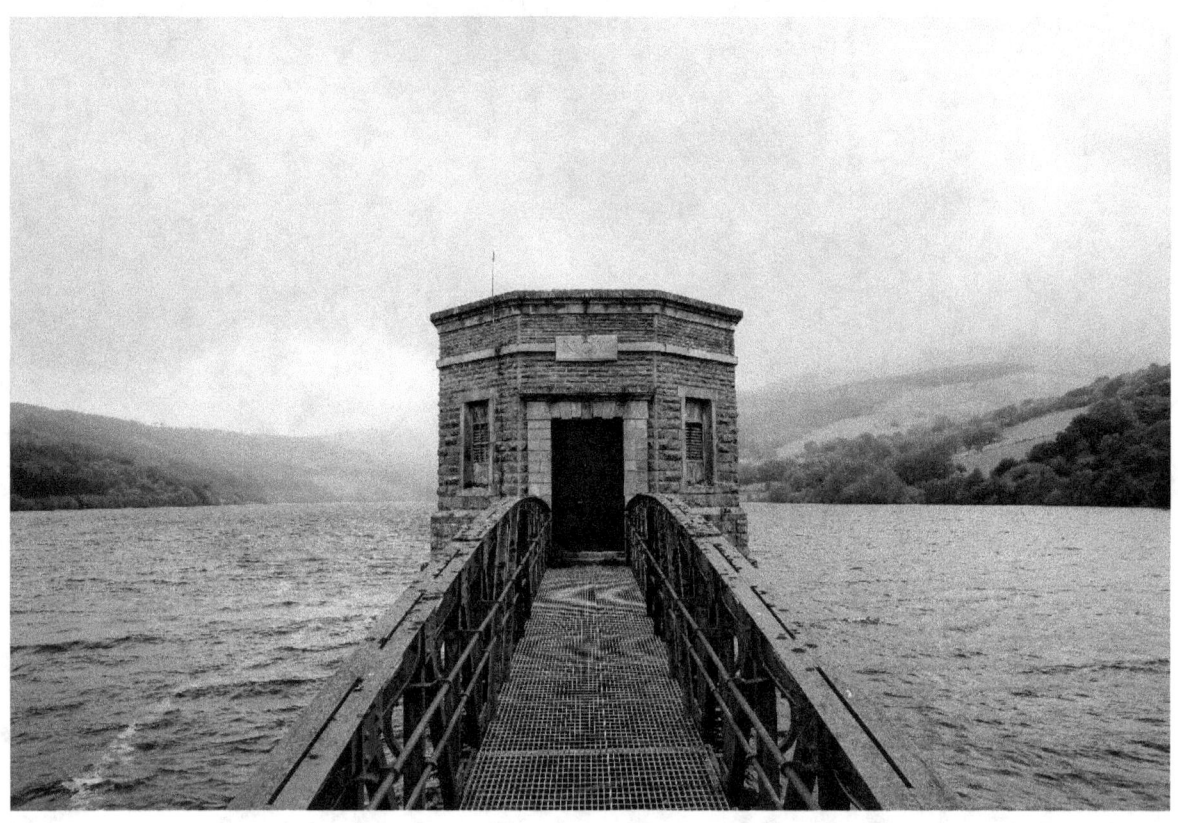

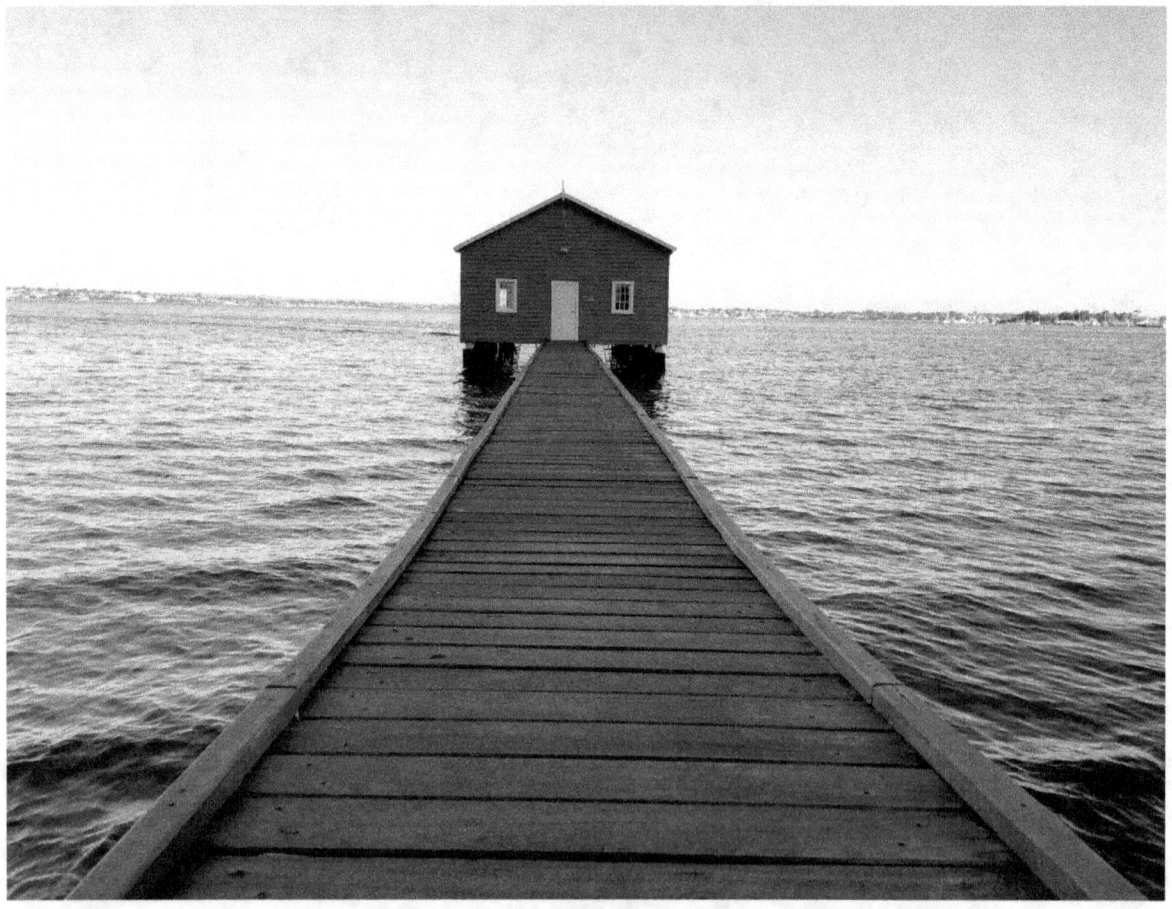

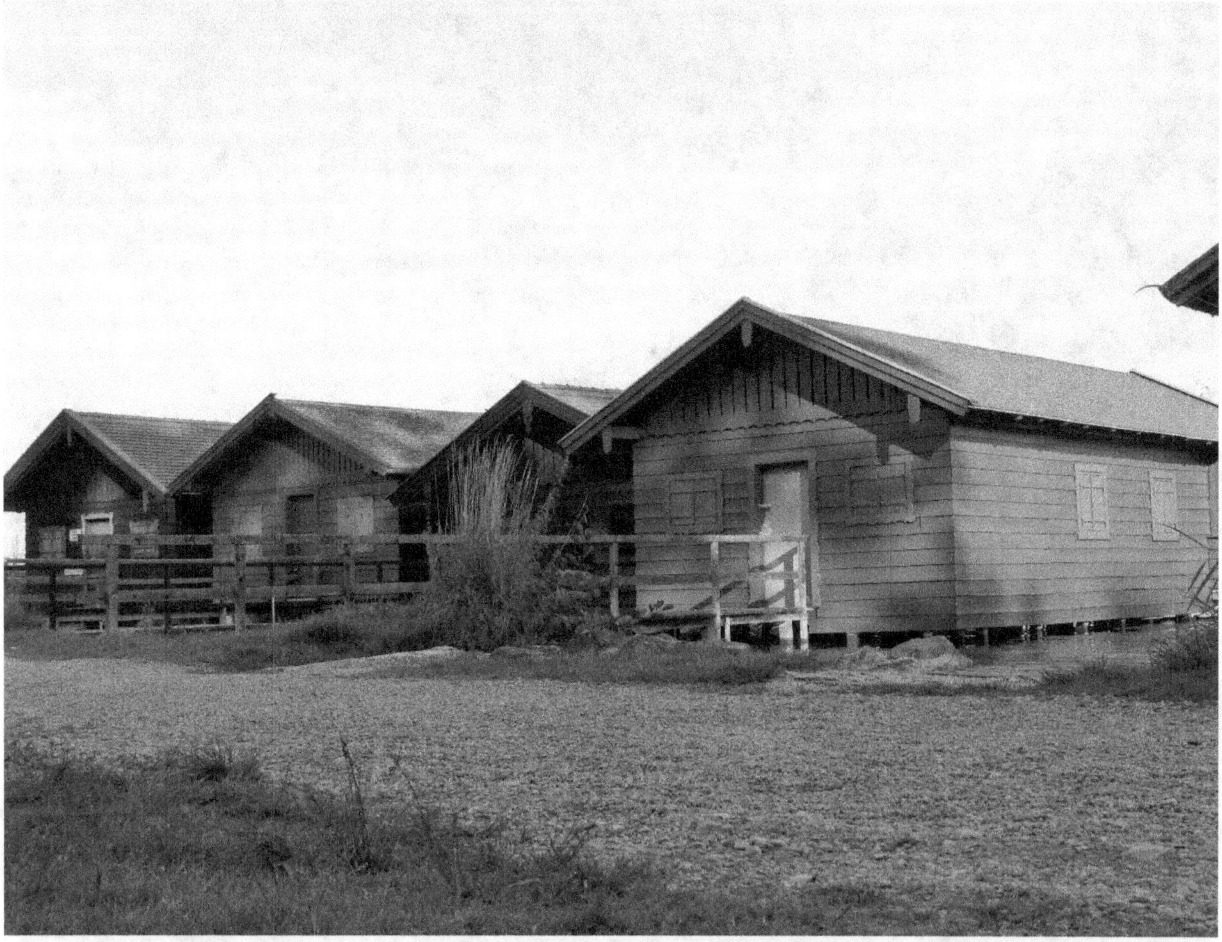

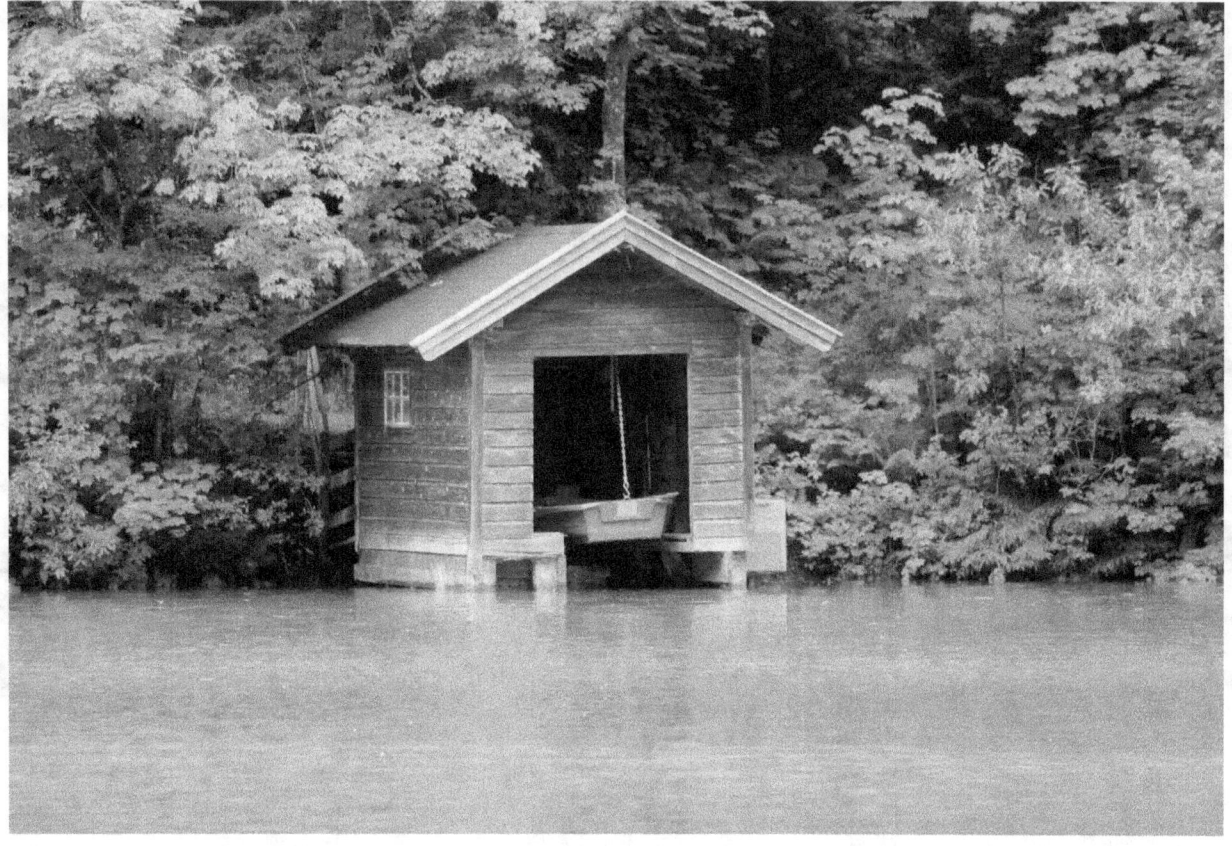

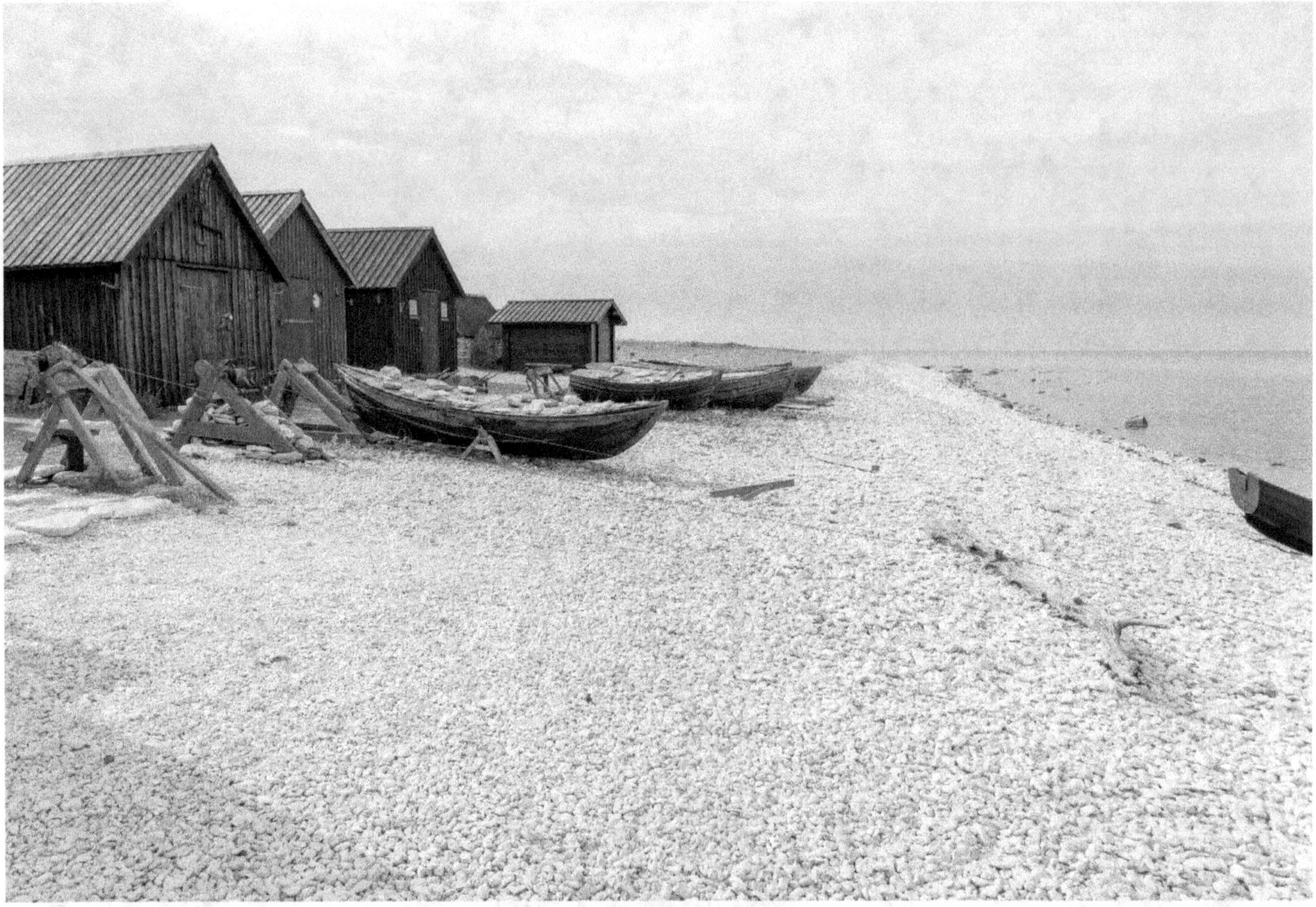

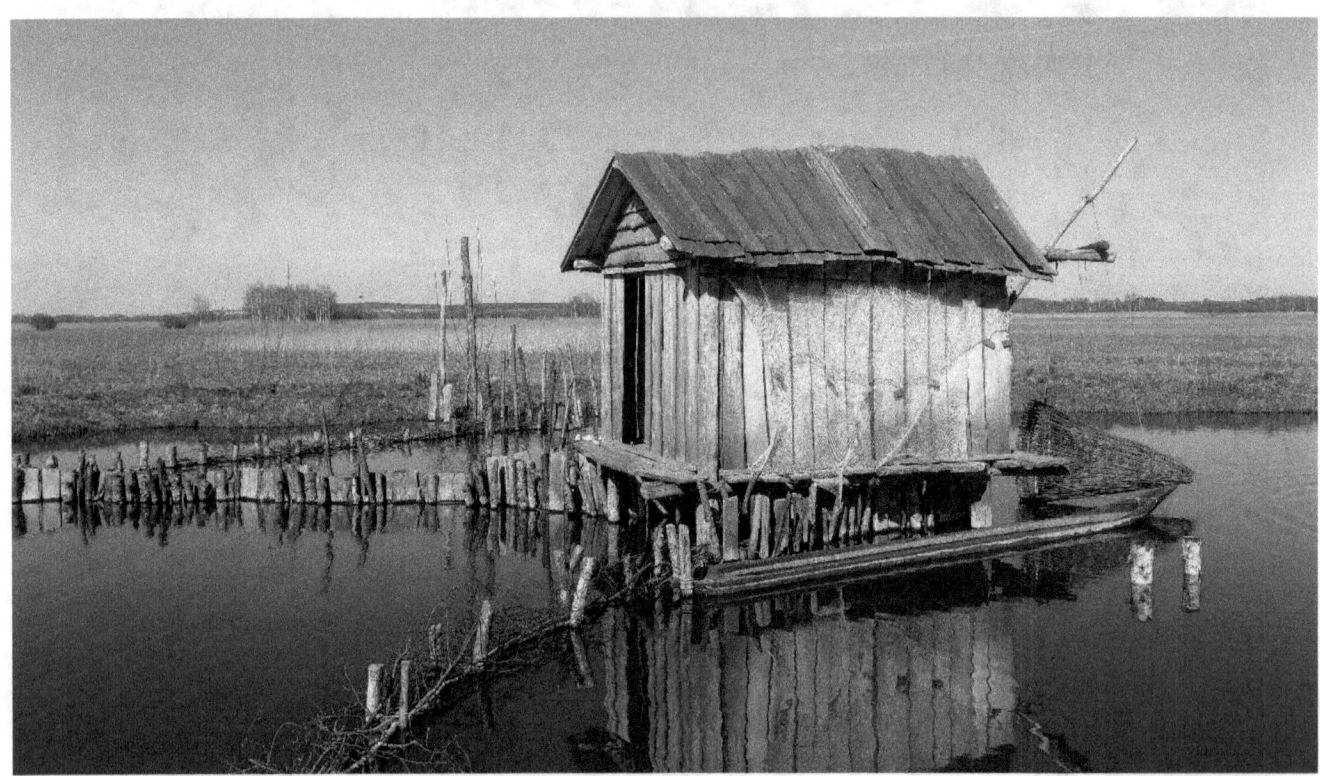

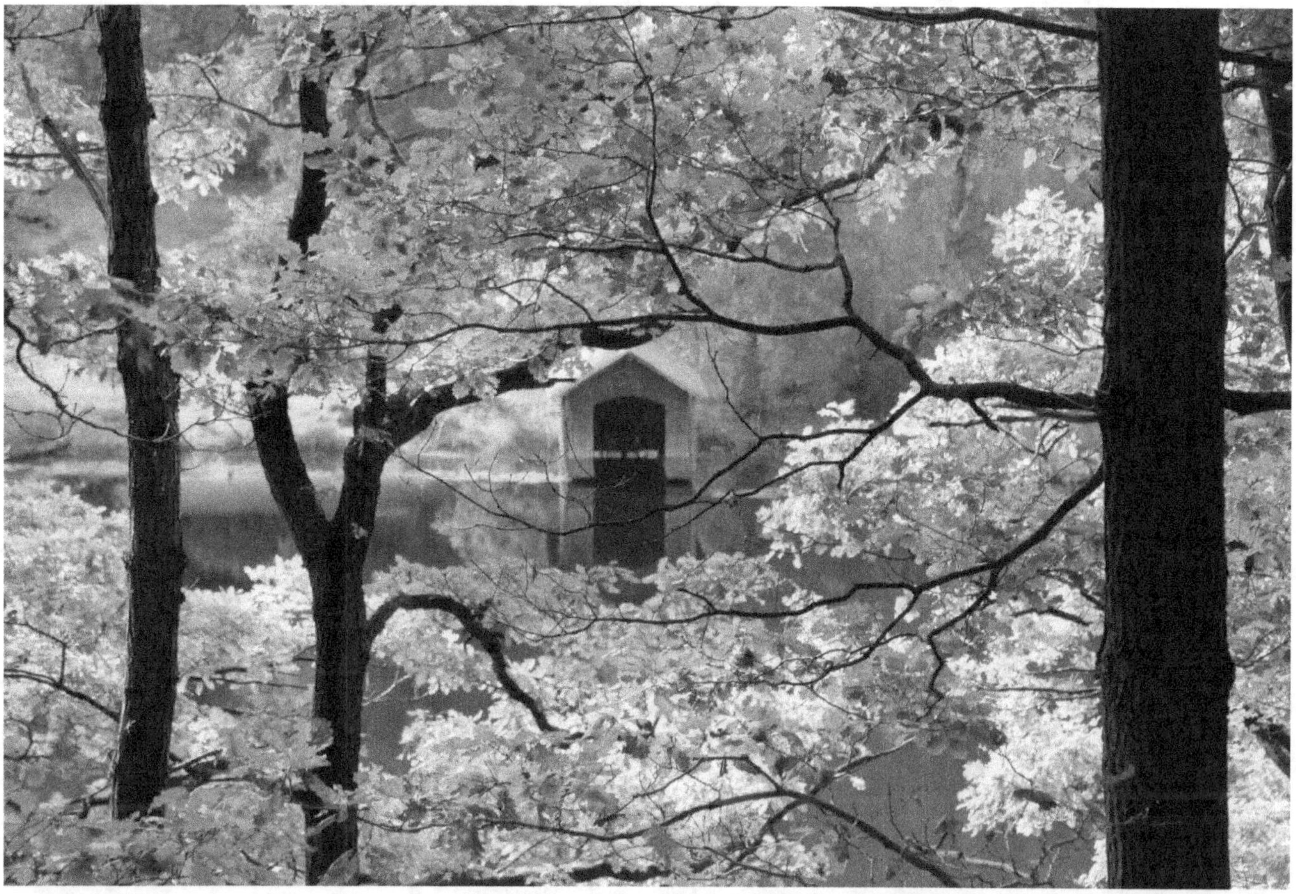

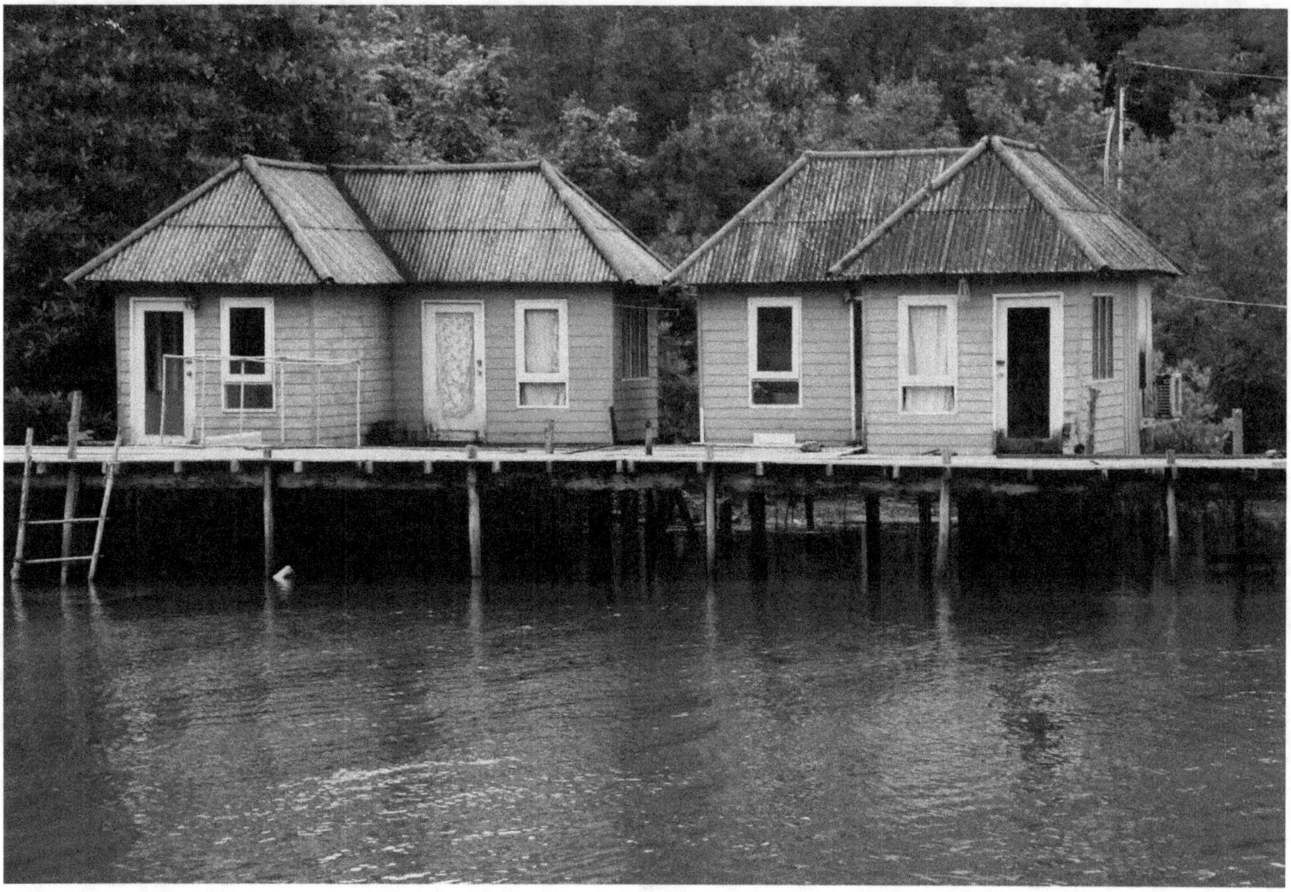

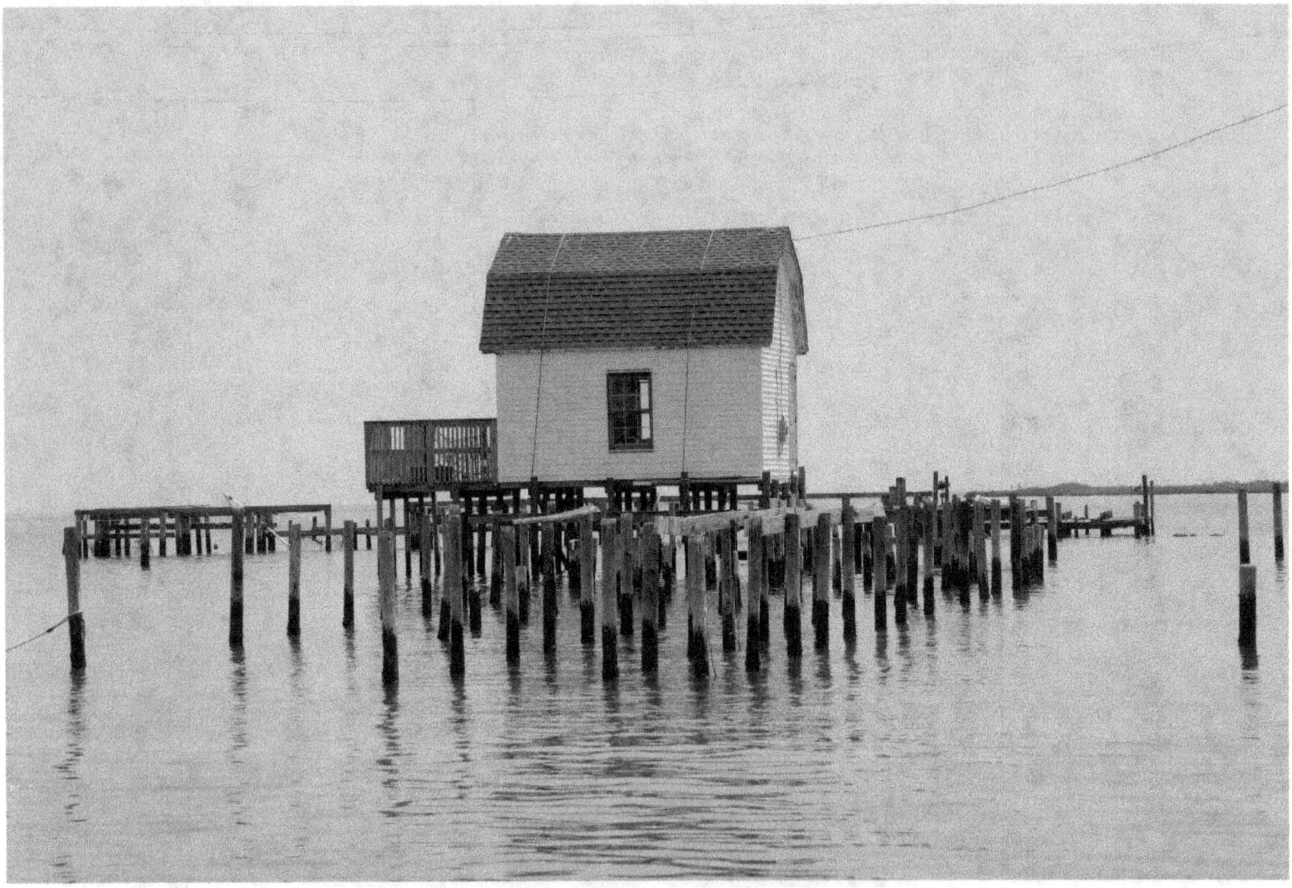

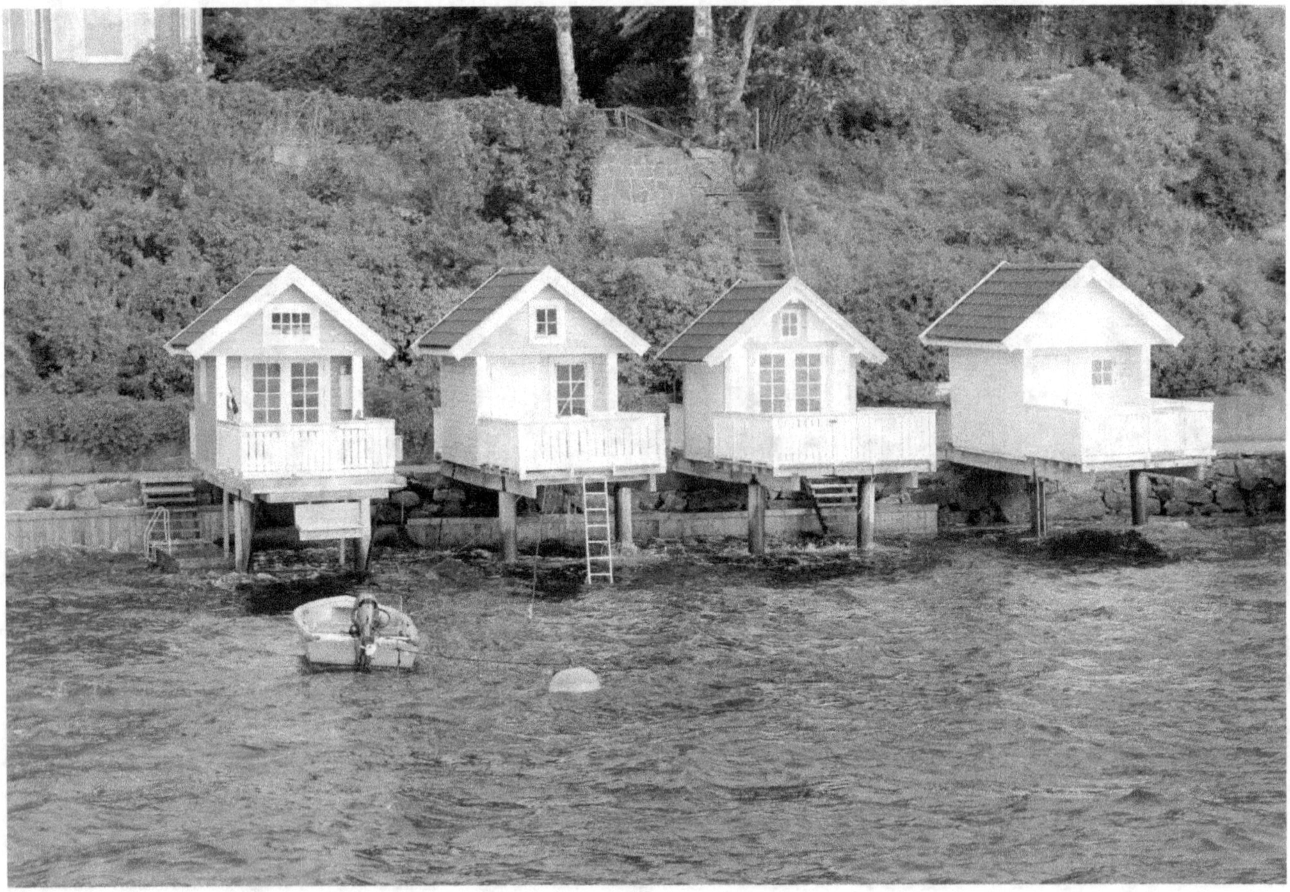

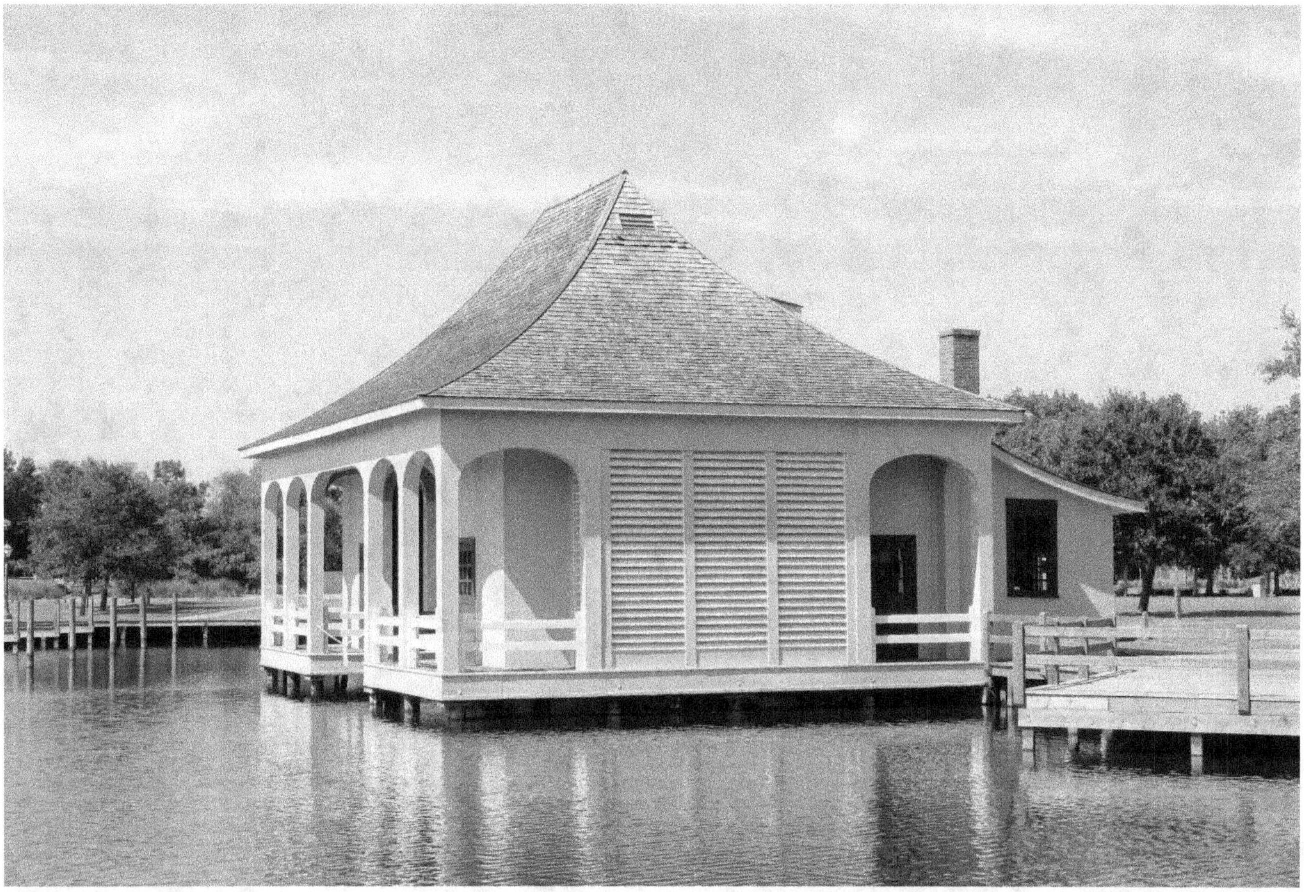

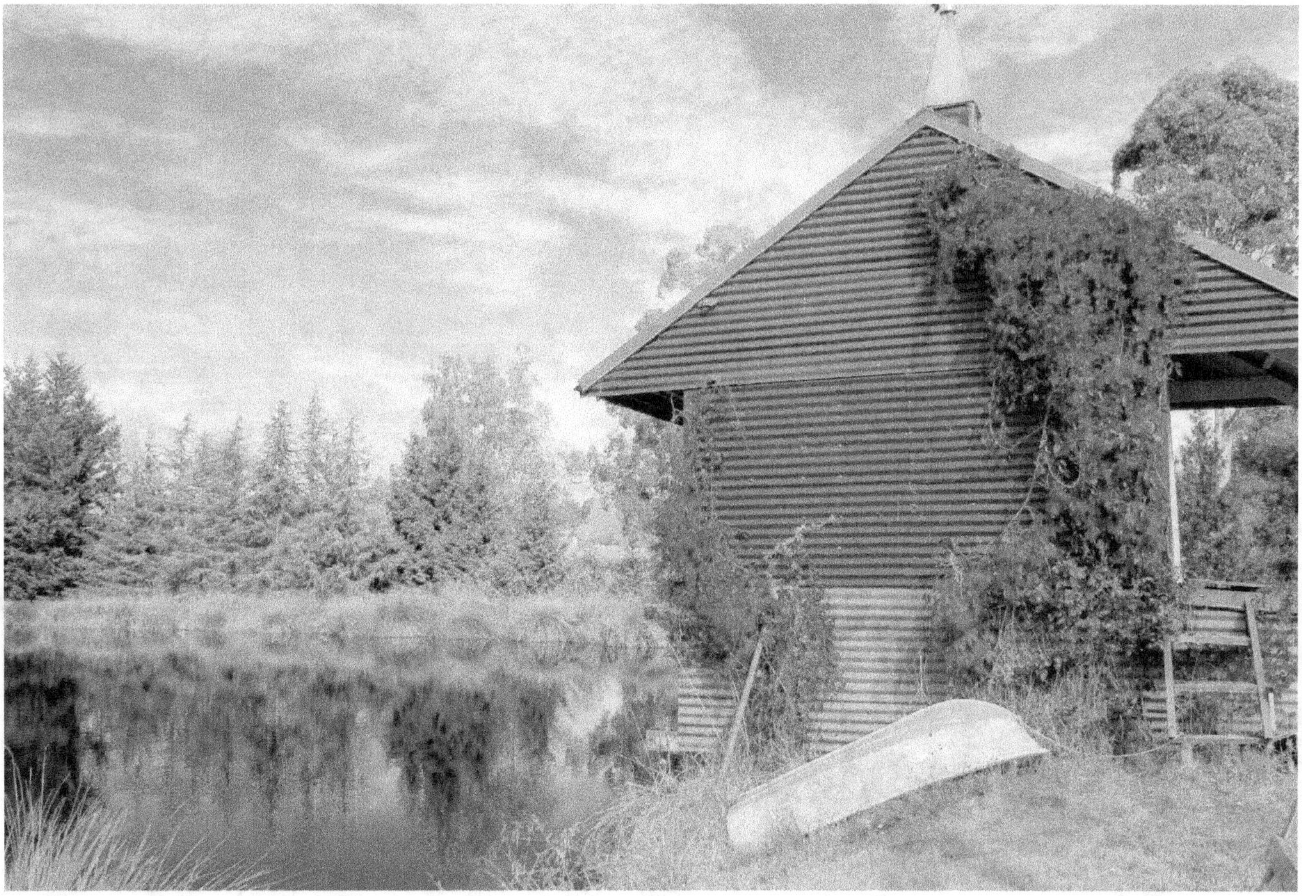

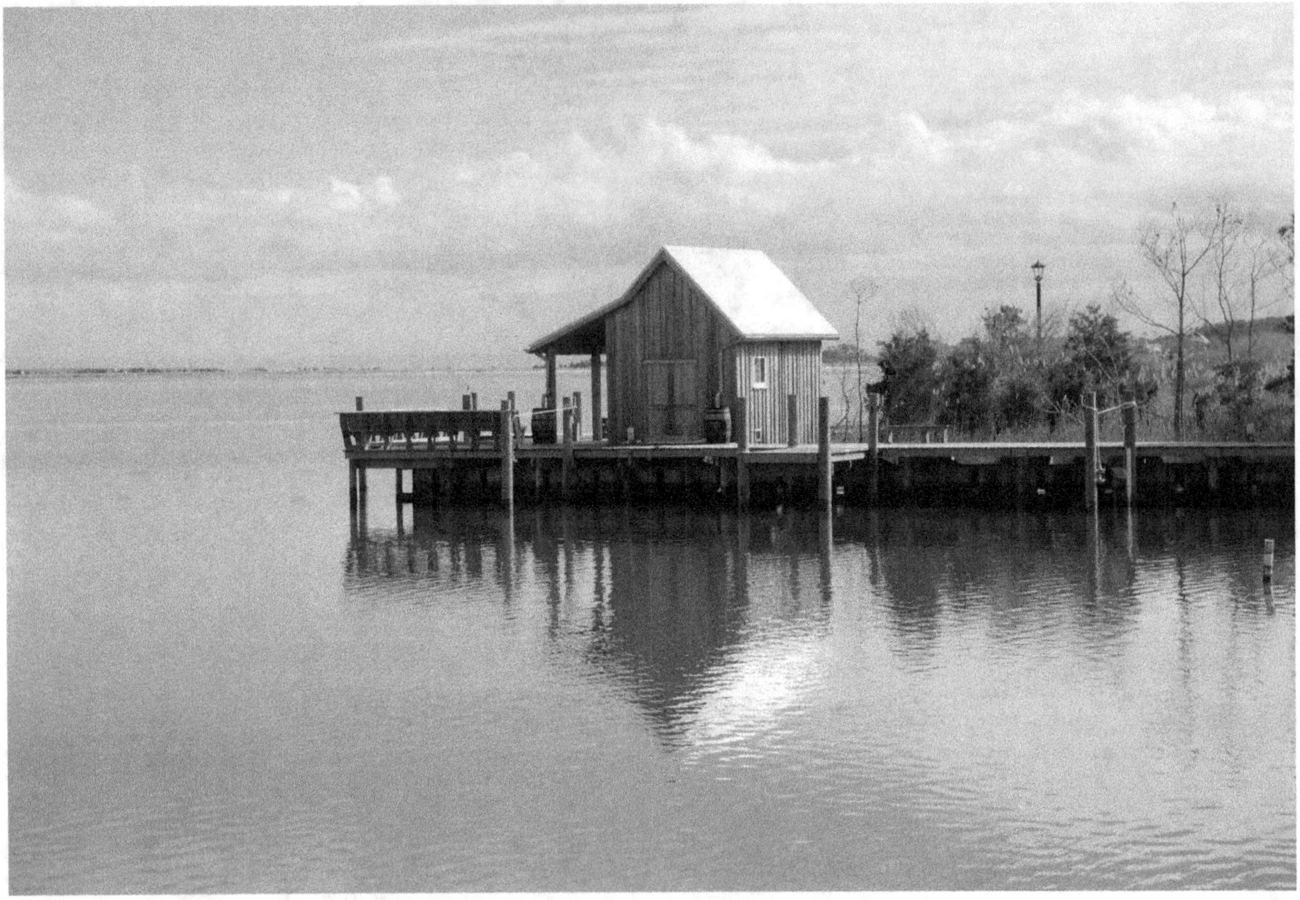

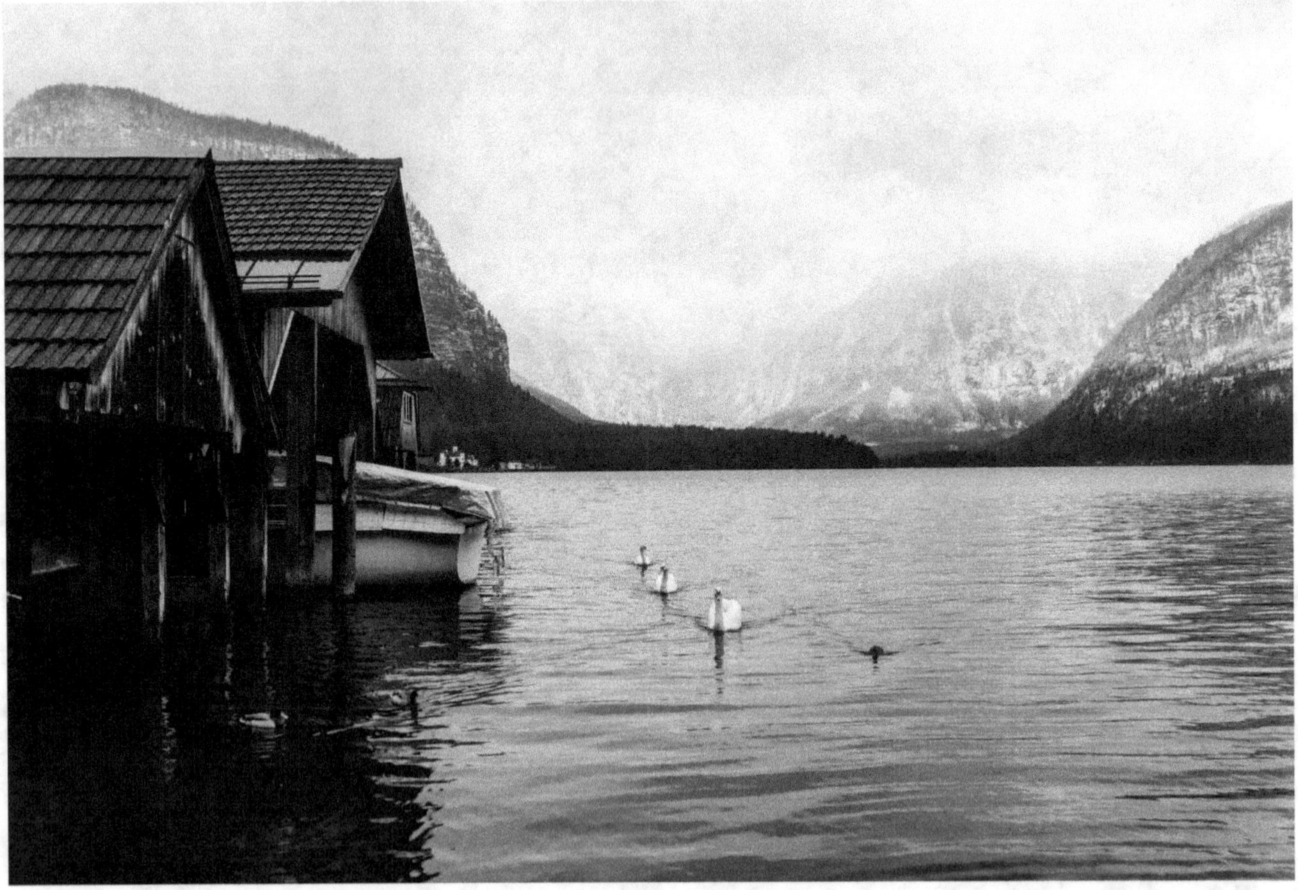

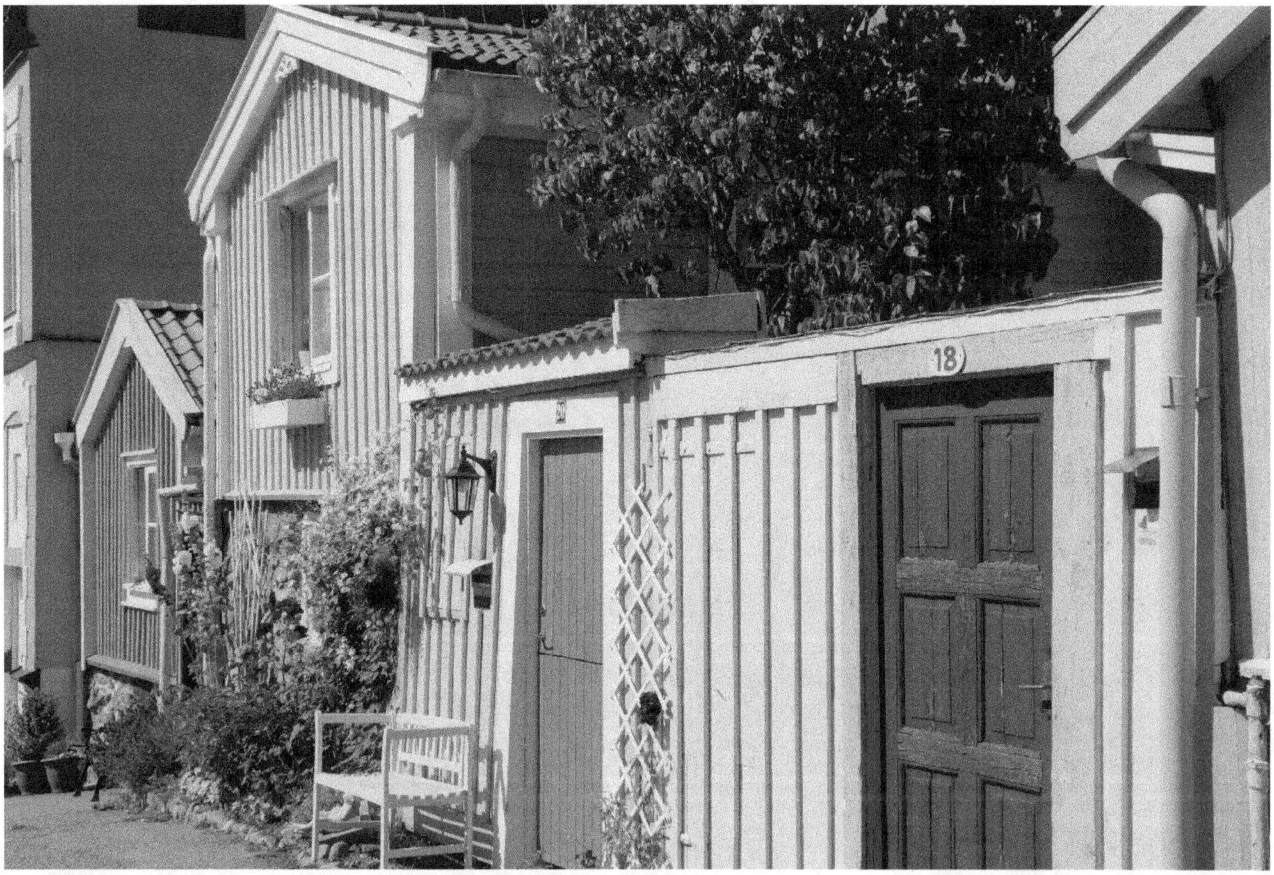
18

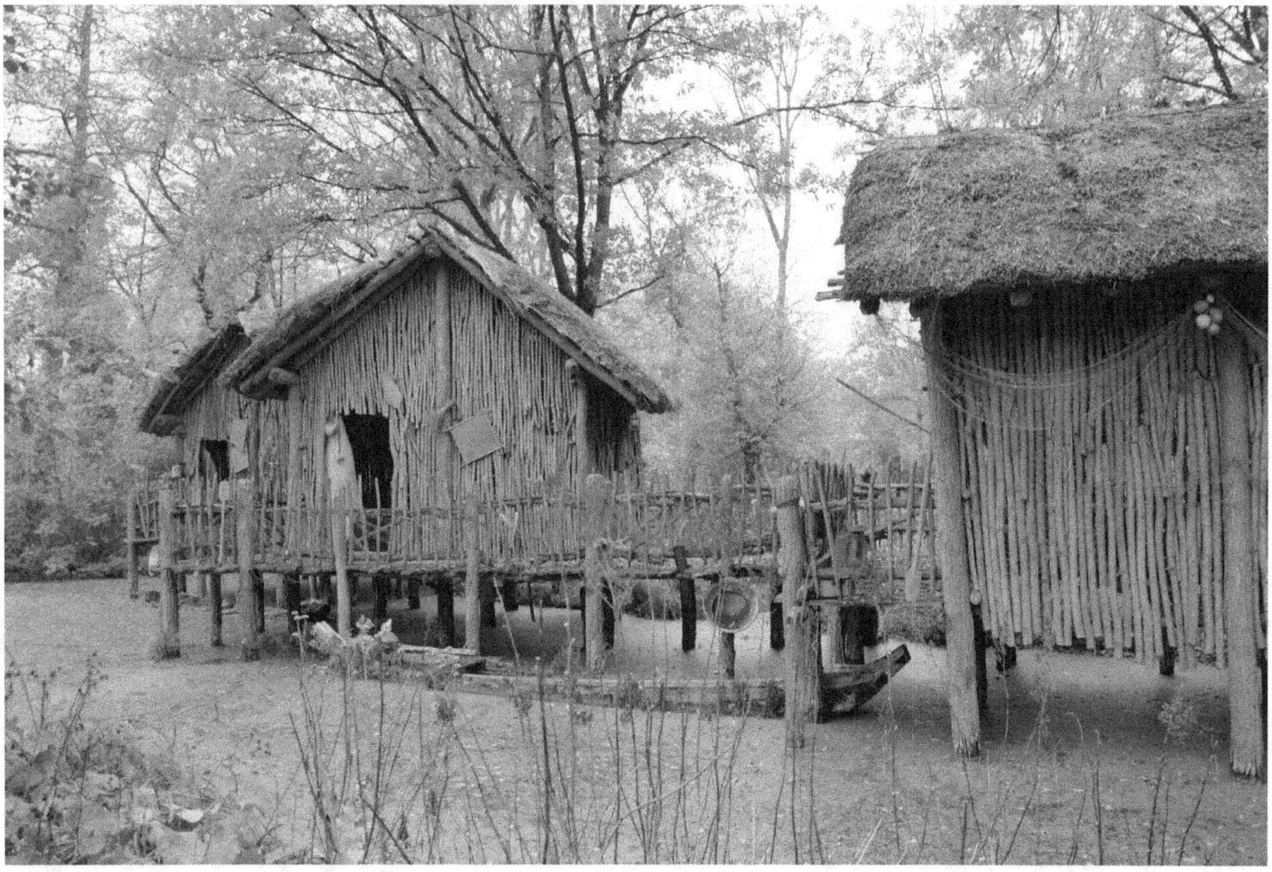

Houseboats

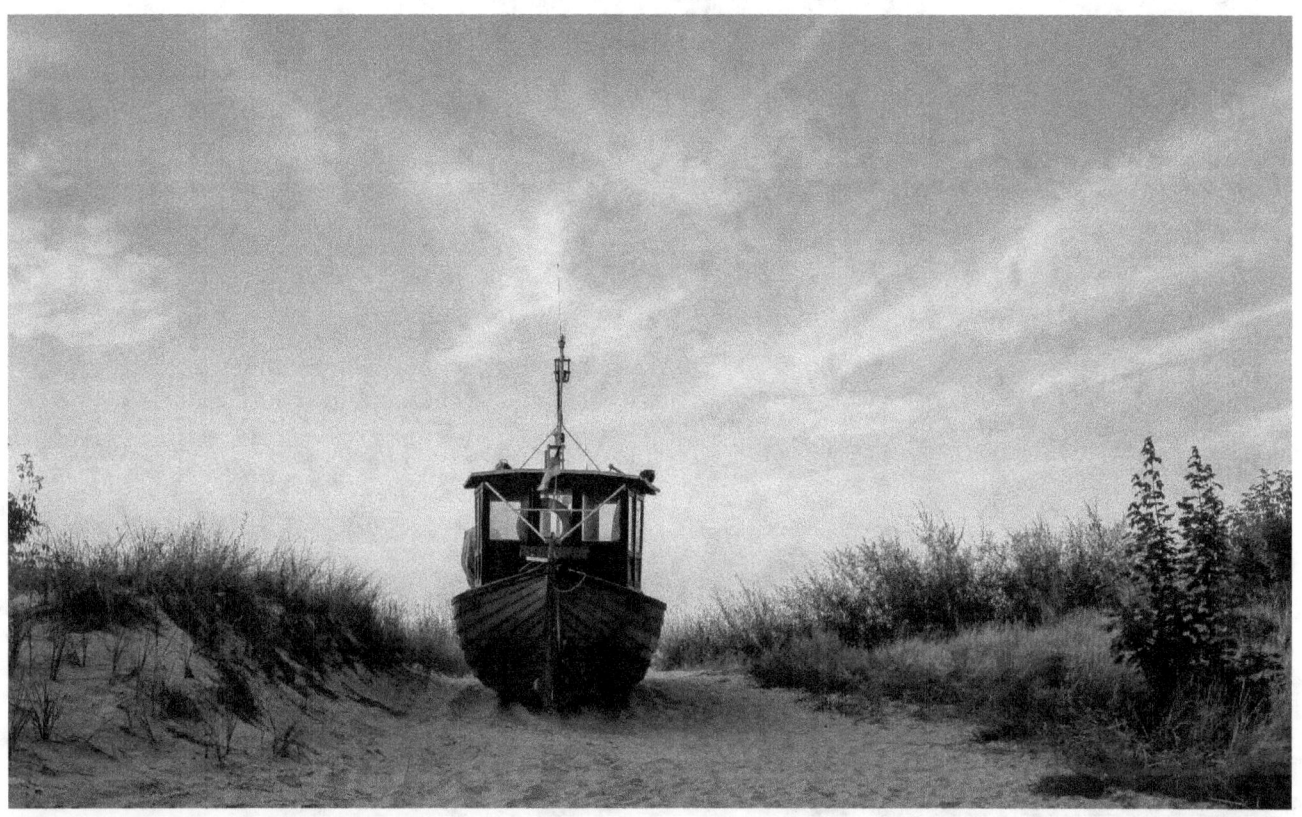

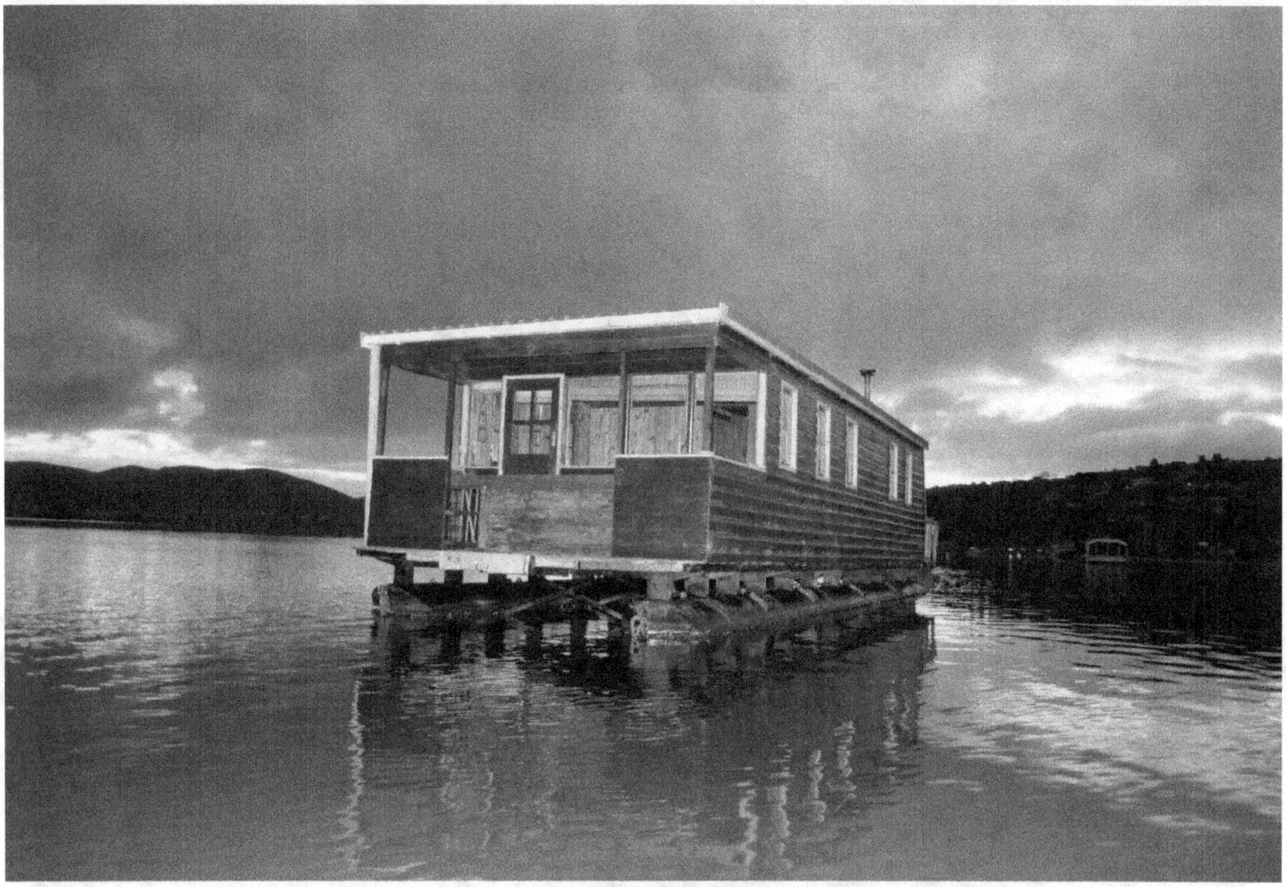

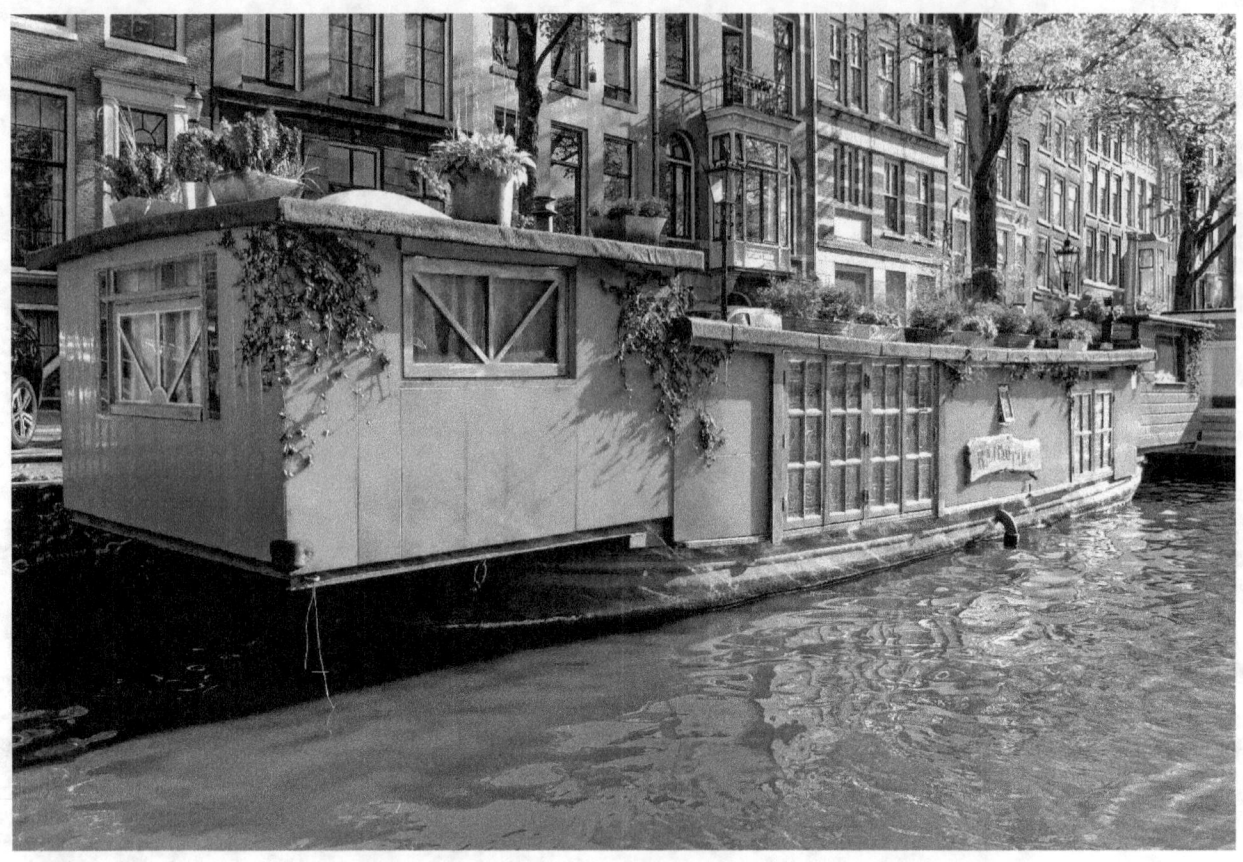

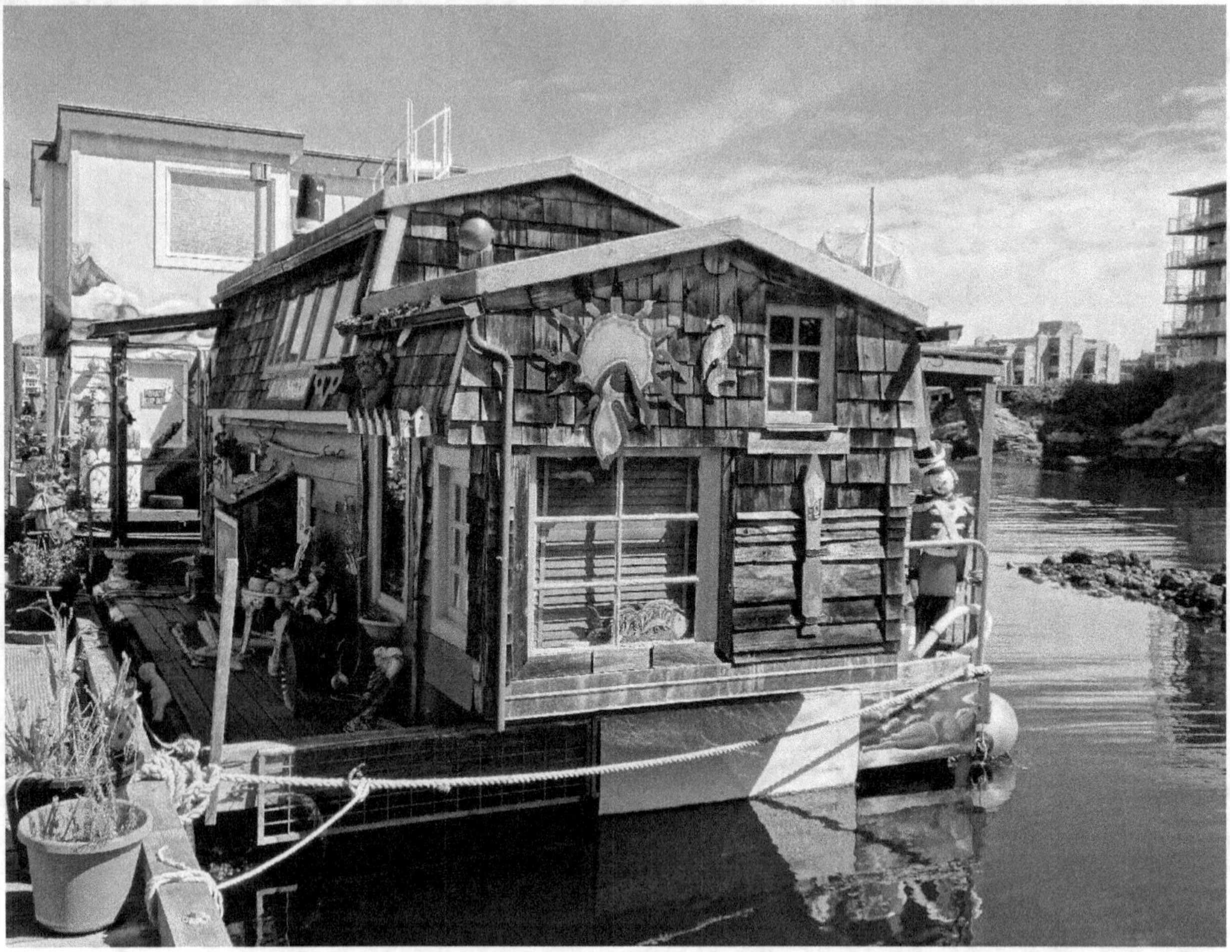

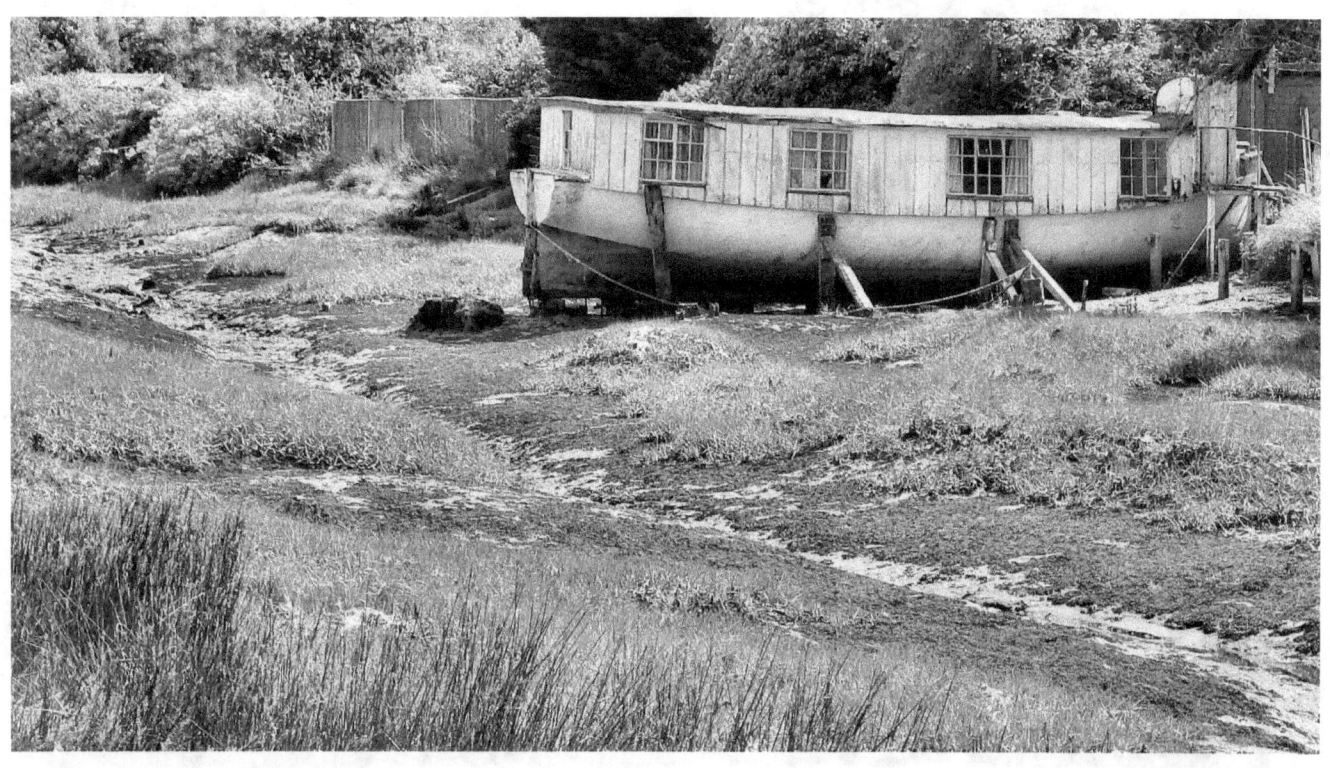

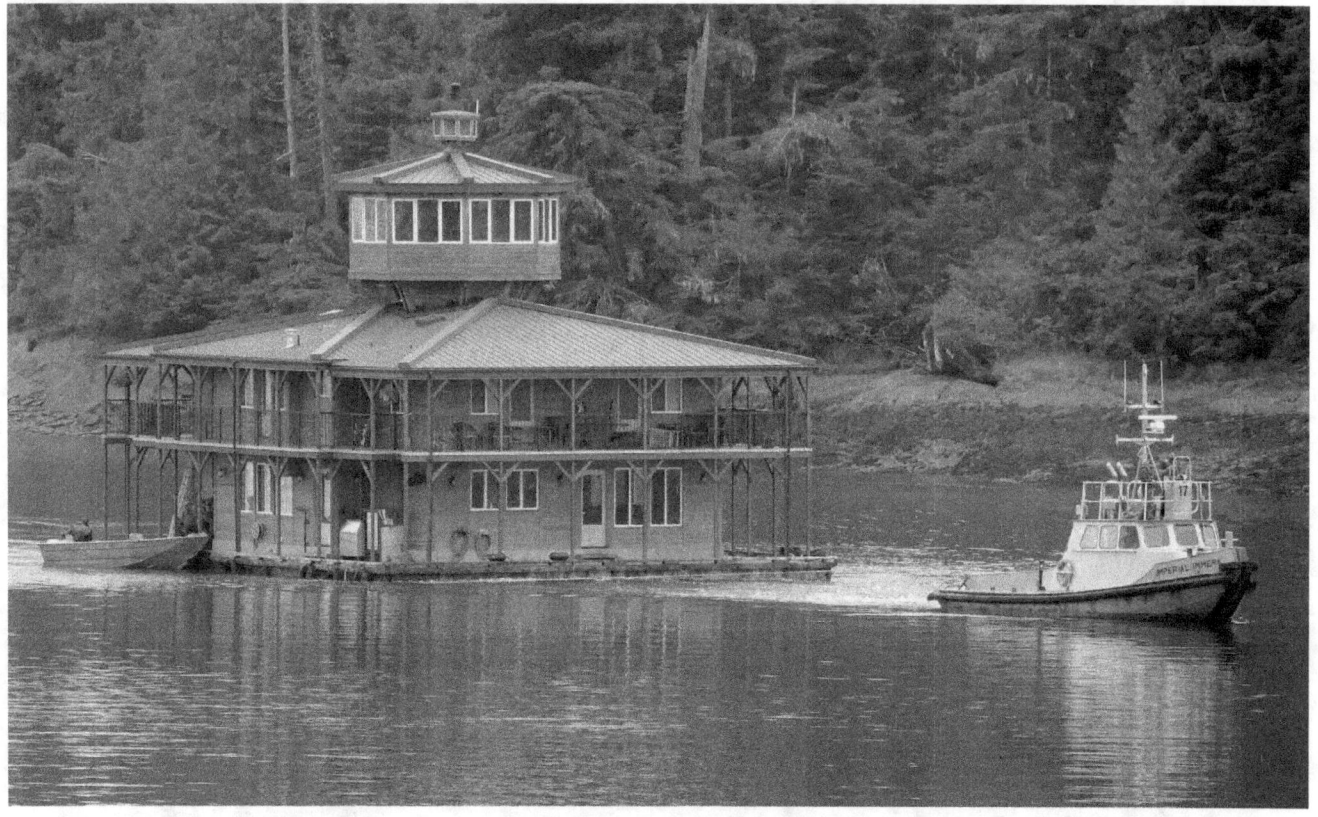

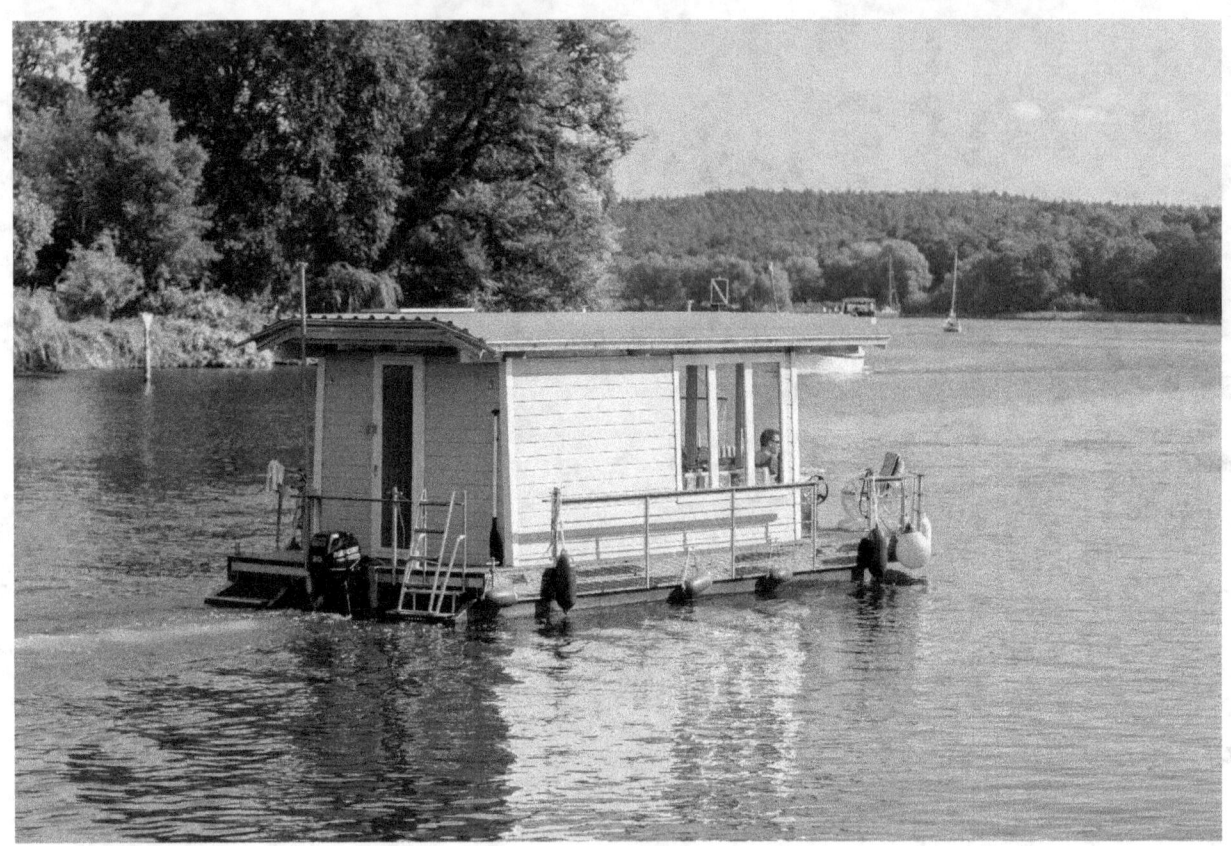

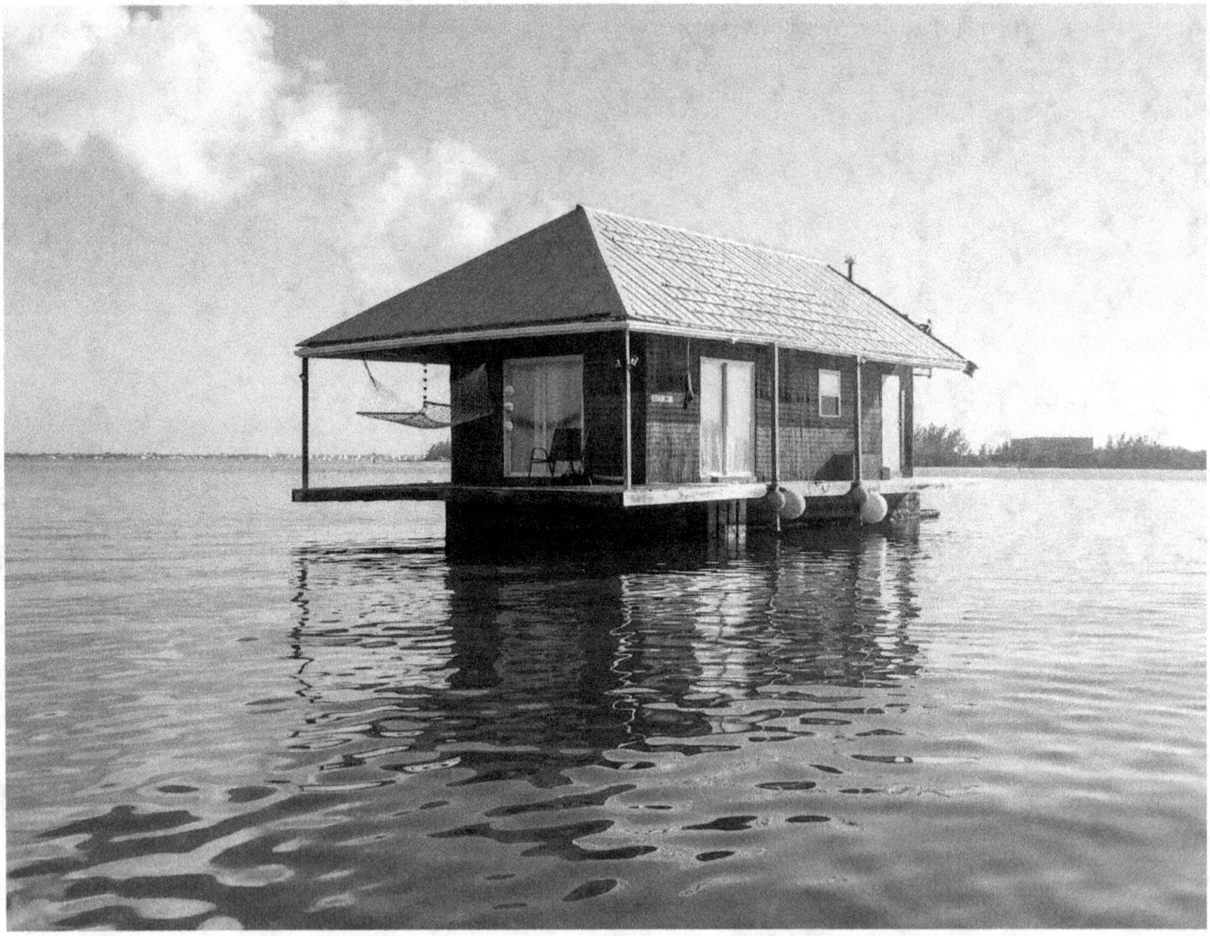

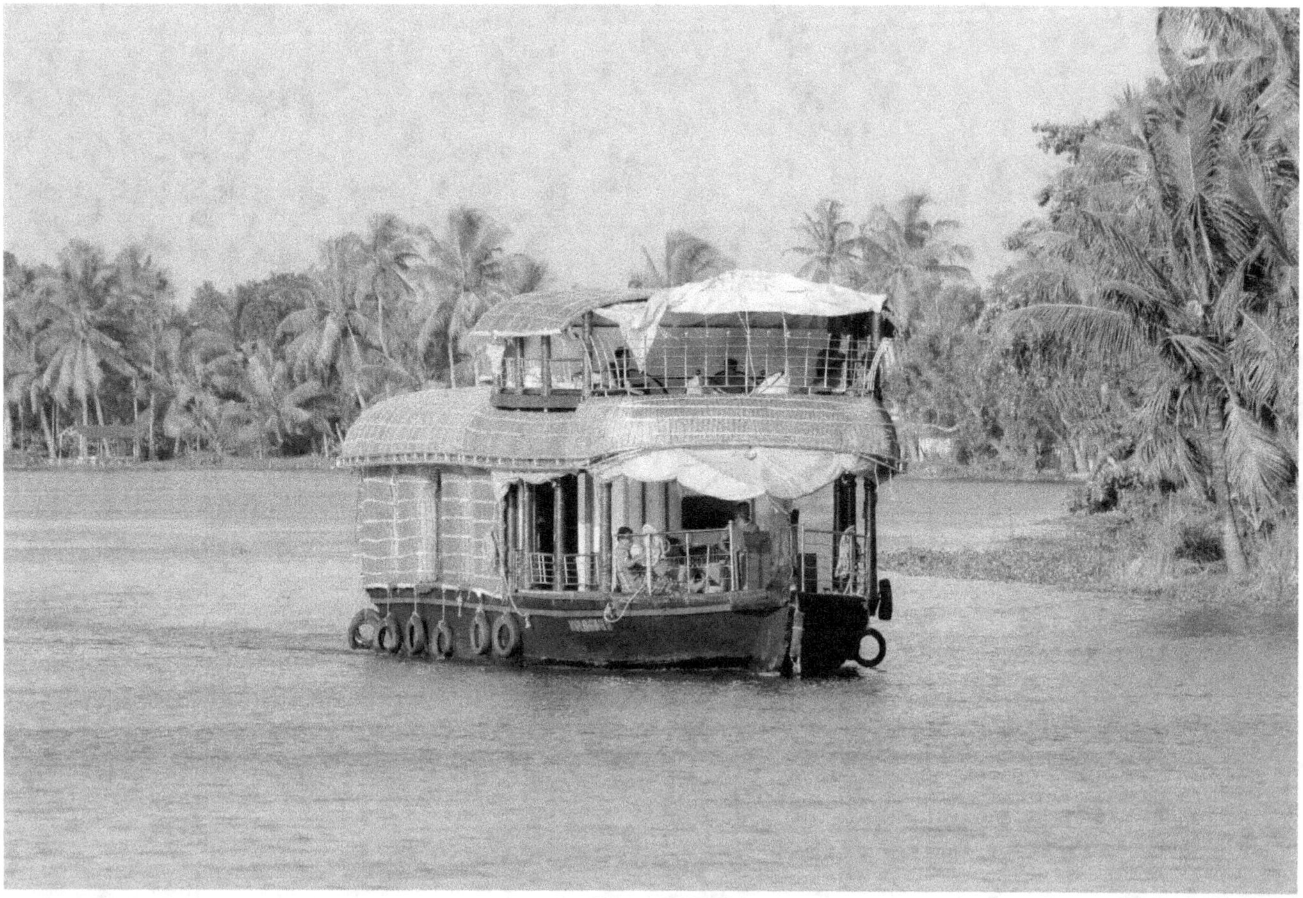

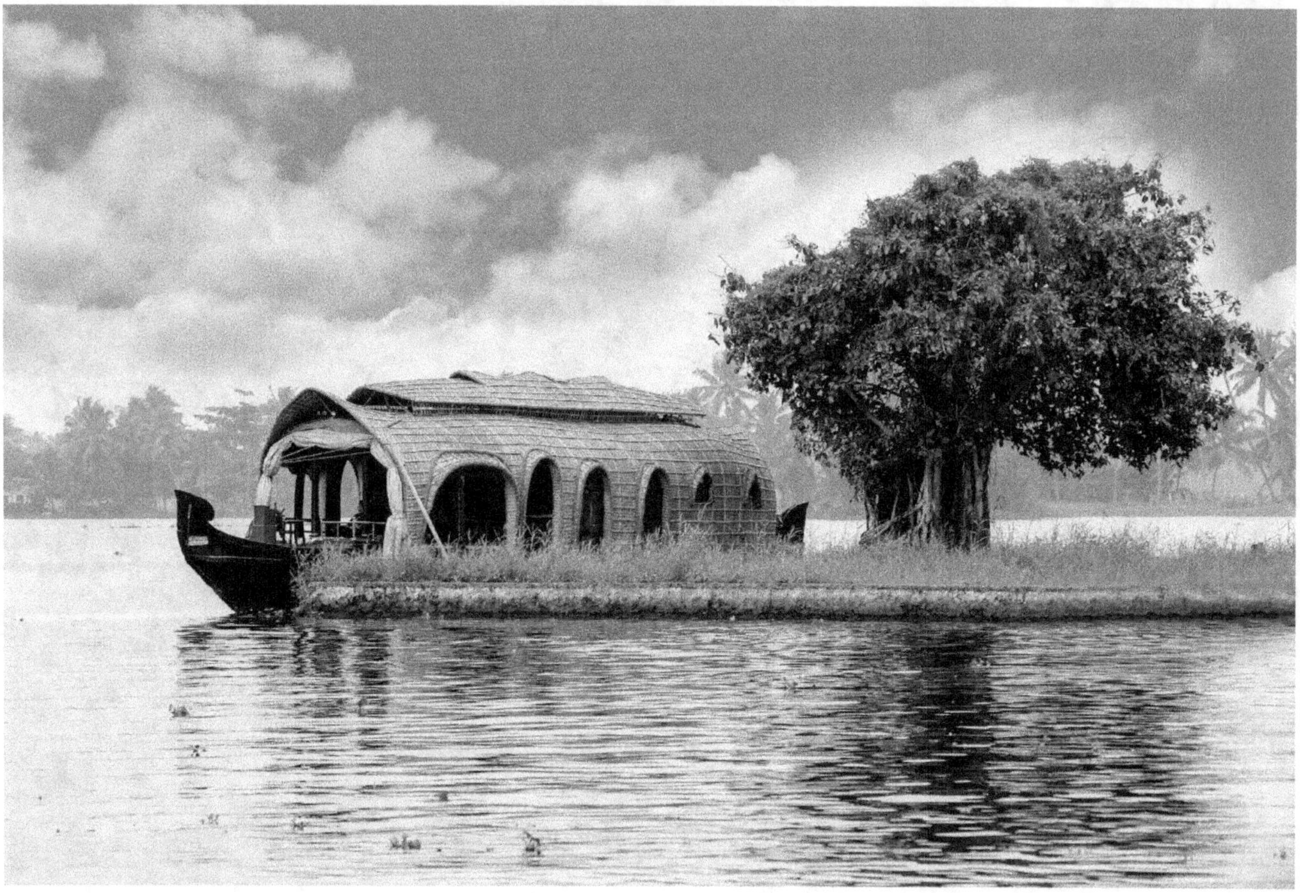

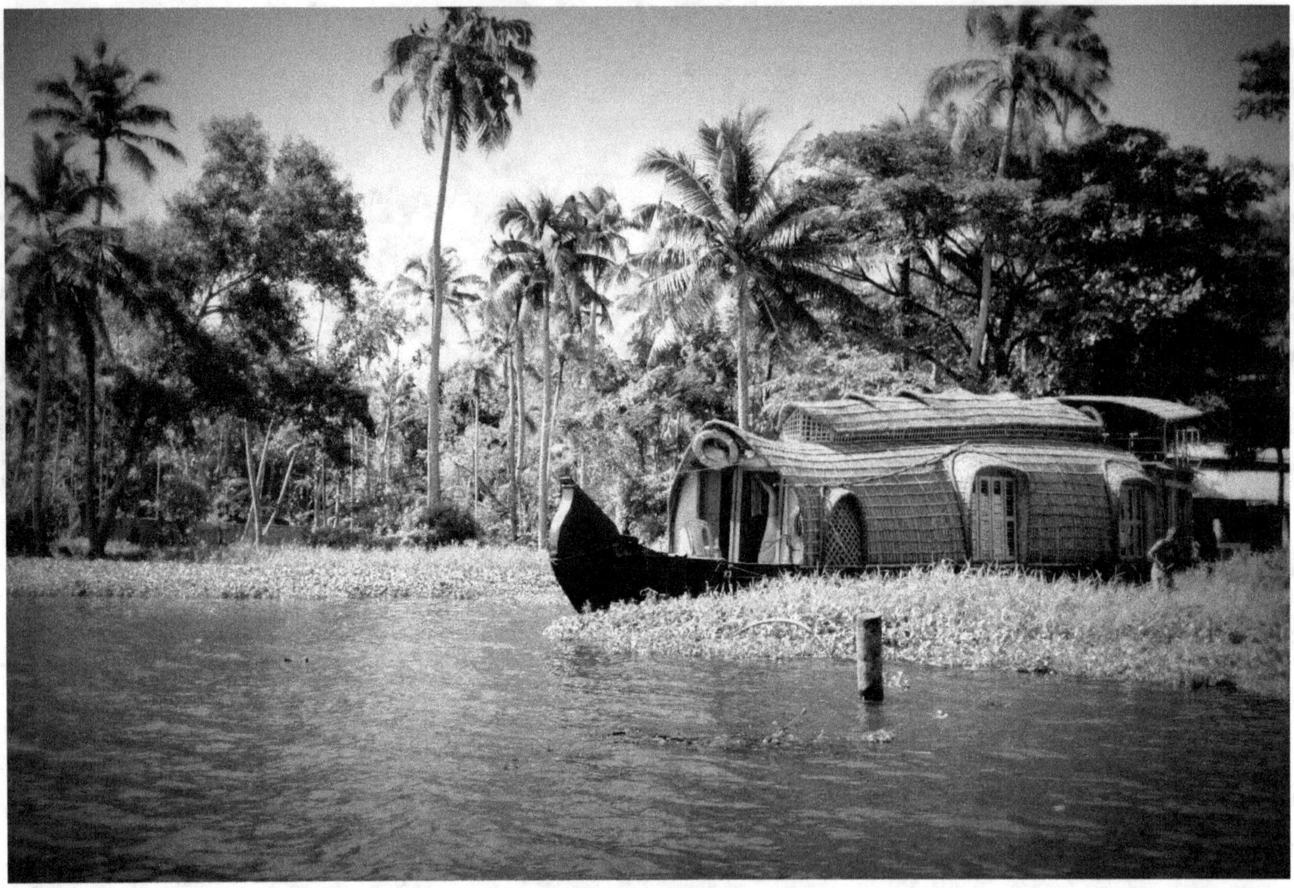

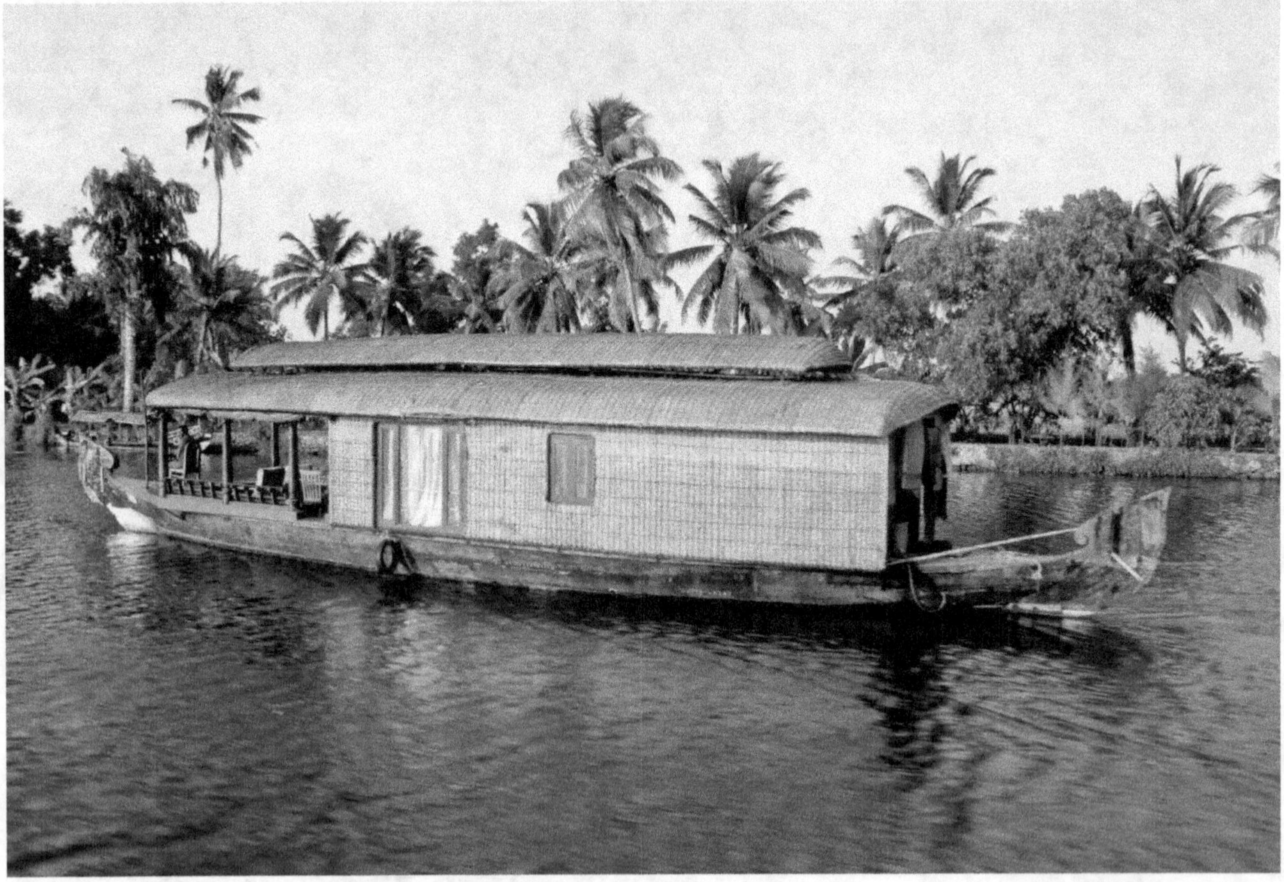

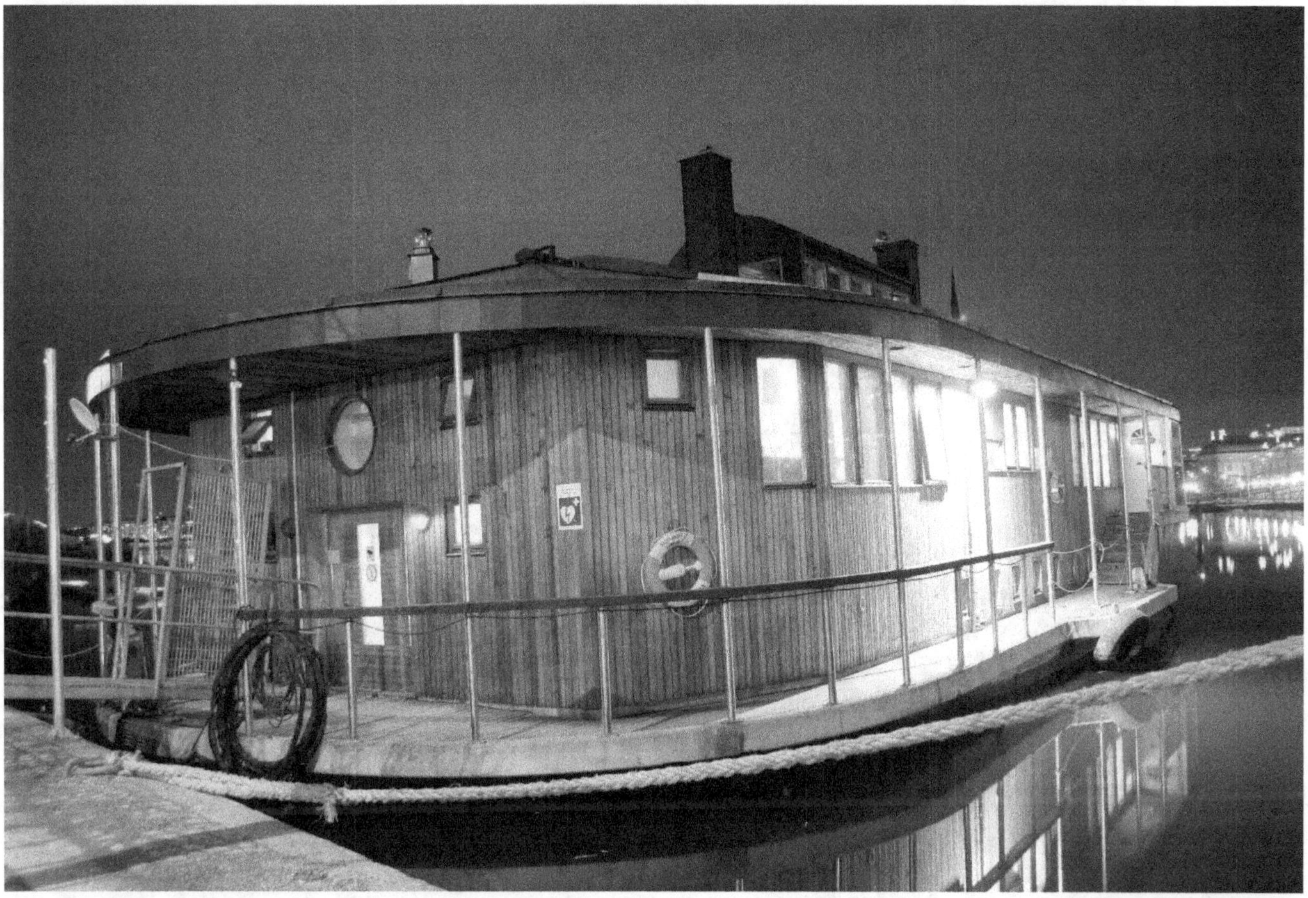

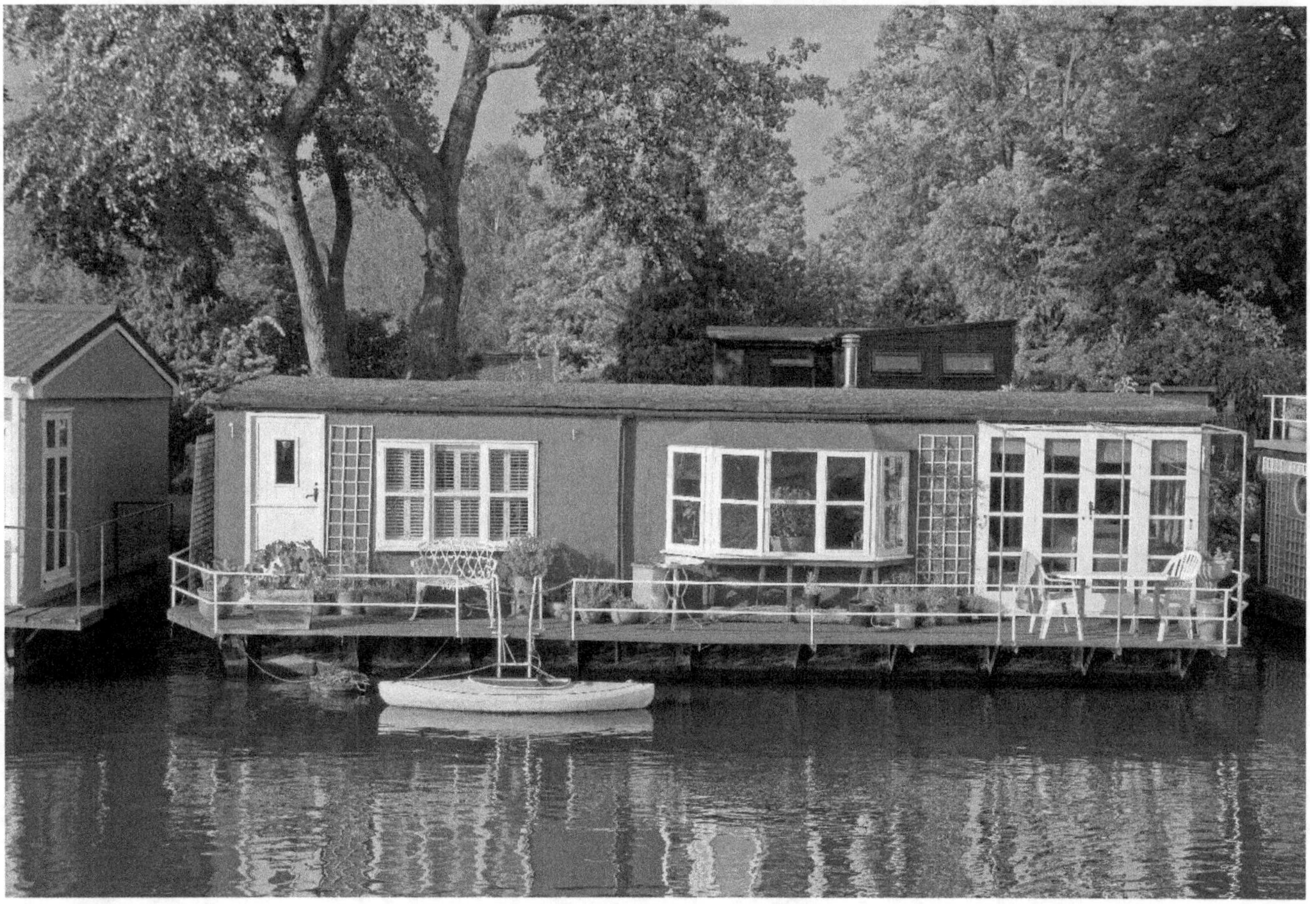

4 SUN

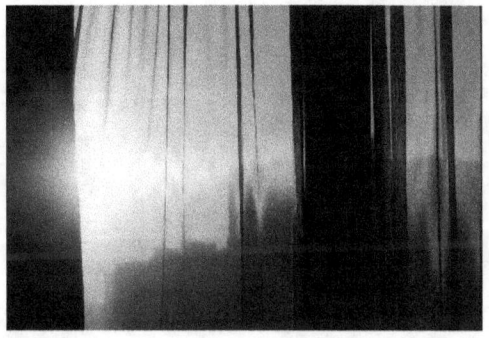

Glass, desert dwellings, African huts

Glass

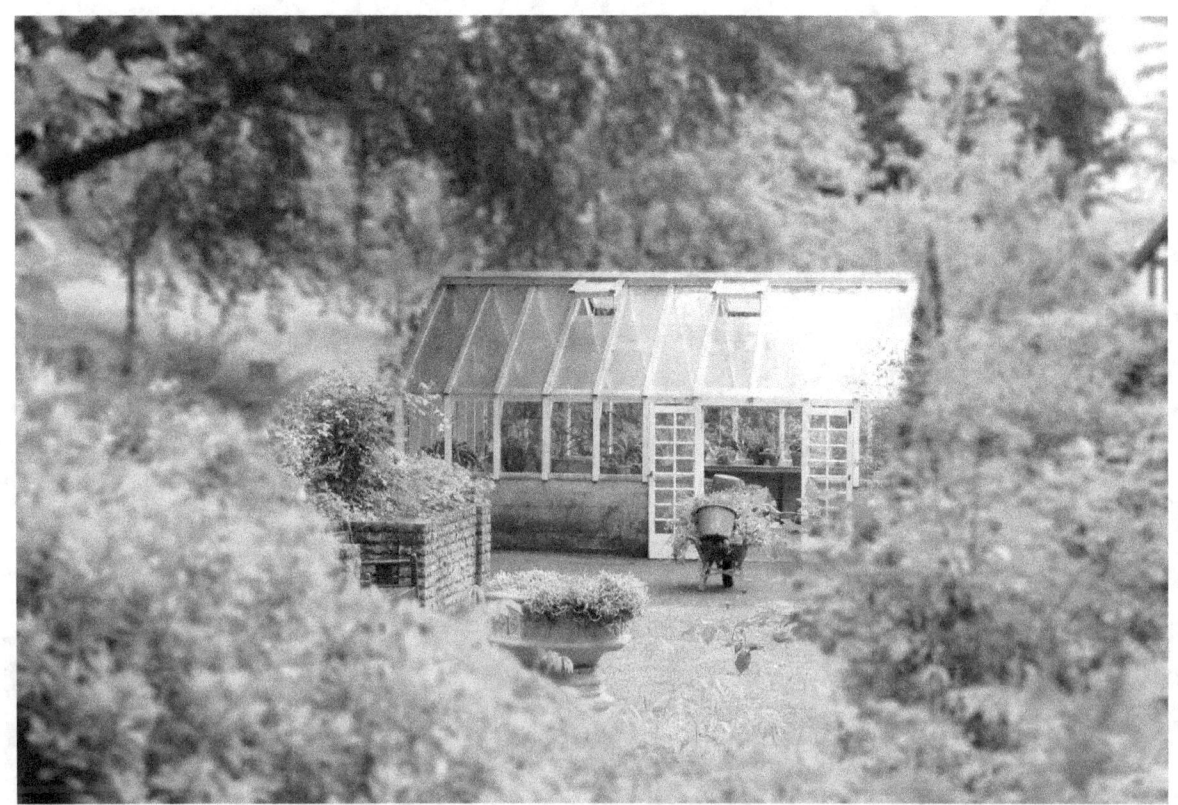

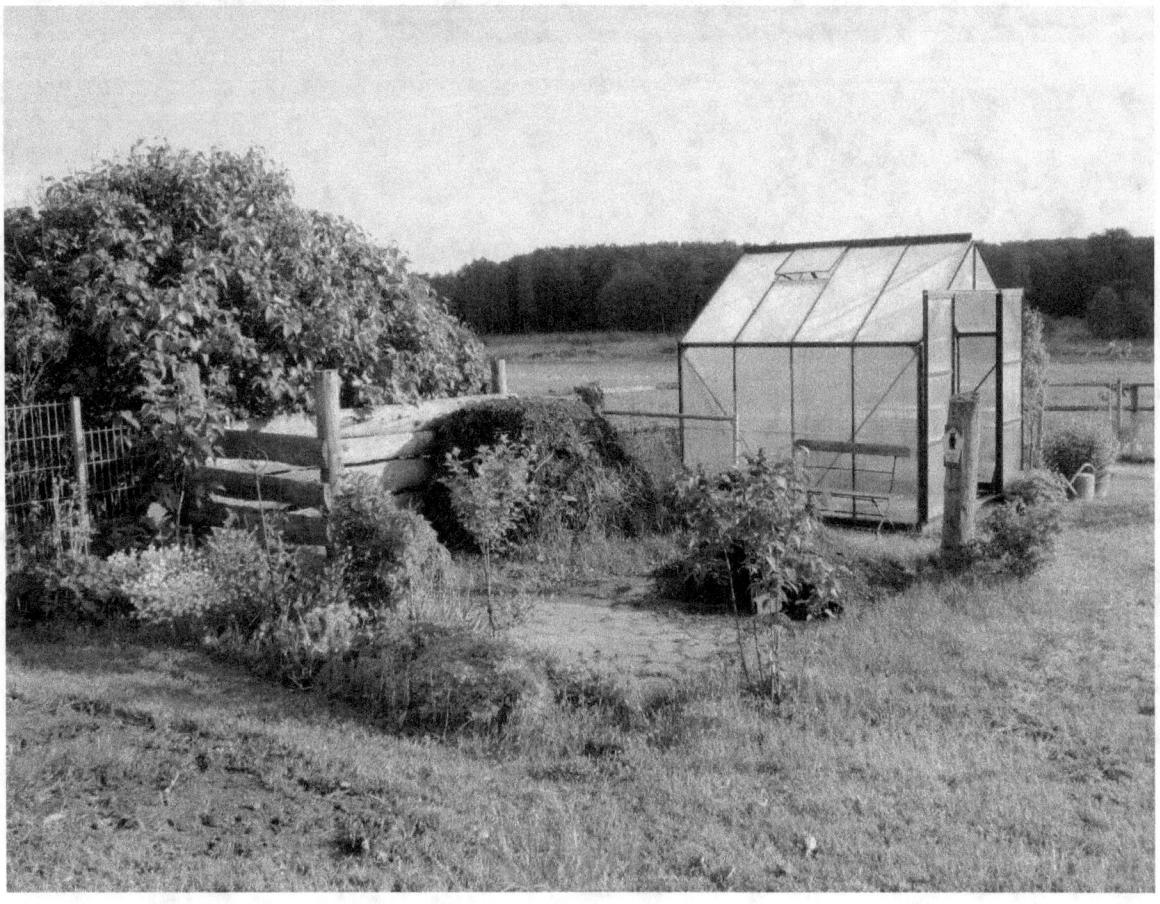

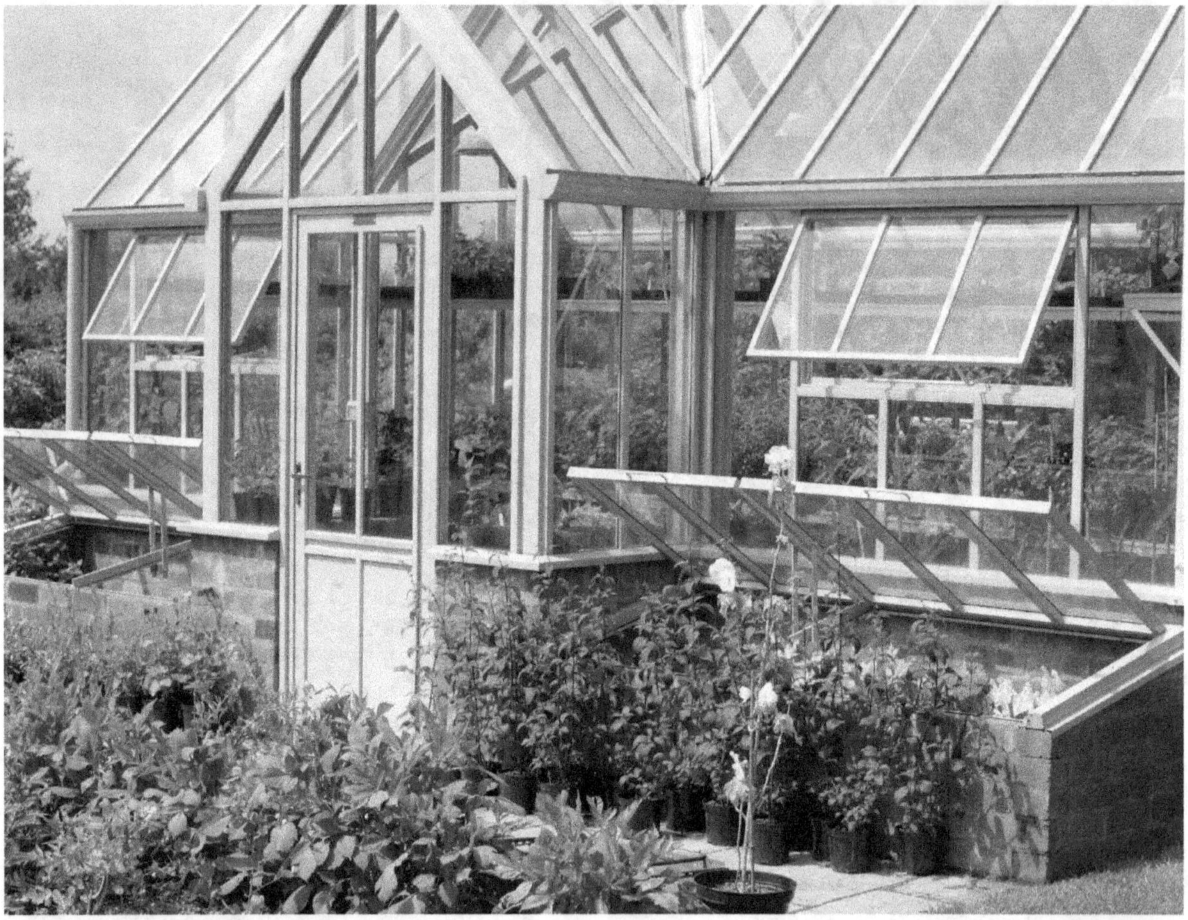

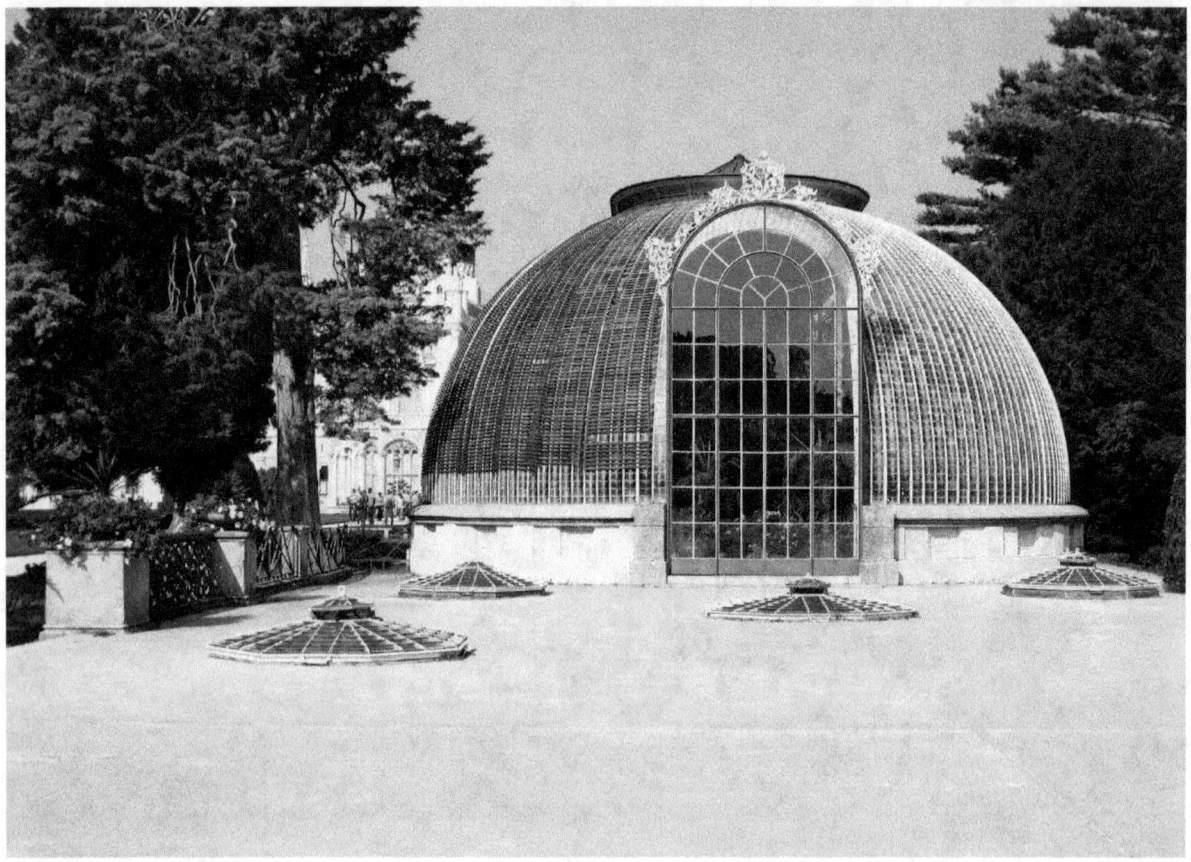

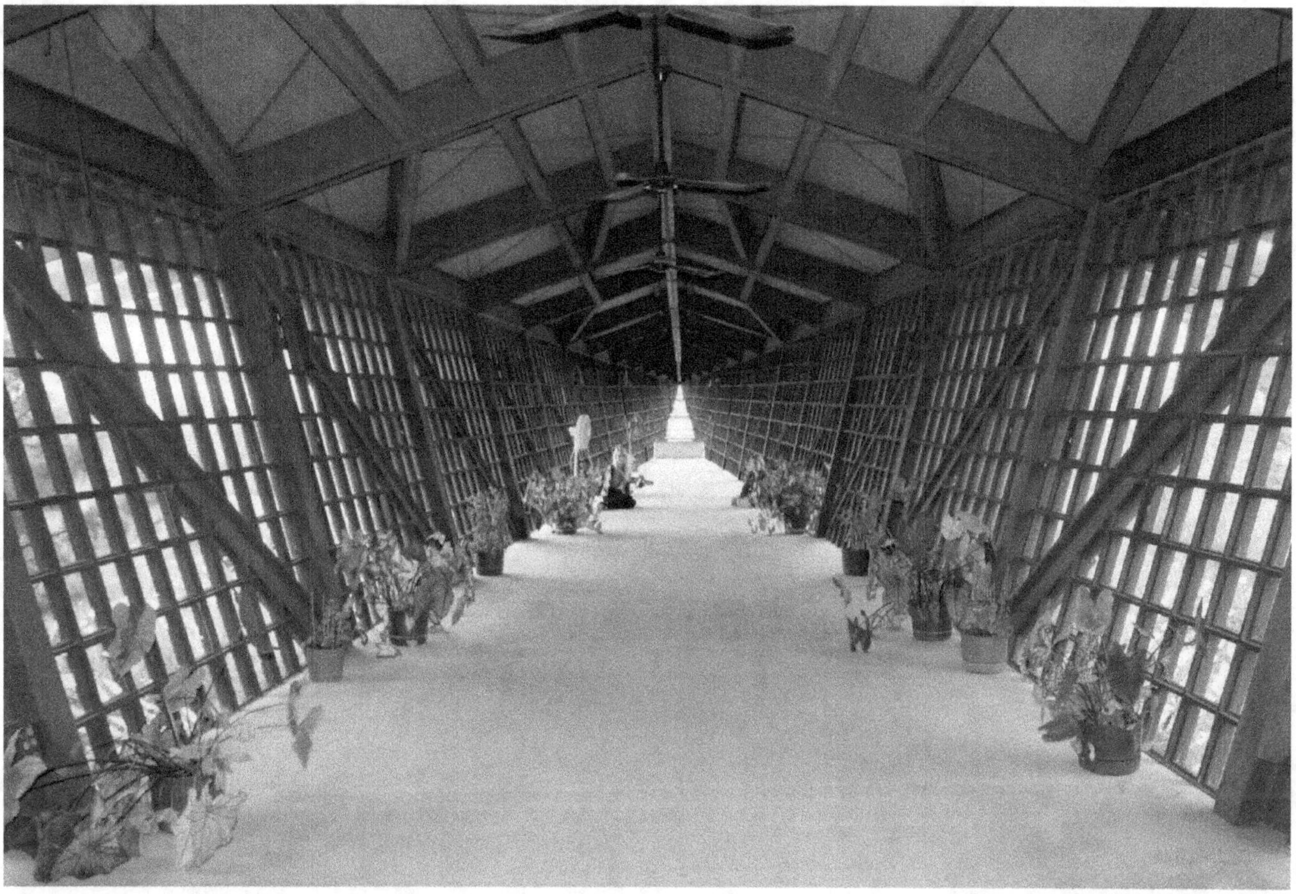

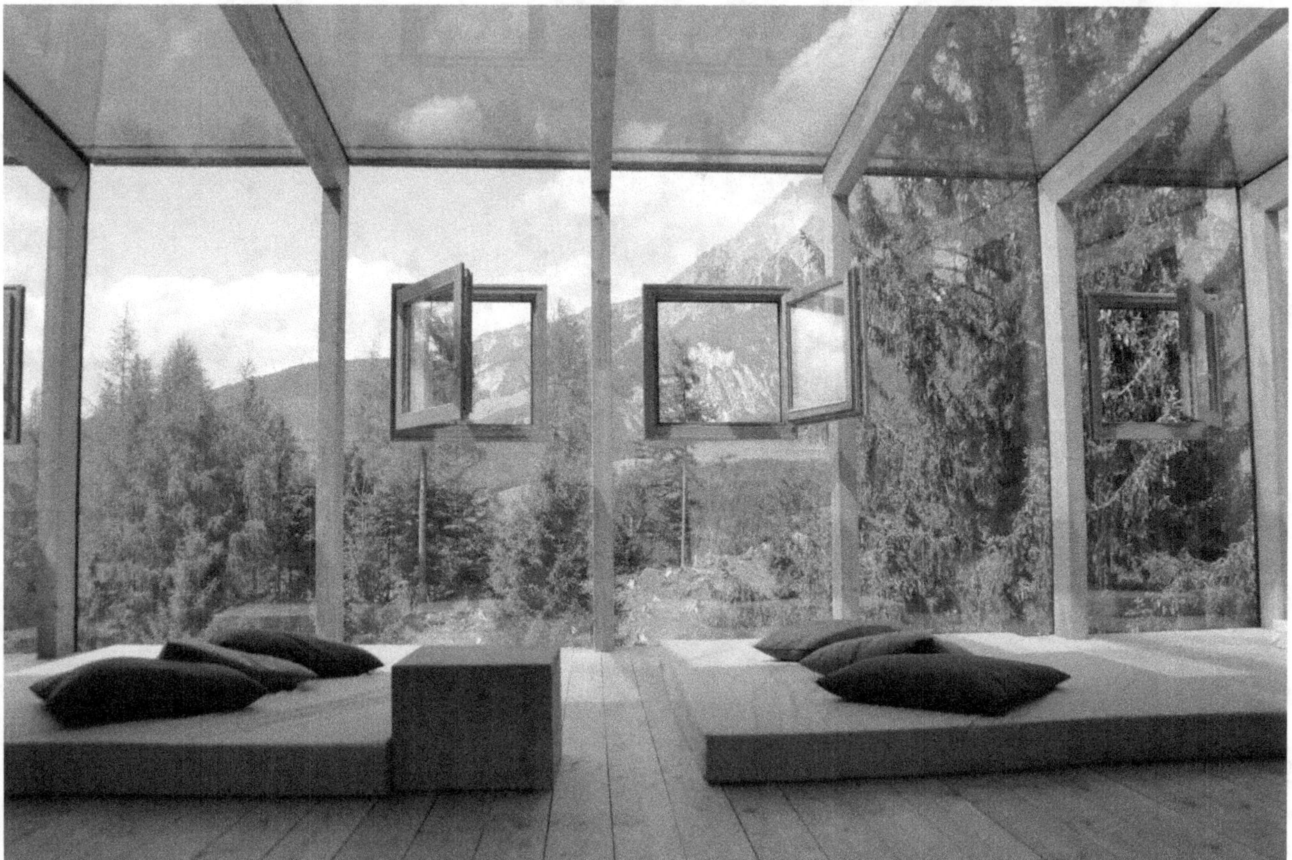

Desert Dwellings

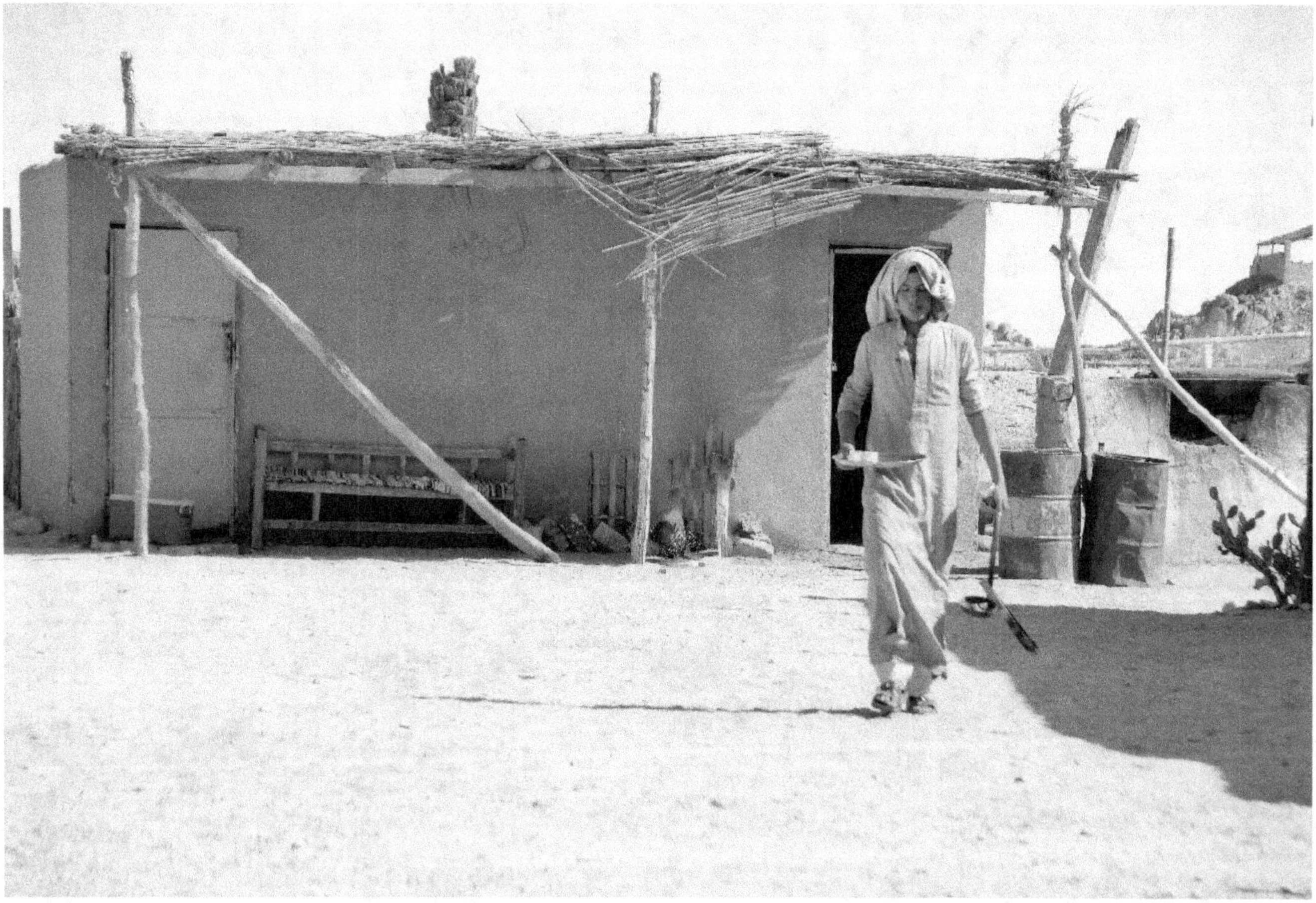

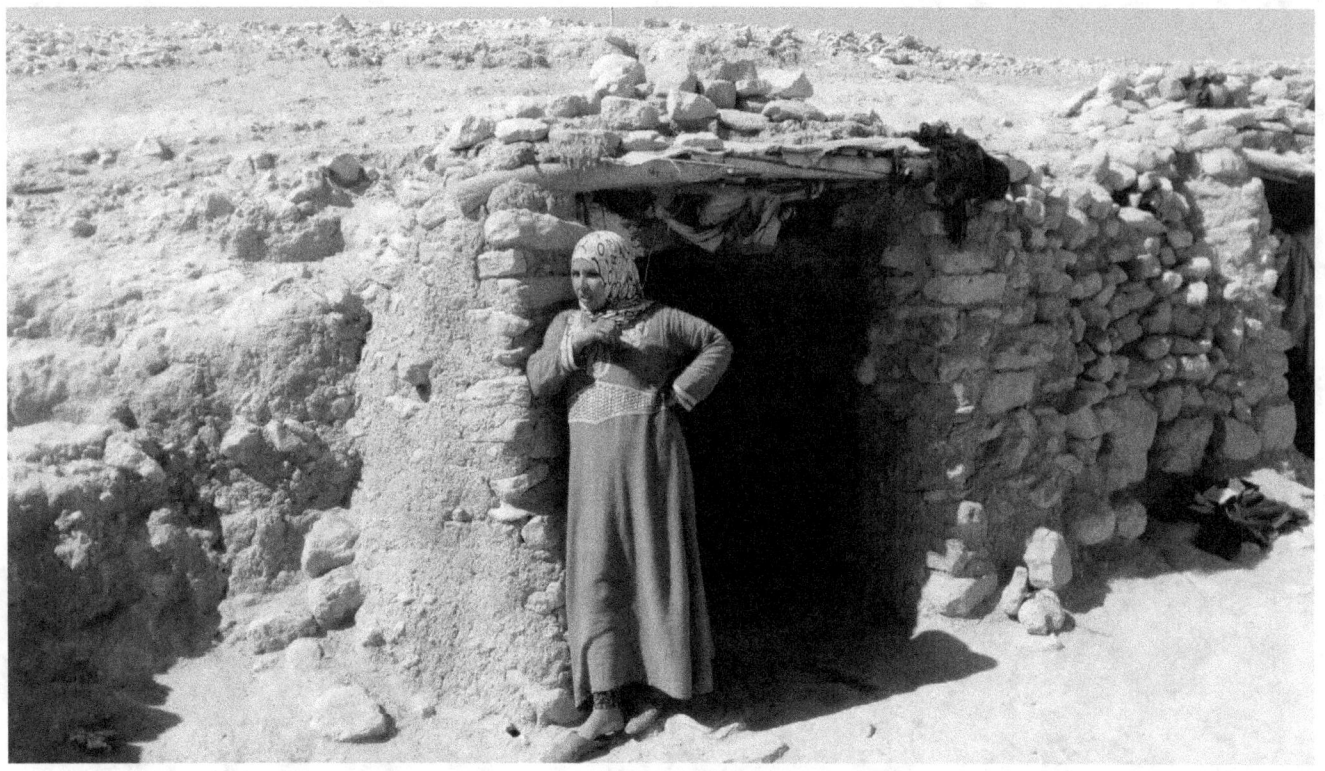

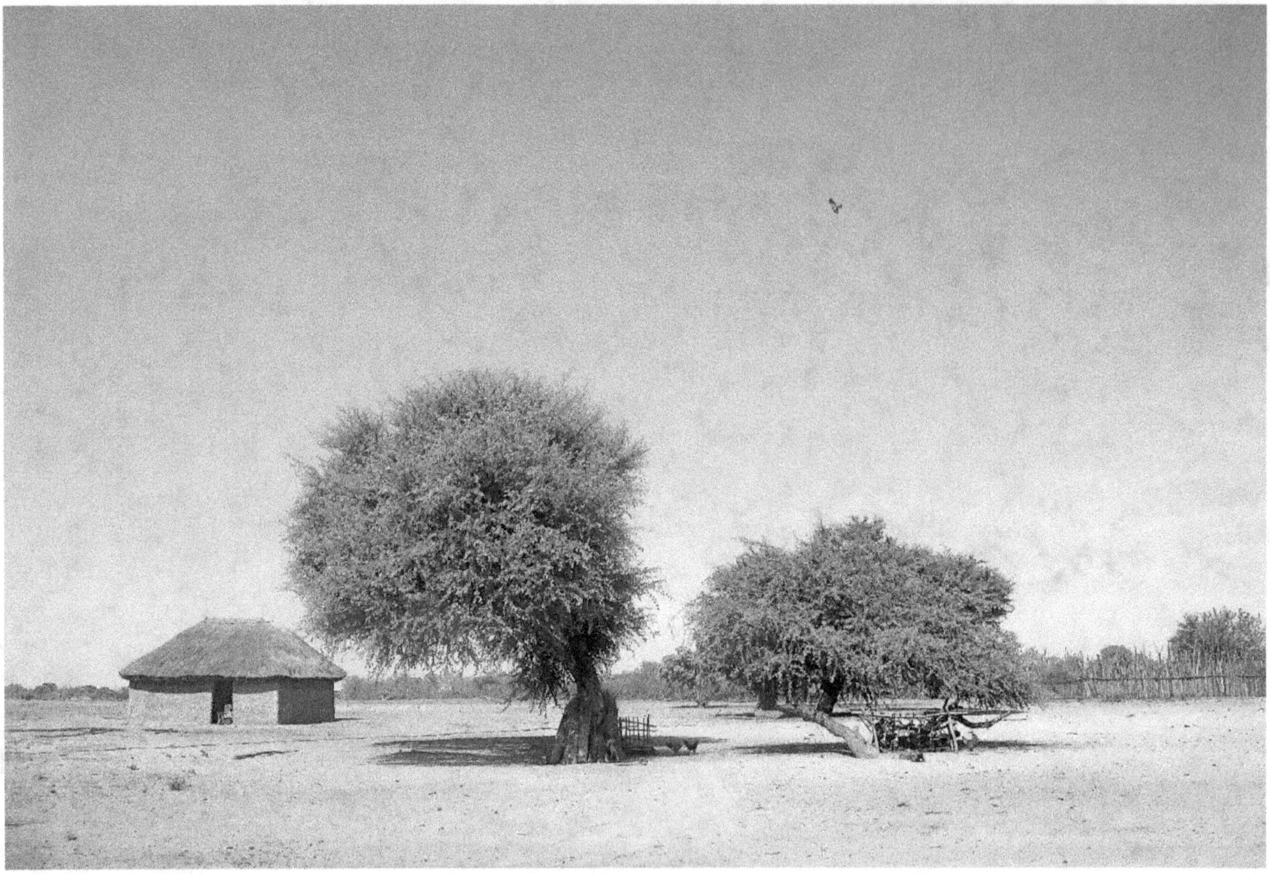

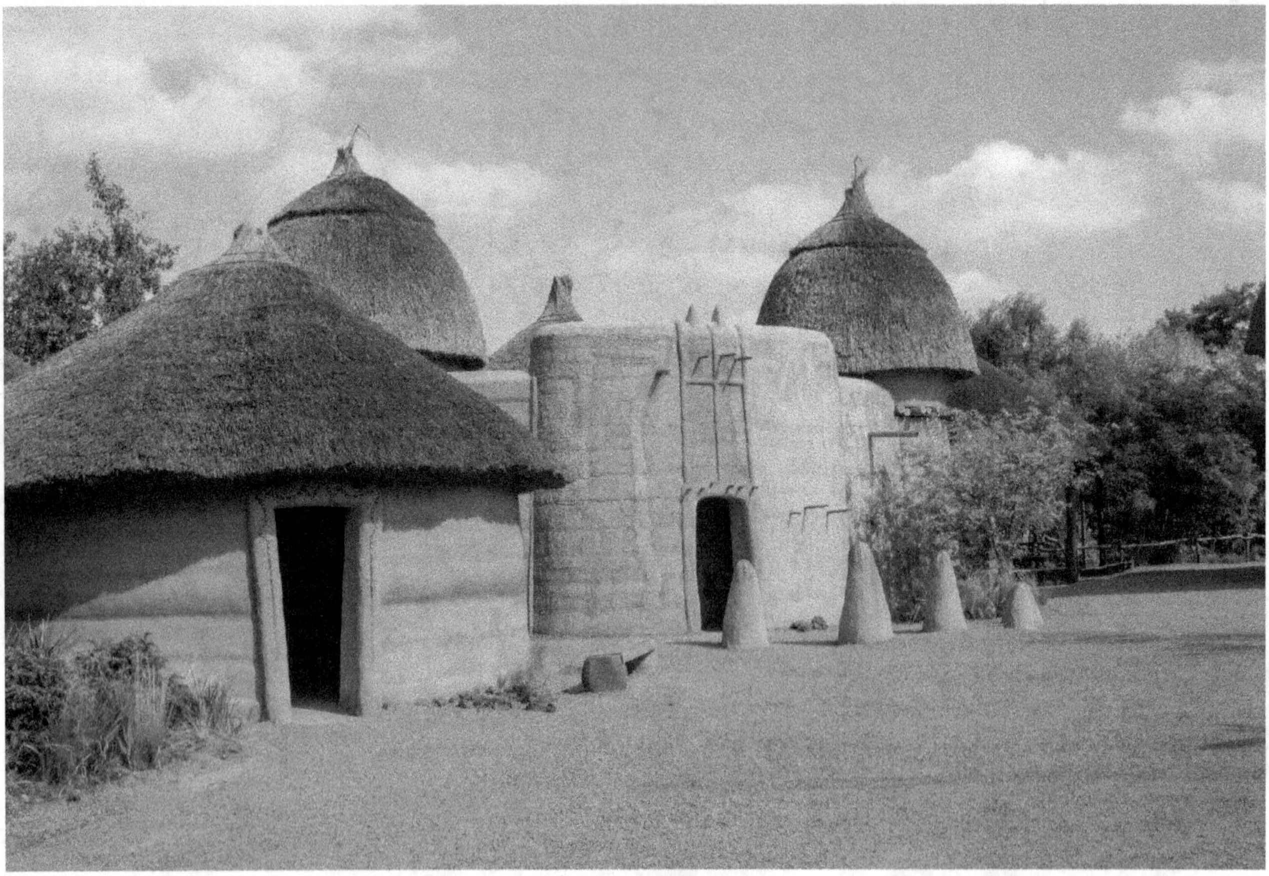

African huts

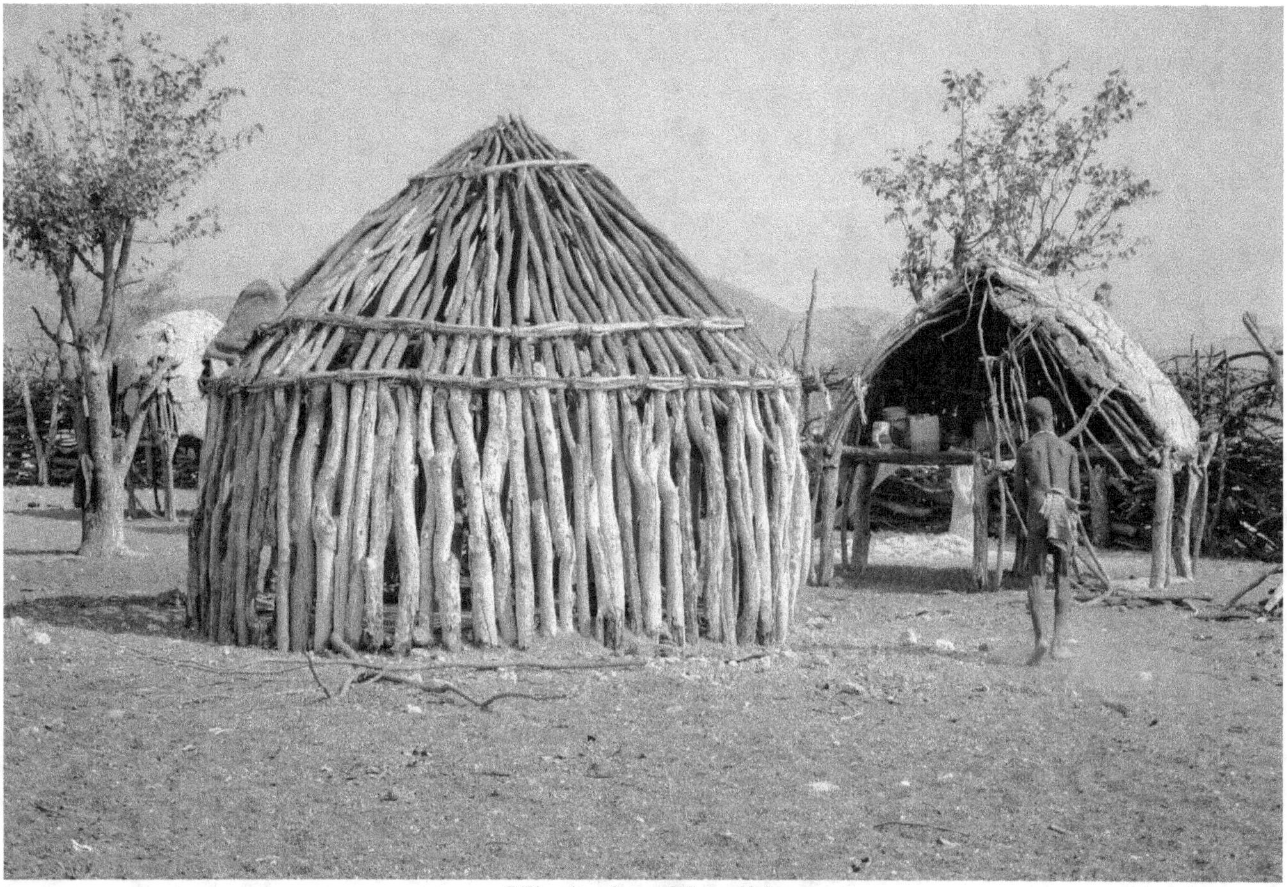

Himba hut, Namibia

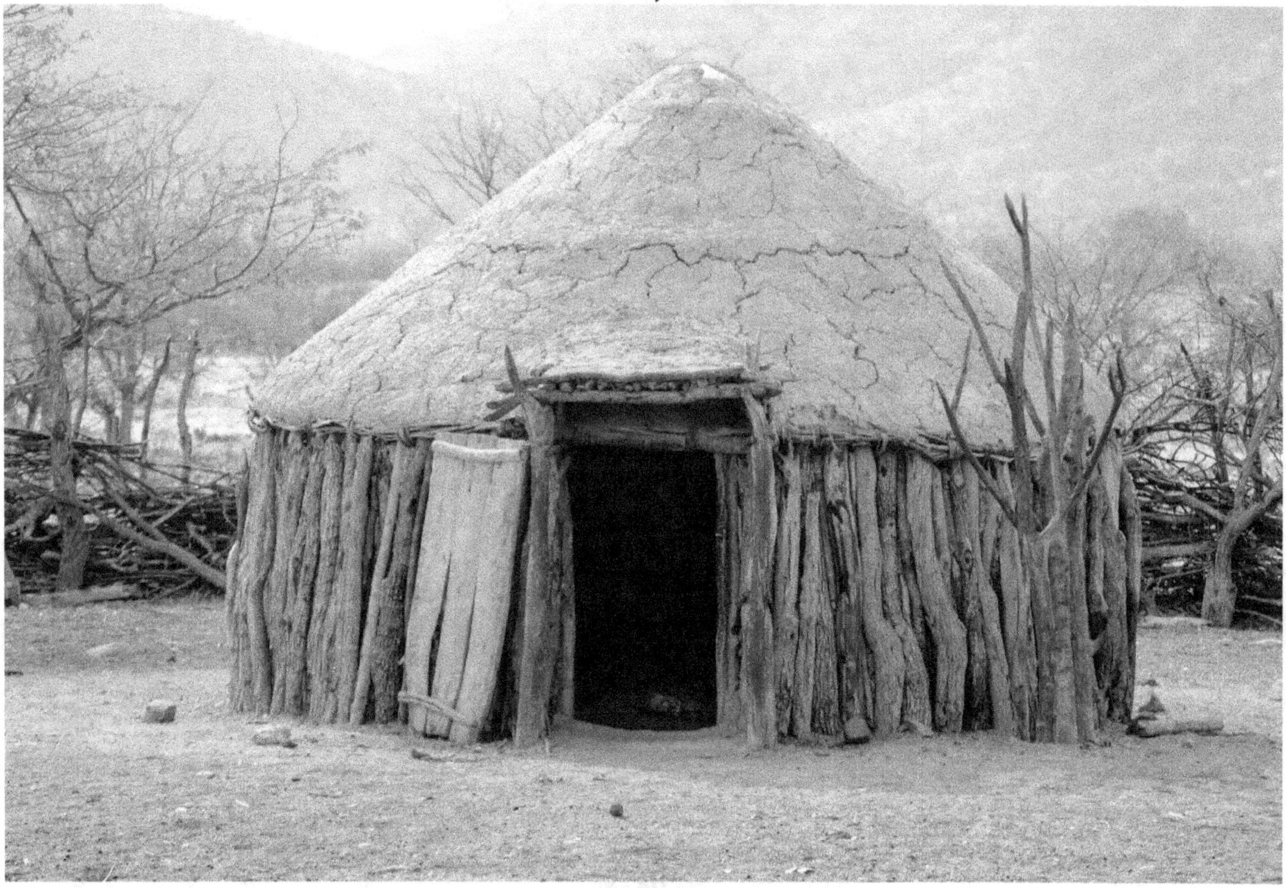

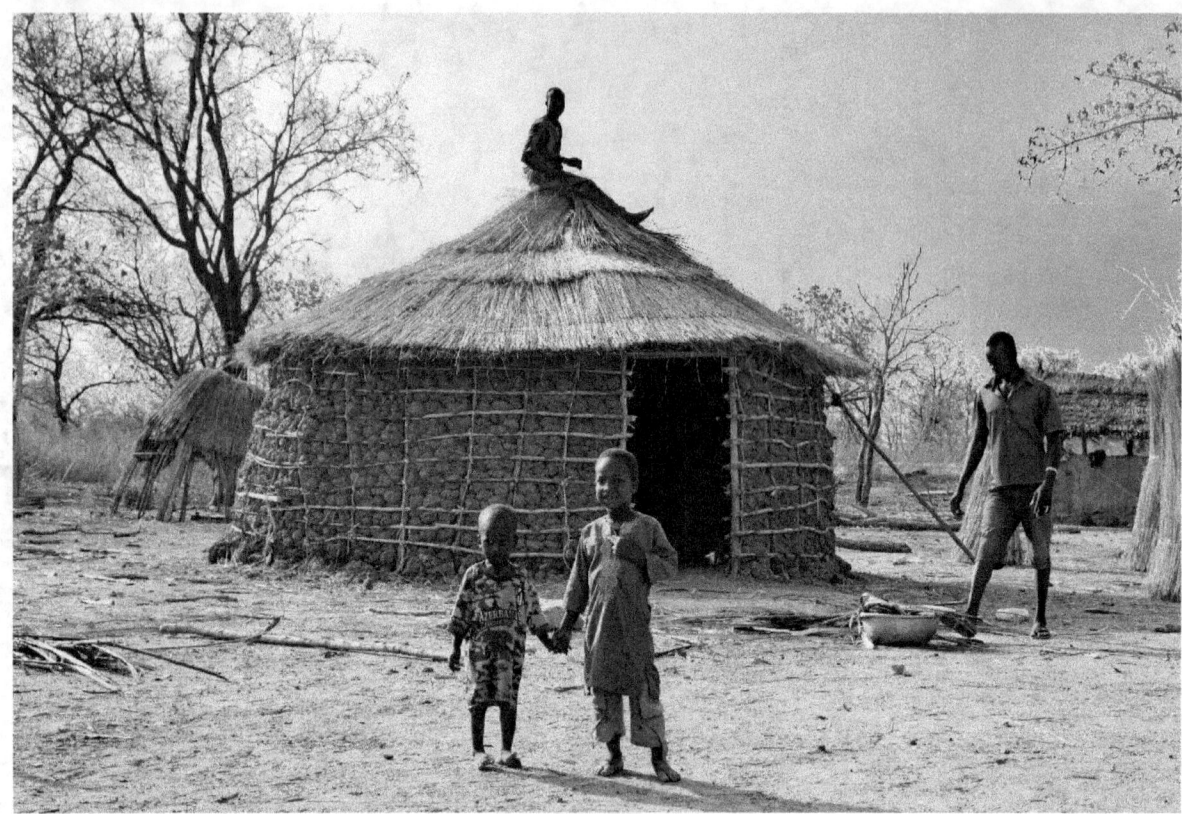

Ghana

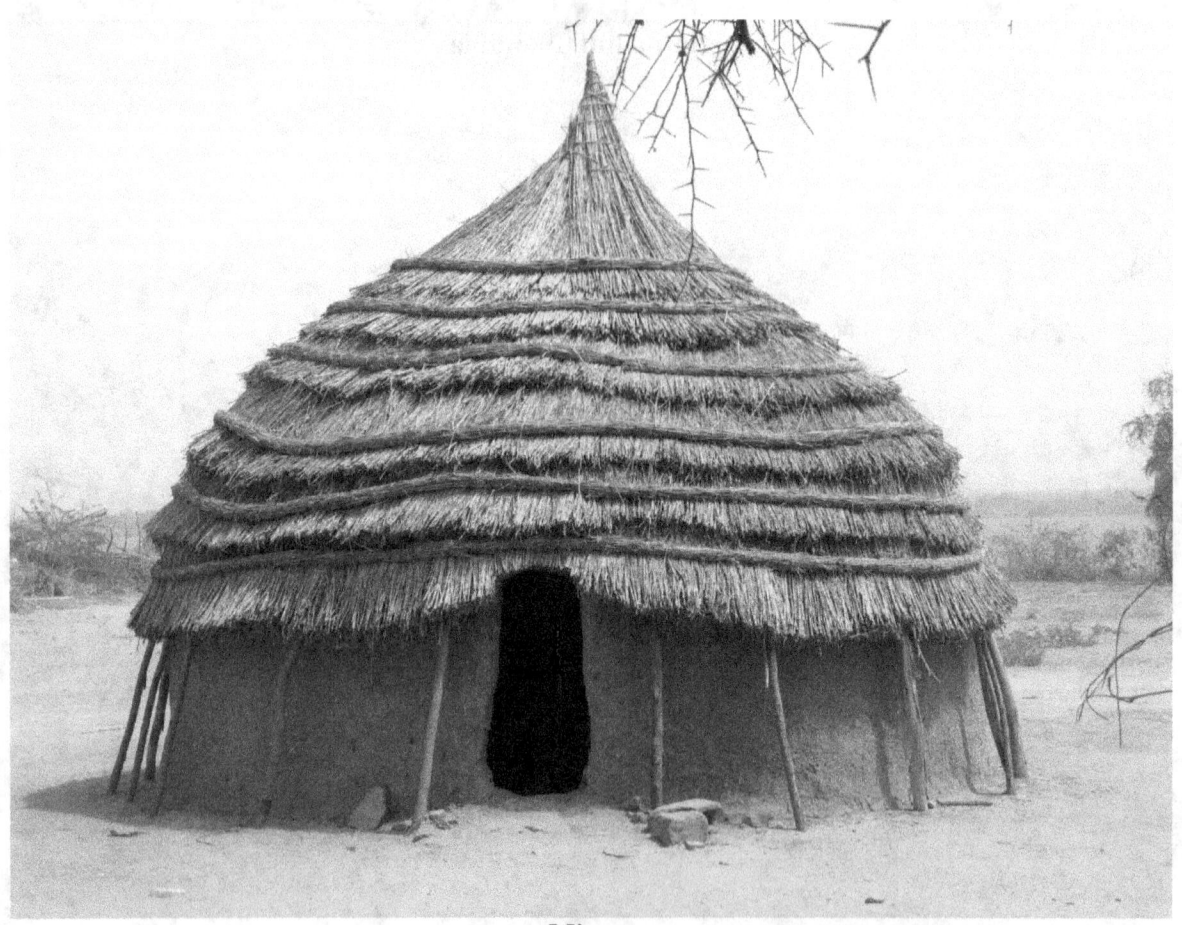

Niger

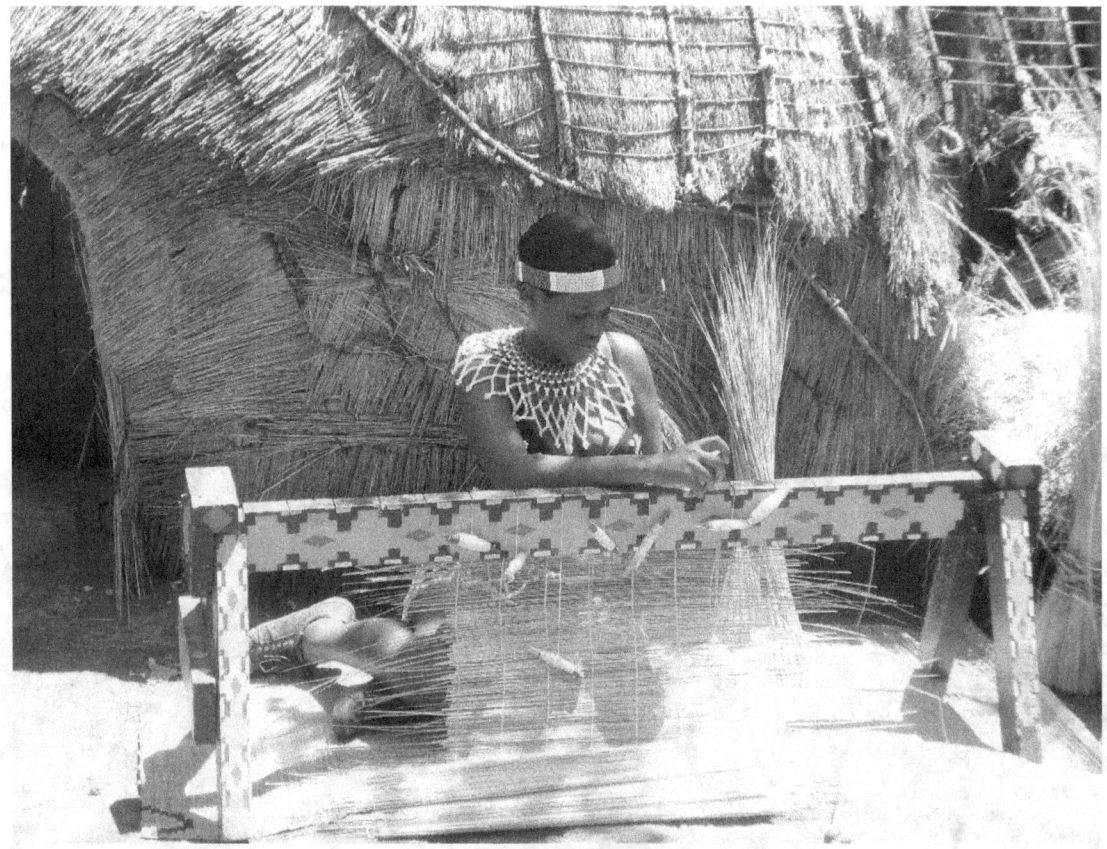

South Africa

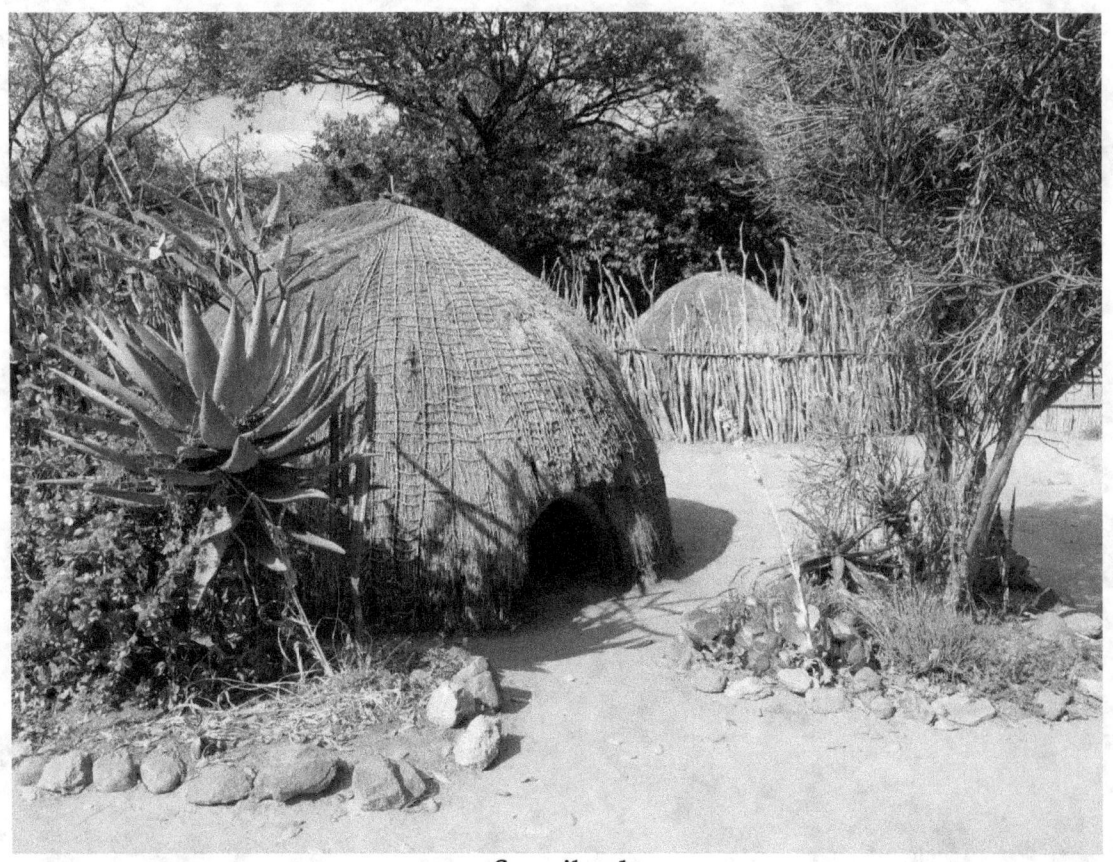

Swaziland

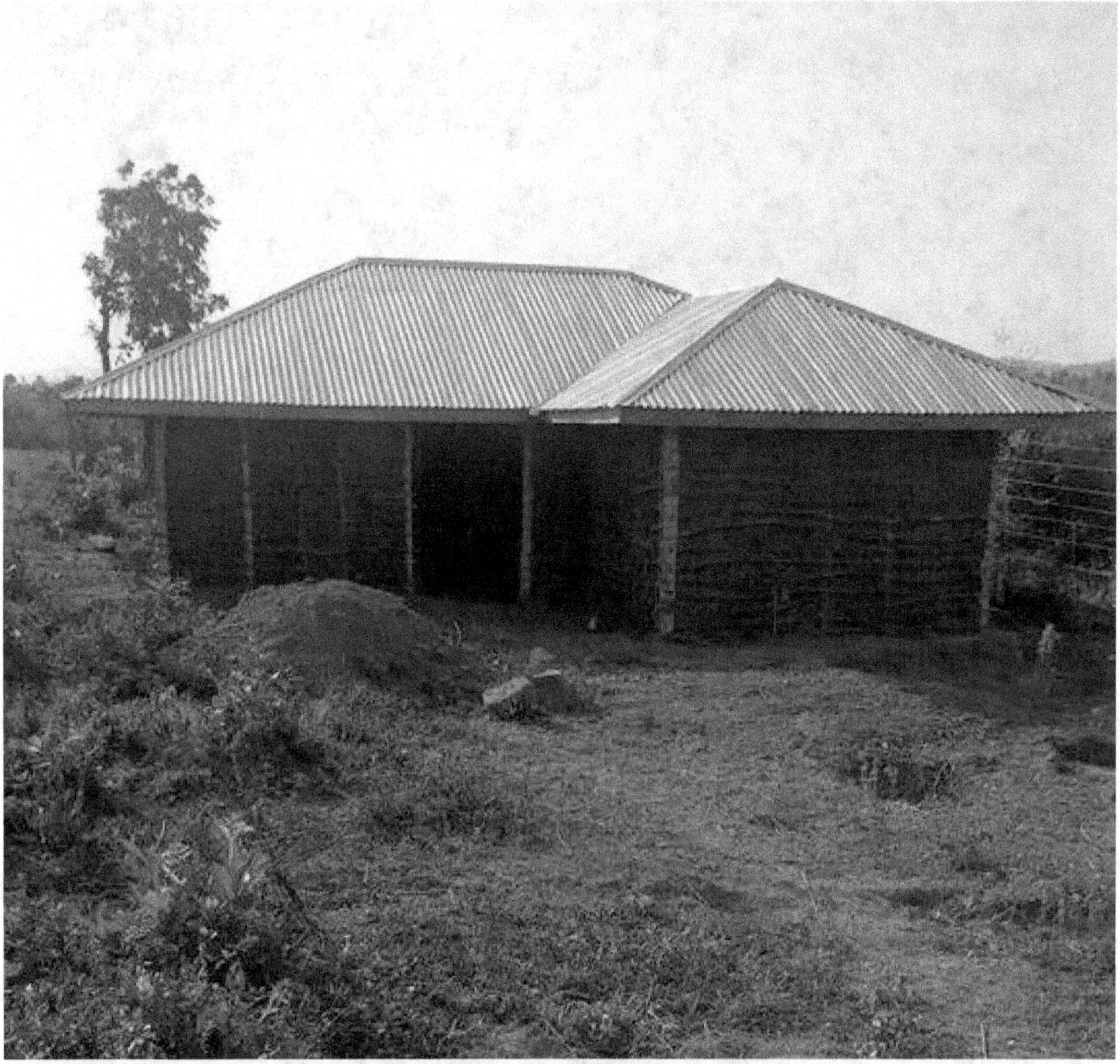

Homa Bay, Kenya

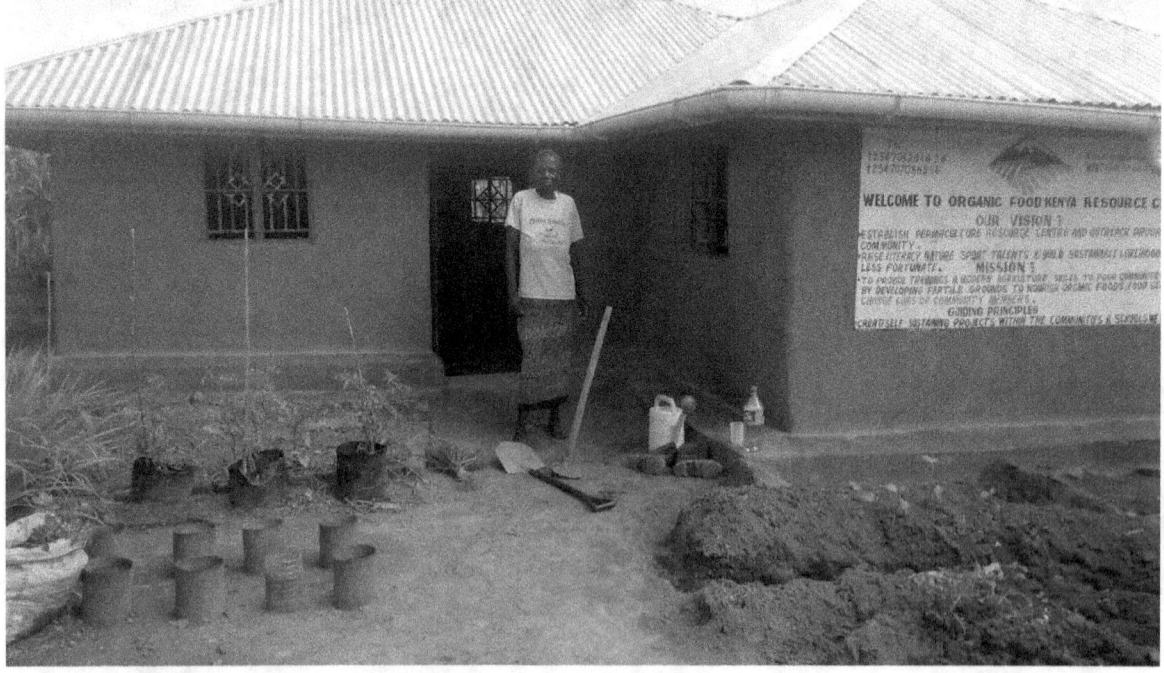

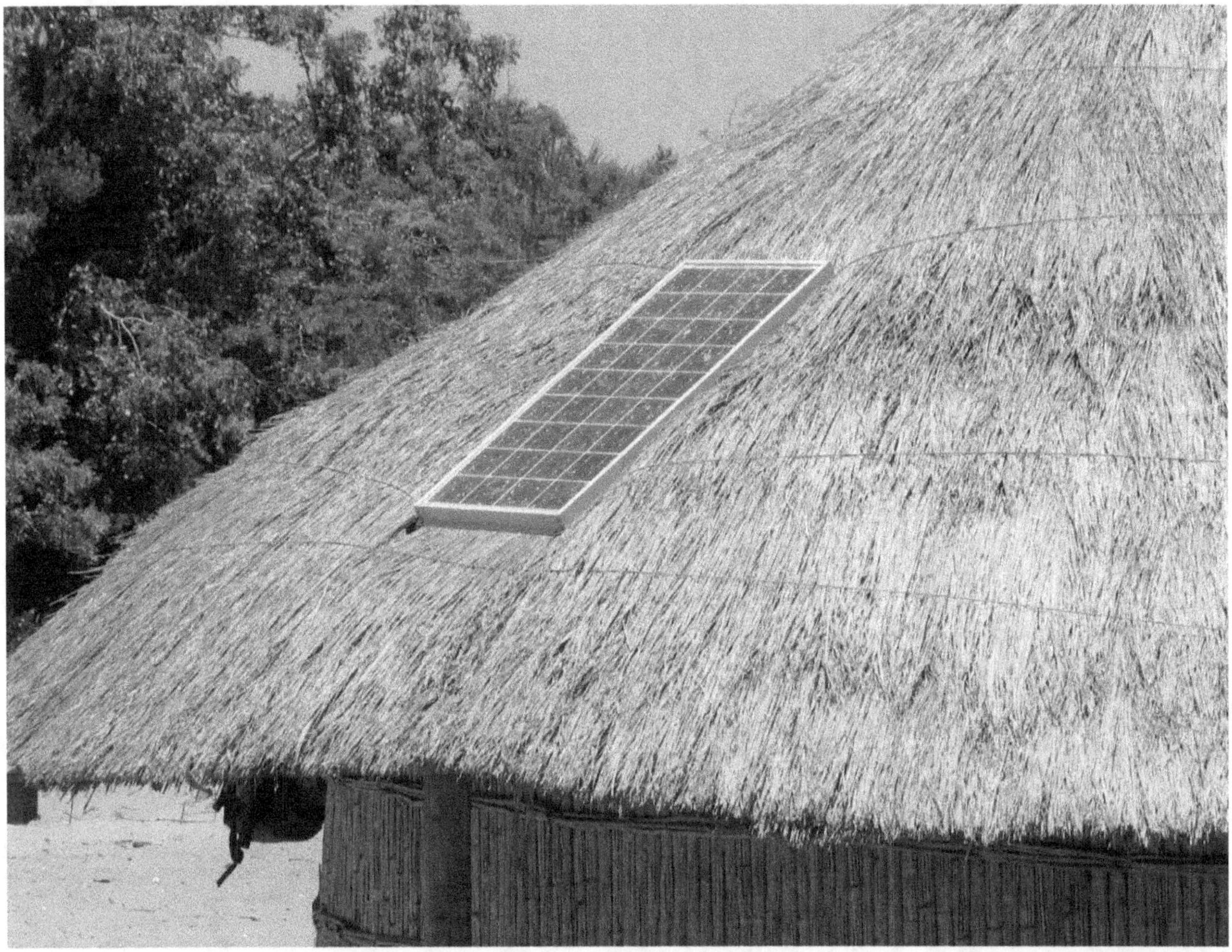

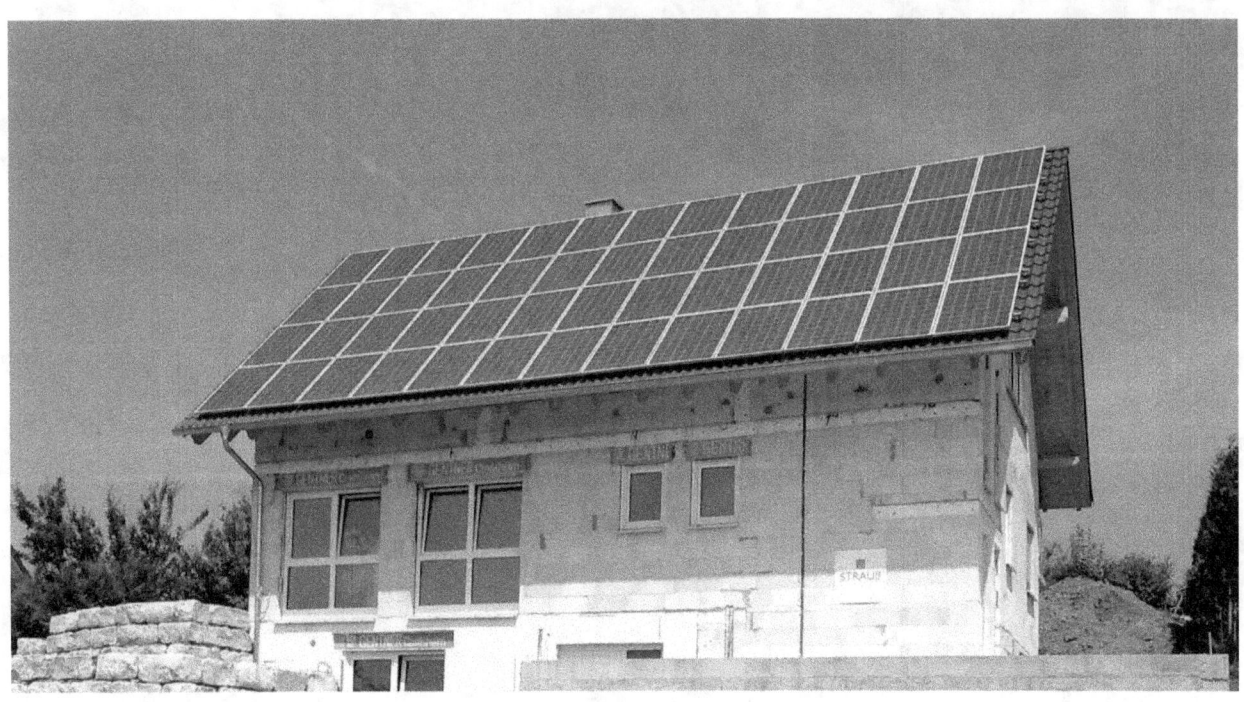

5 SKY

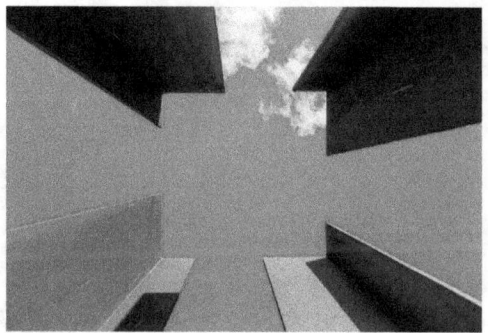

Homes on piers or stilts, chapels, towers, and lighthouses

Piers & Stilts

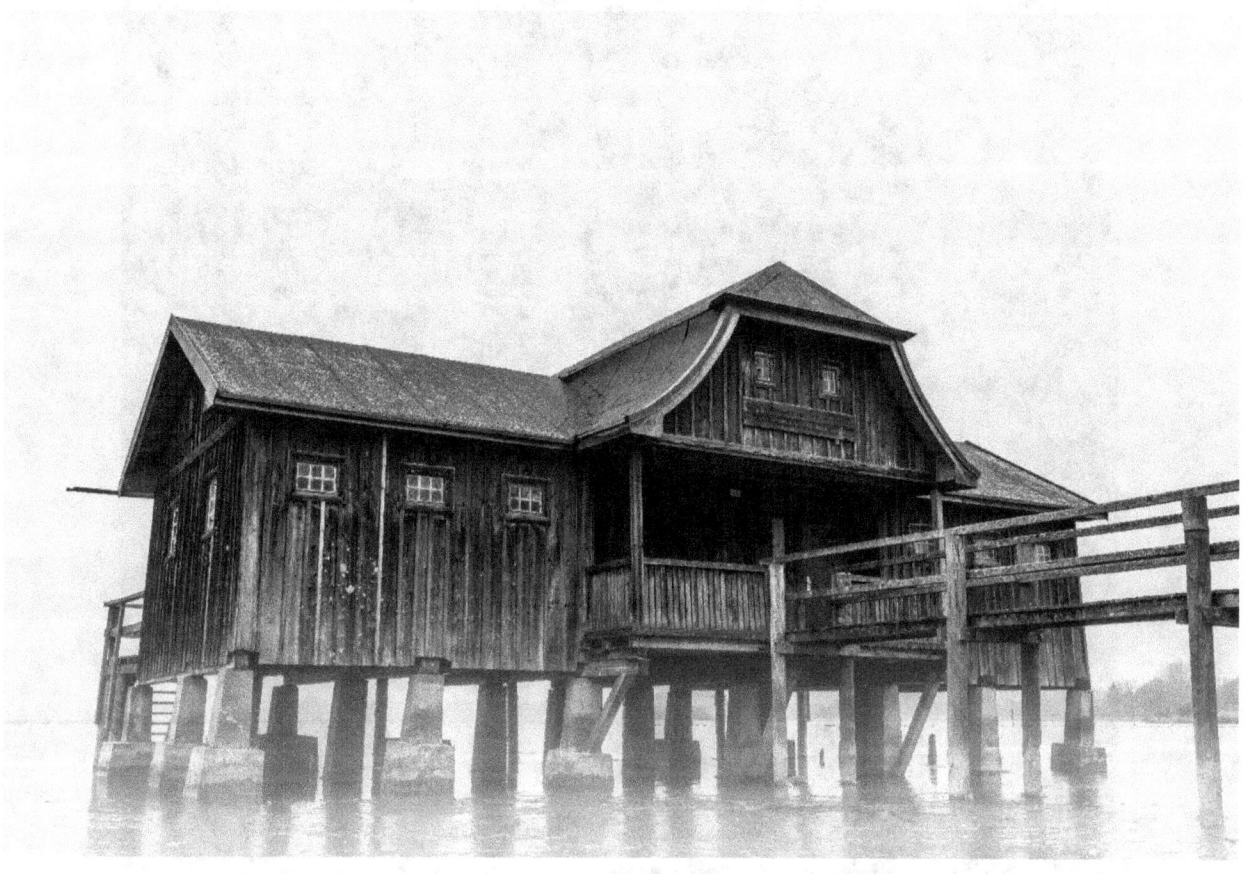

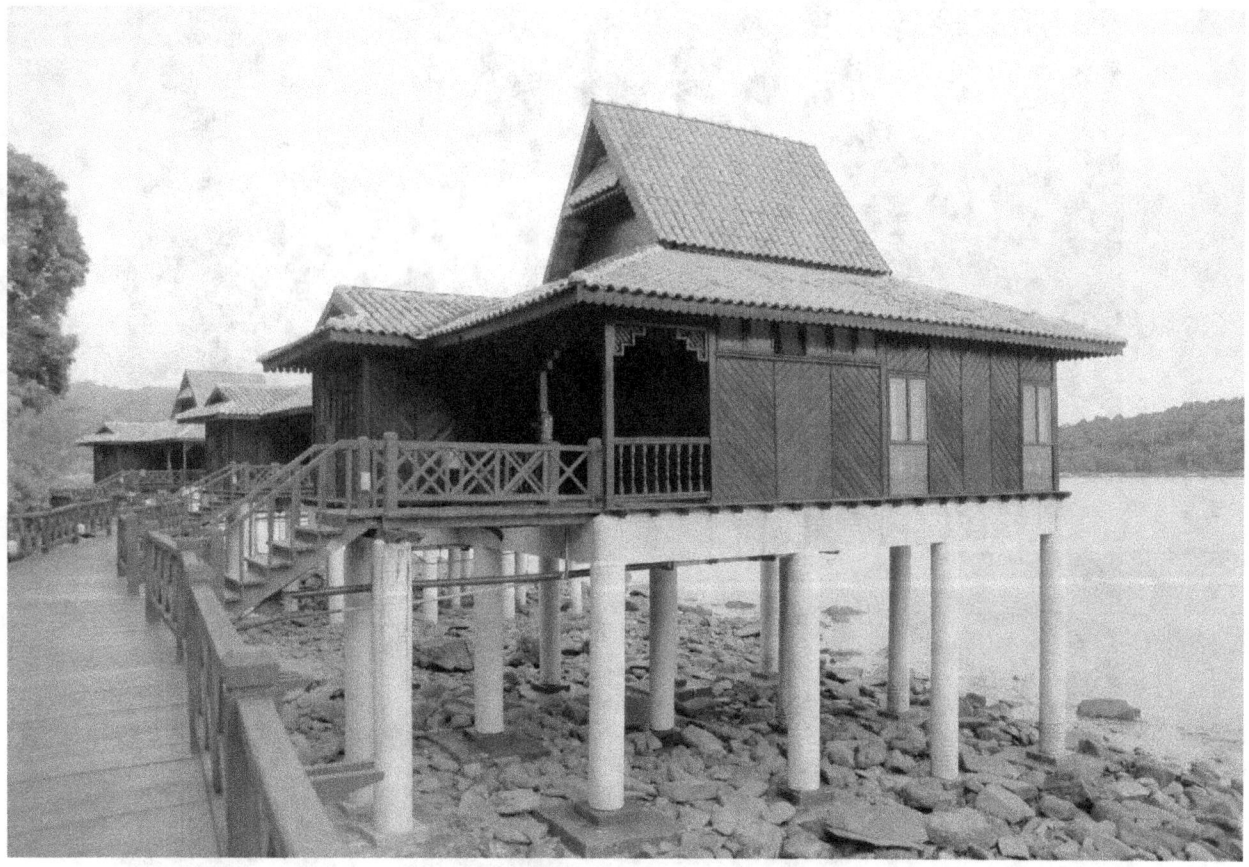

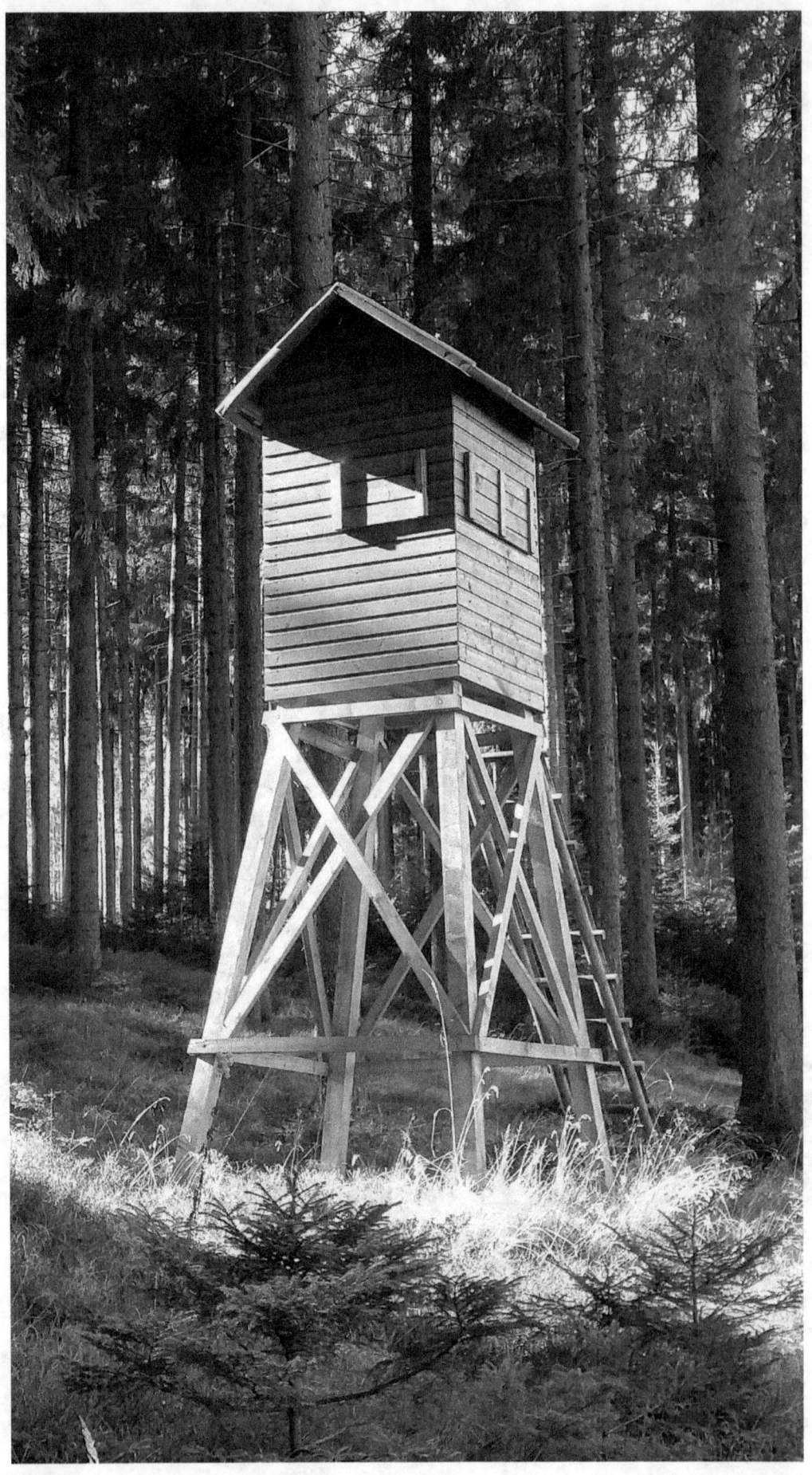

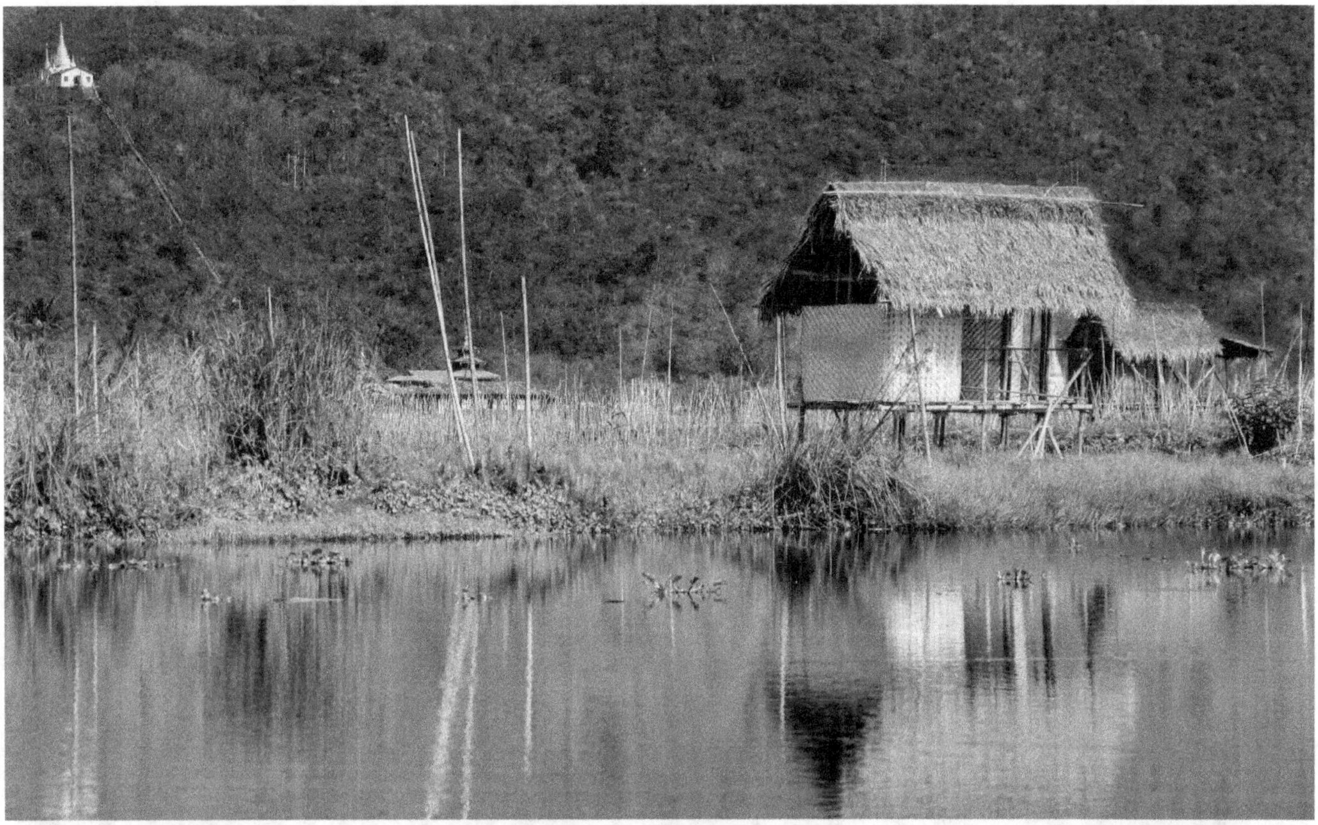

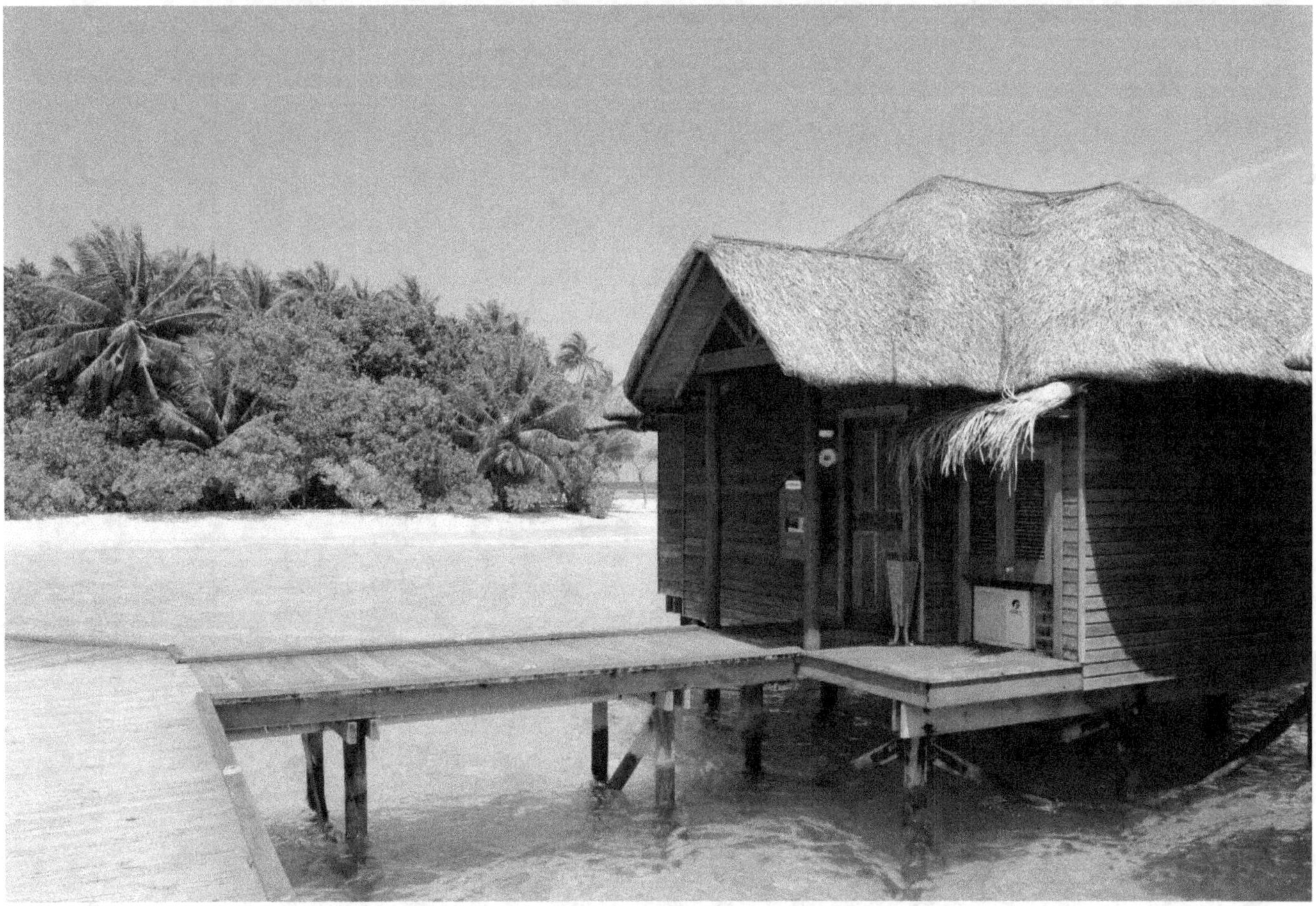

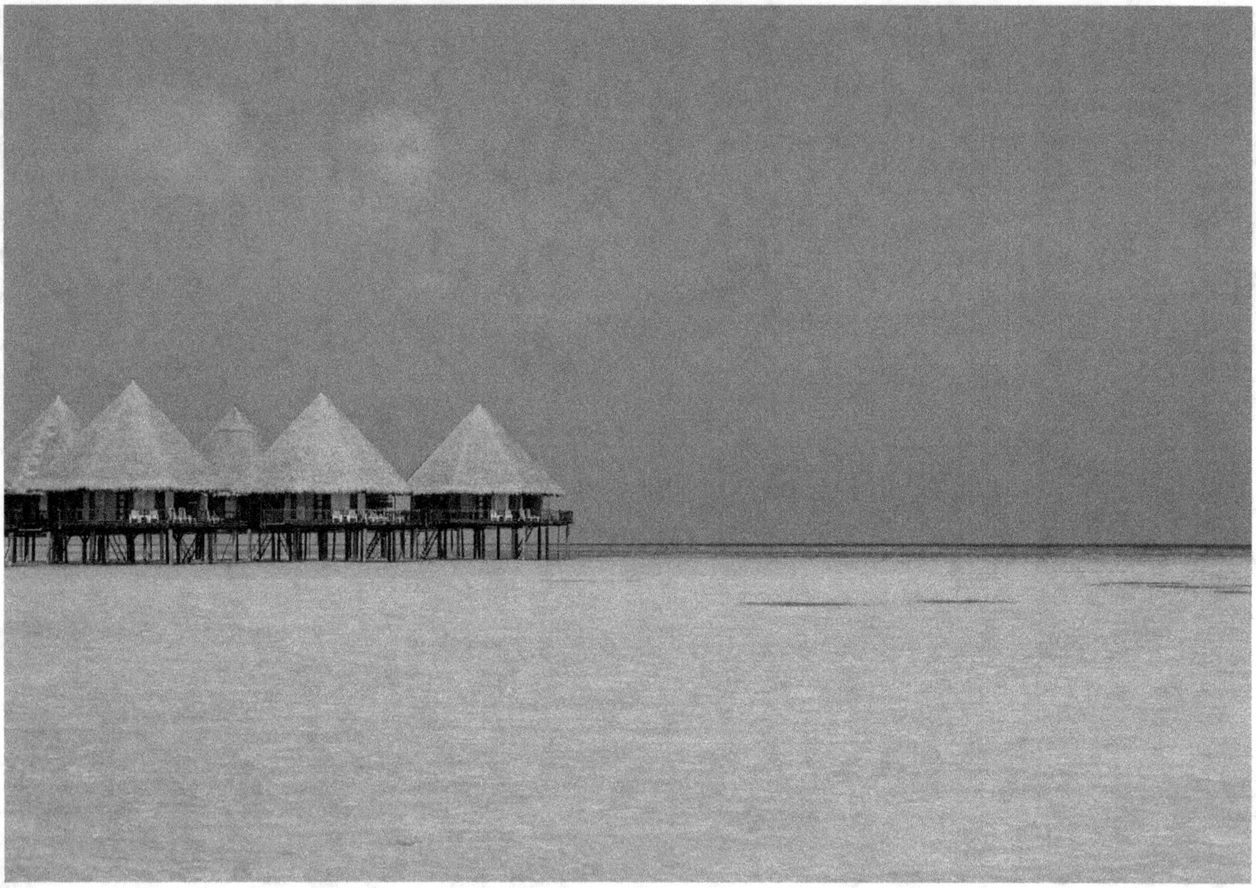

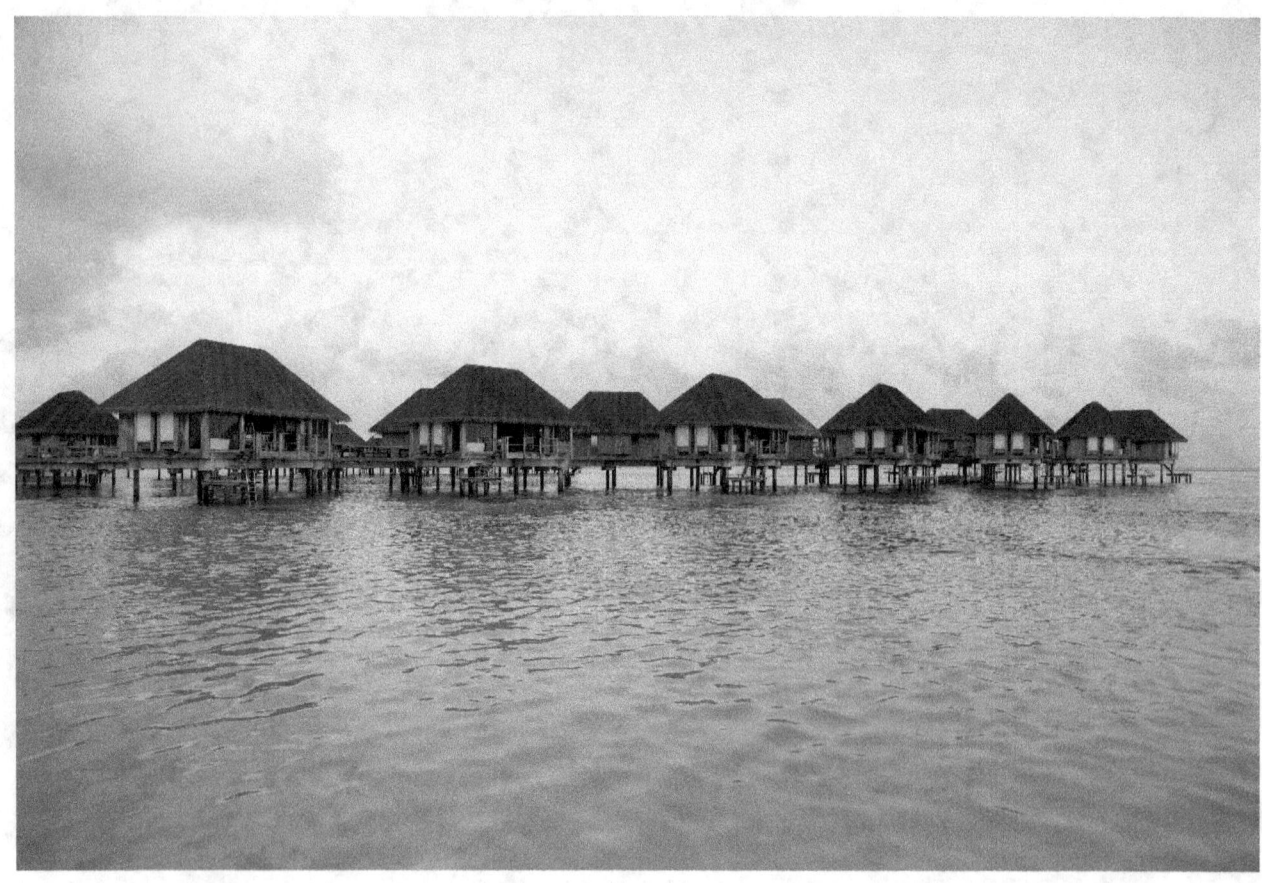

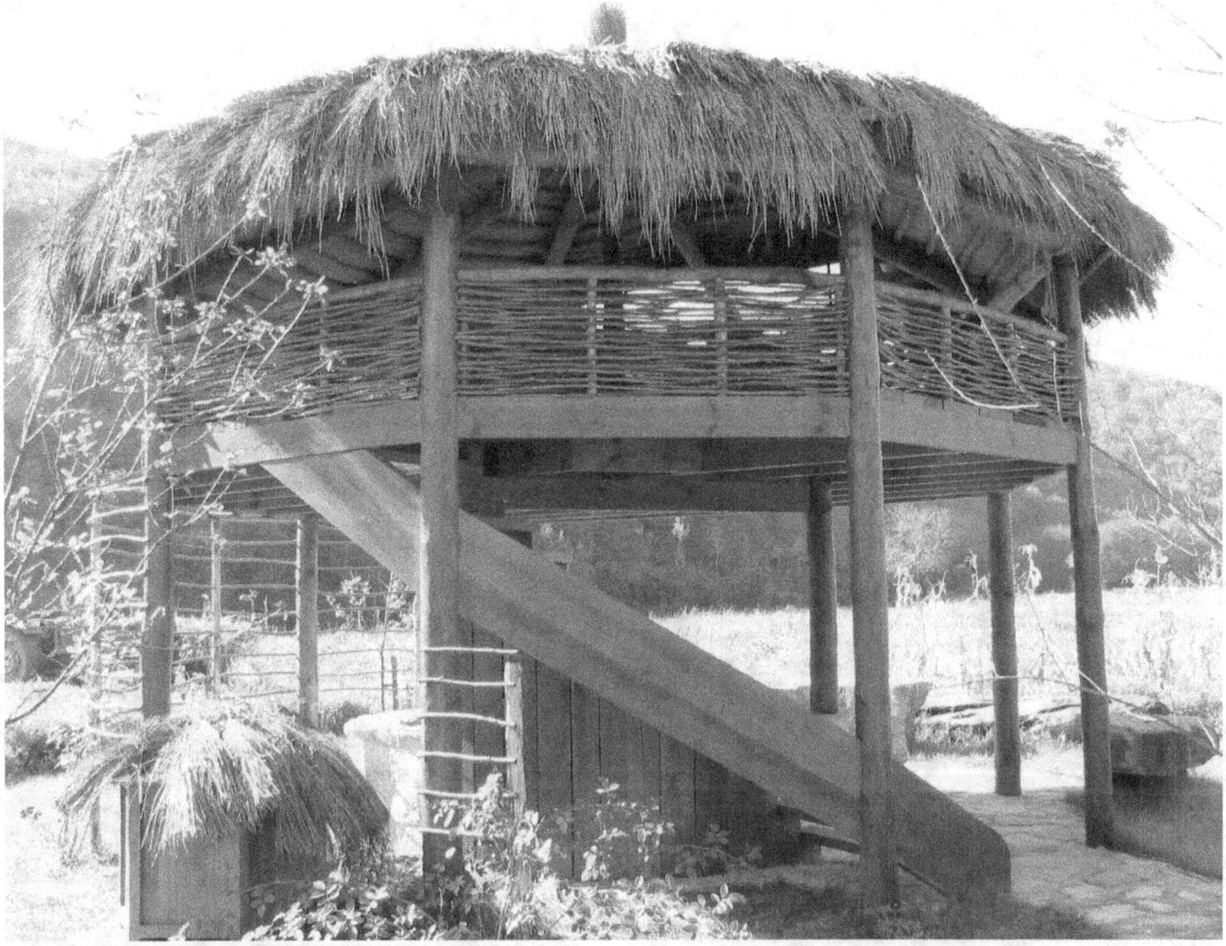

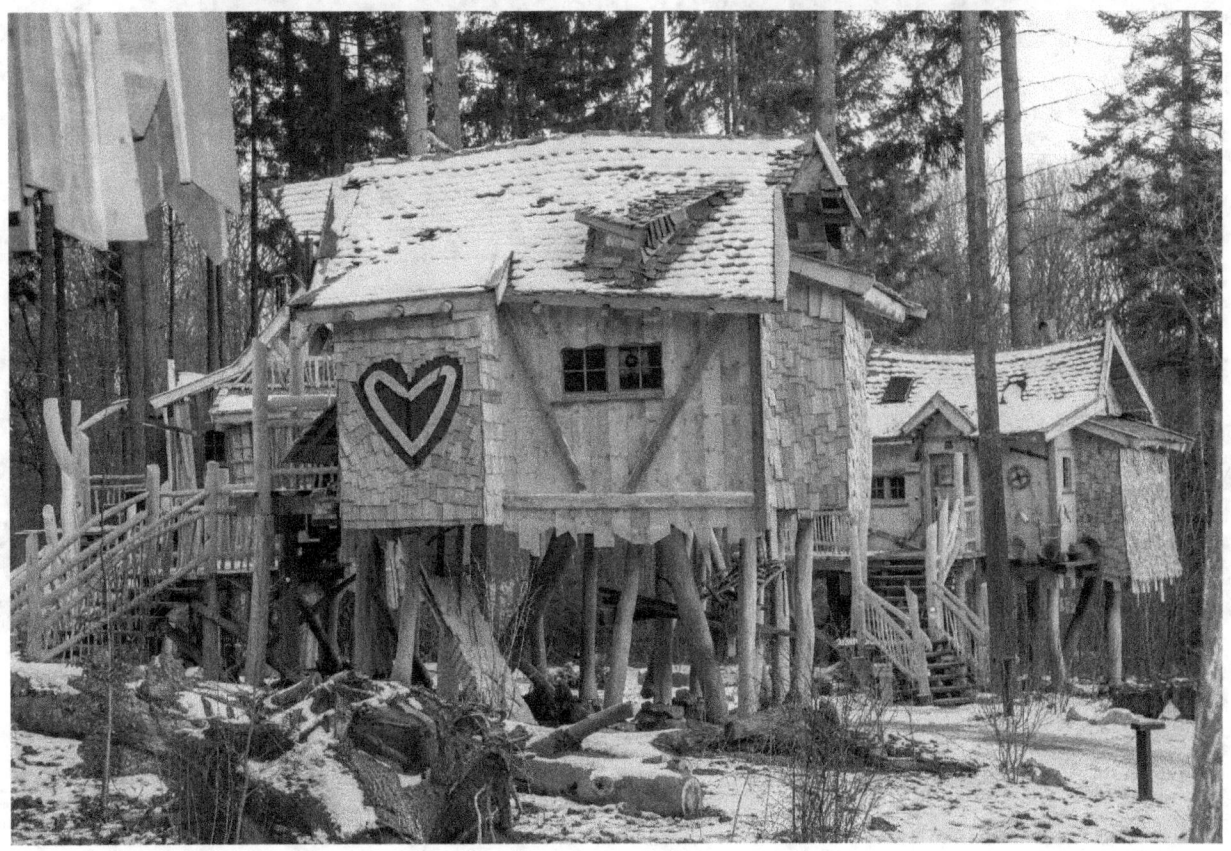

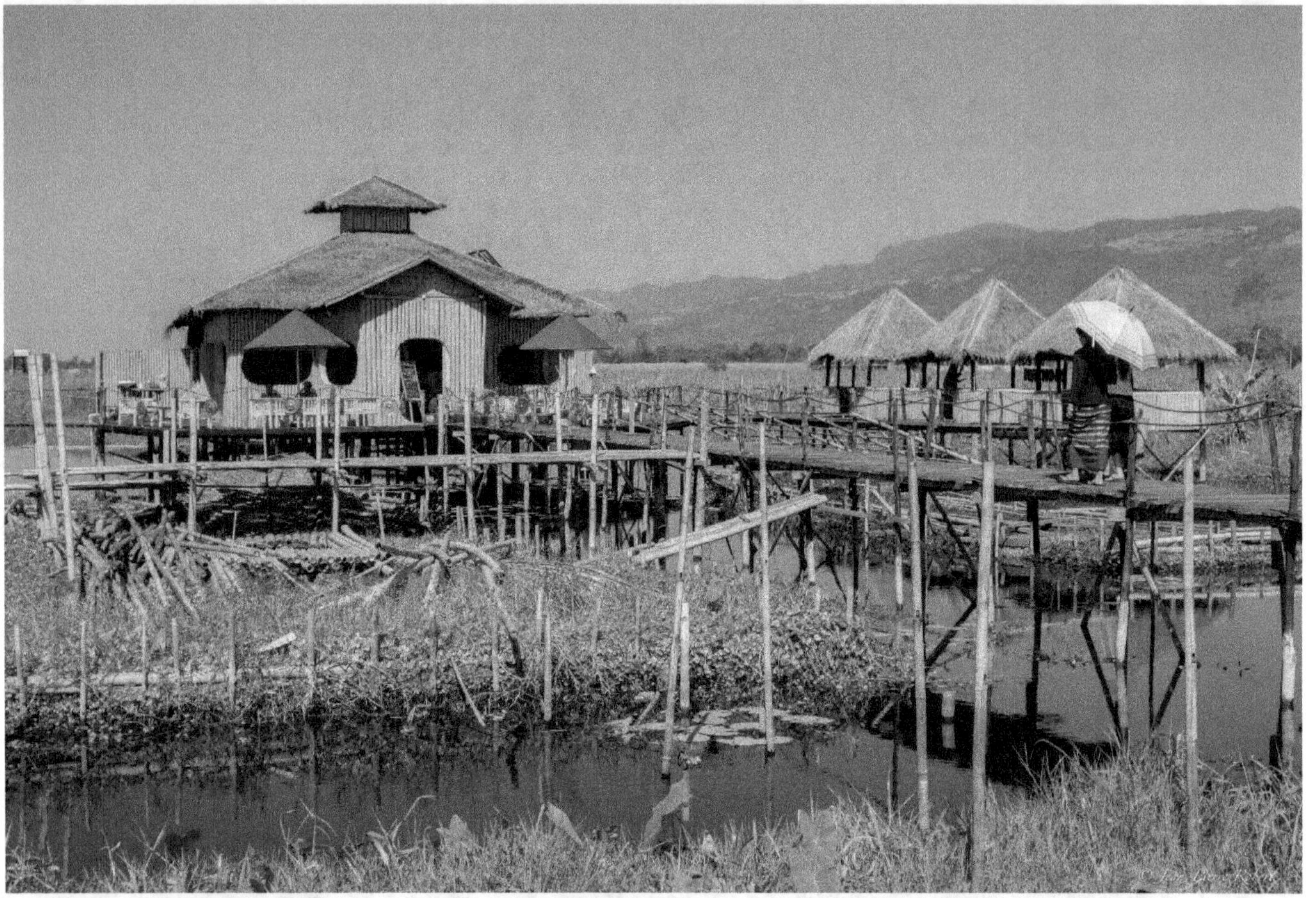

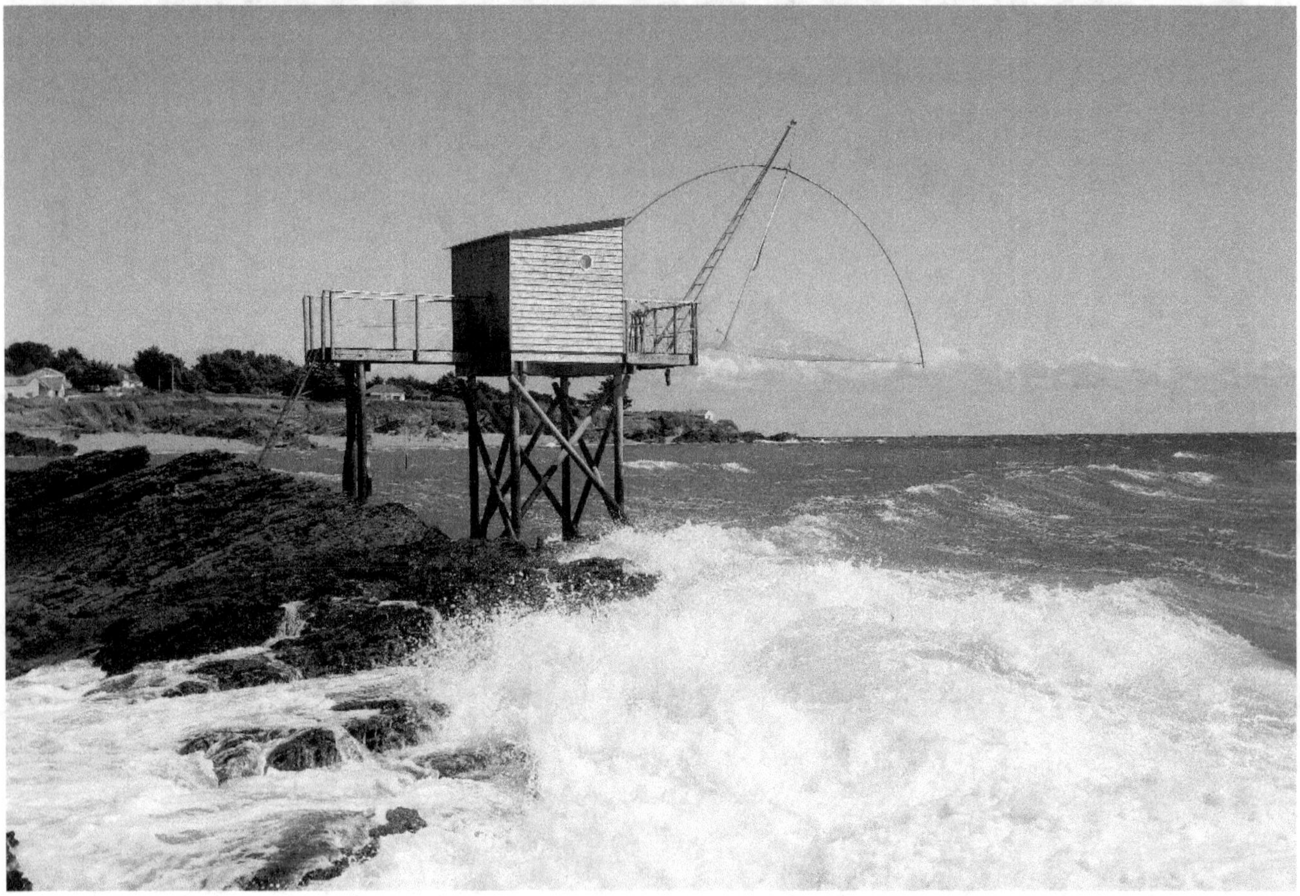

Chapels

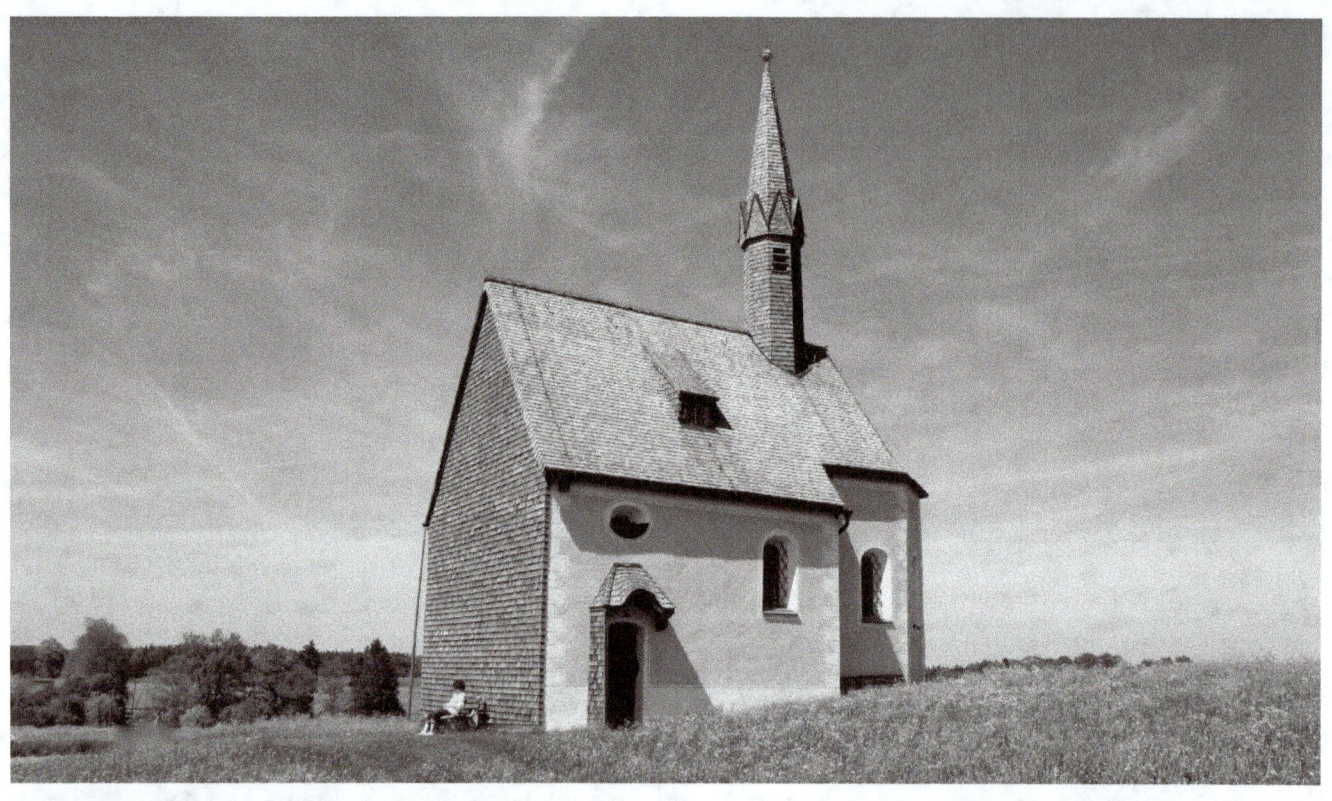

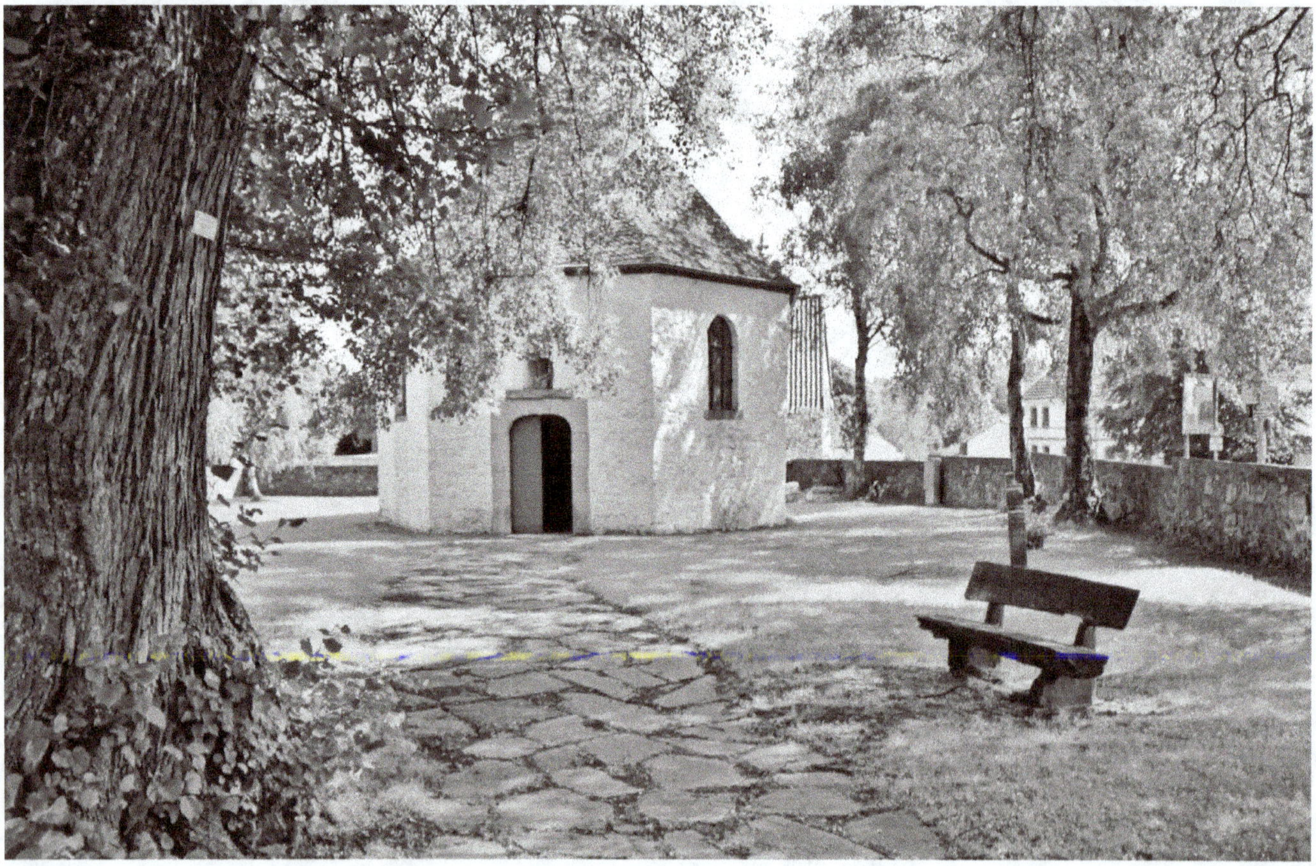

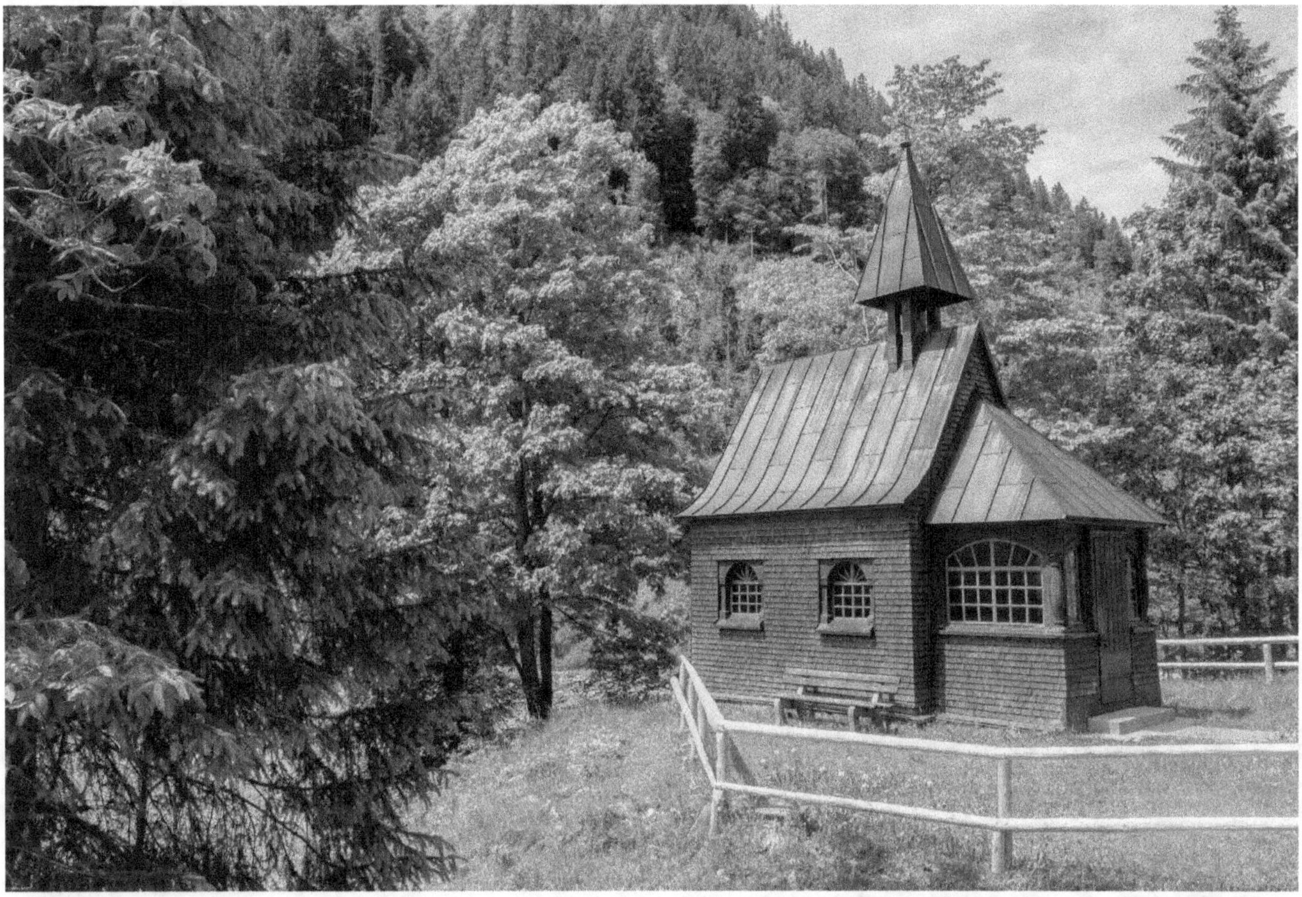

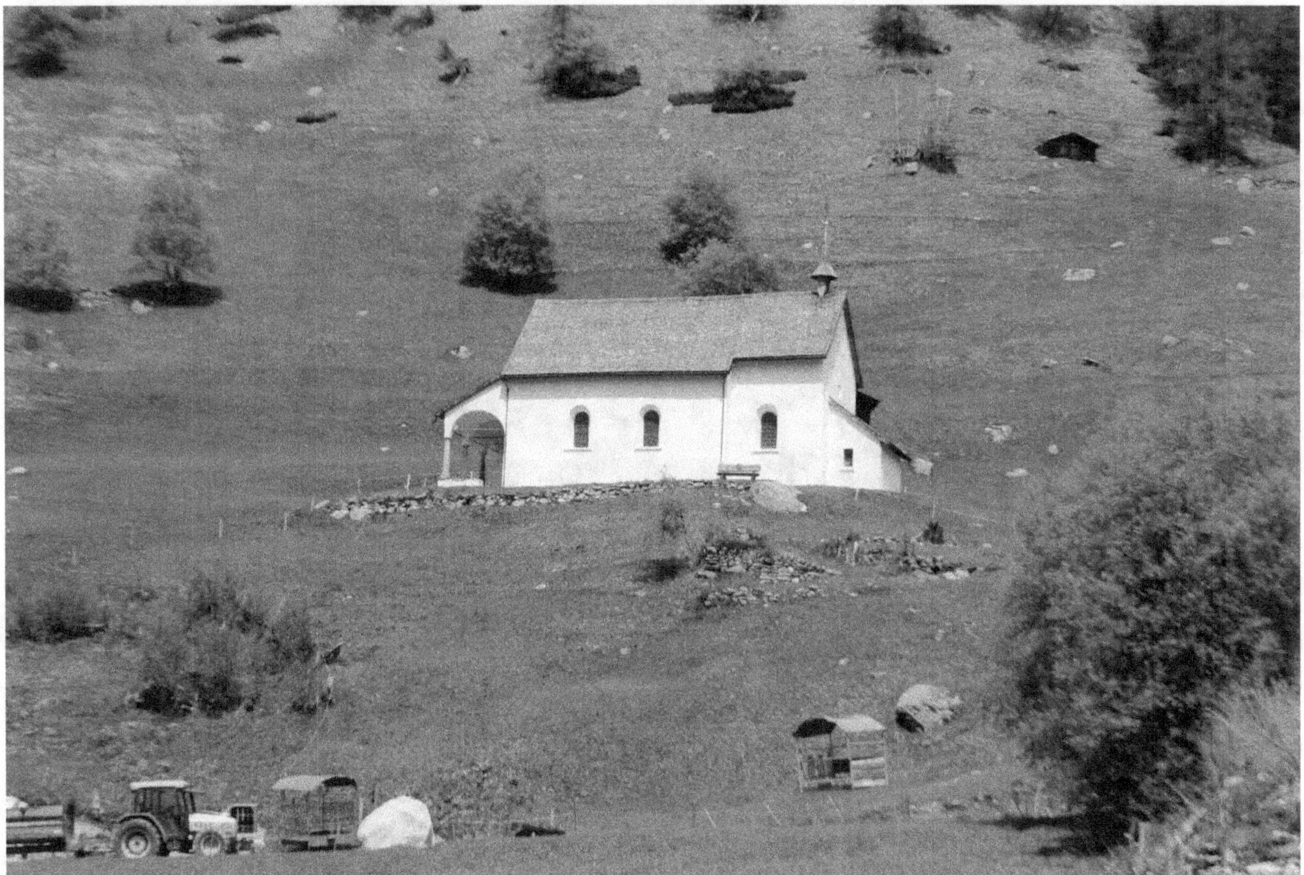

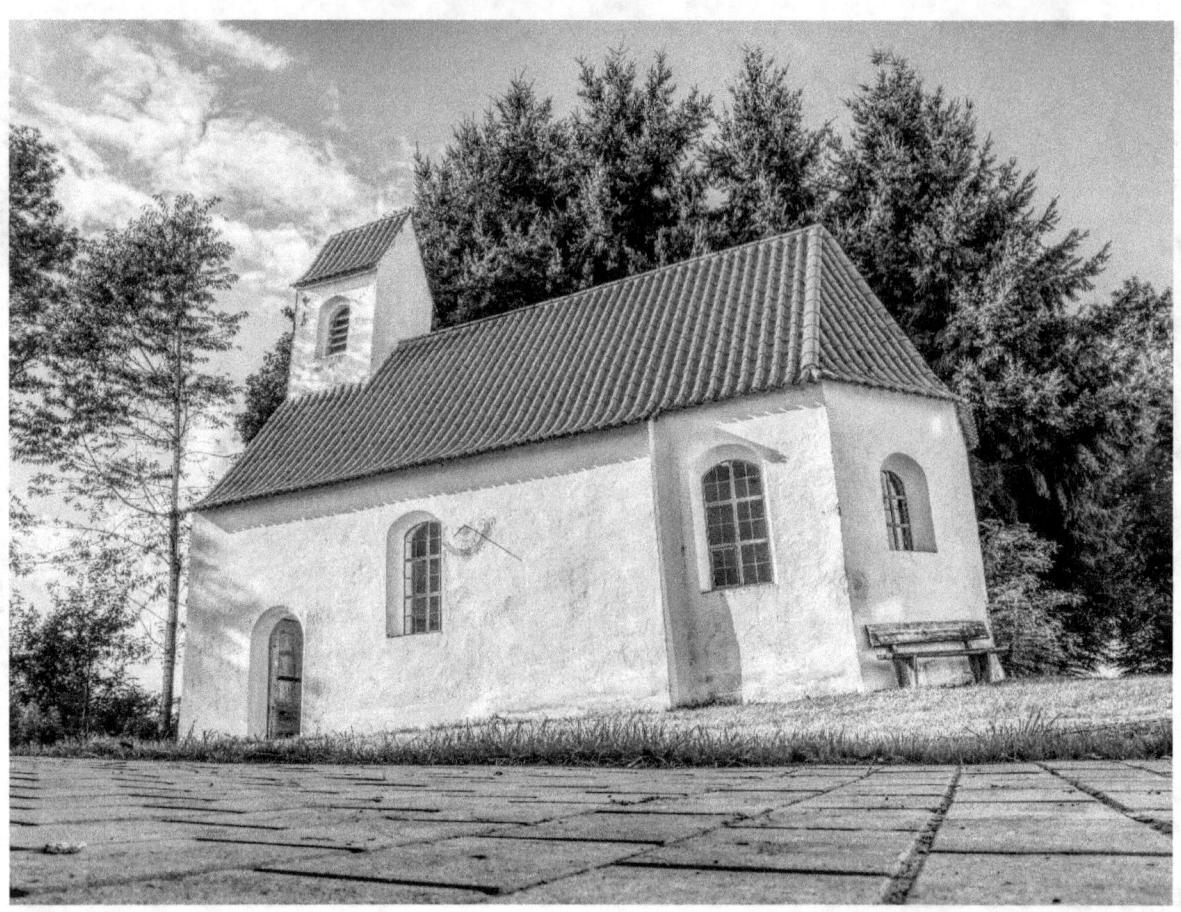

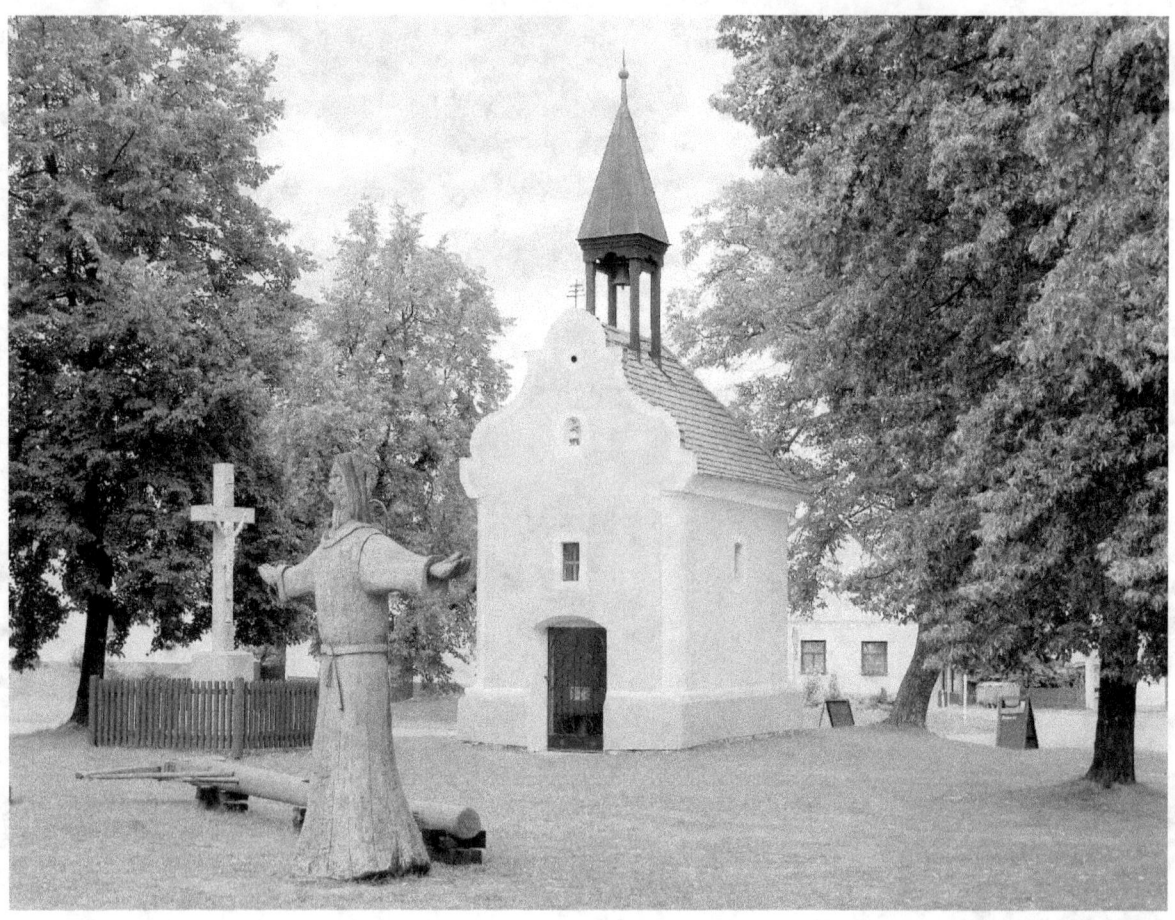

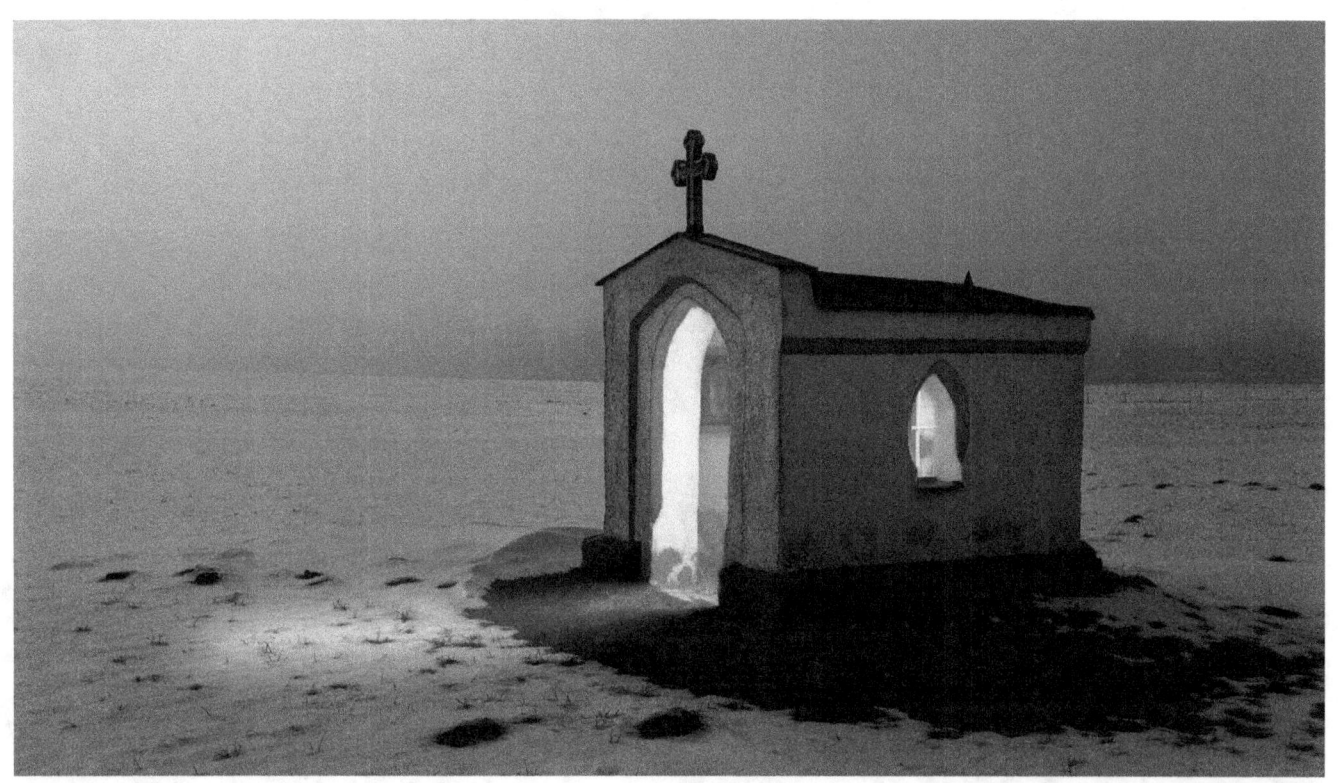

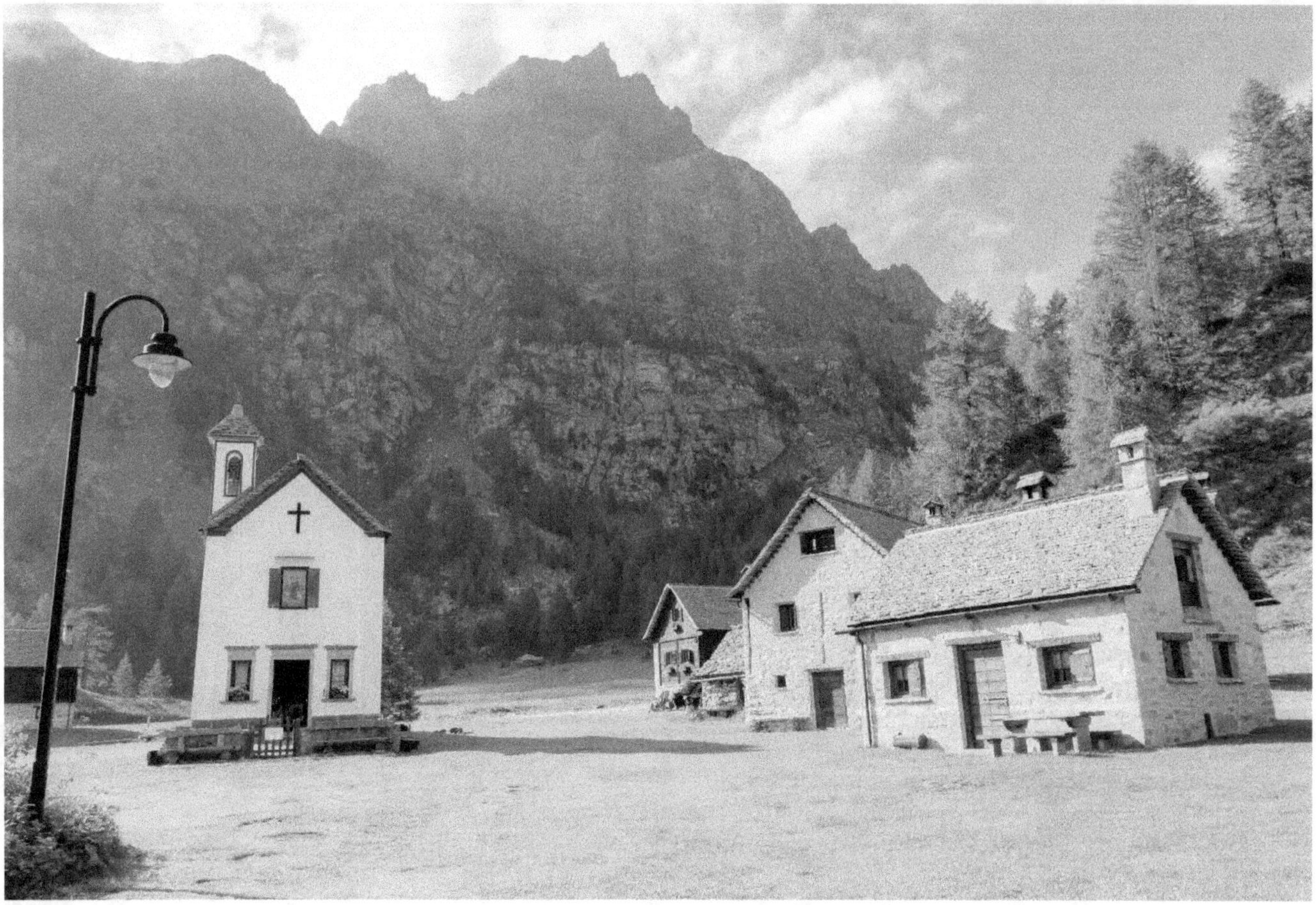

Towers

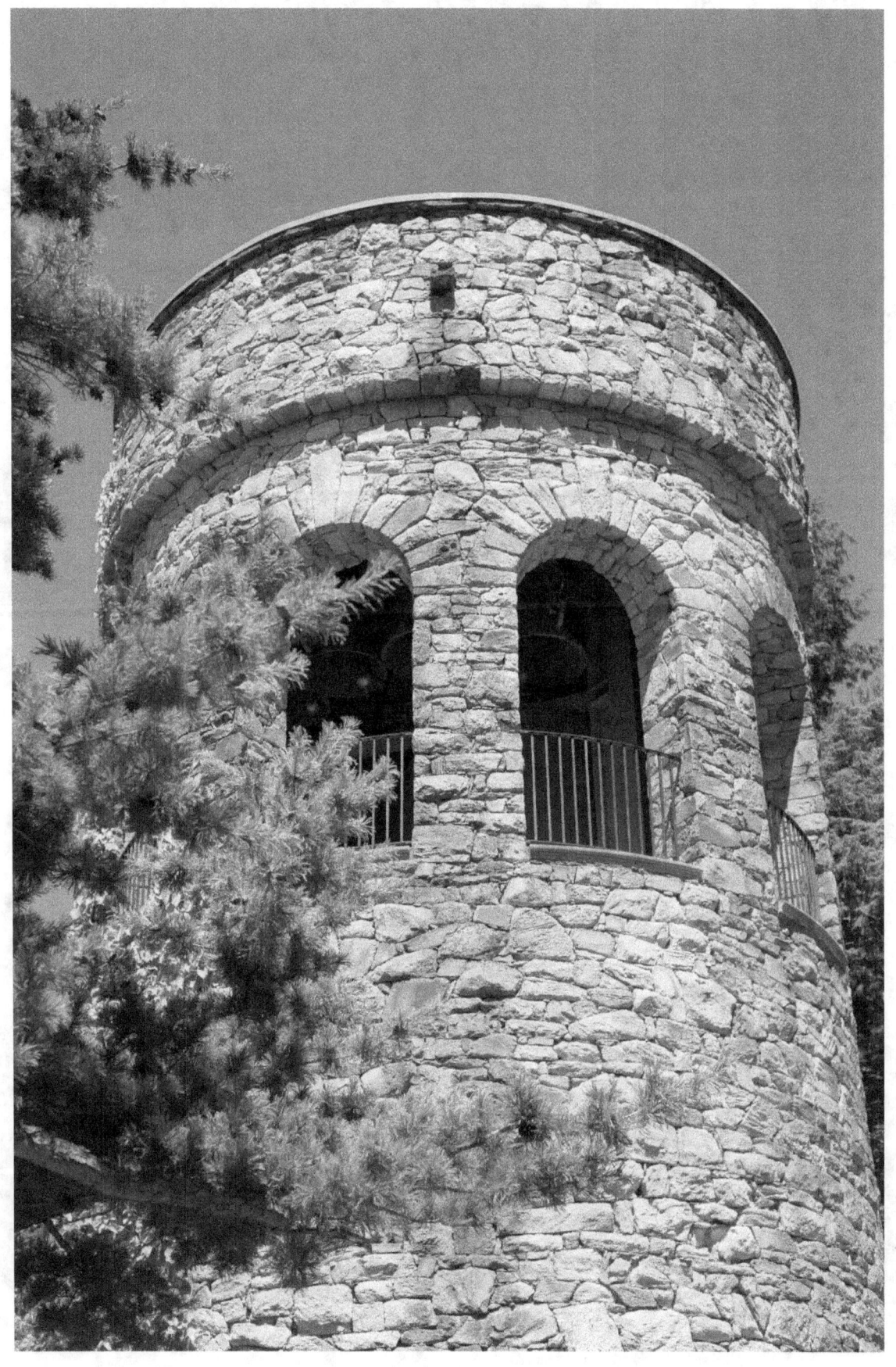

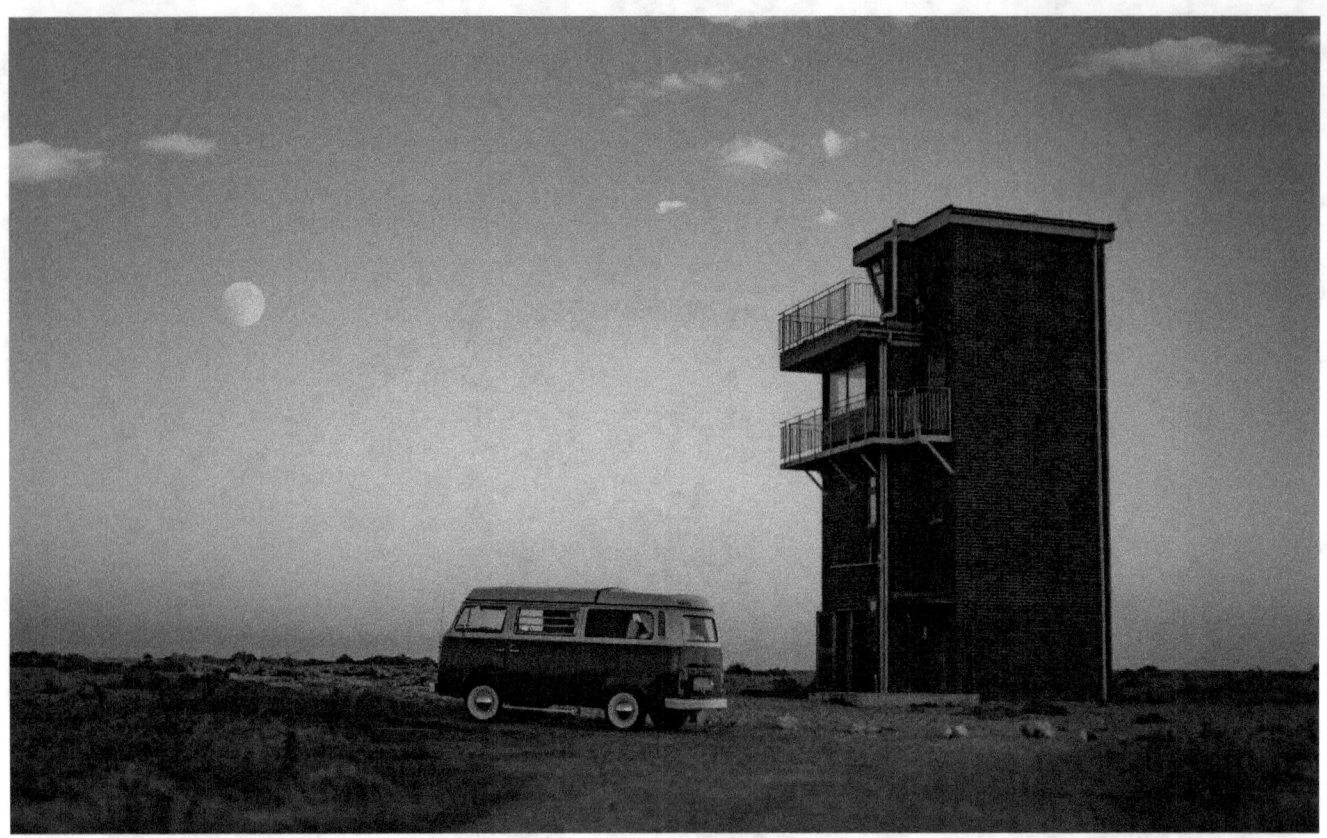

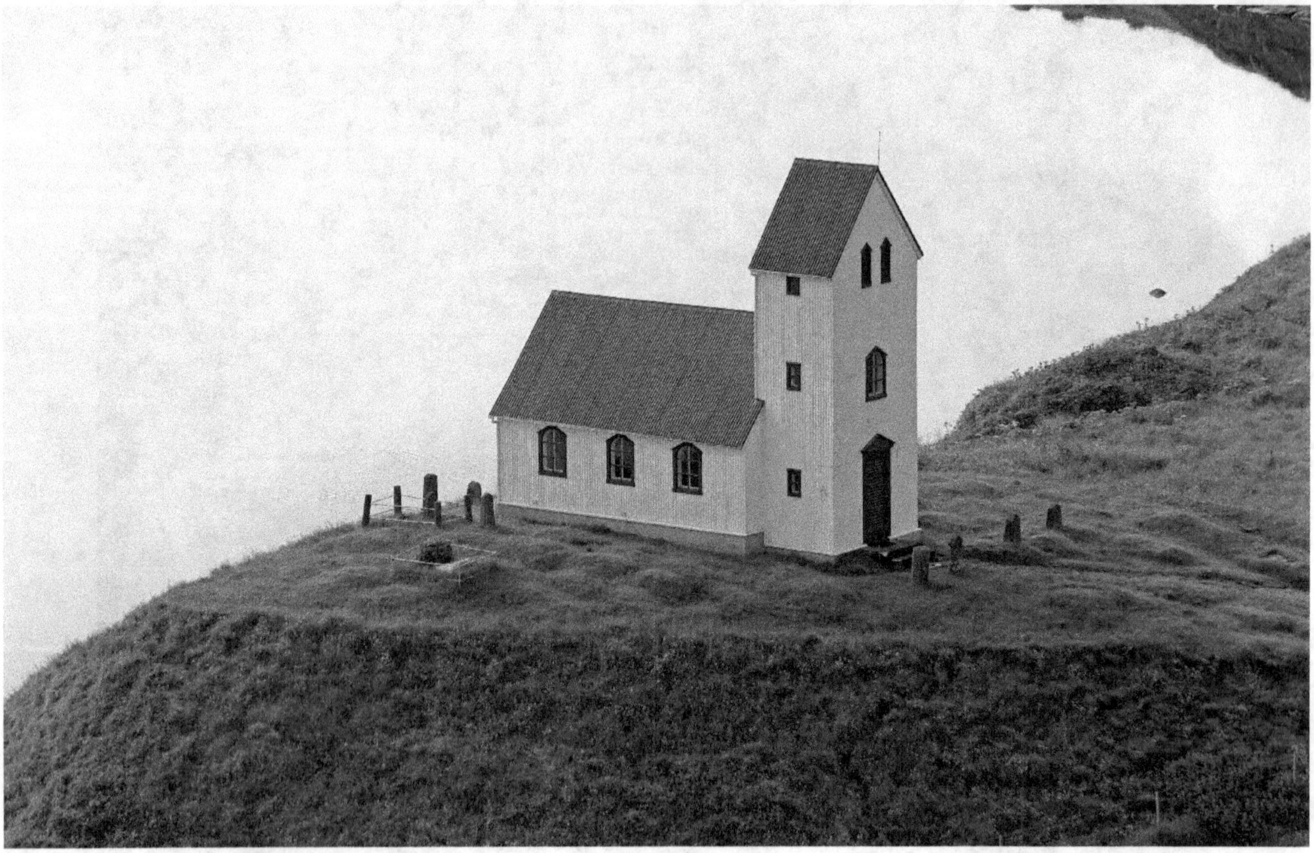

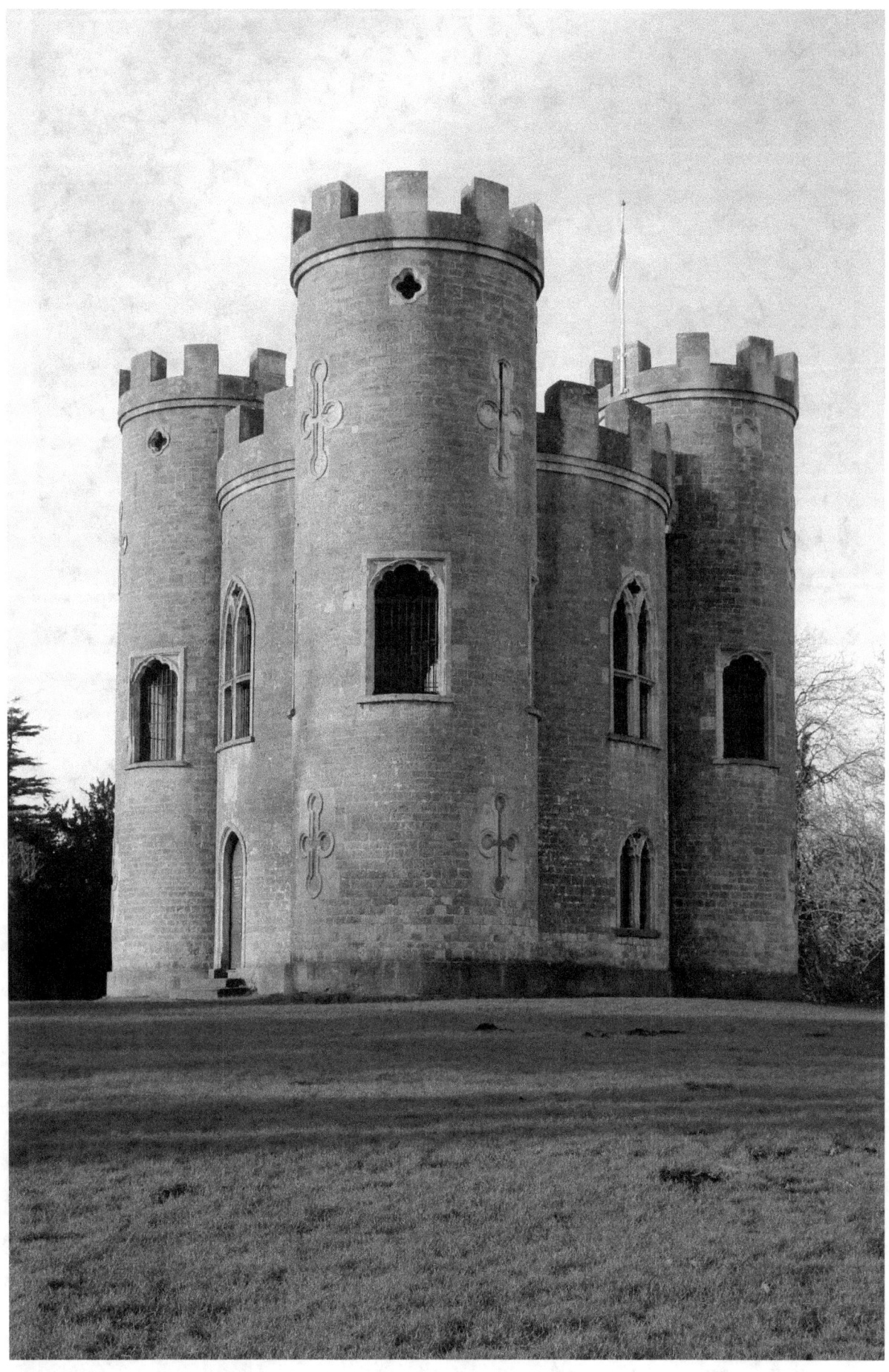

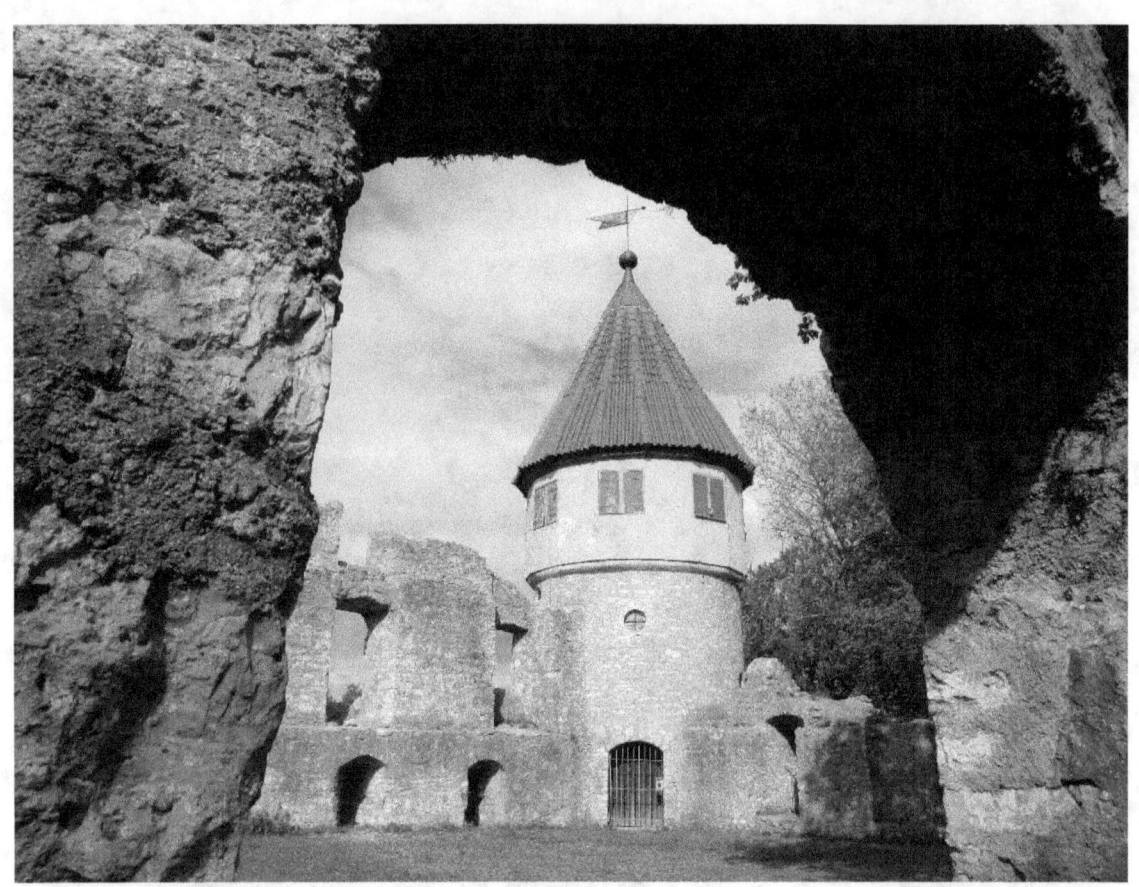

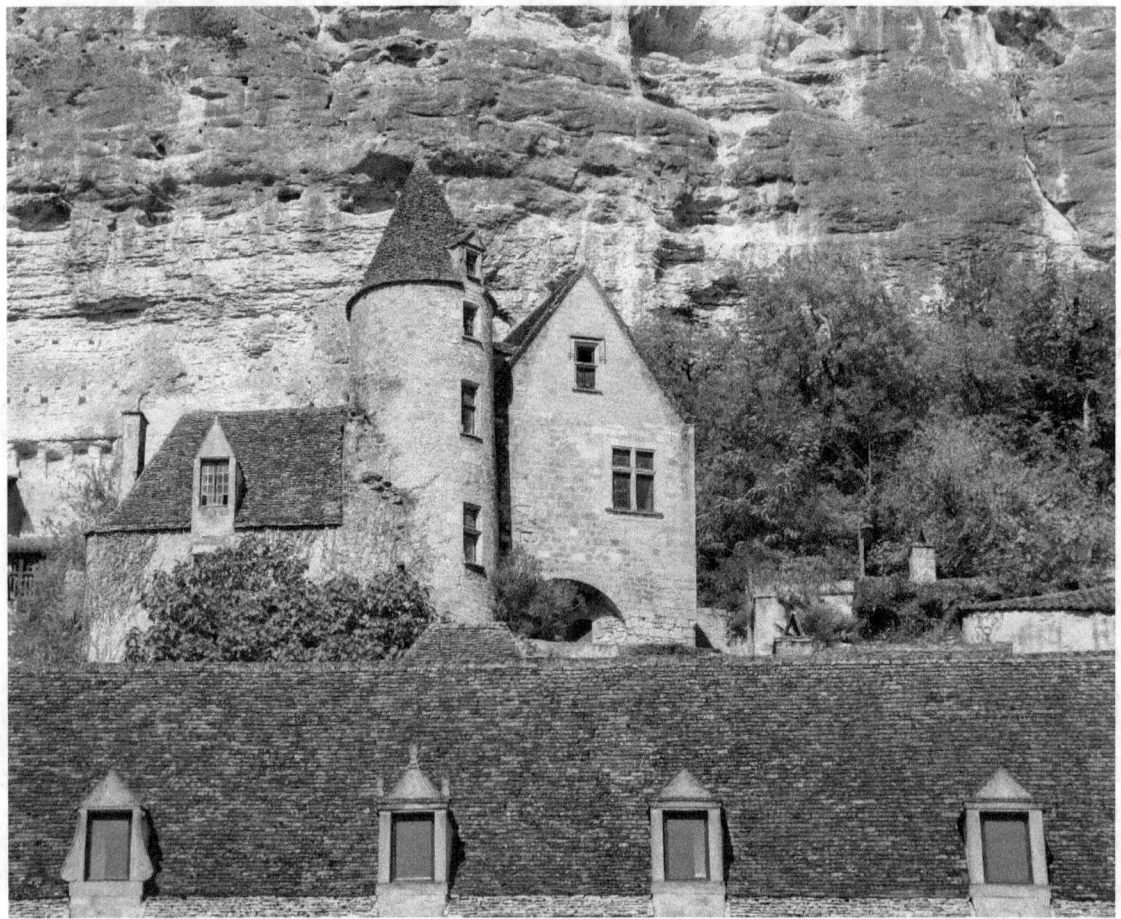

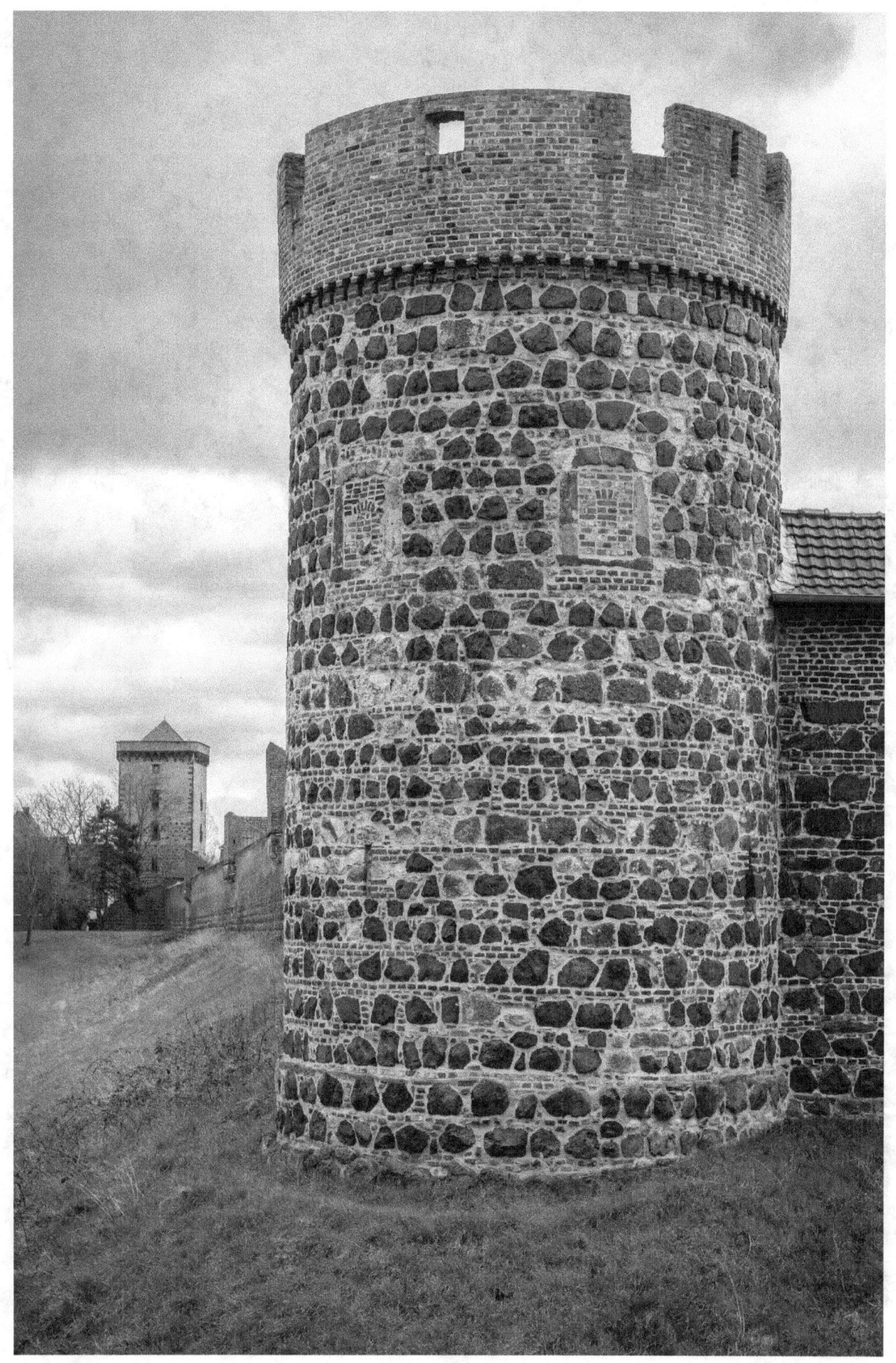

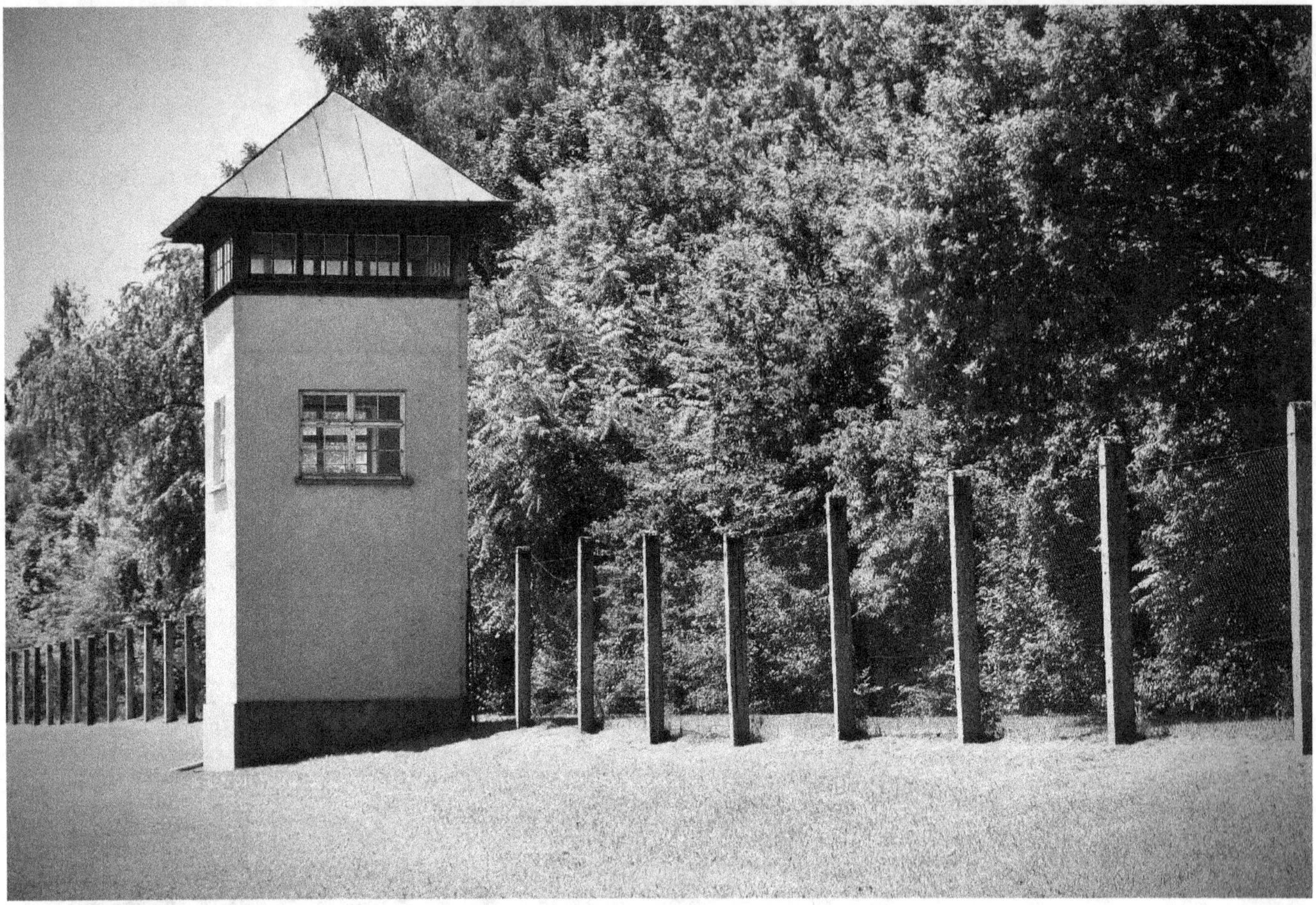

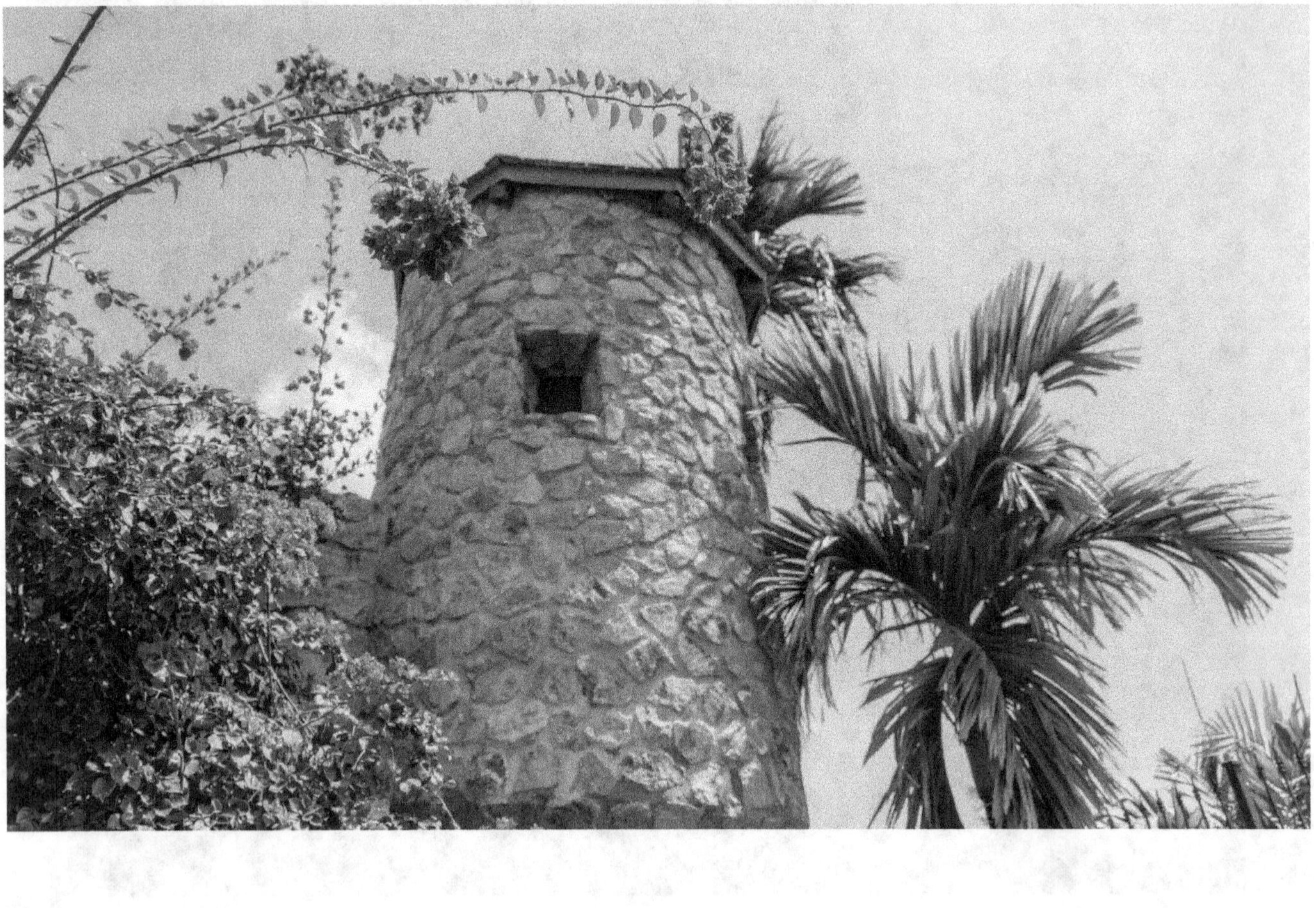

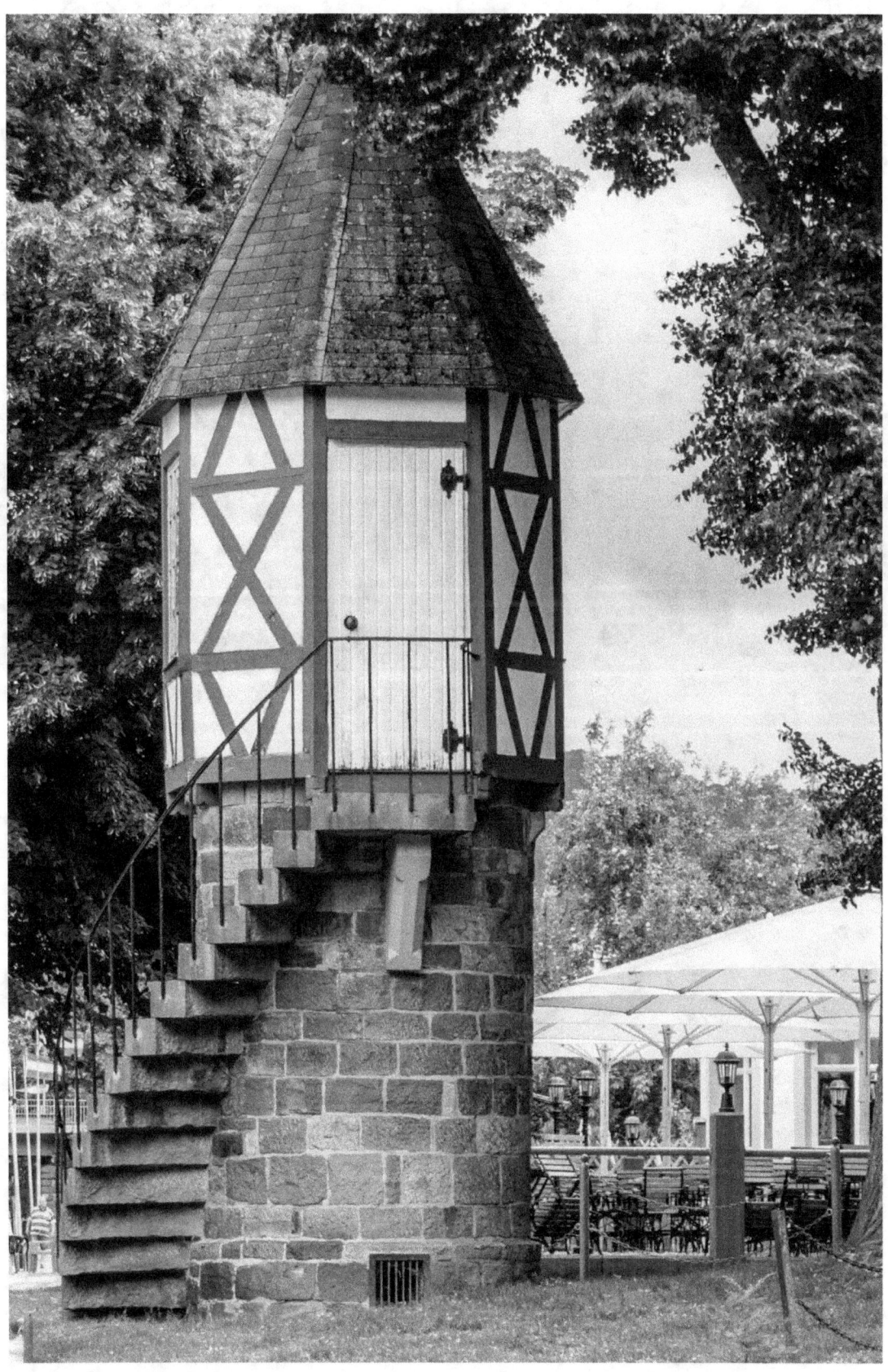

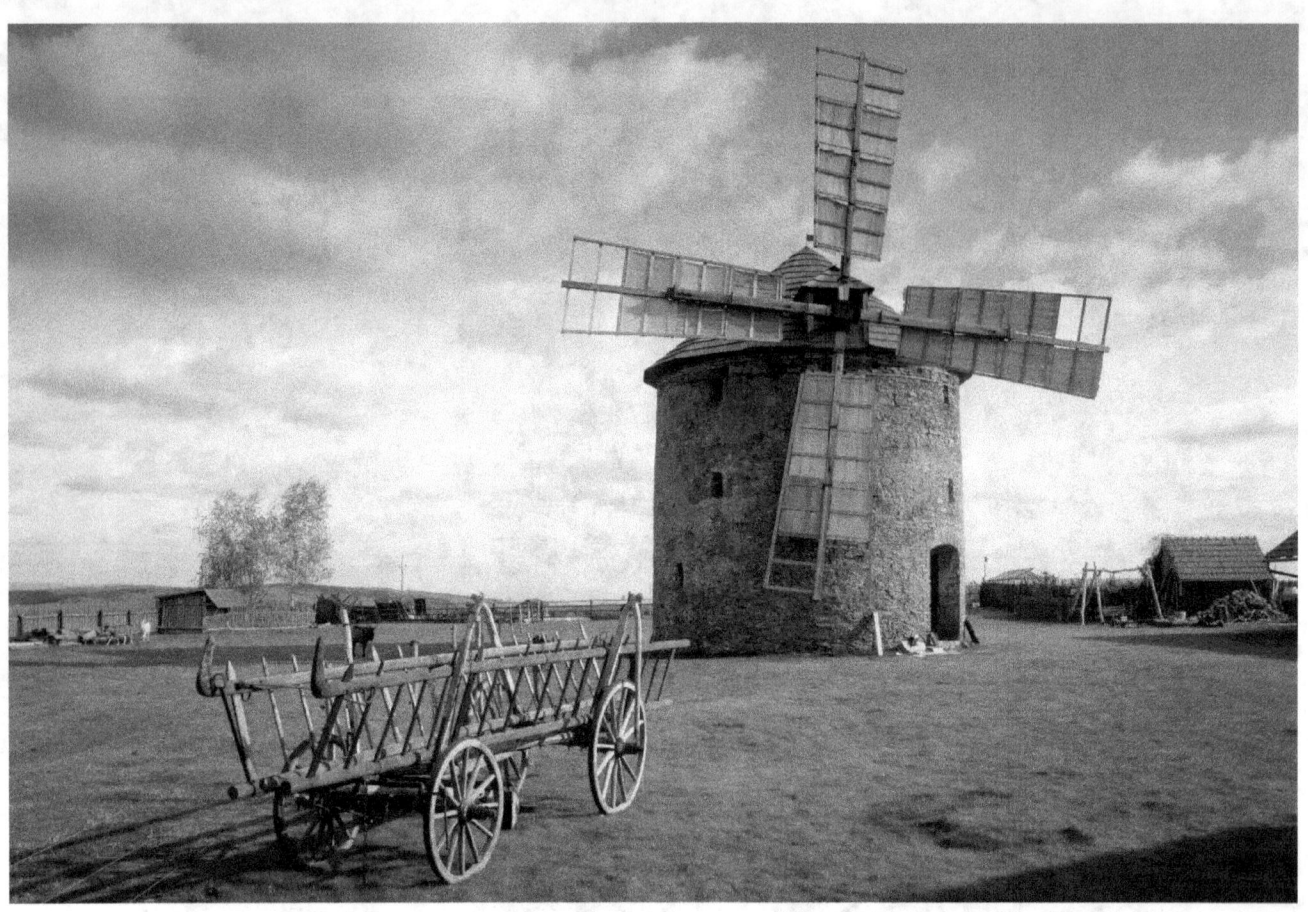

Lighthouses

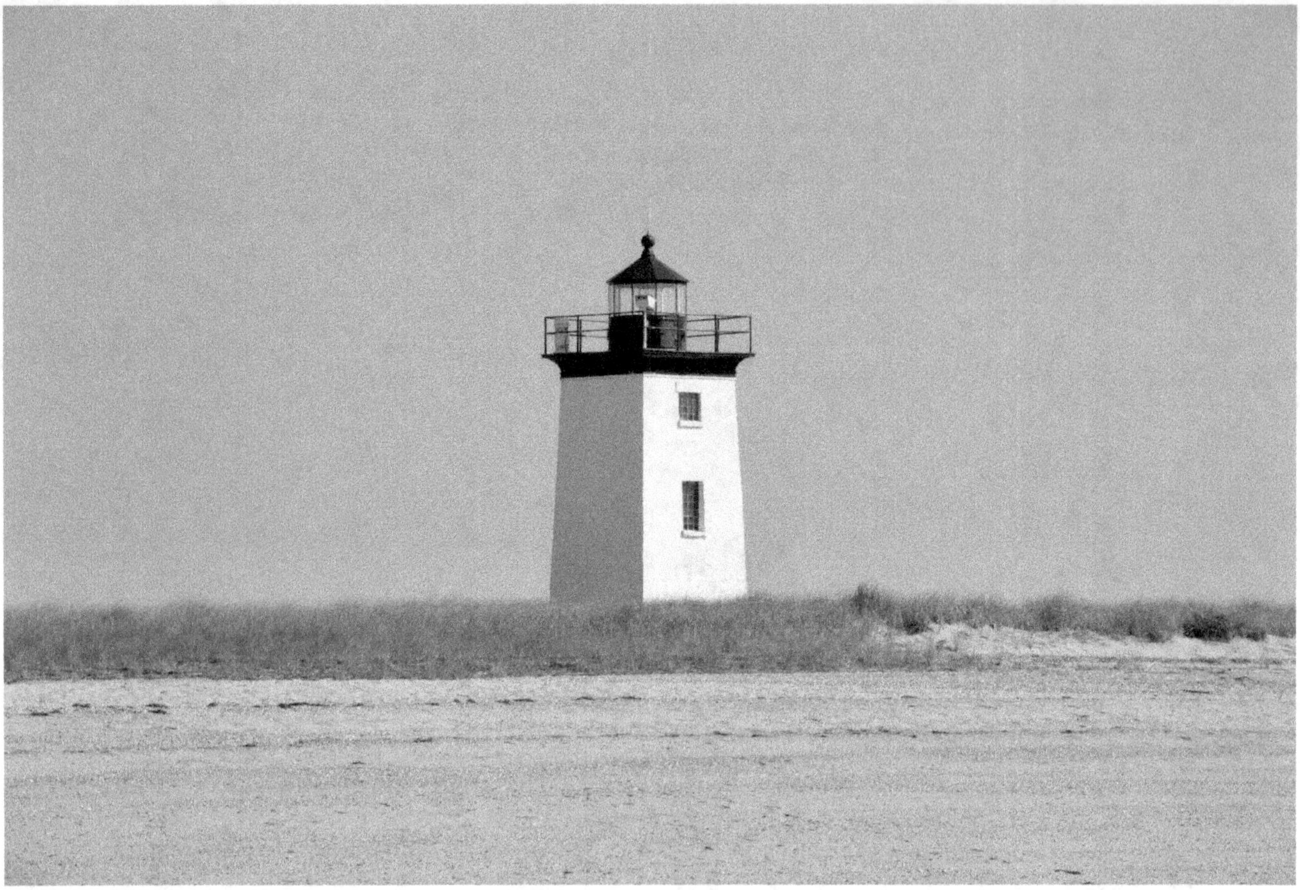

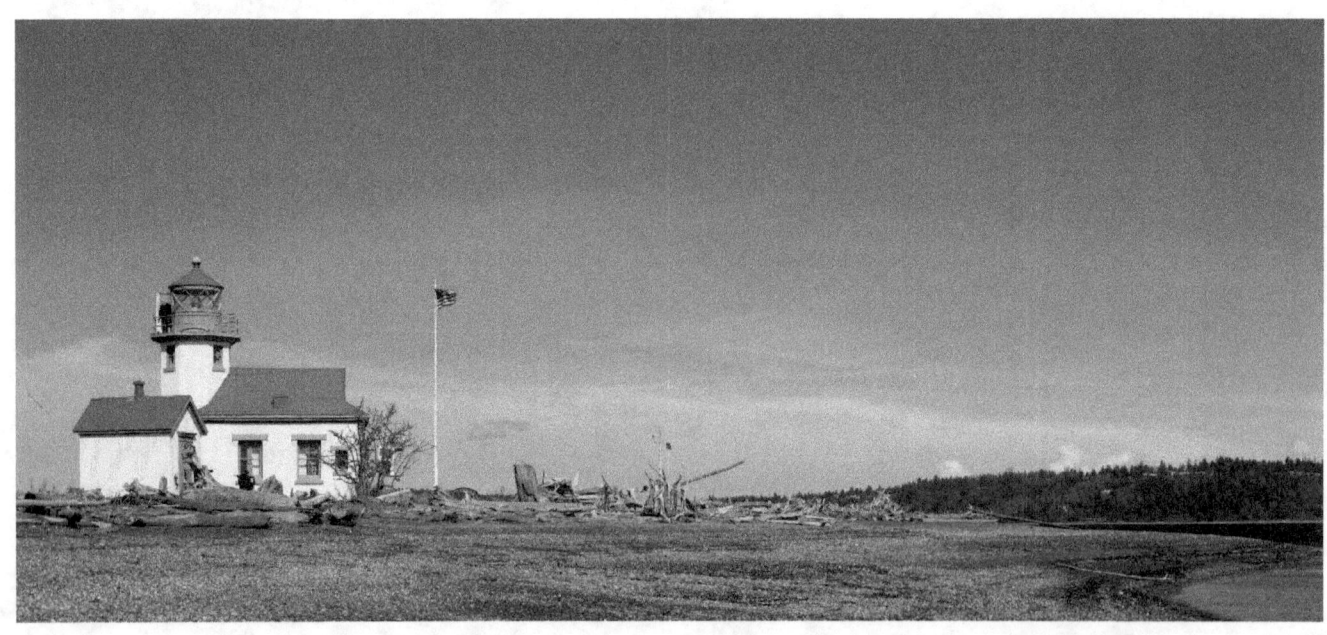

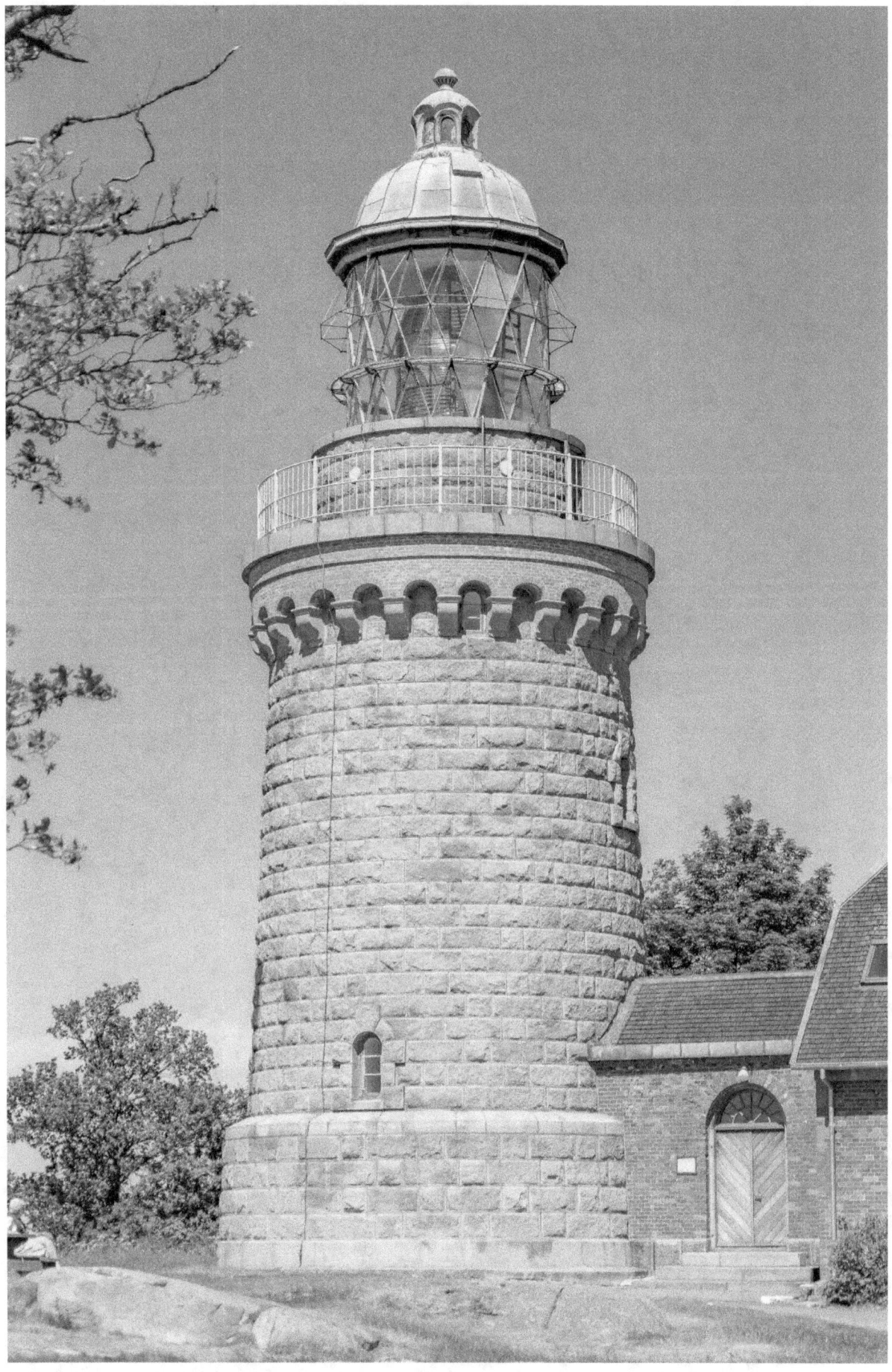

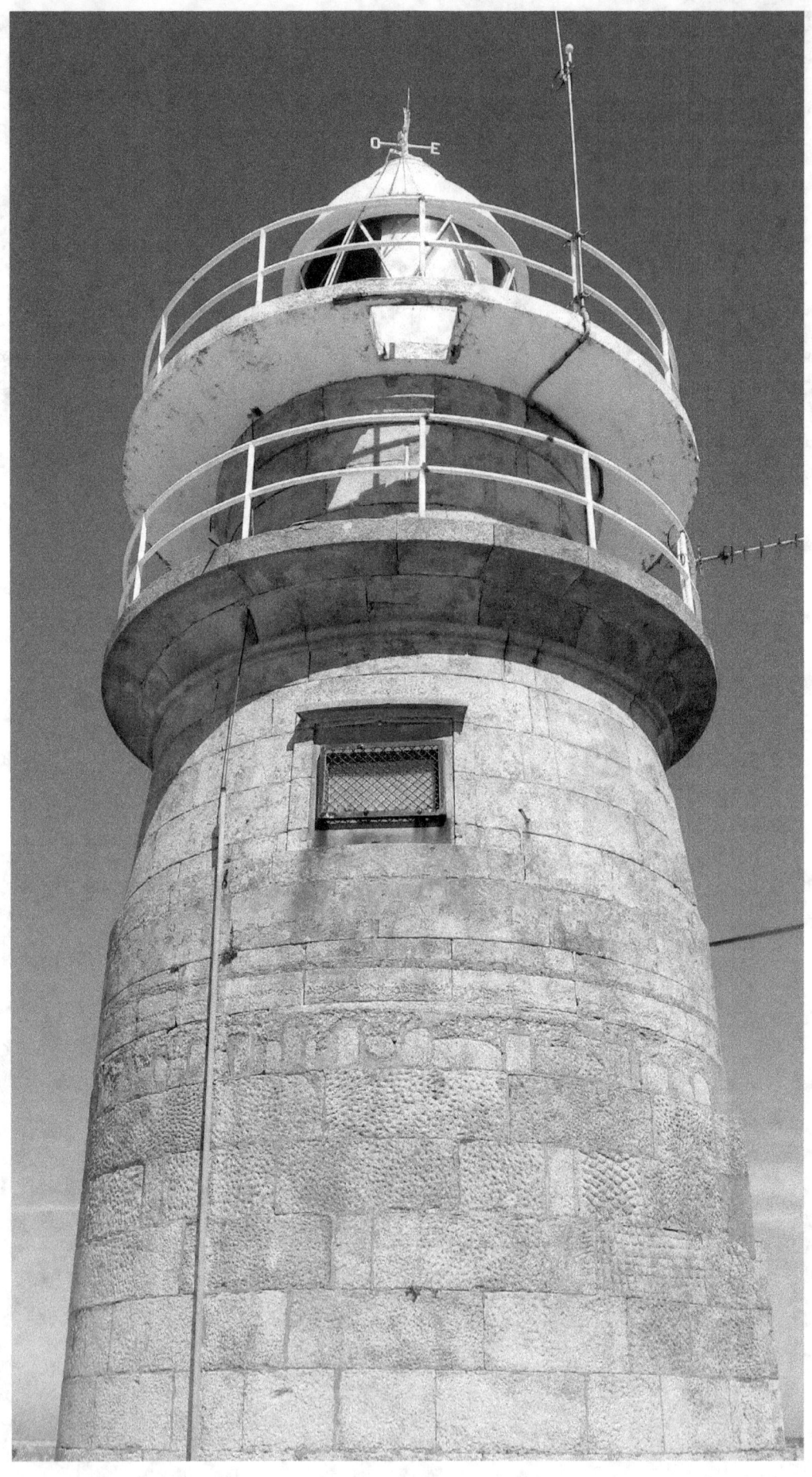

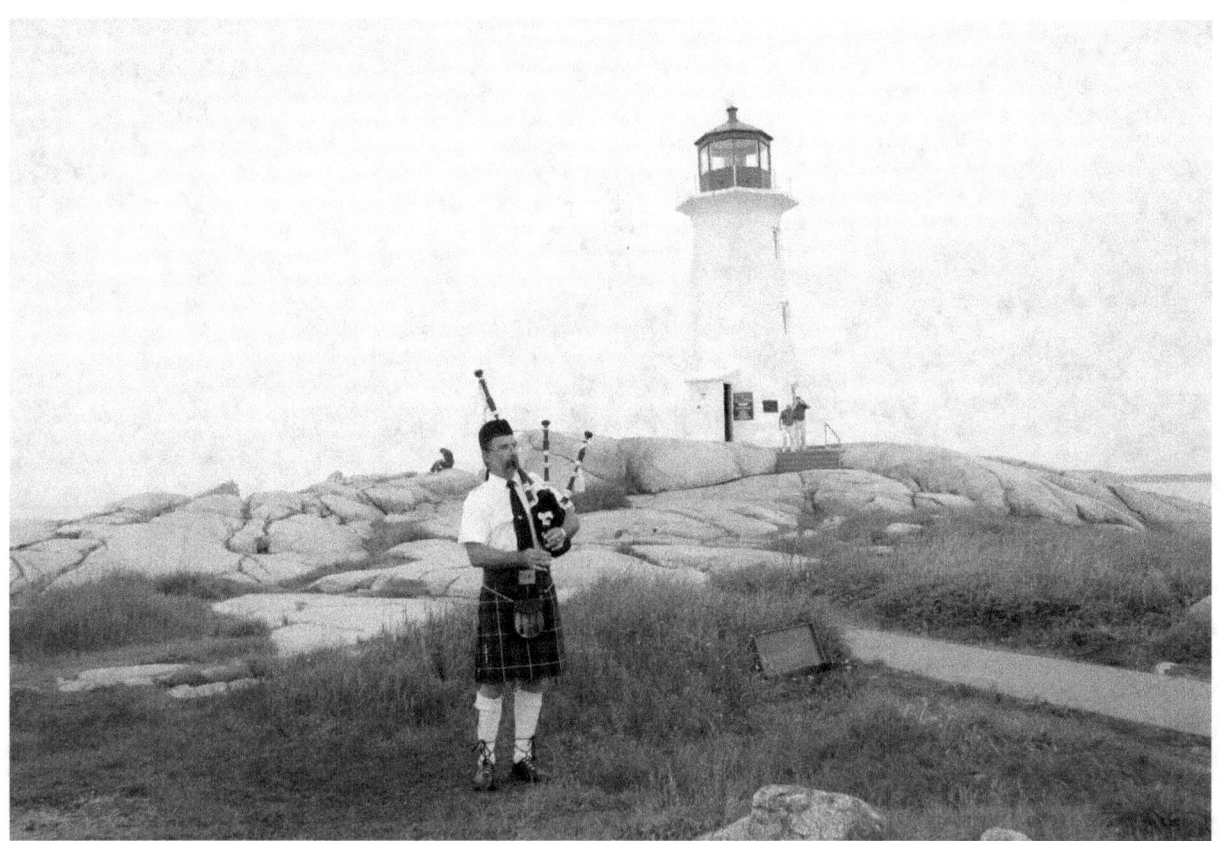

Peggy's Cove, Nova Scotia

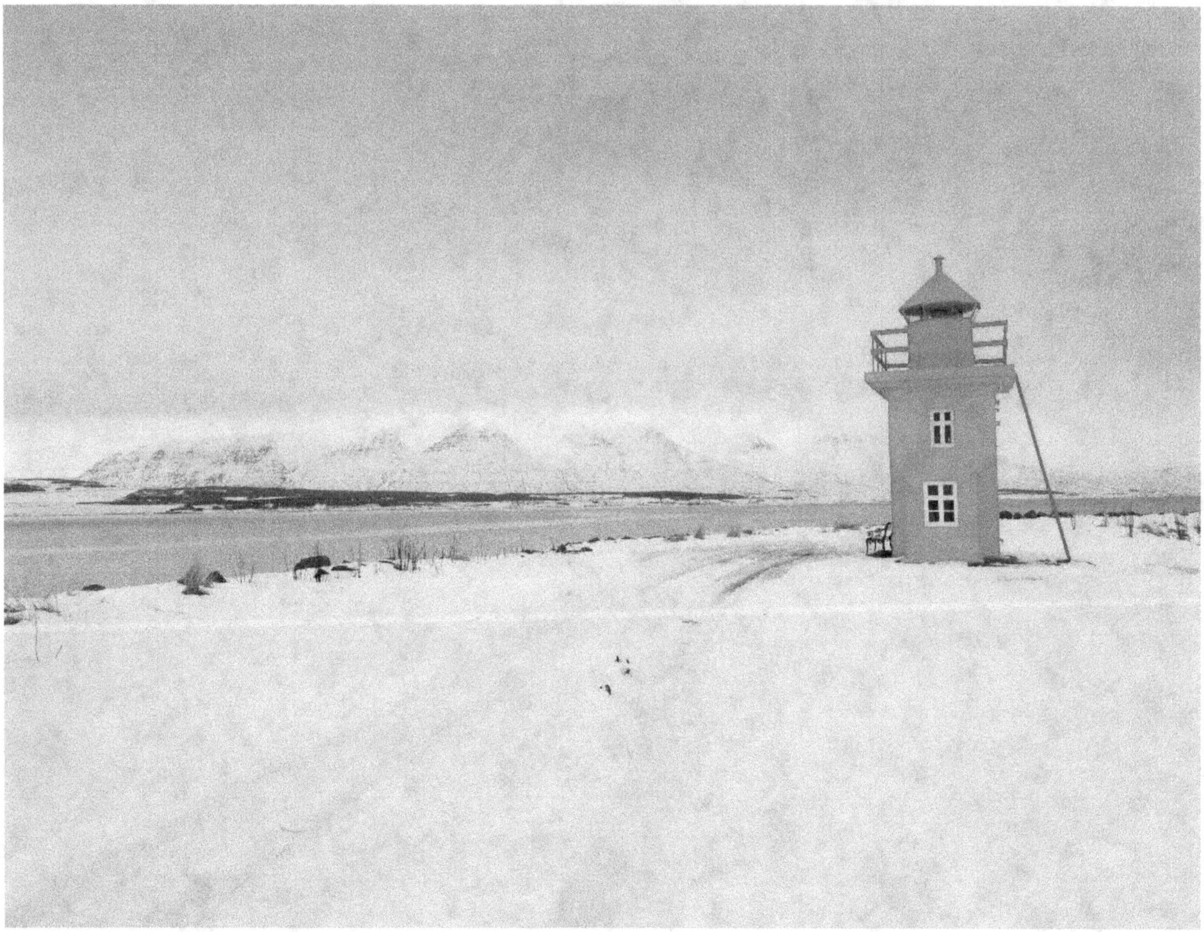

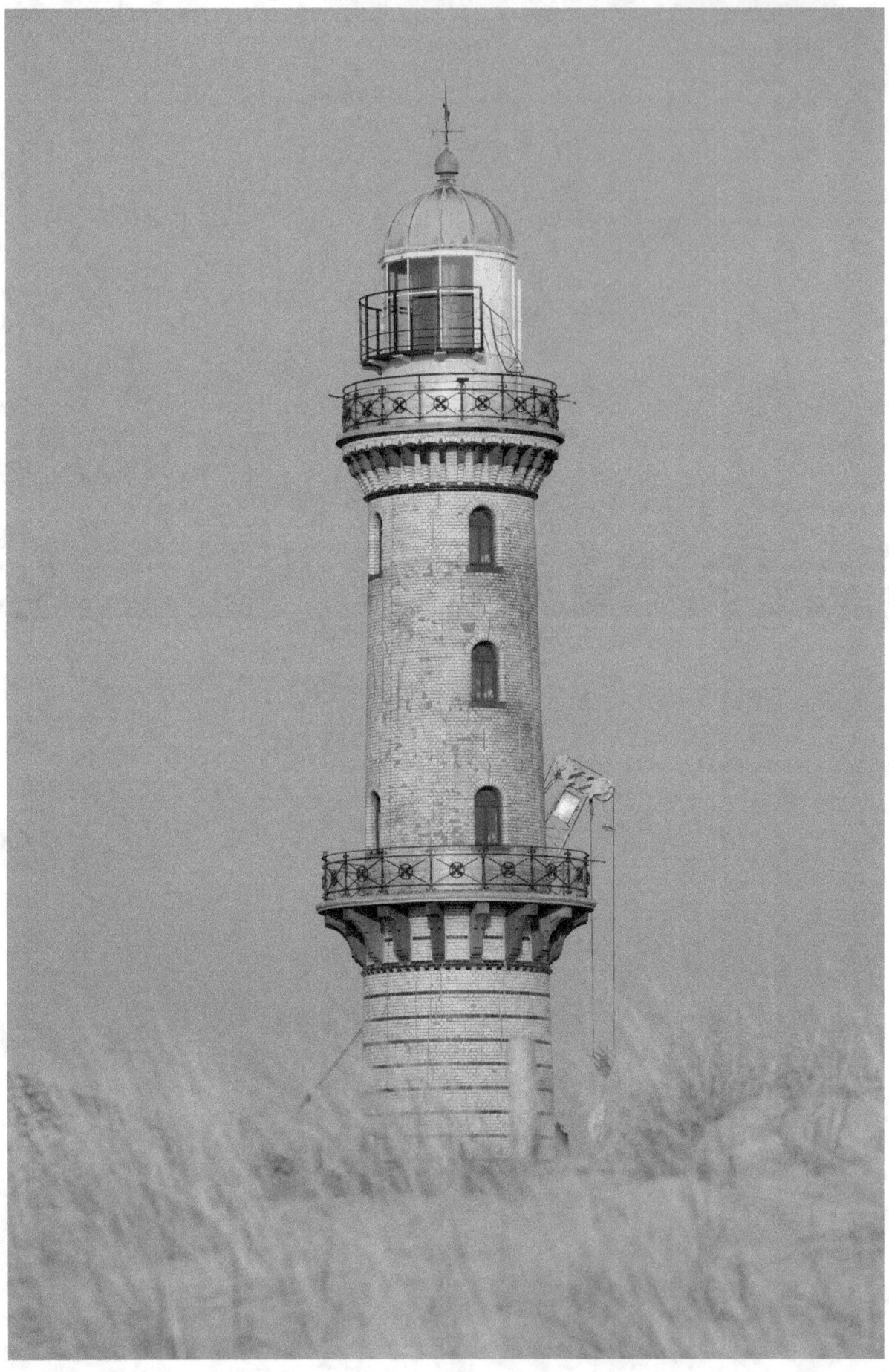

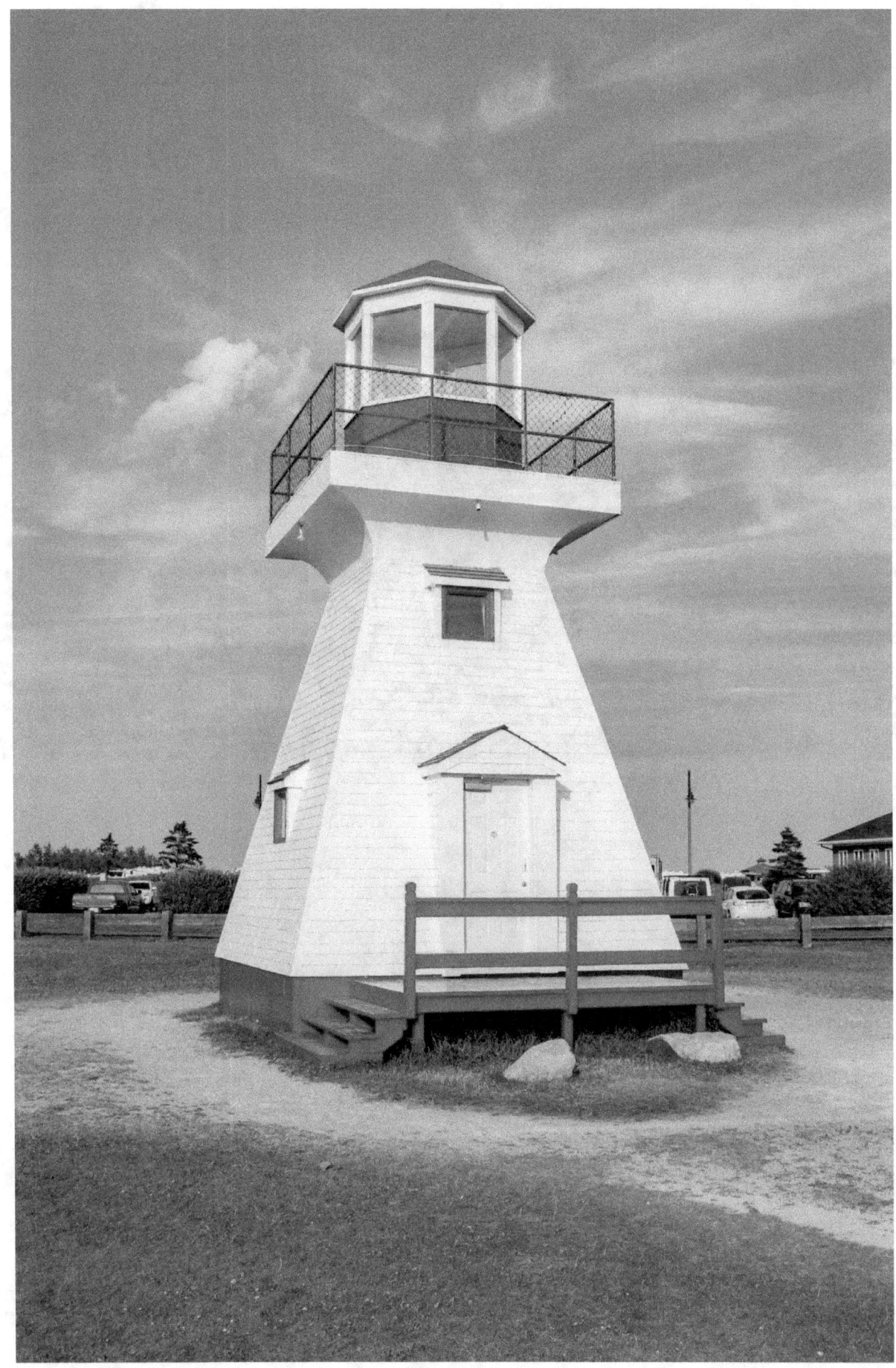

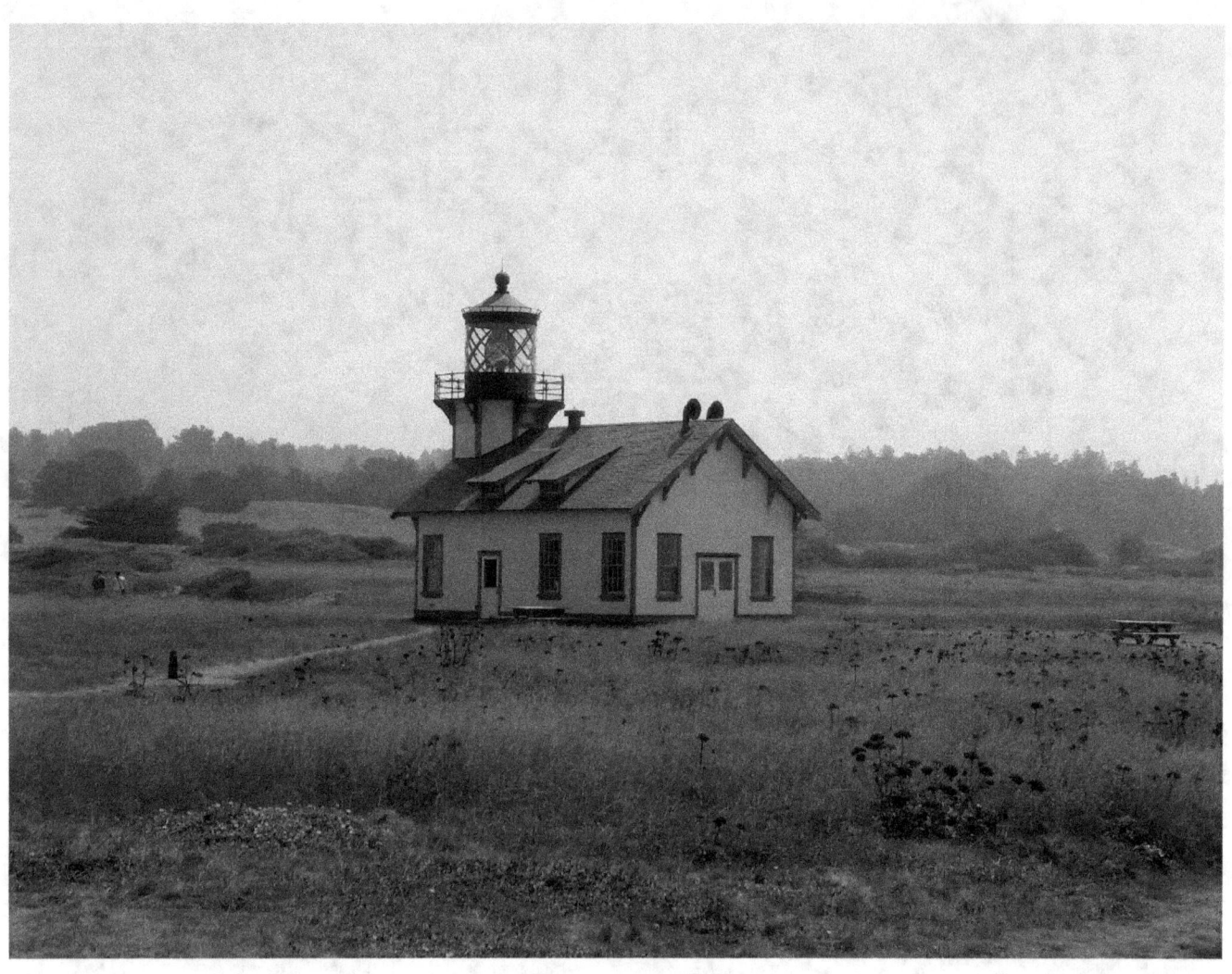

This page is intentionally left blank

6 WOOD

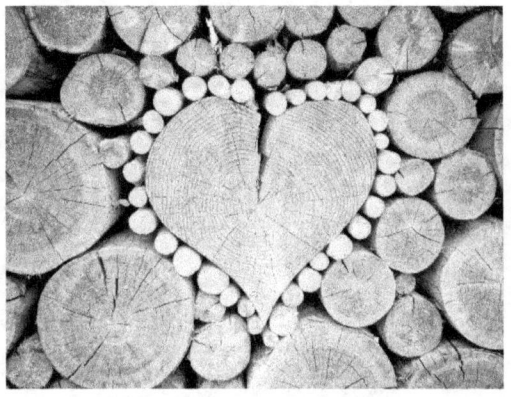

Log cabins, wooden homes, bungalows, row houses

Log Cabins

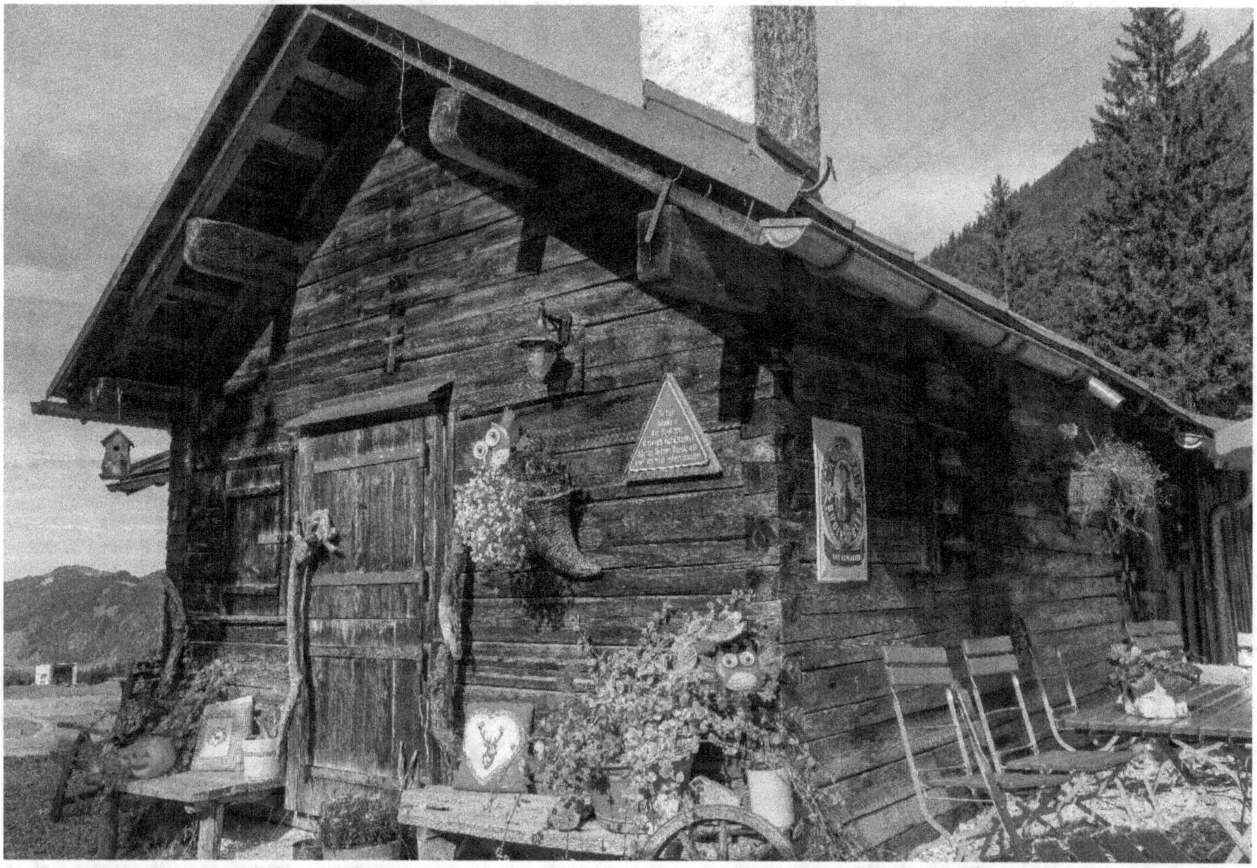

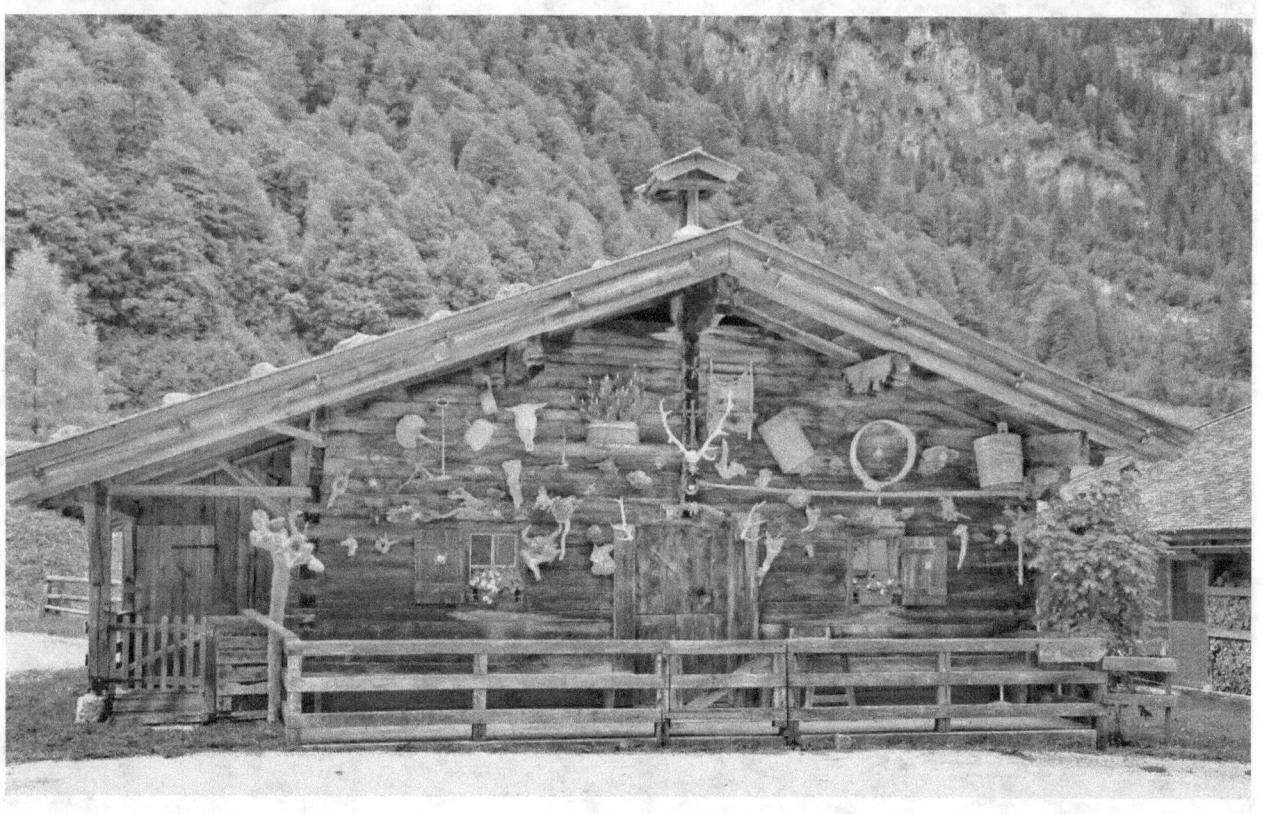

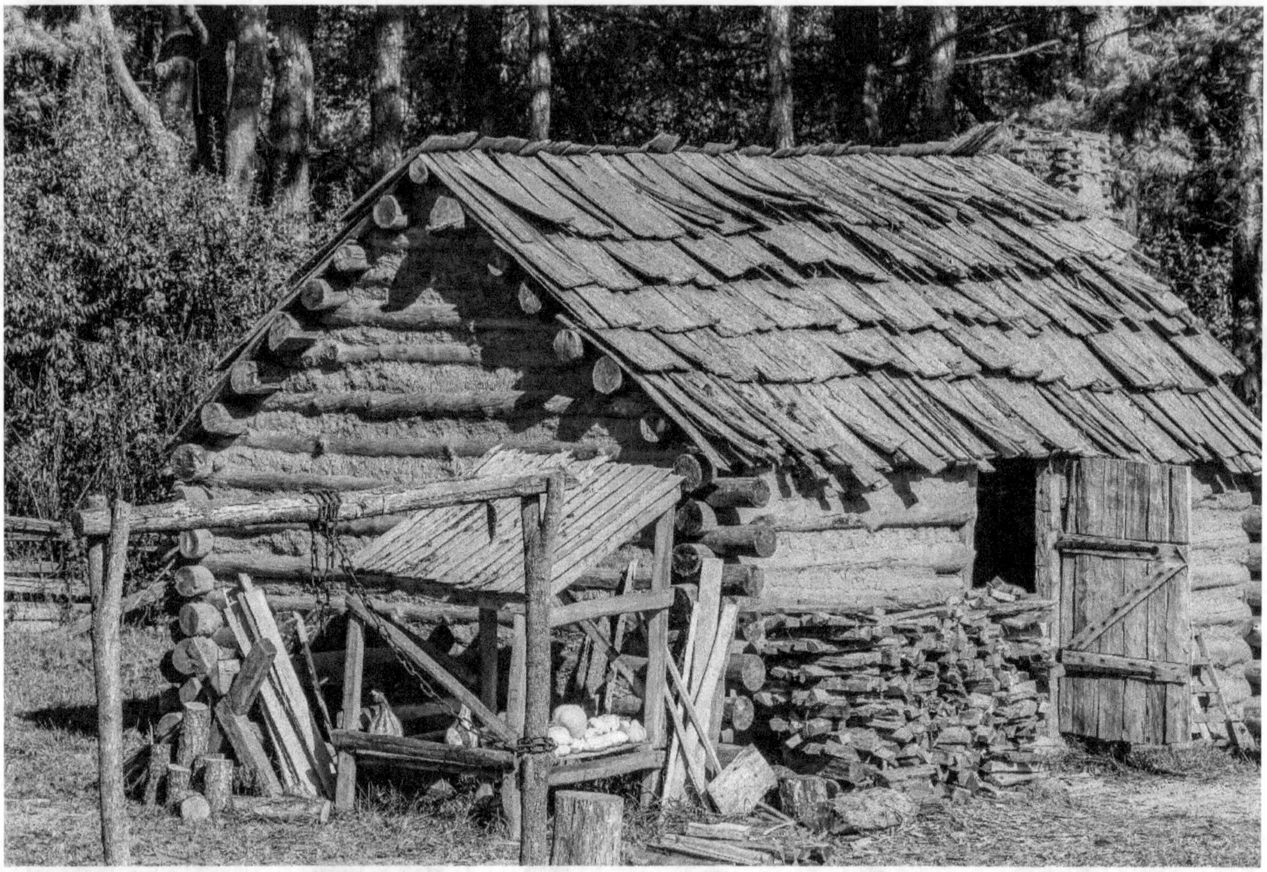

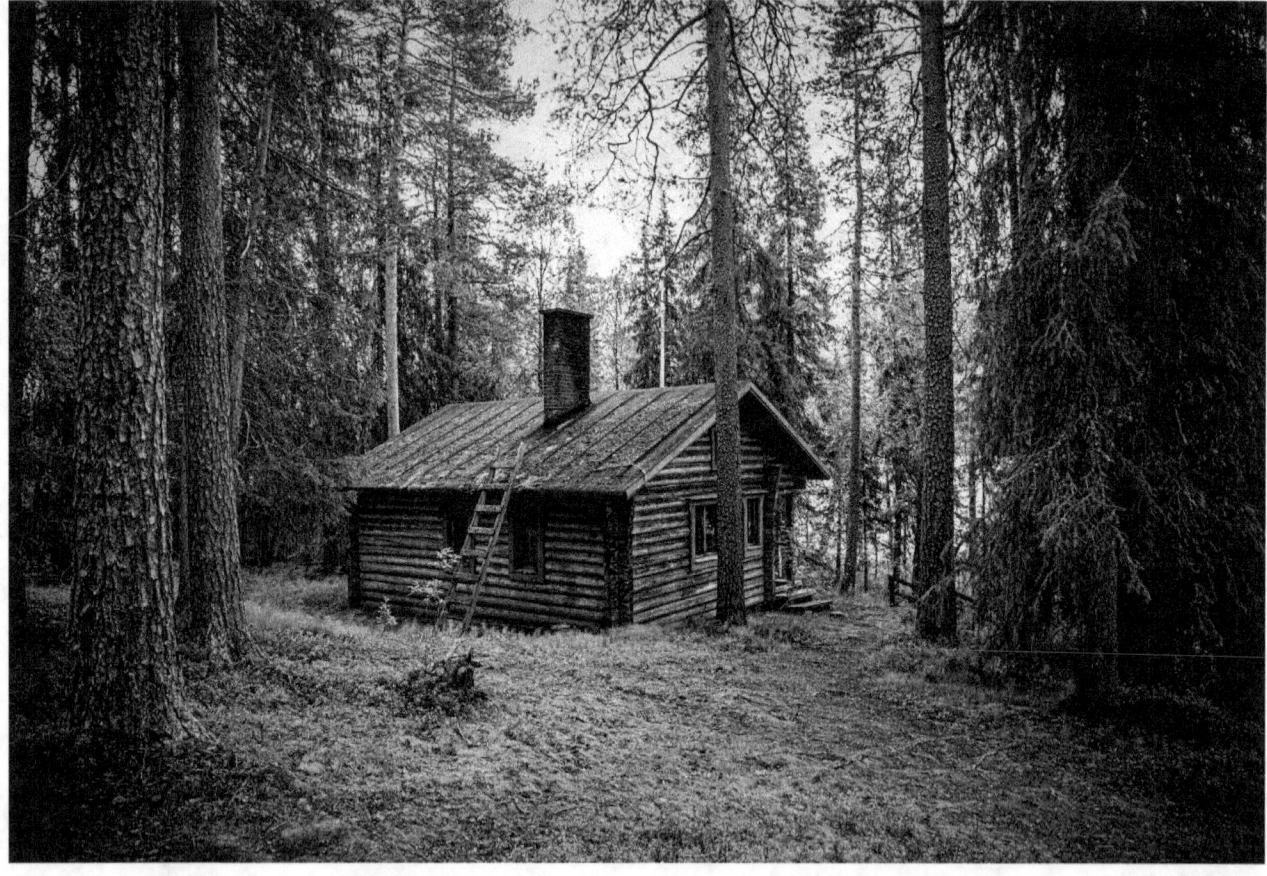

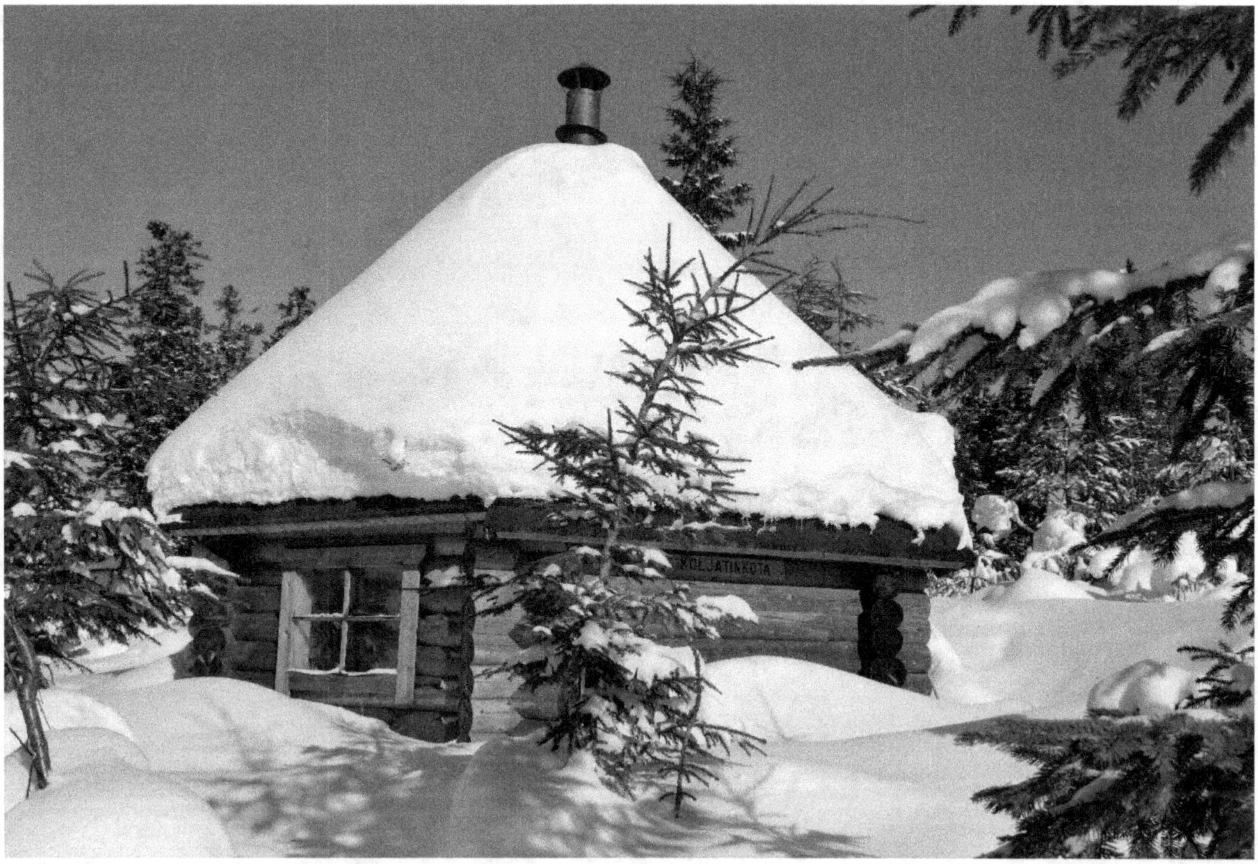

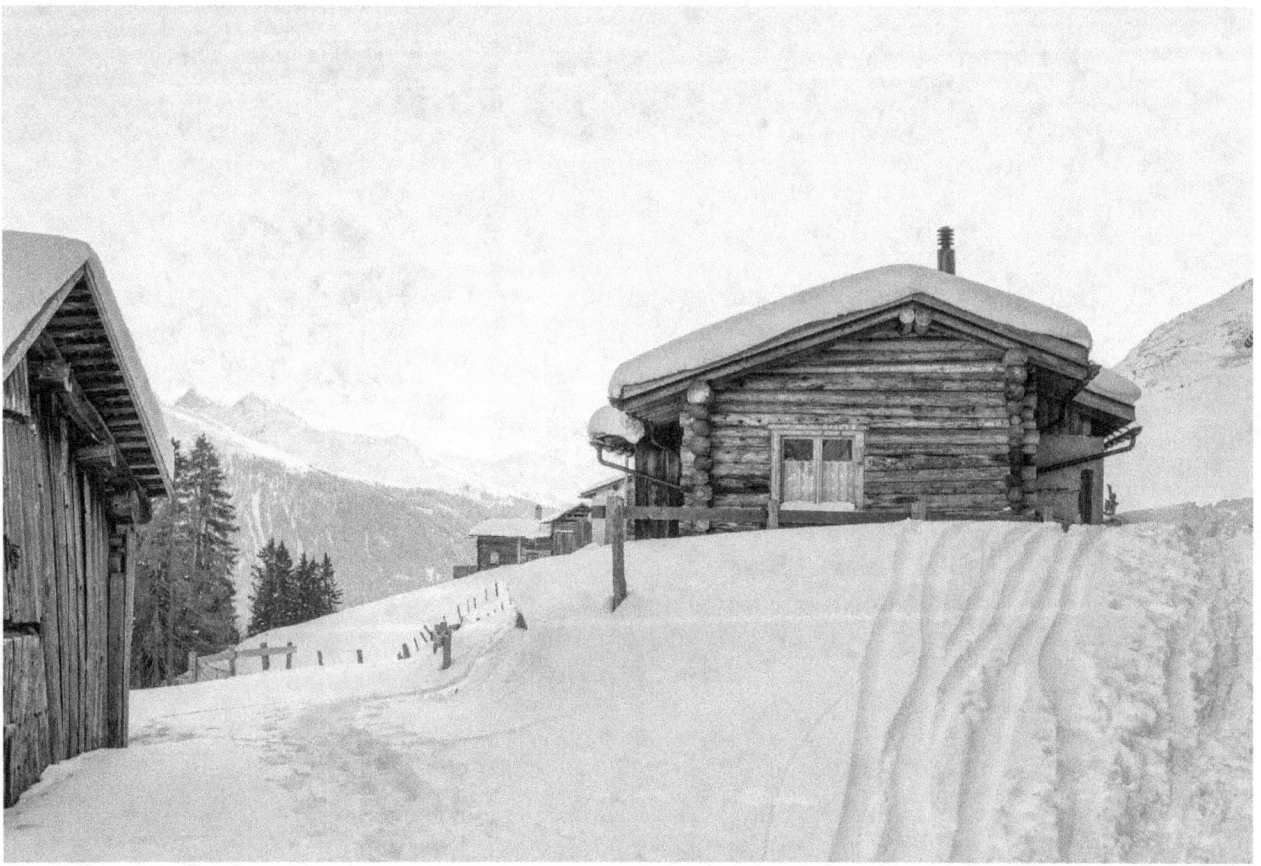

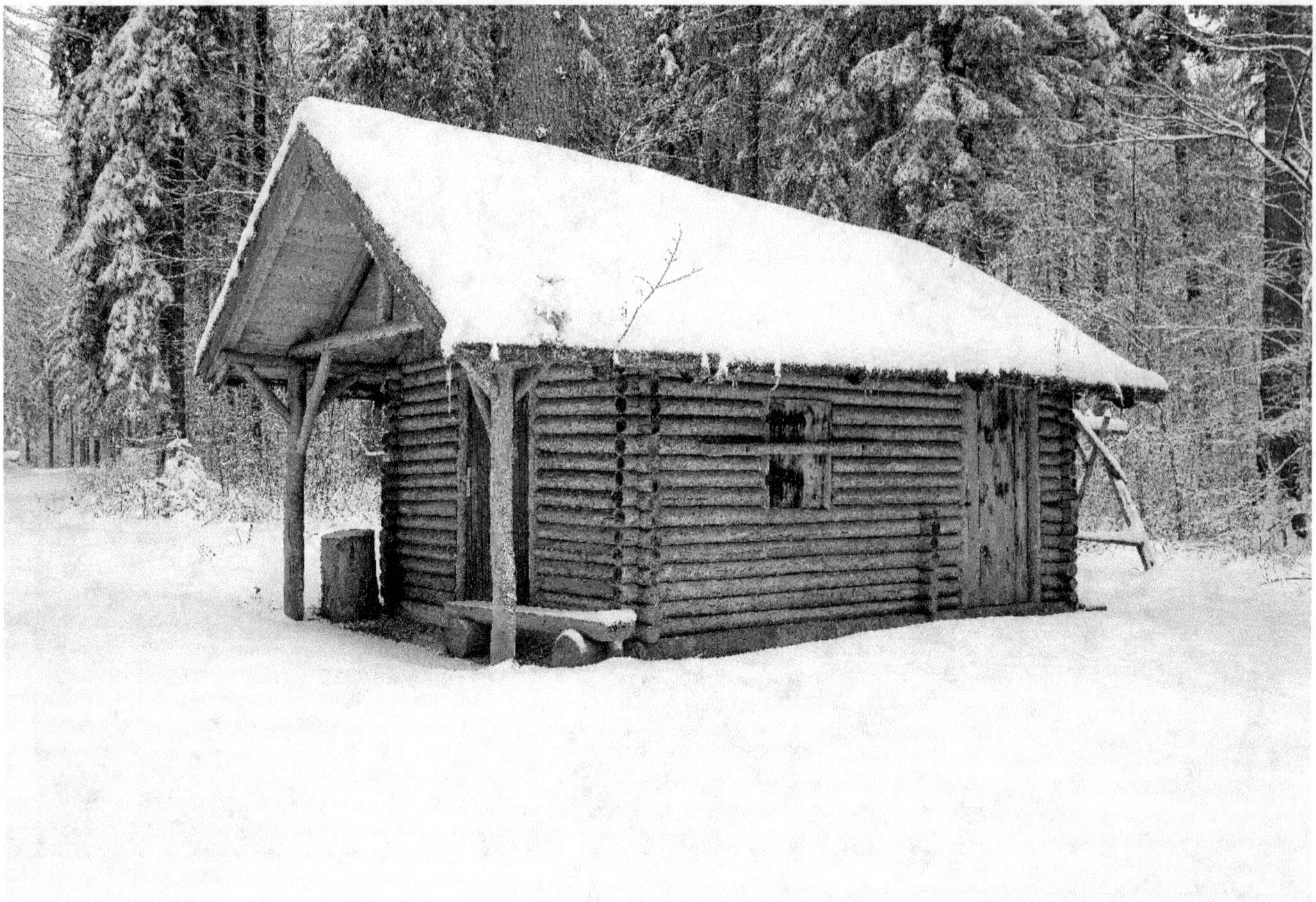

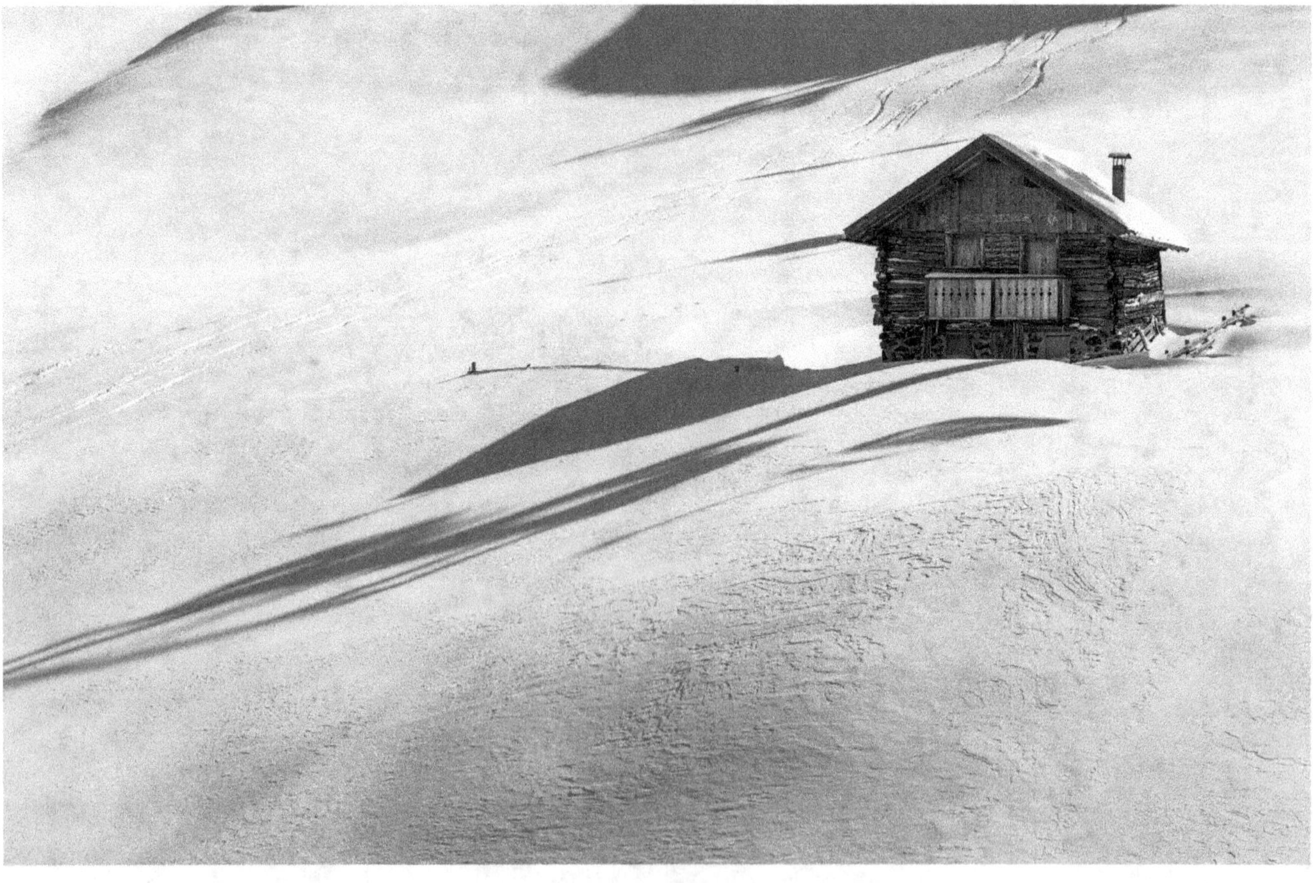

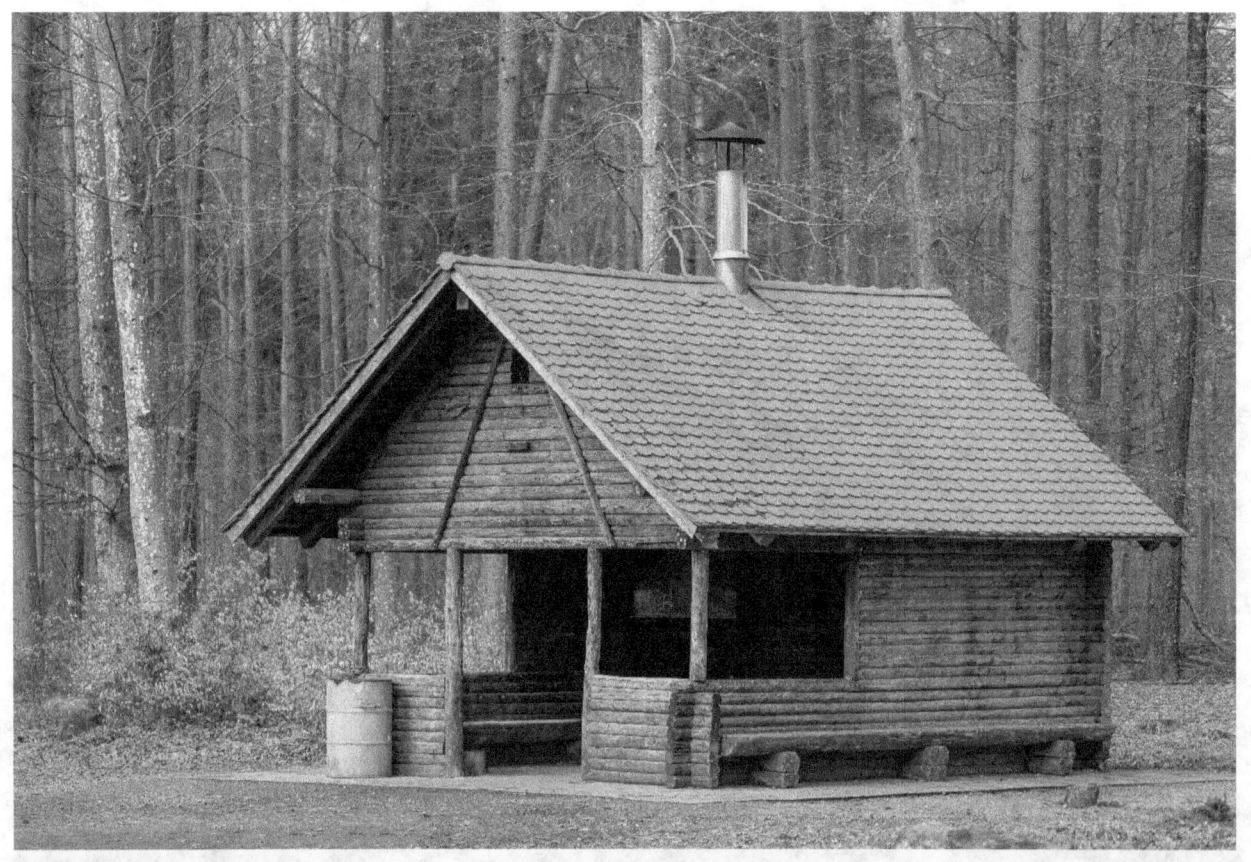

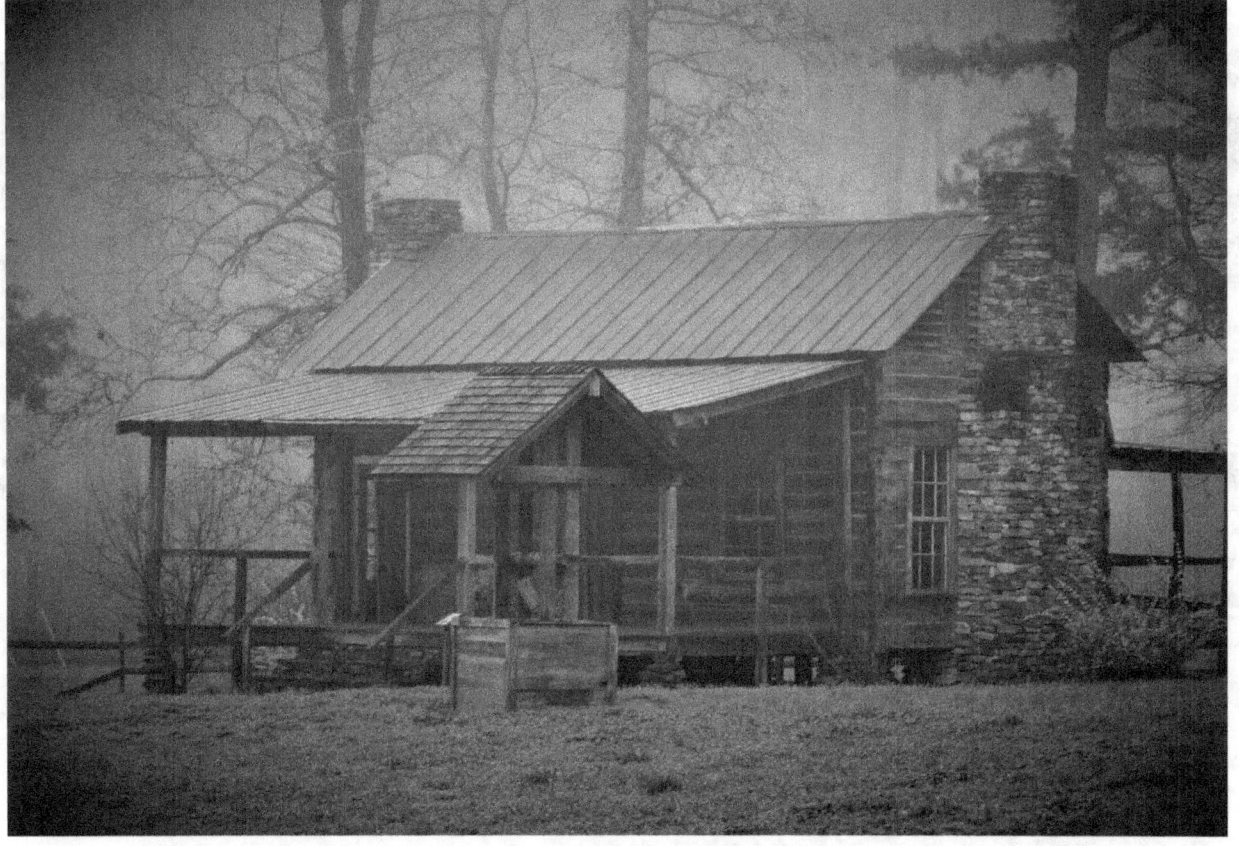

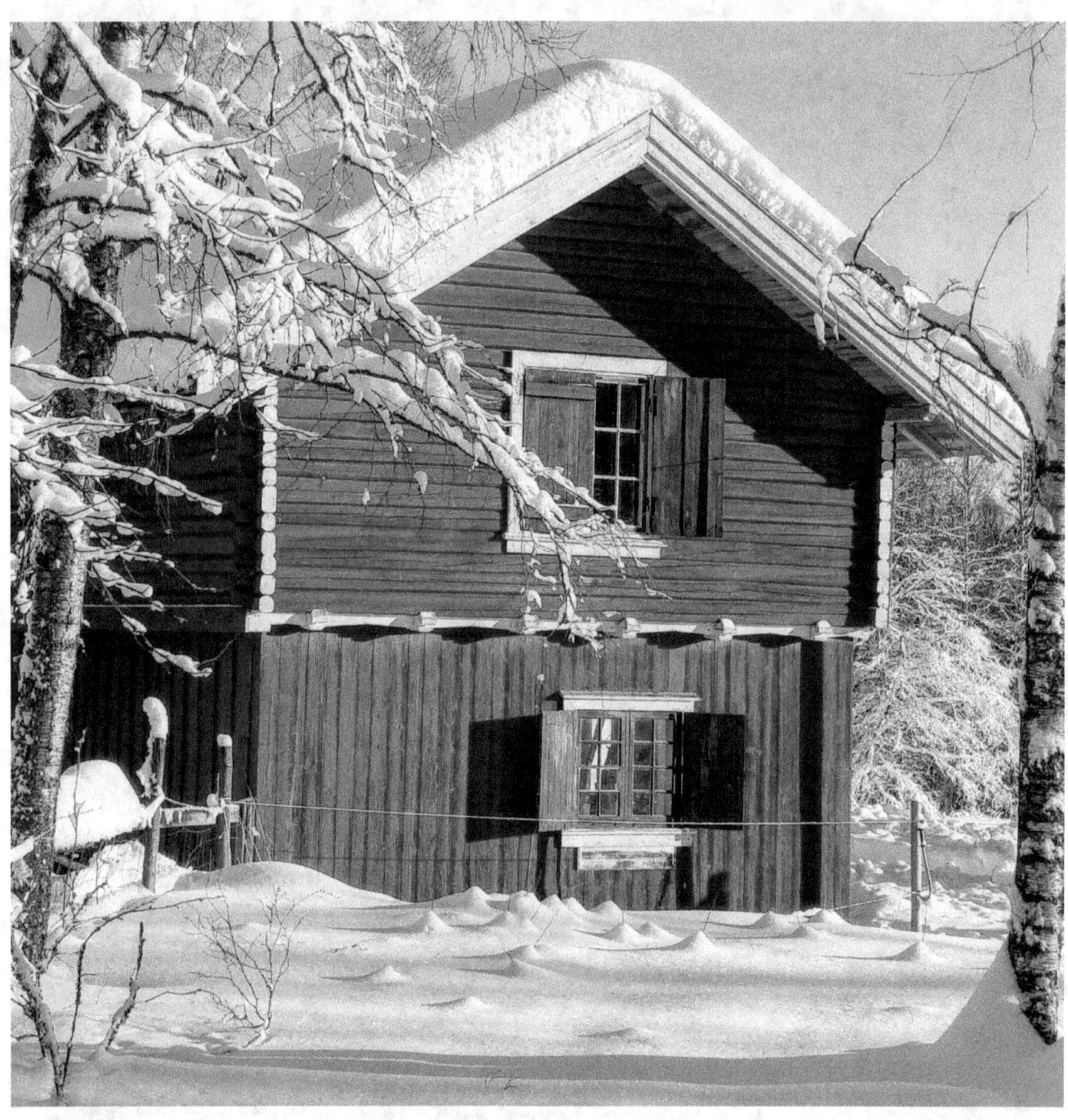

Wood Homes

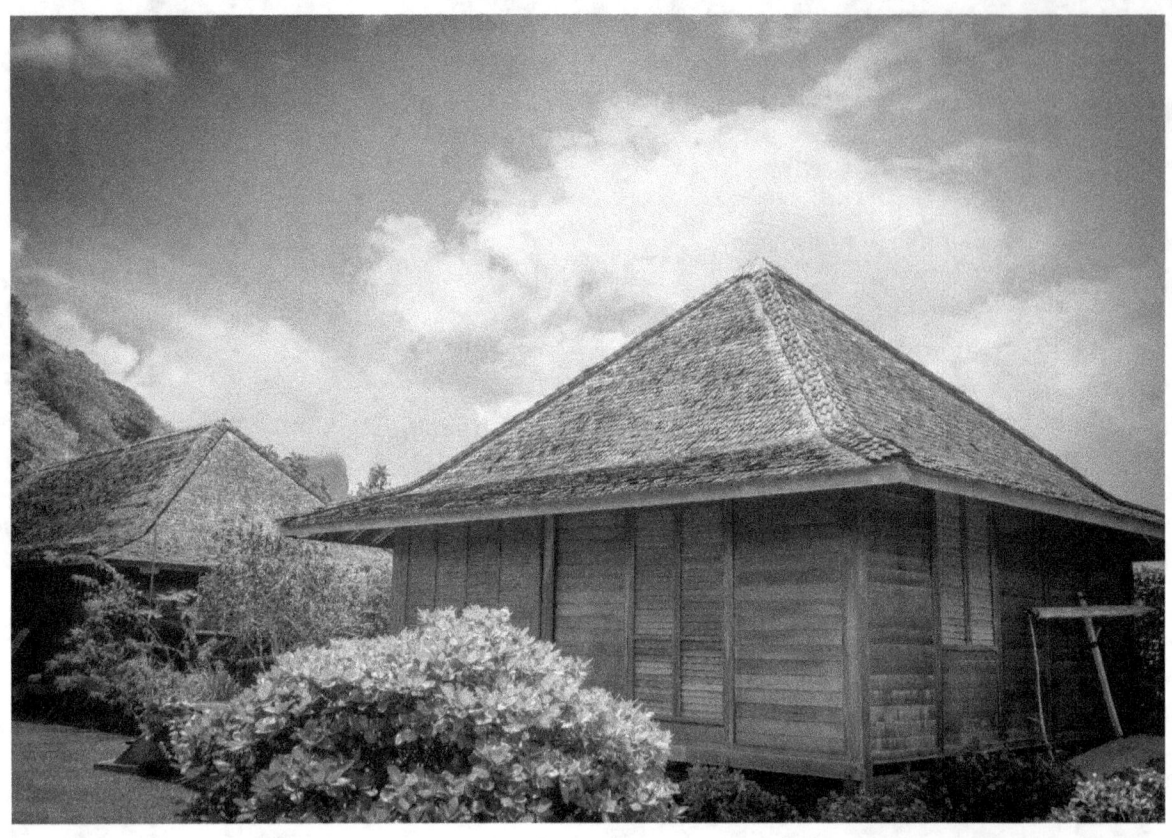

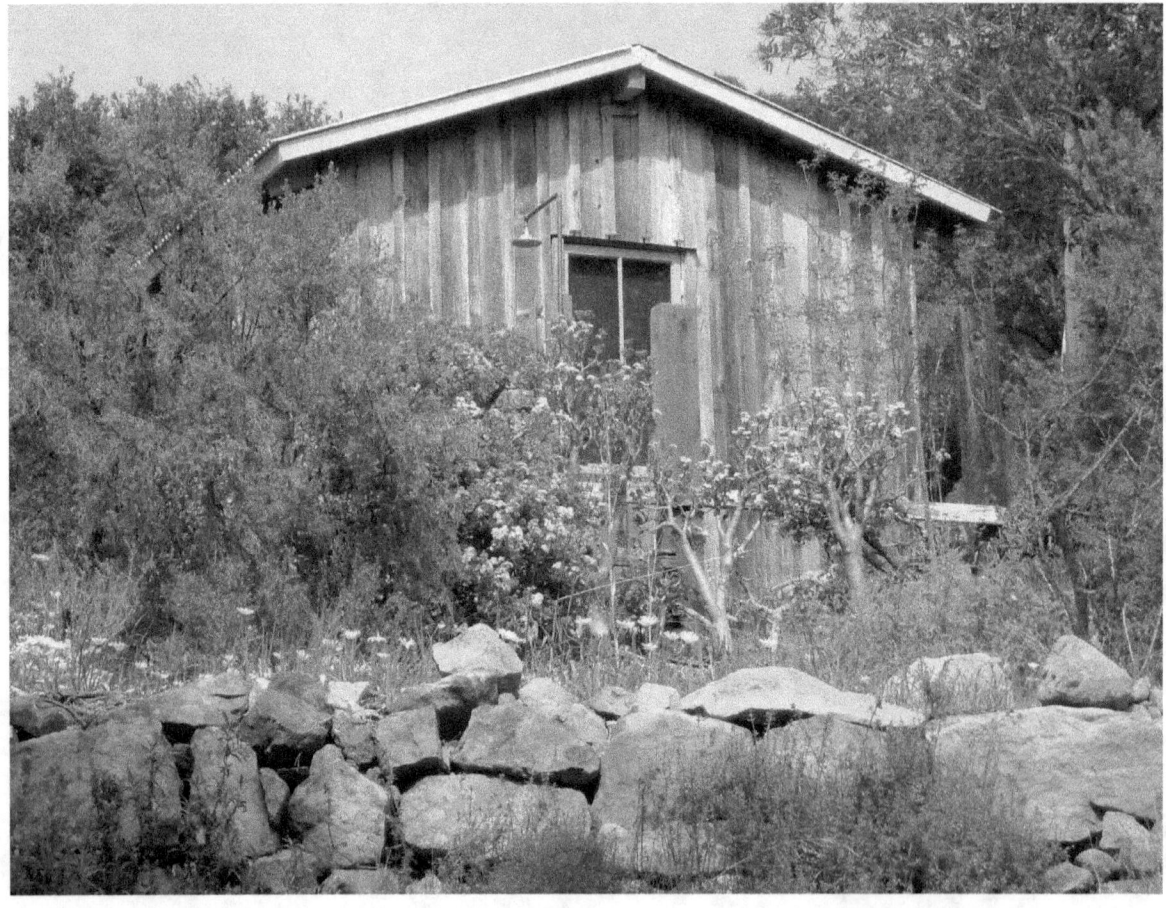

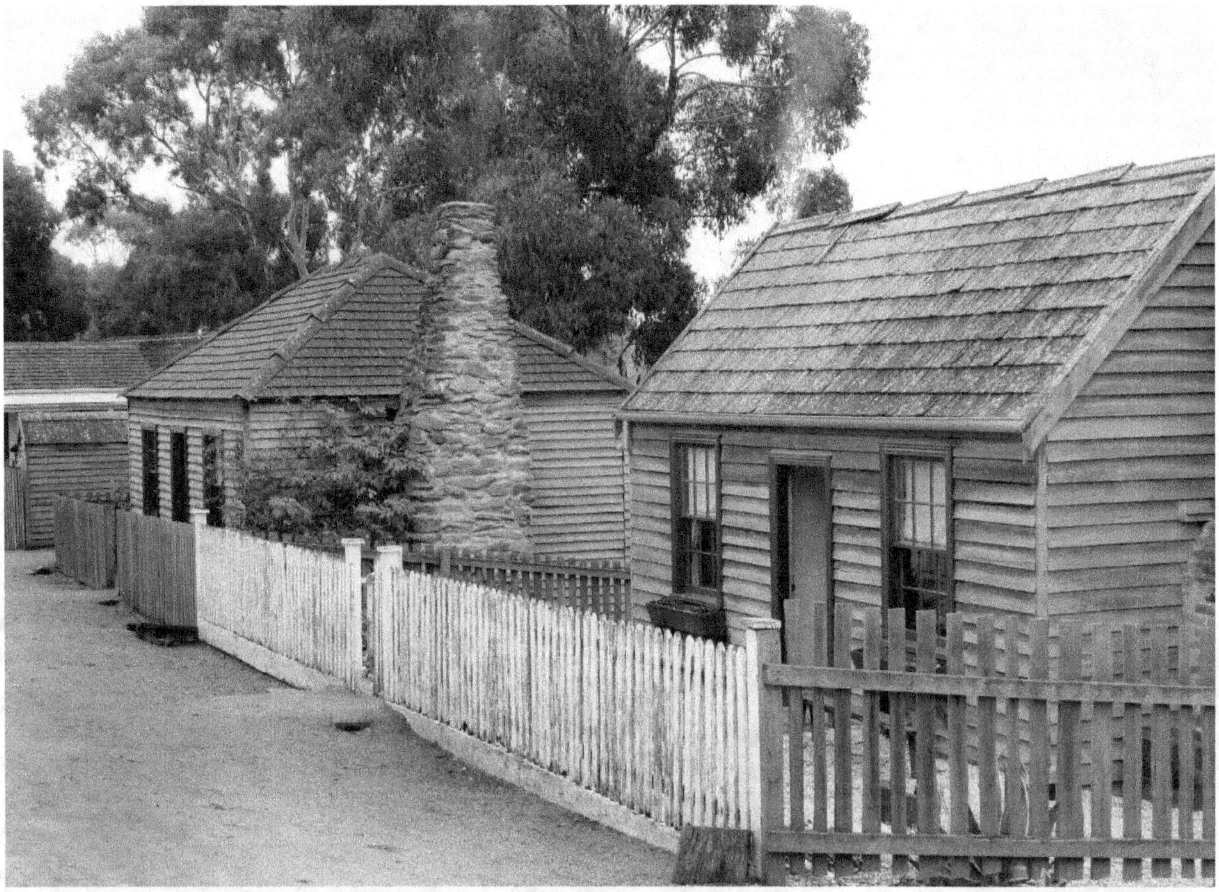

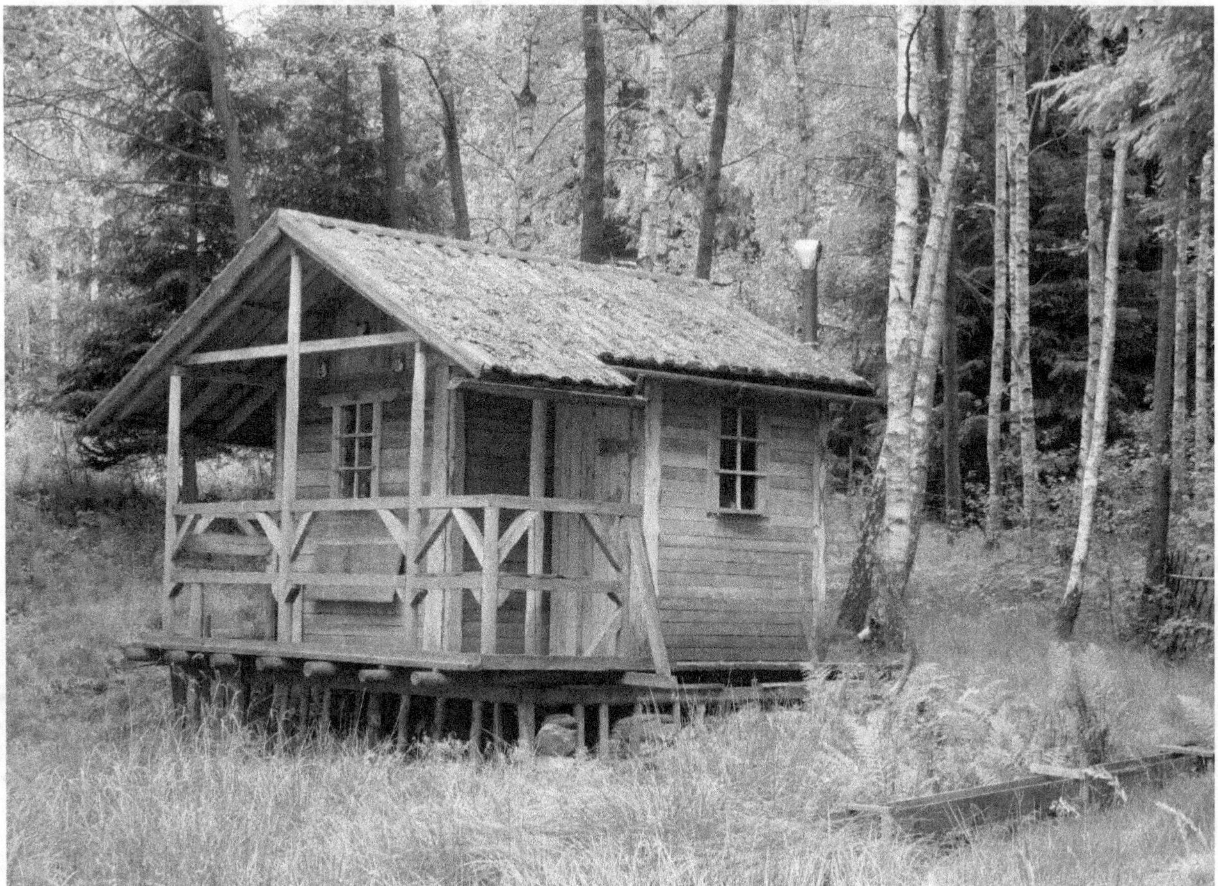

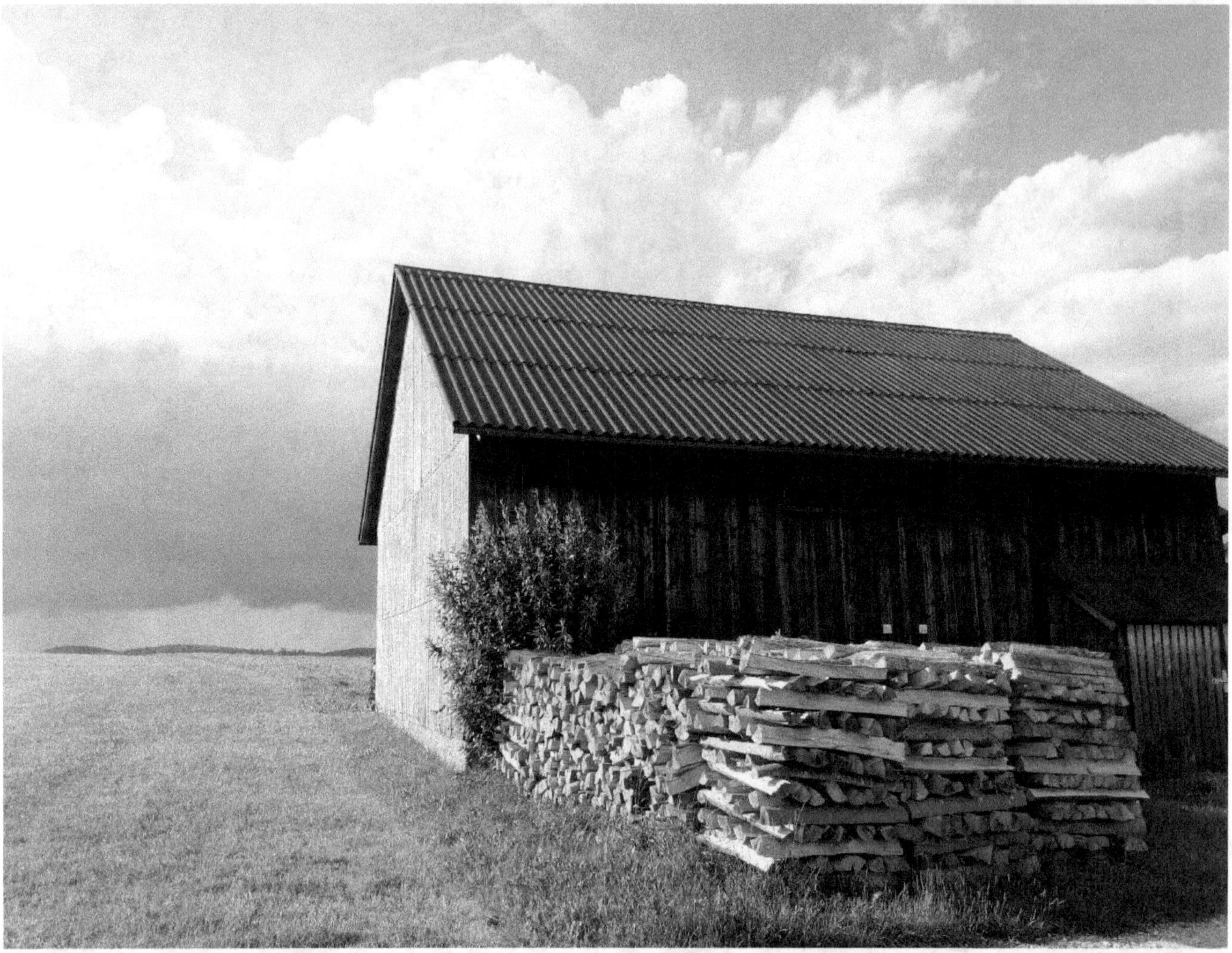

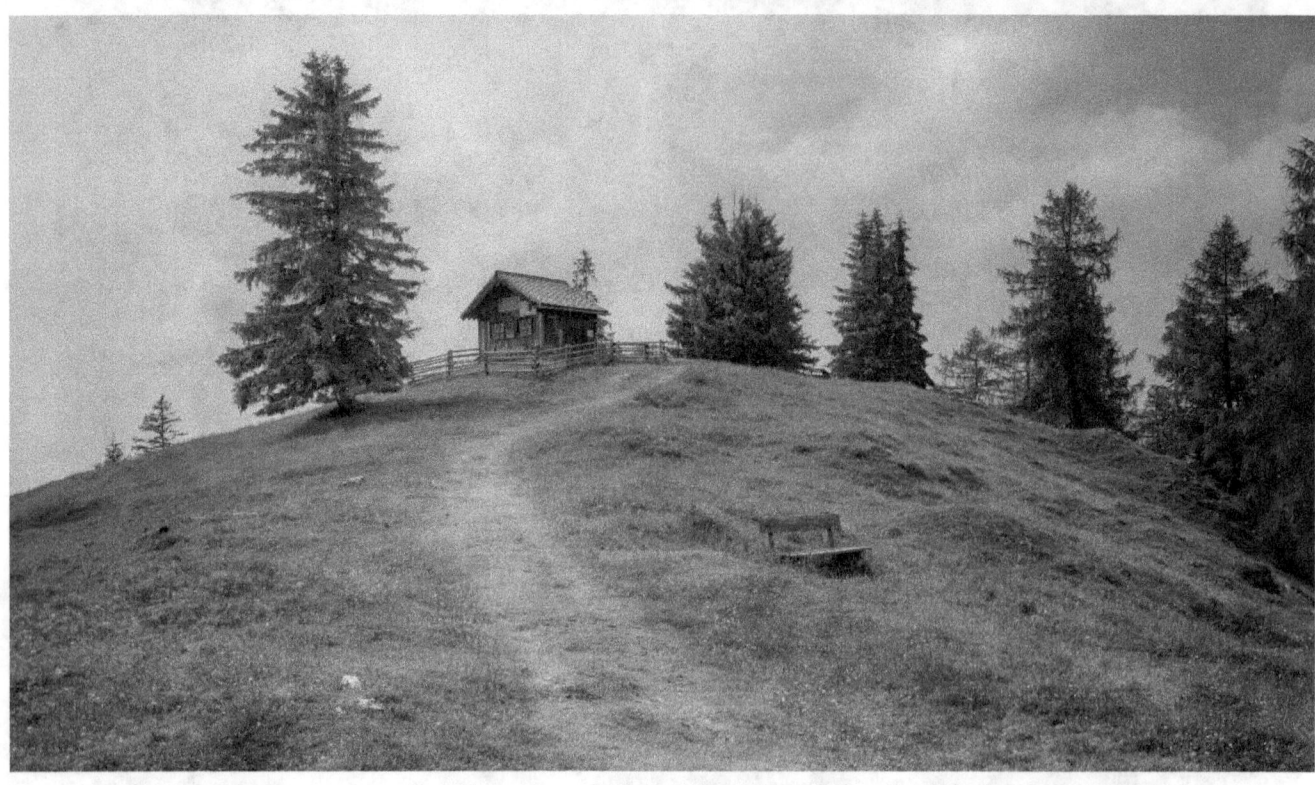

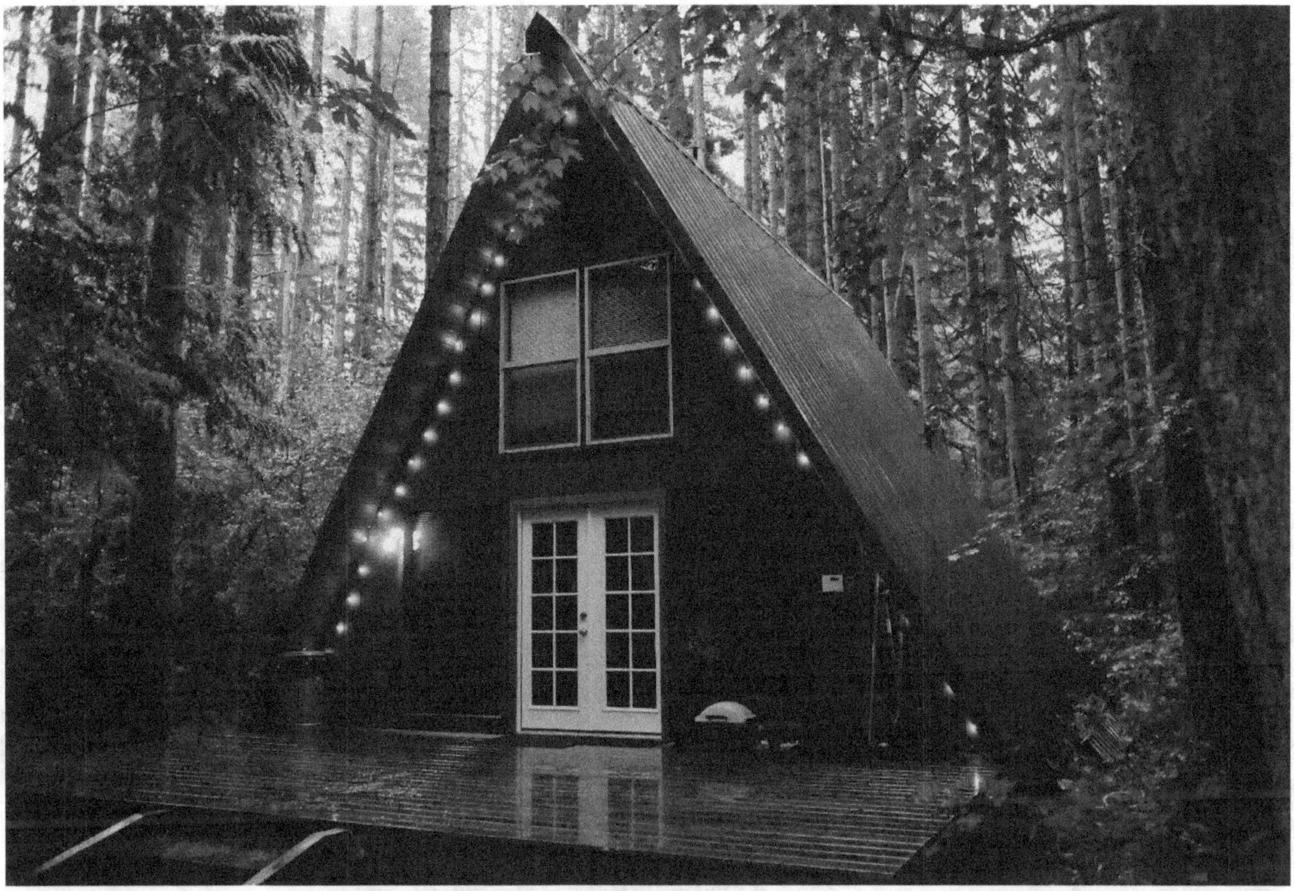

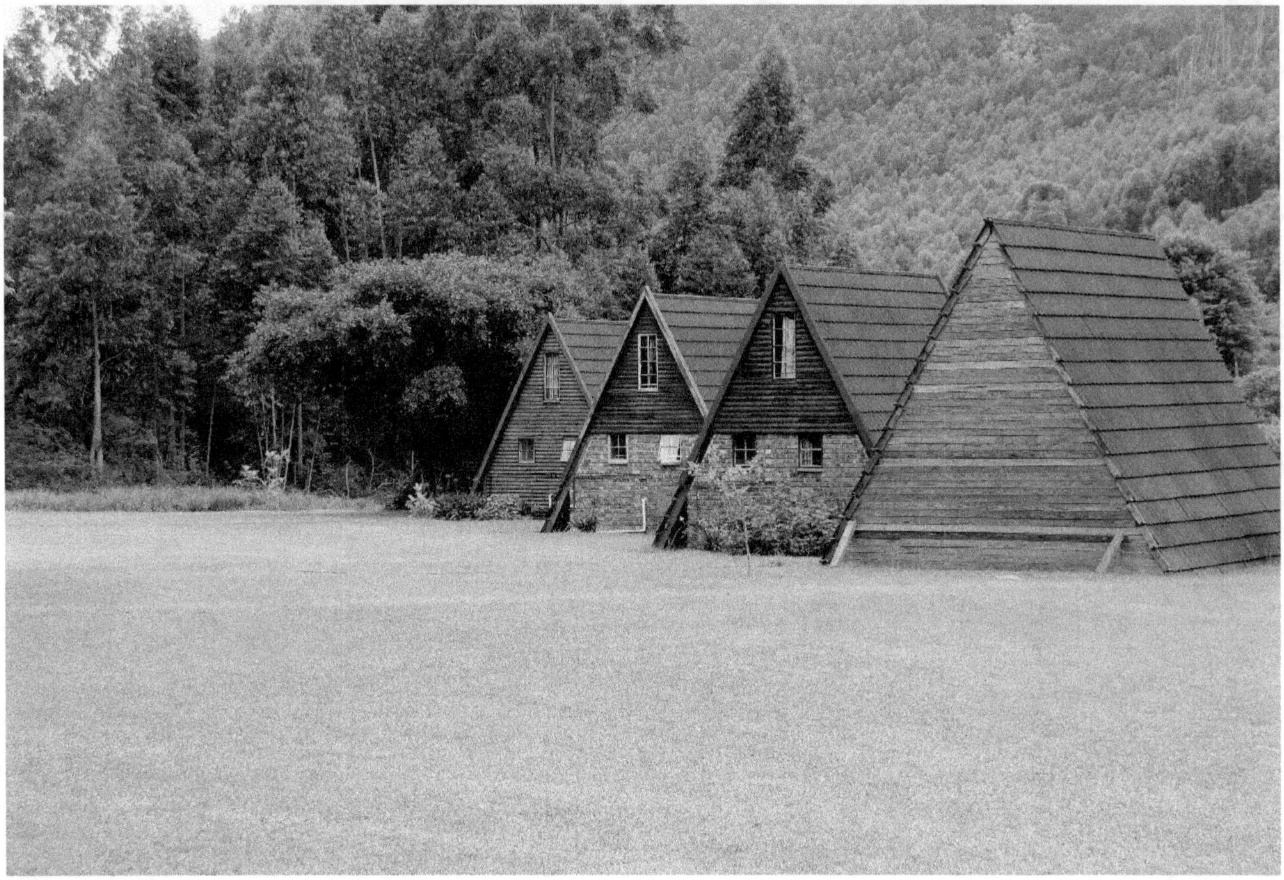

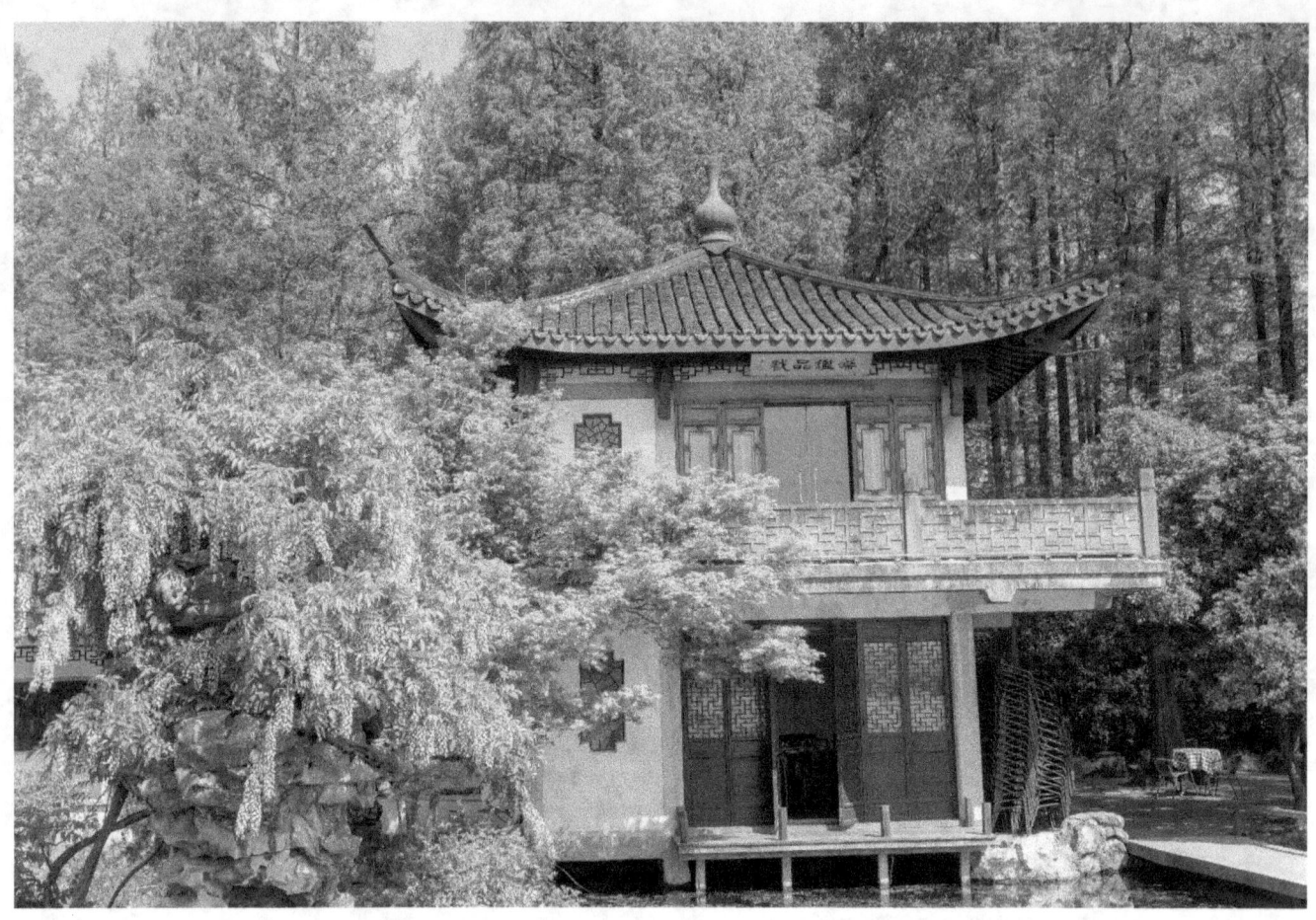

Bungalows

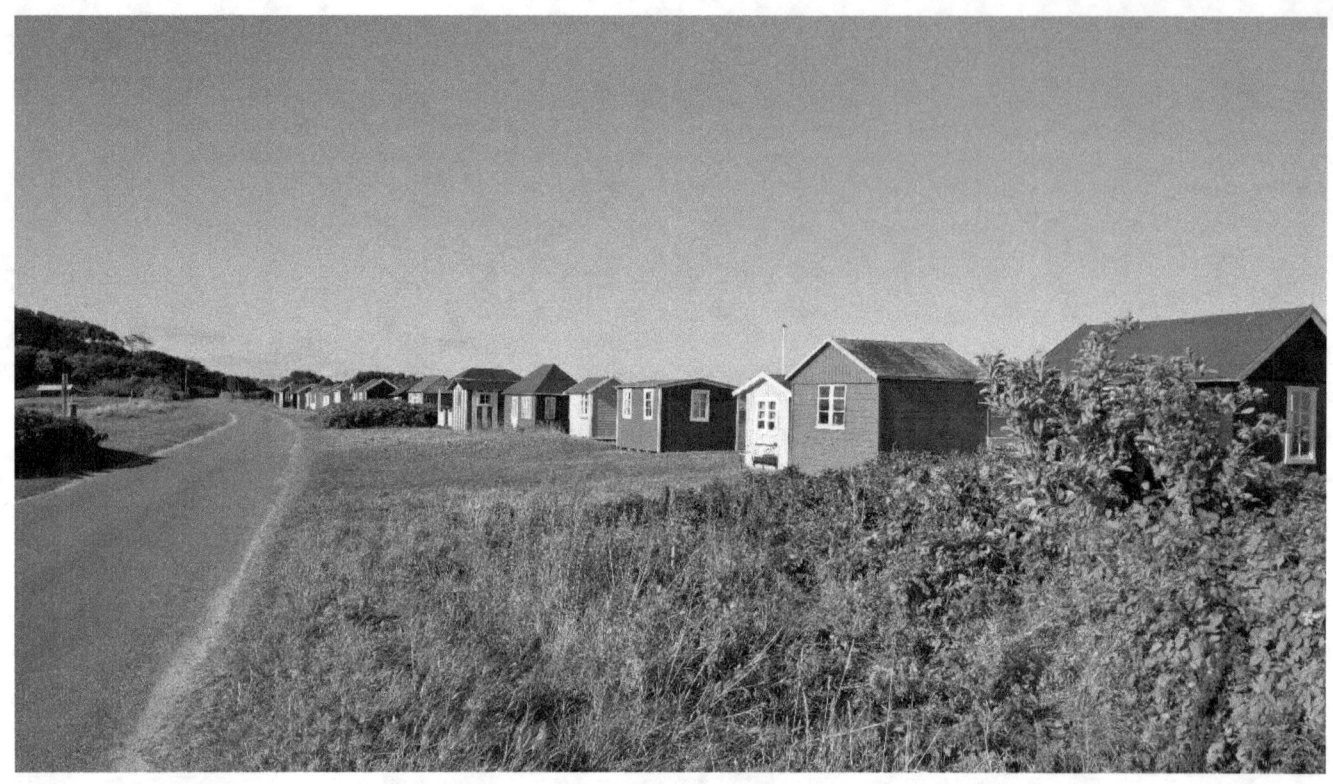

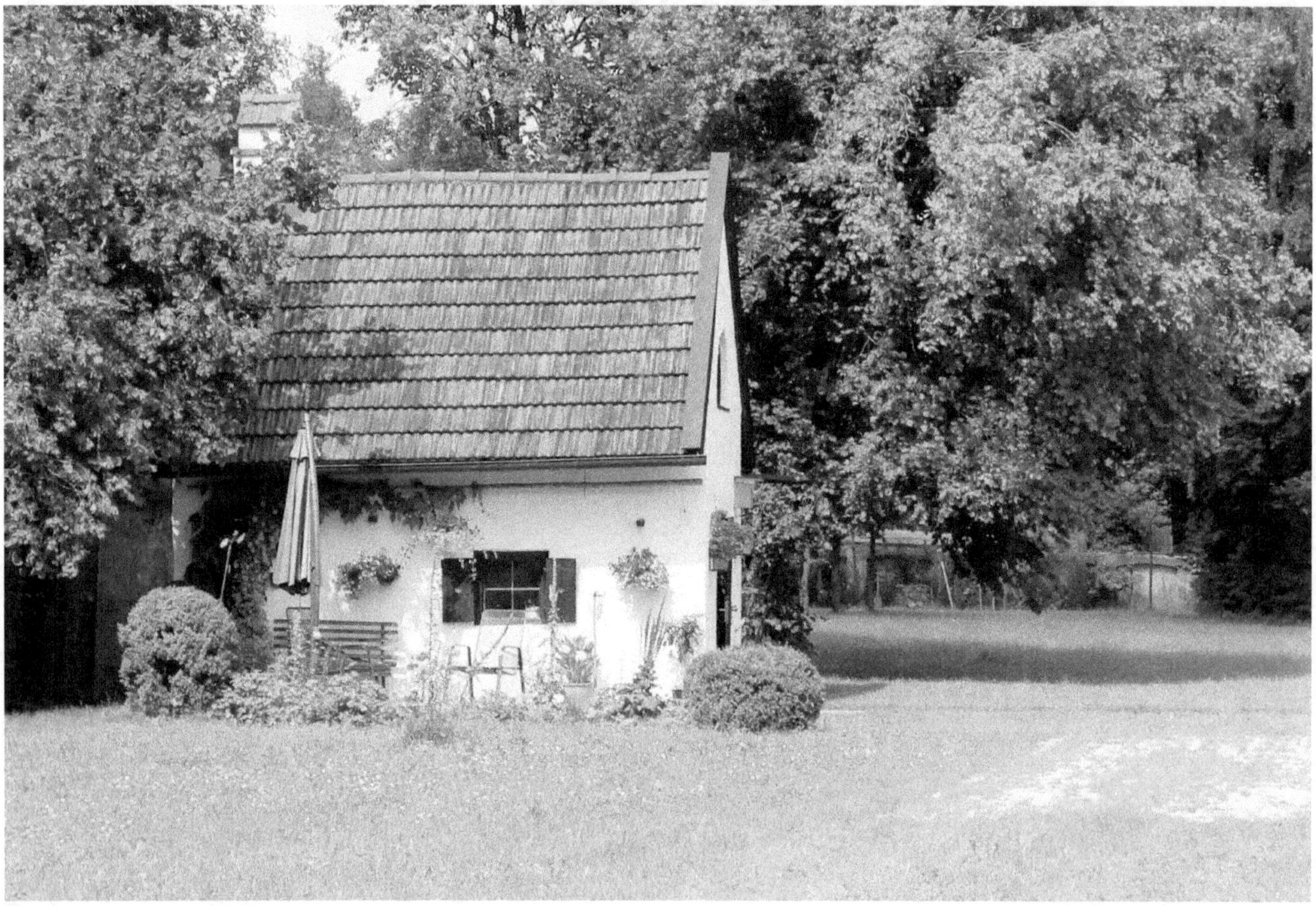

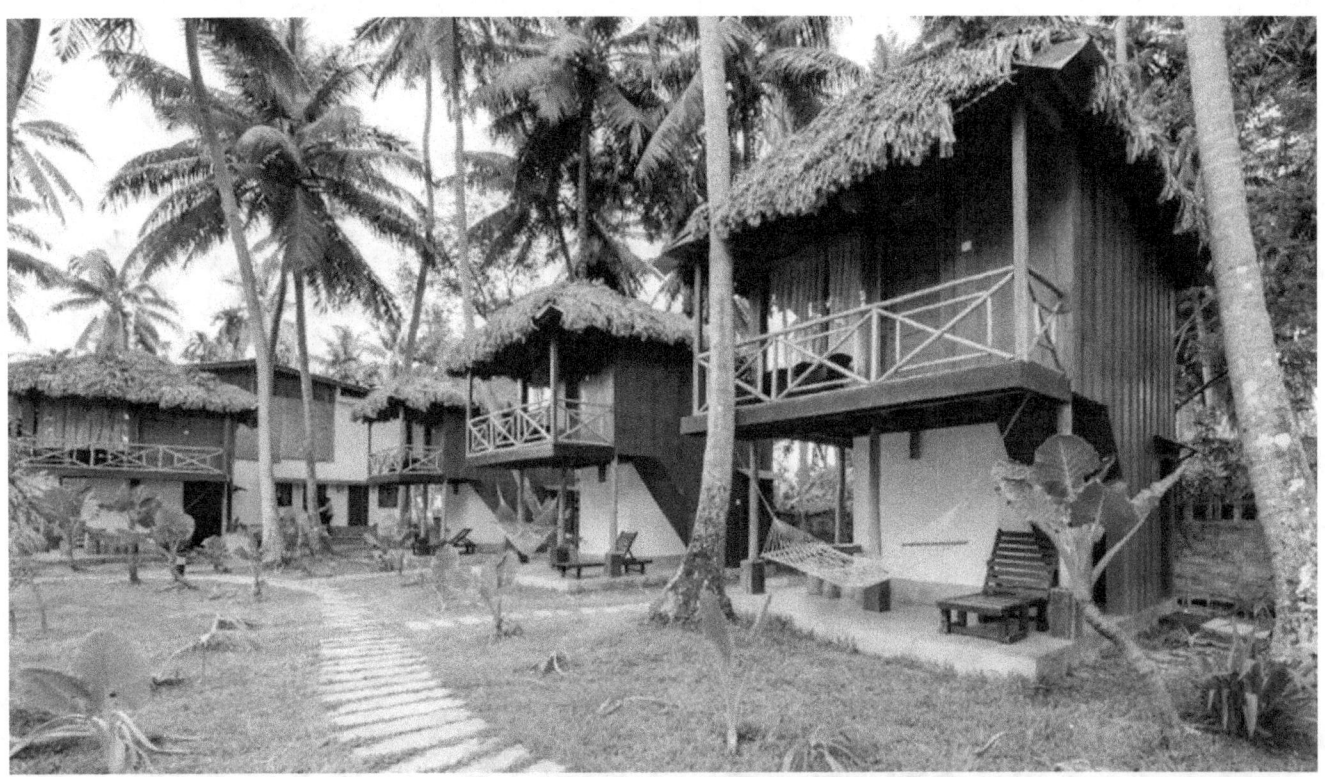

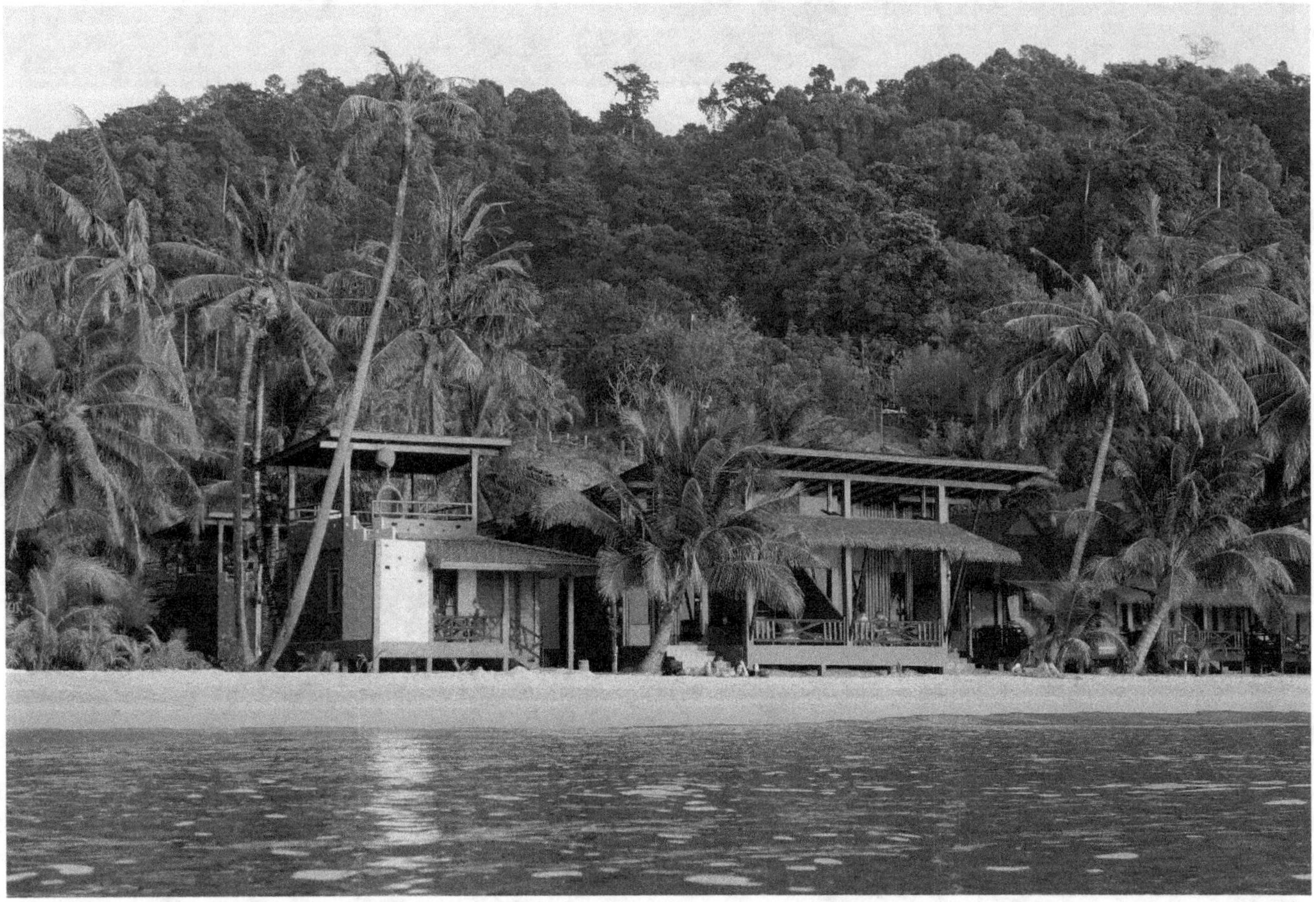

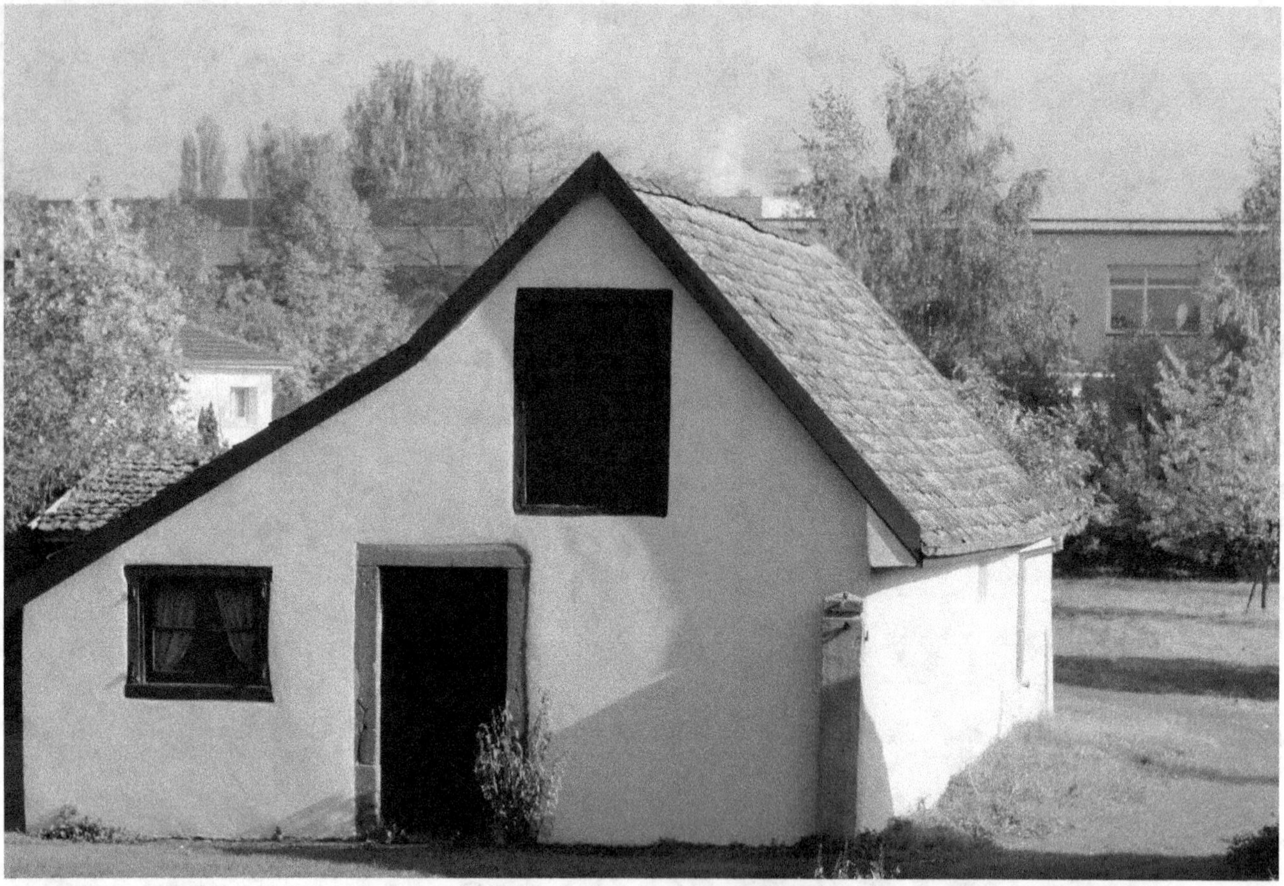

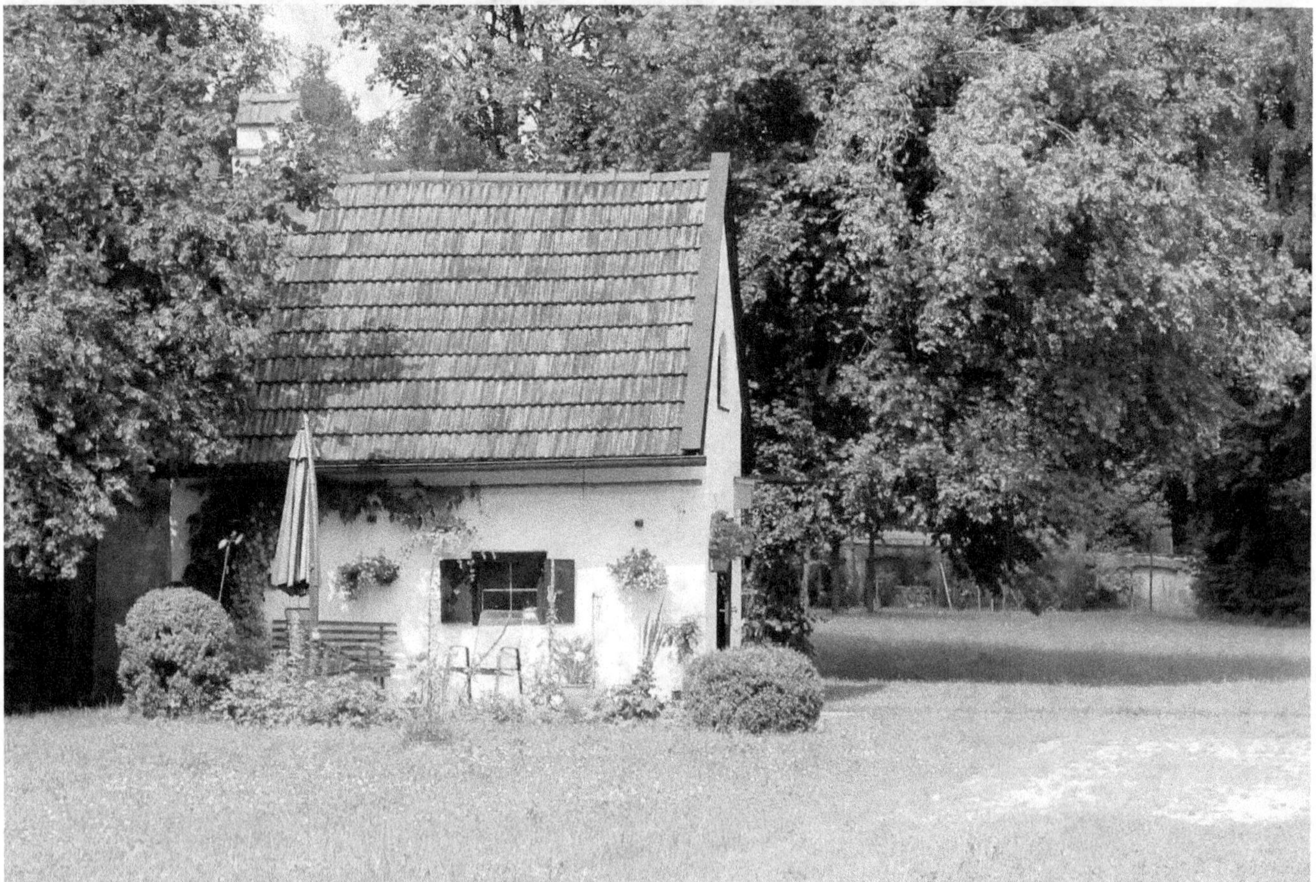

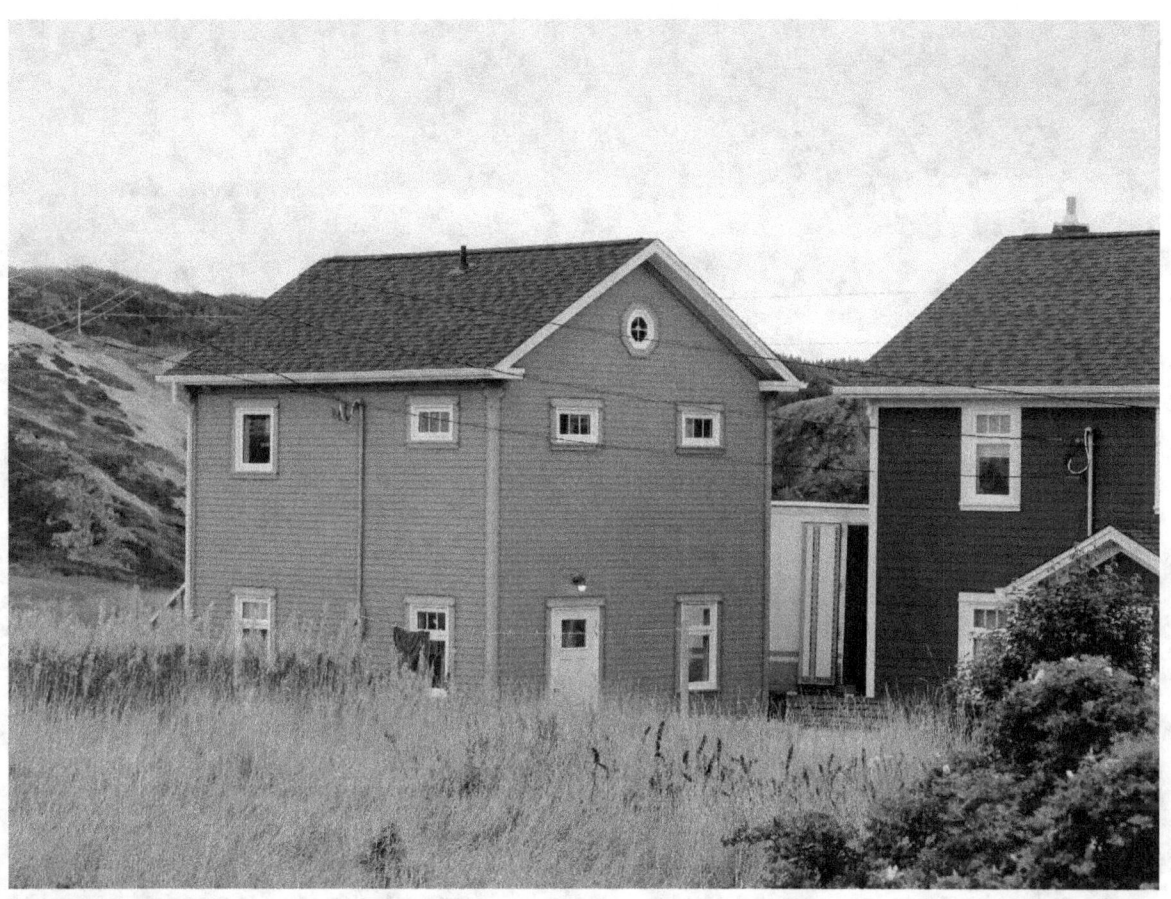

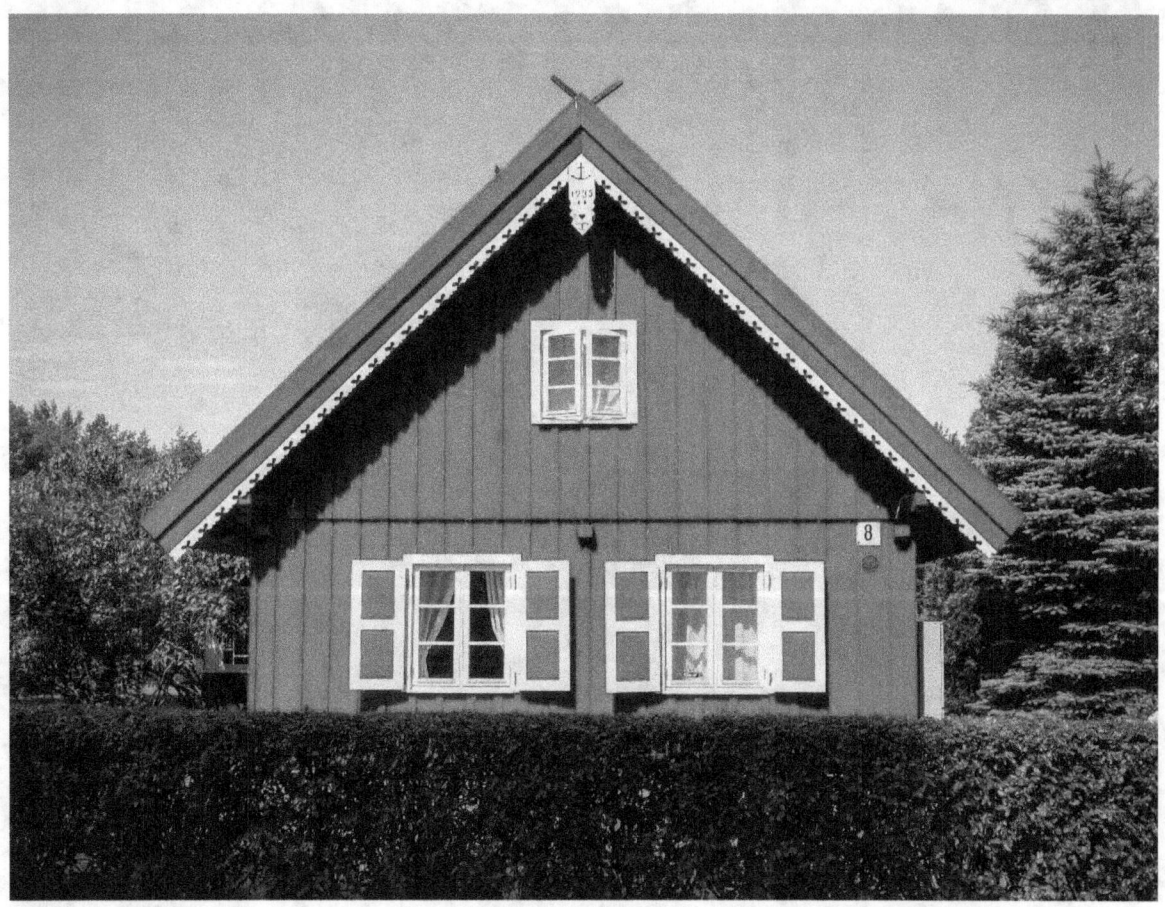

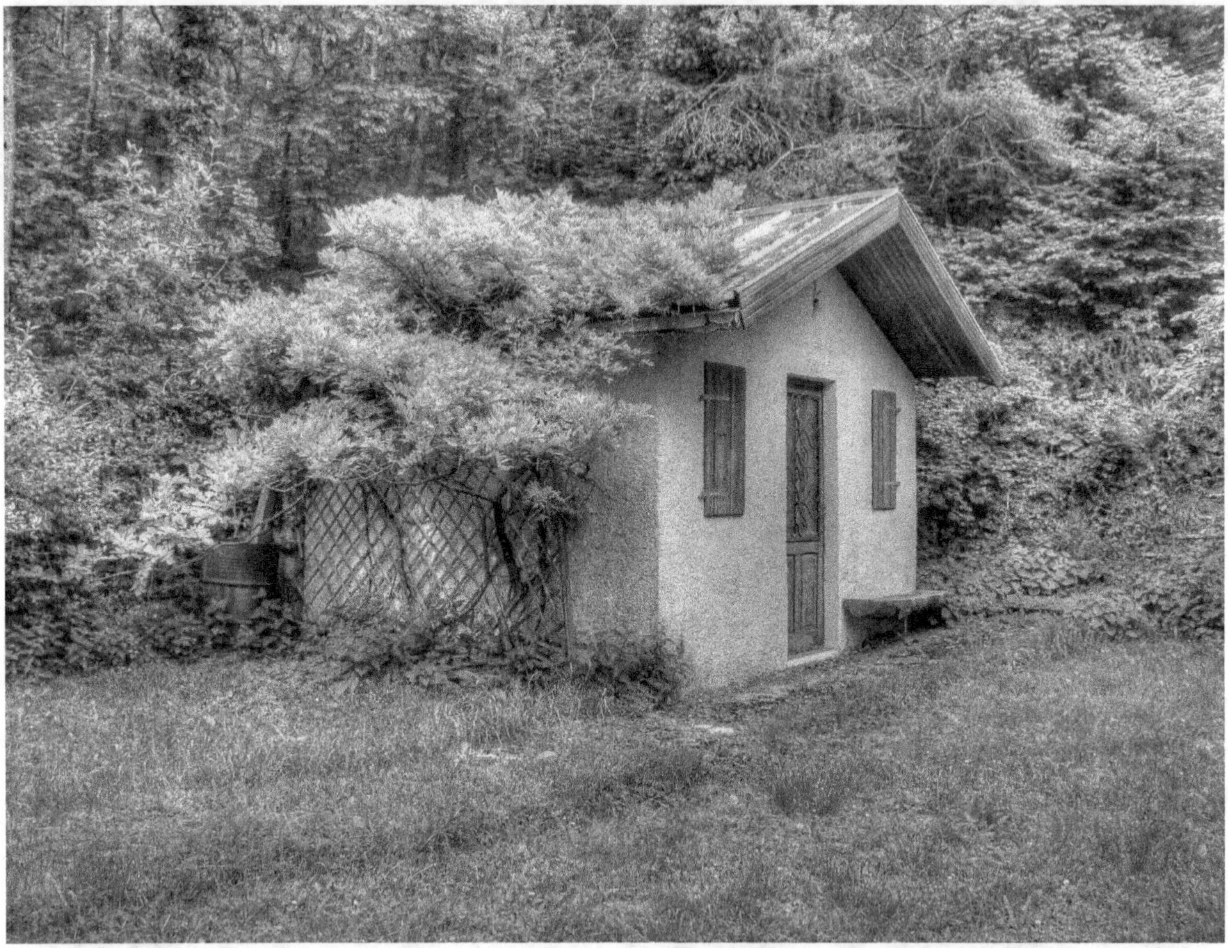

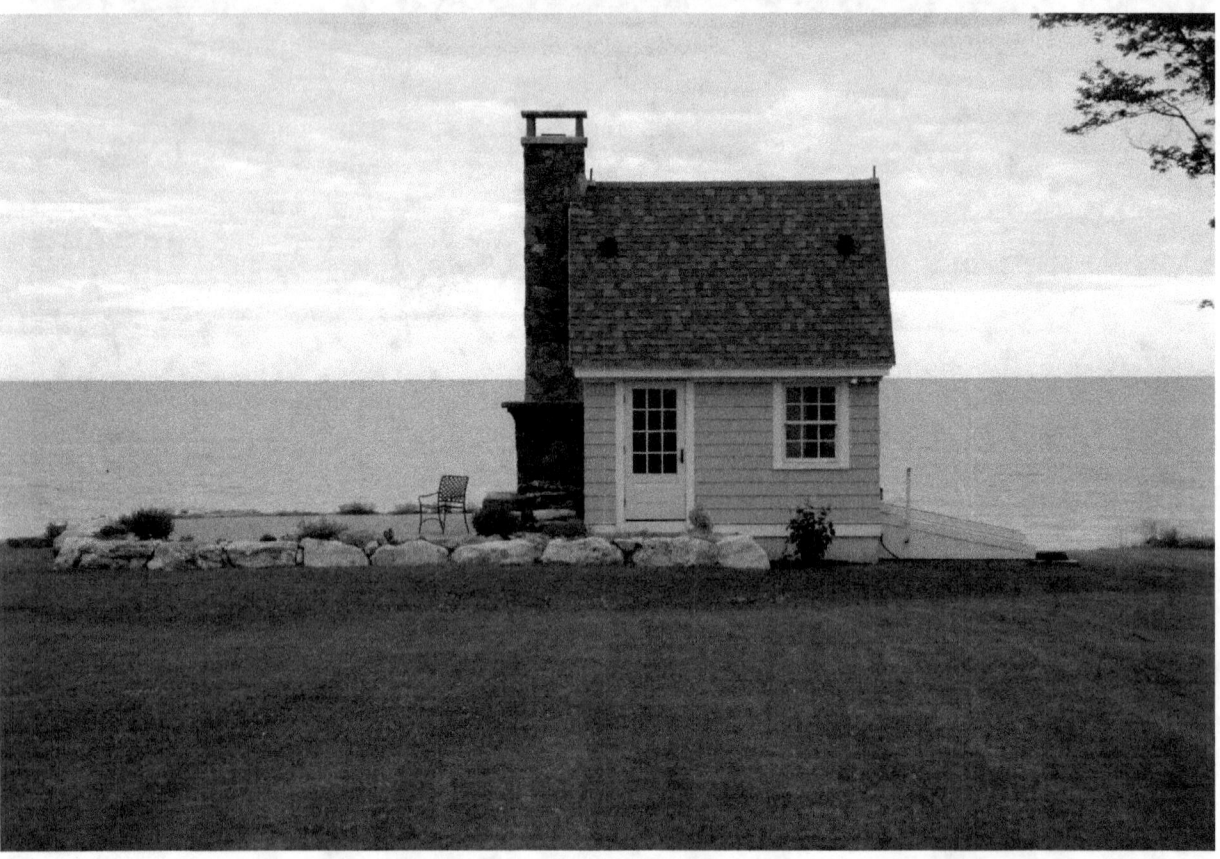

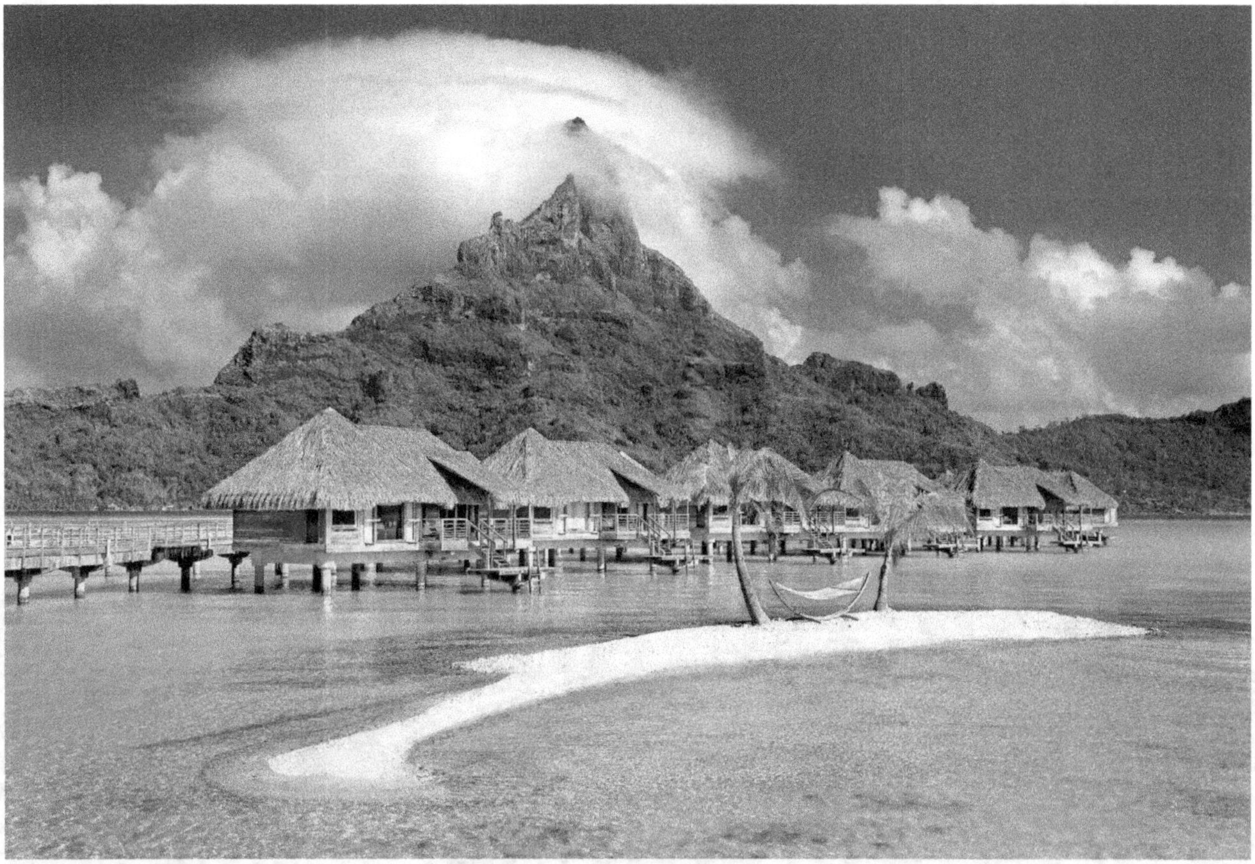

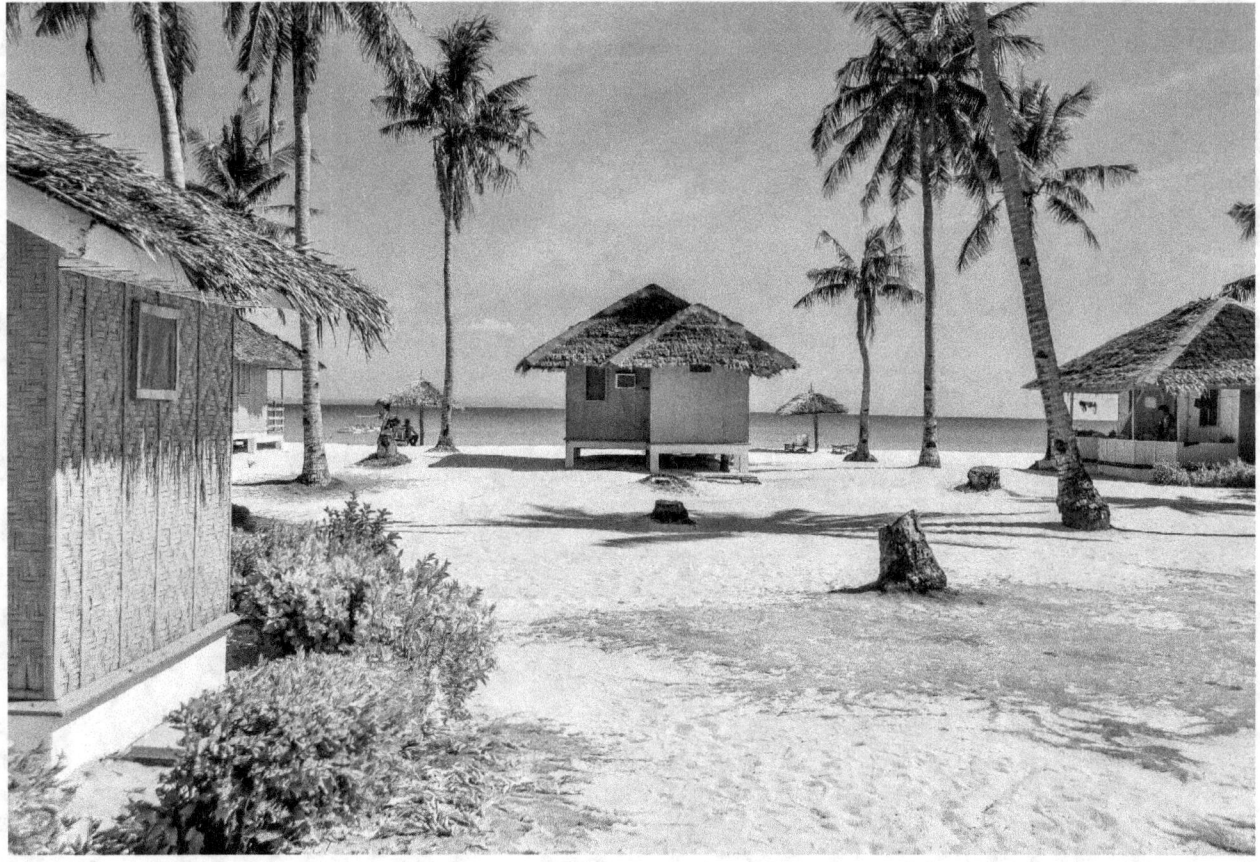

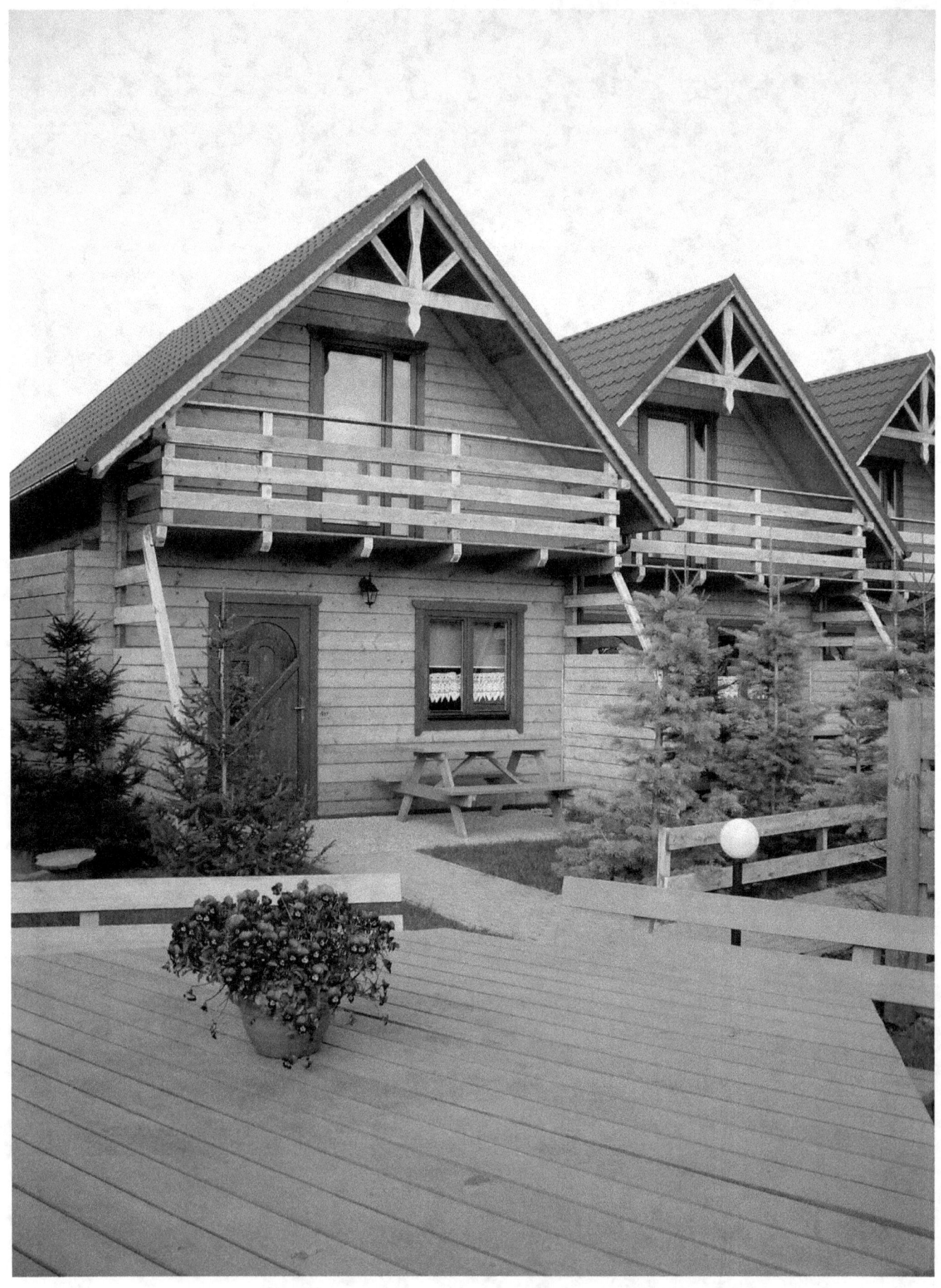

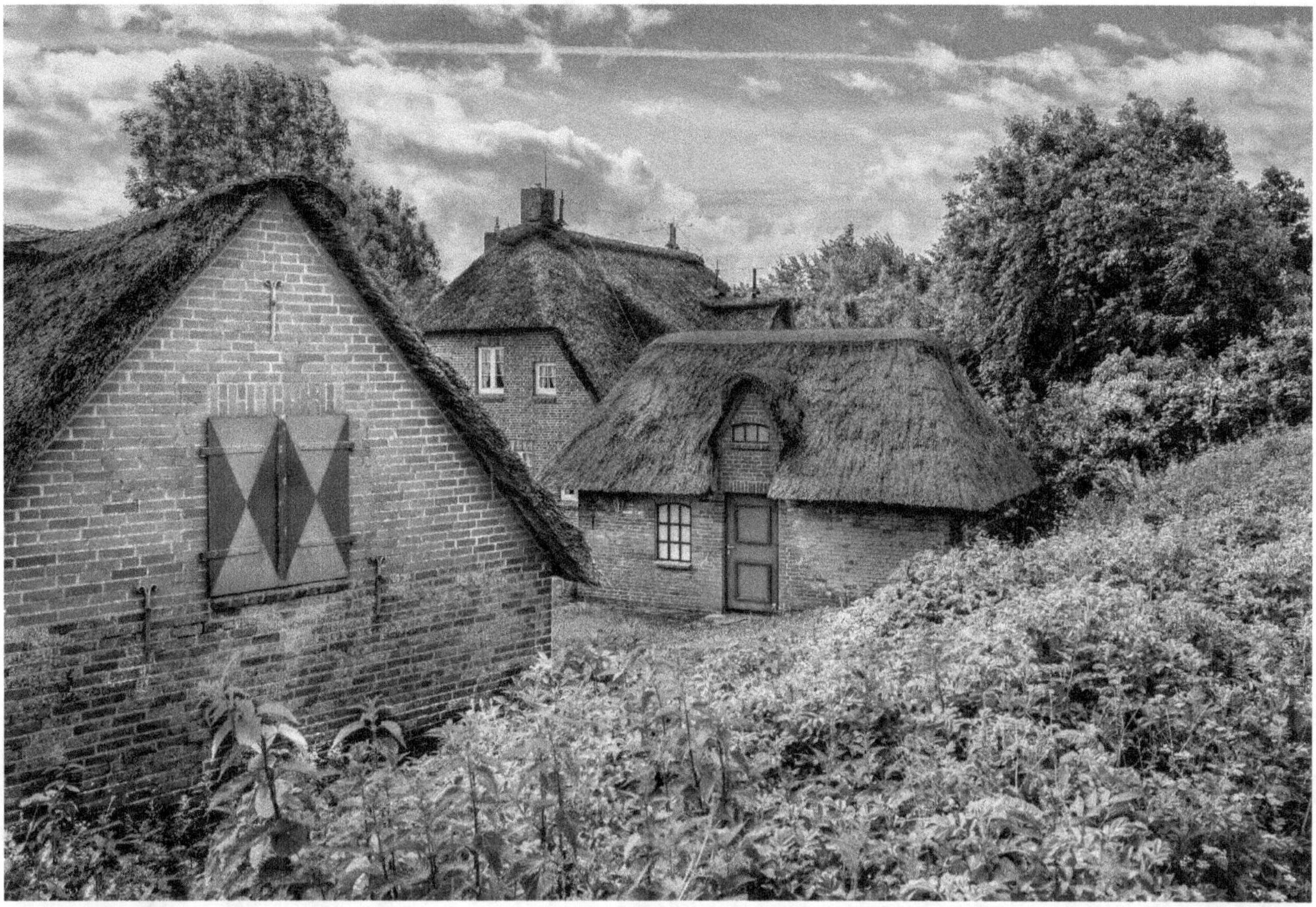

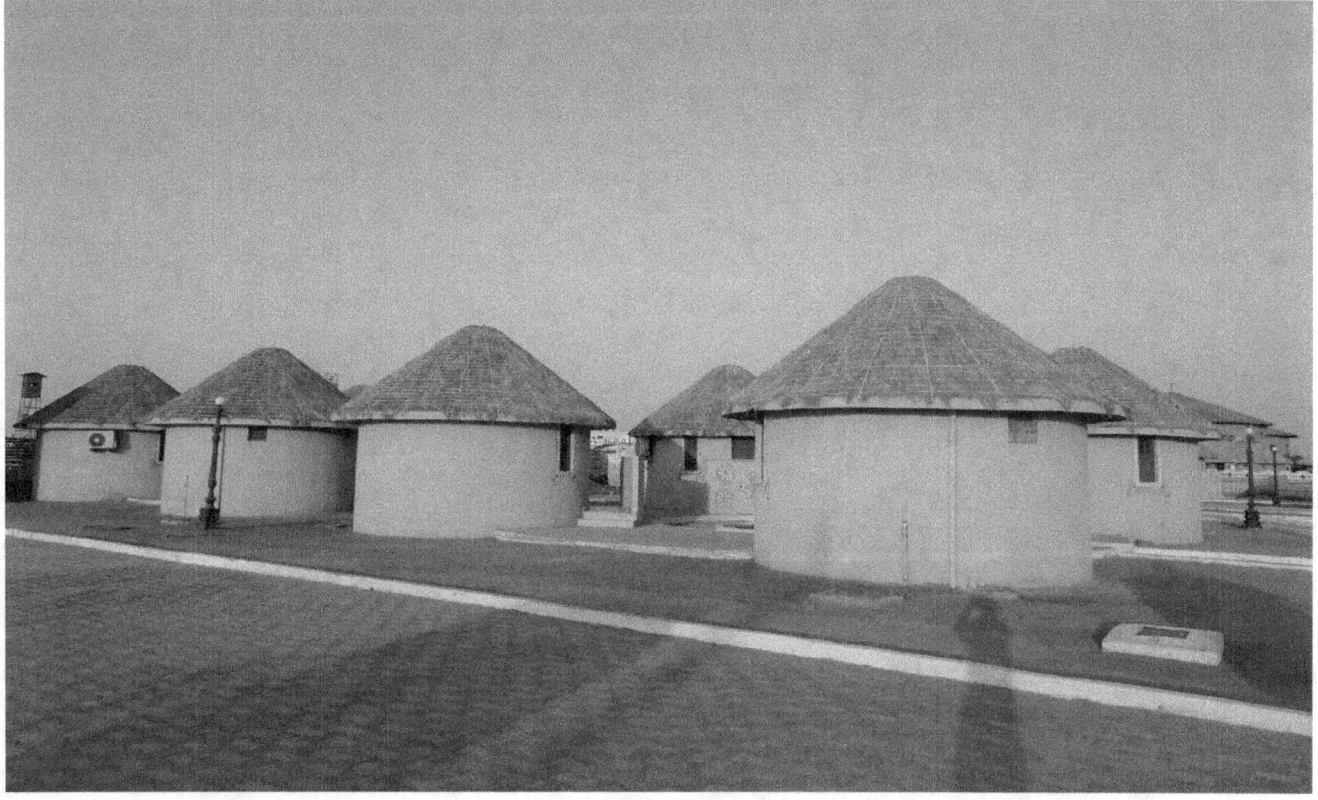

Row Houses

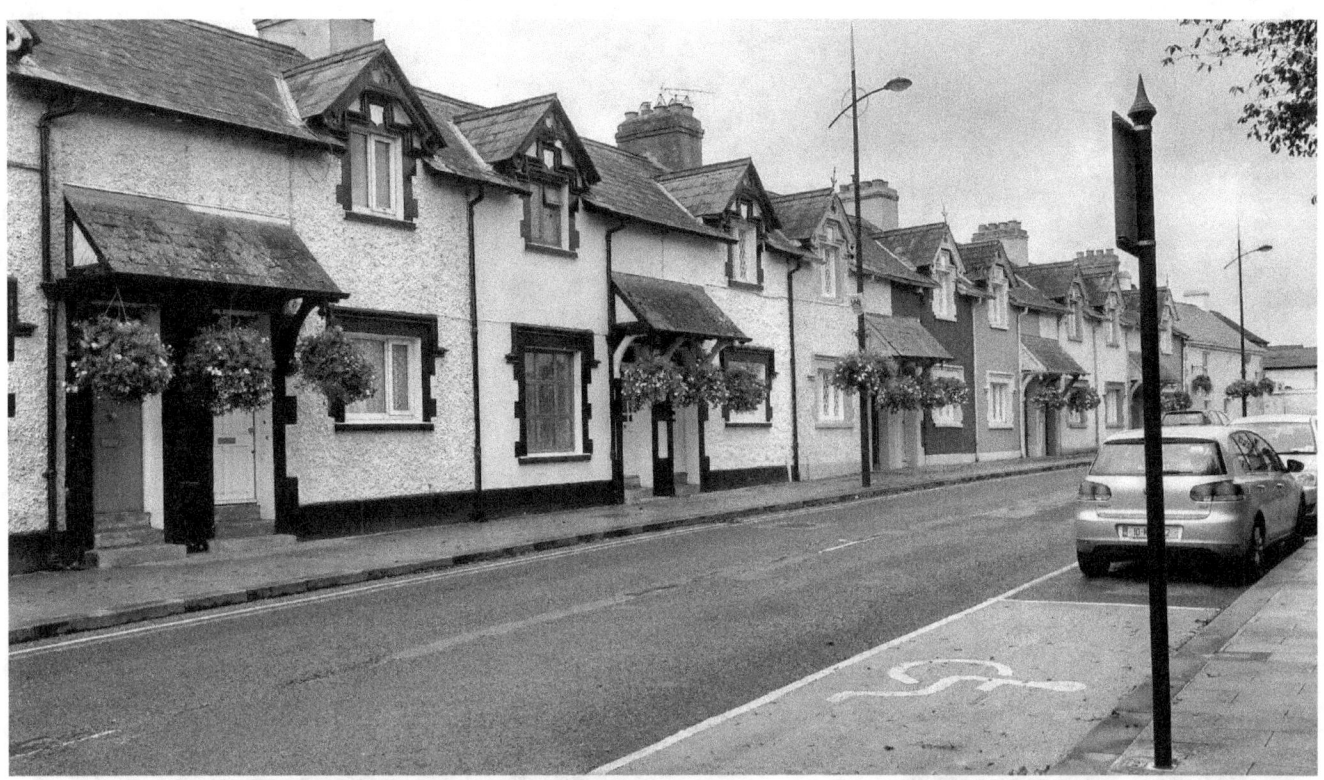

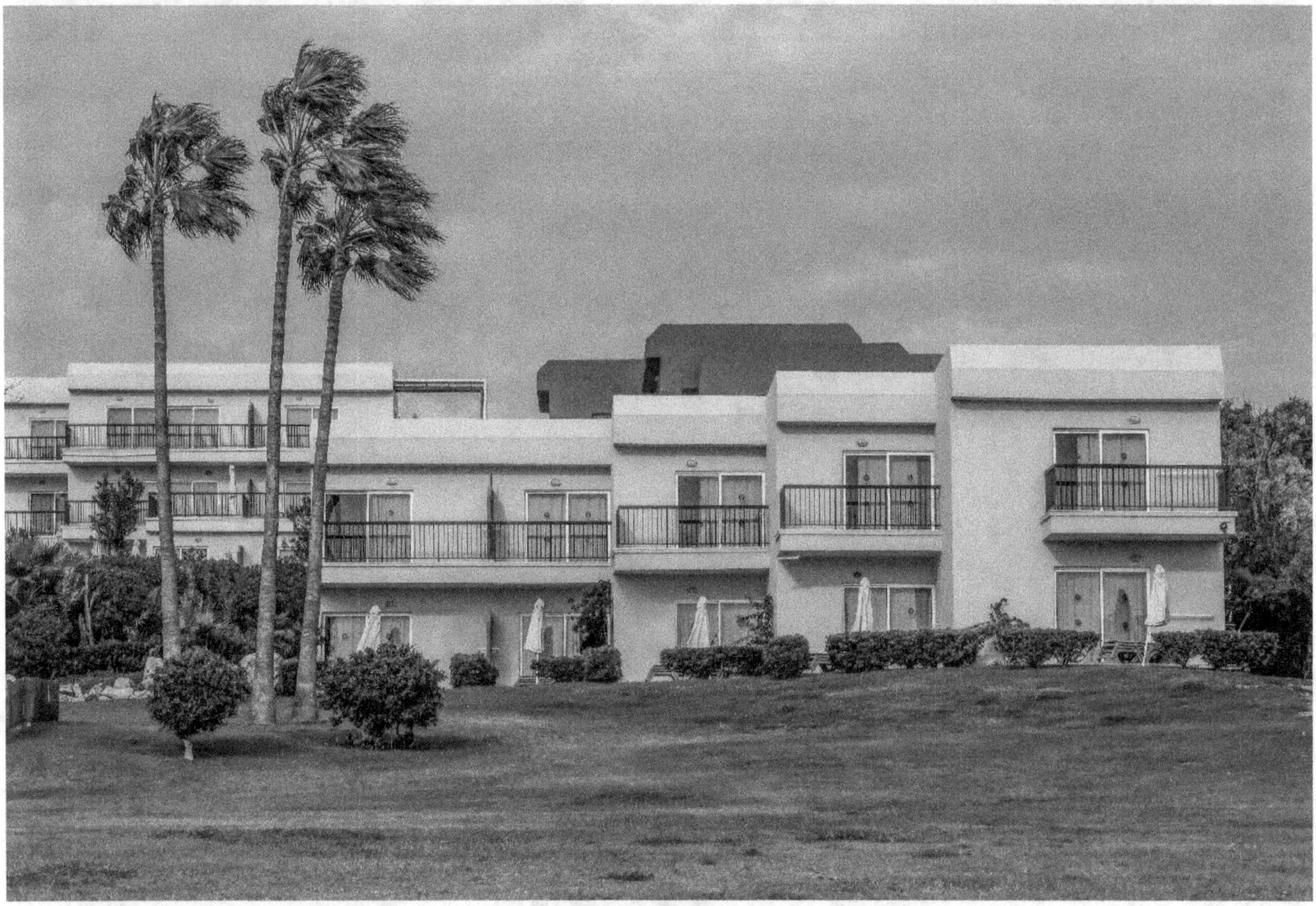

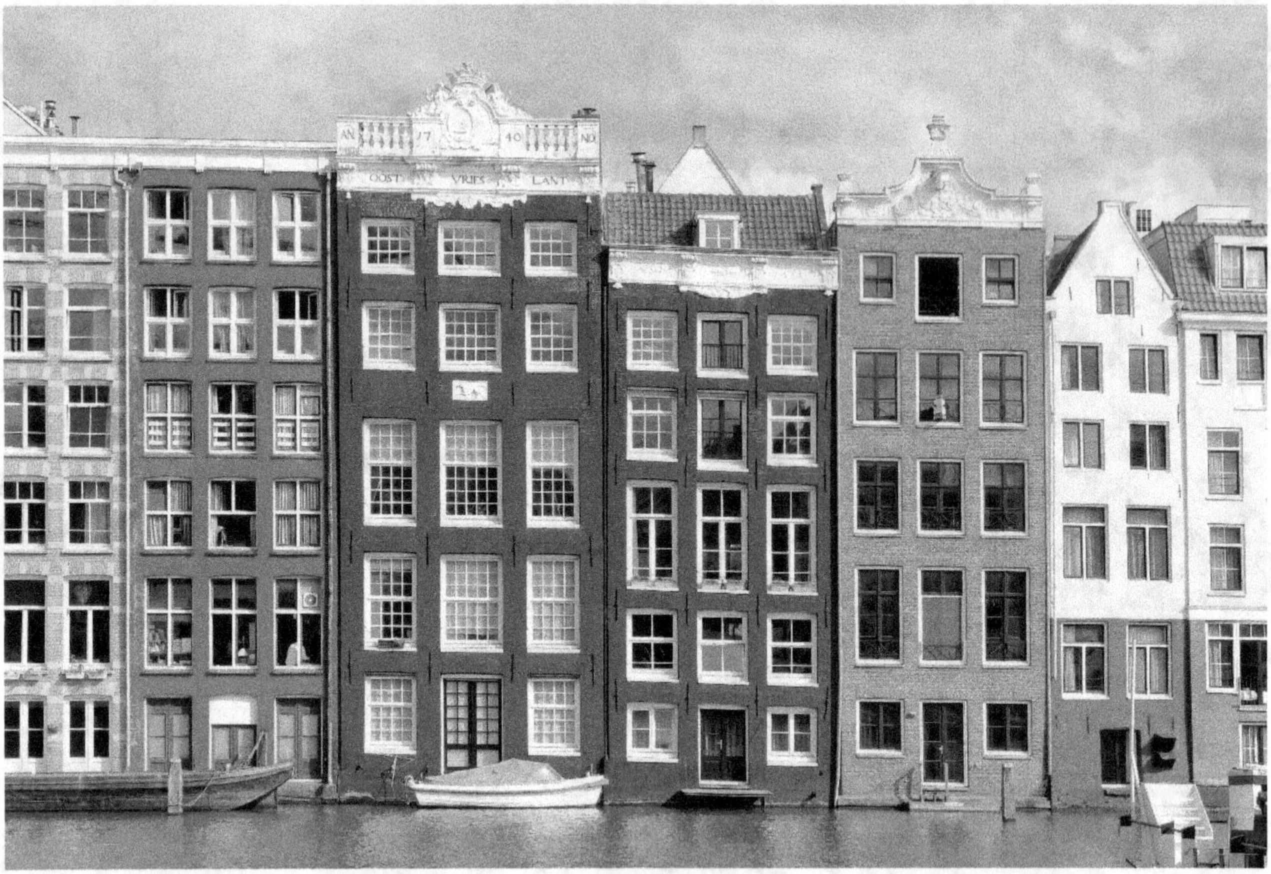
AN 17 40 NO
OOST VRIES LANT

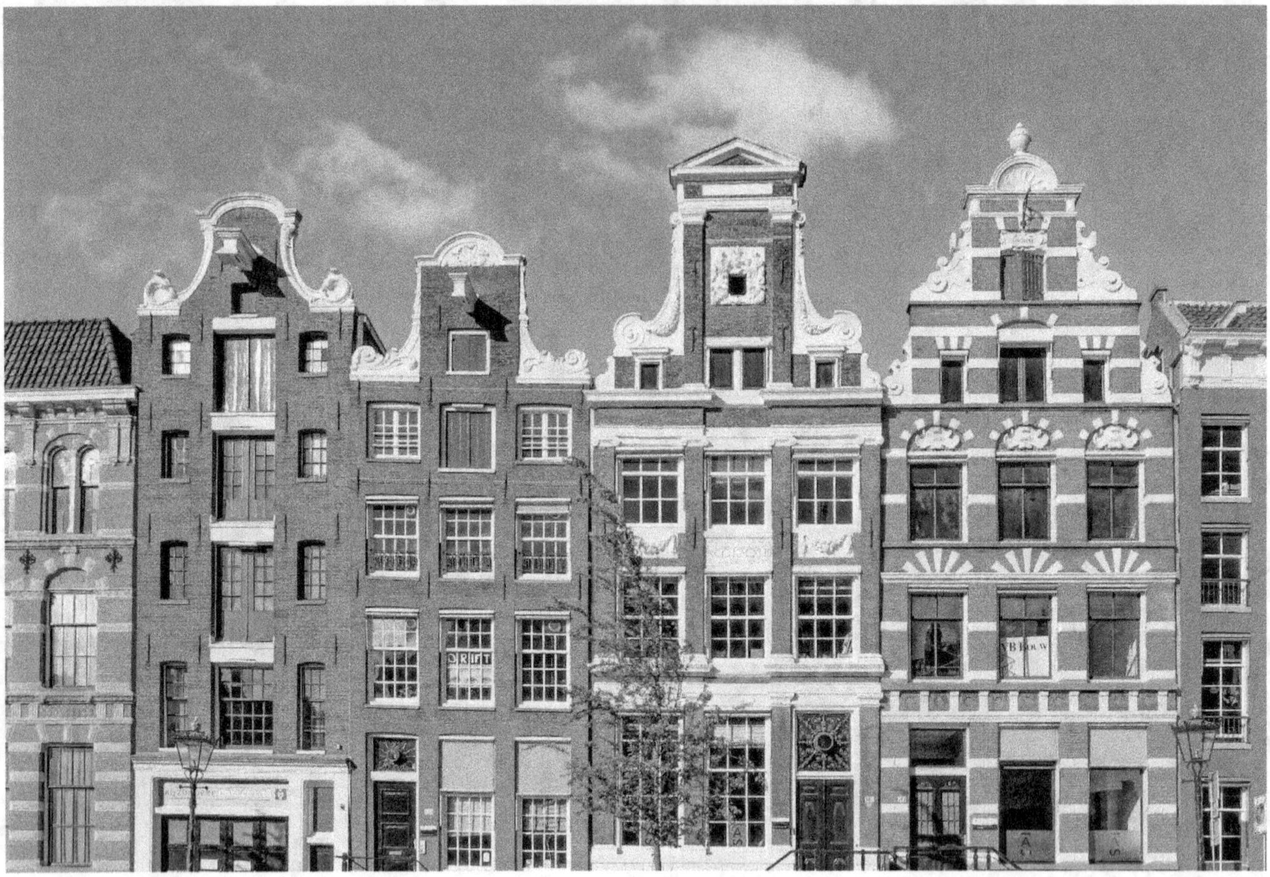

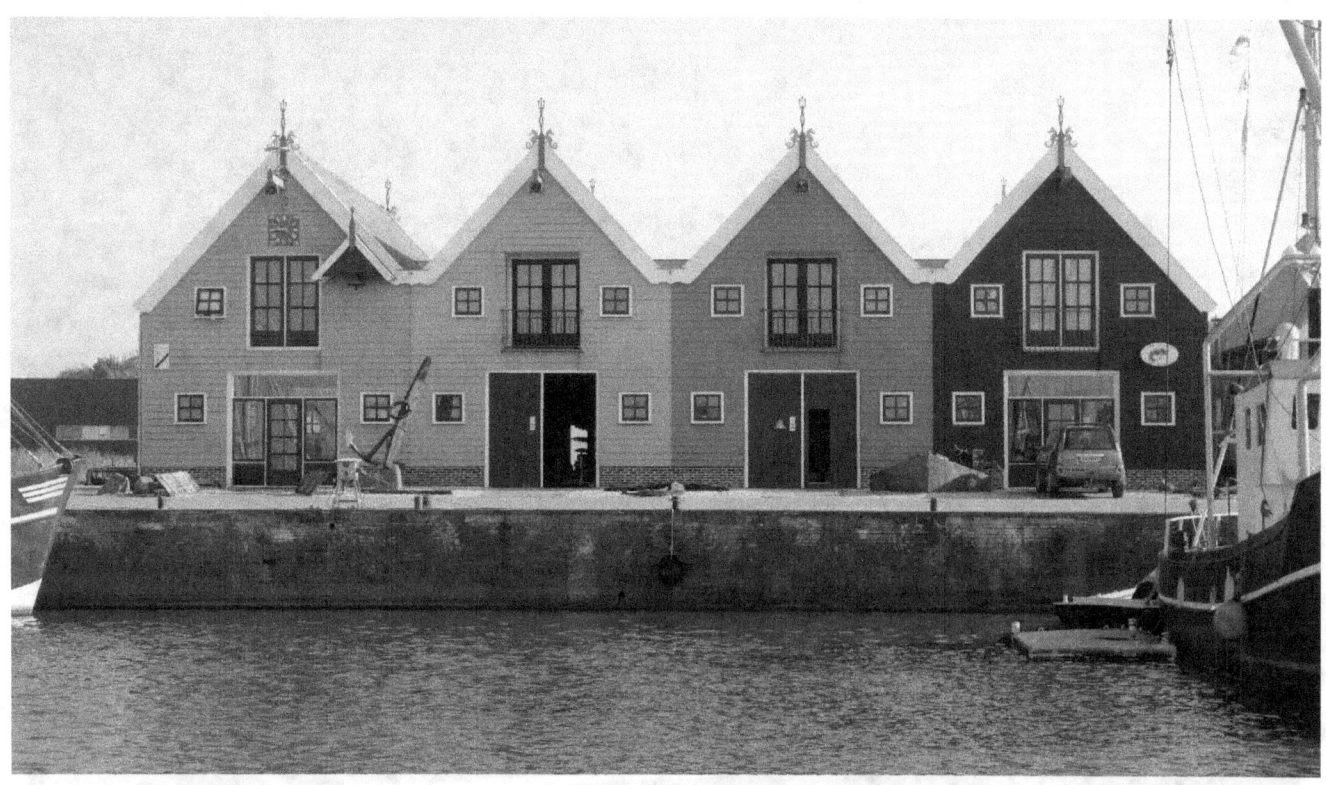

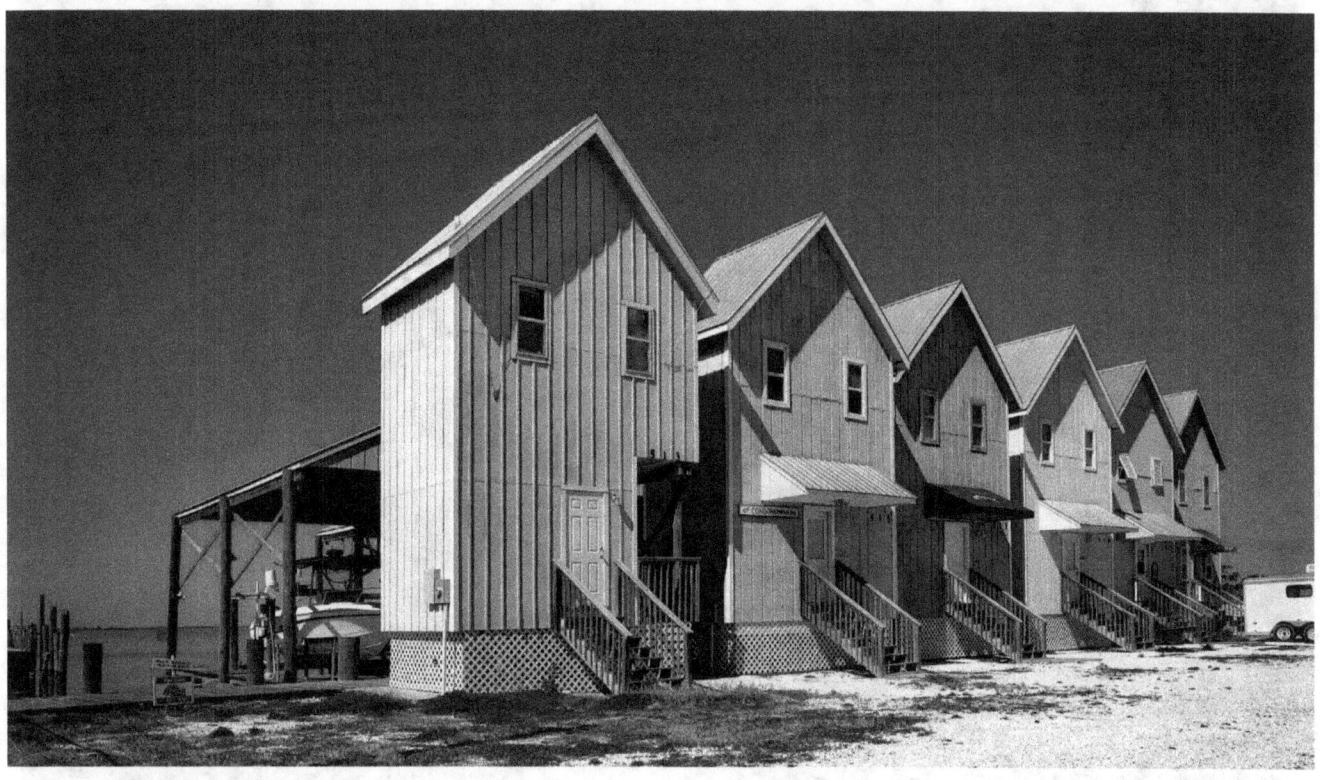

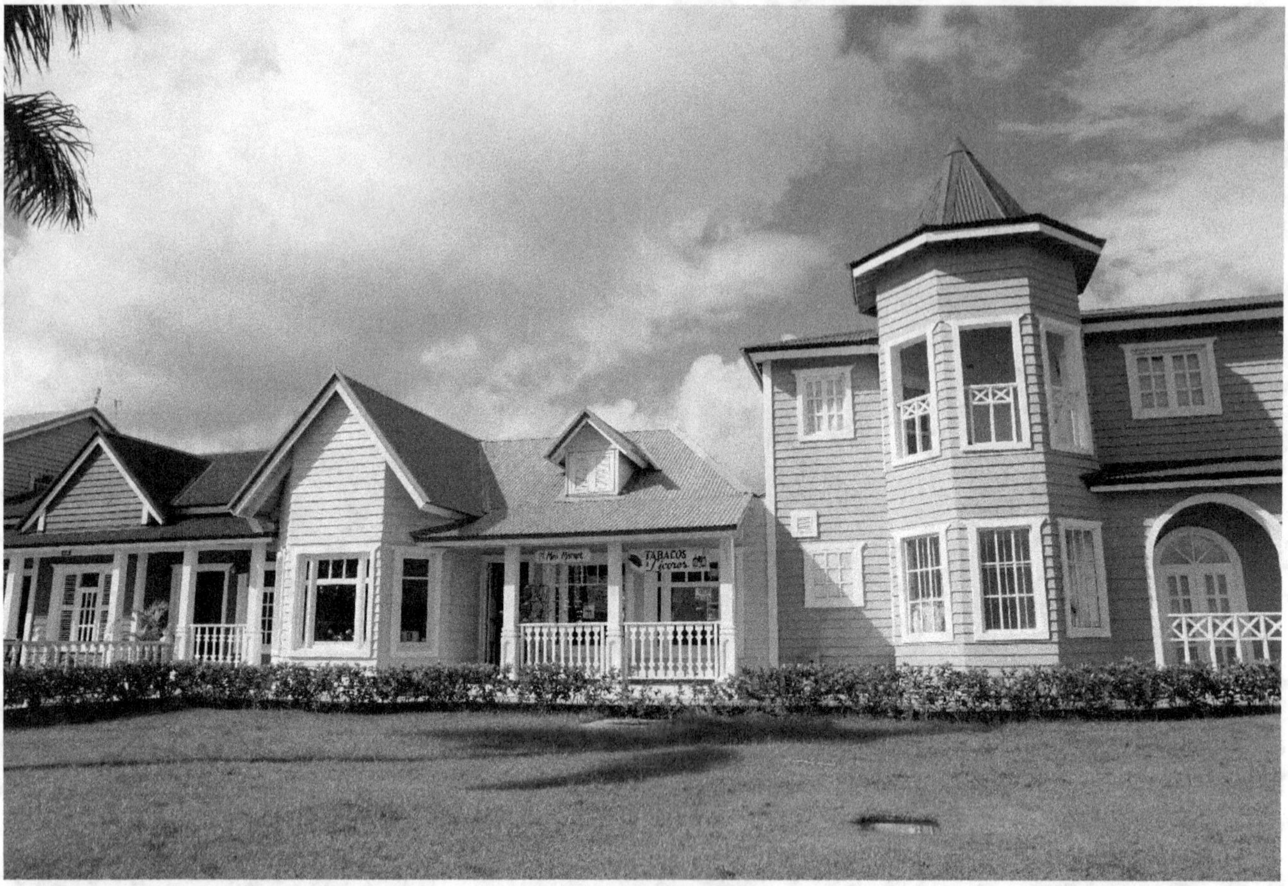

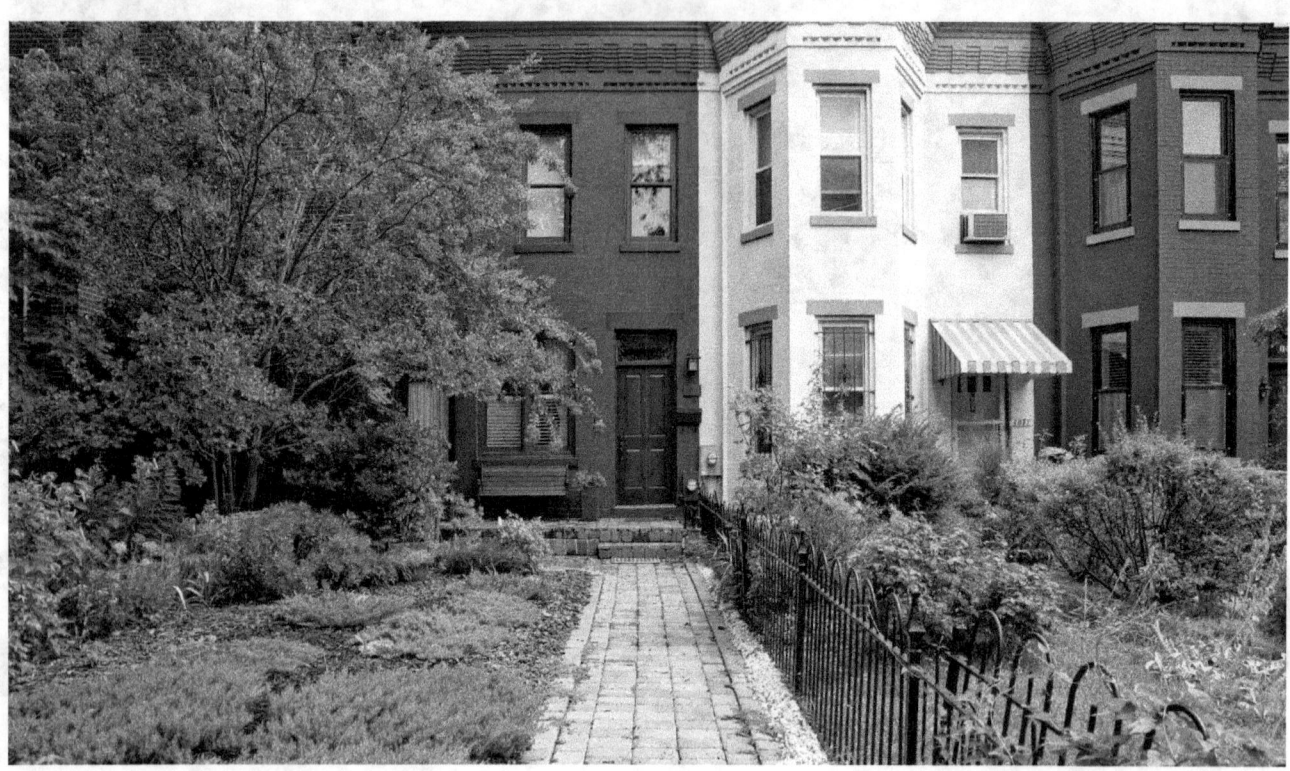

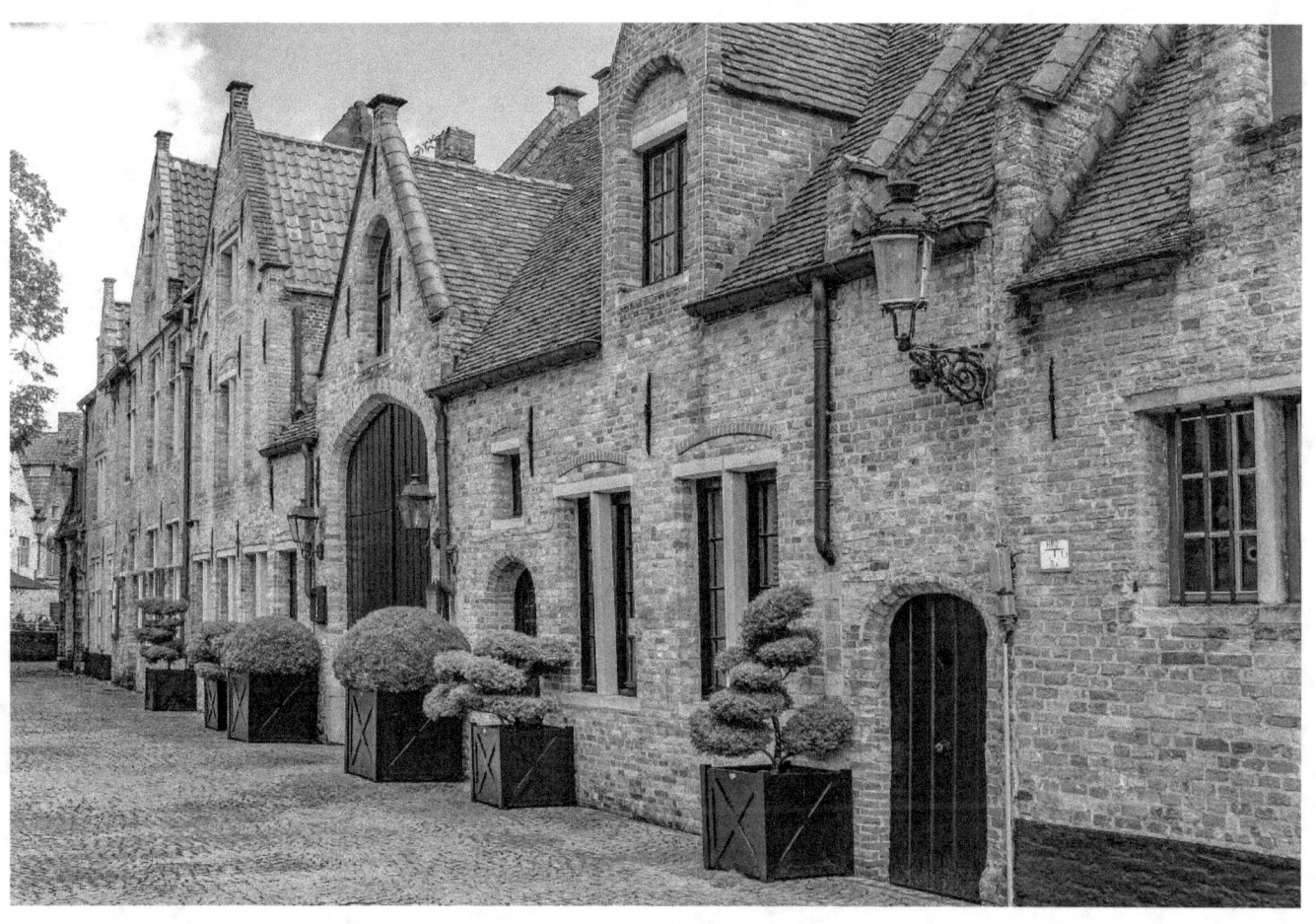

7 PLANTS

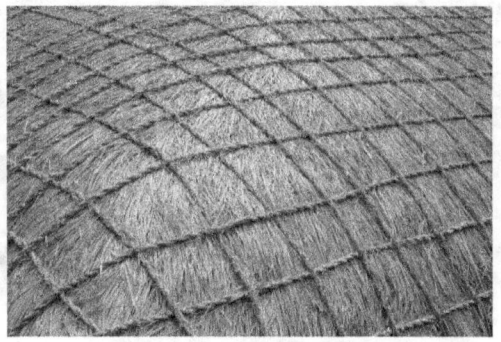

Thatch, reeds and vines

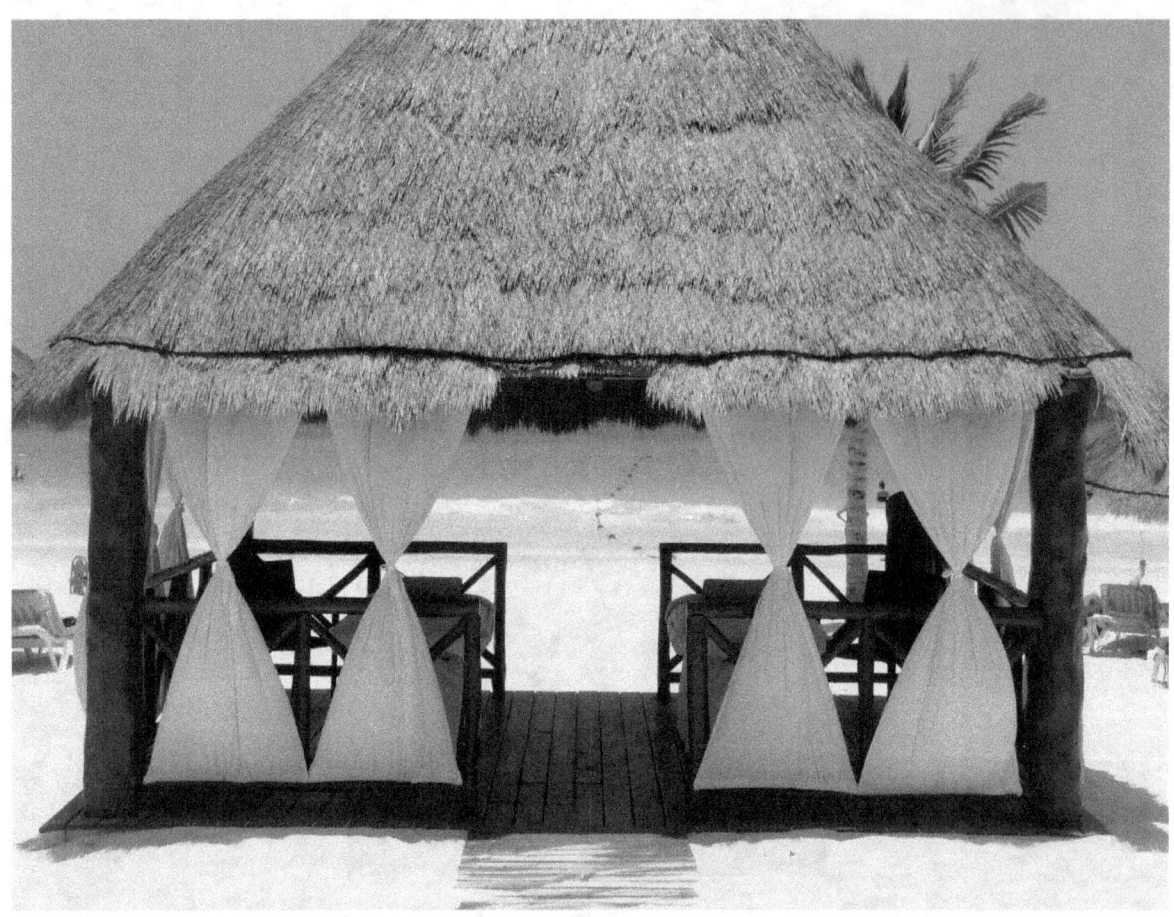

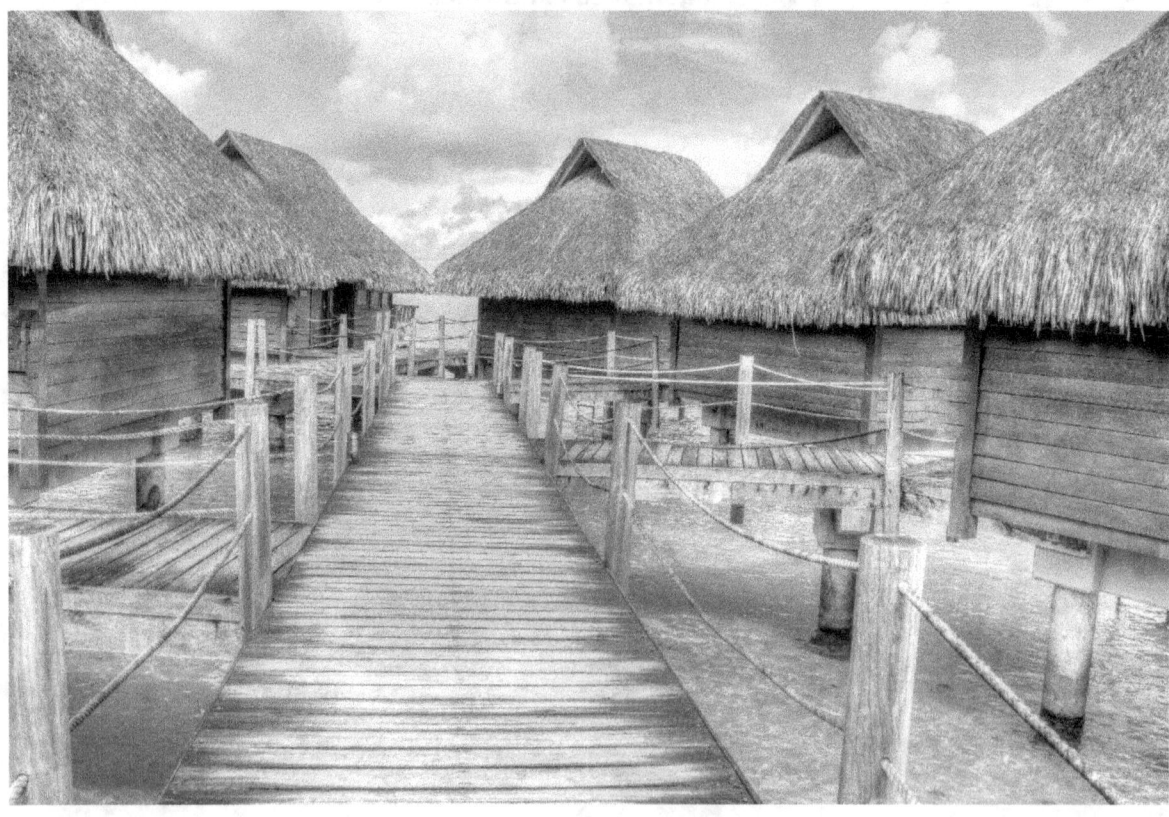

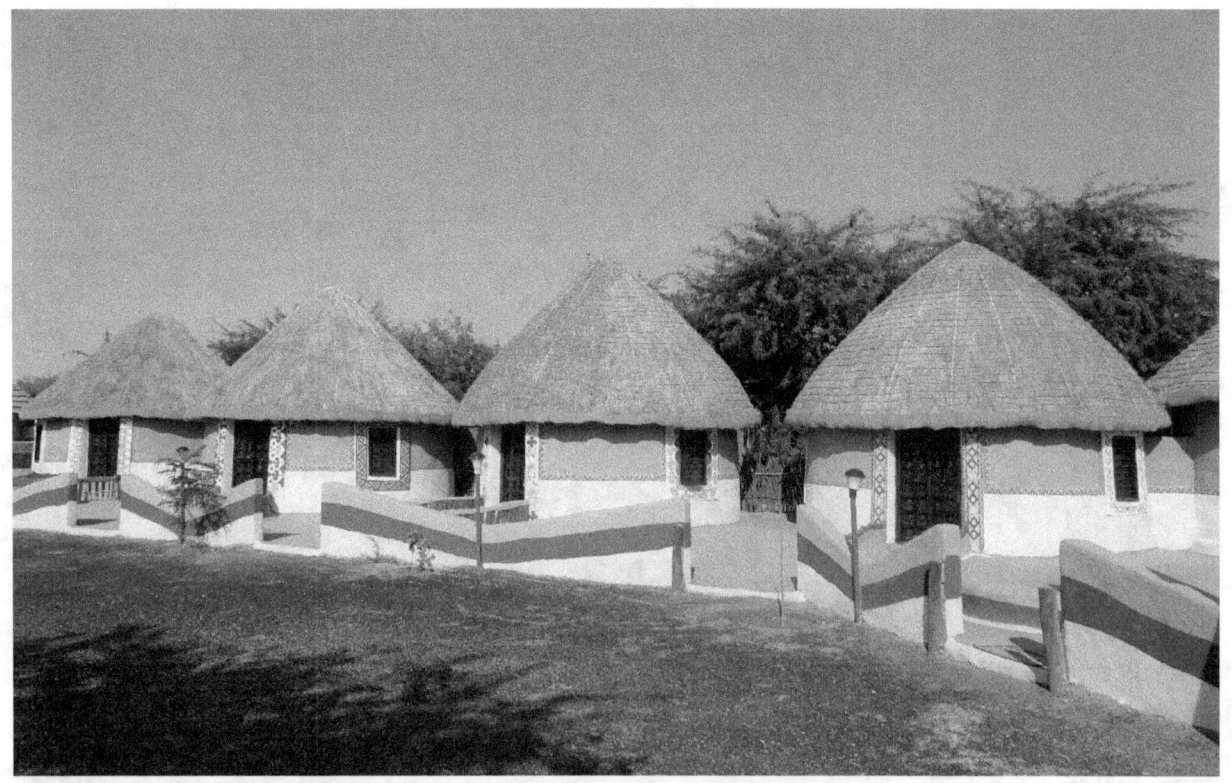

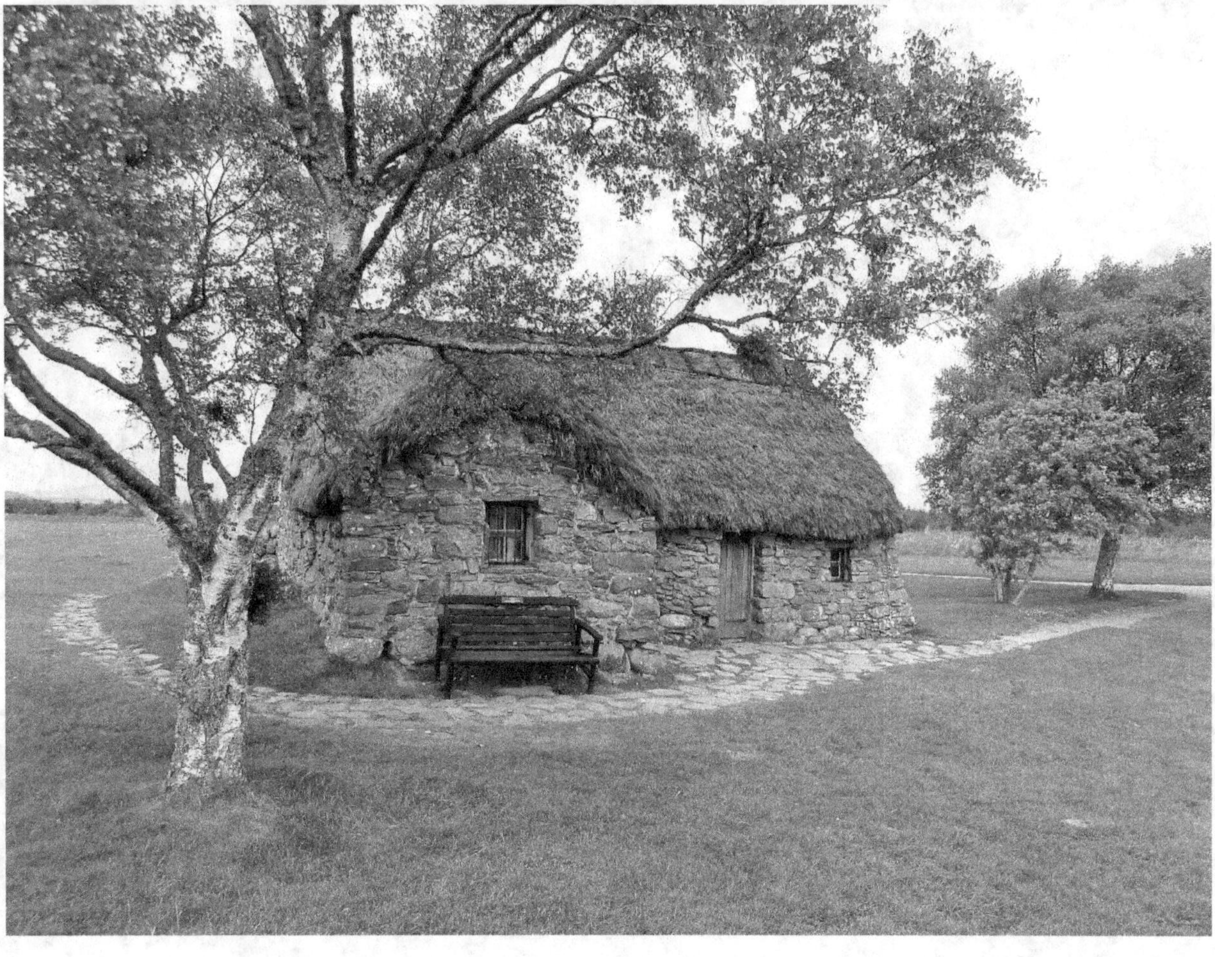

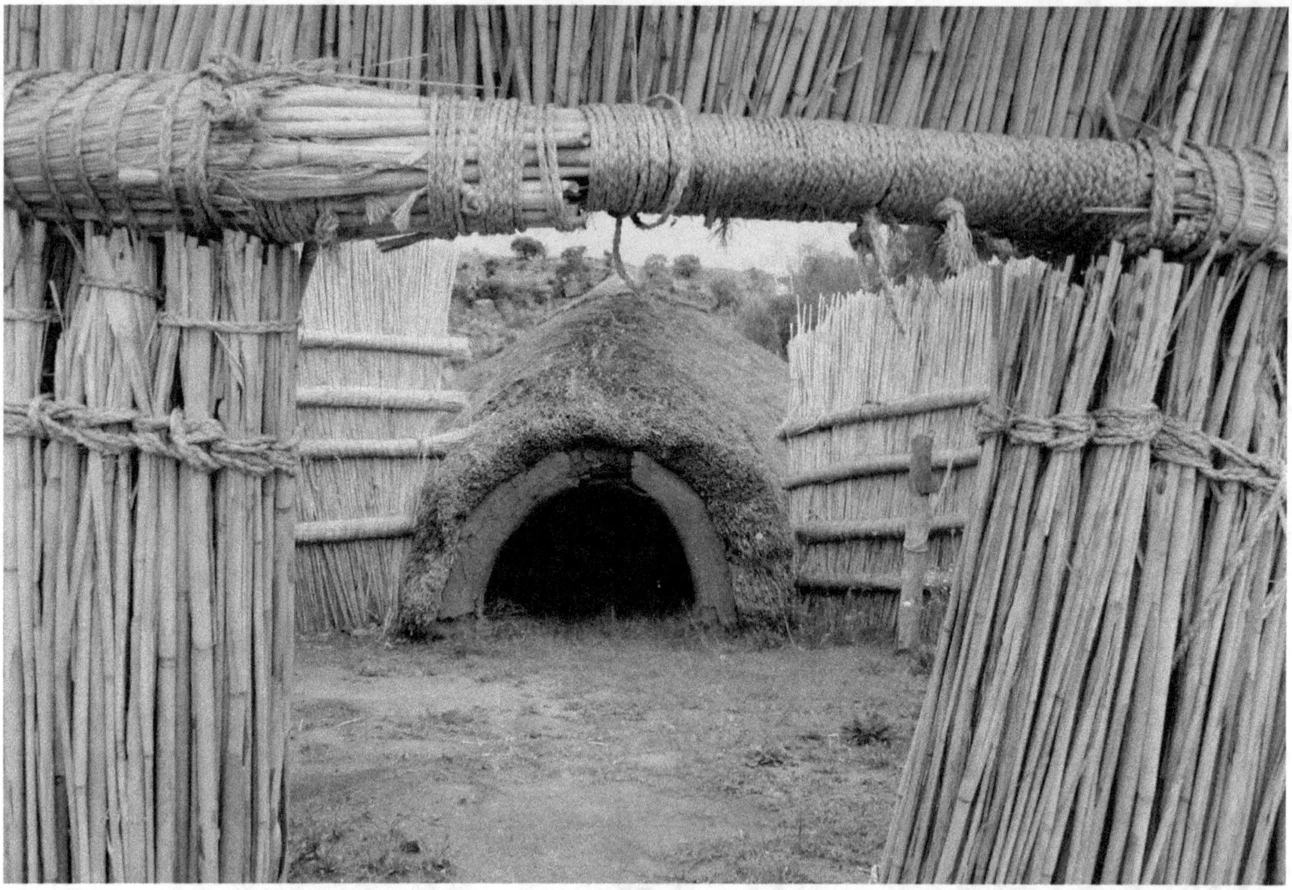

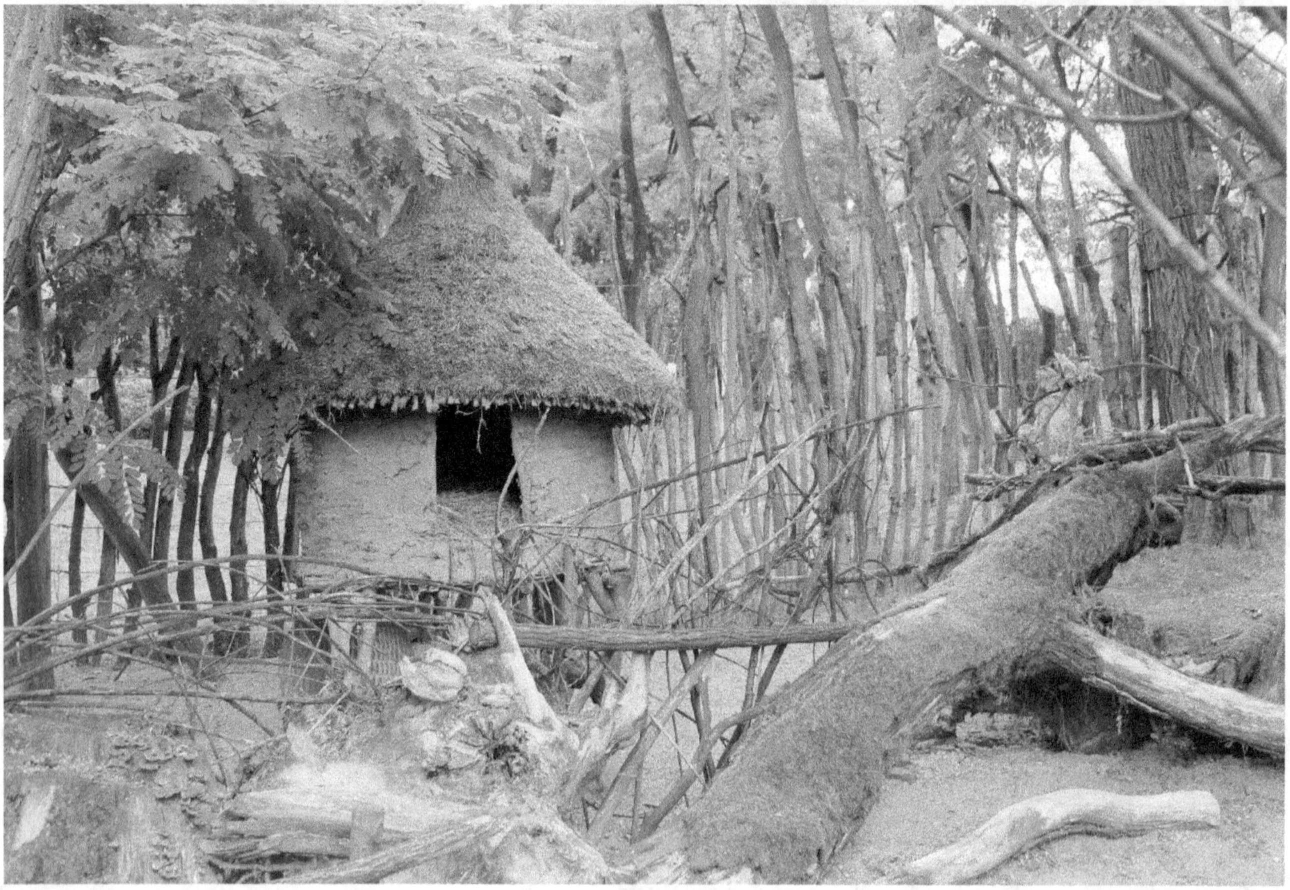

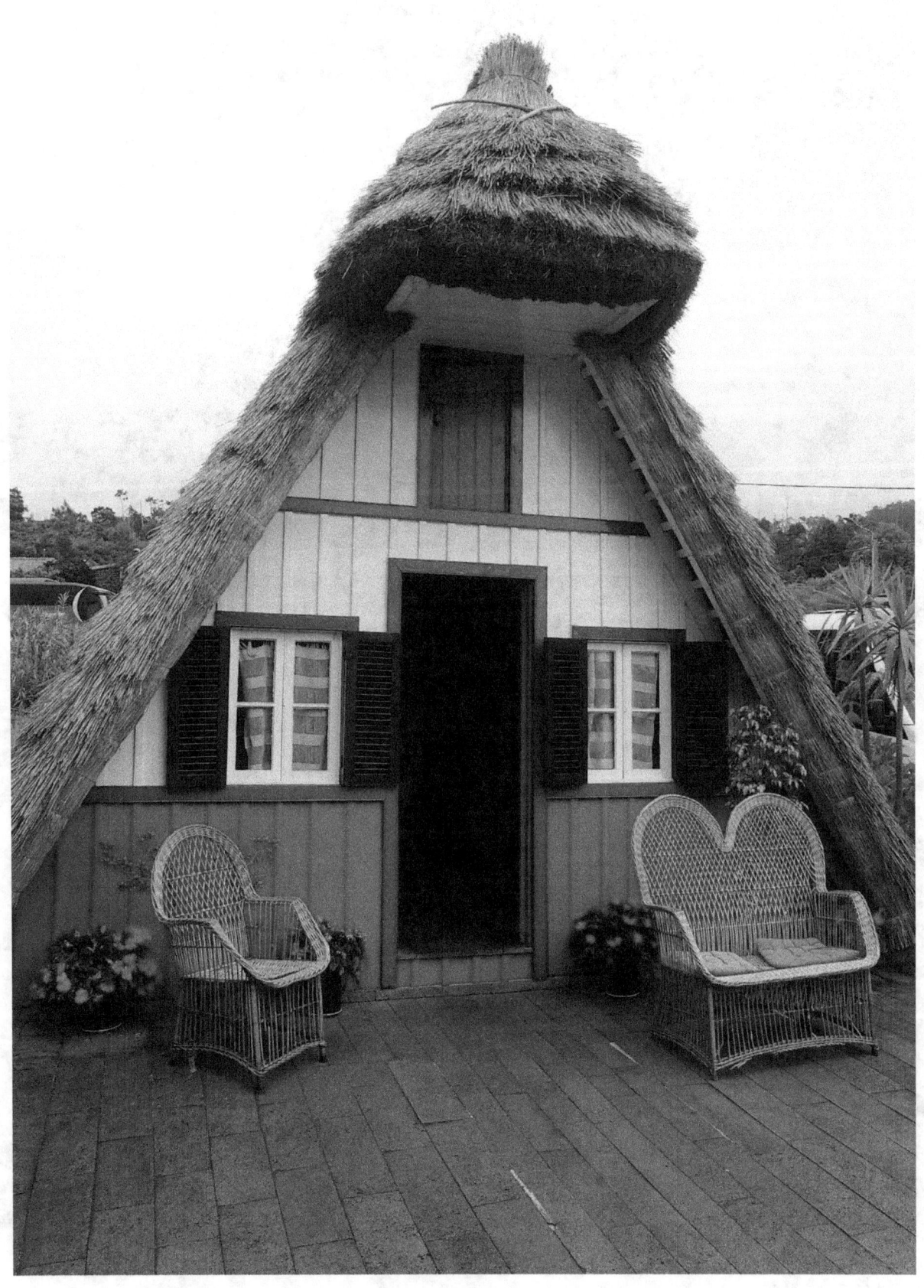

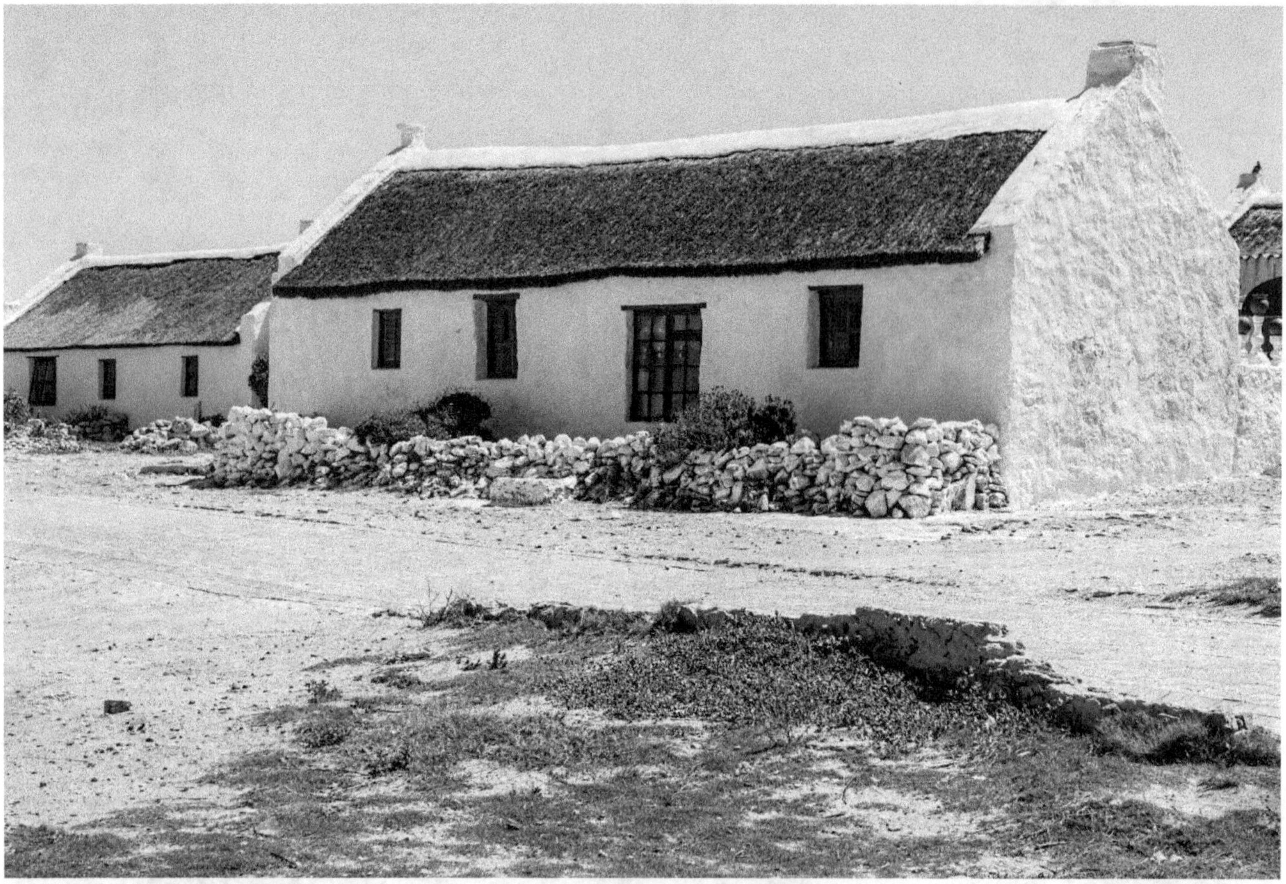

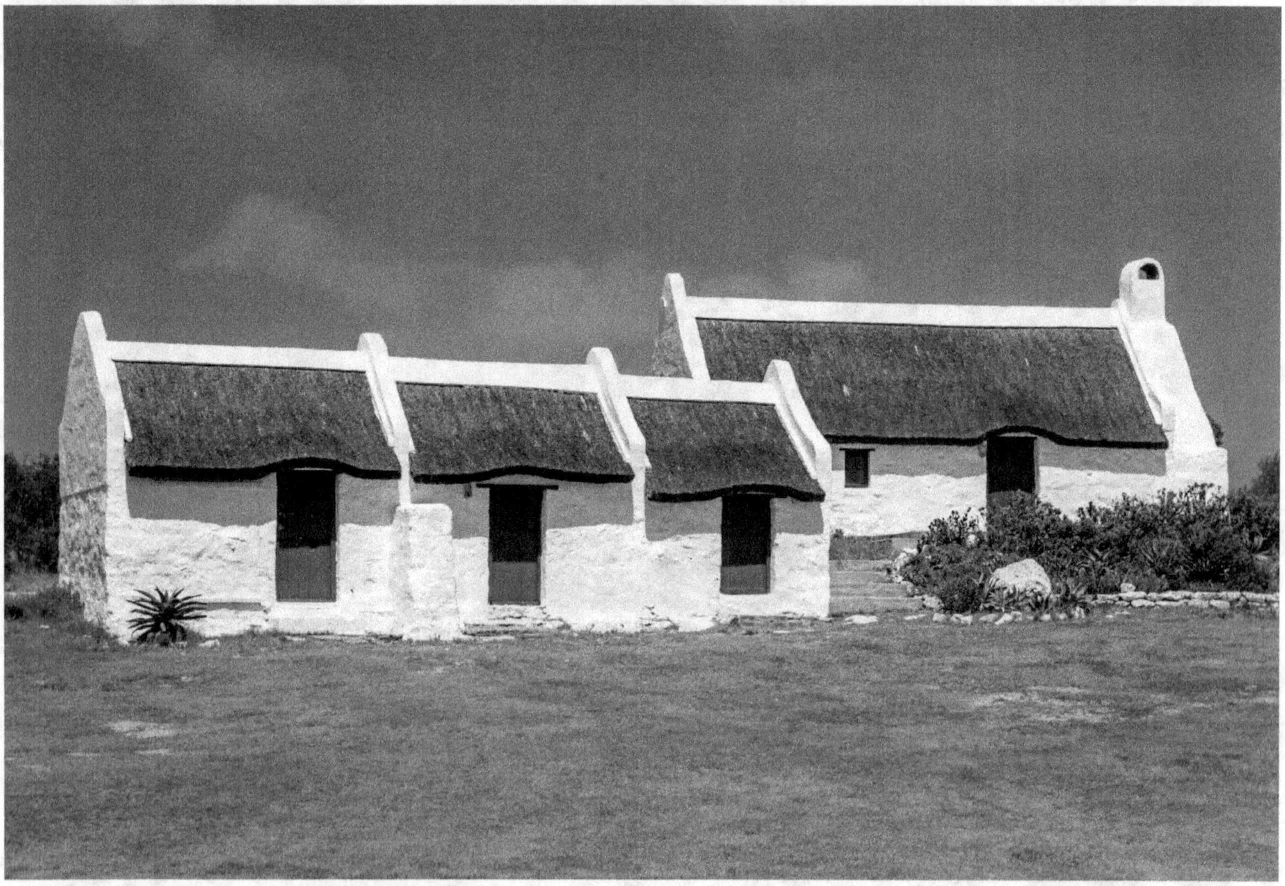

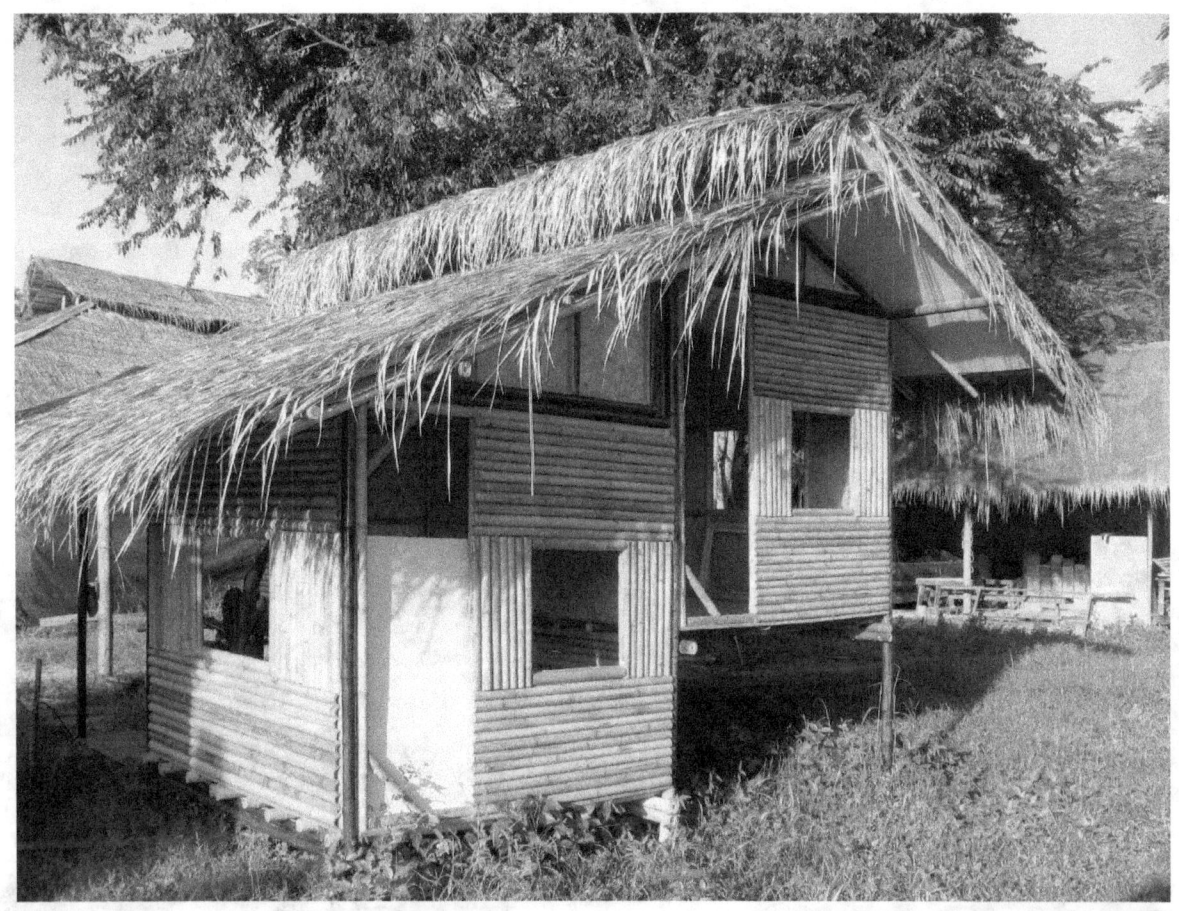

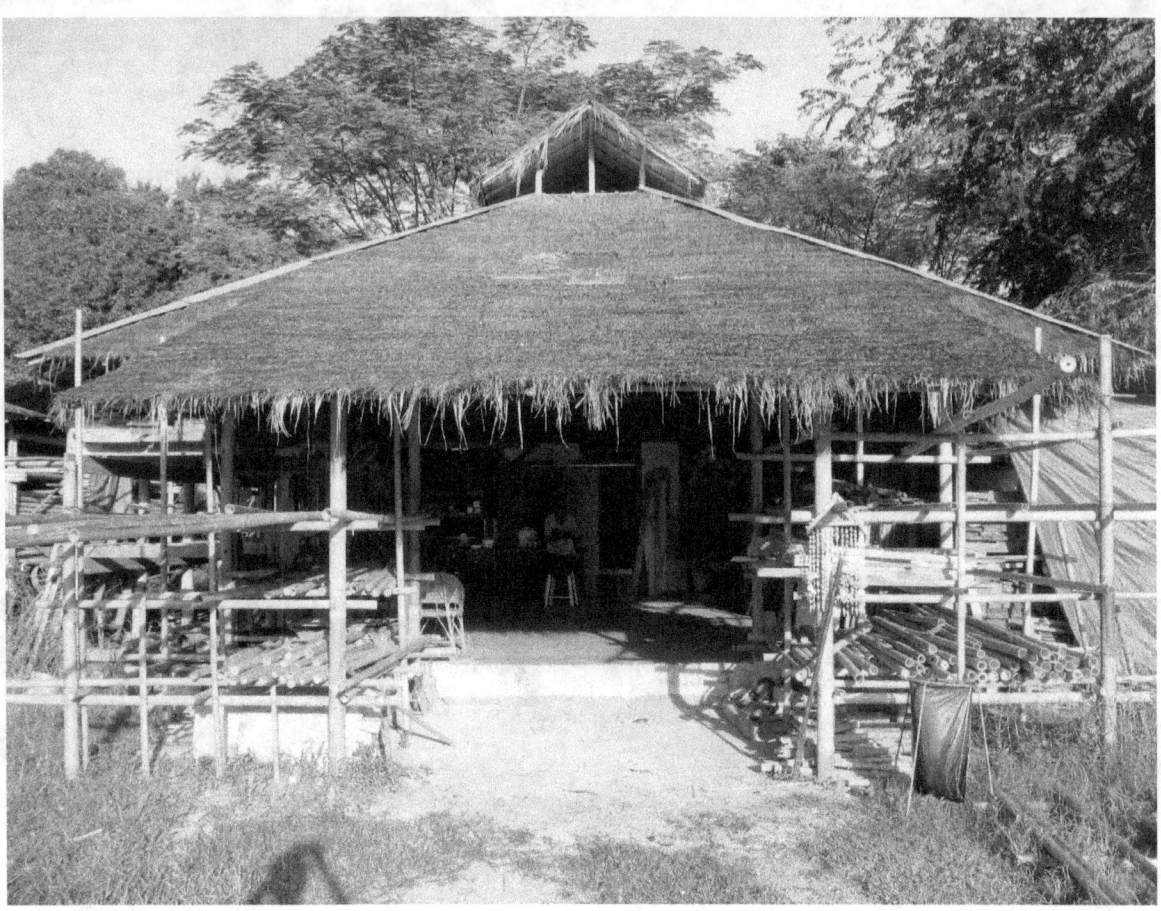

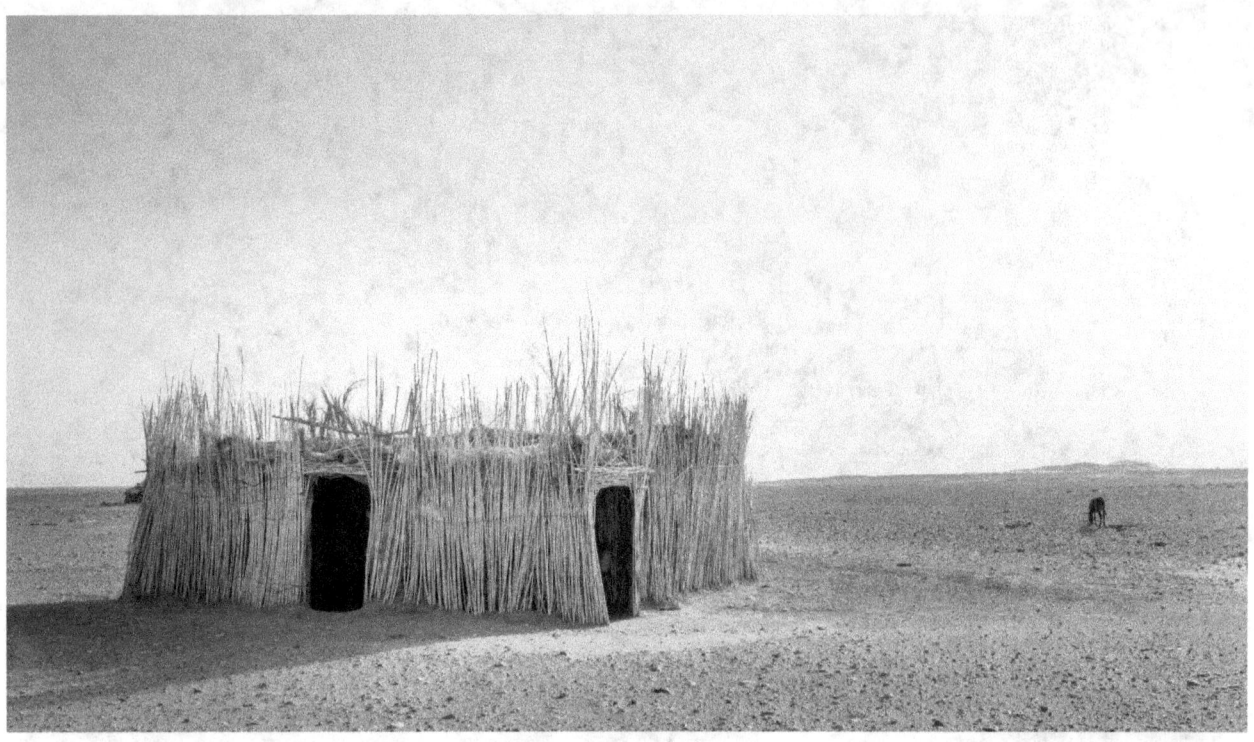

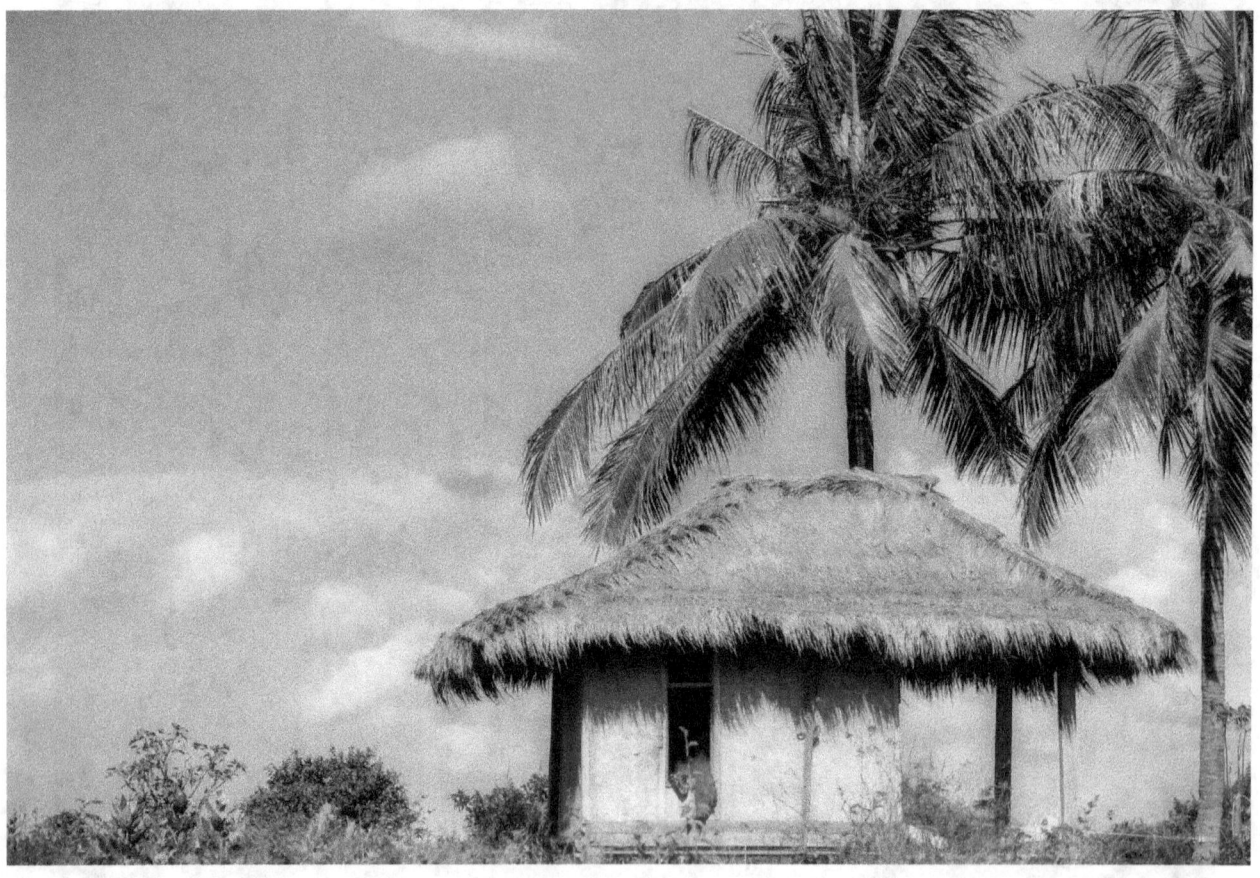

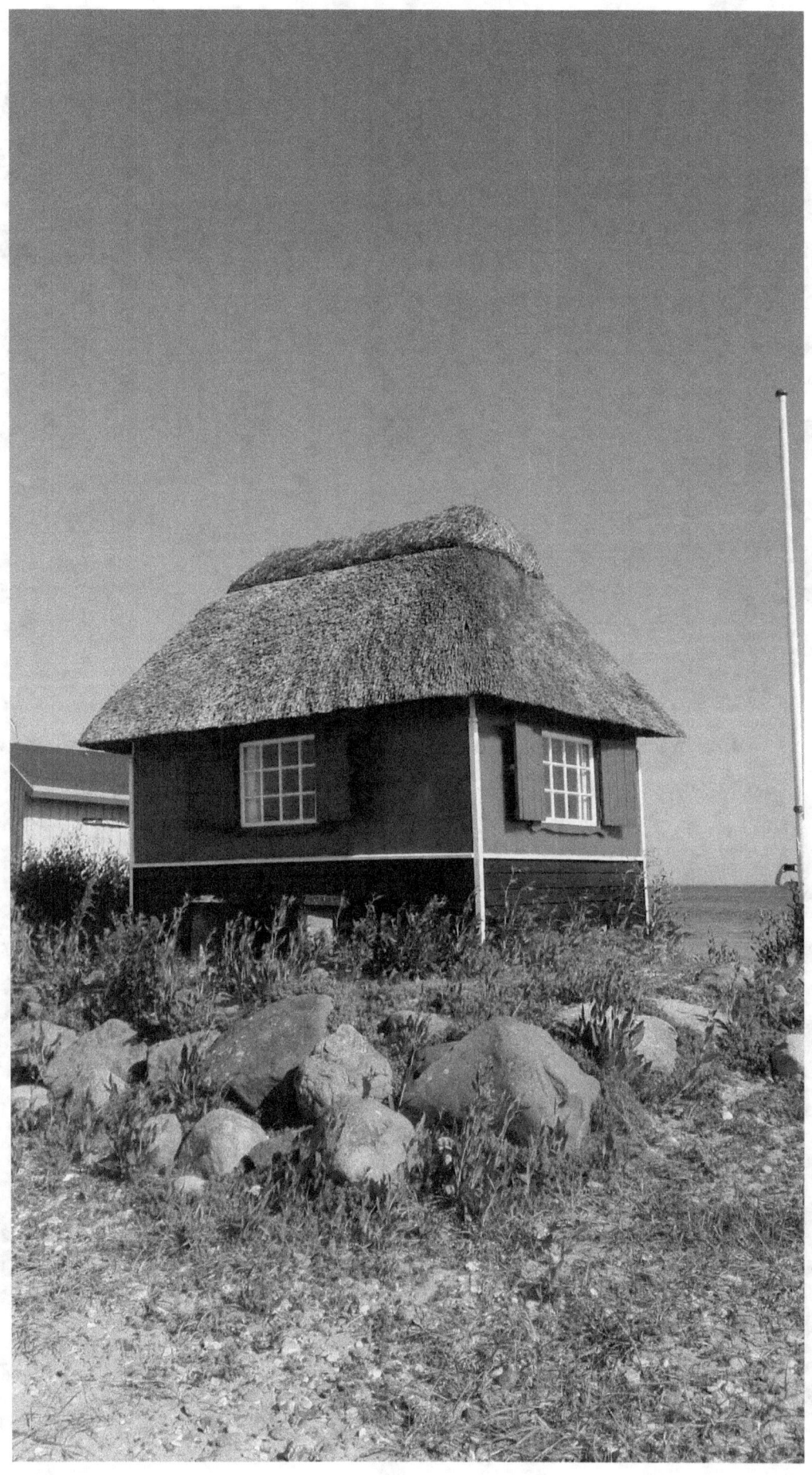

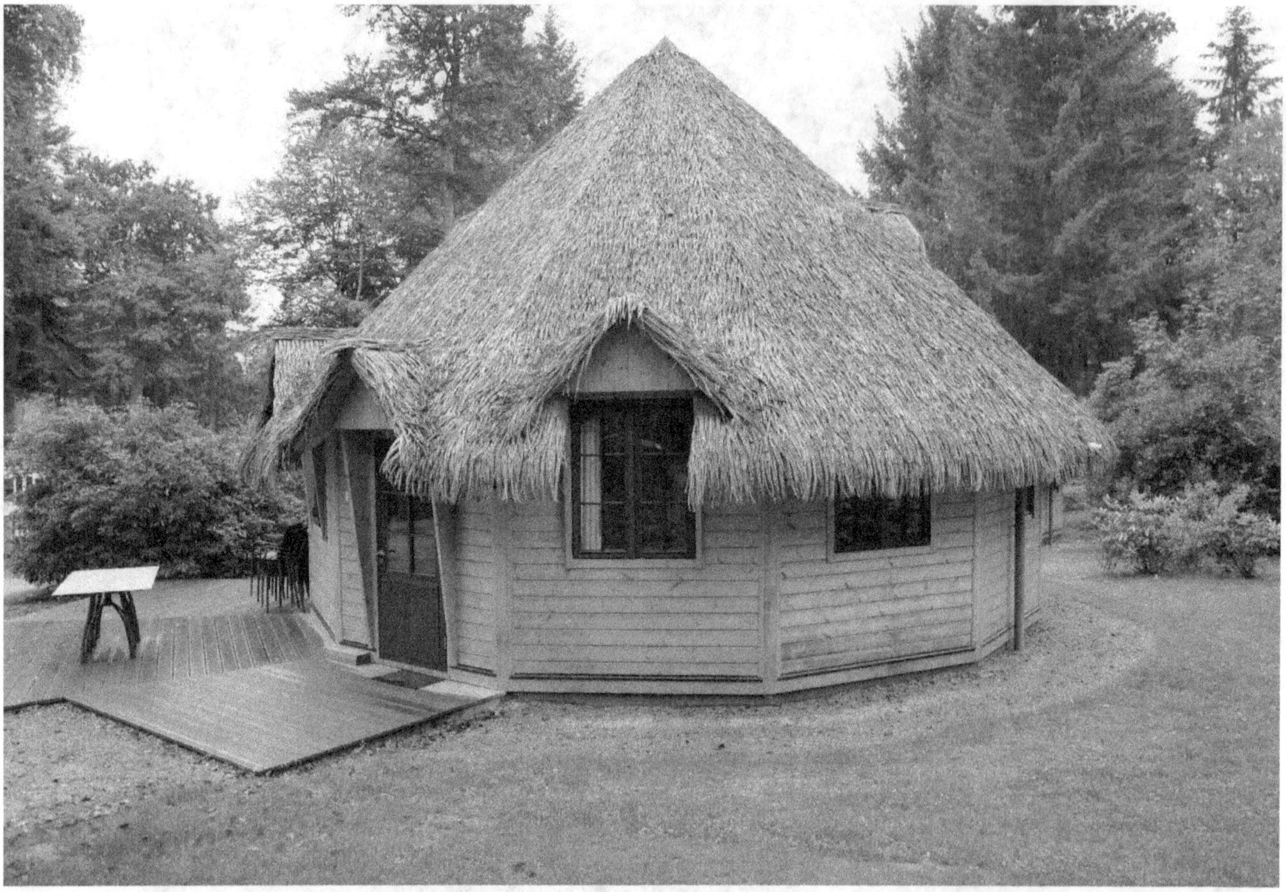

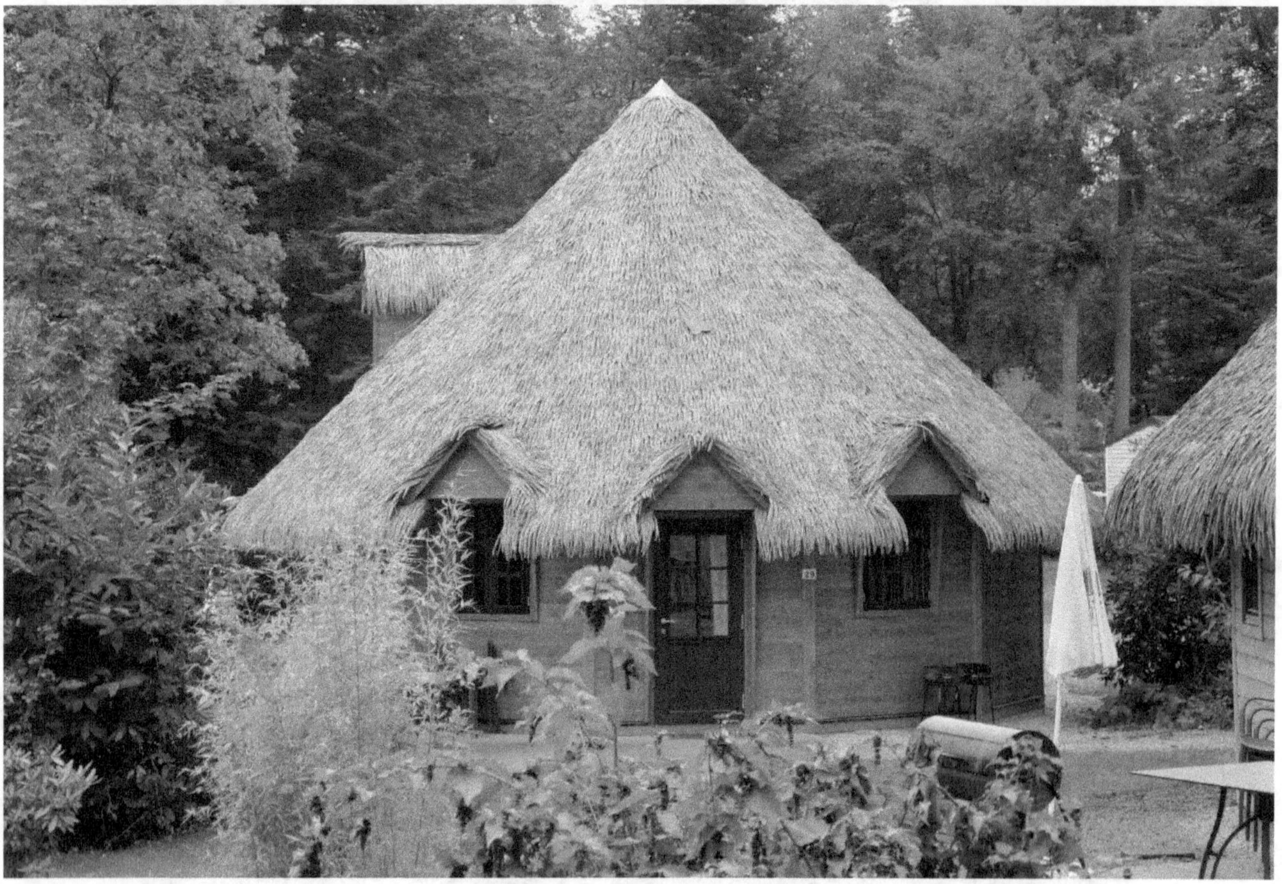

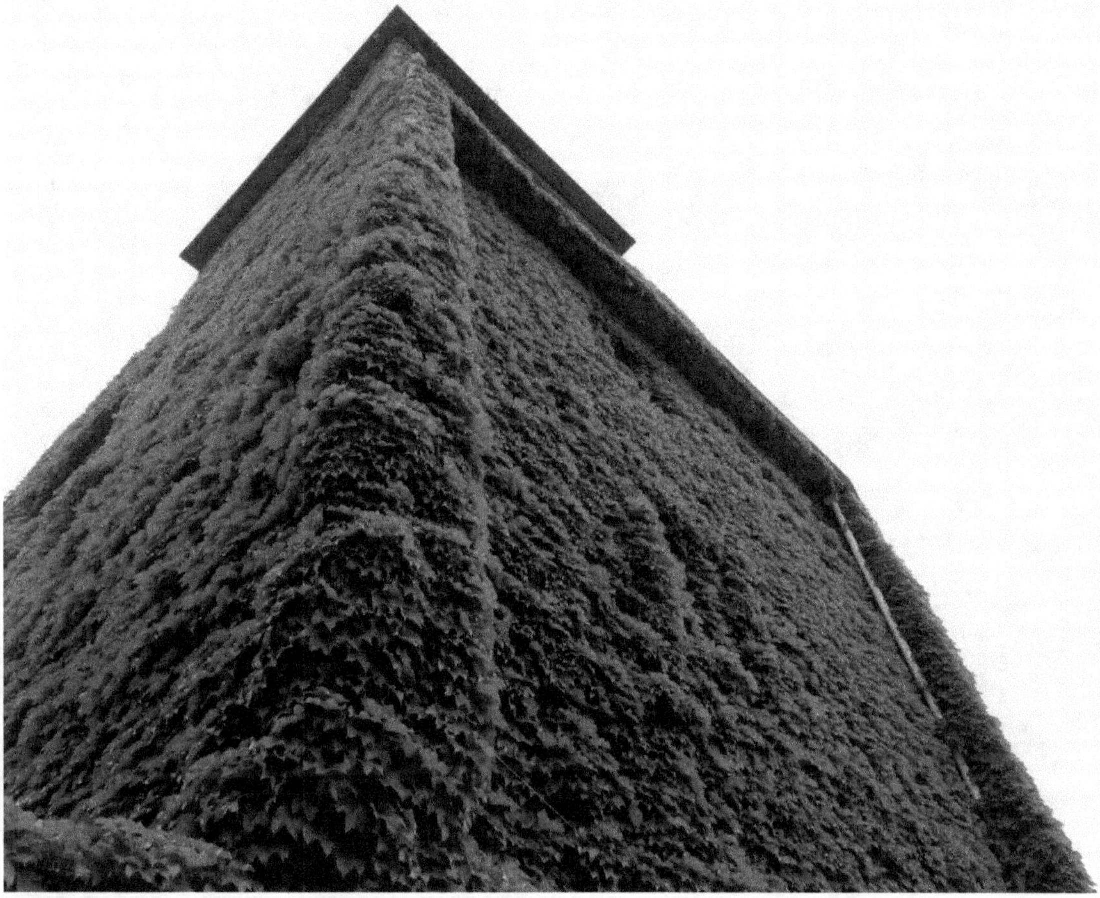

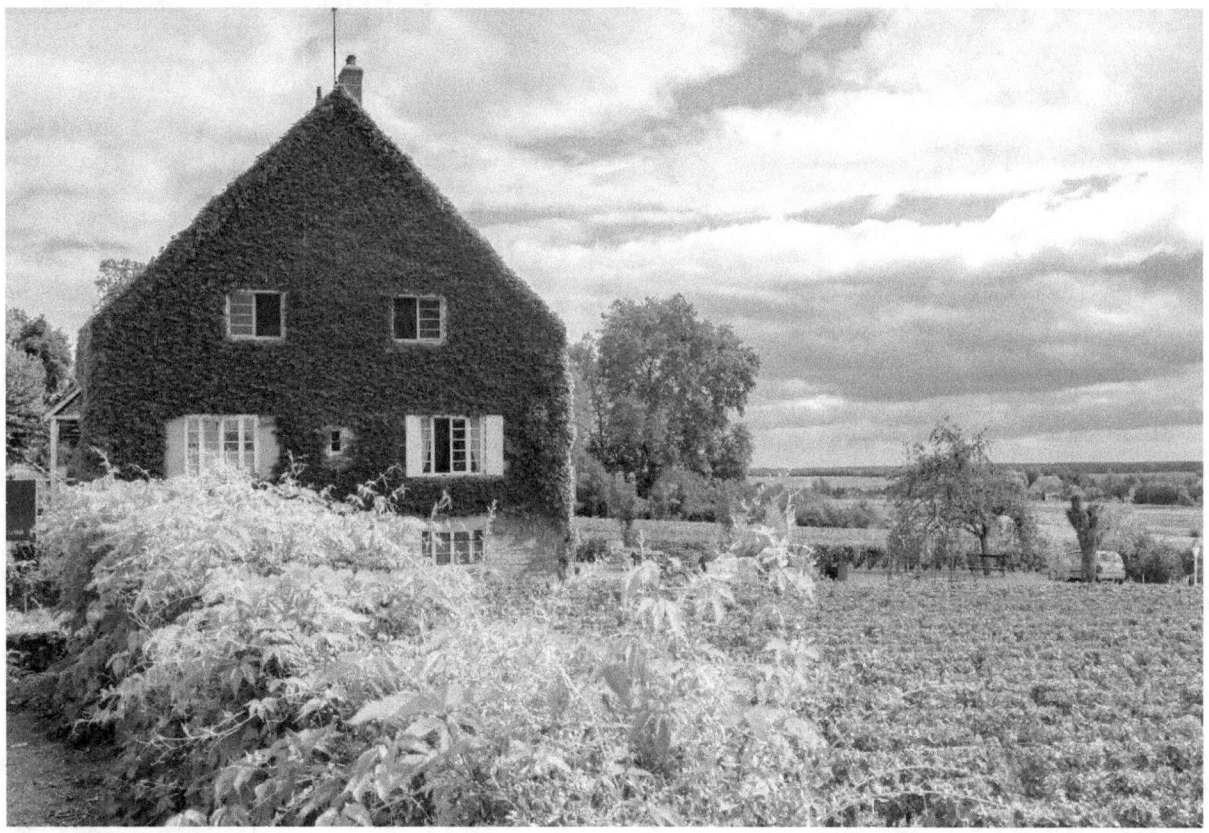

8 SKINS

Yurts, tipis and wigwams

Yurts

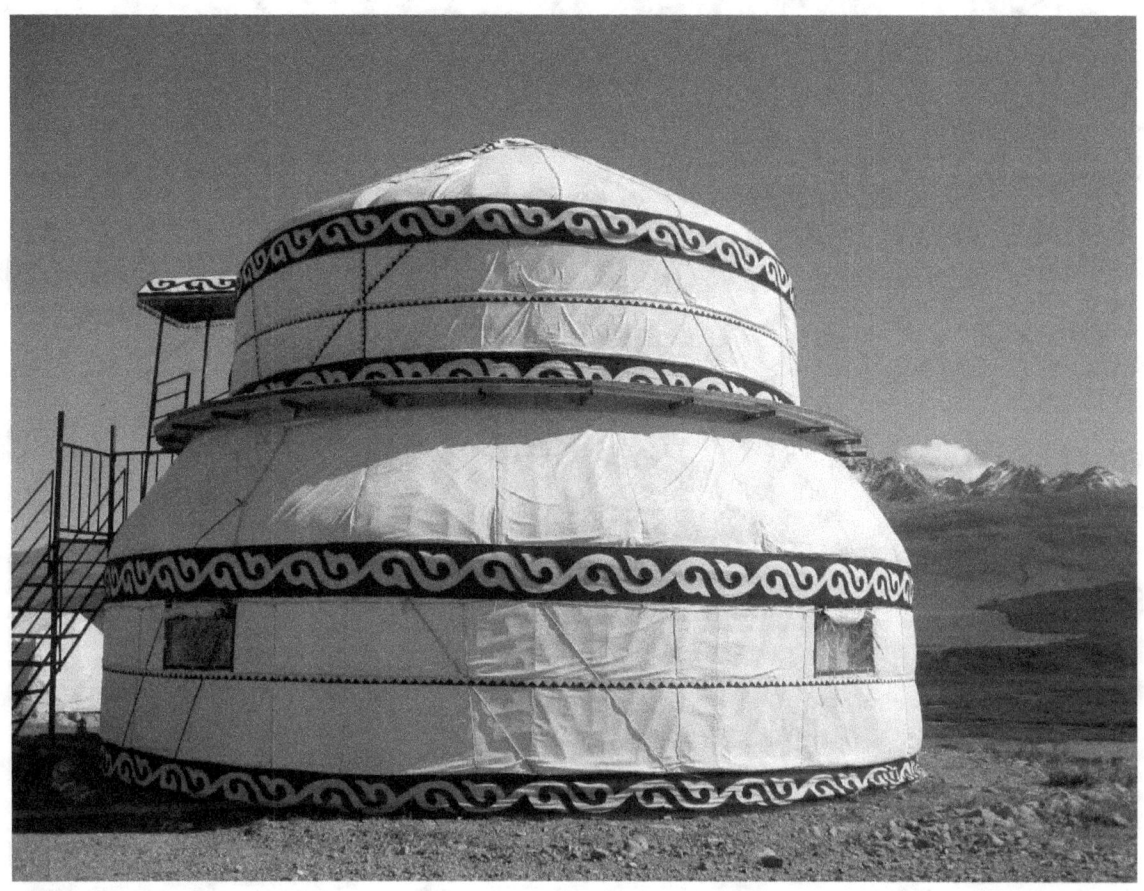

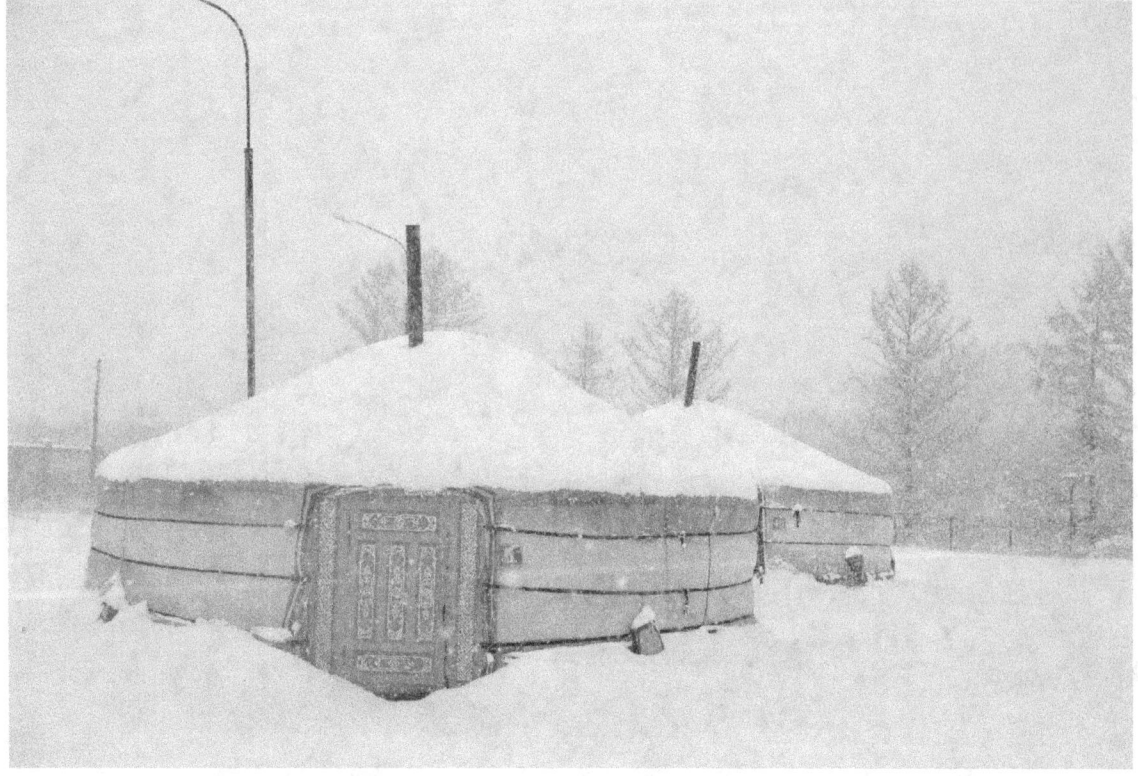

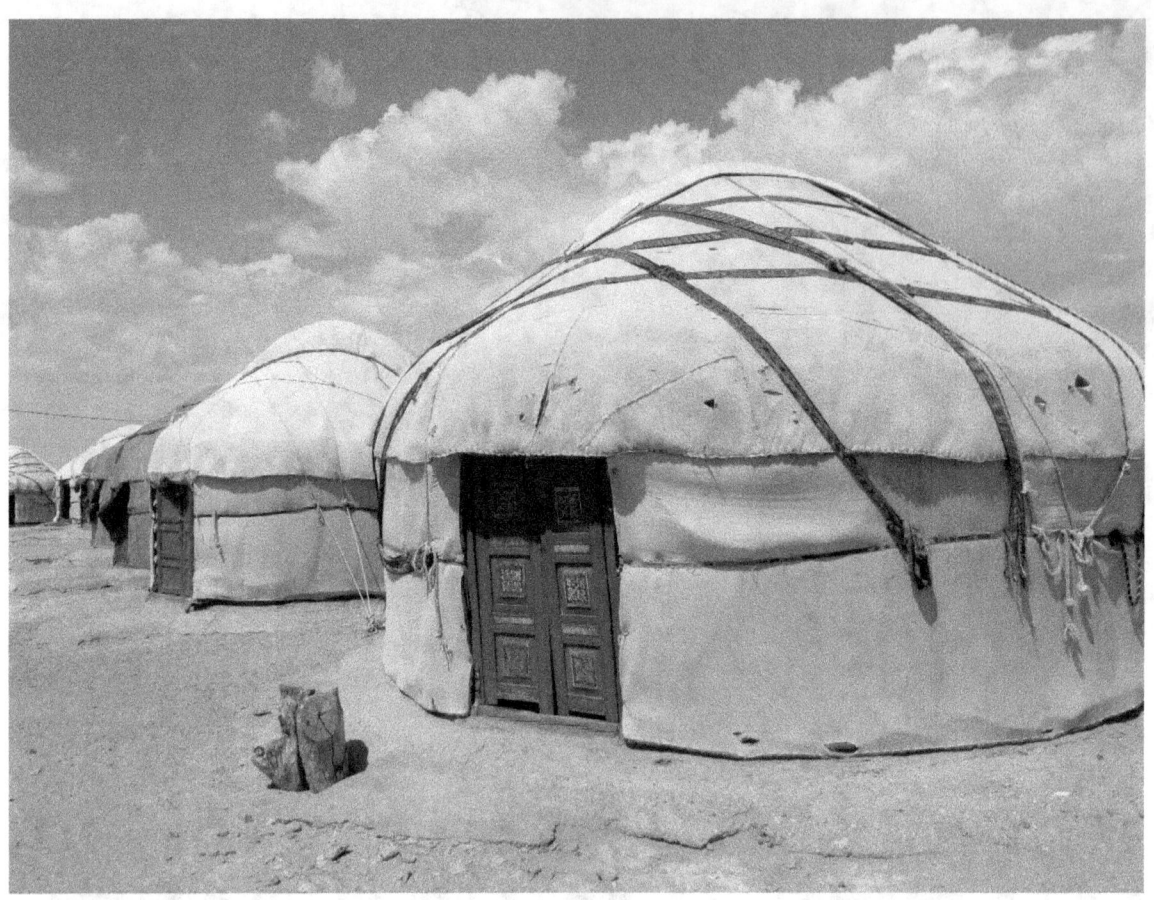

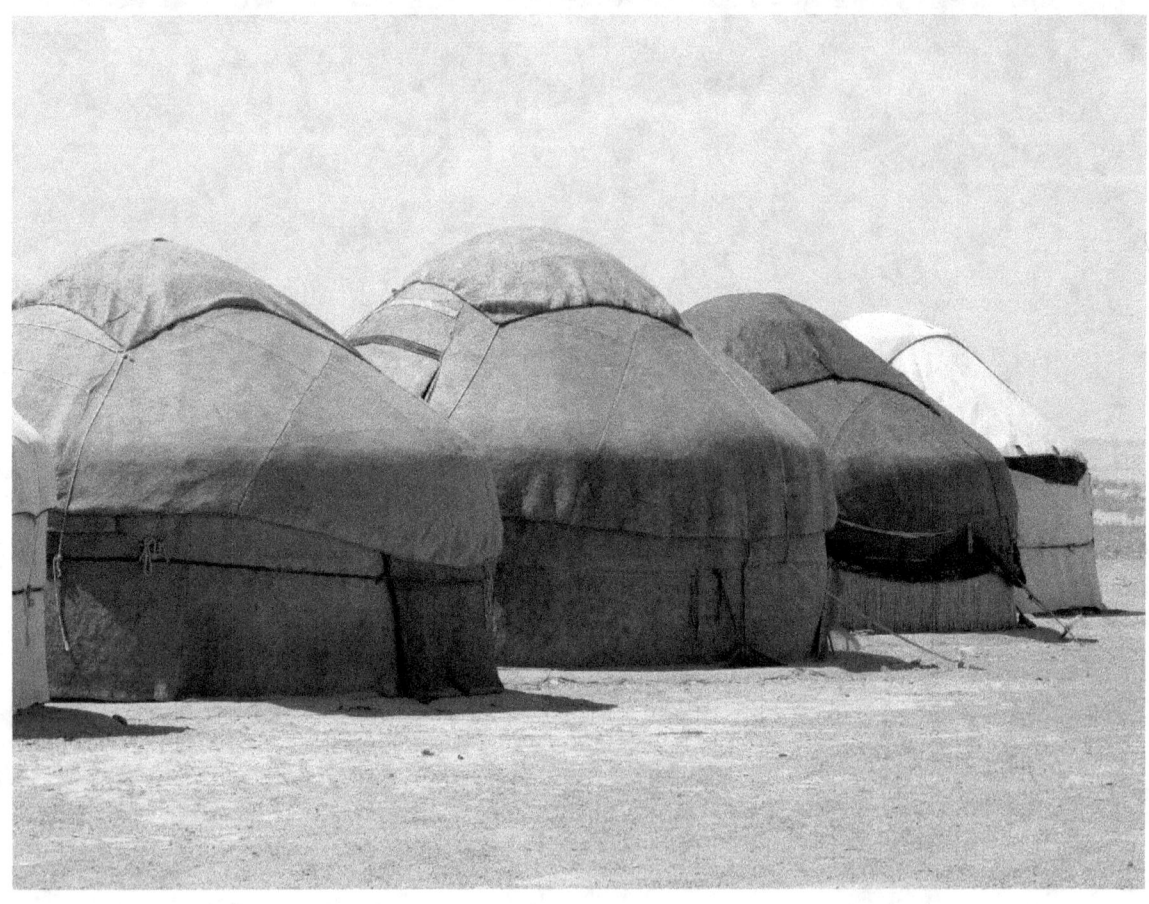

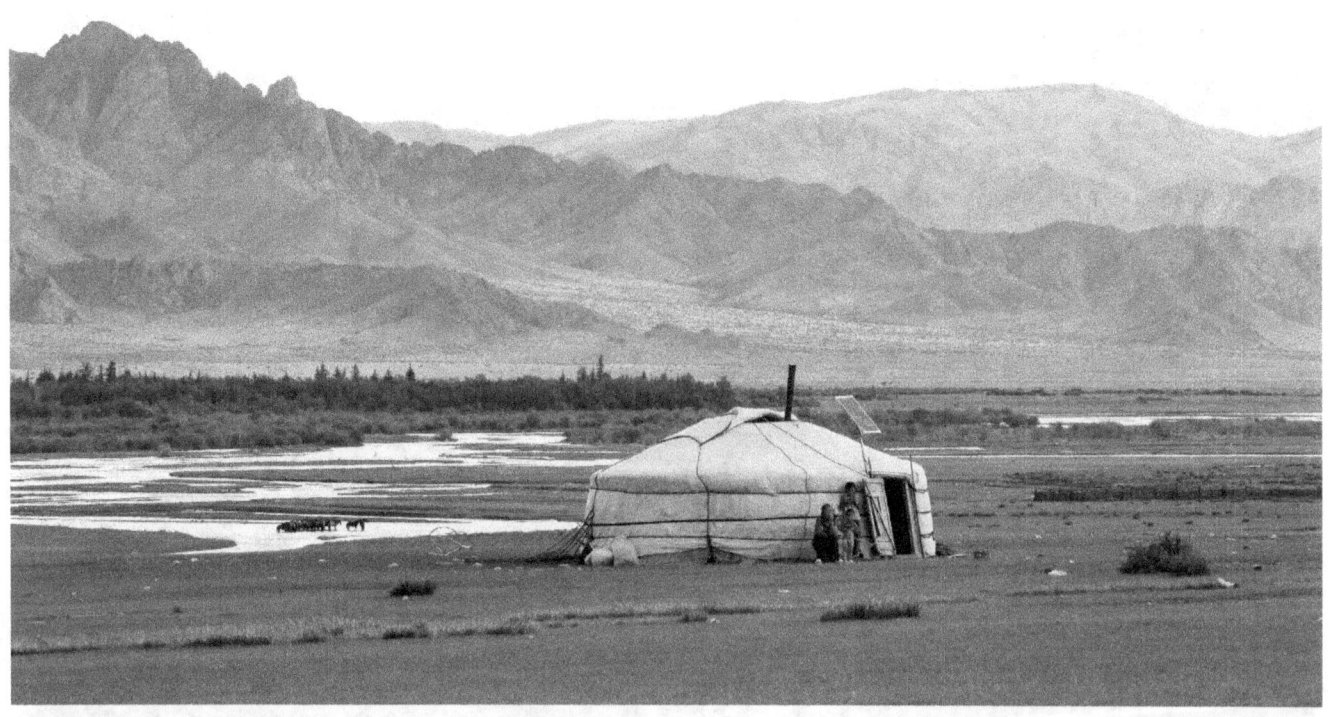

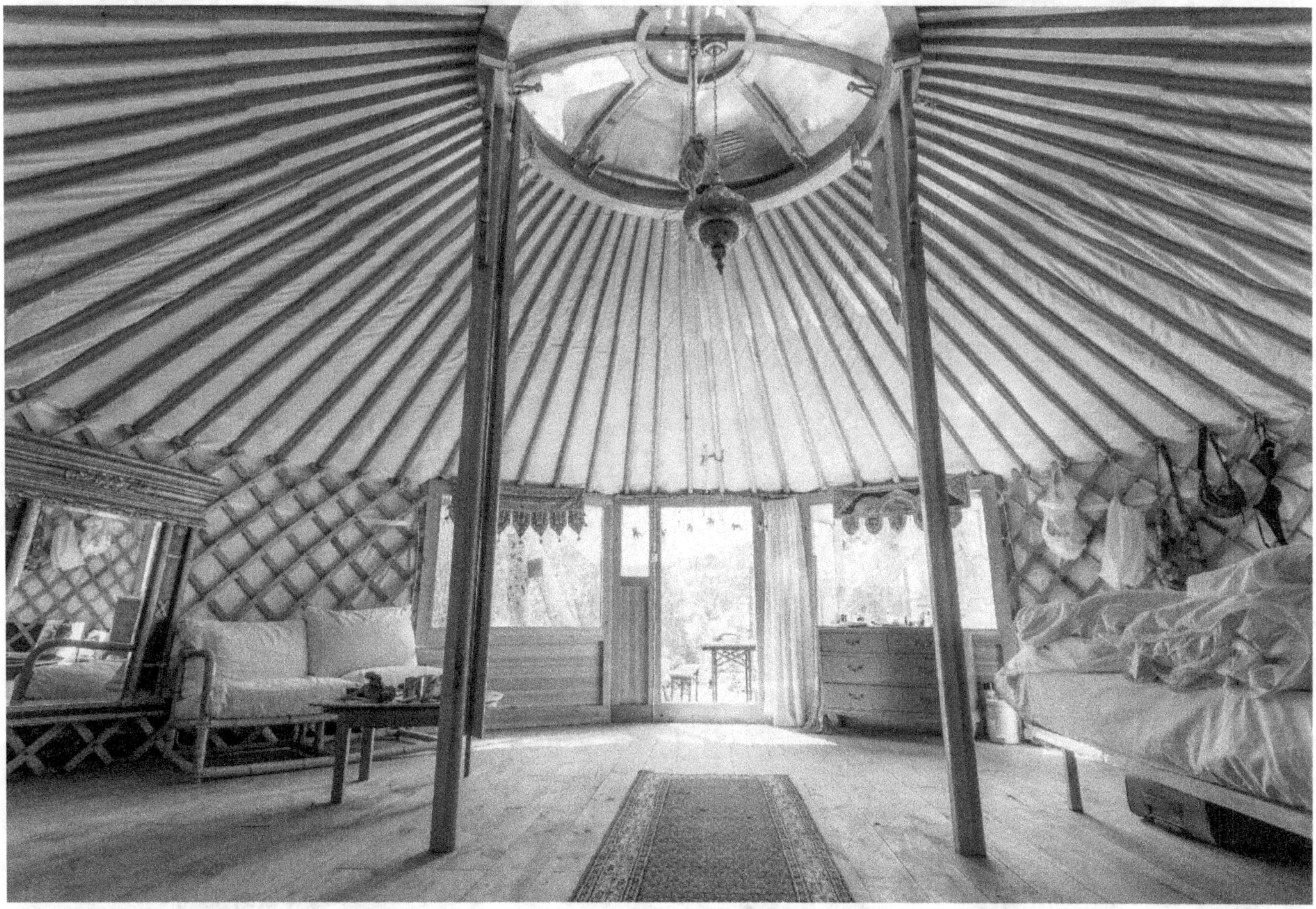

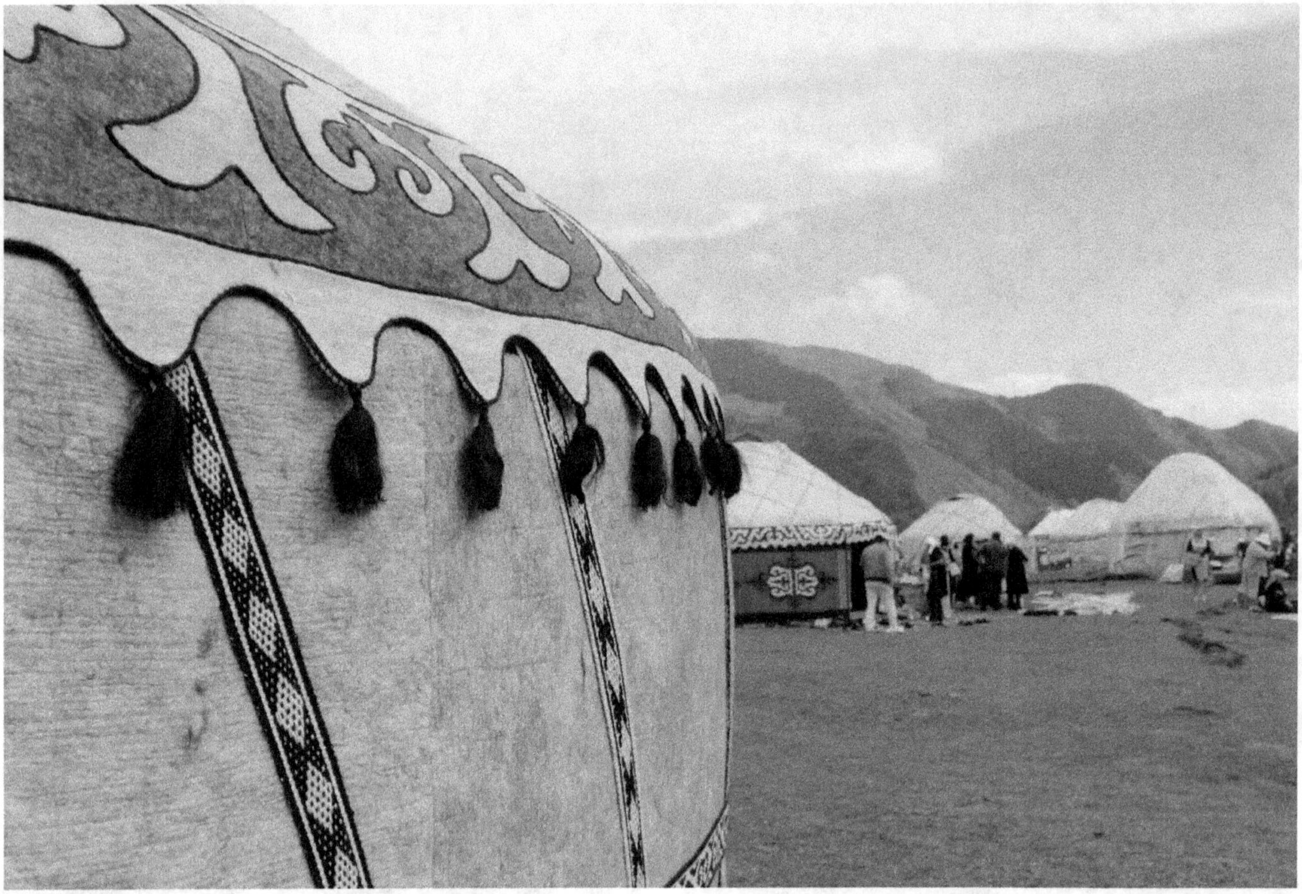

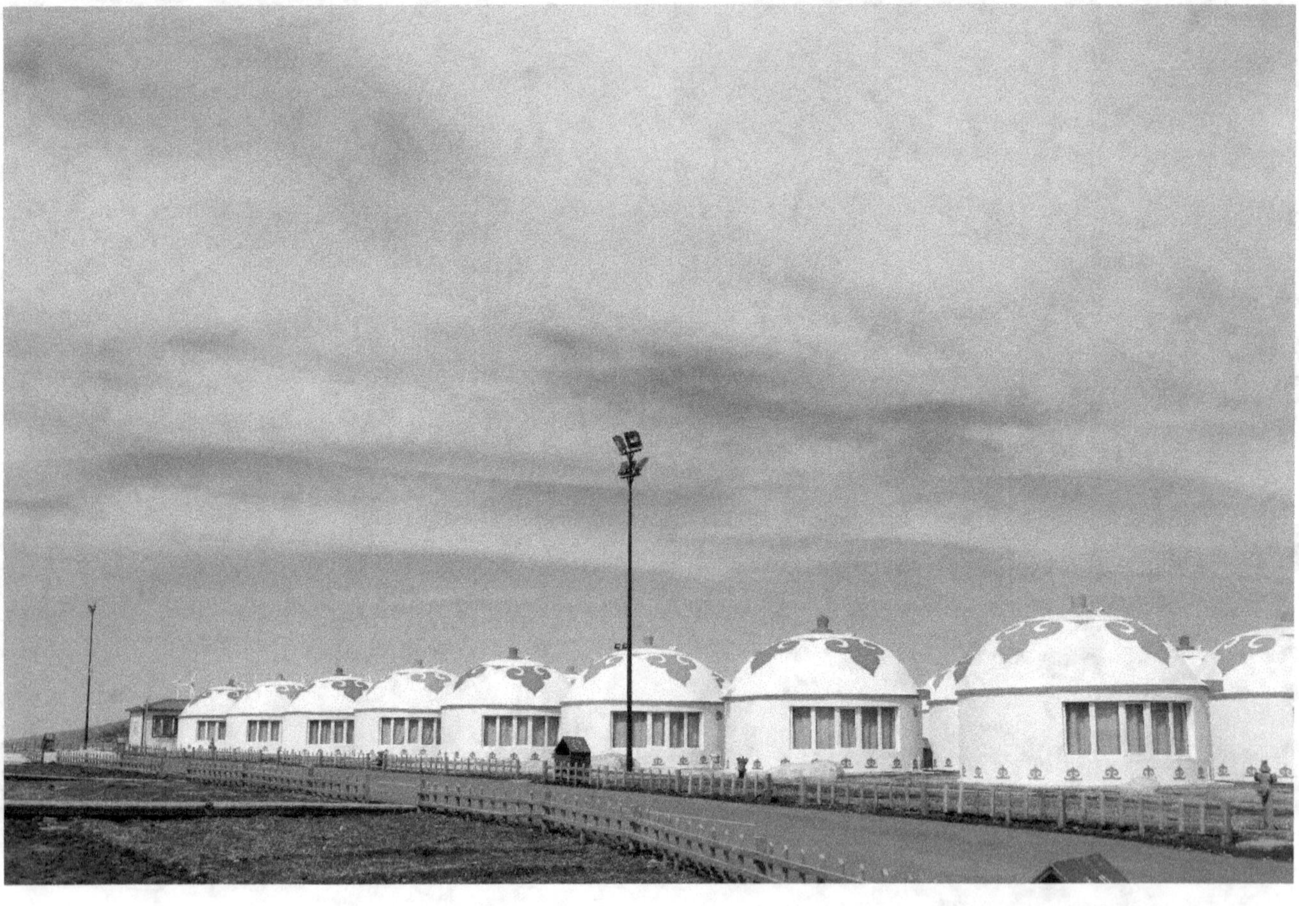

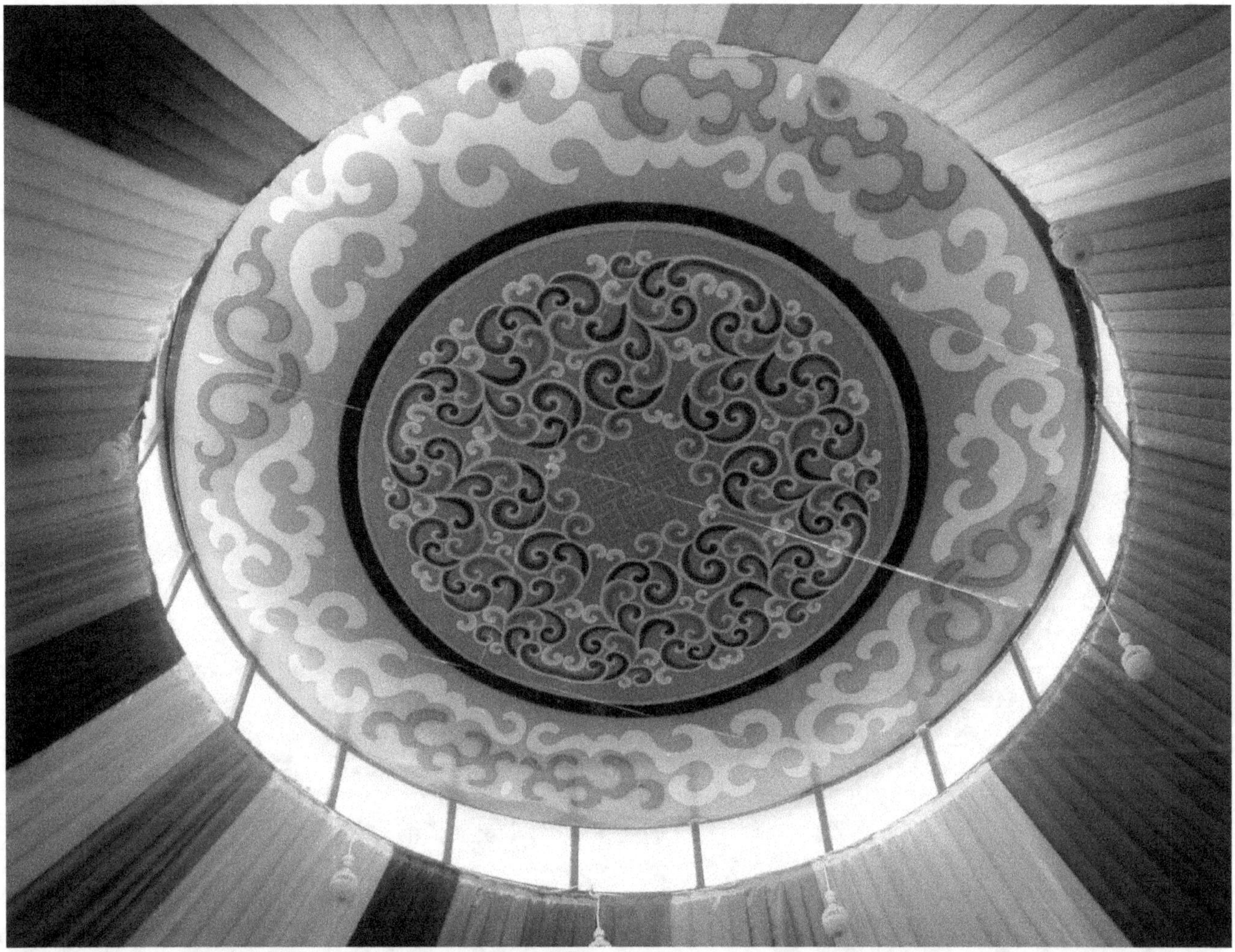

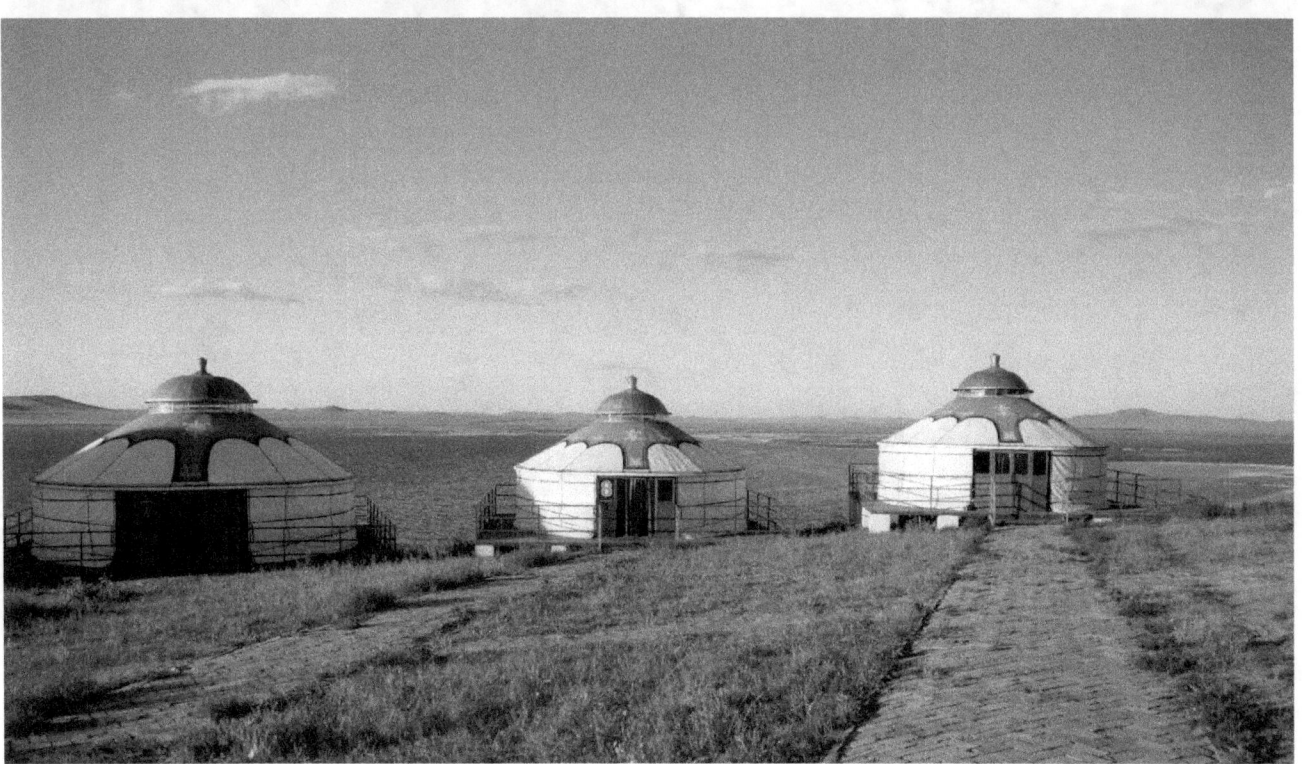

Tipis & Wigwams

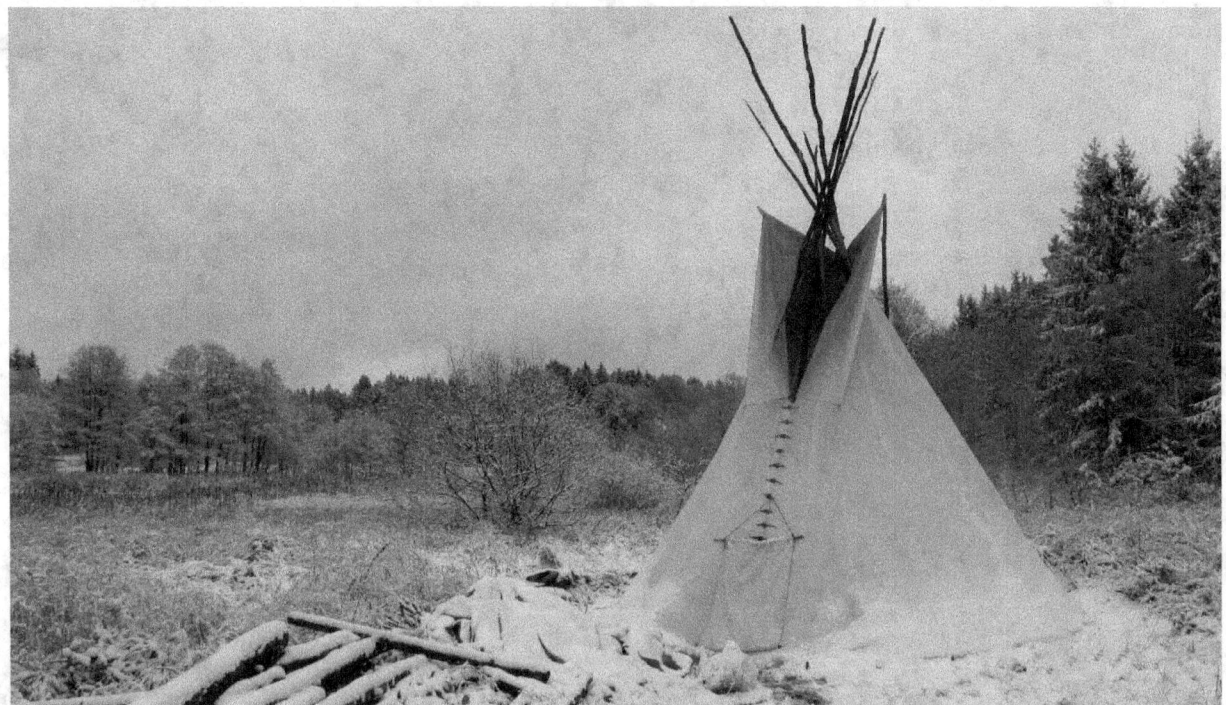

Tipis built by Native Peoples in North America

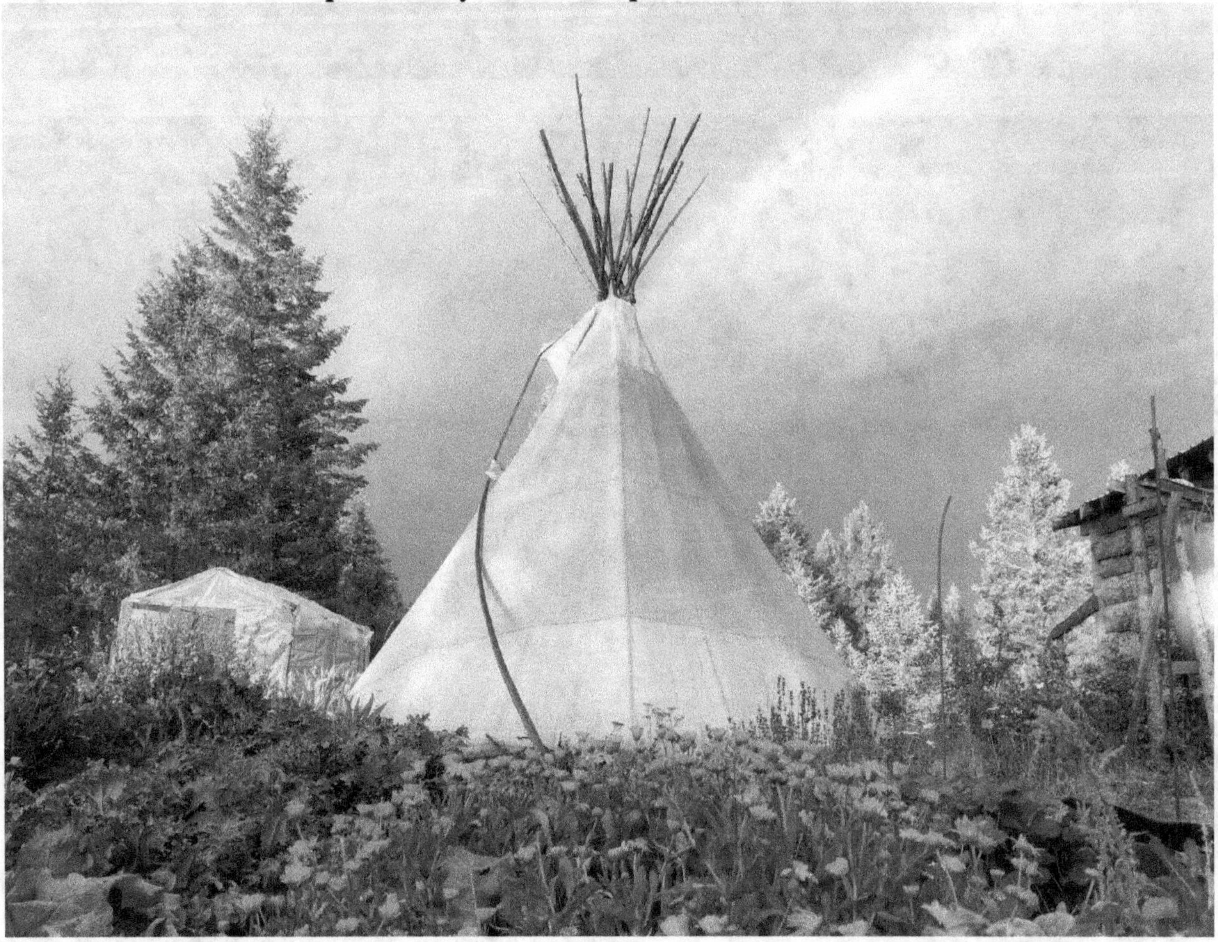

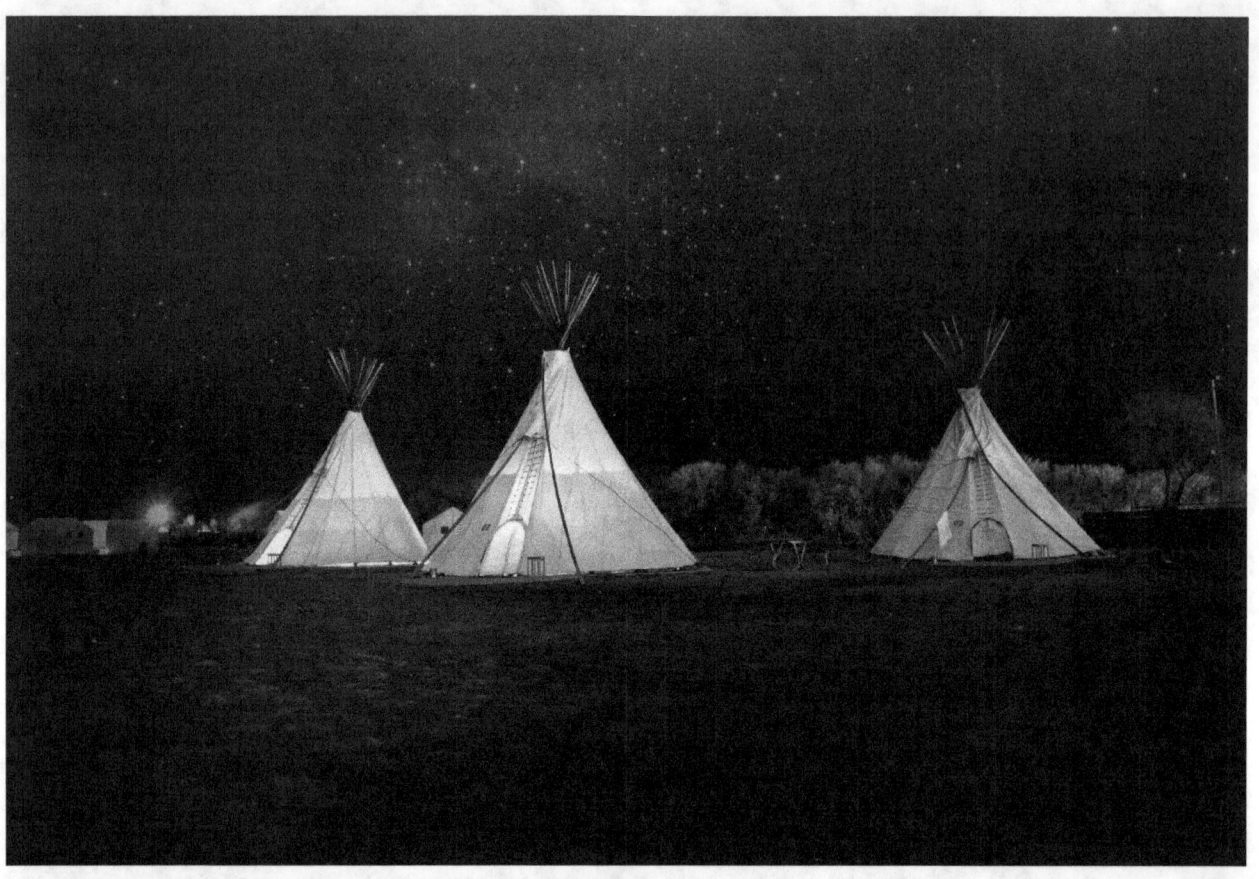

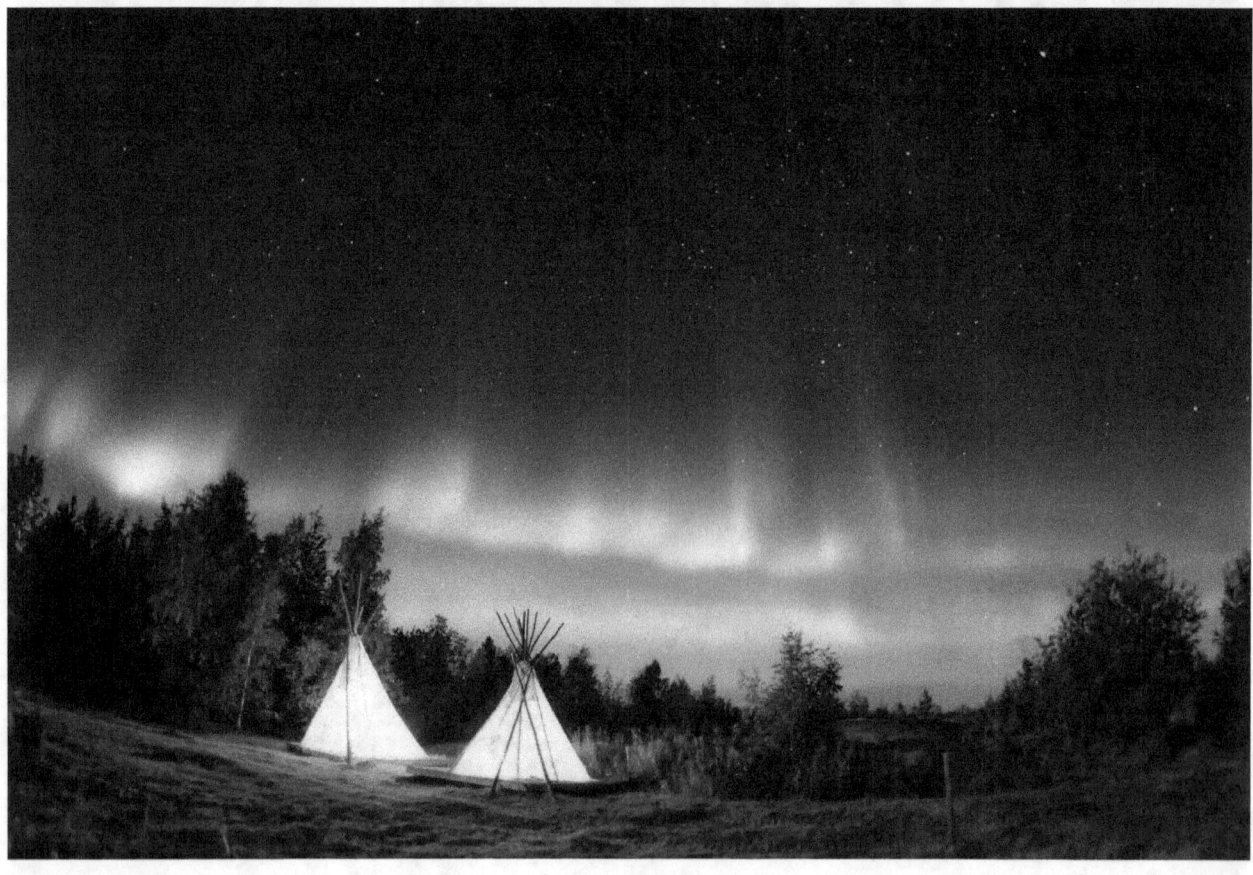

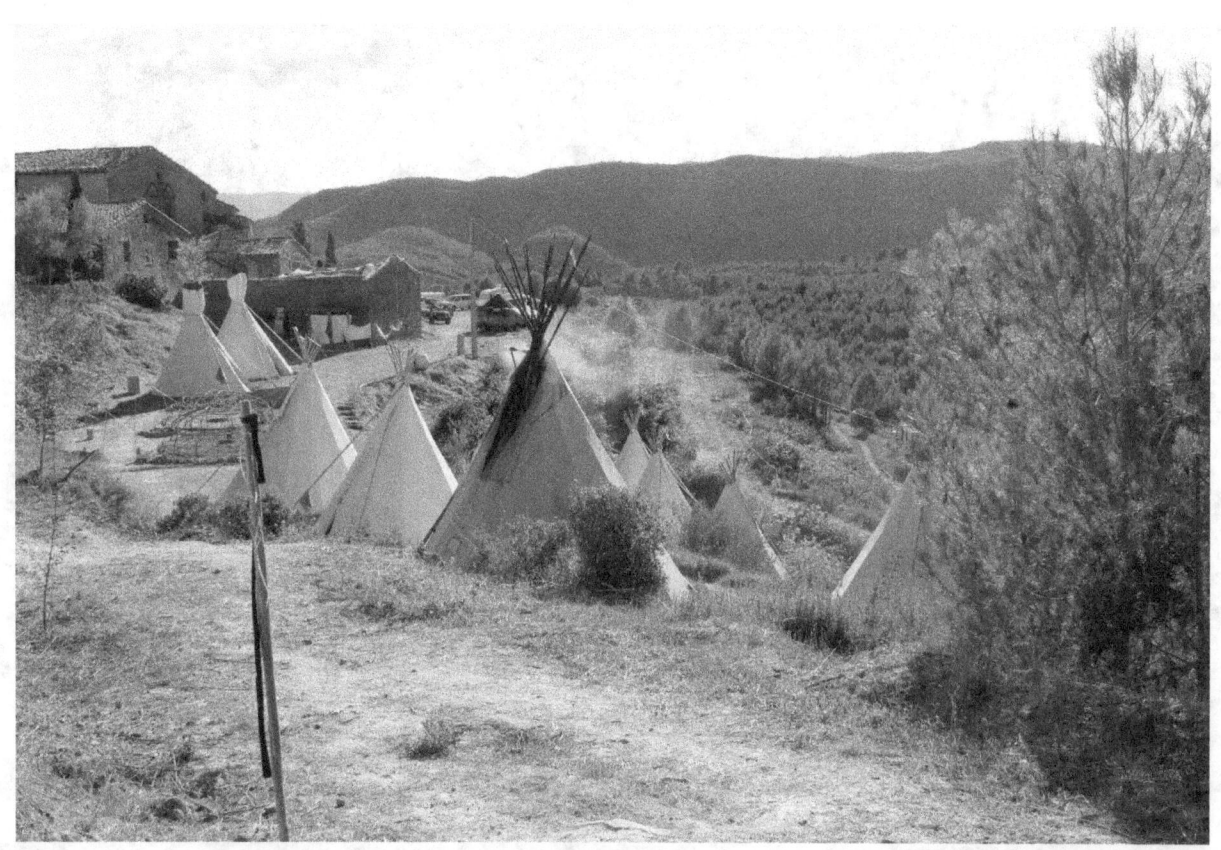

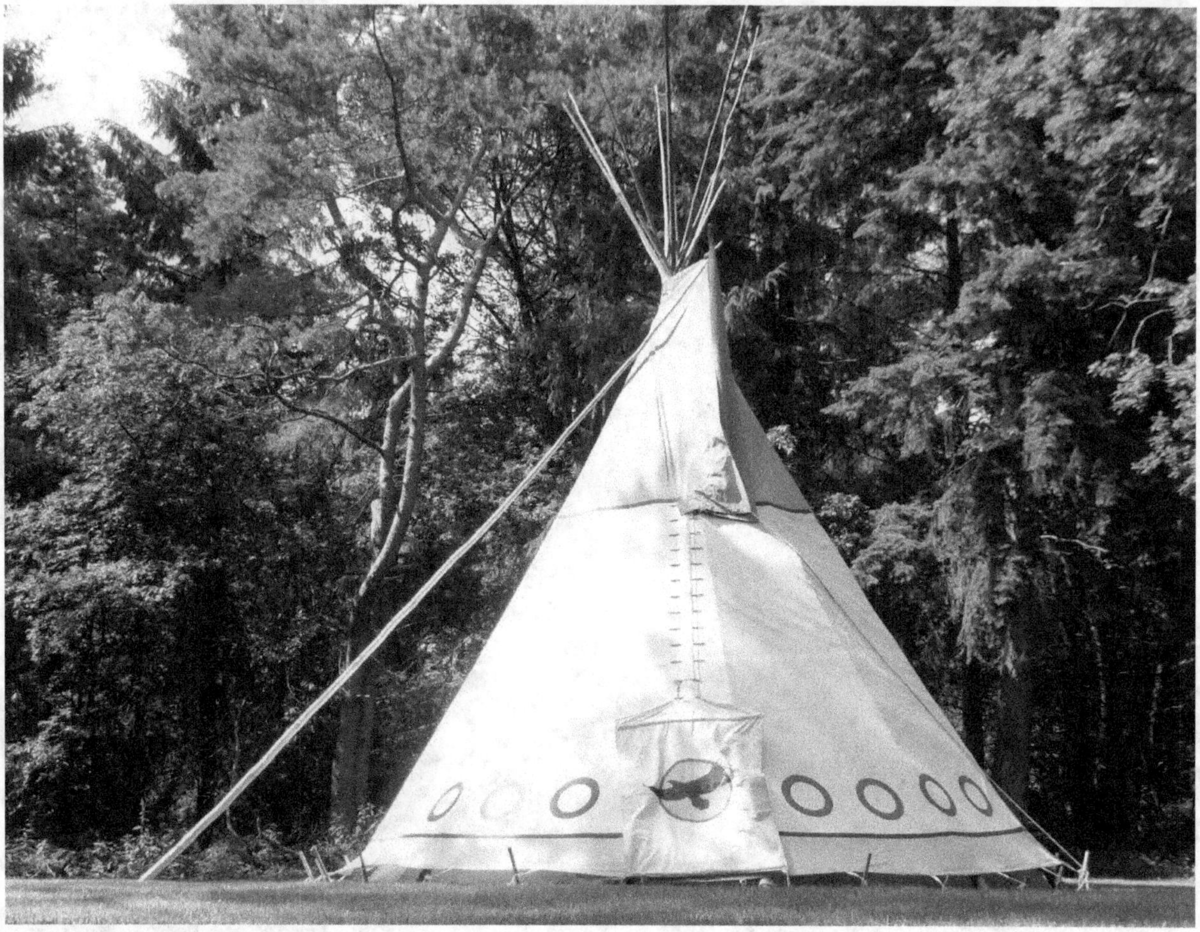

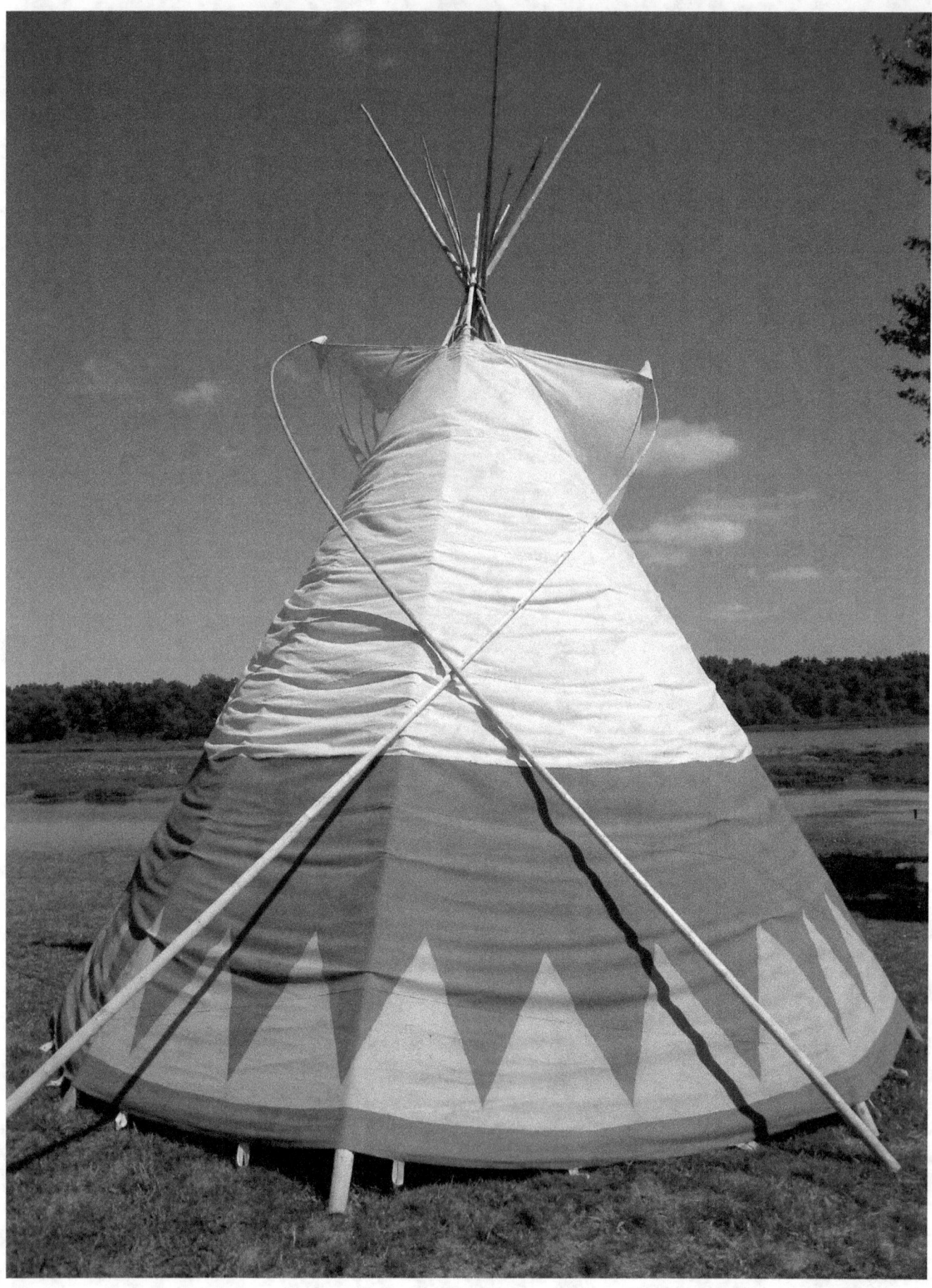

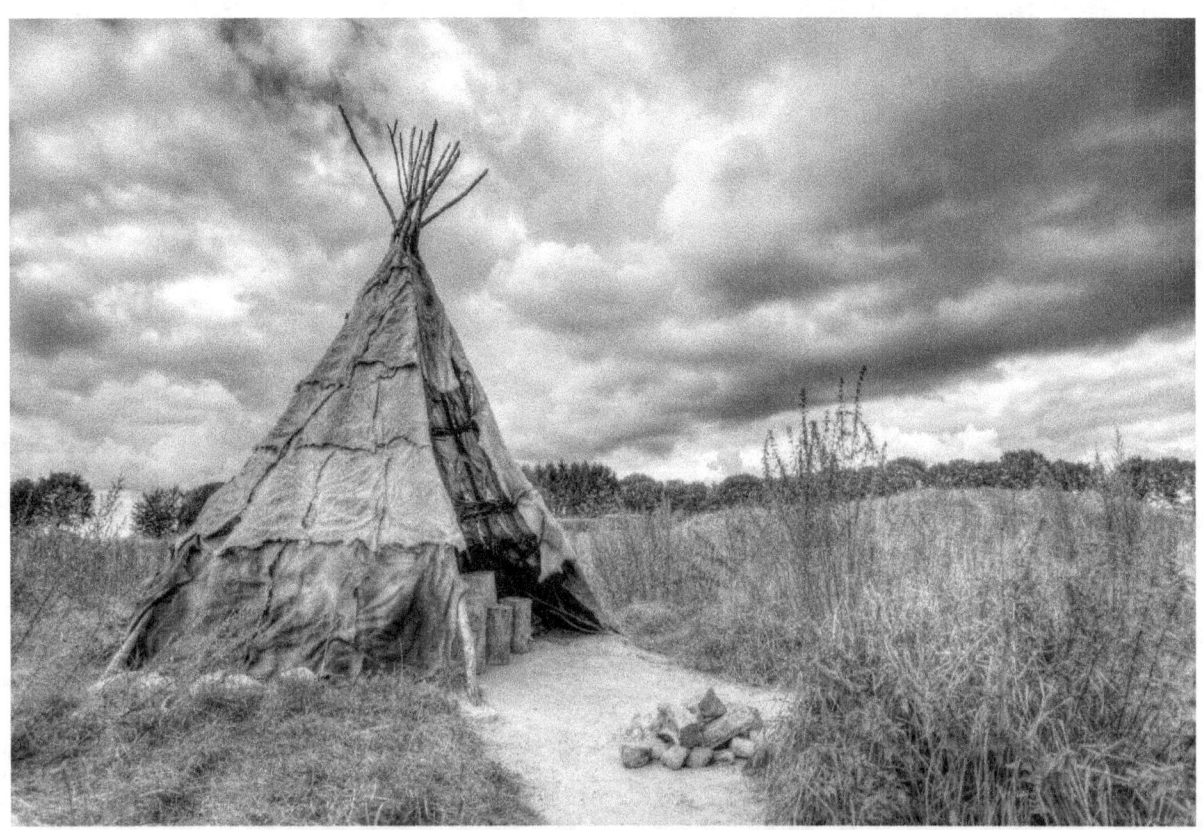

Wigwam home of the Northeastern Tribes

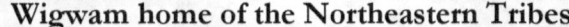

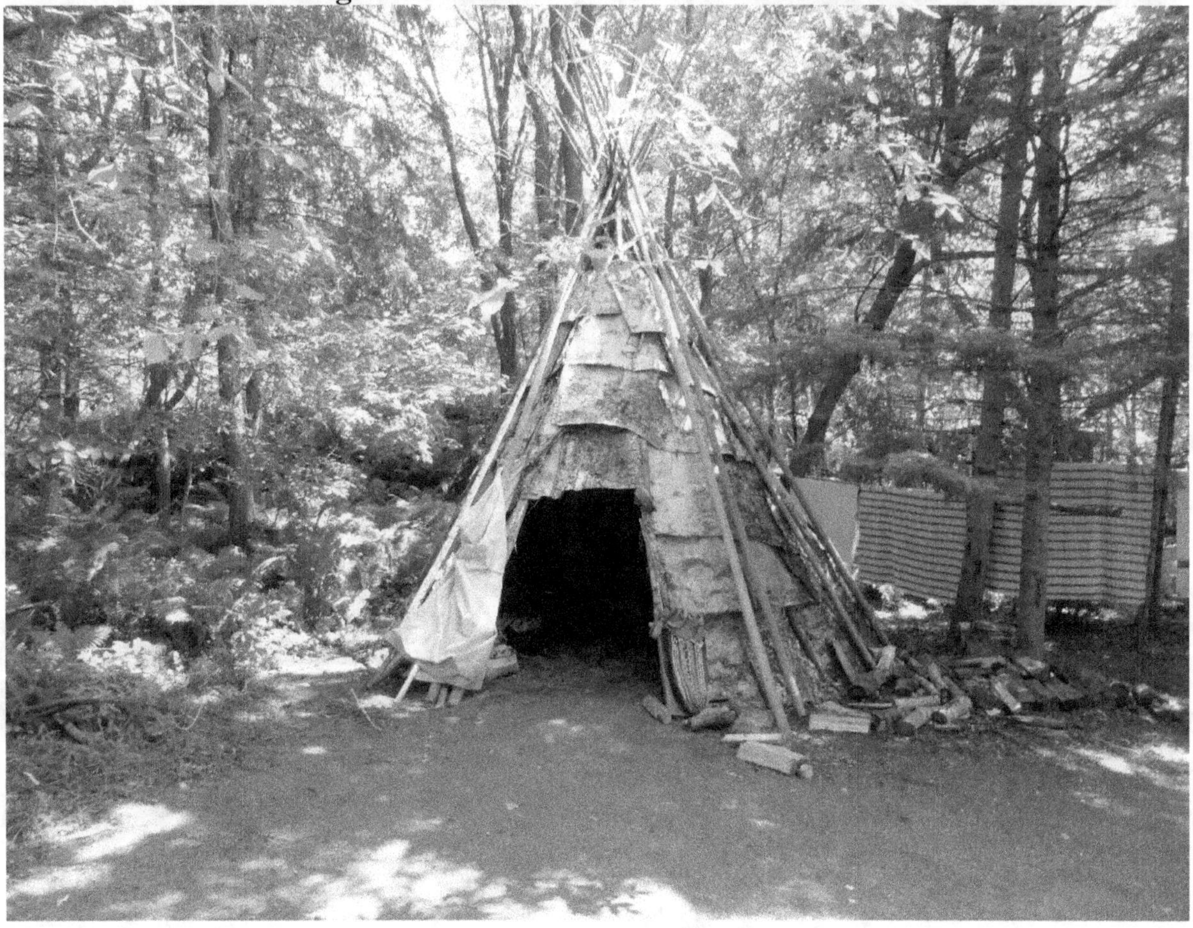

9 PLAY

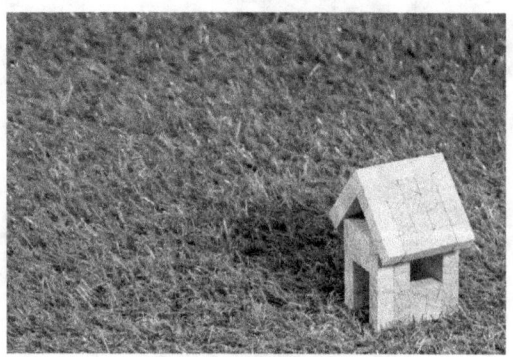

Playhouses and treehouses

Playhouses

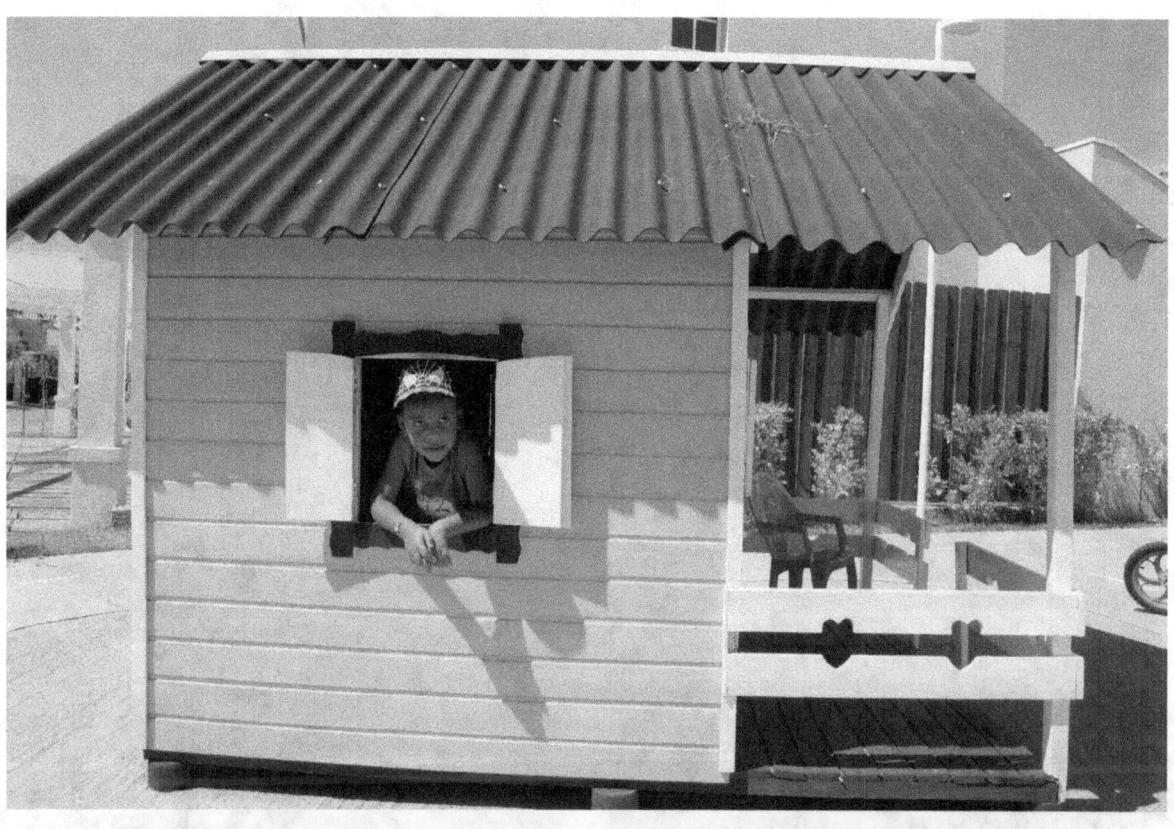

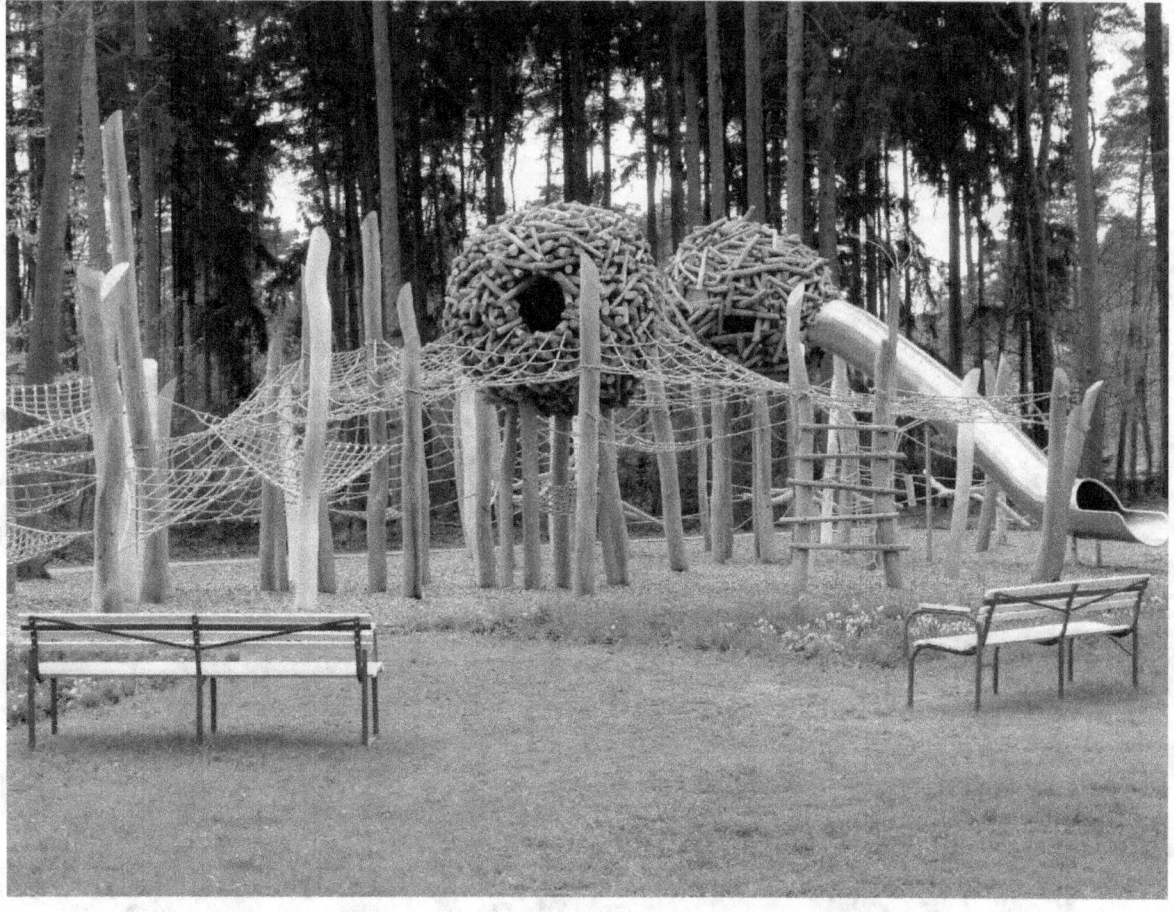

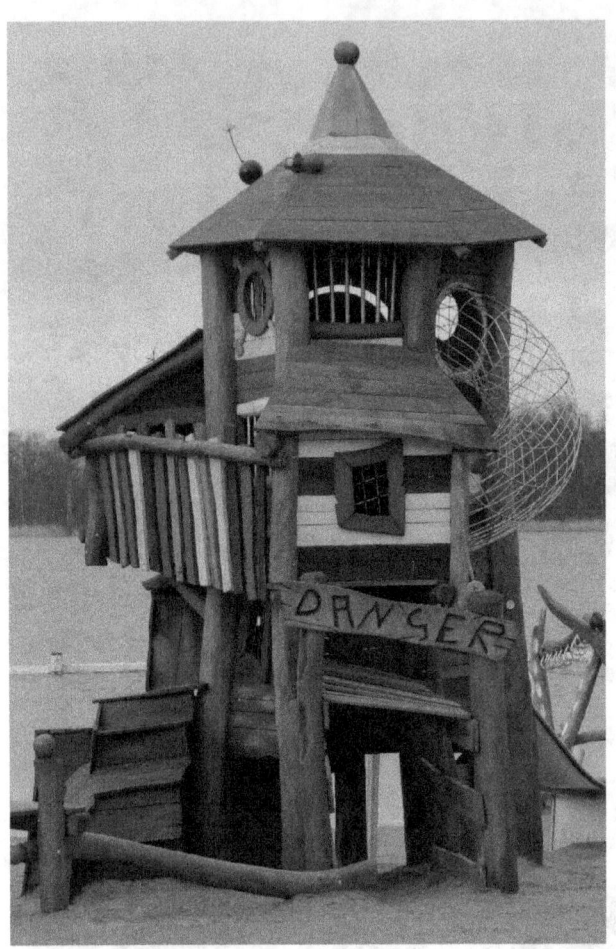
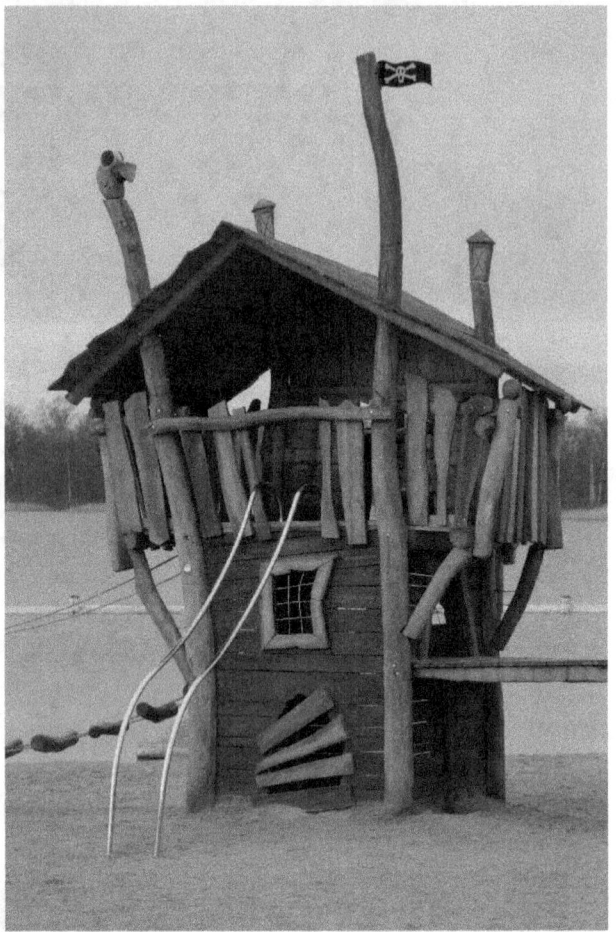
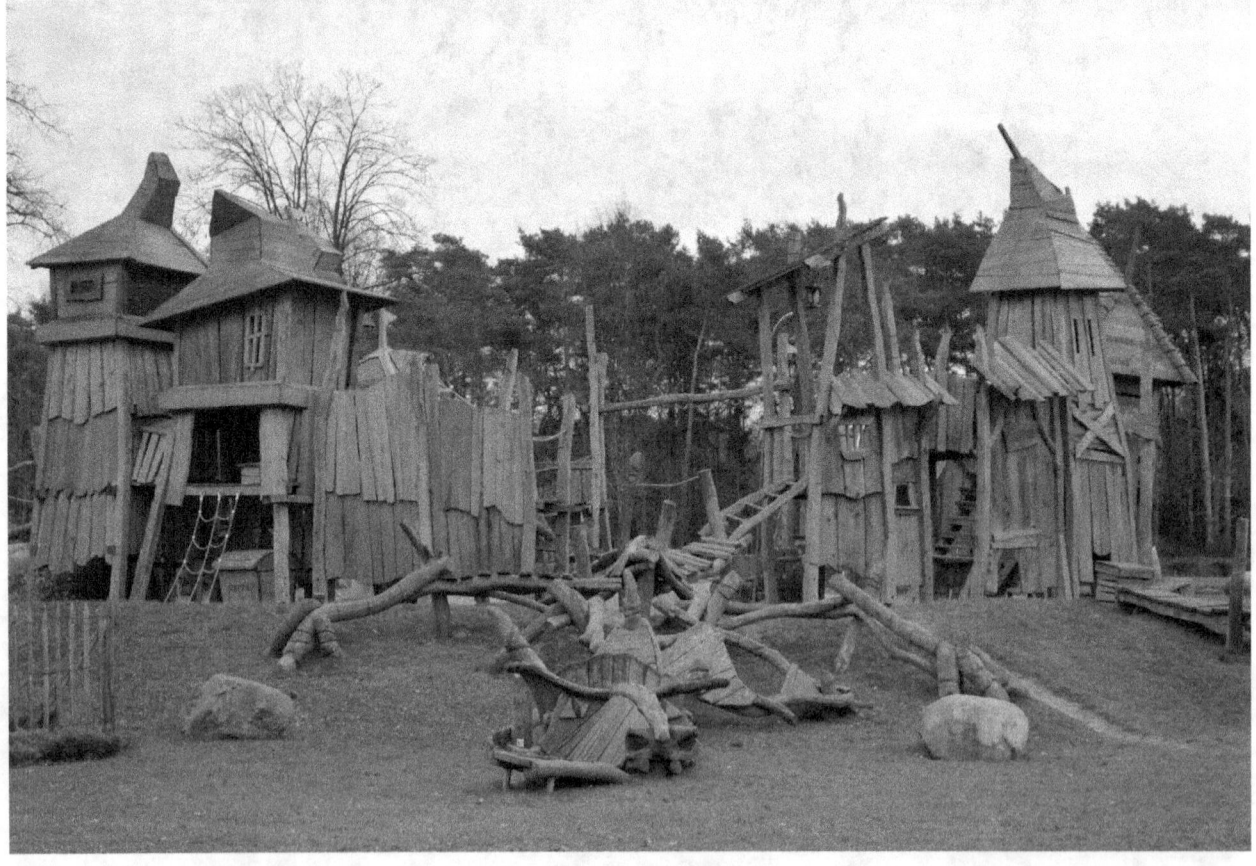

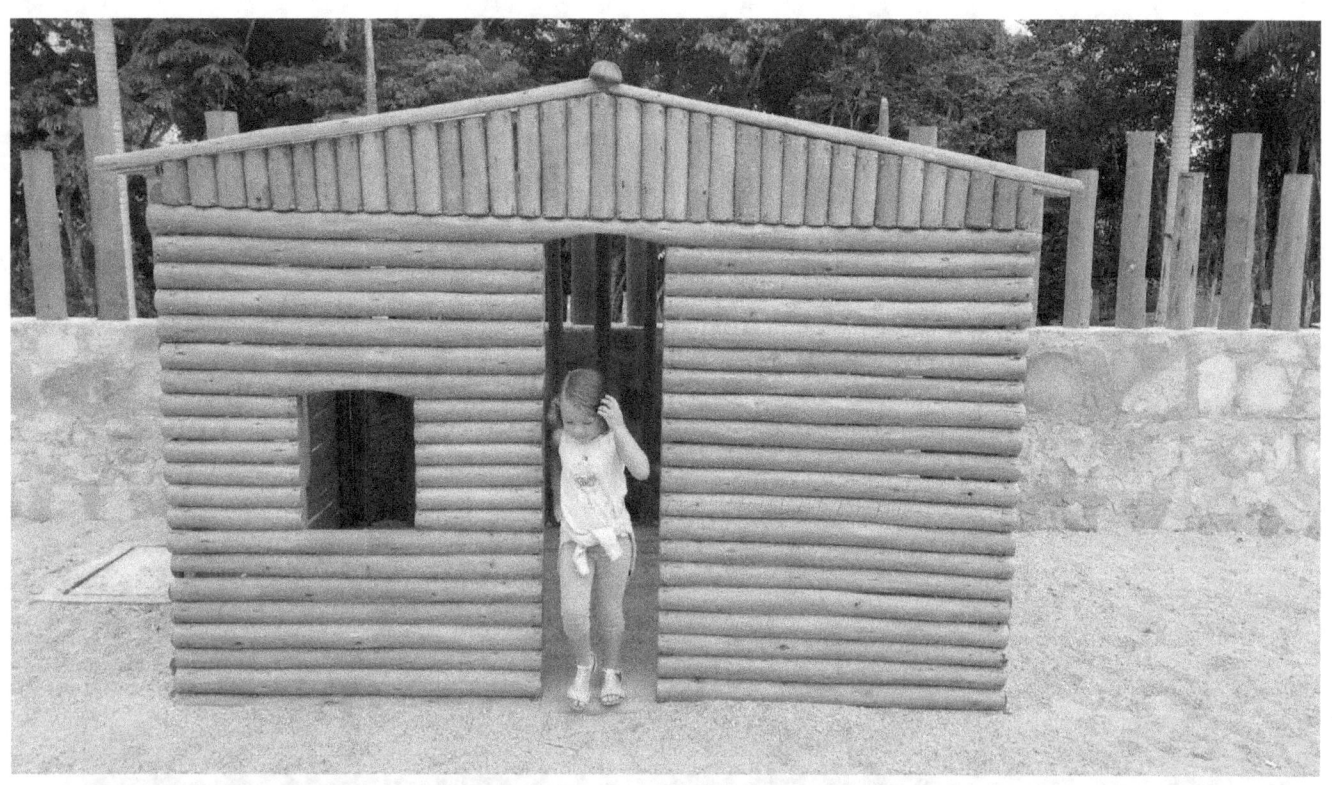

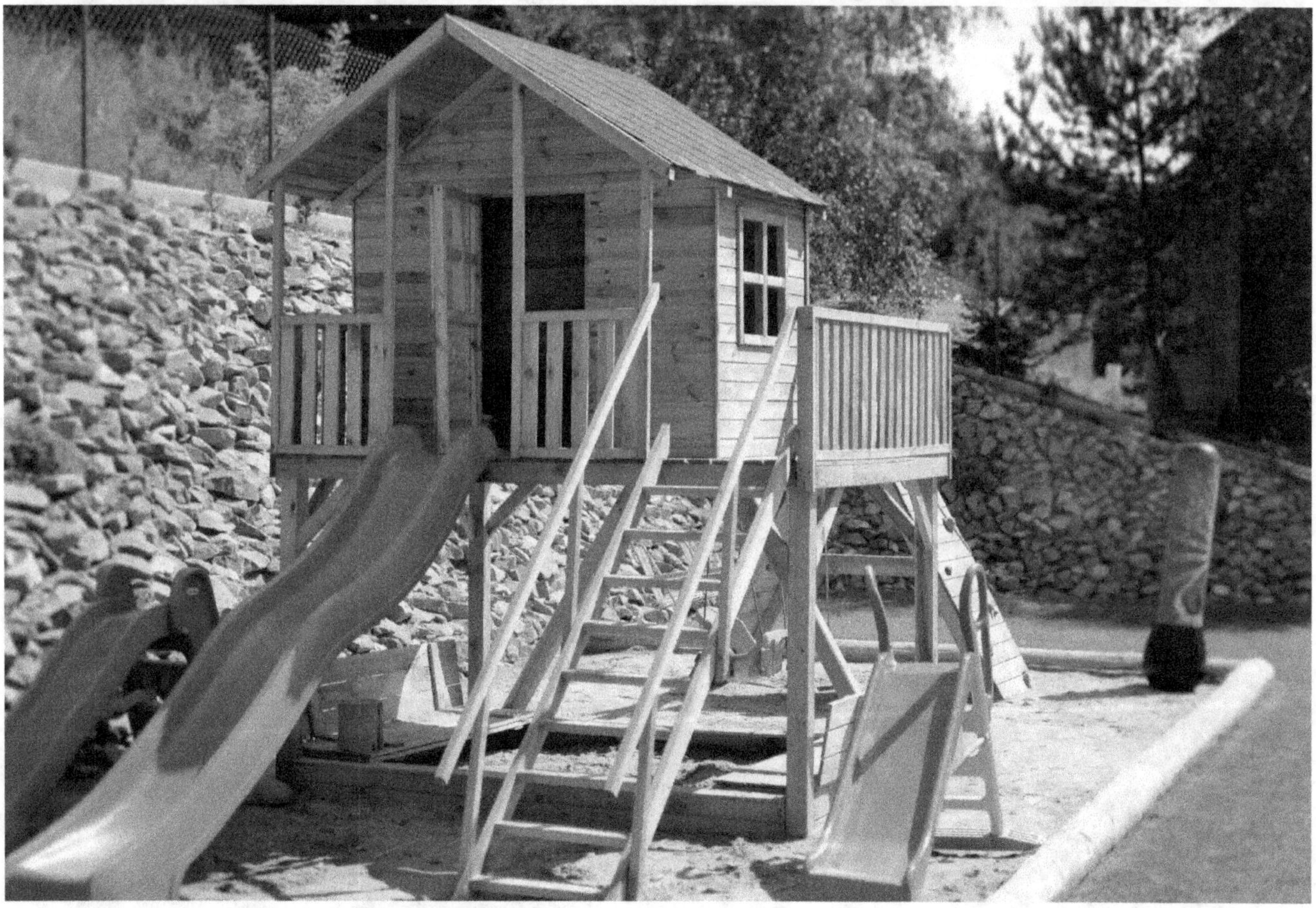

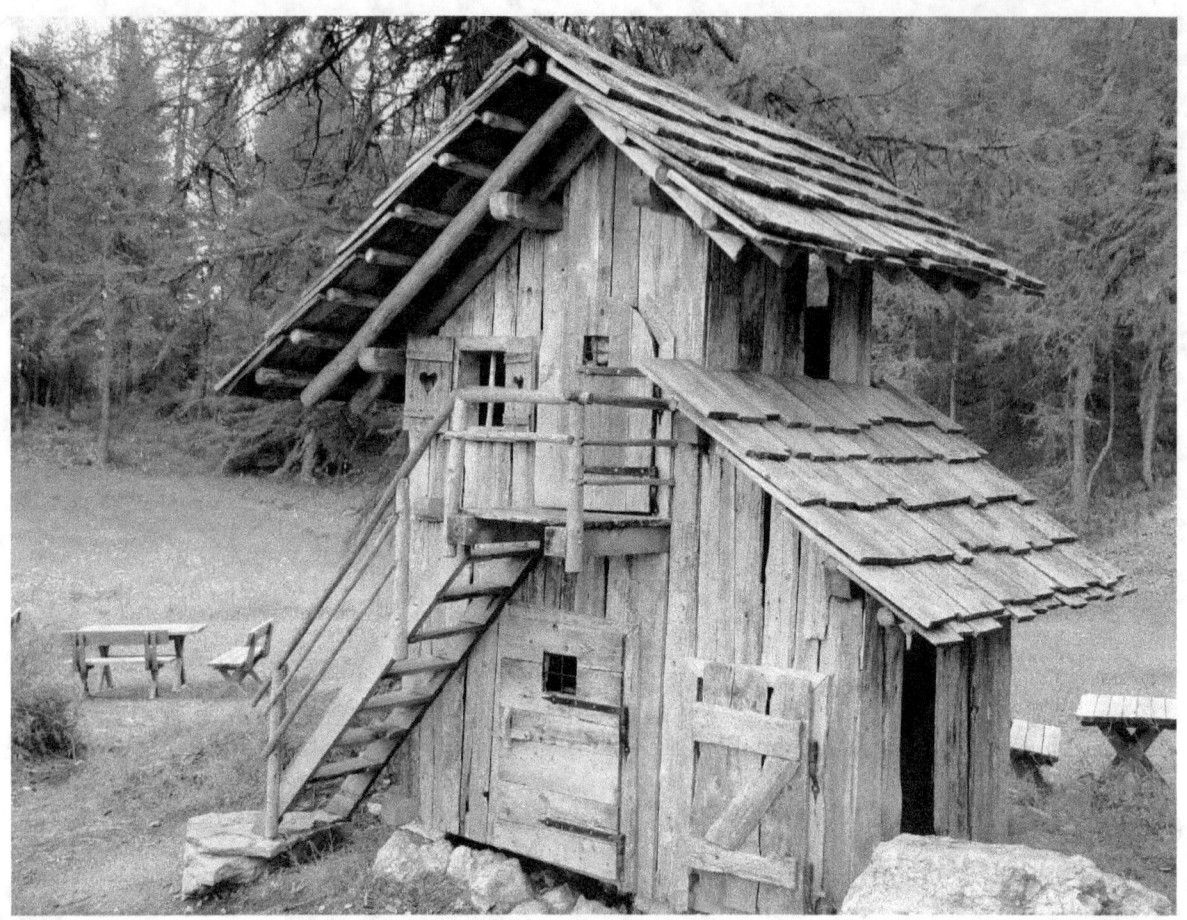

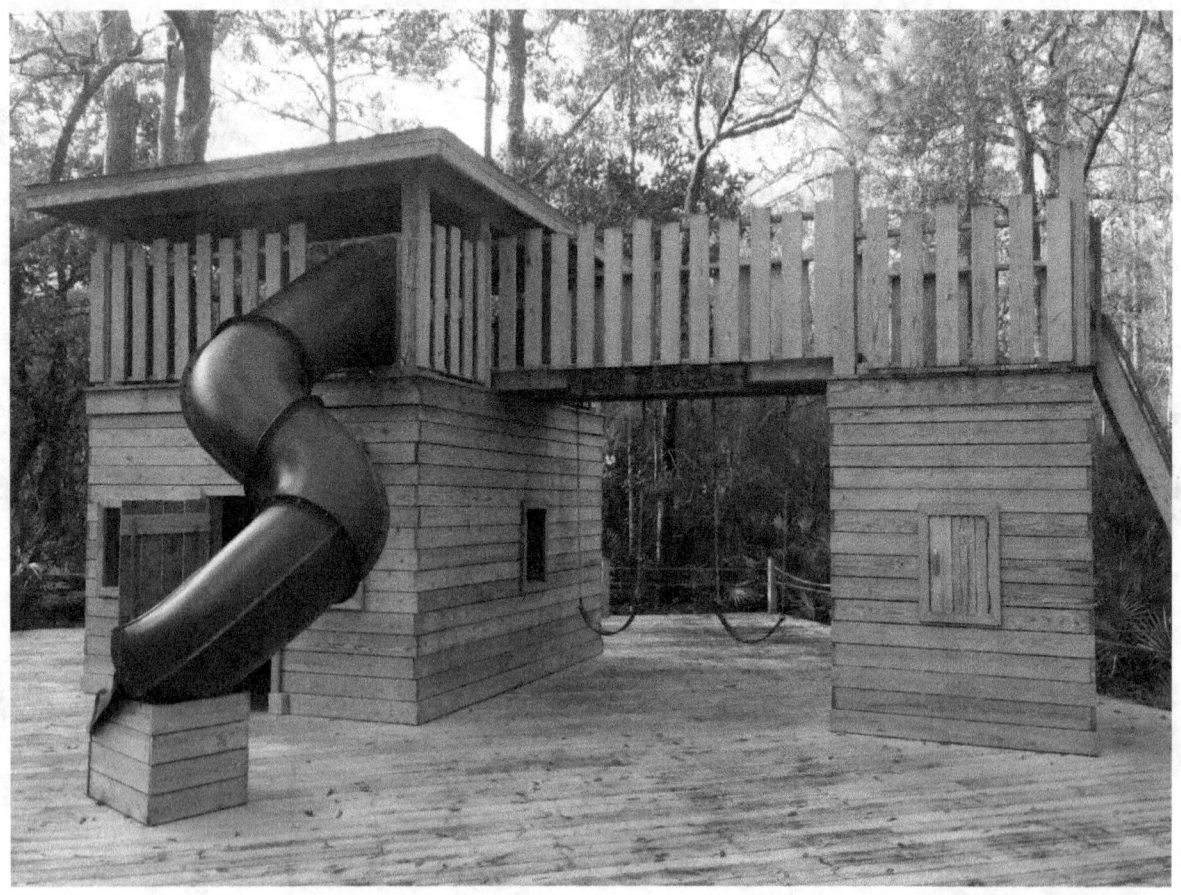

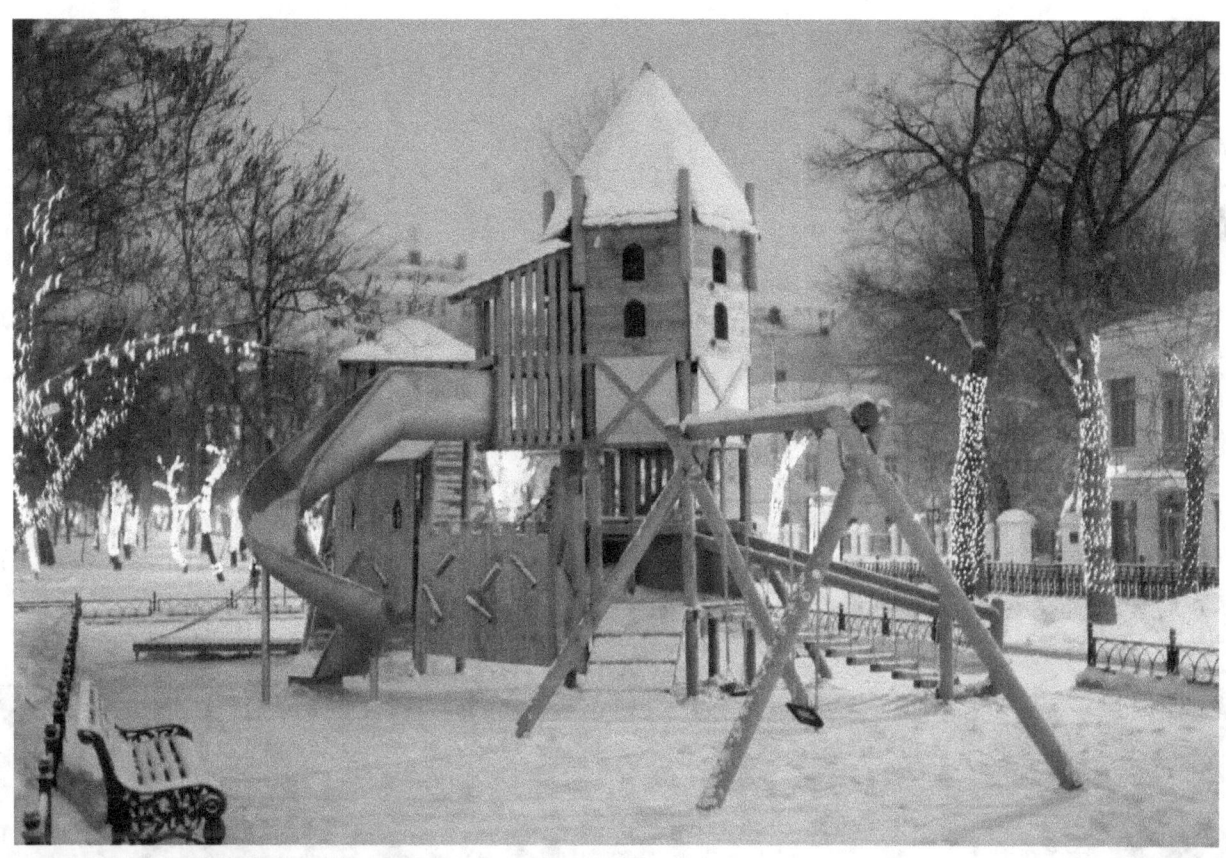

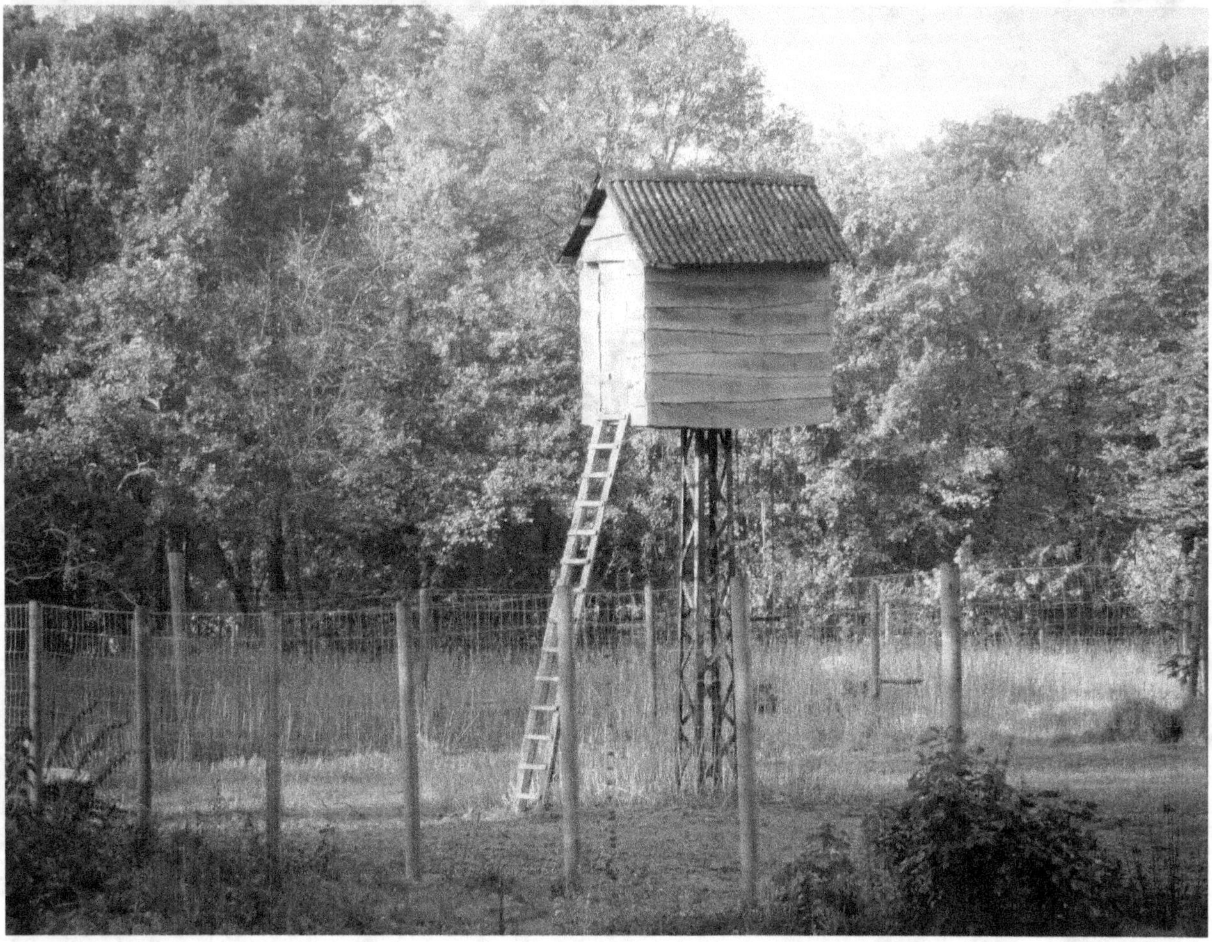

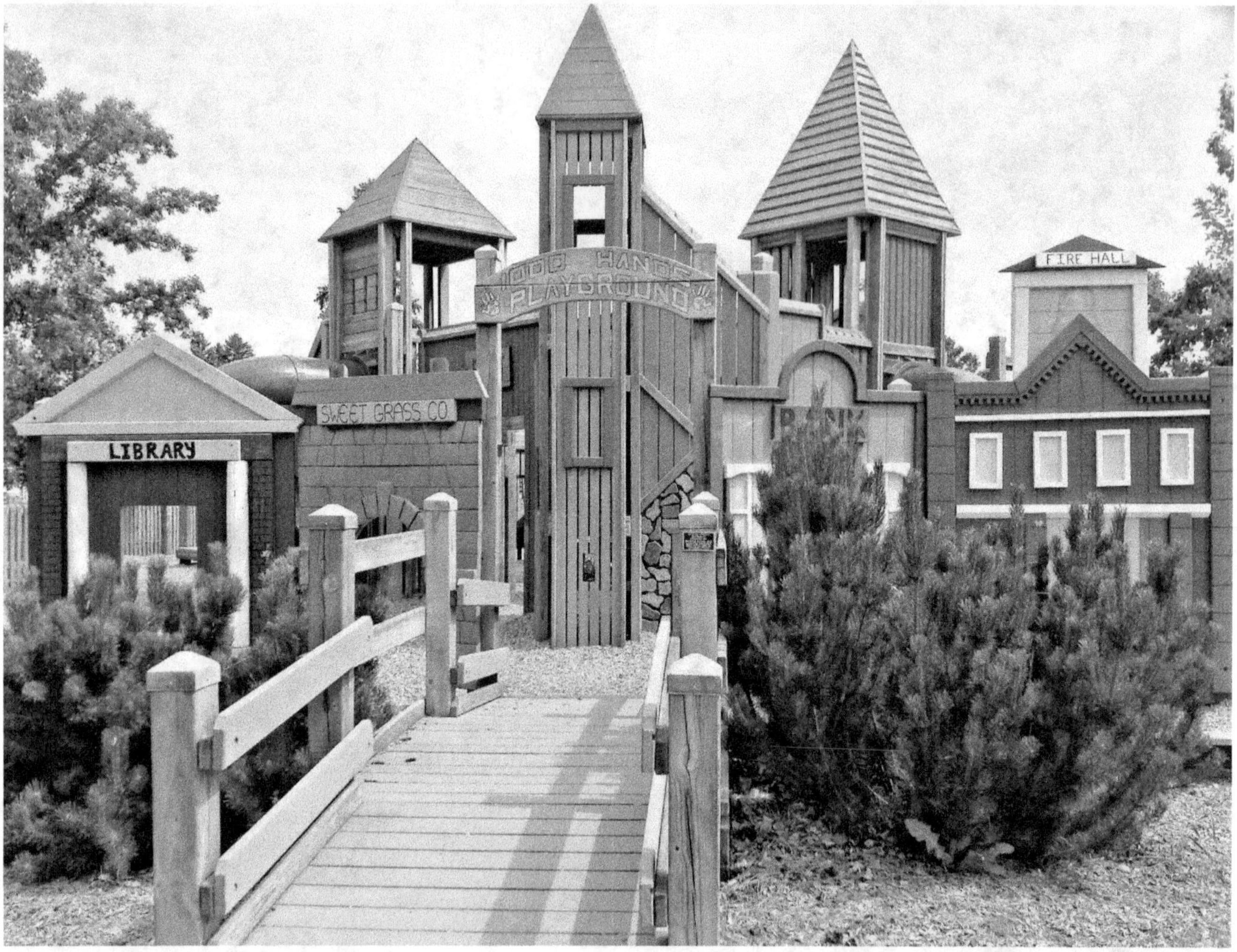

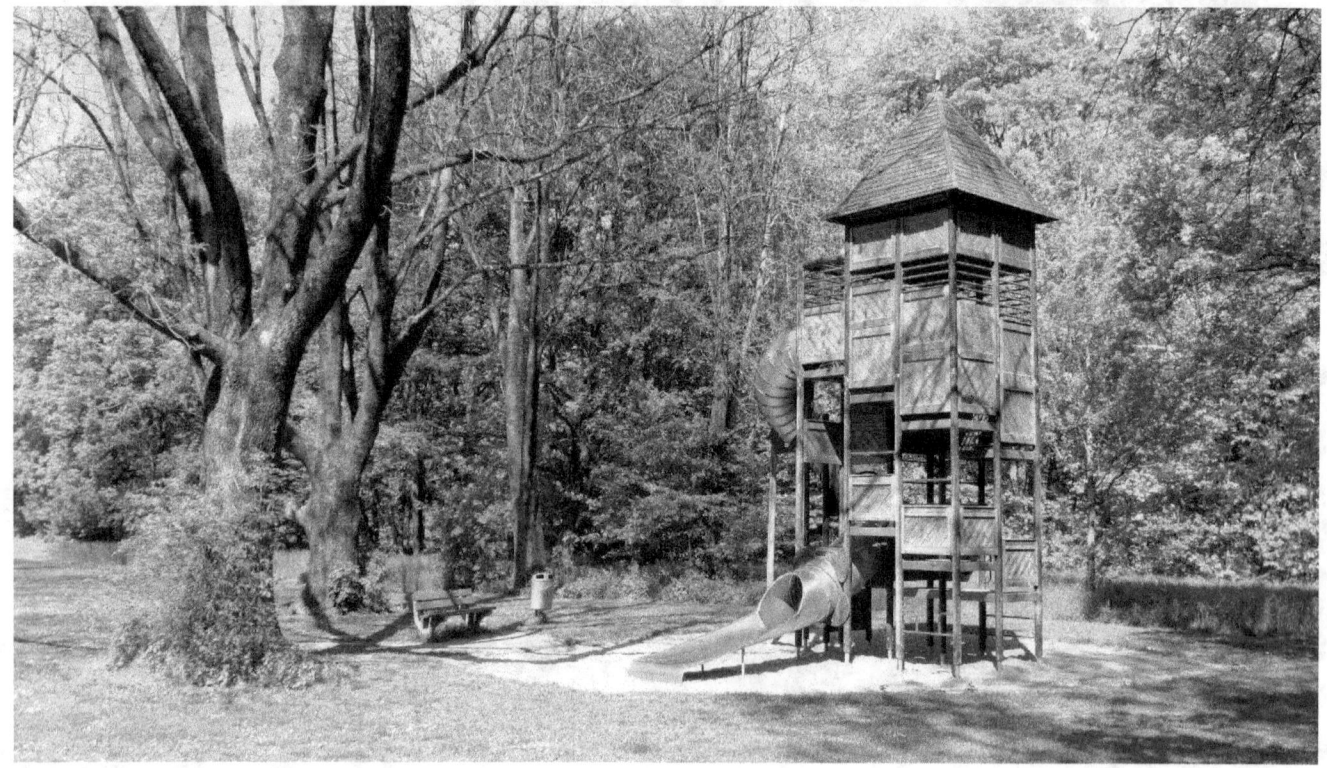

Treehouses

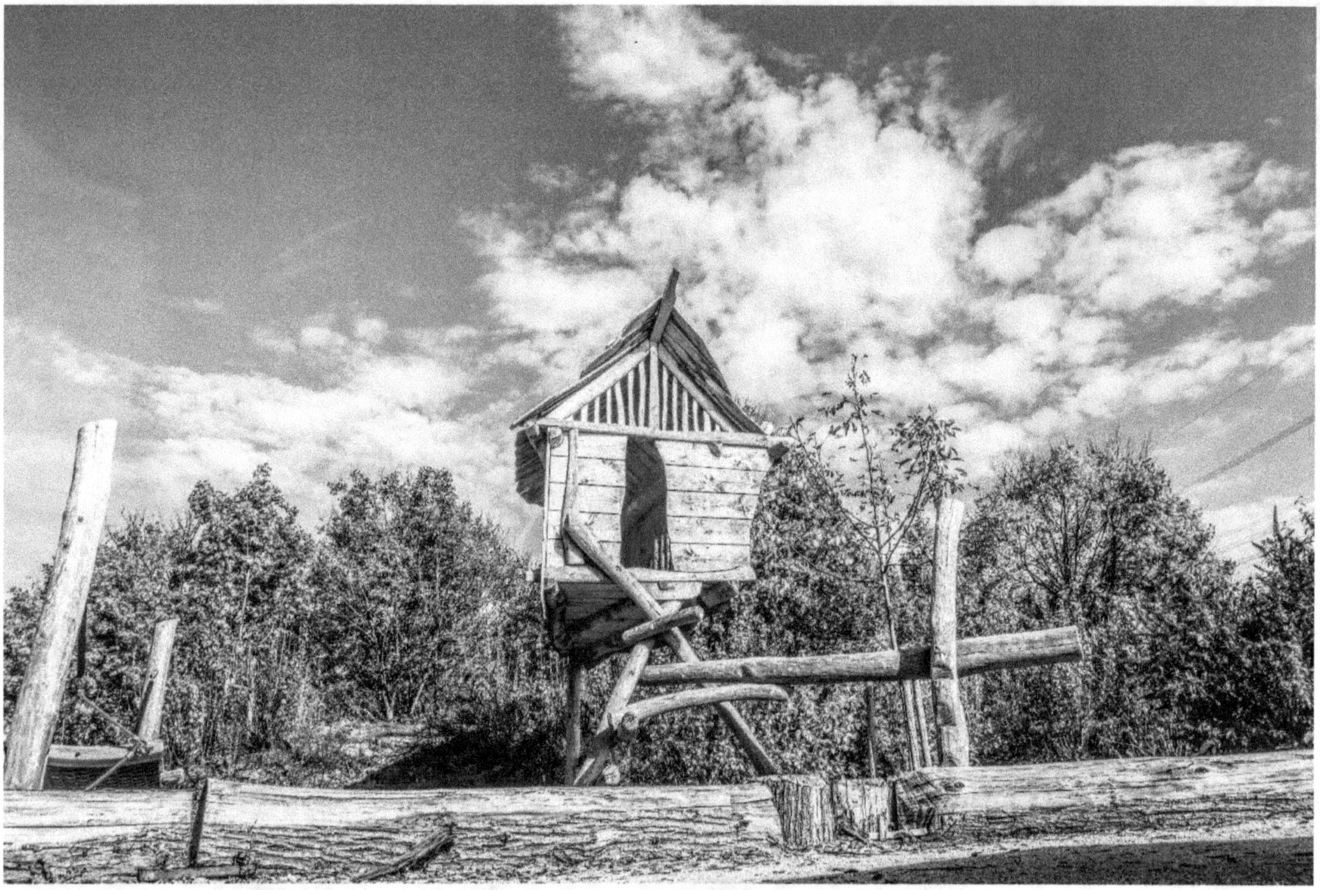

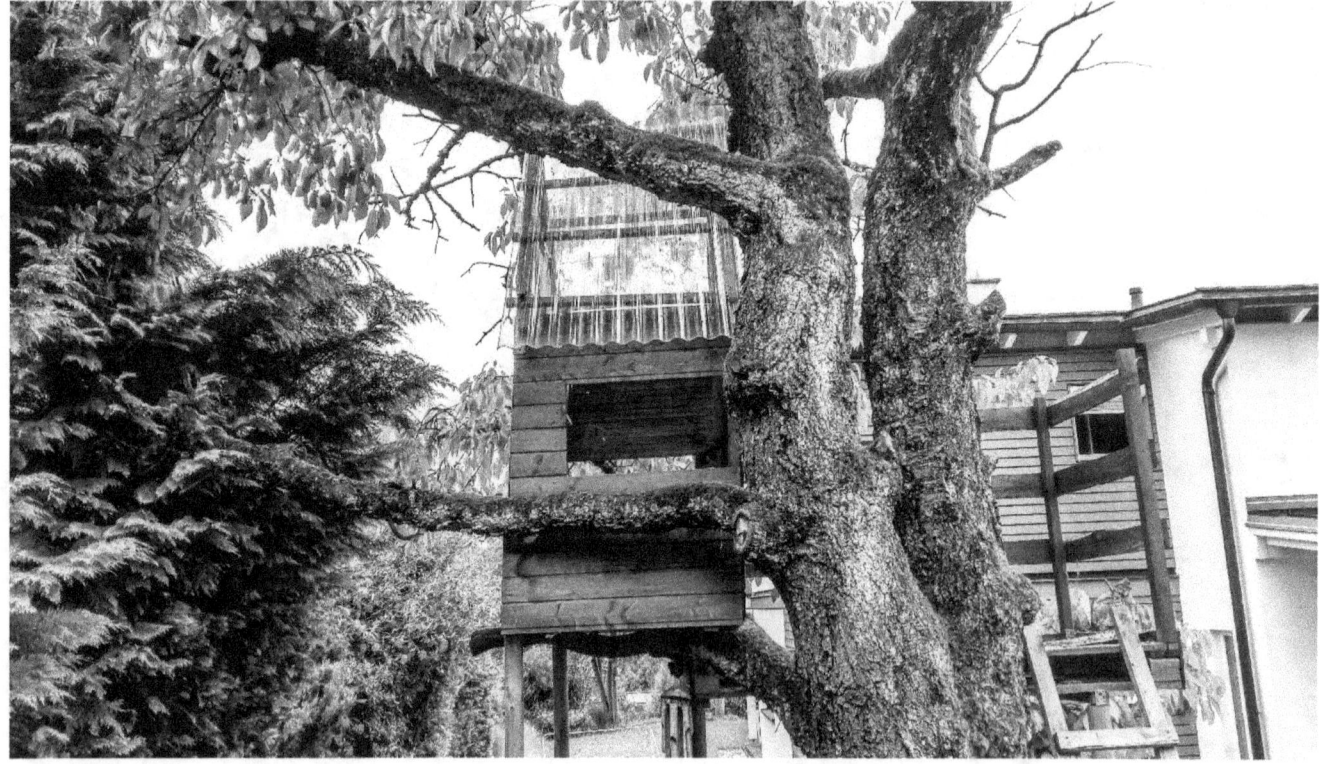

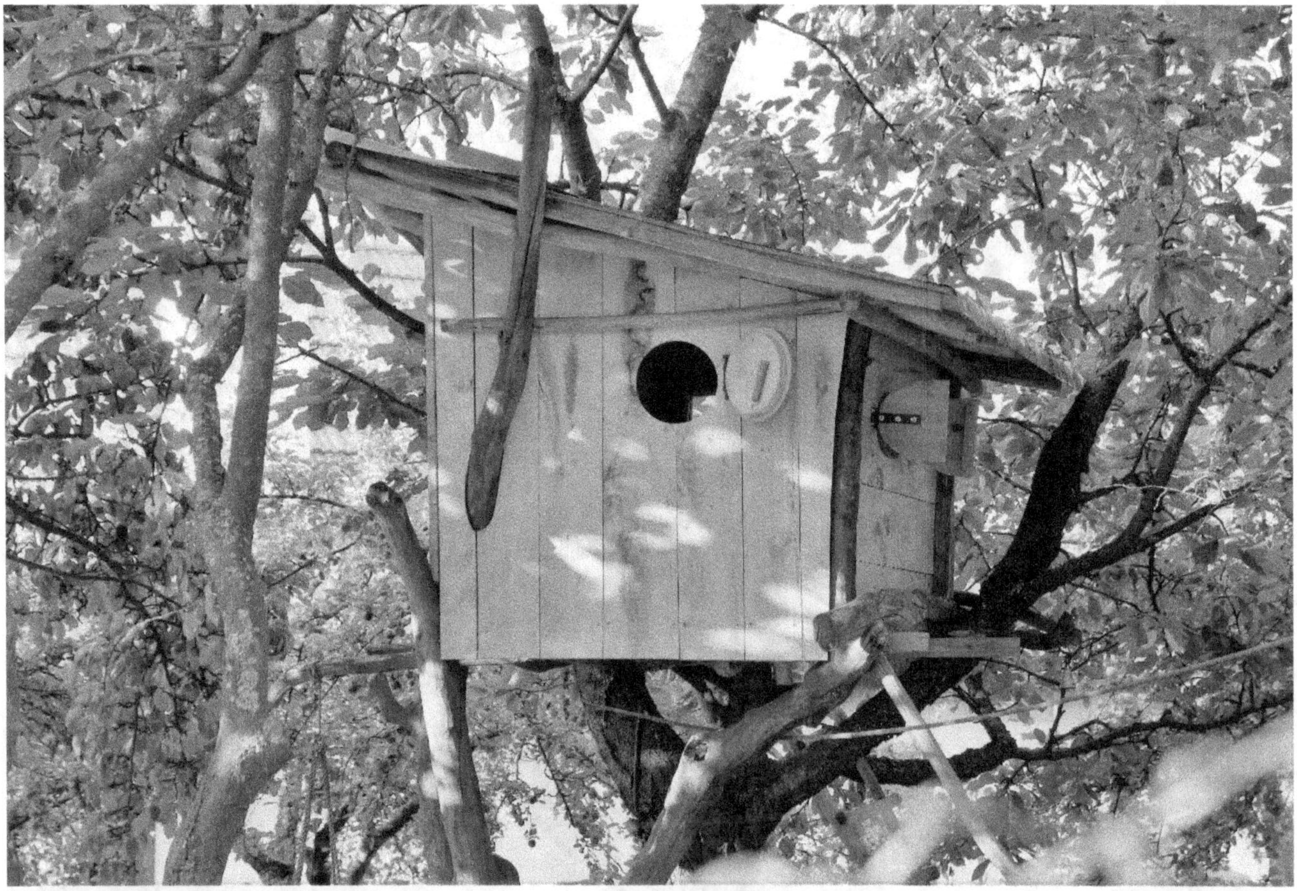

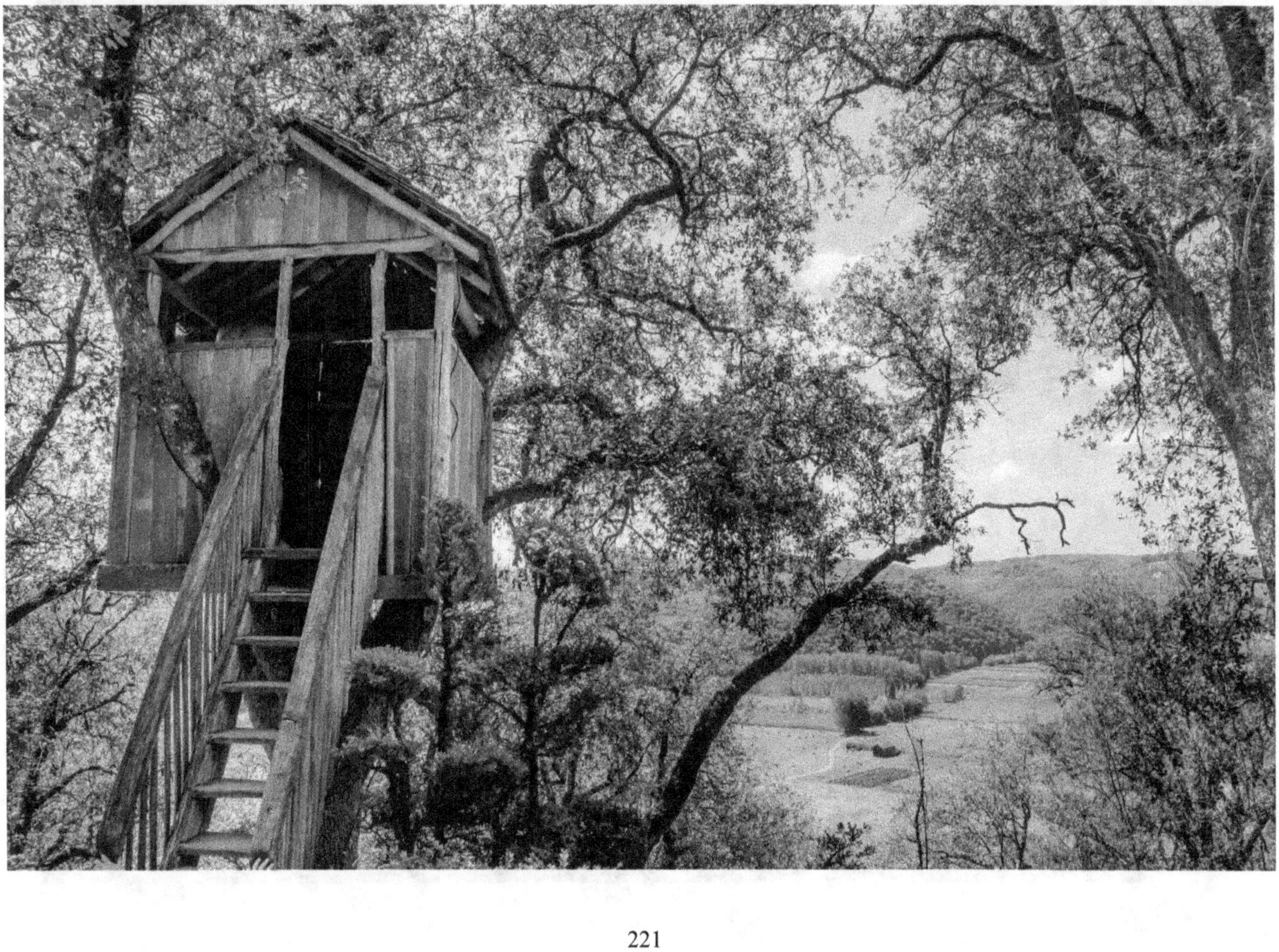

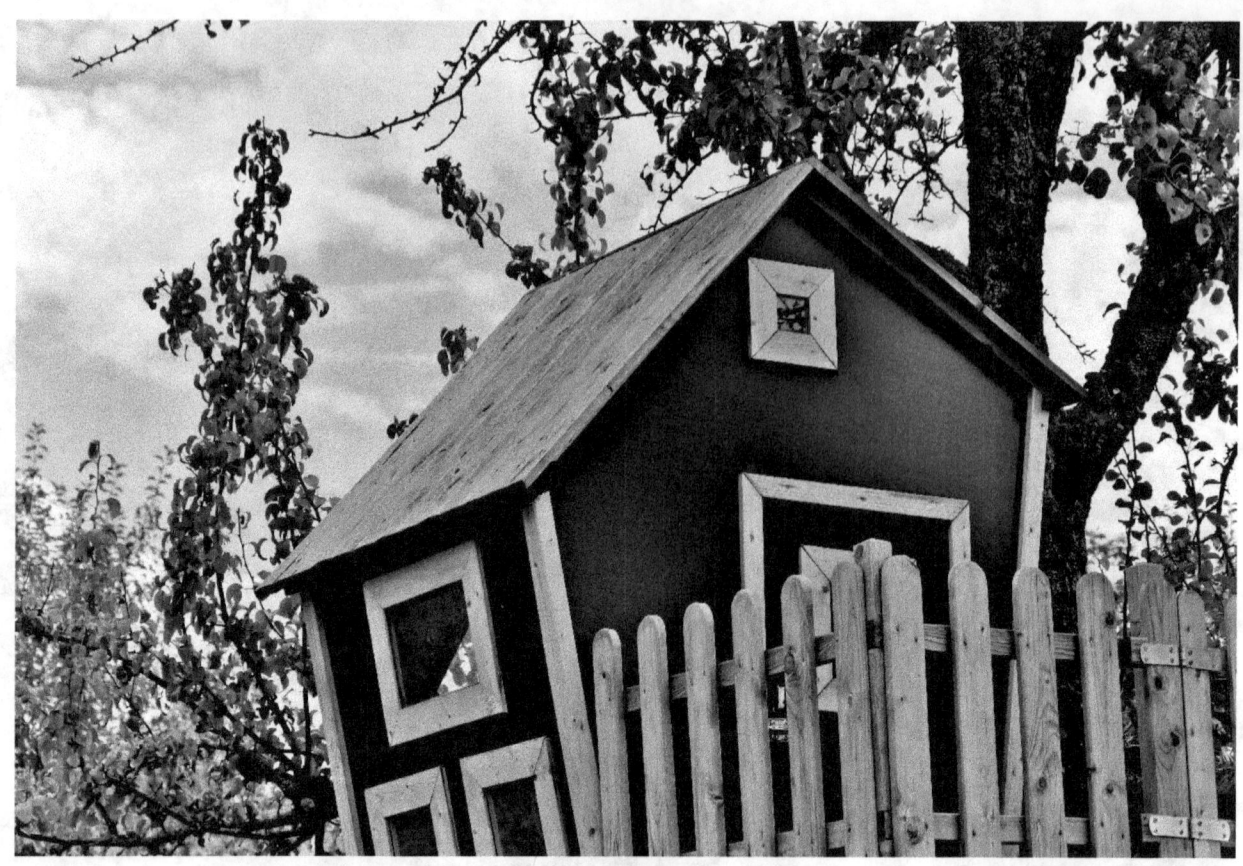

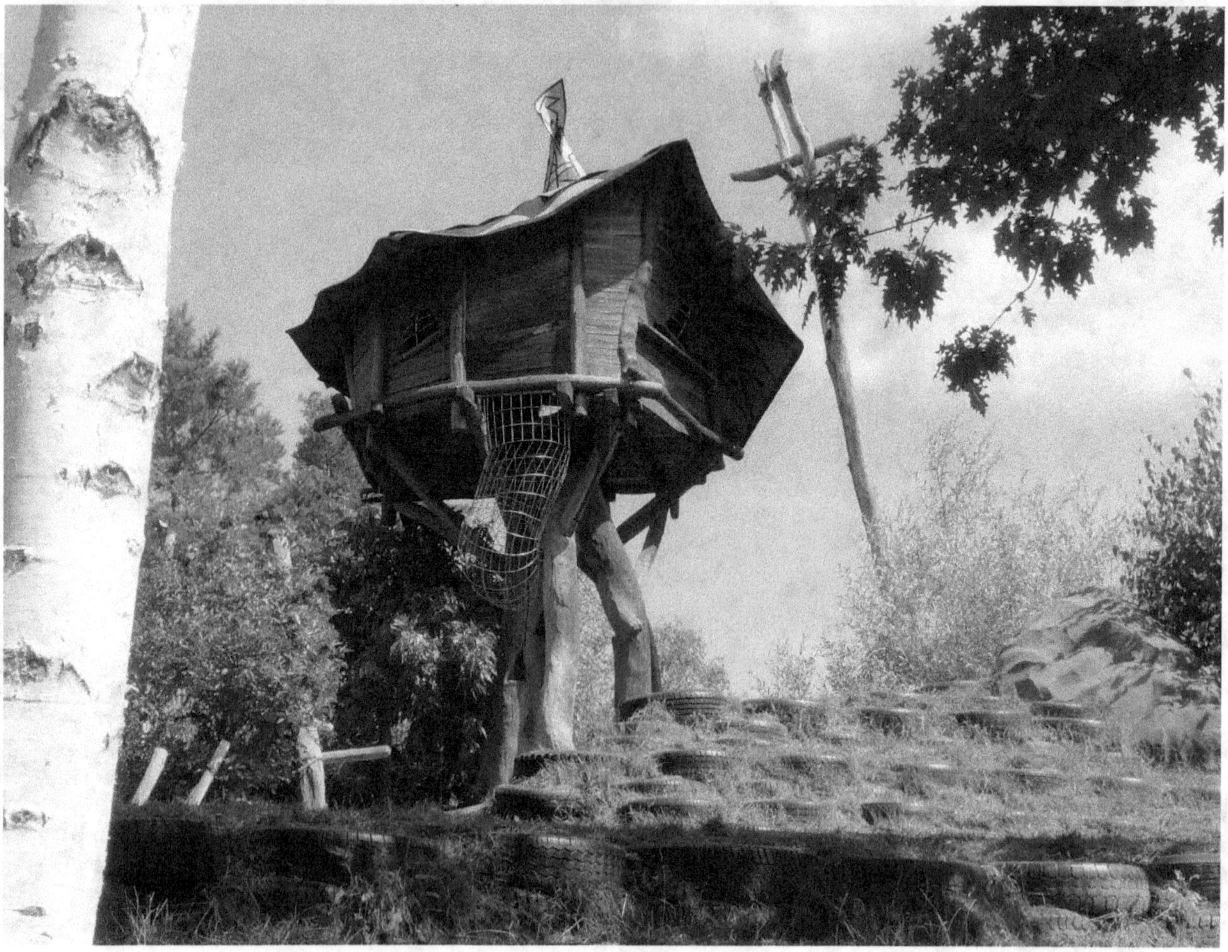

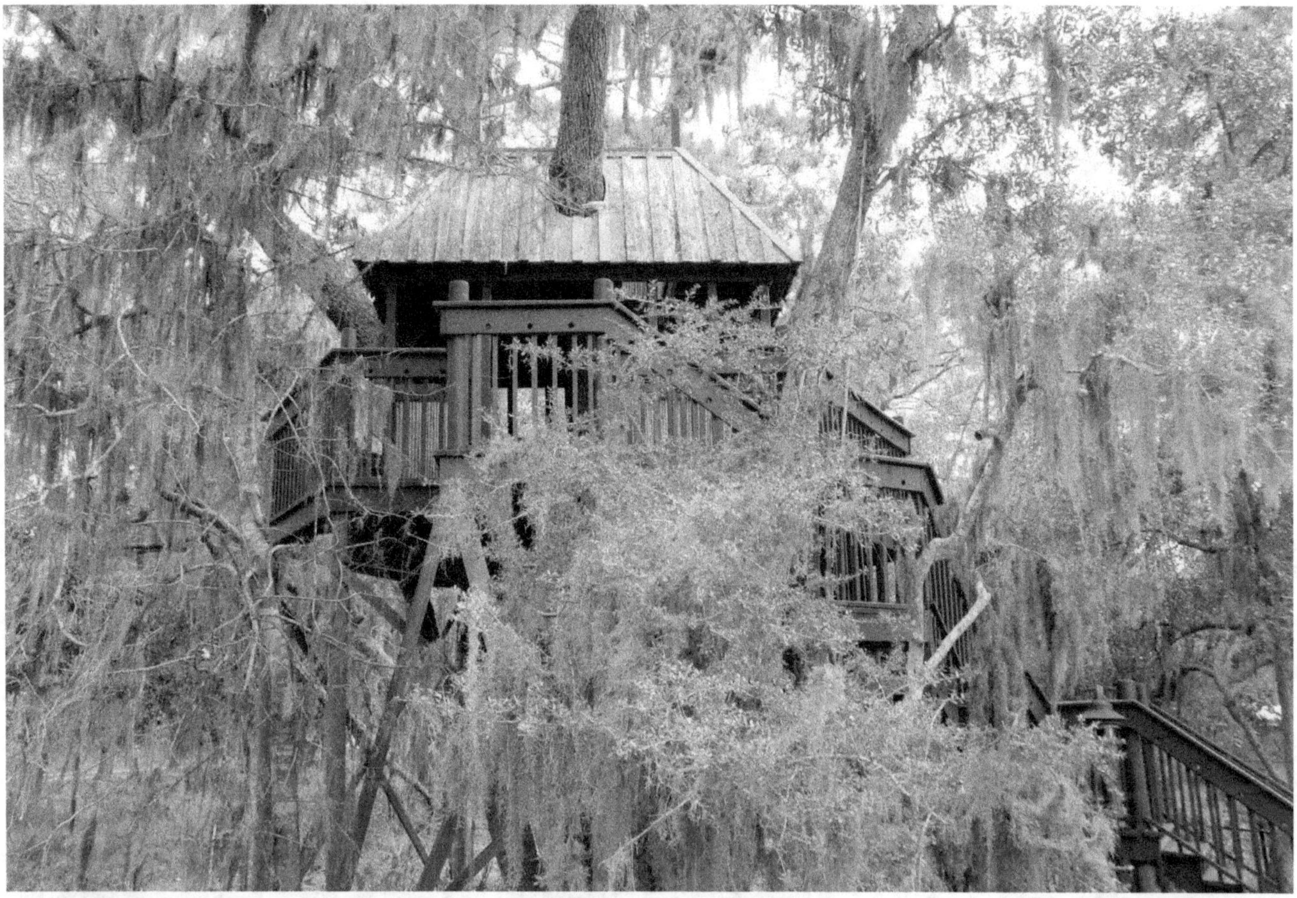

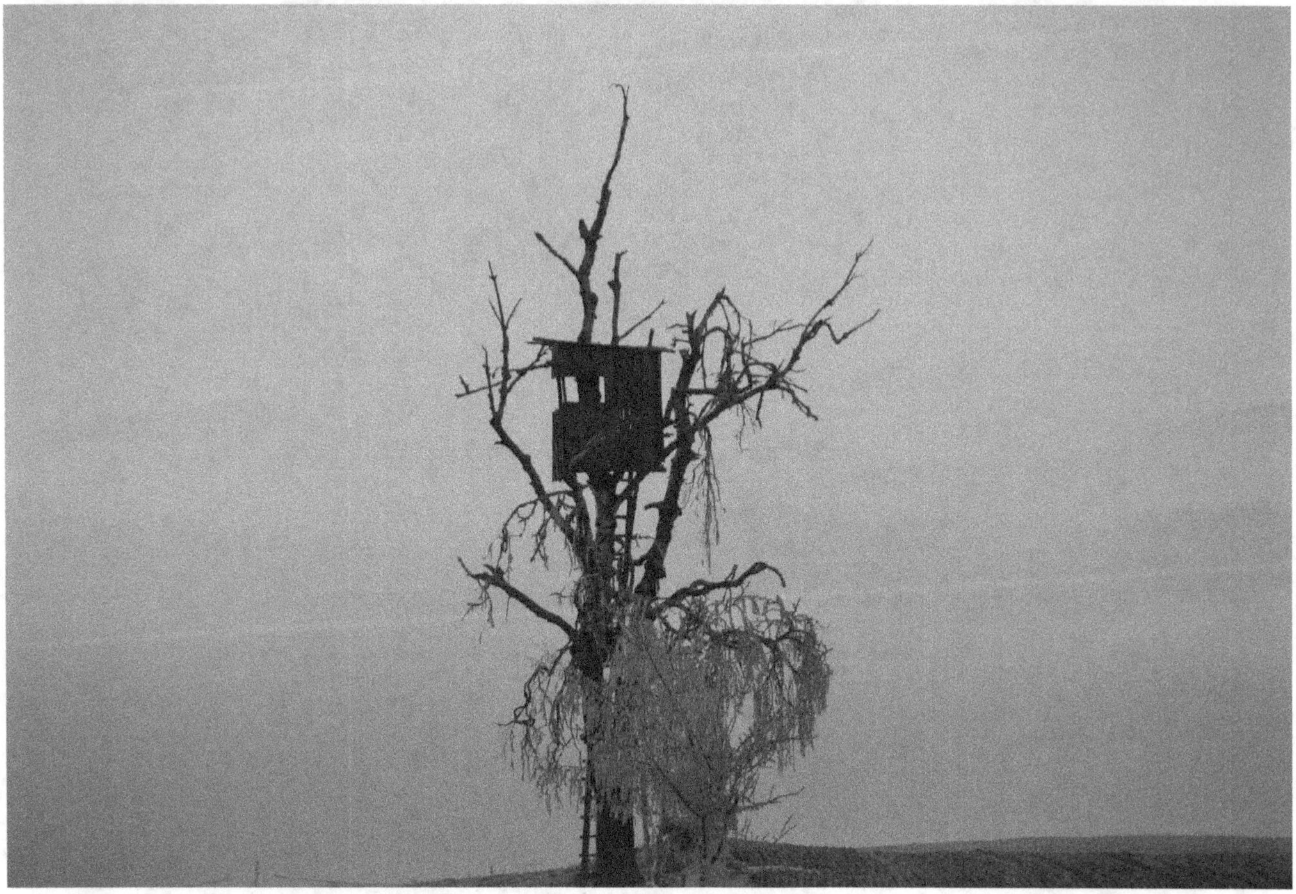

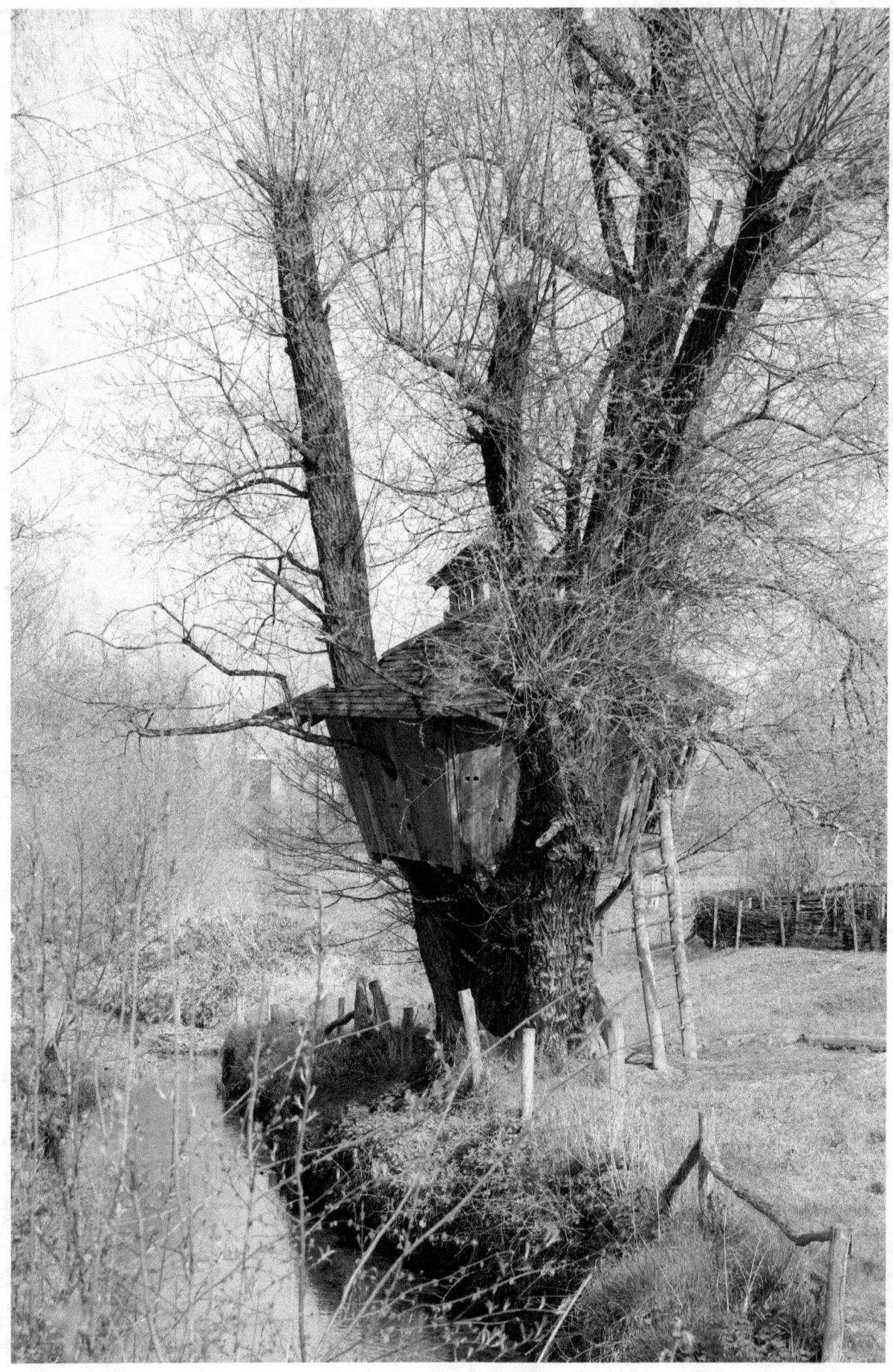

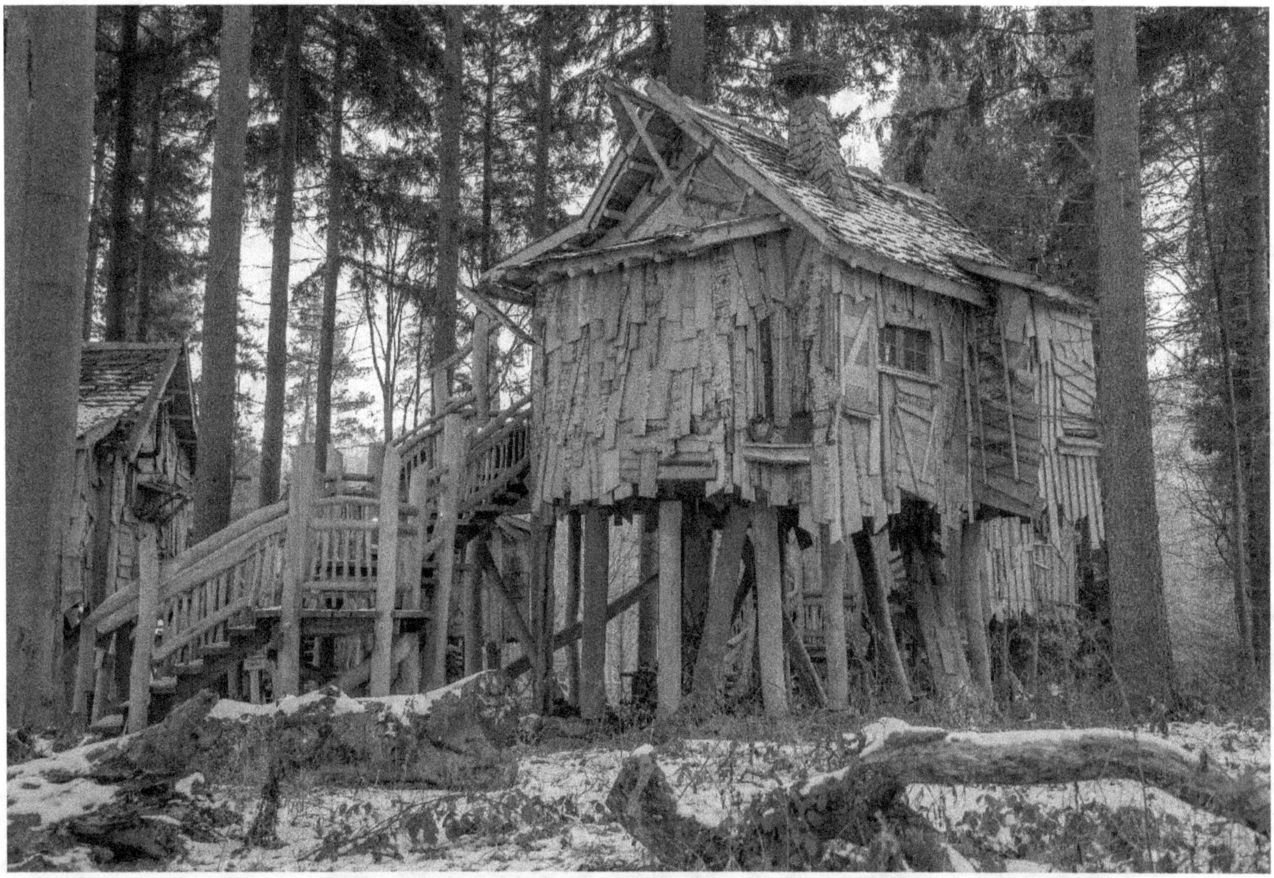

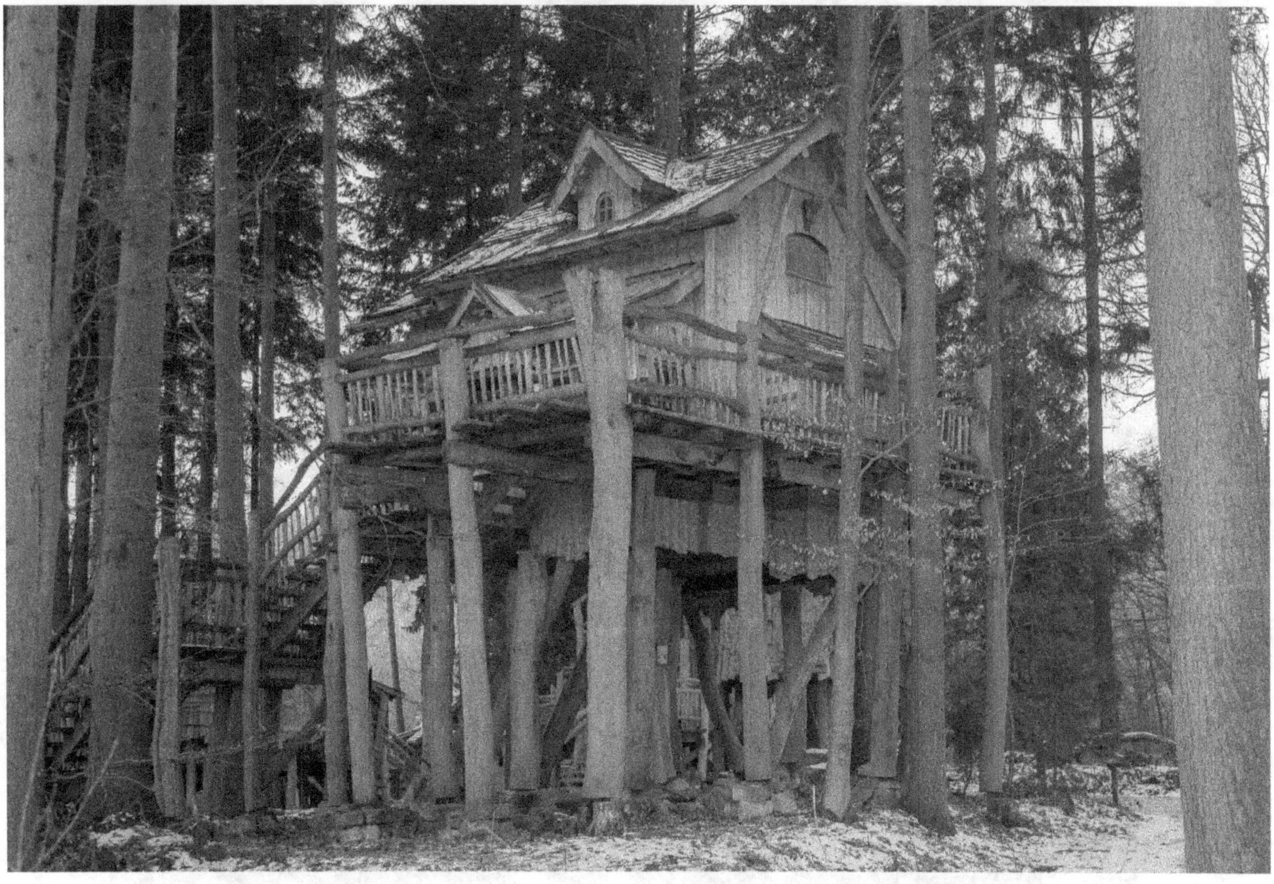

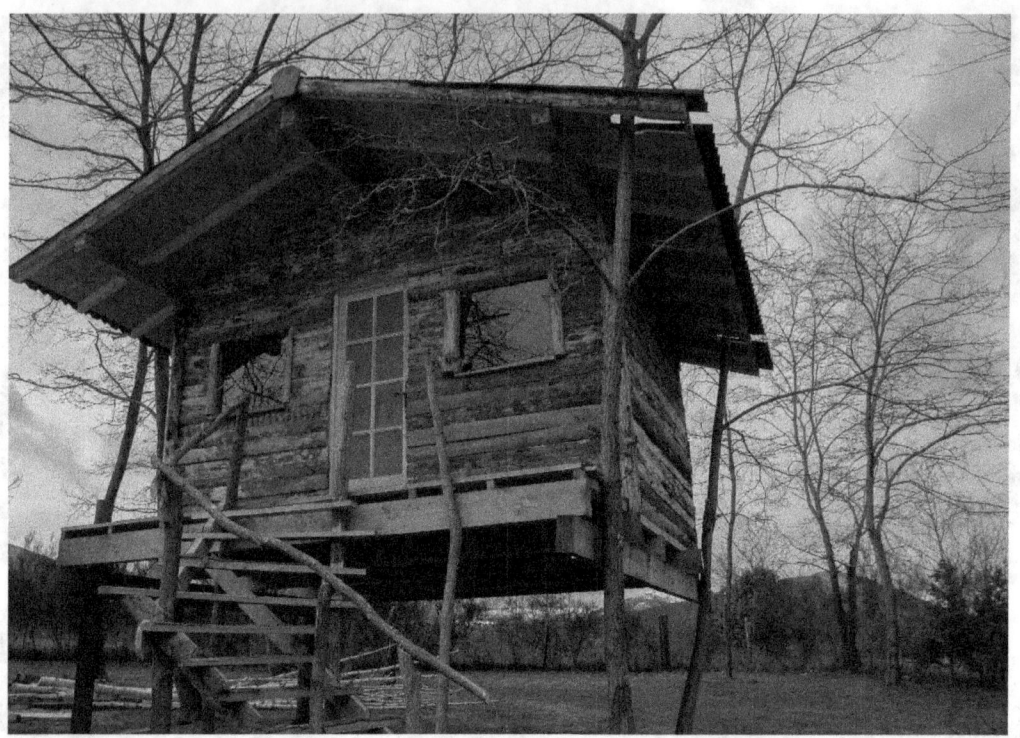

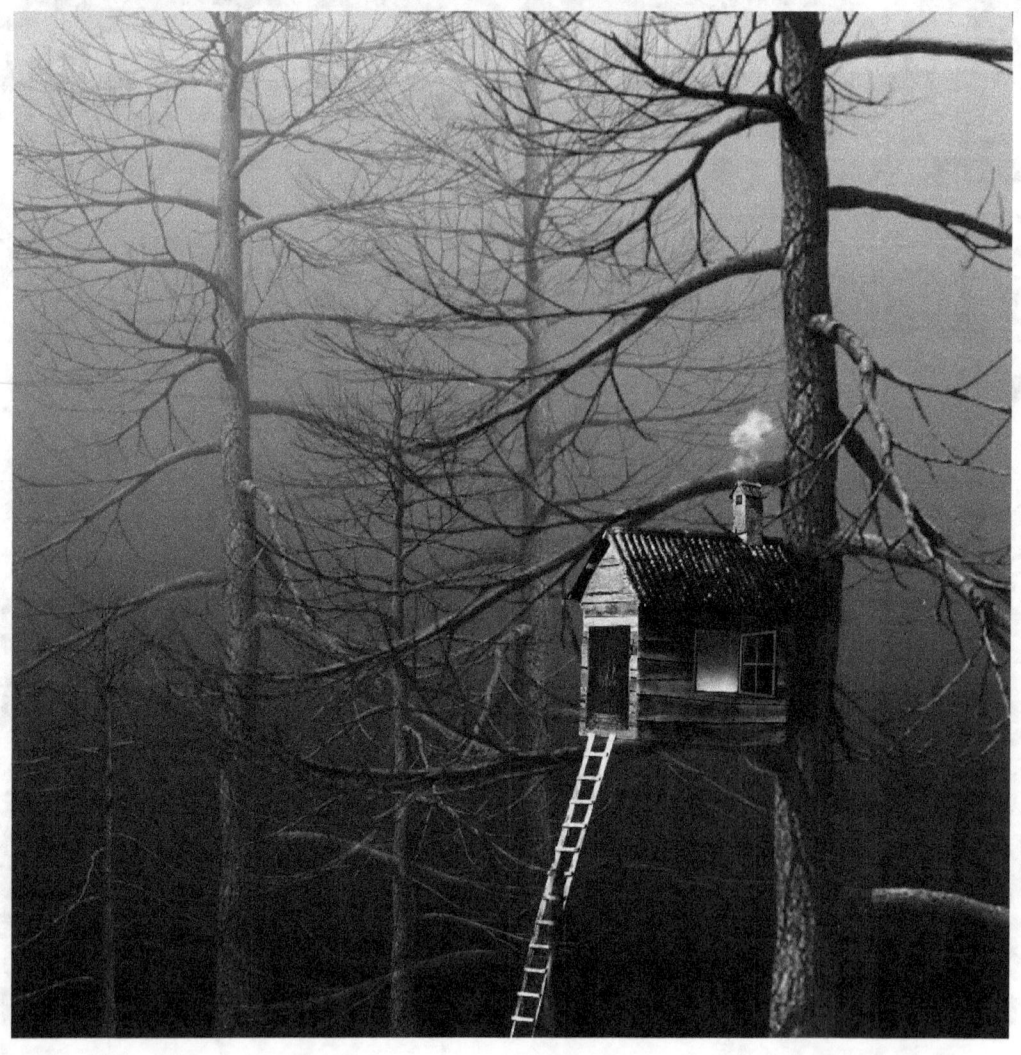

This page is intentionally left blank

10 OLD

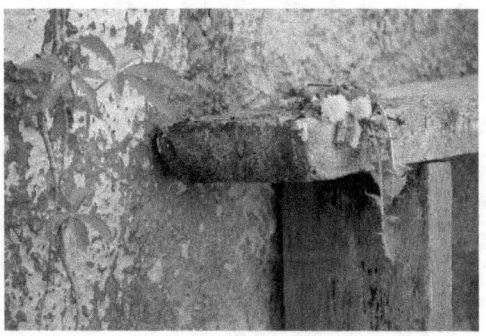

Old and worn, ruins (major rehab?), ideas for arches, free junk huts, and abandoned buildings

Old

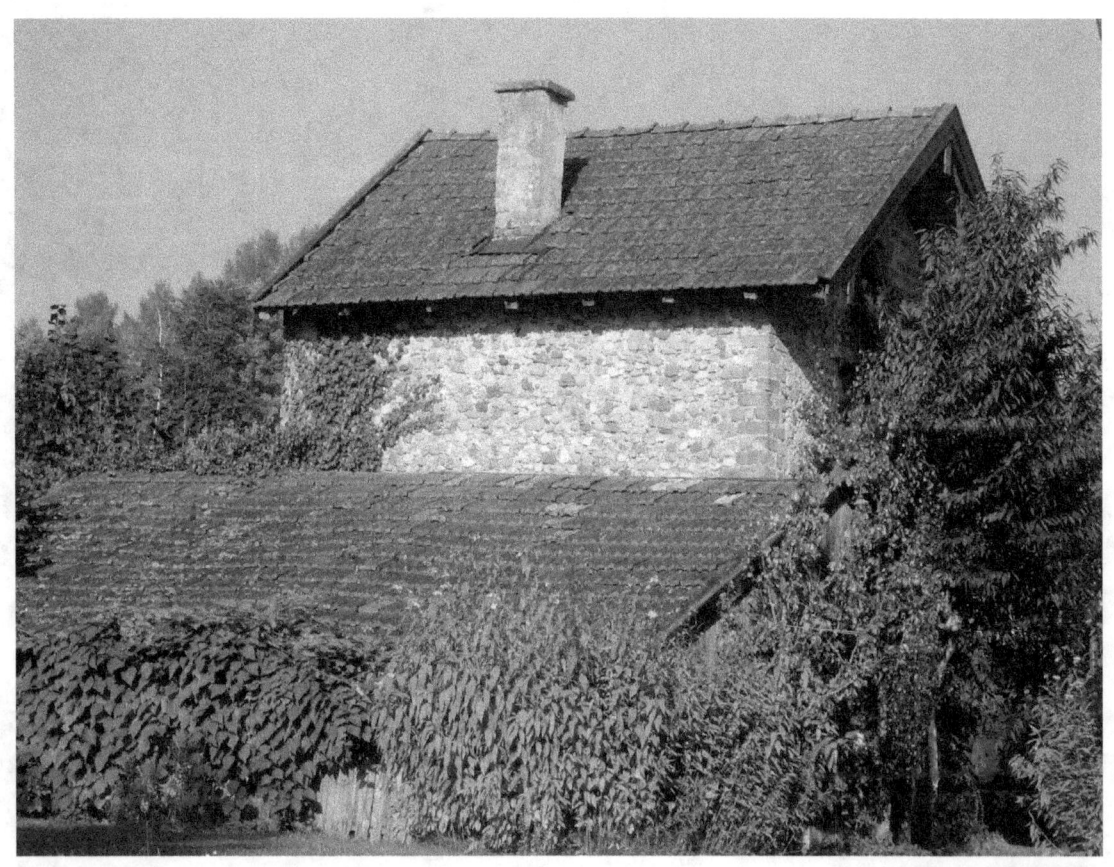

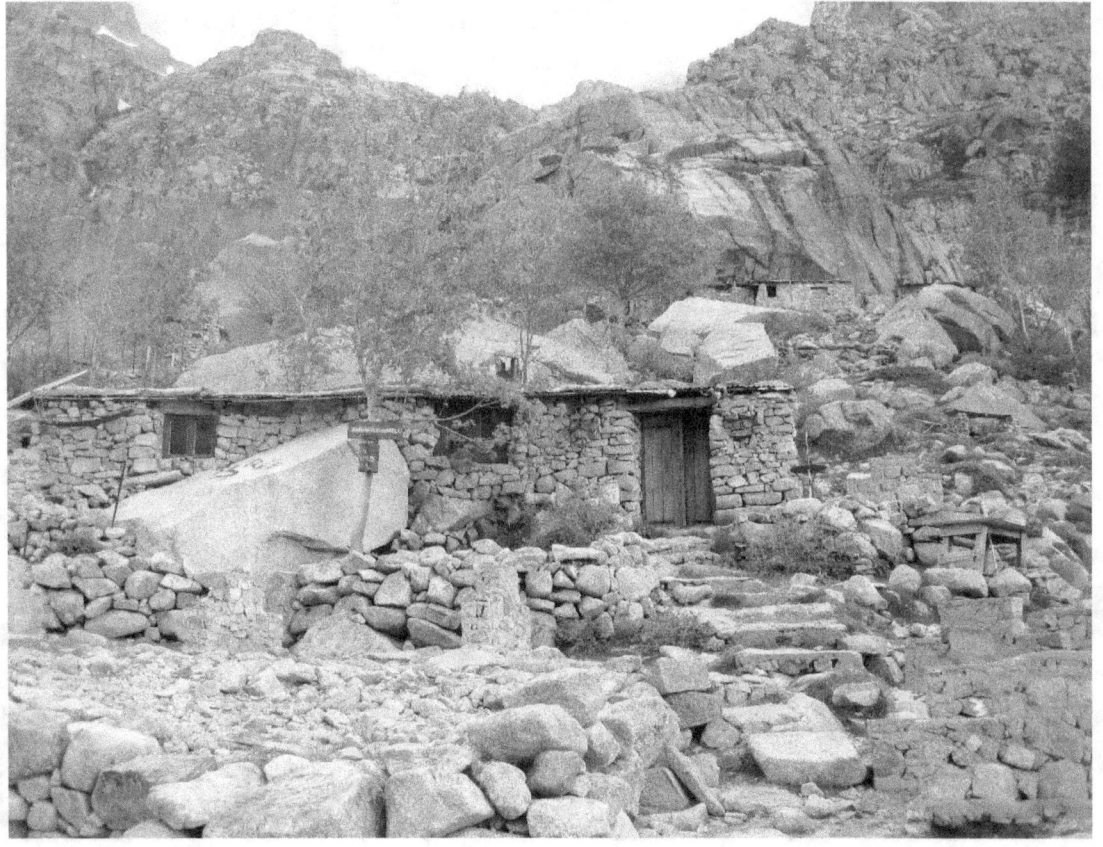

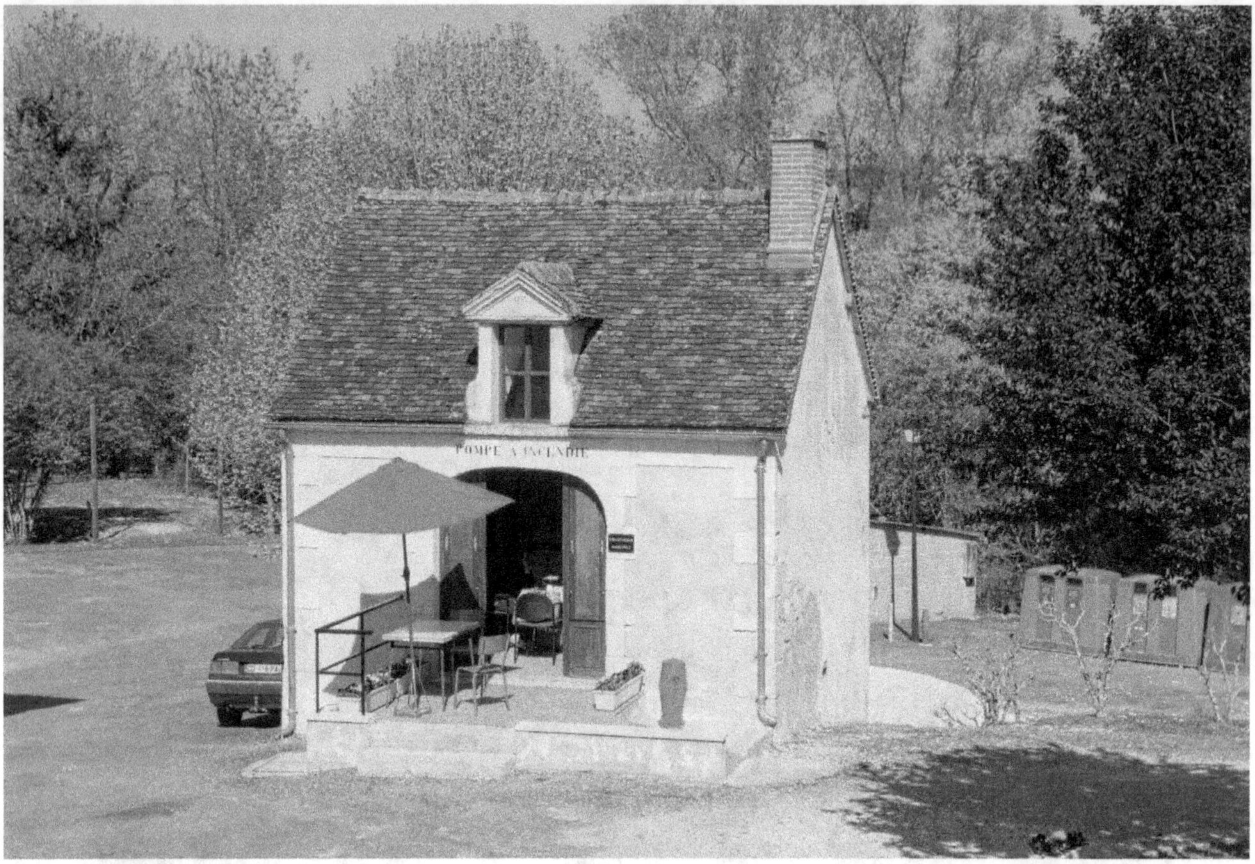

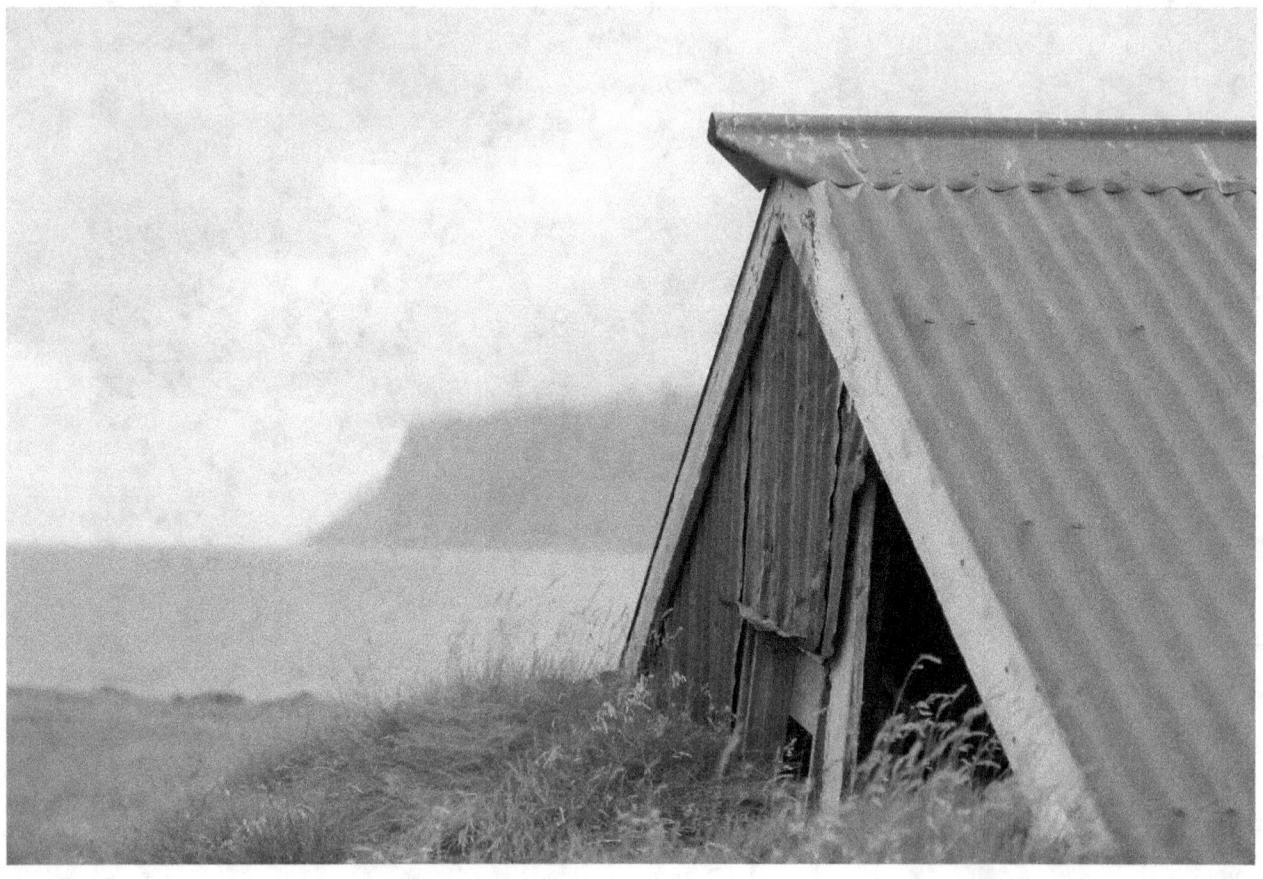

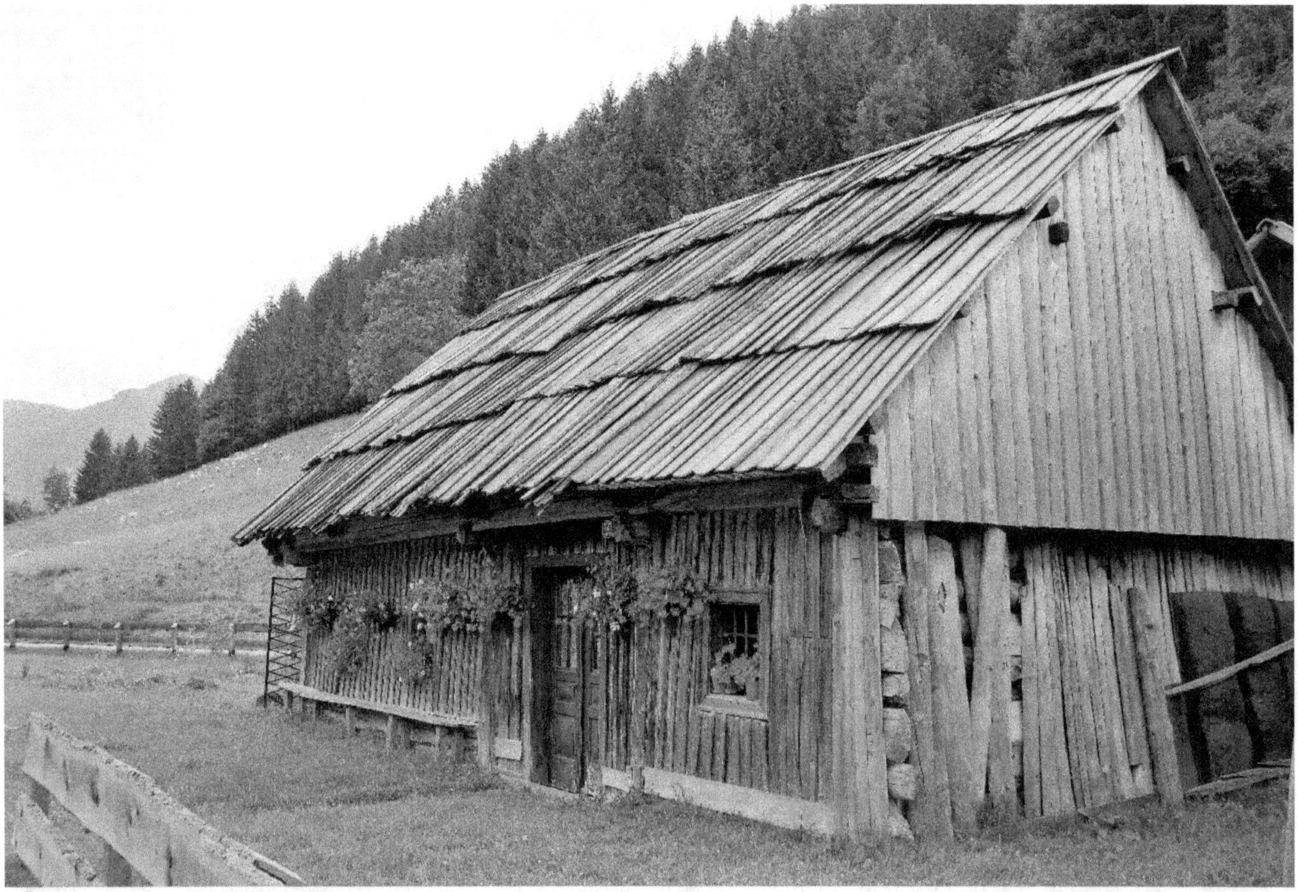

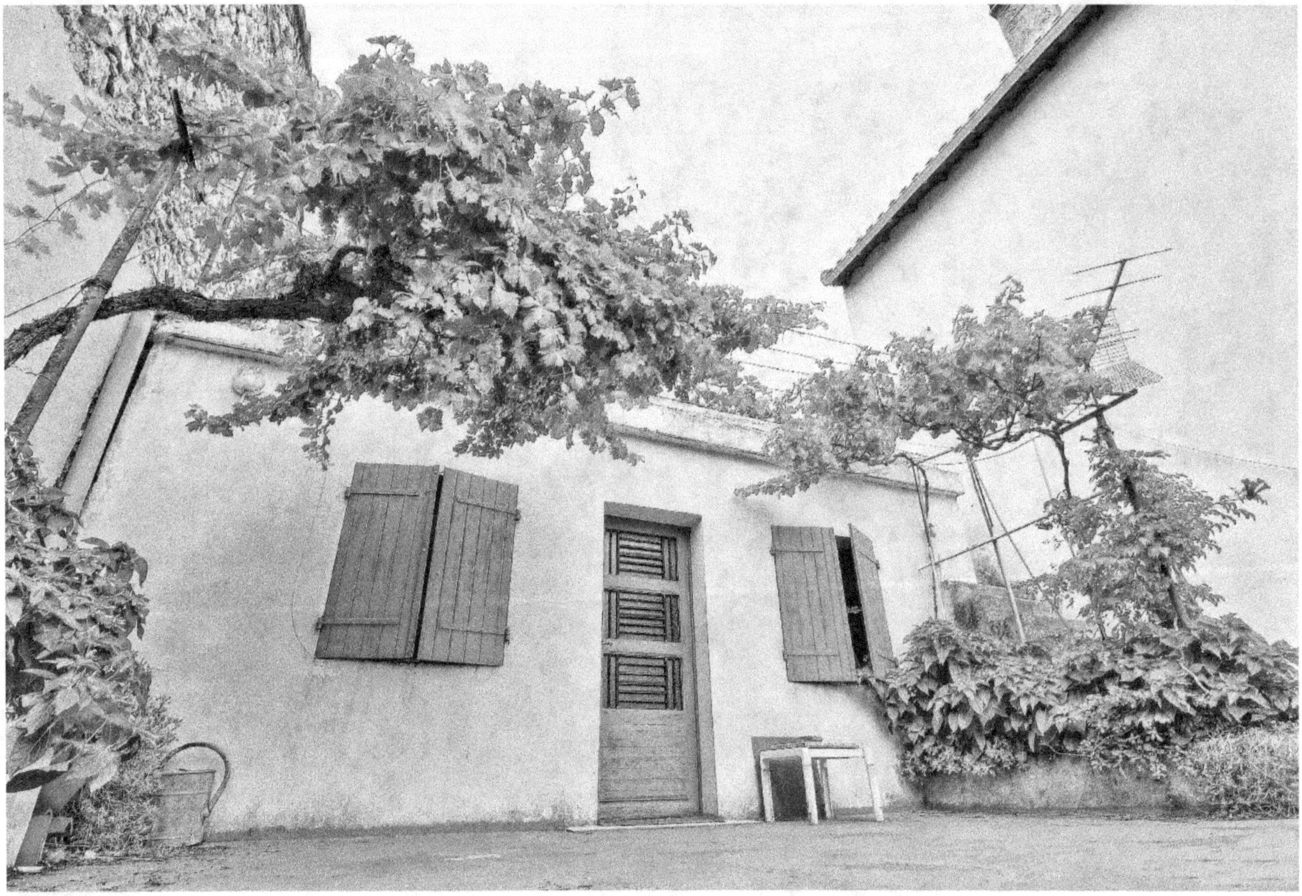

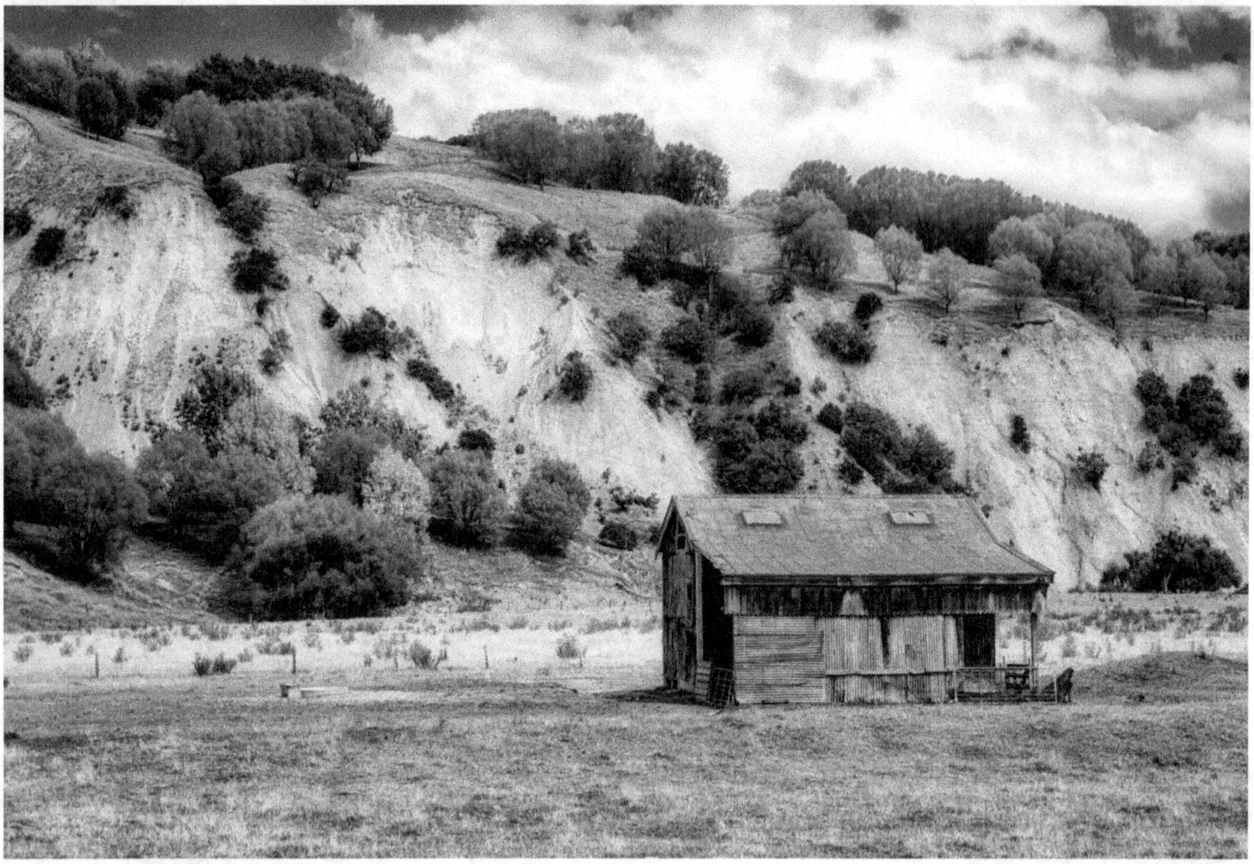

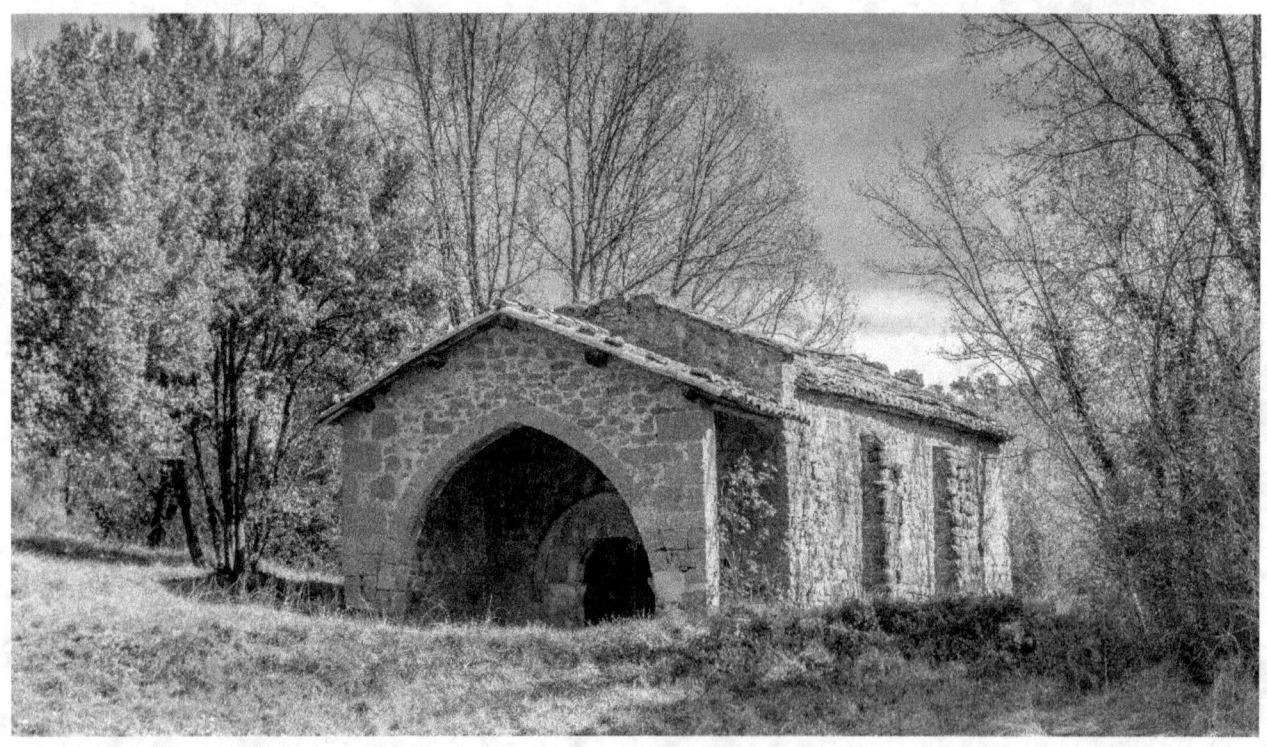

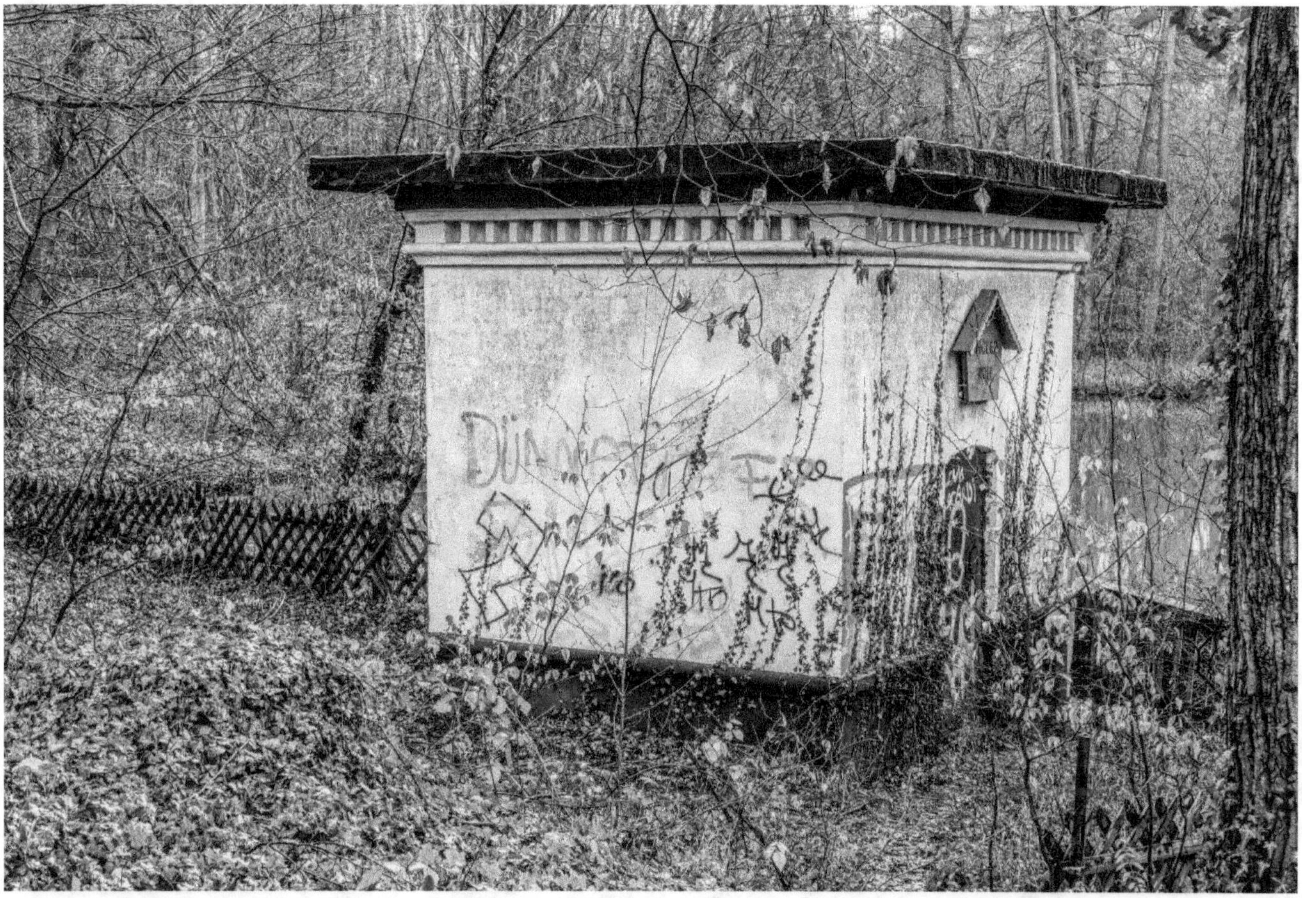

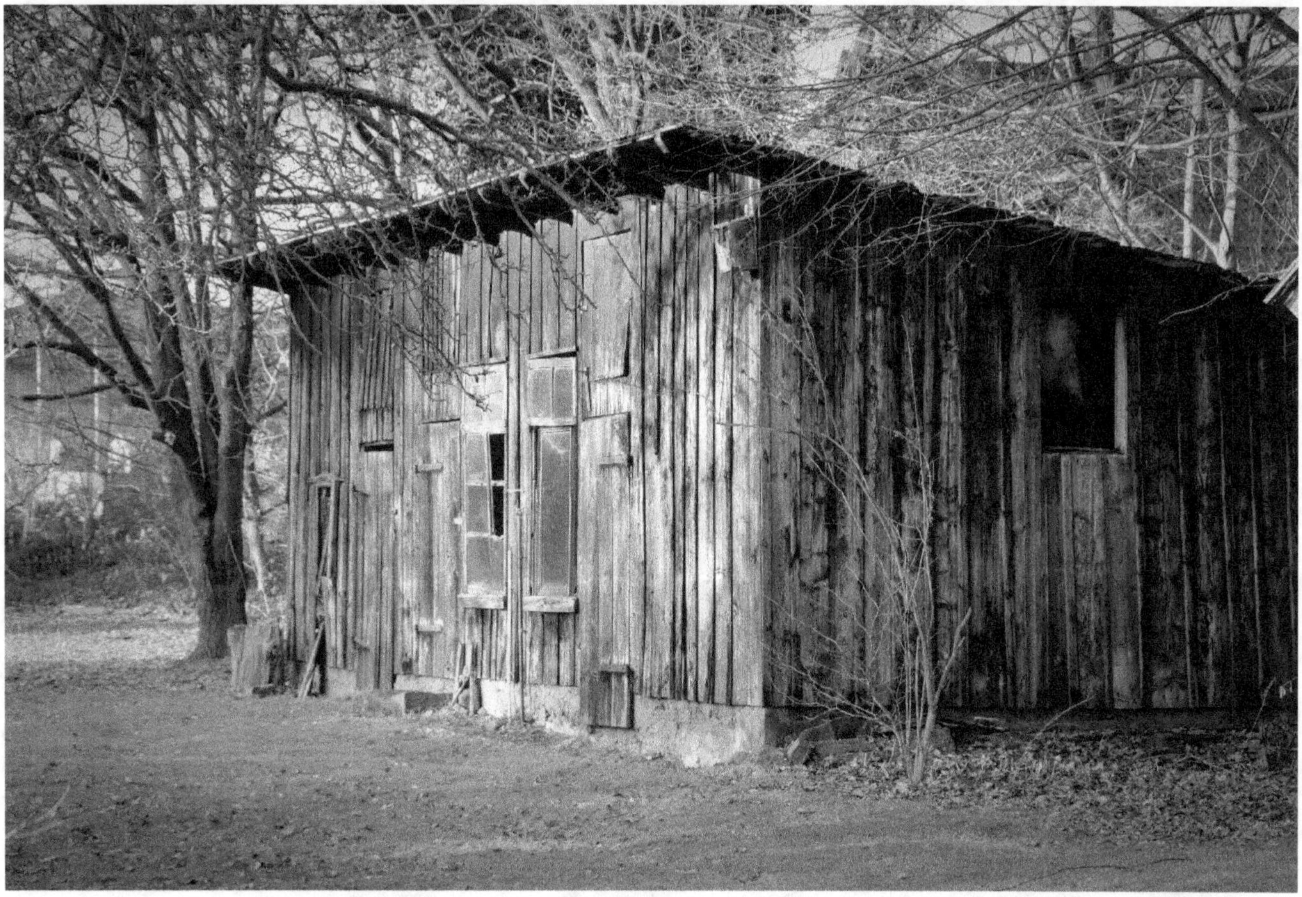

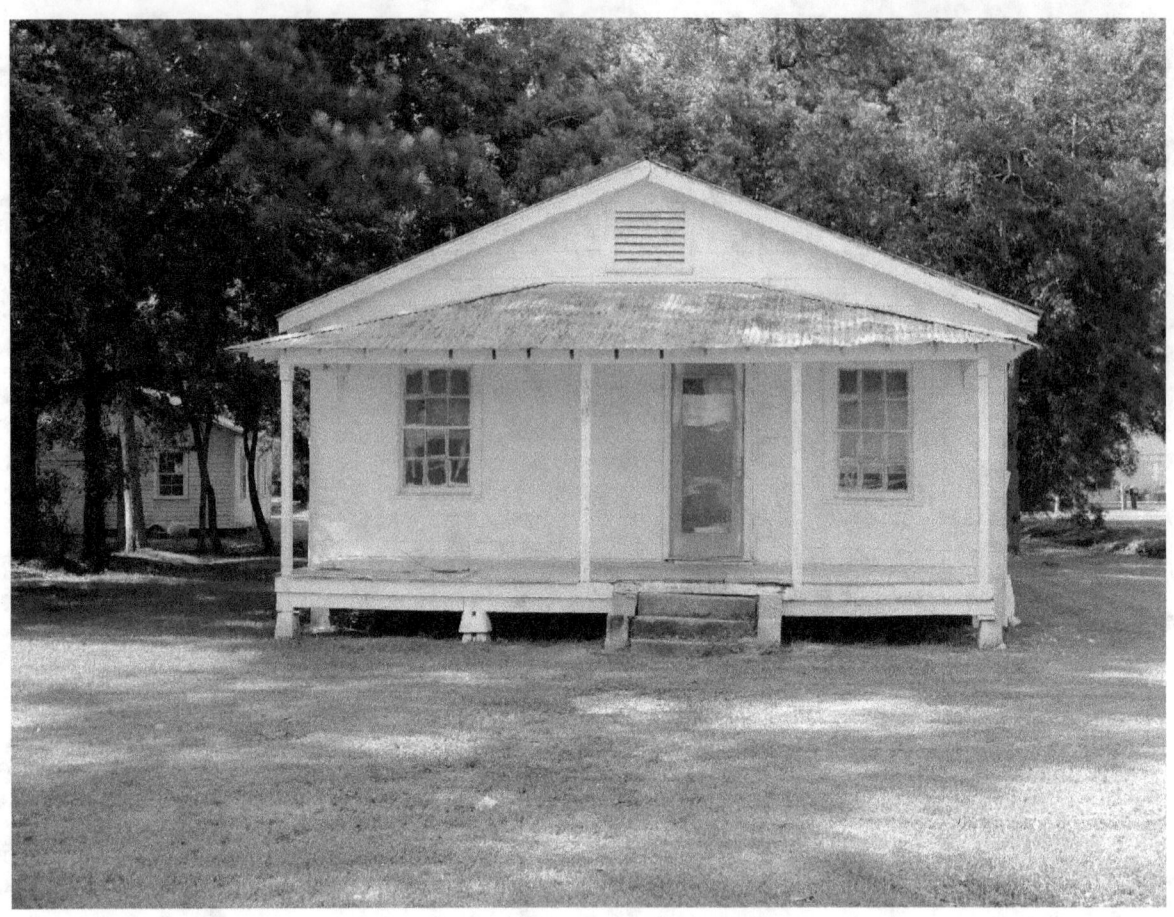

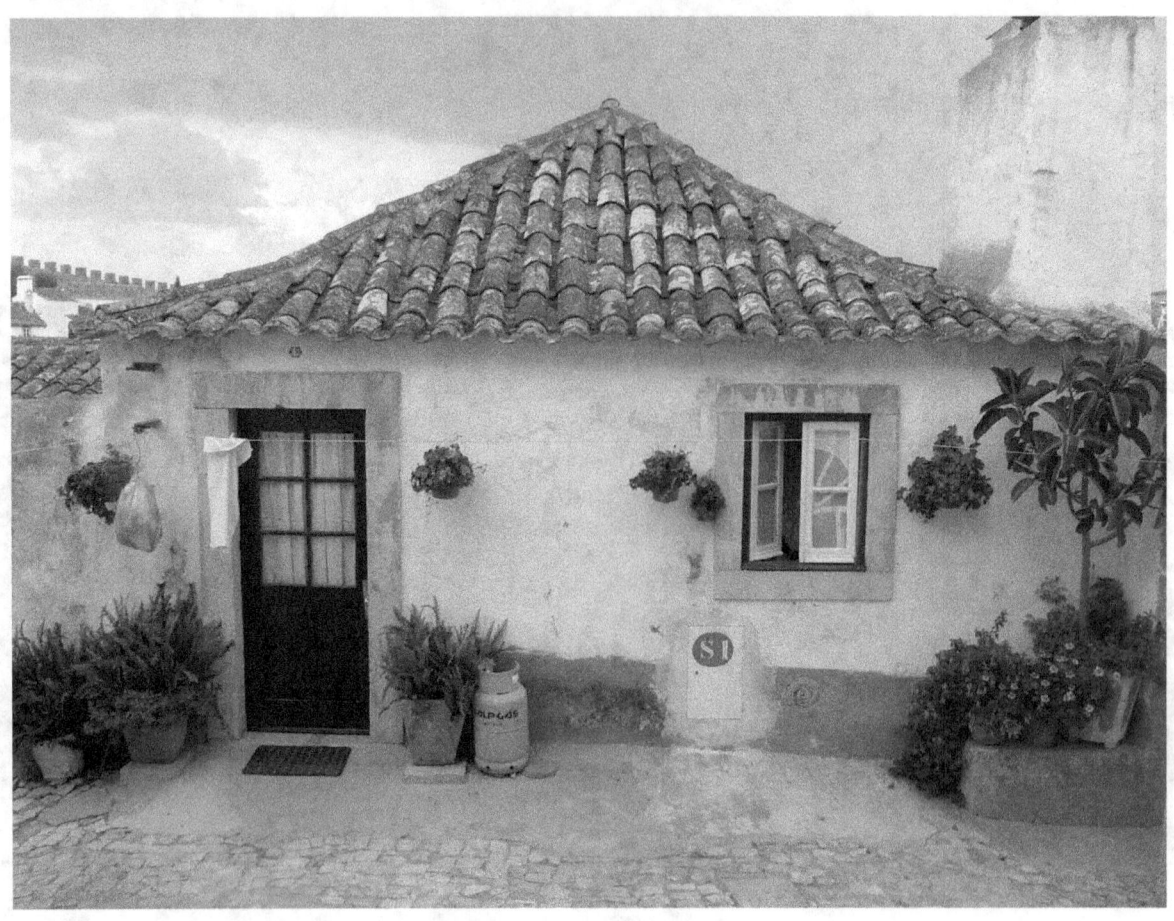

Ruins

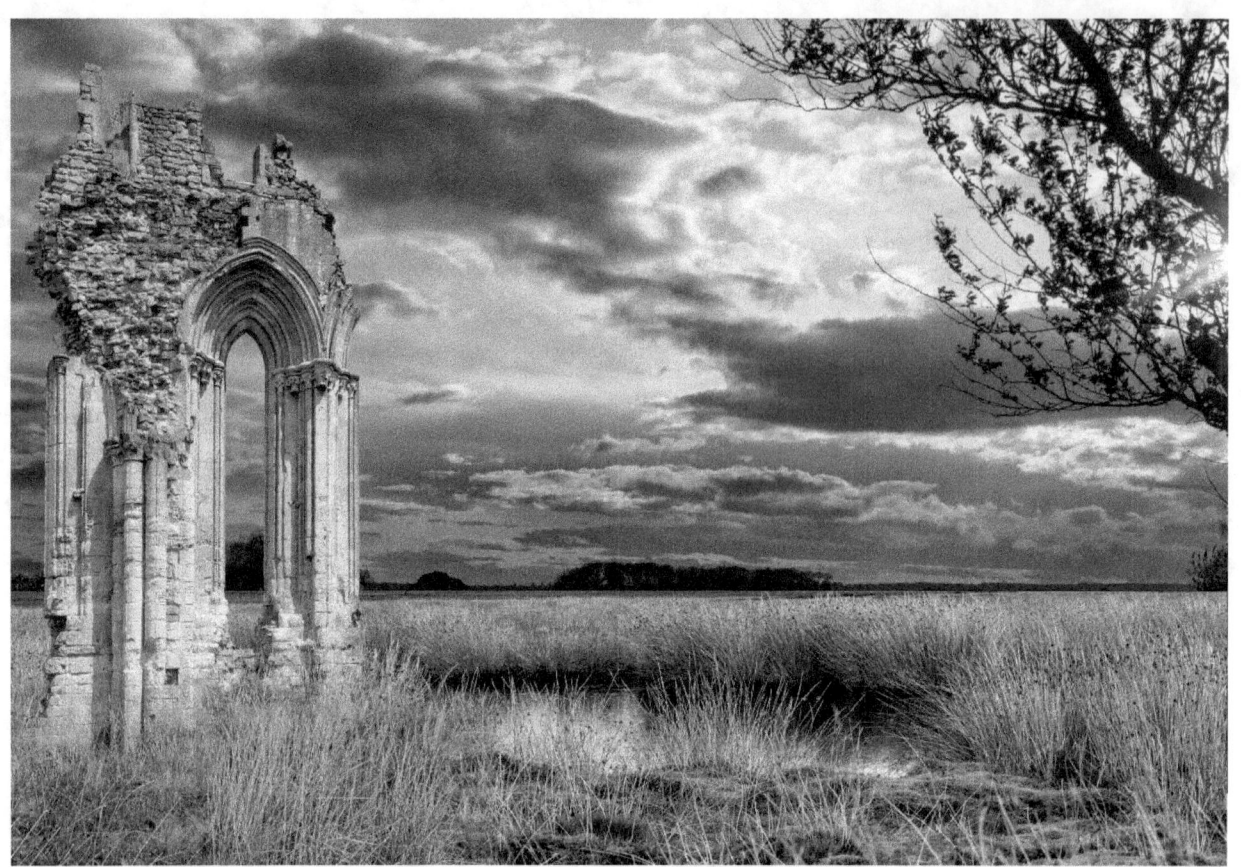

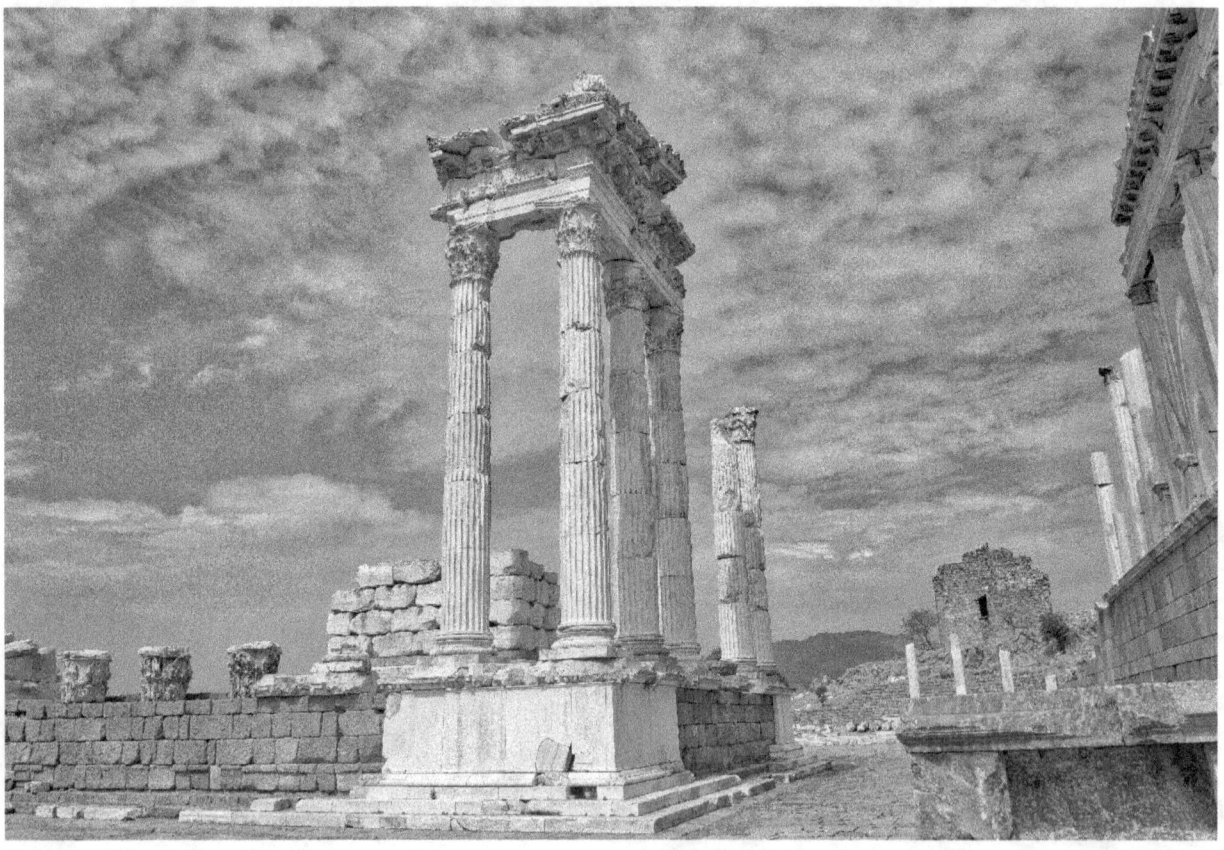

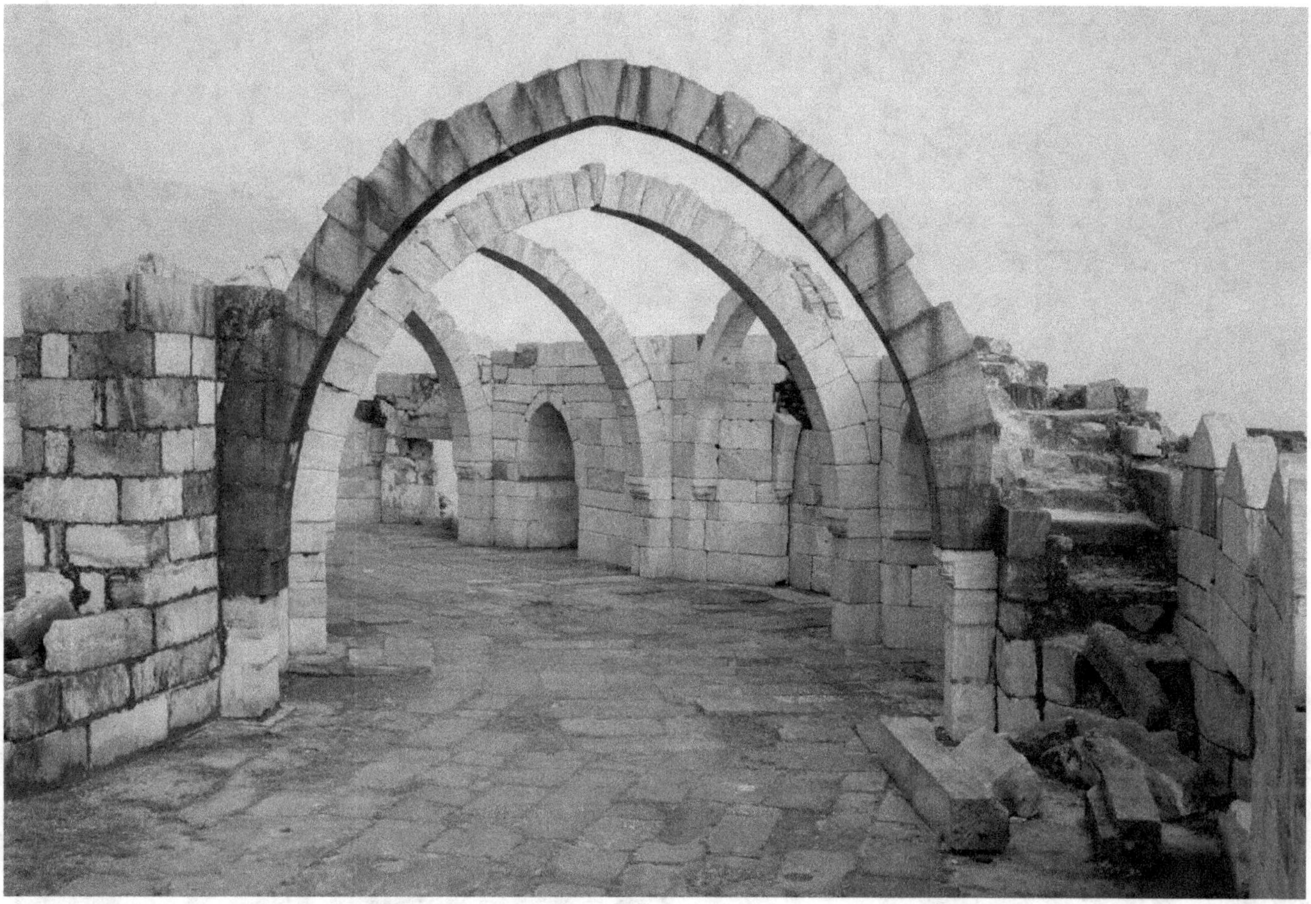

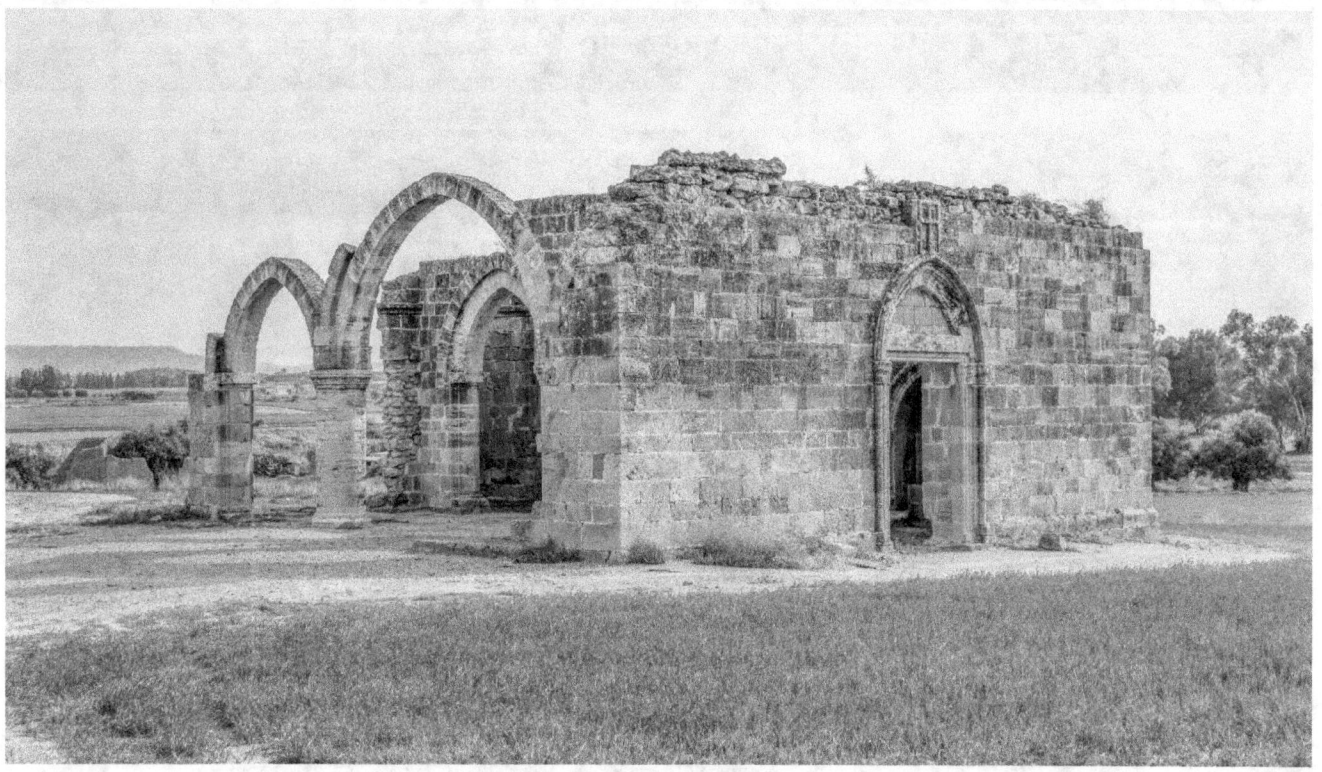

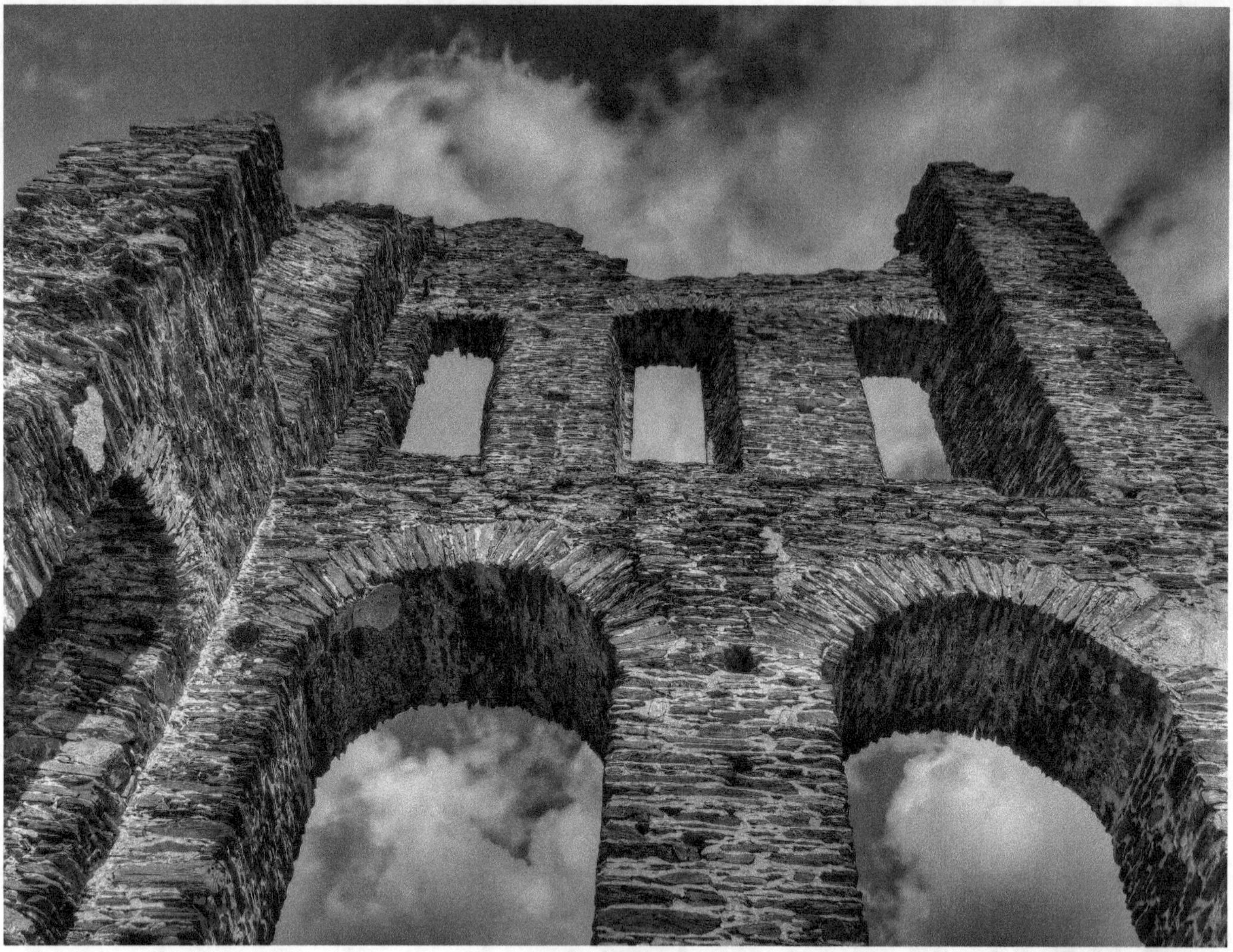

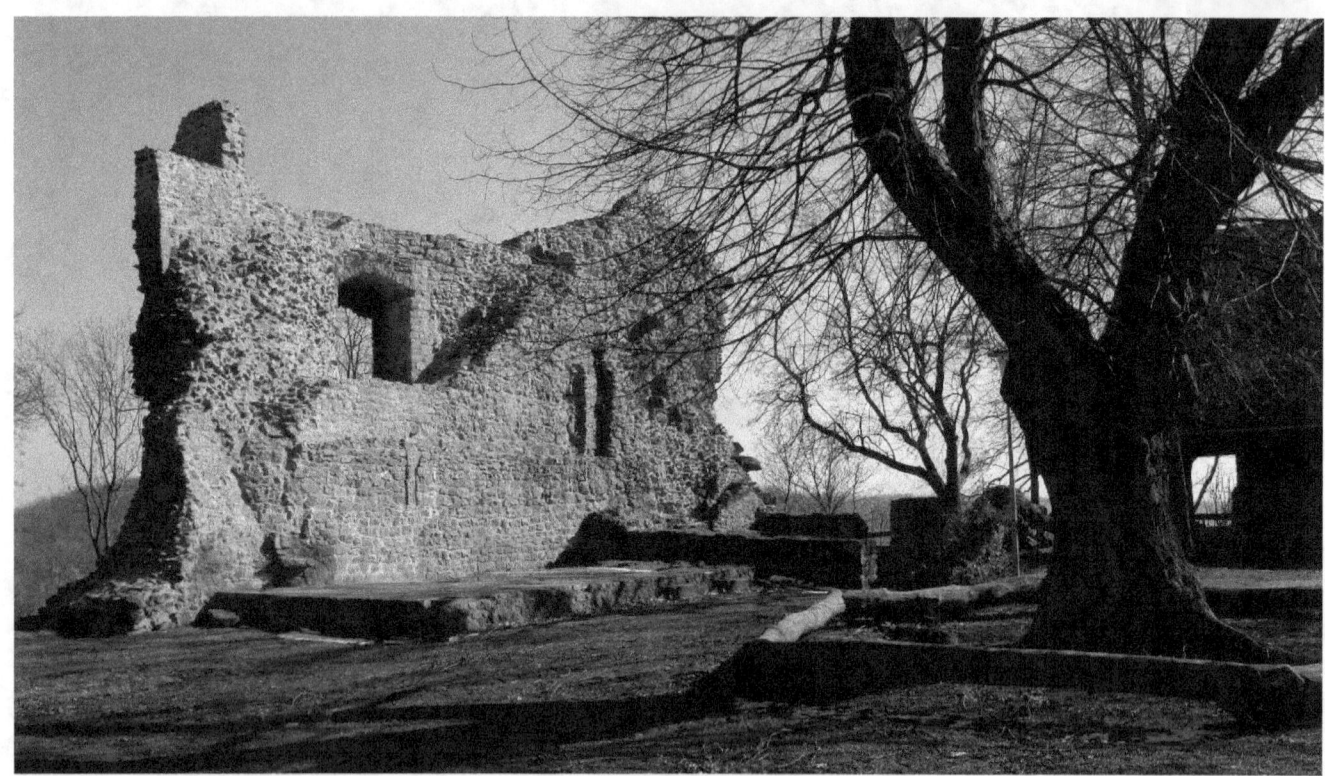

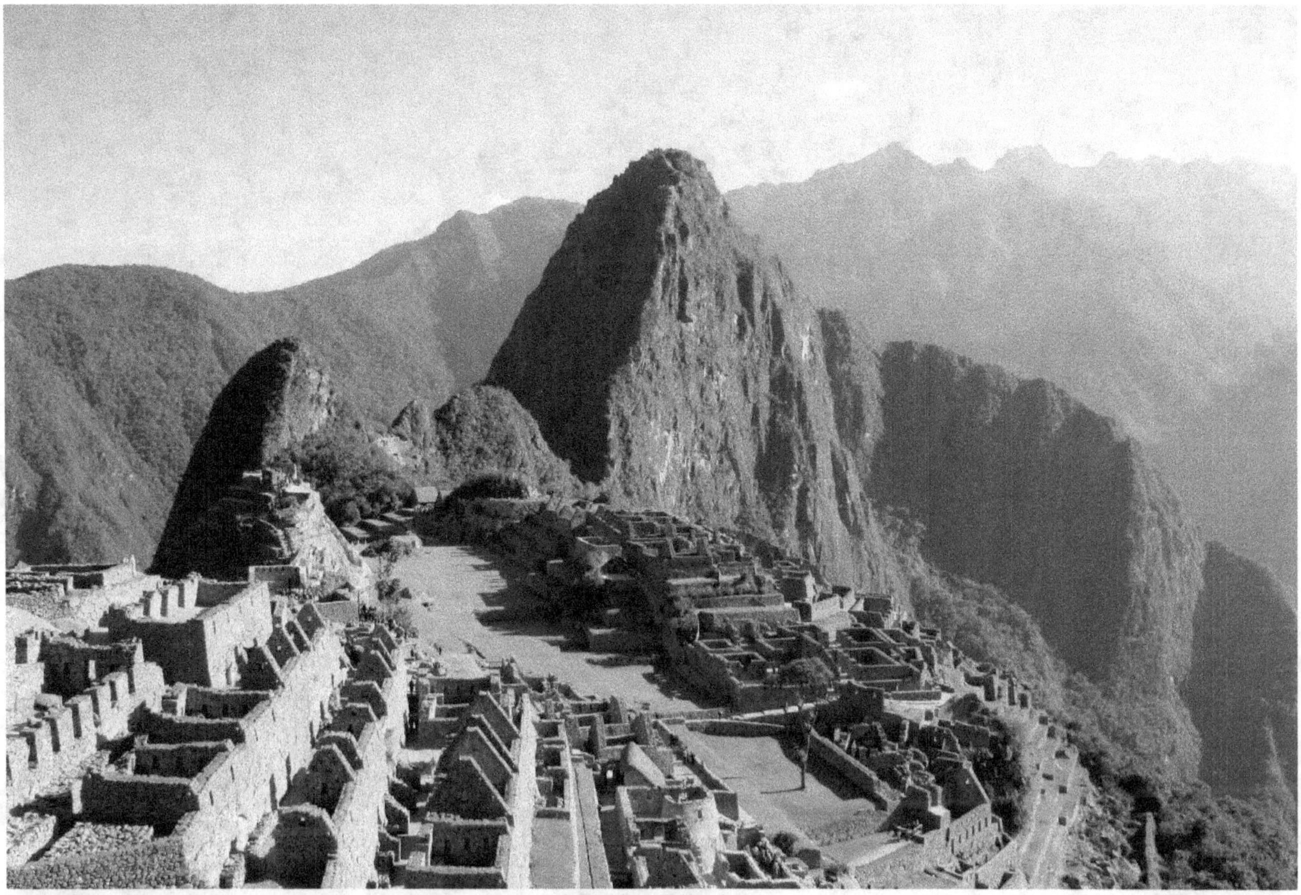

Machu Picchu

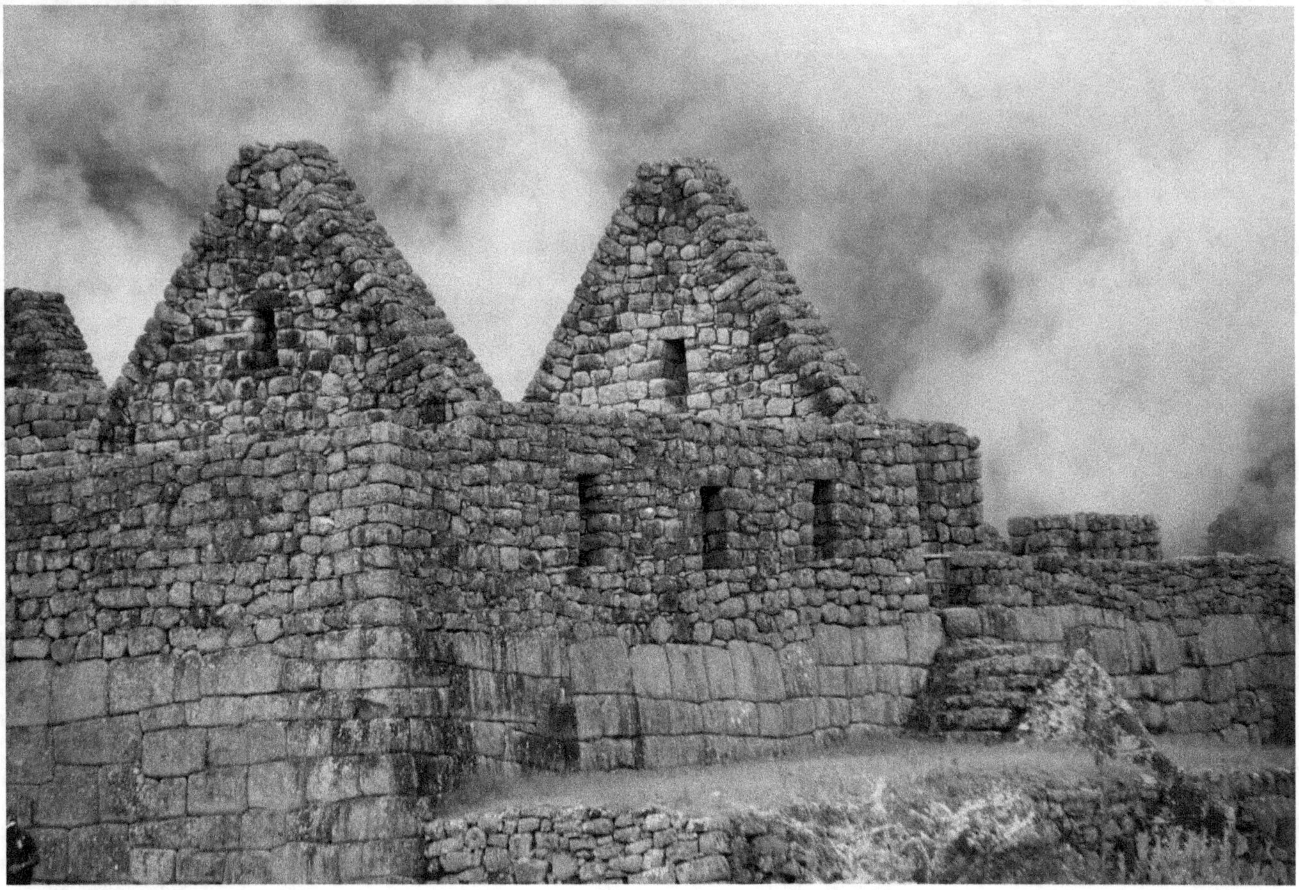

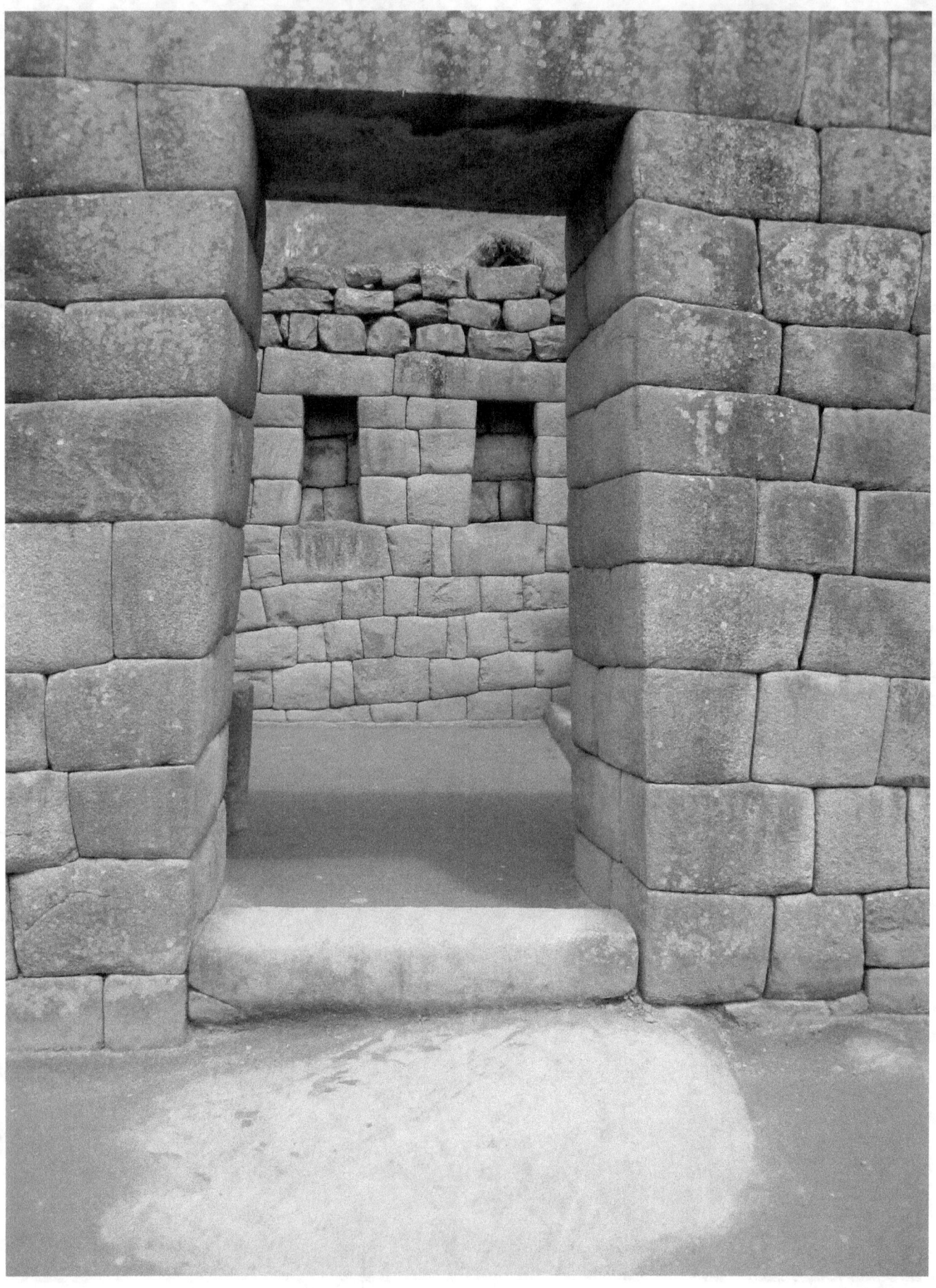

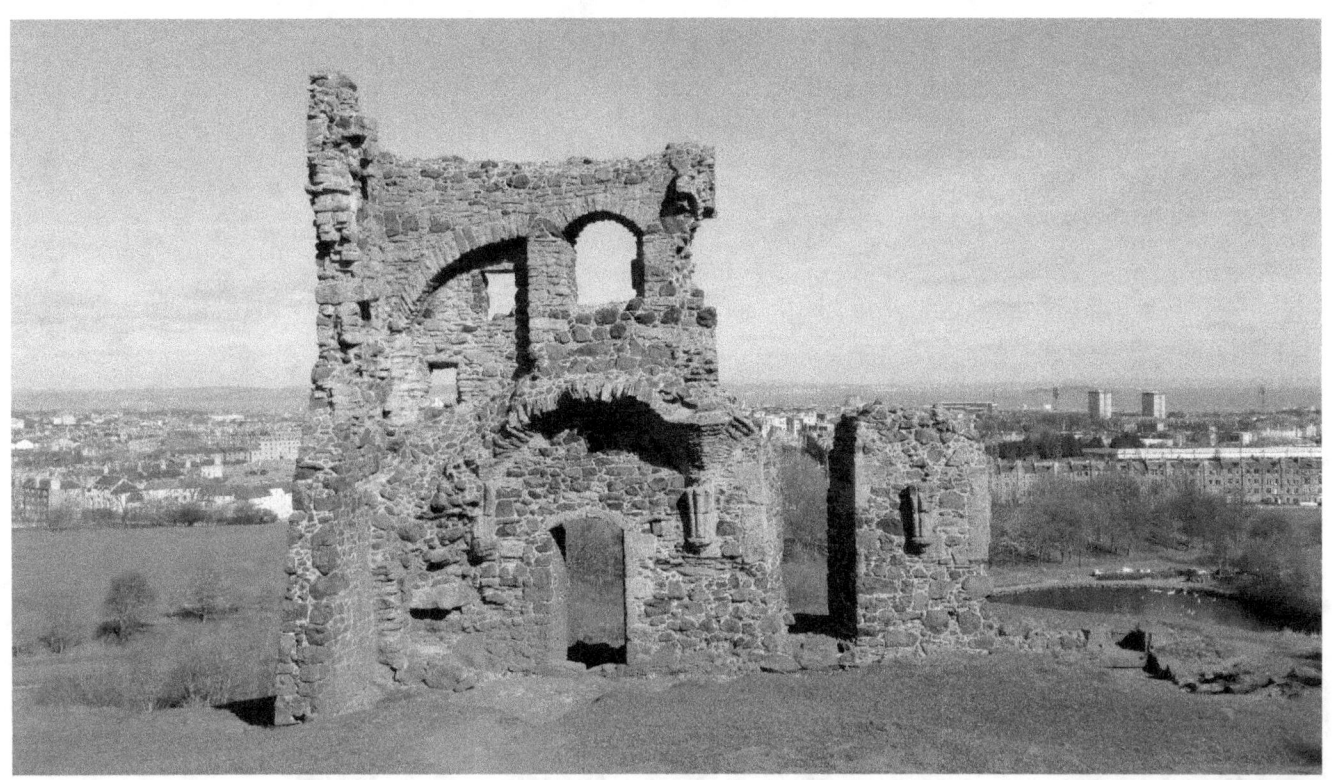

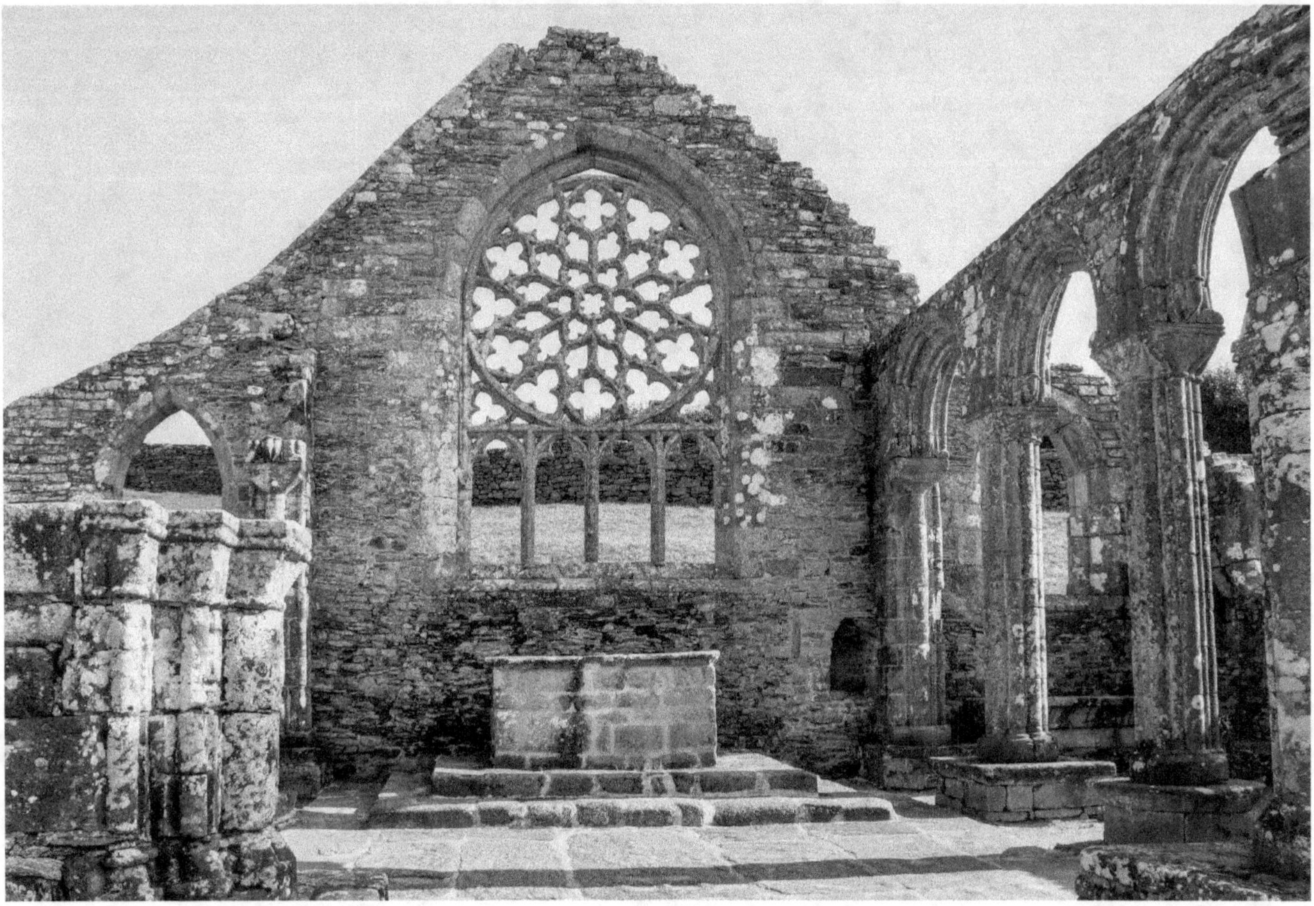

Arches

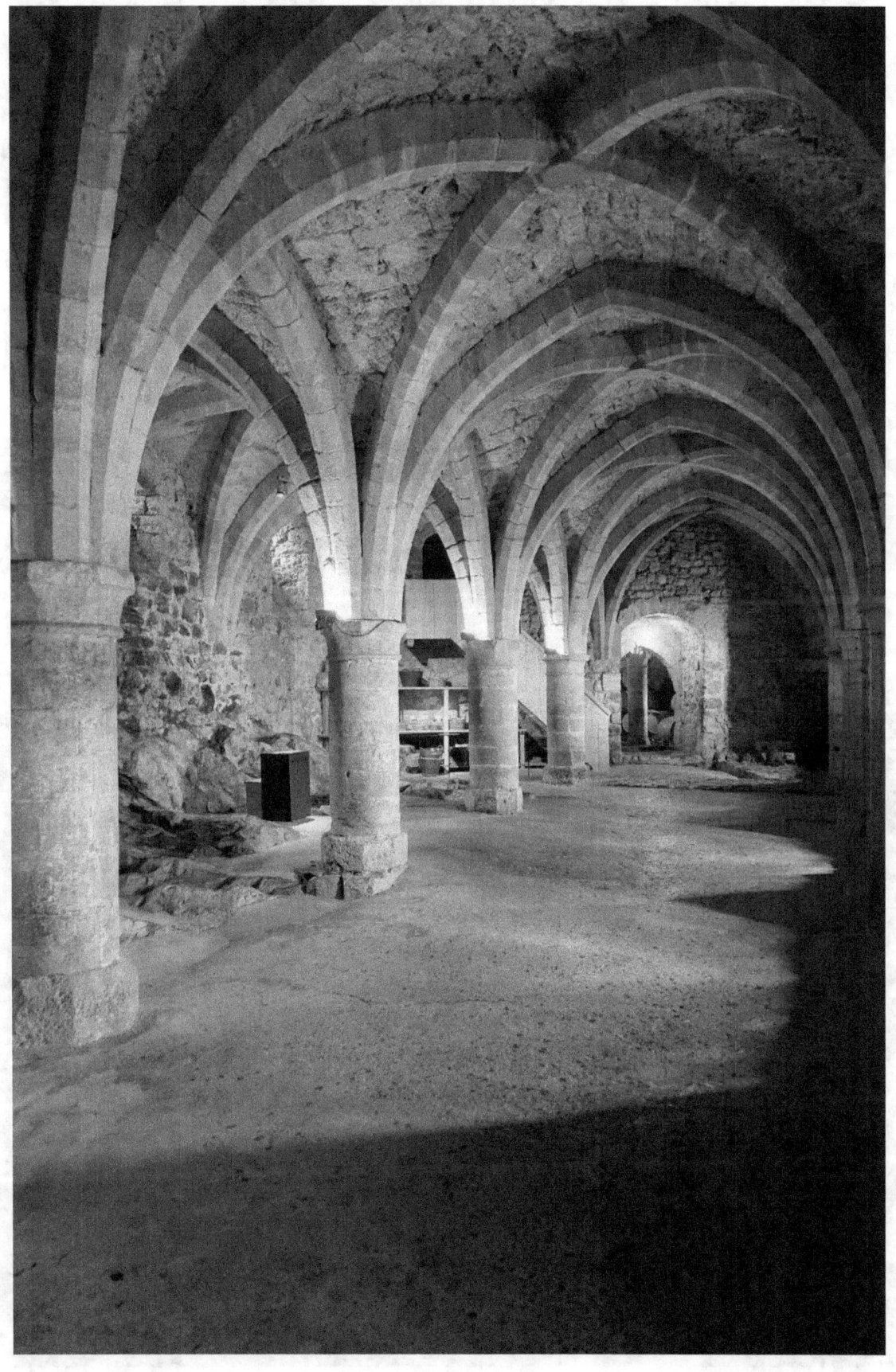

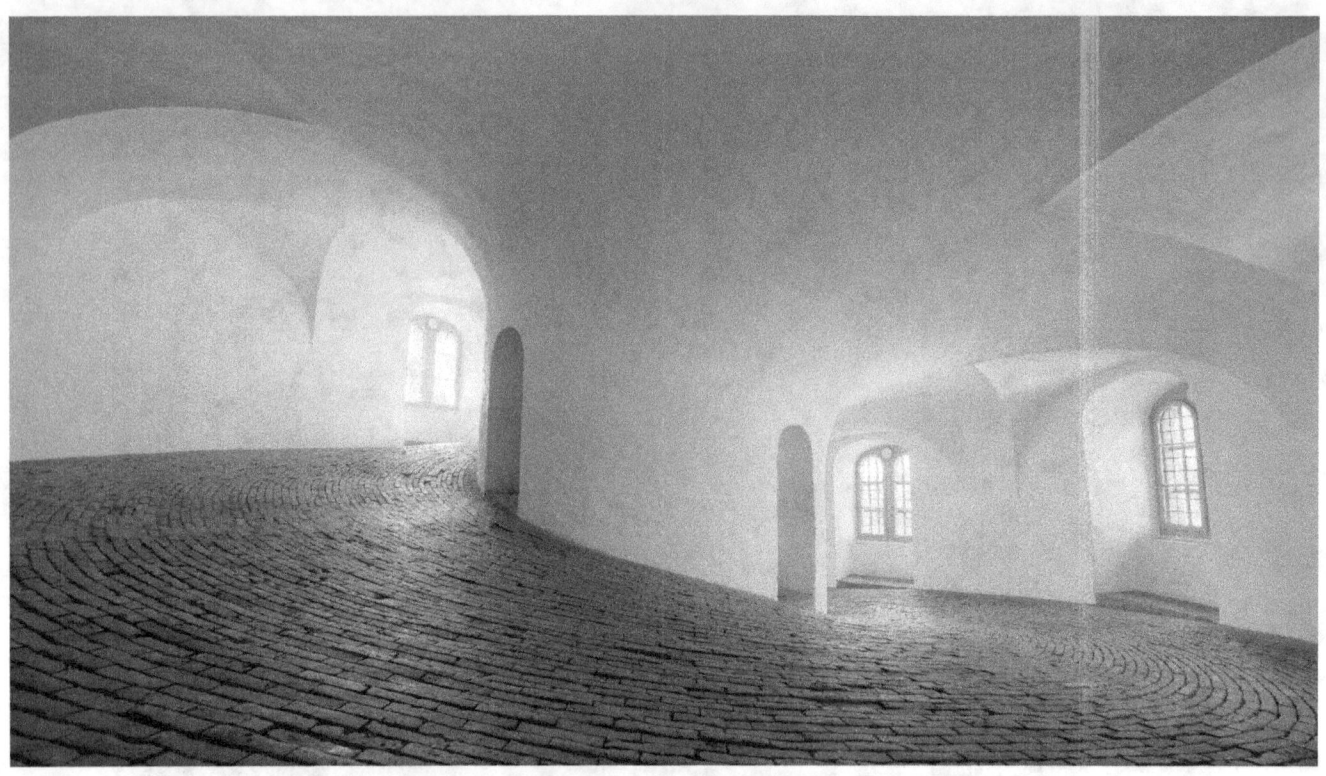

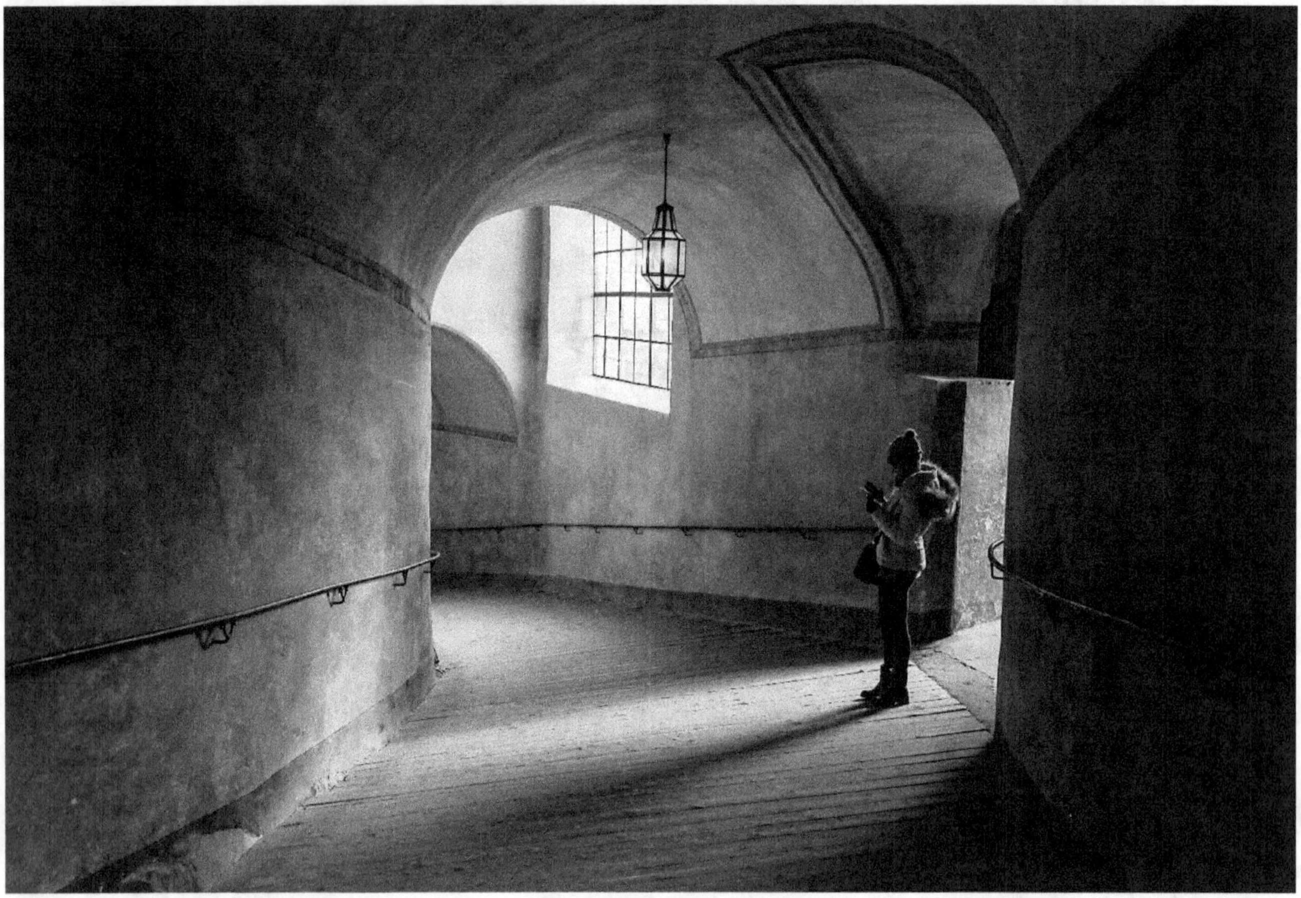

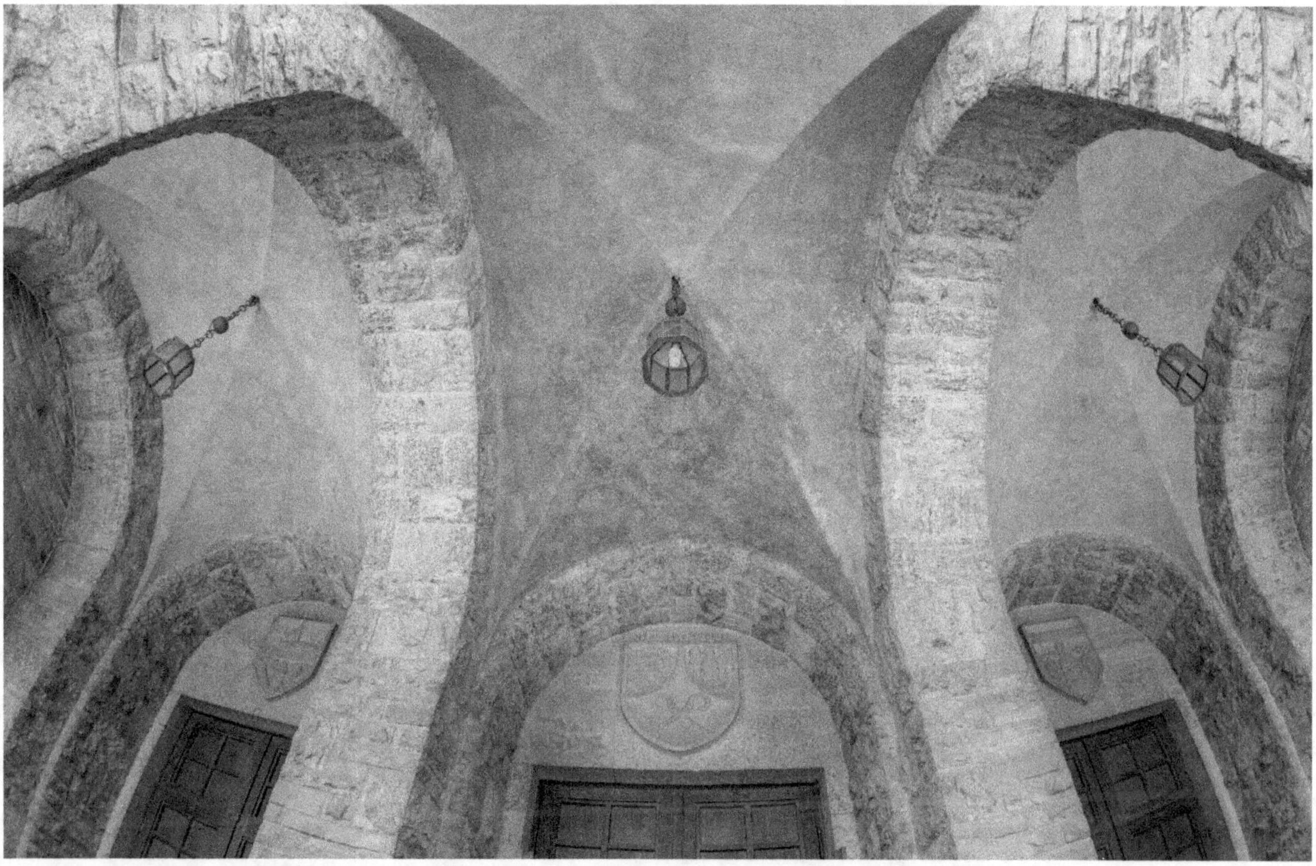

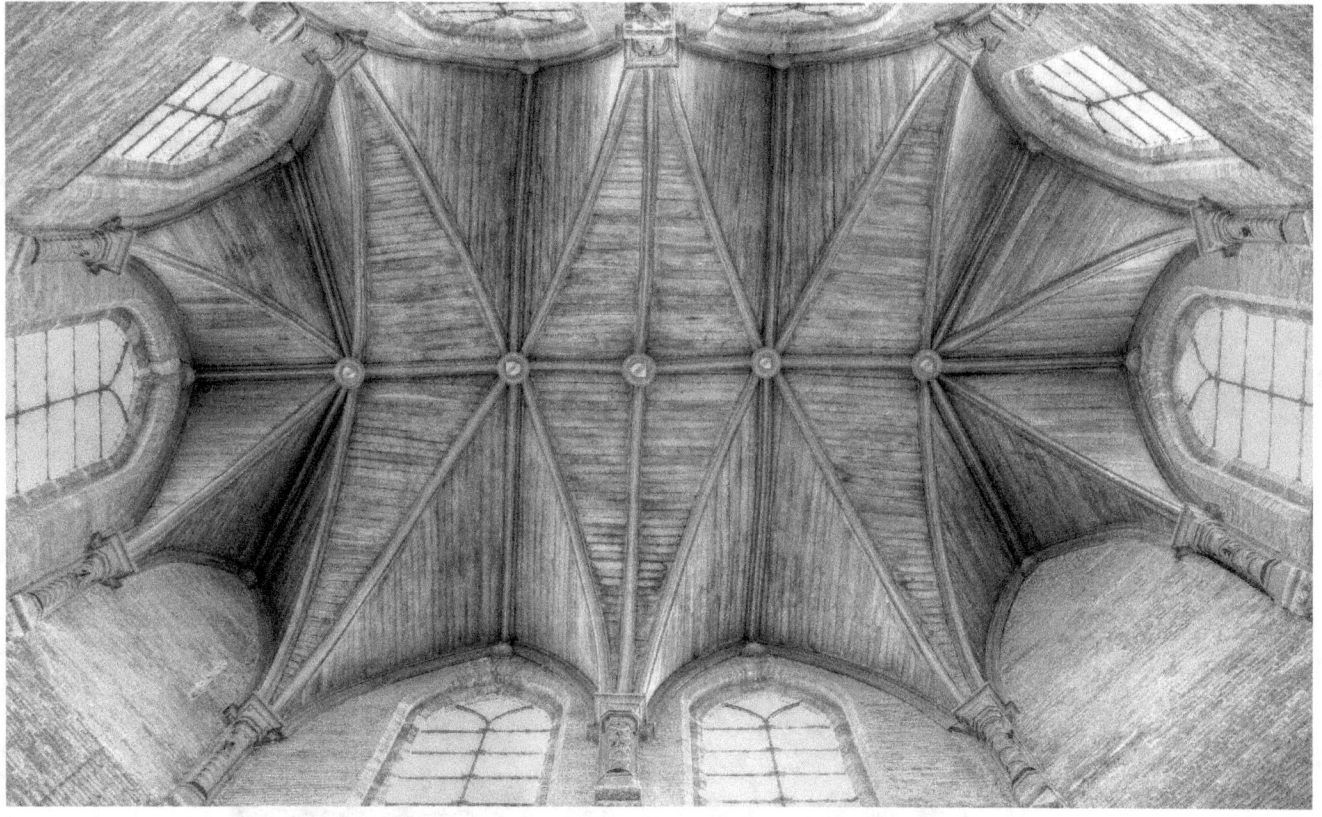

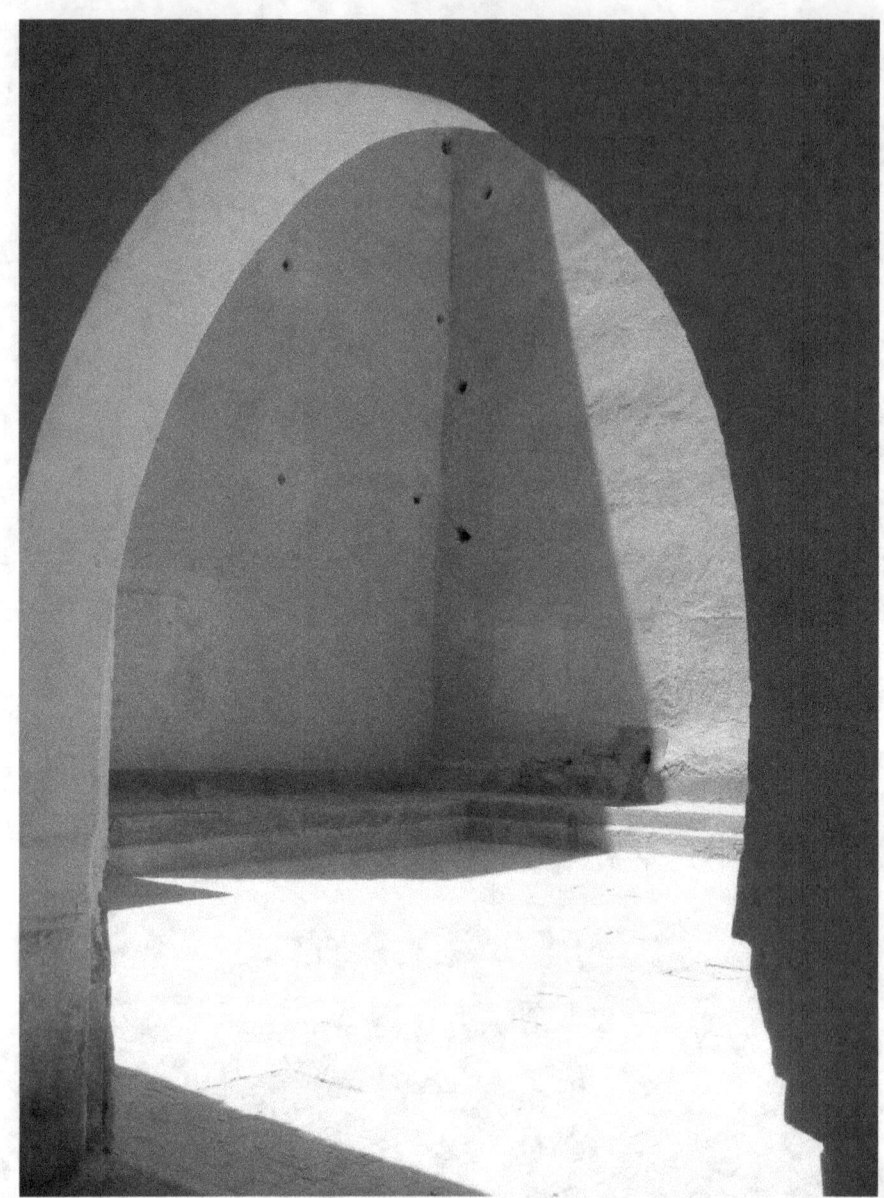

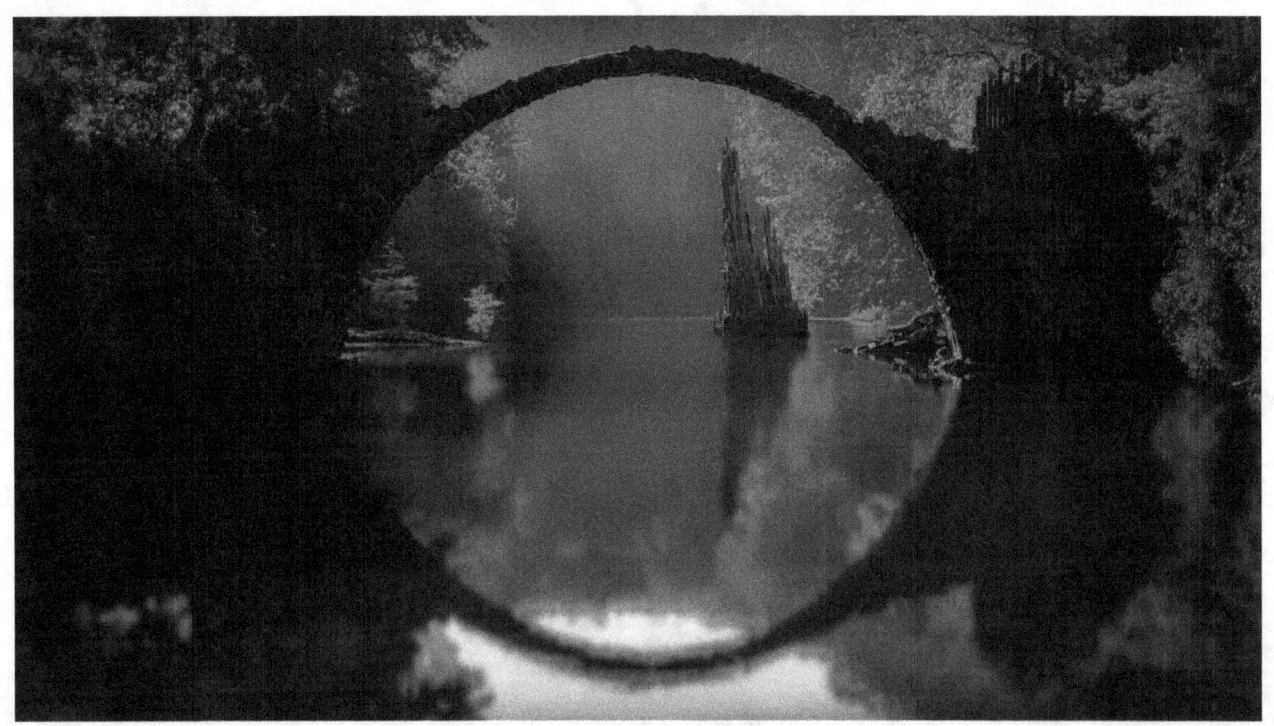

Free Junk Huts

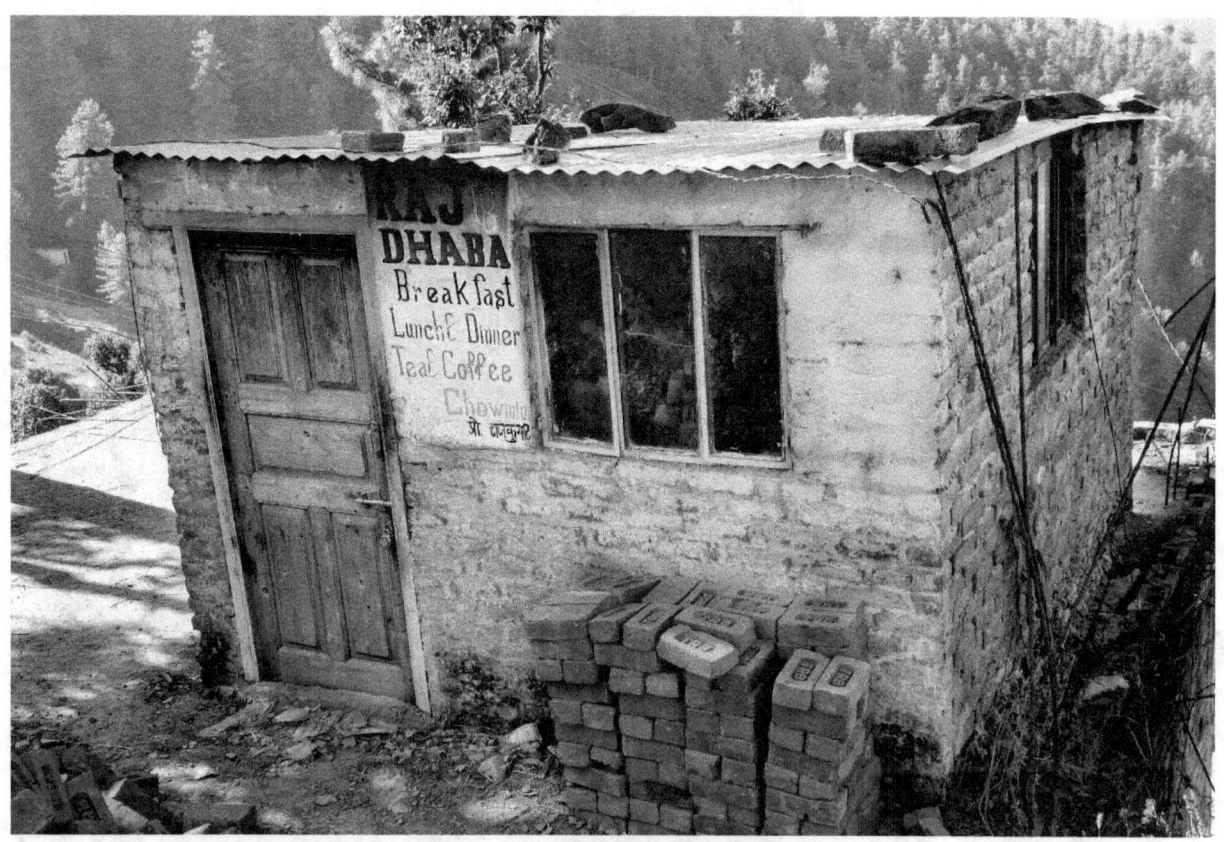

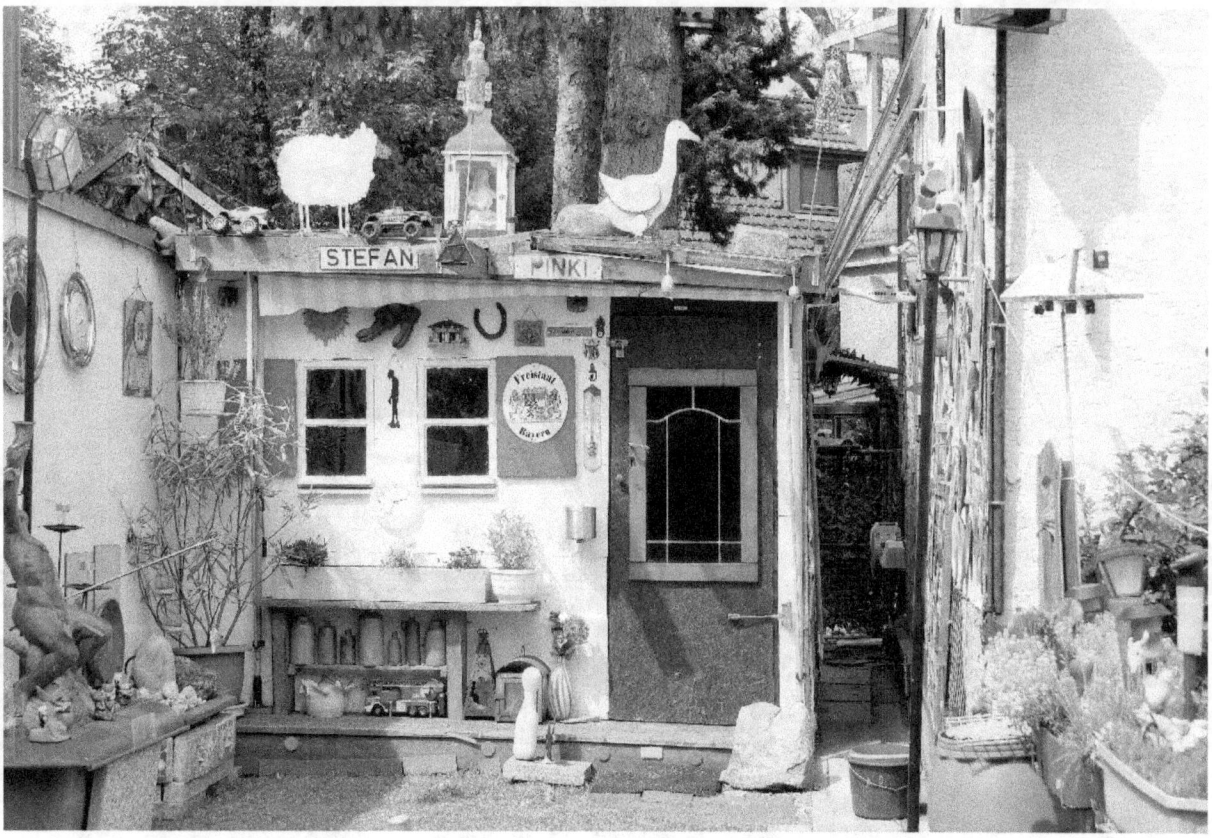

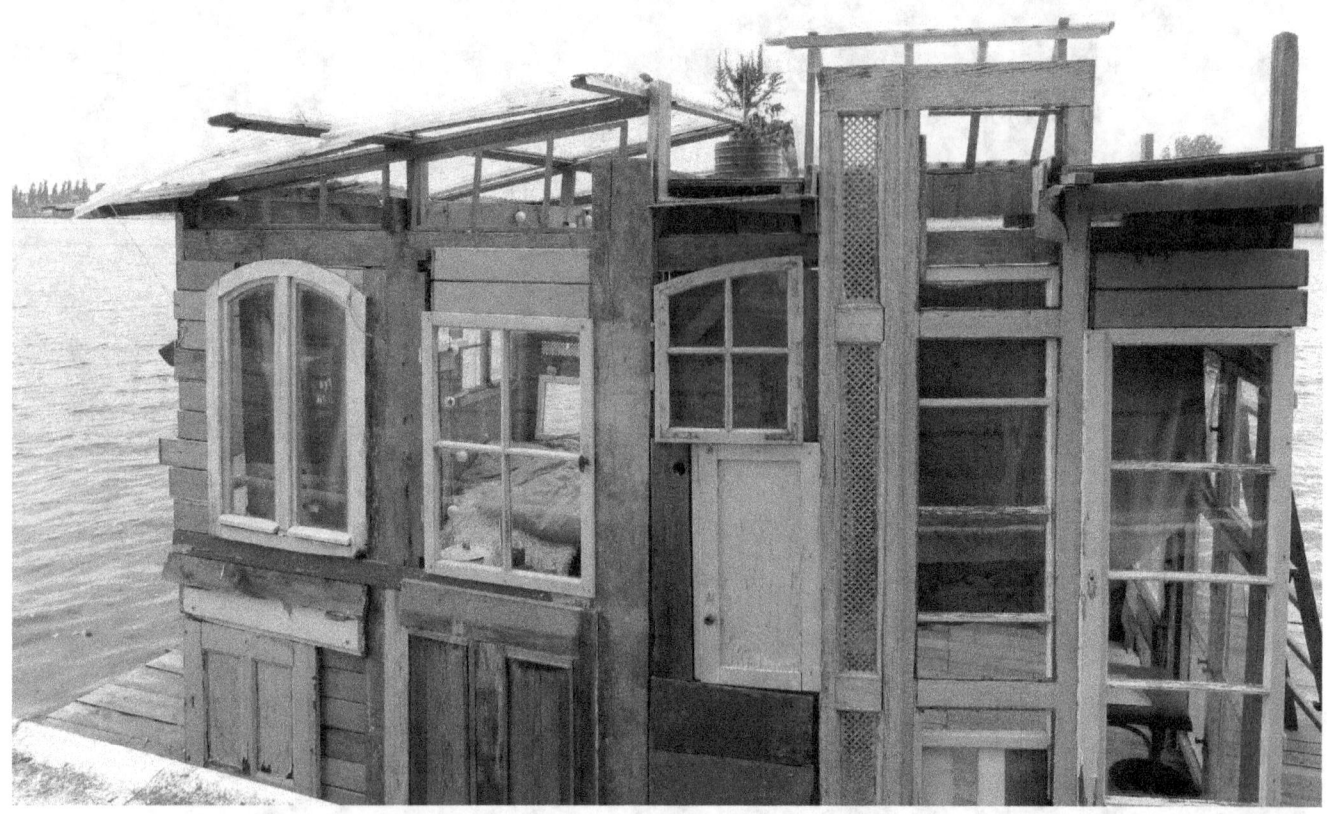

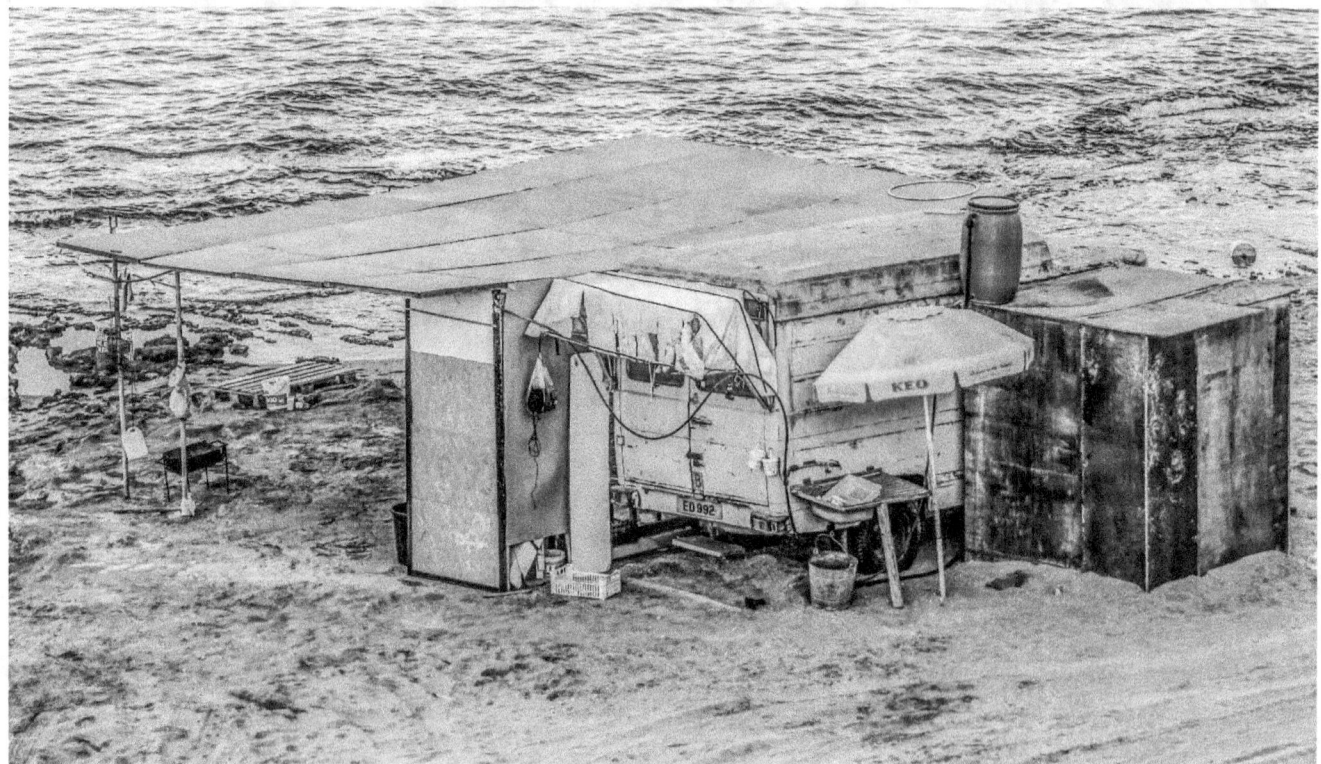

Abandoned

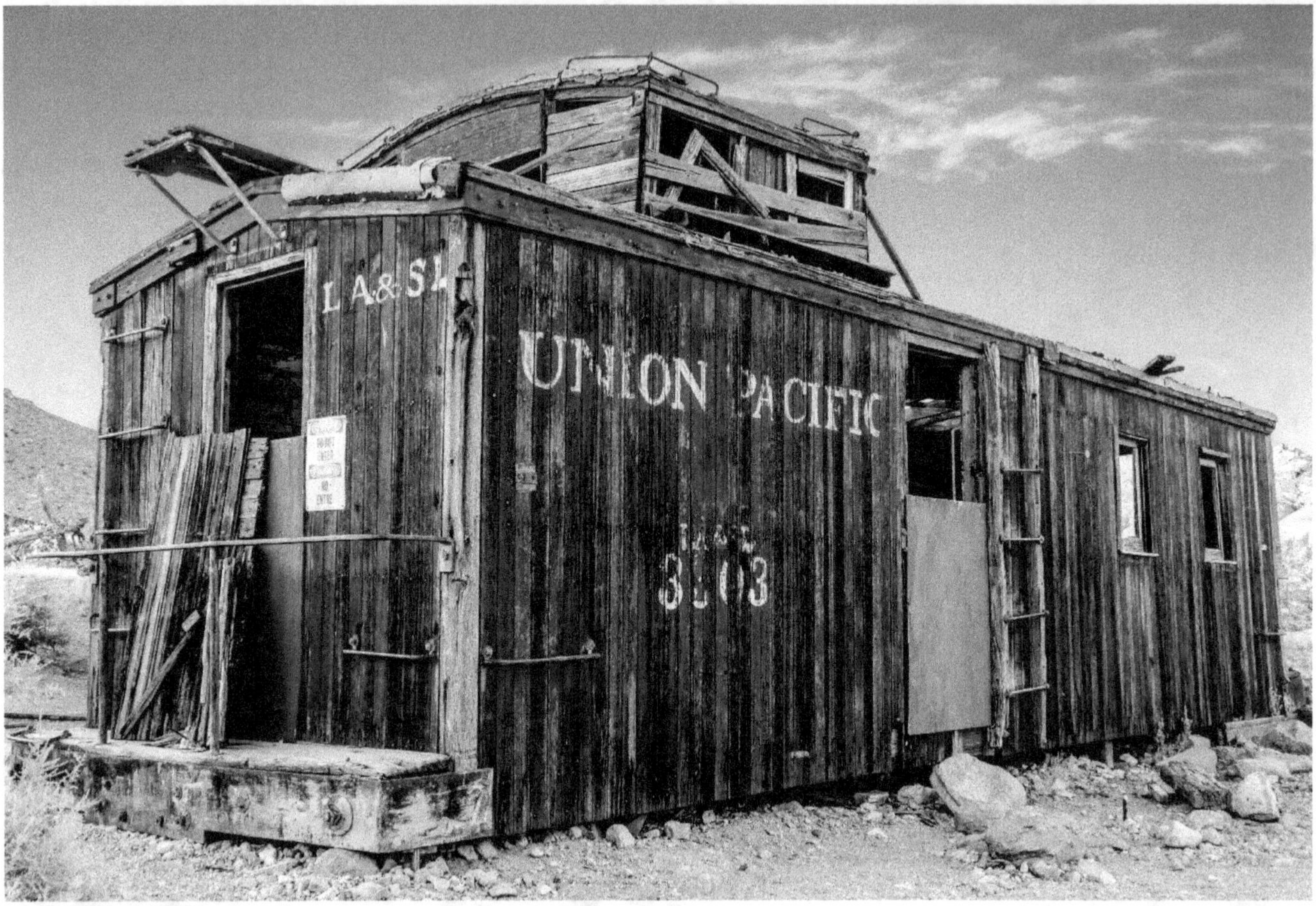

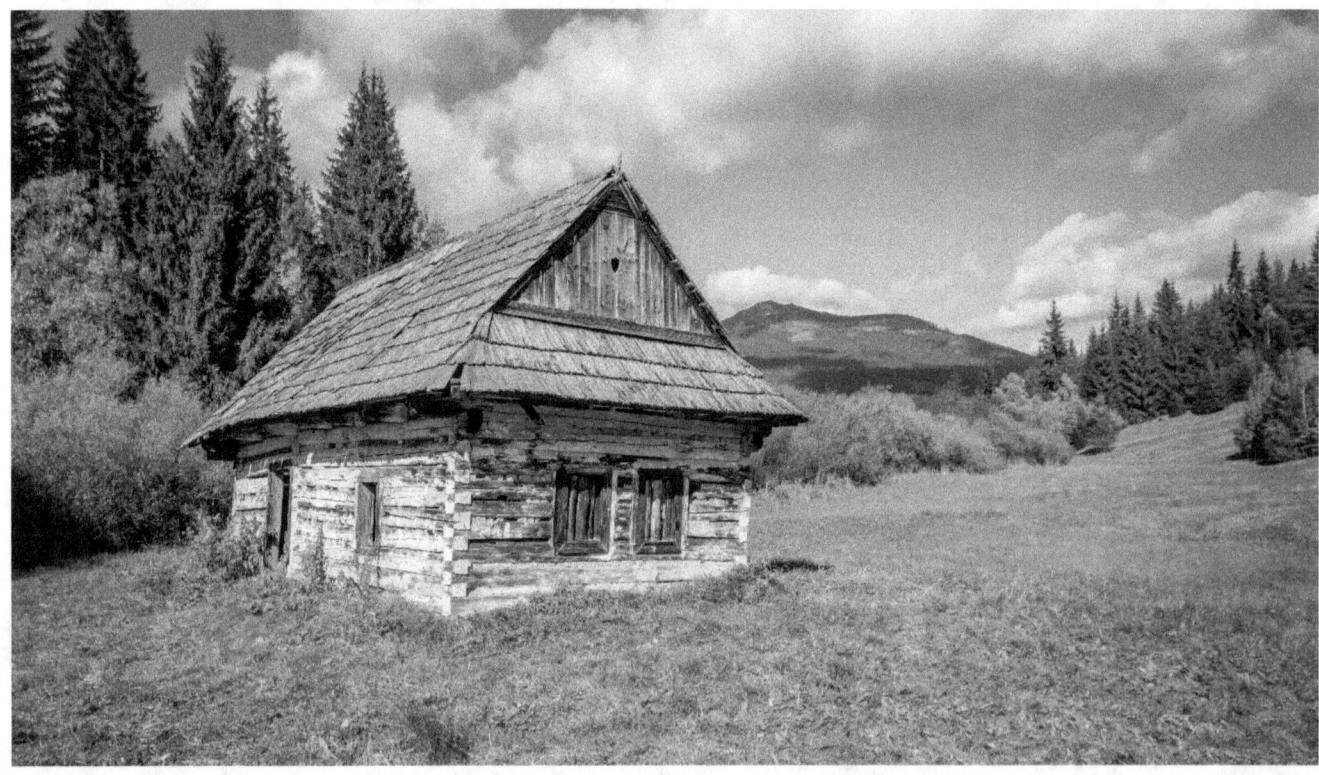

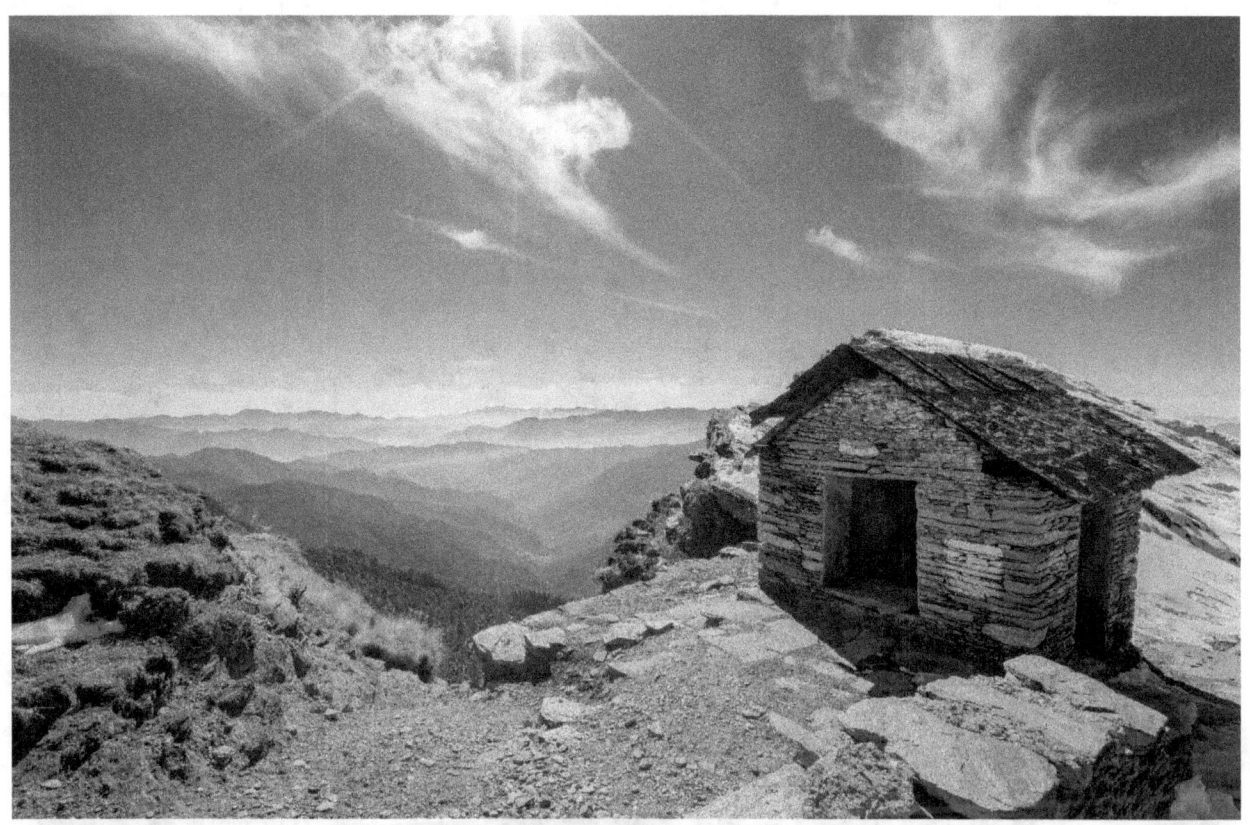

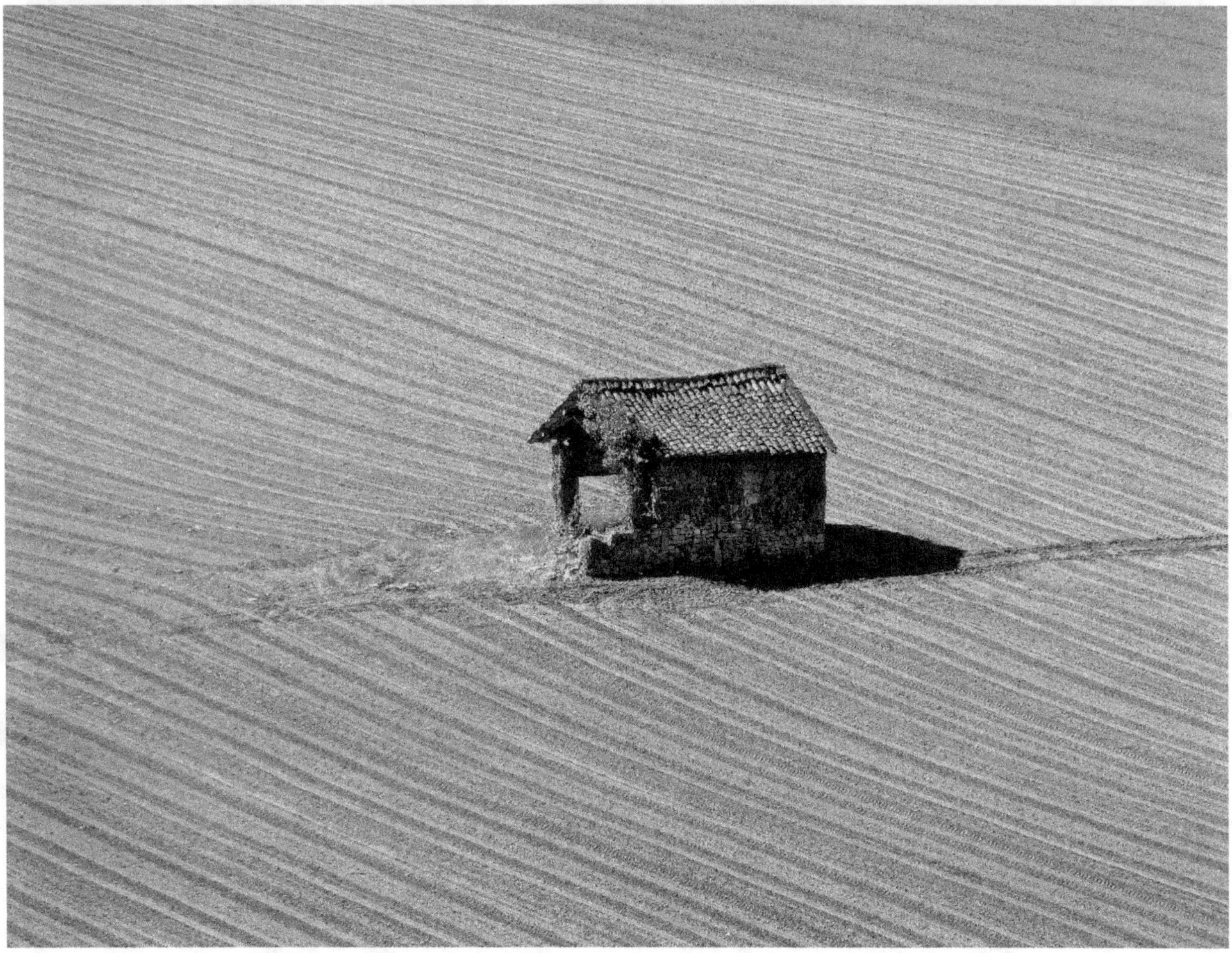

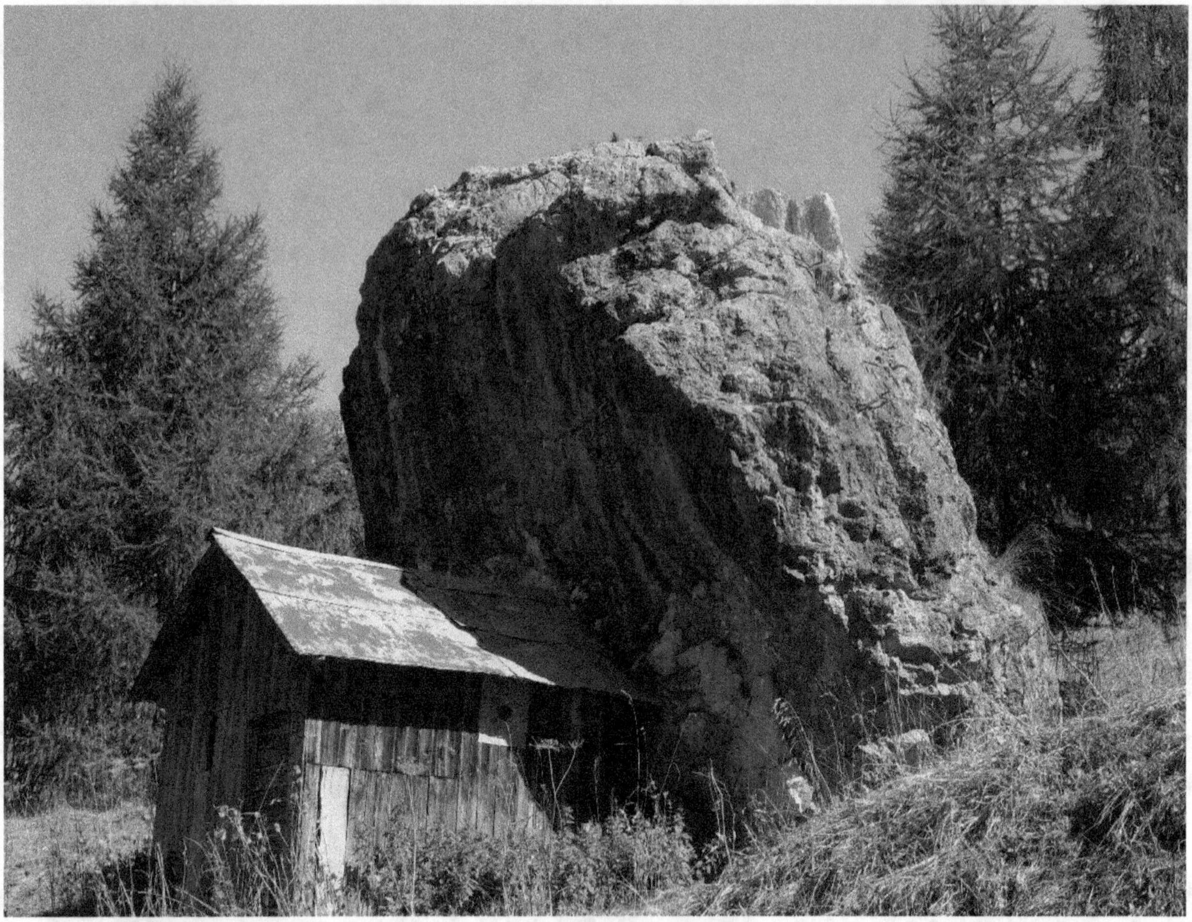

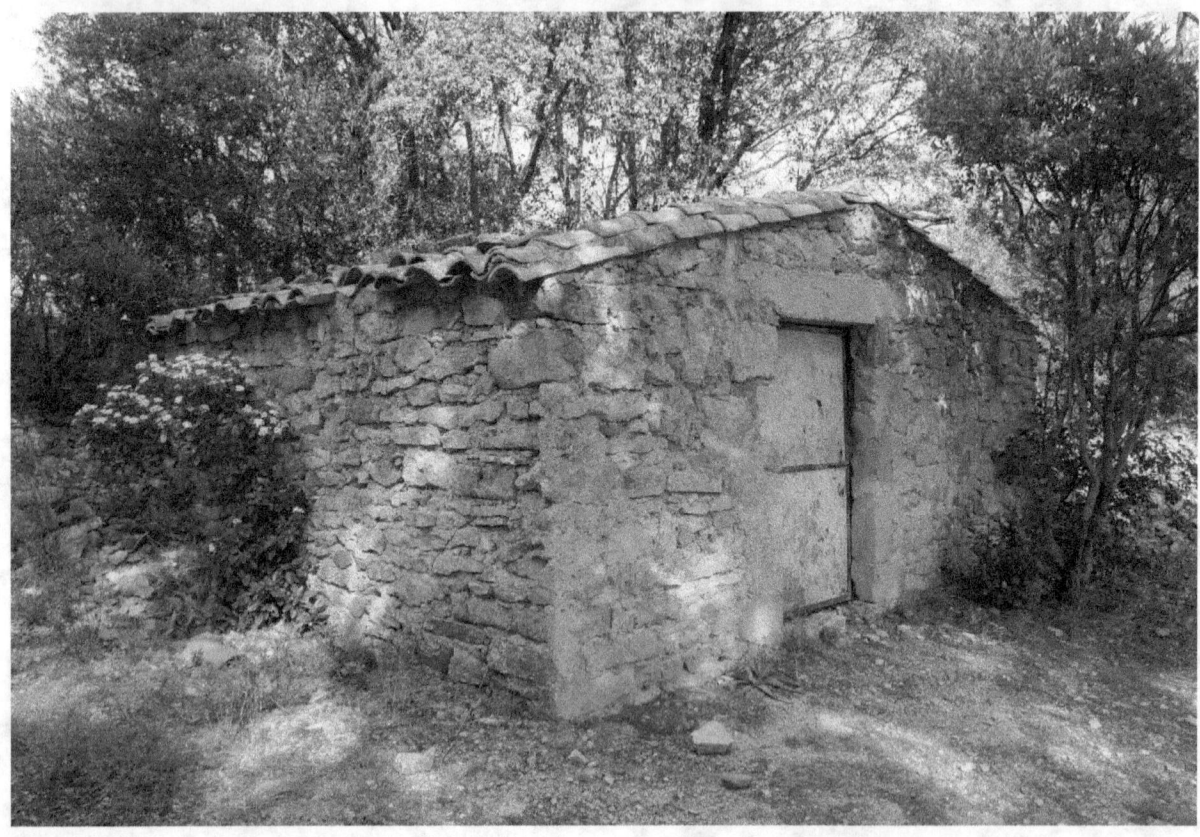

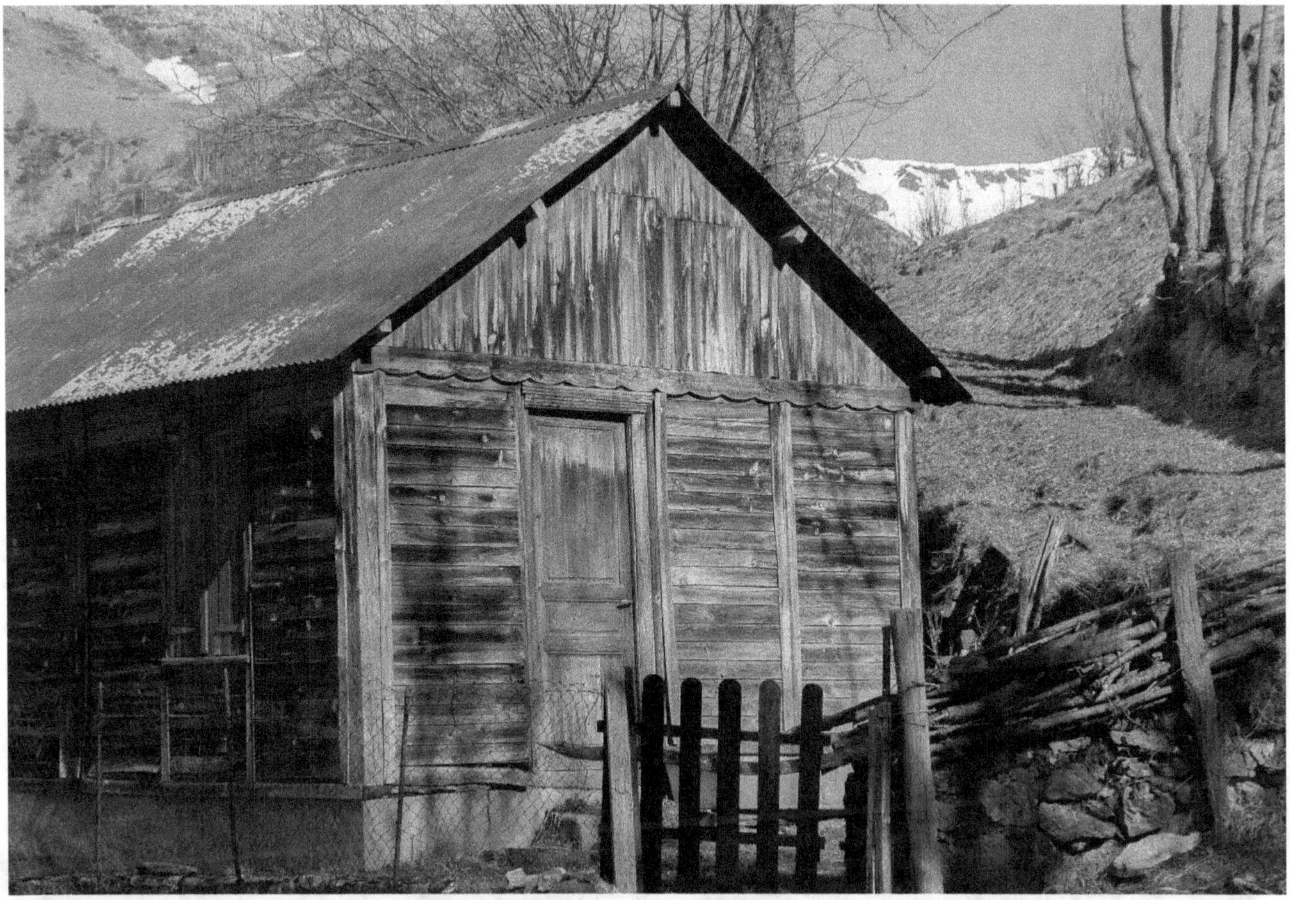

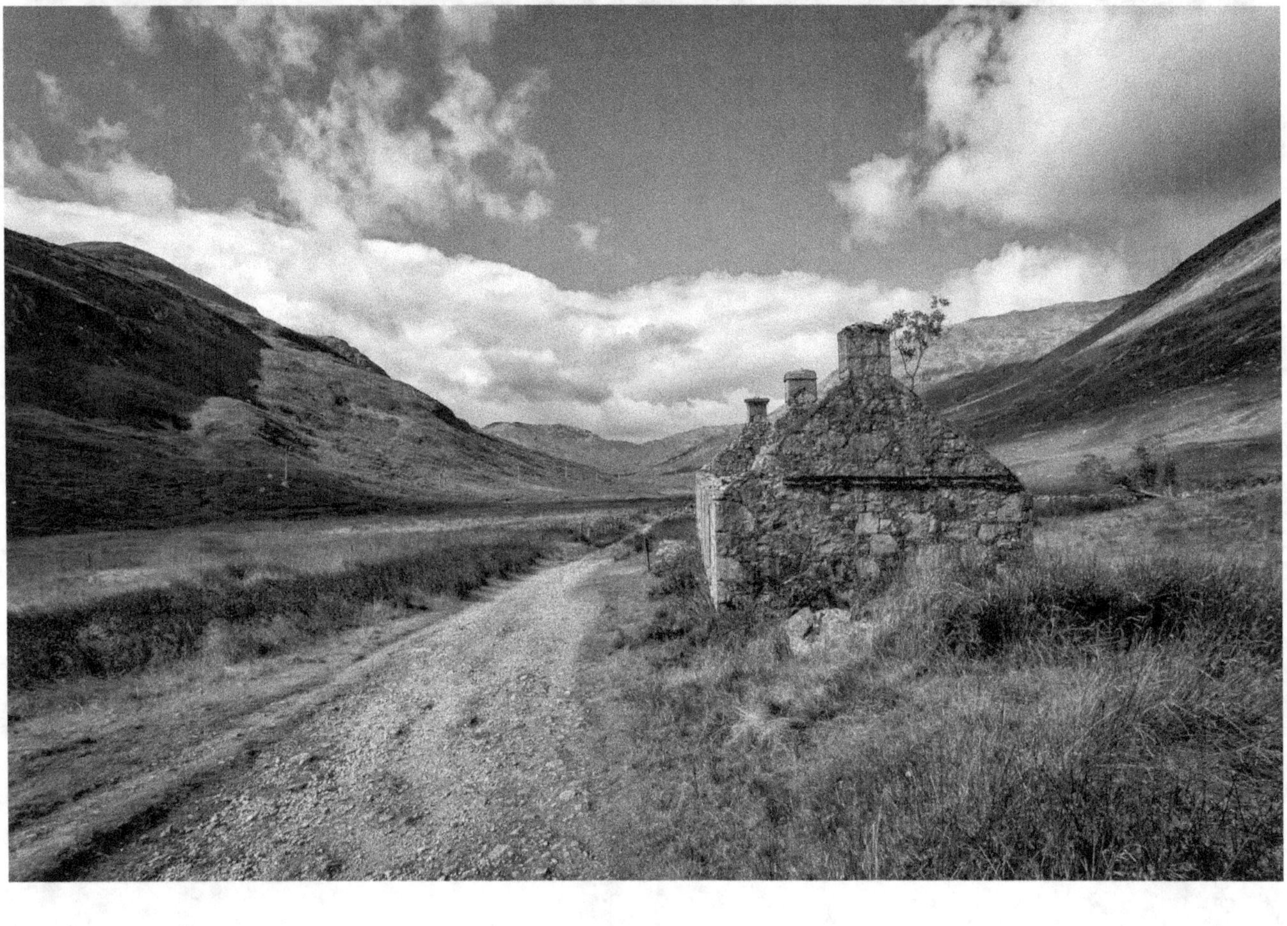

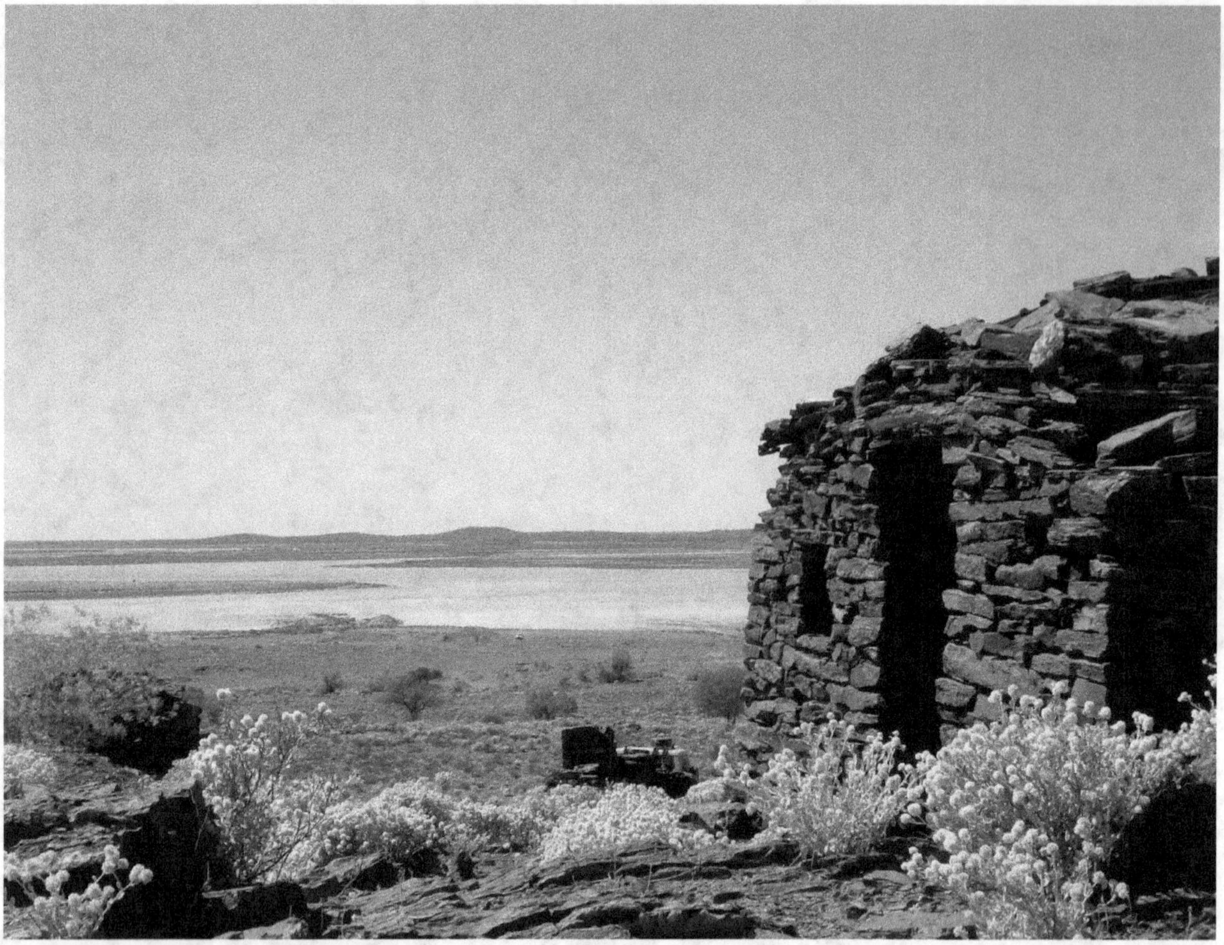

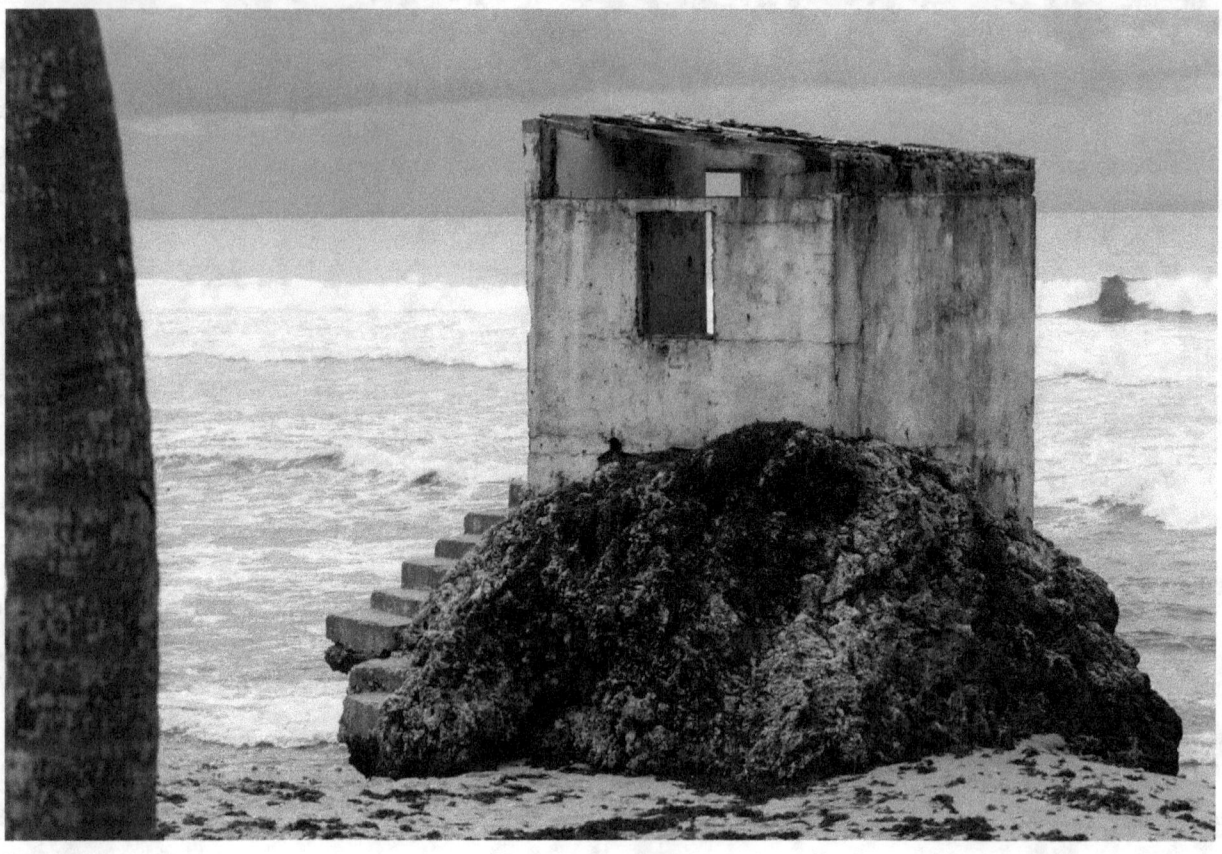

This page is intentionally left blank

11 OTHER

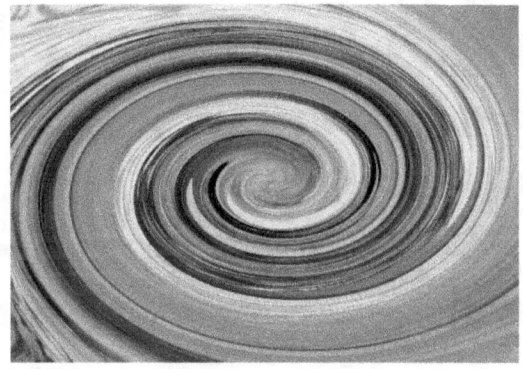

Whimsical, other stuff, little homes on wheels, gazebos and outdoor, privies, domes, and sheds

Whimsical

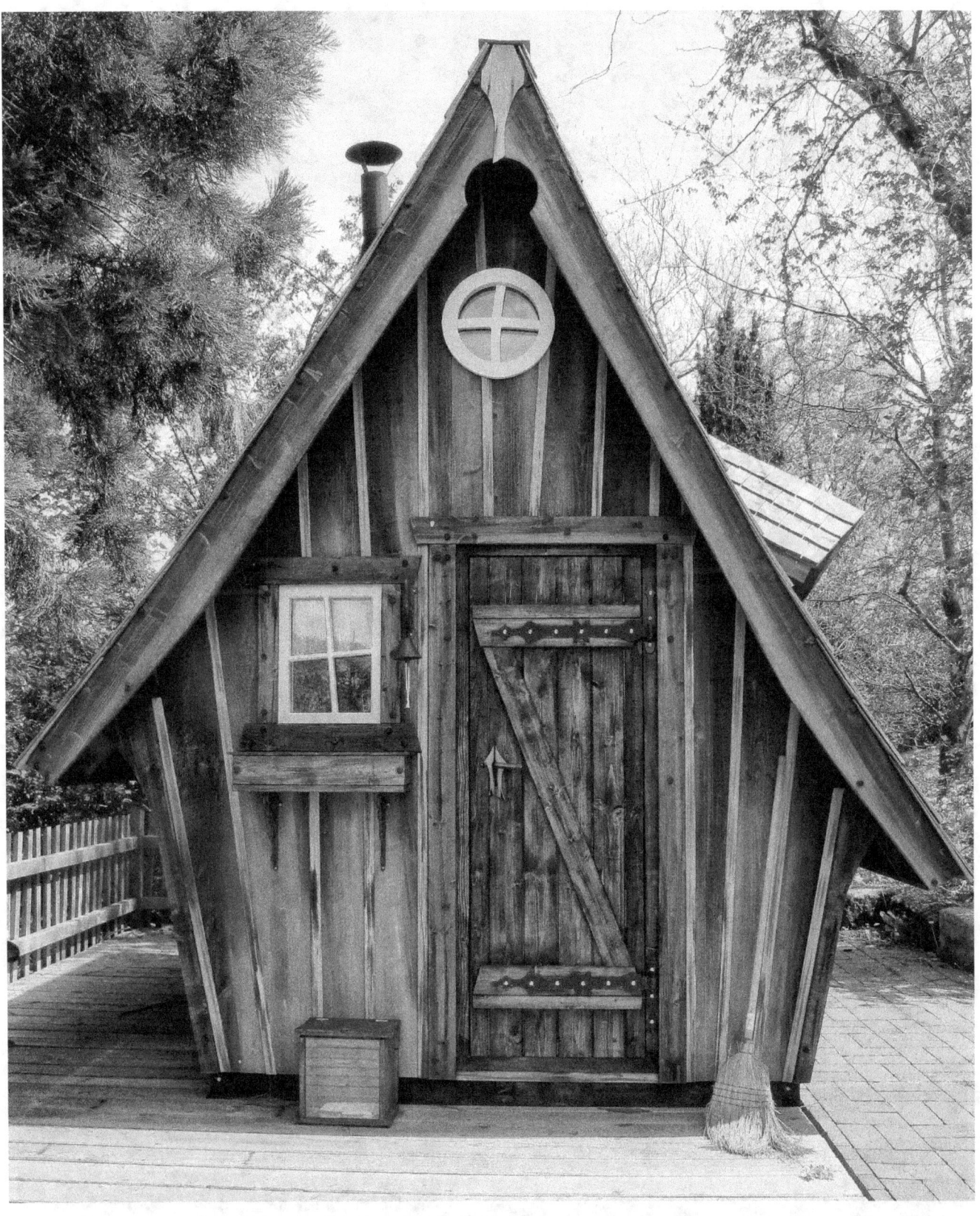

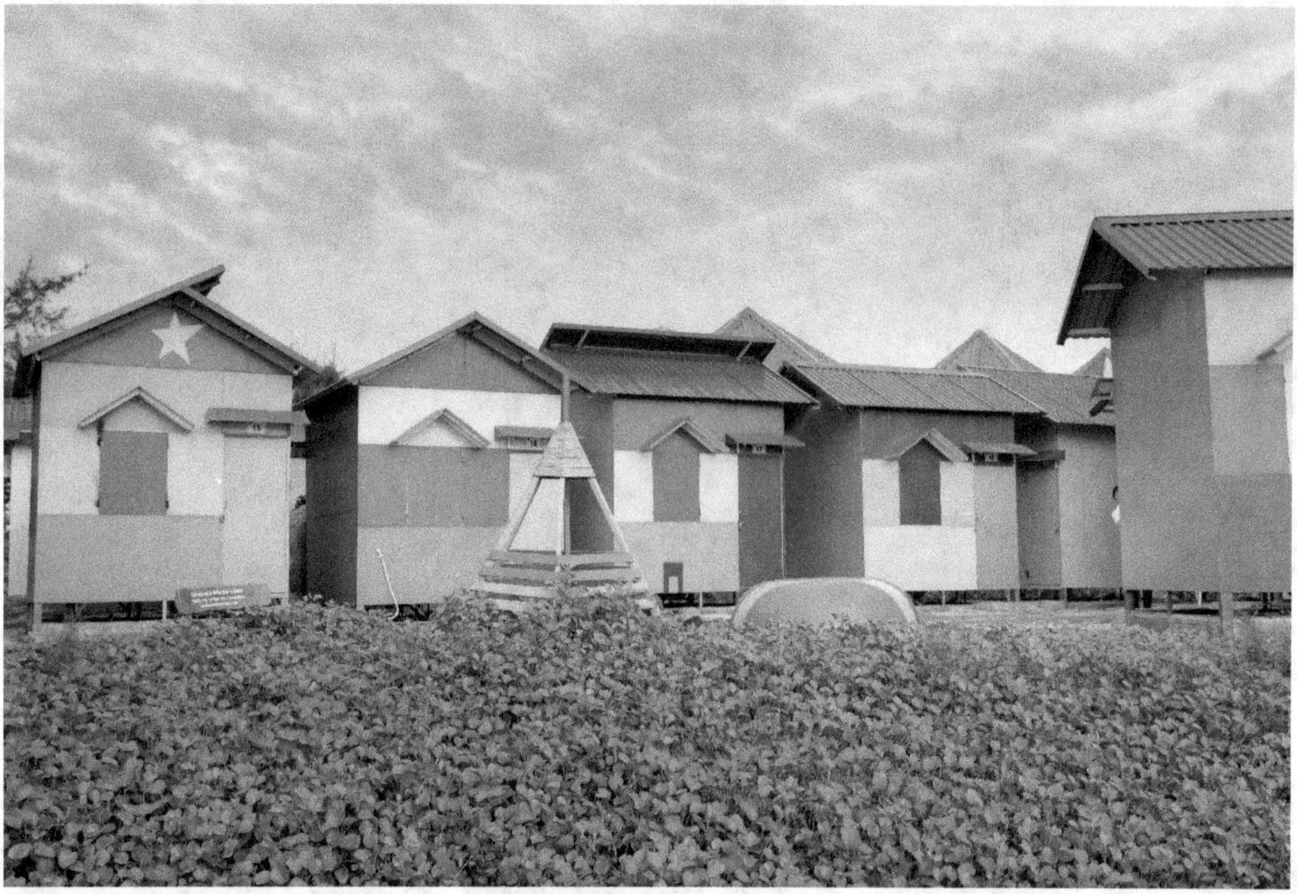

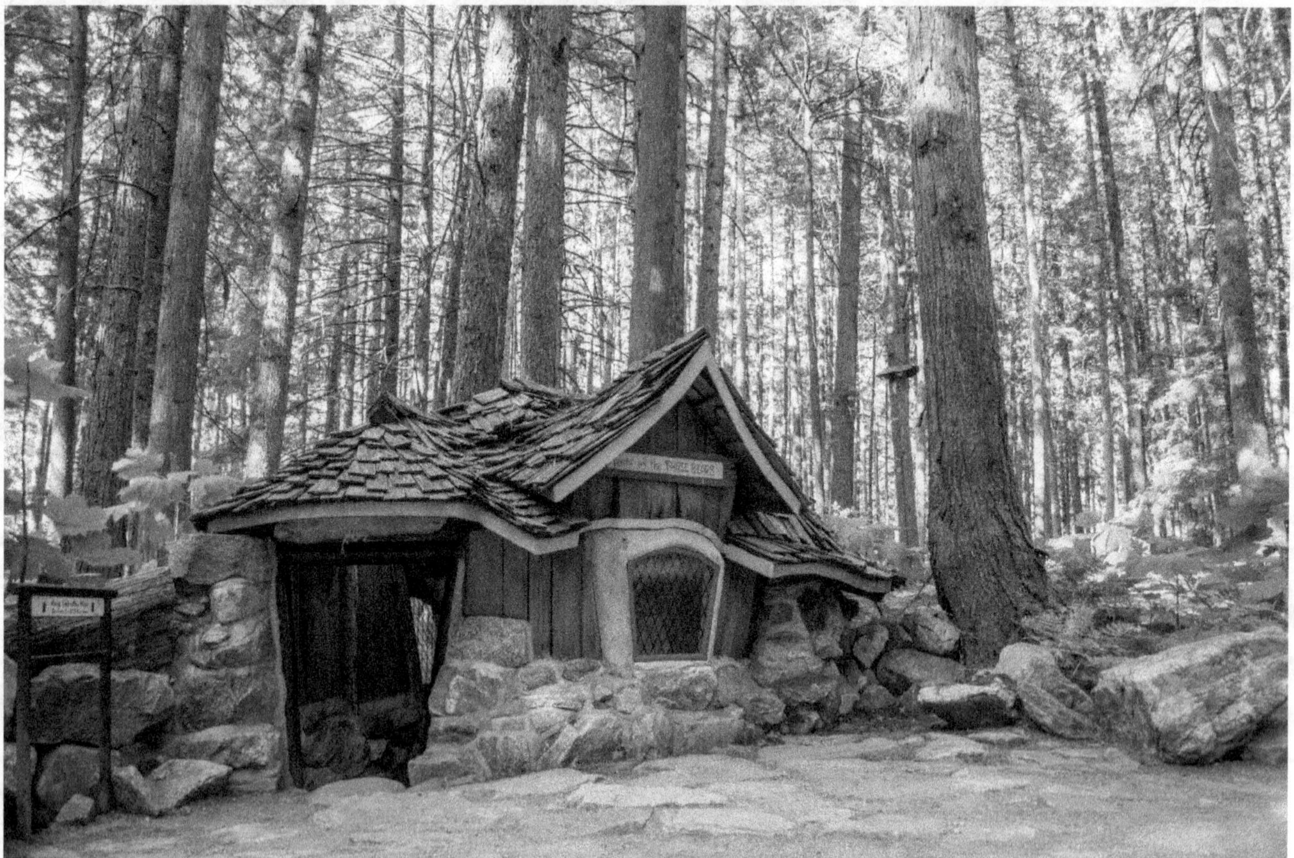

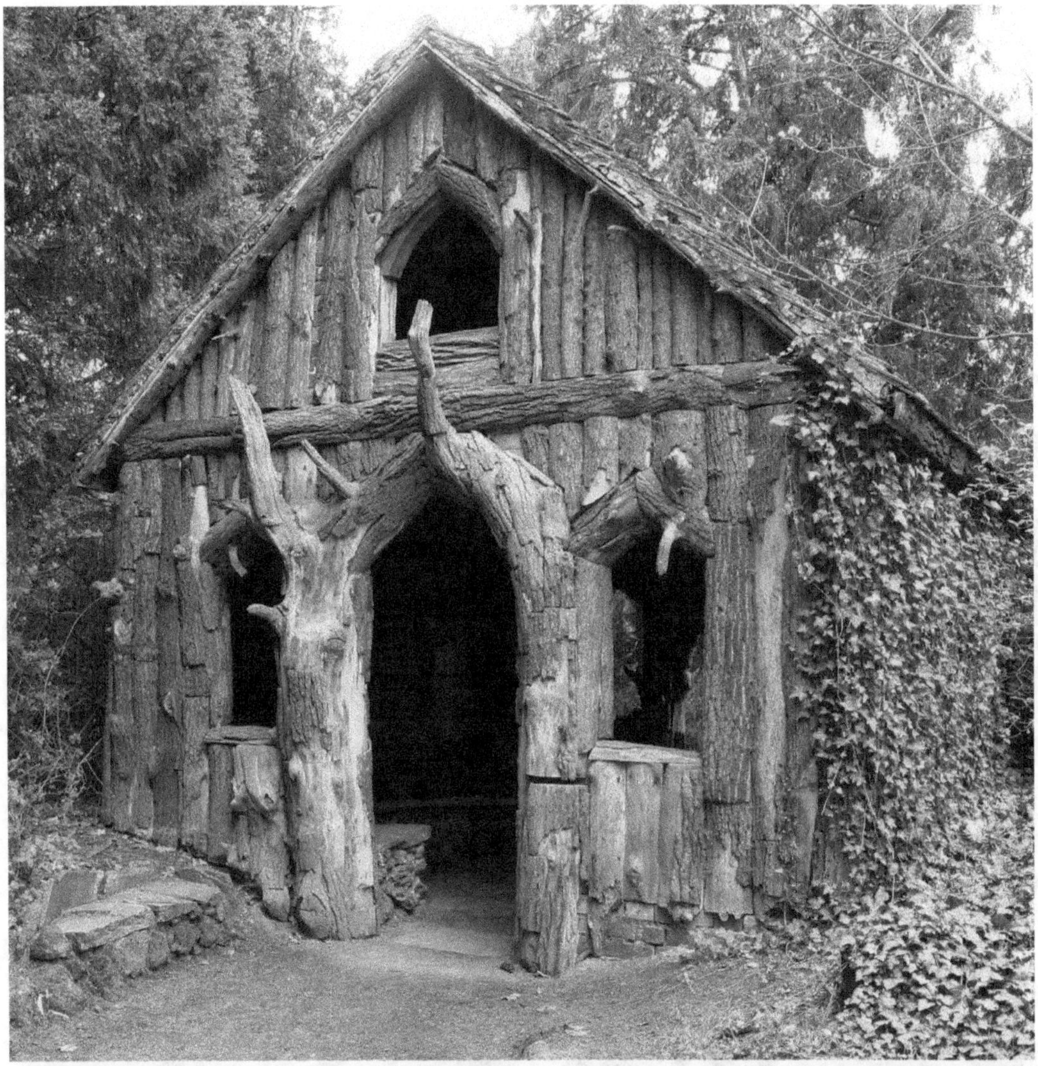

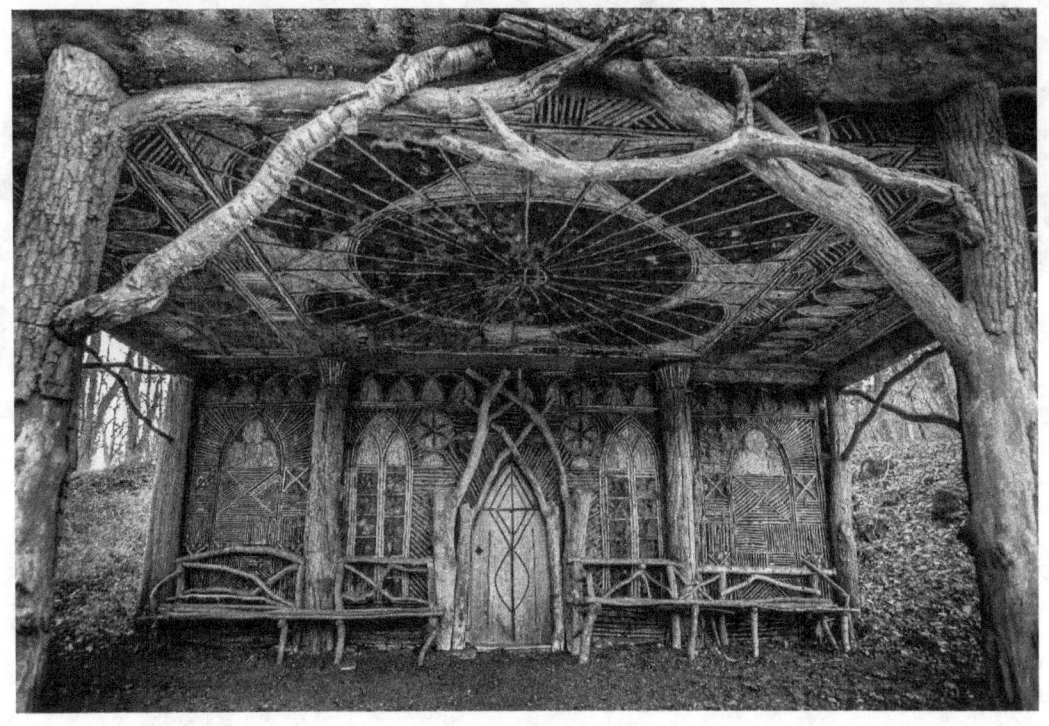

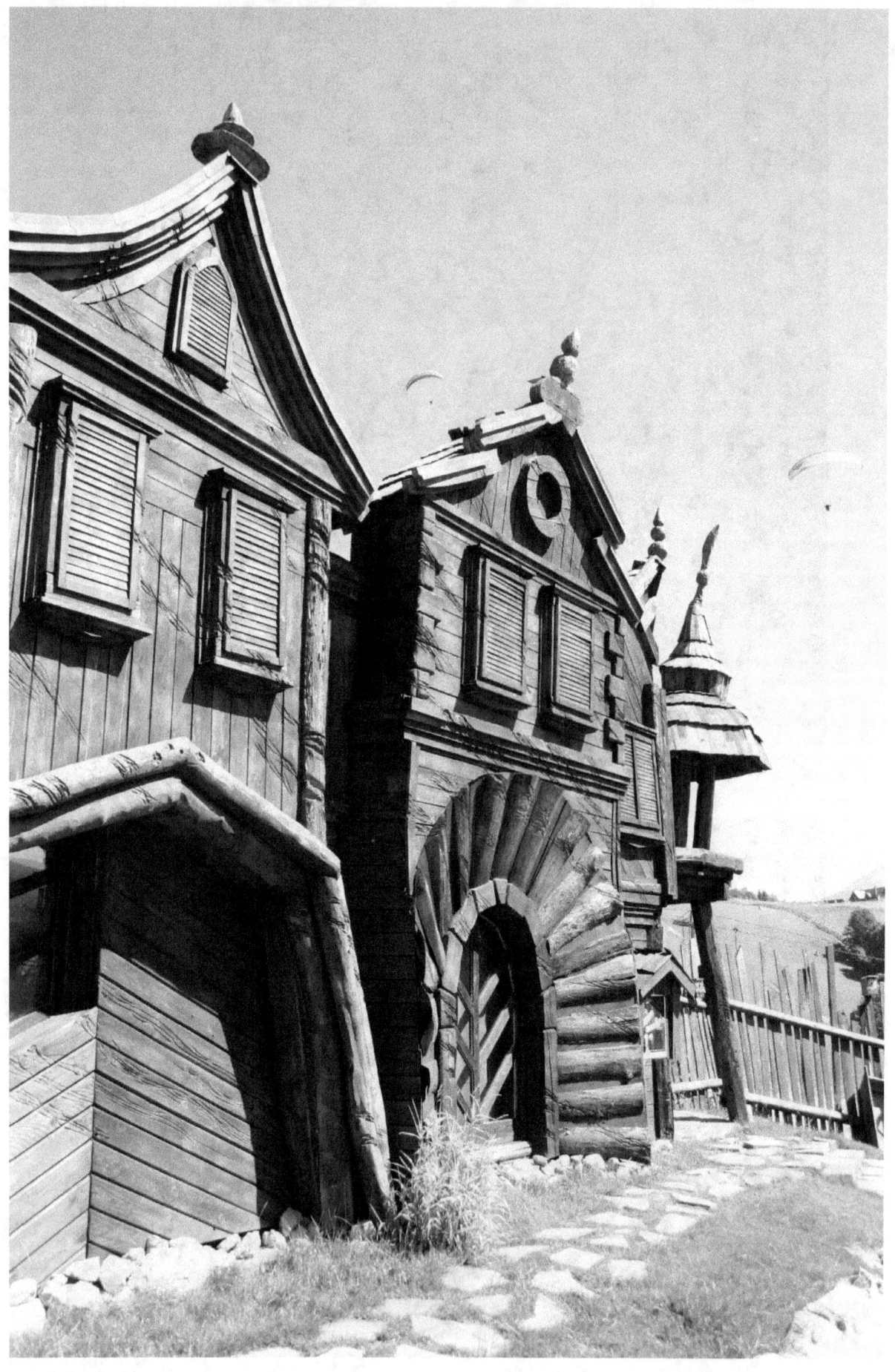

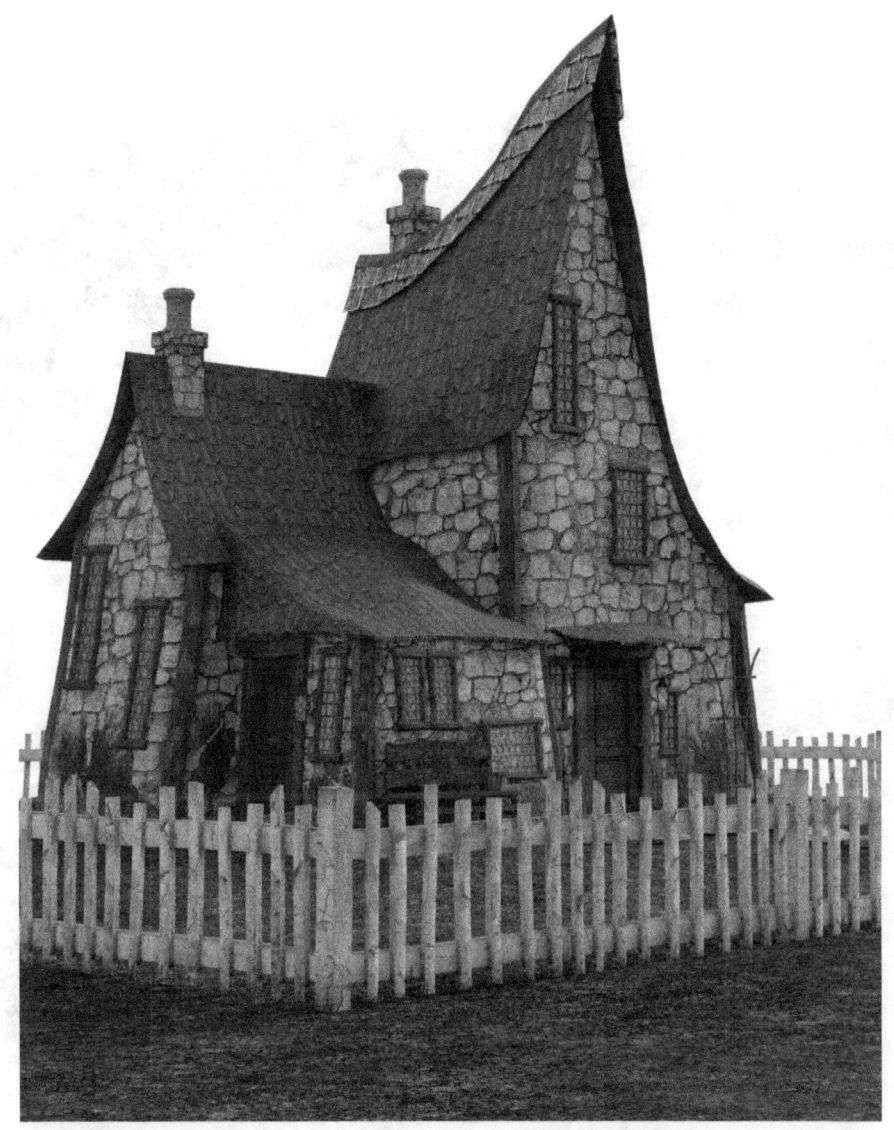

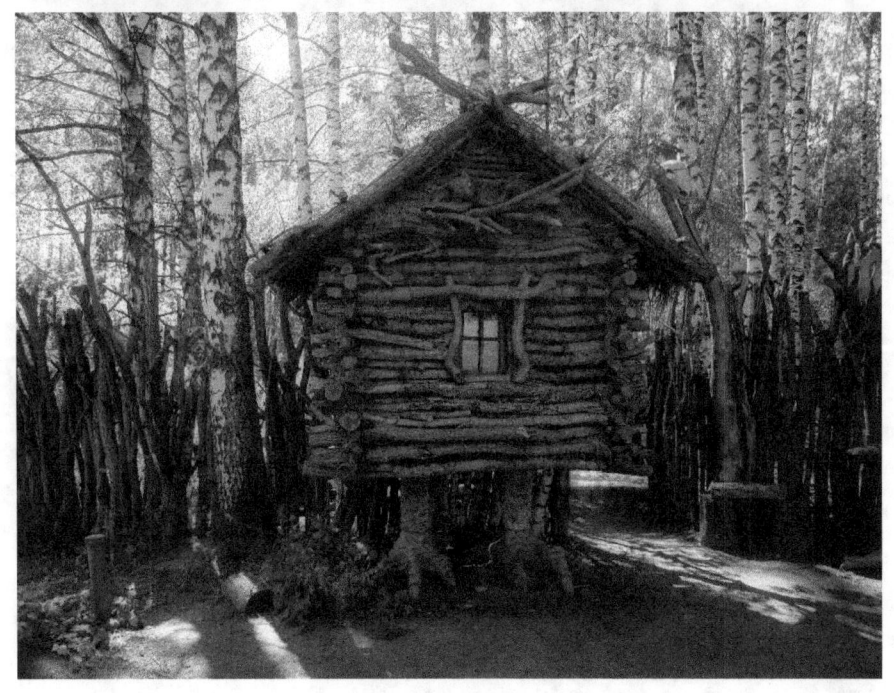

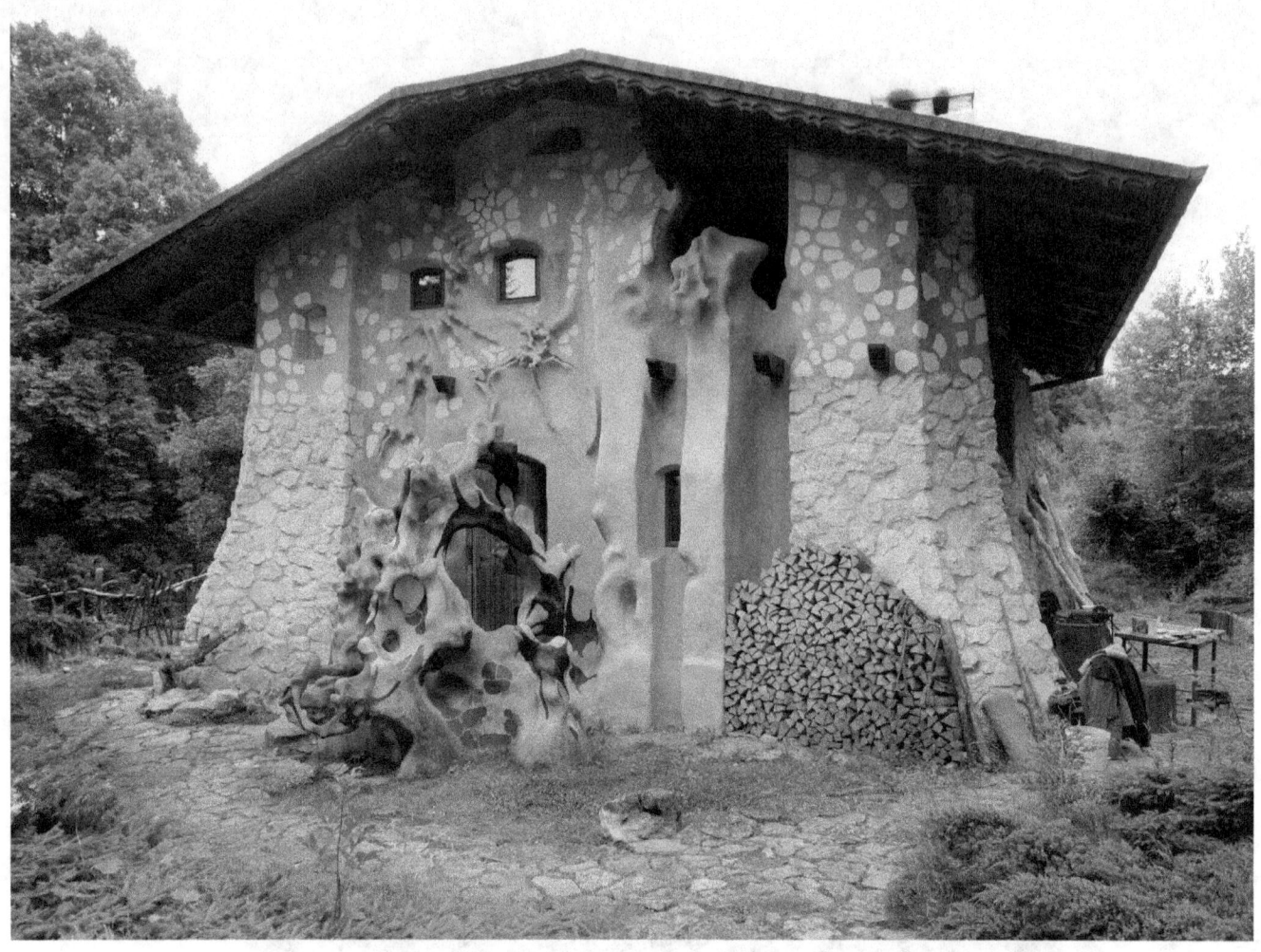

Other Stuff

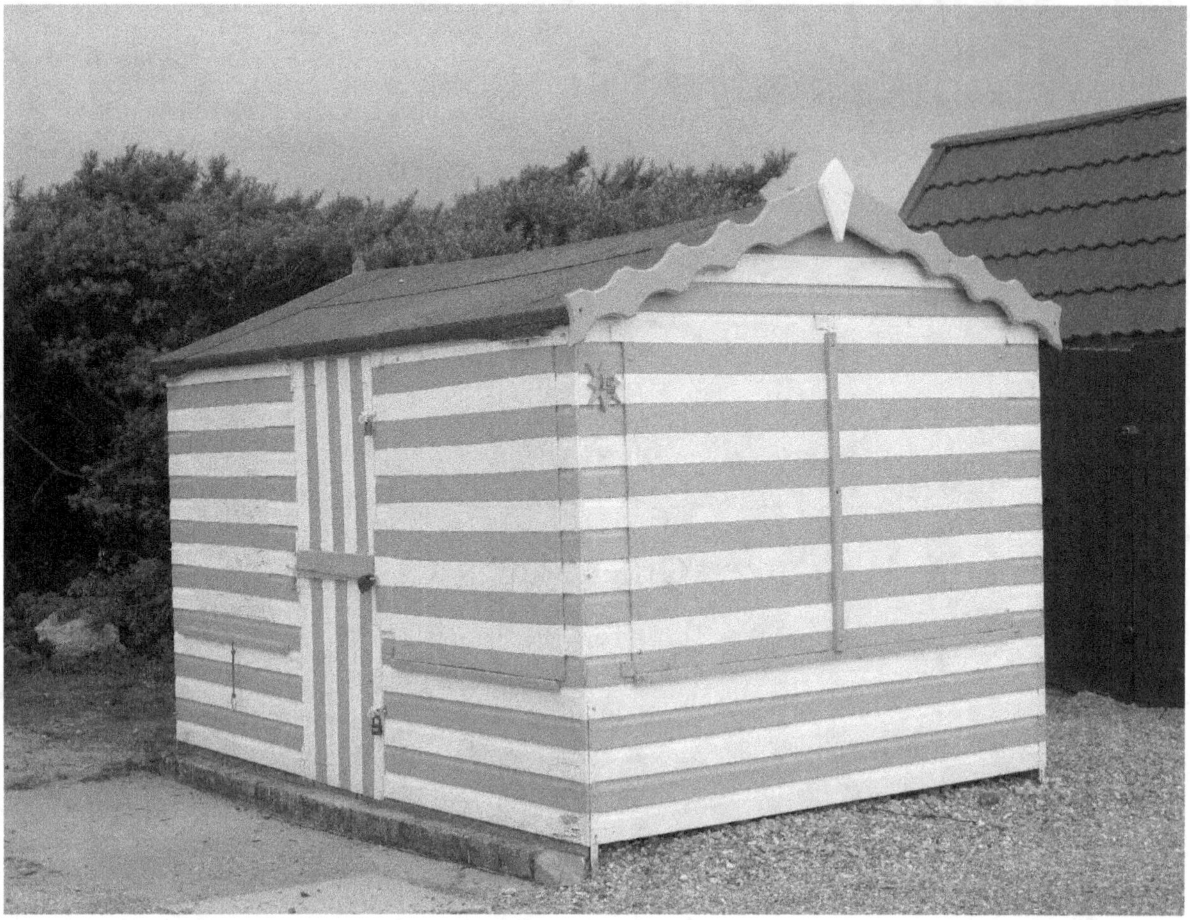

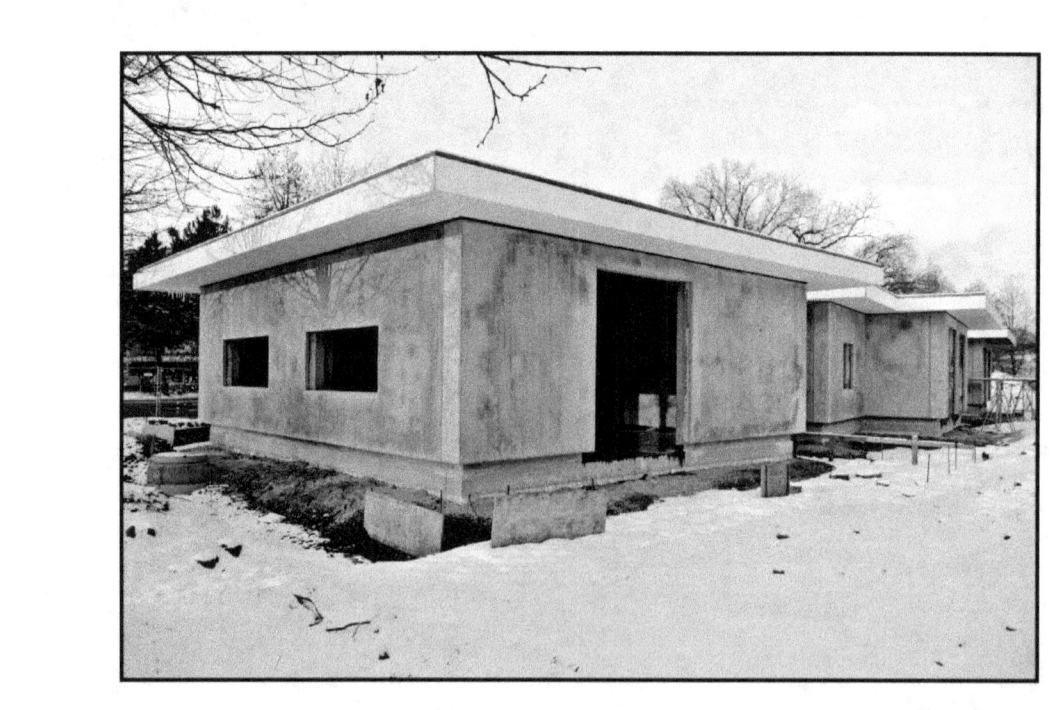

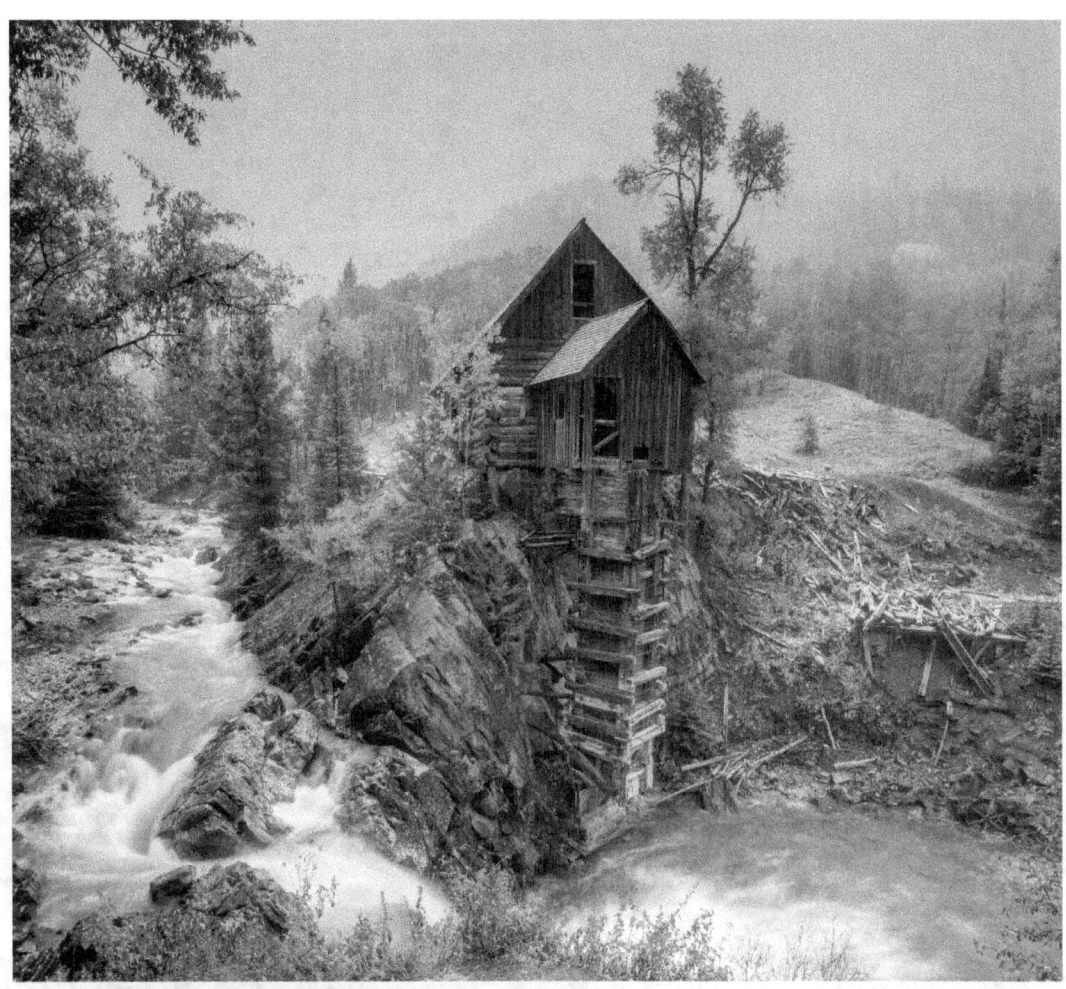

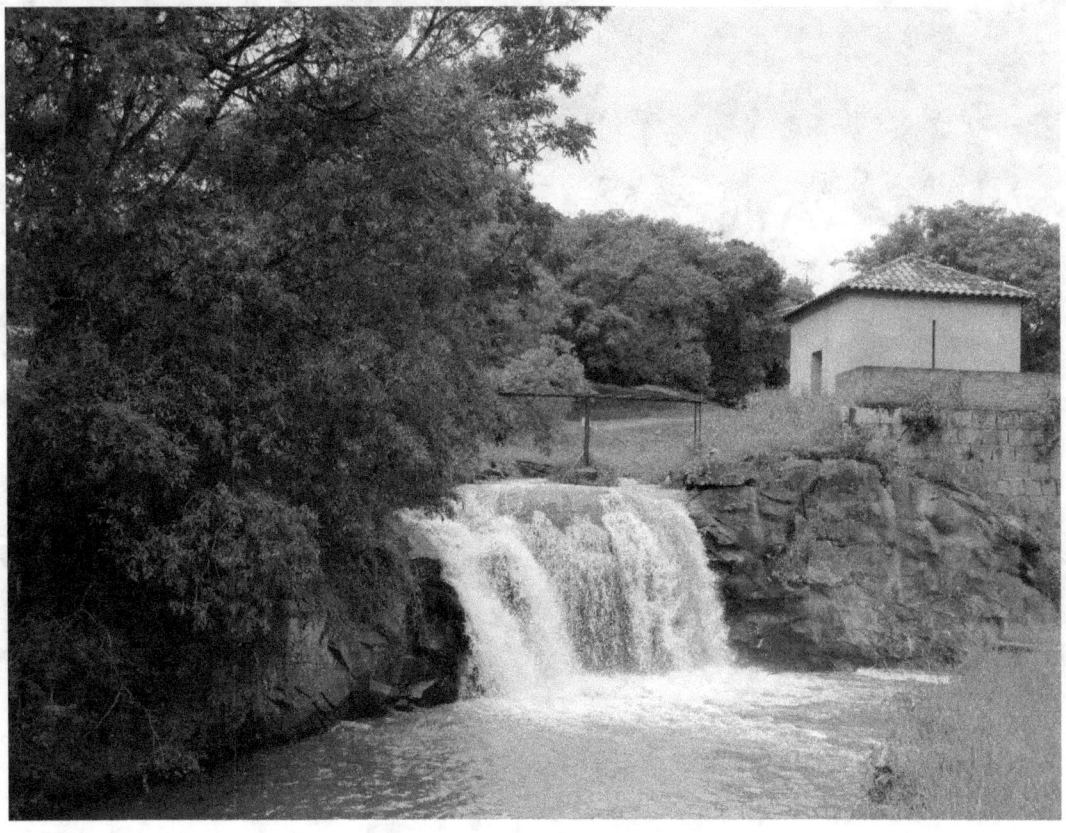

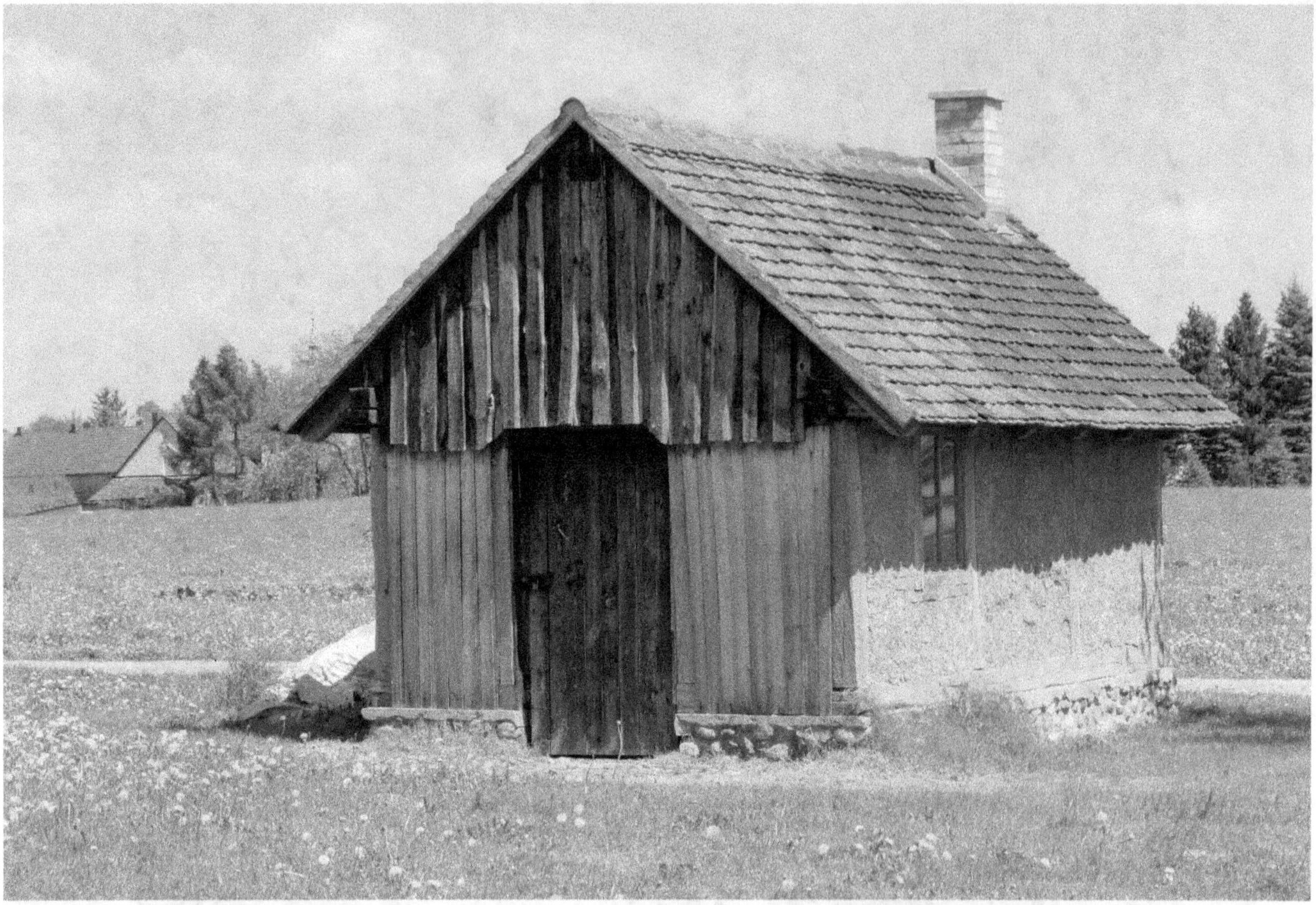

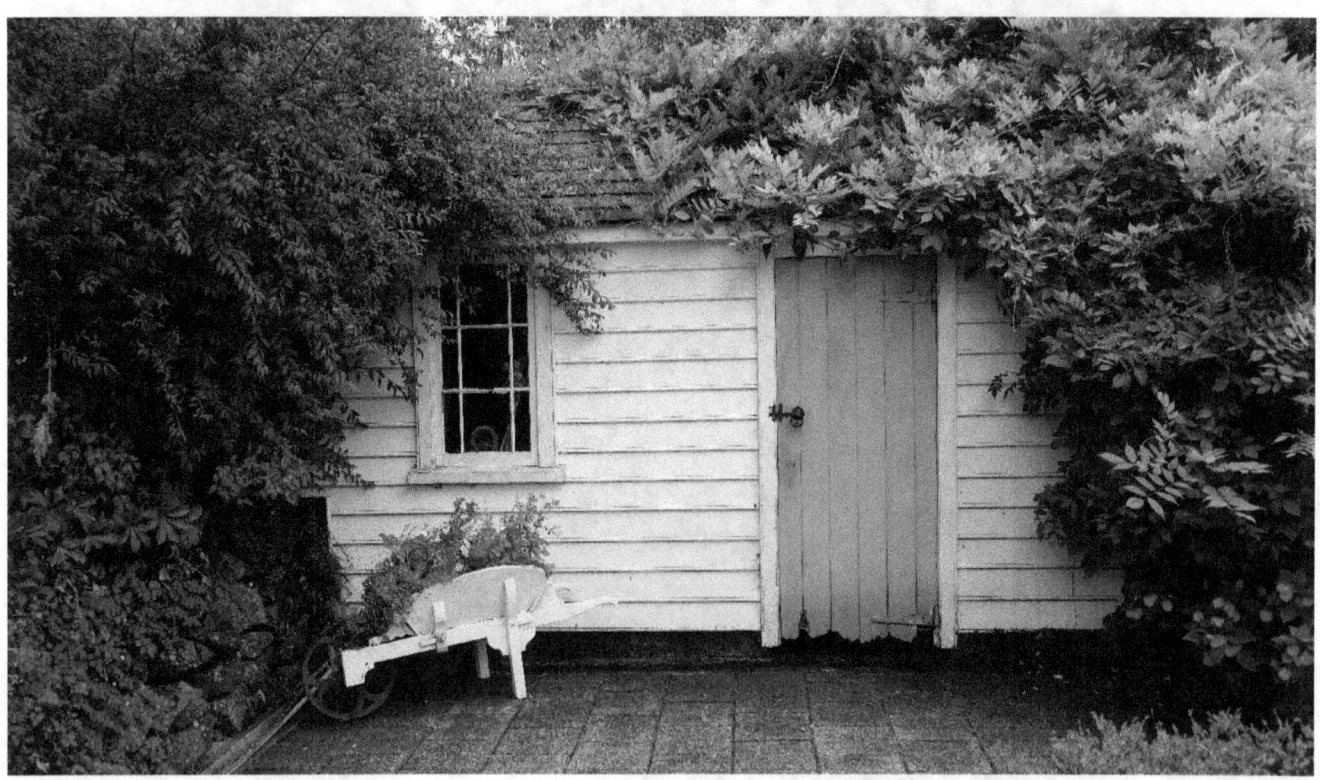

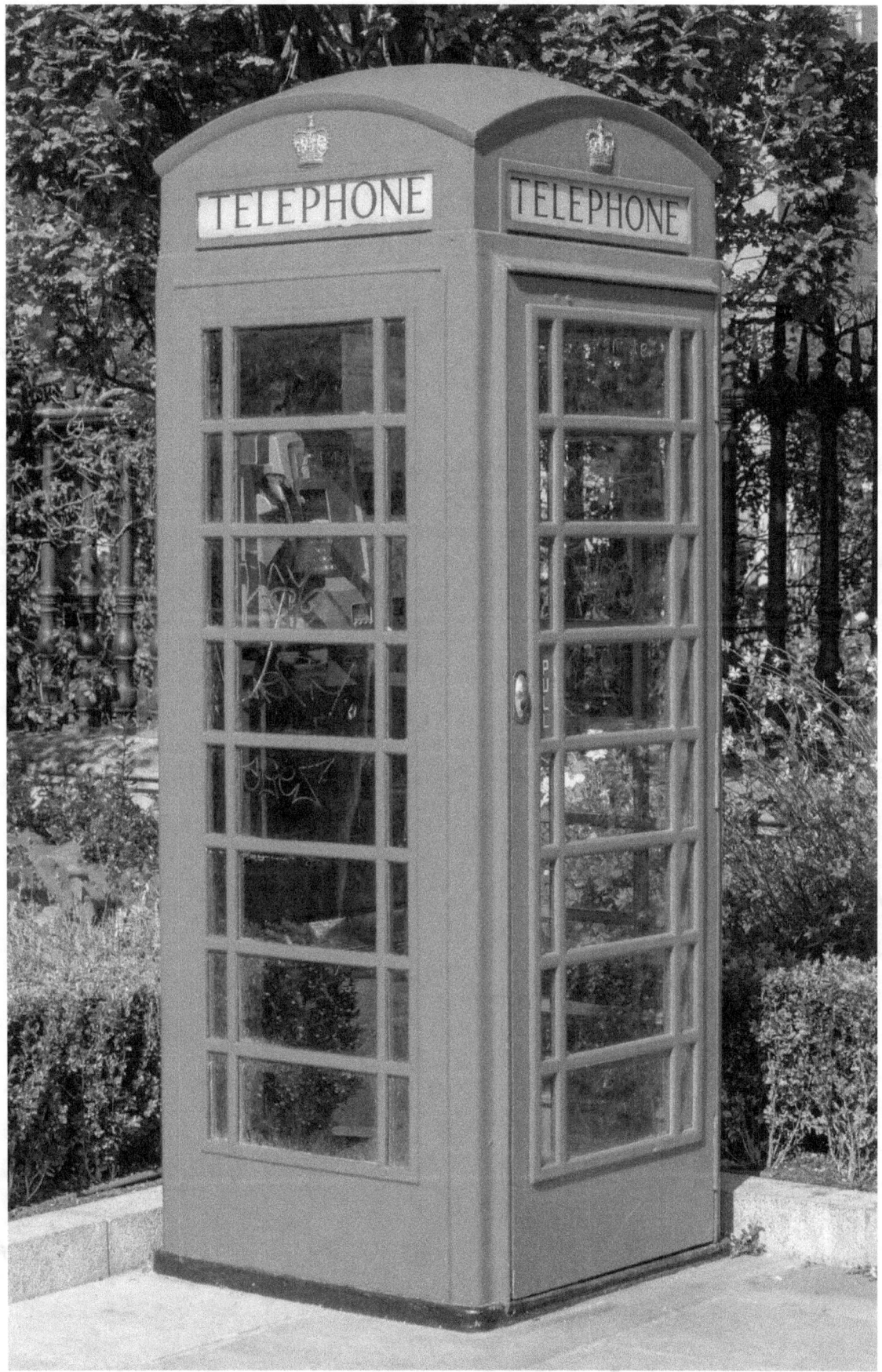

Superman used these as a changing house <wink>

Wheels

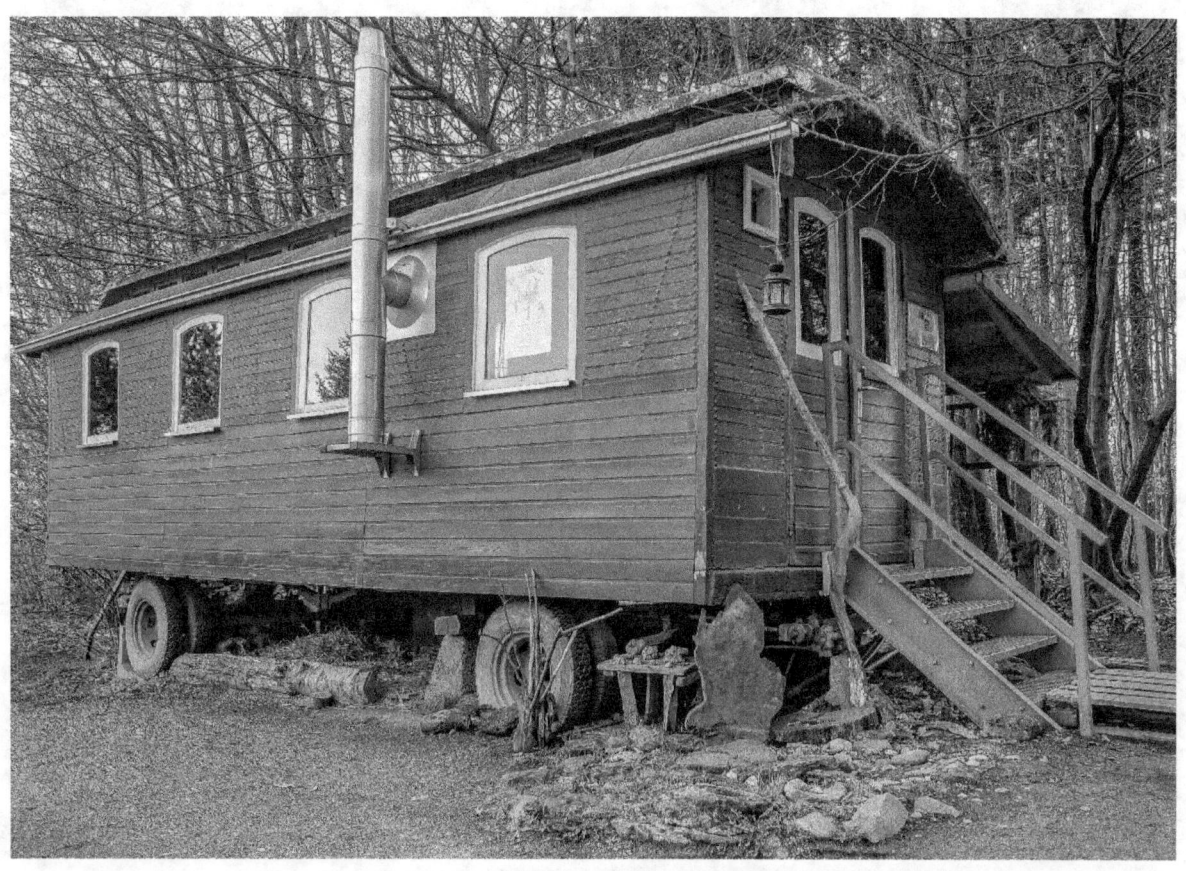

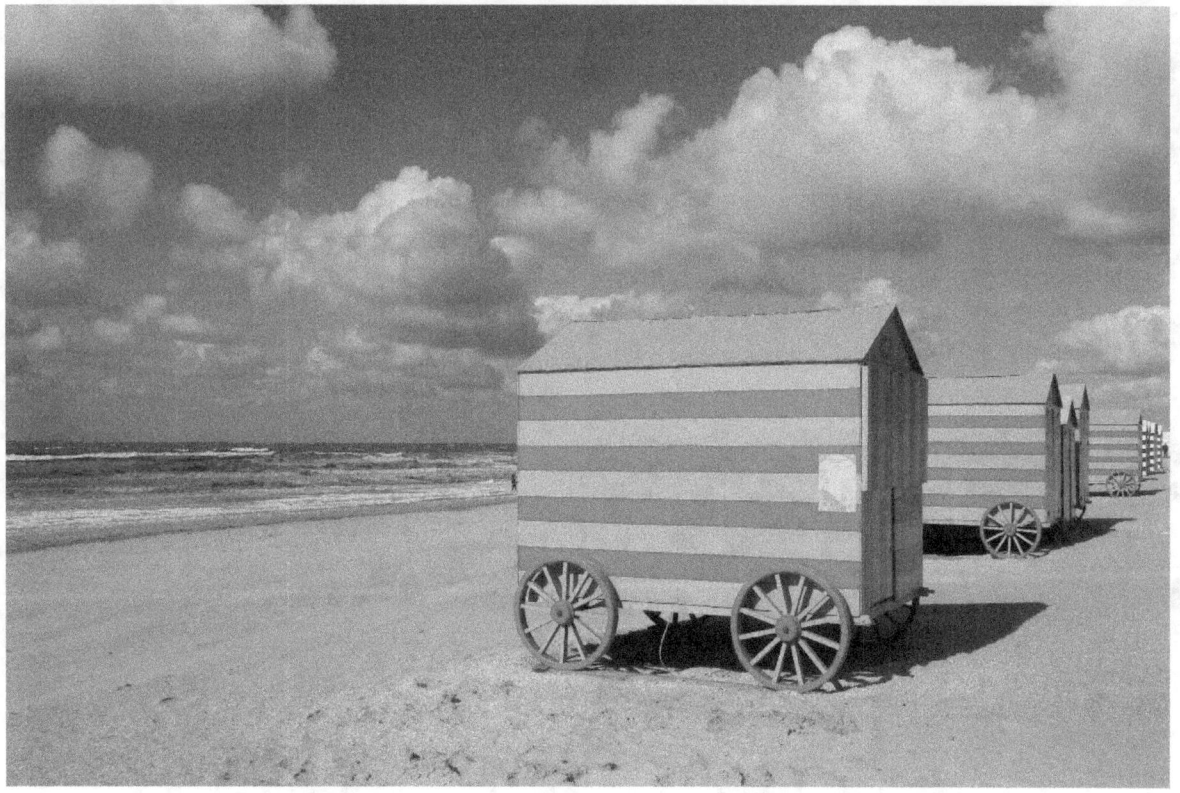

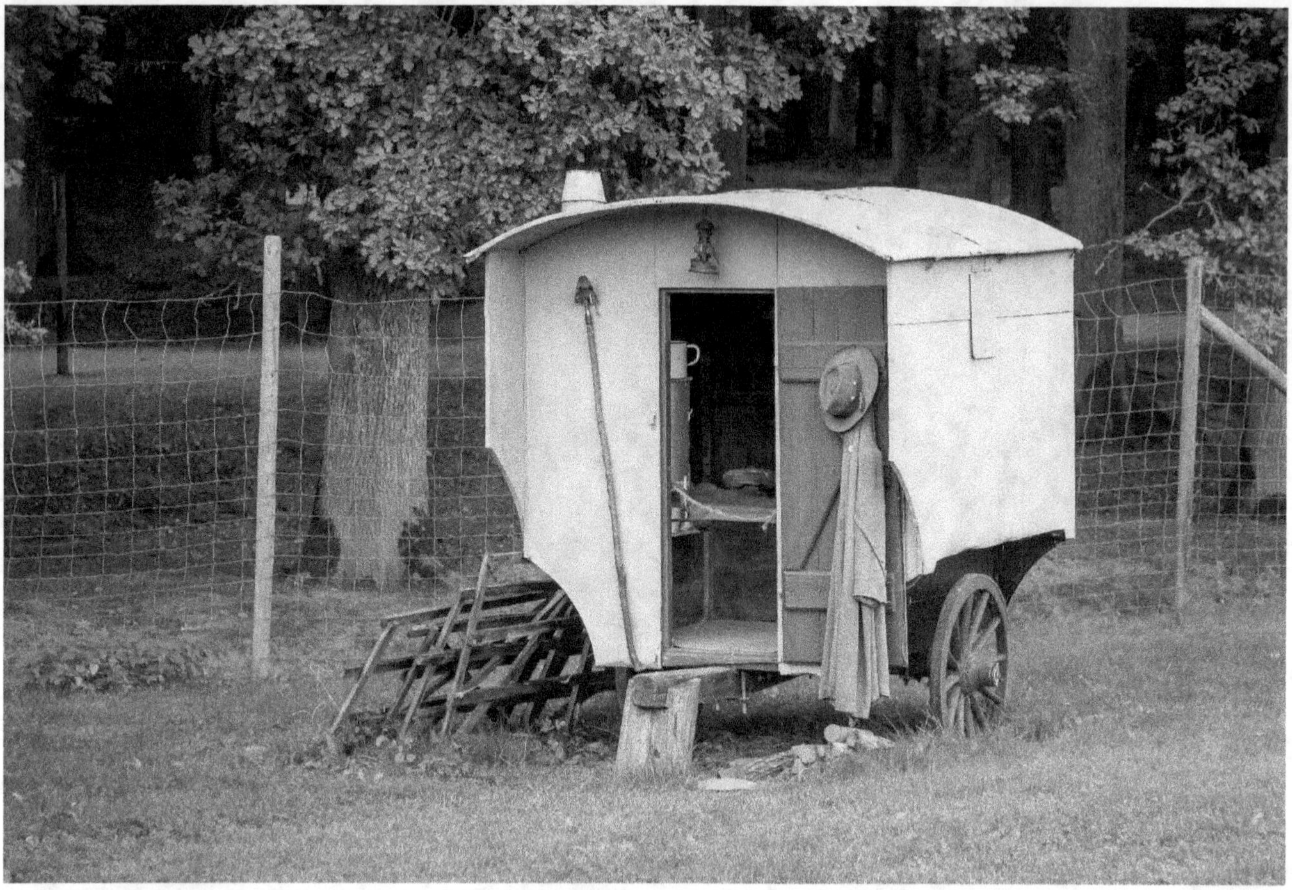

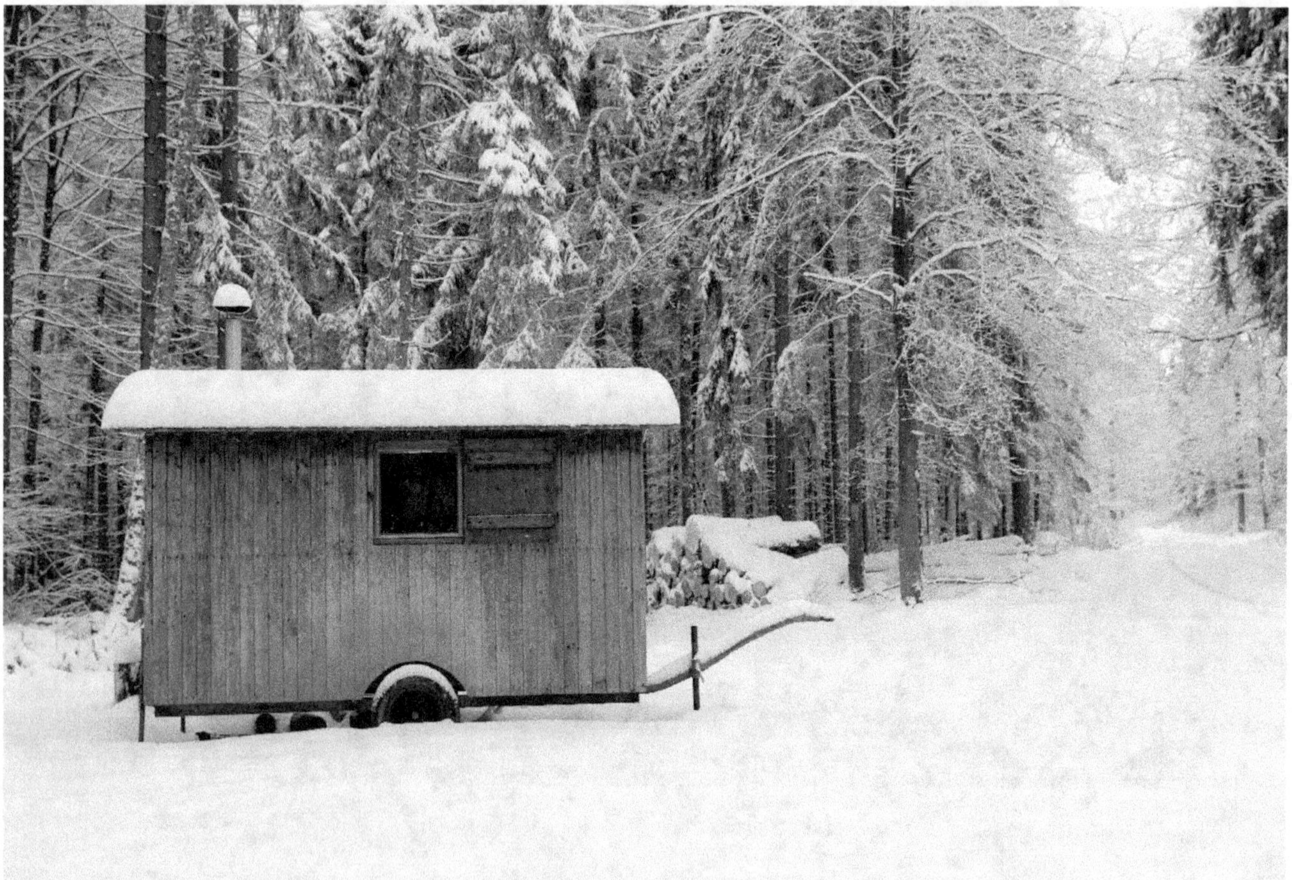

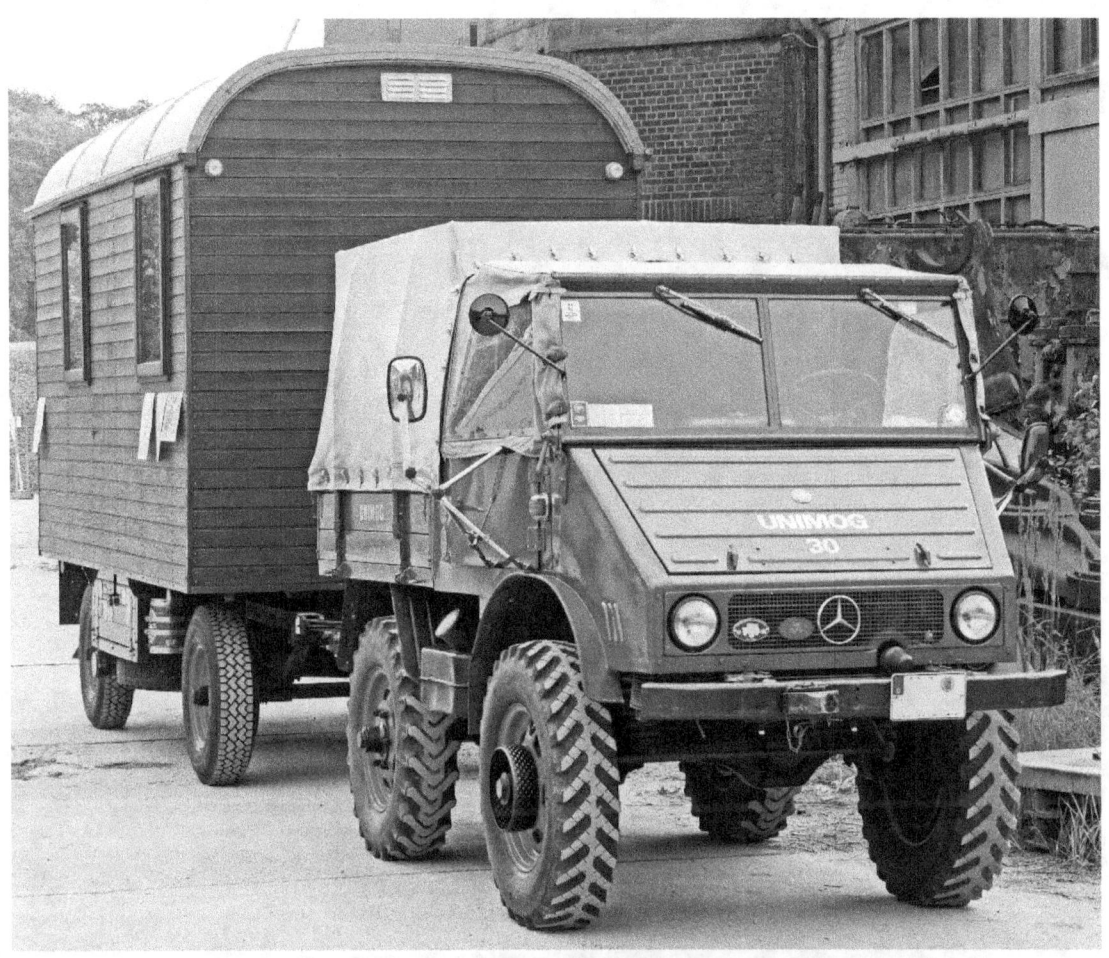

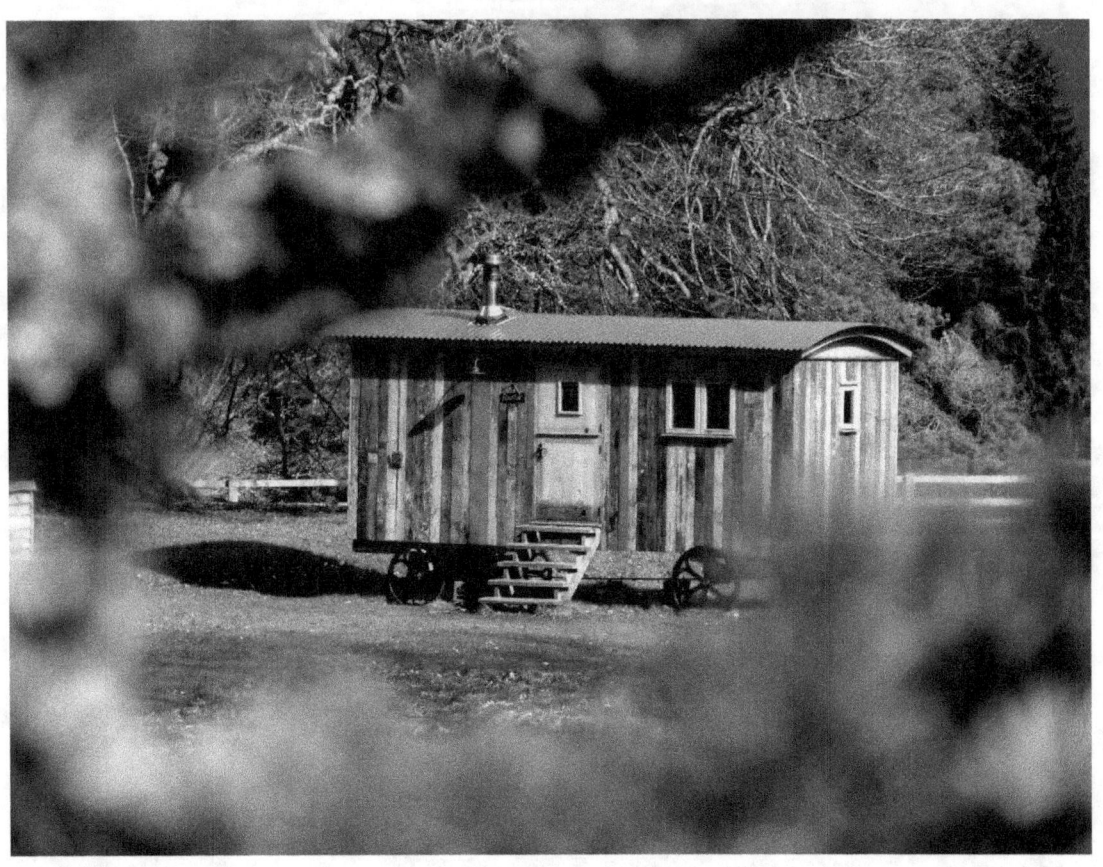

Gazebos & Outdoor Structures

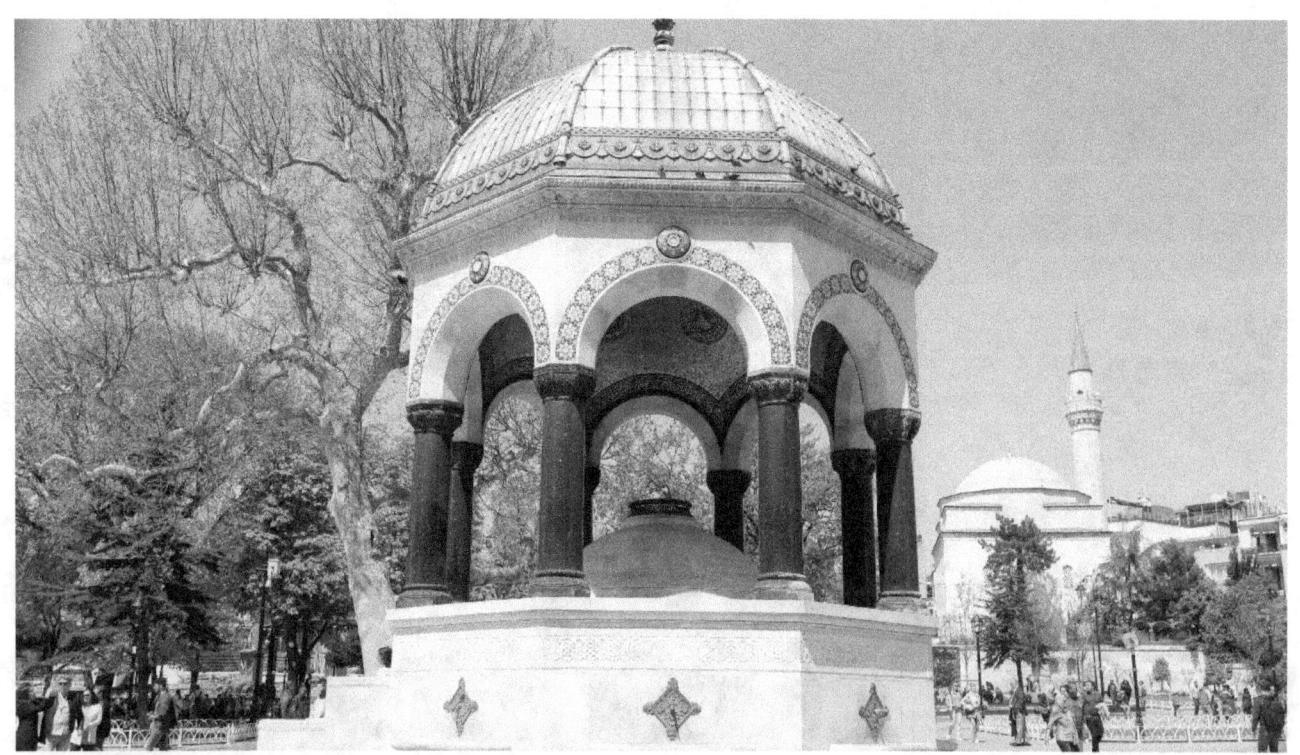

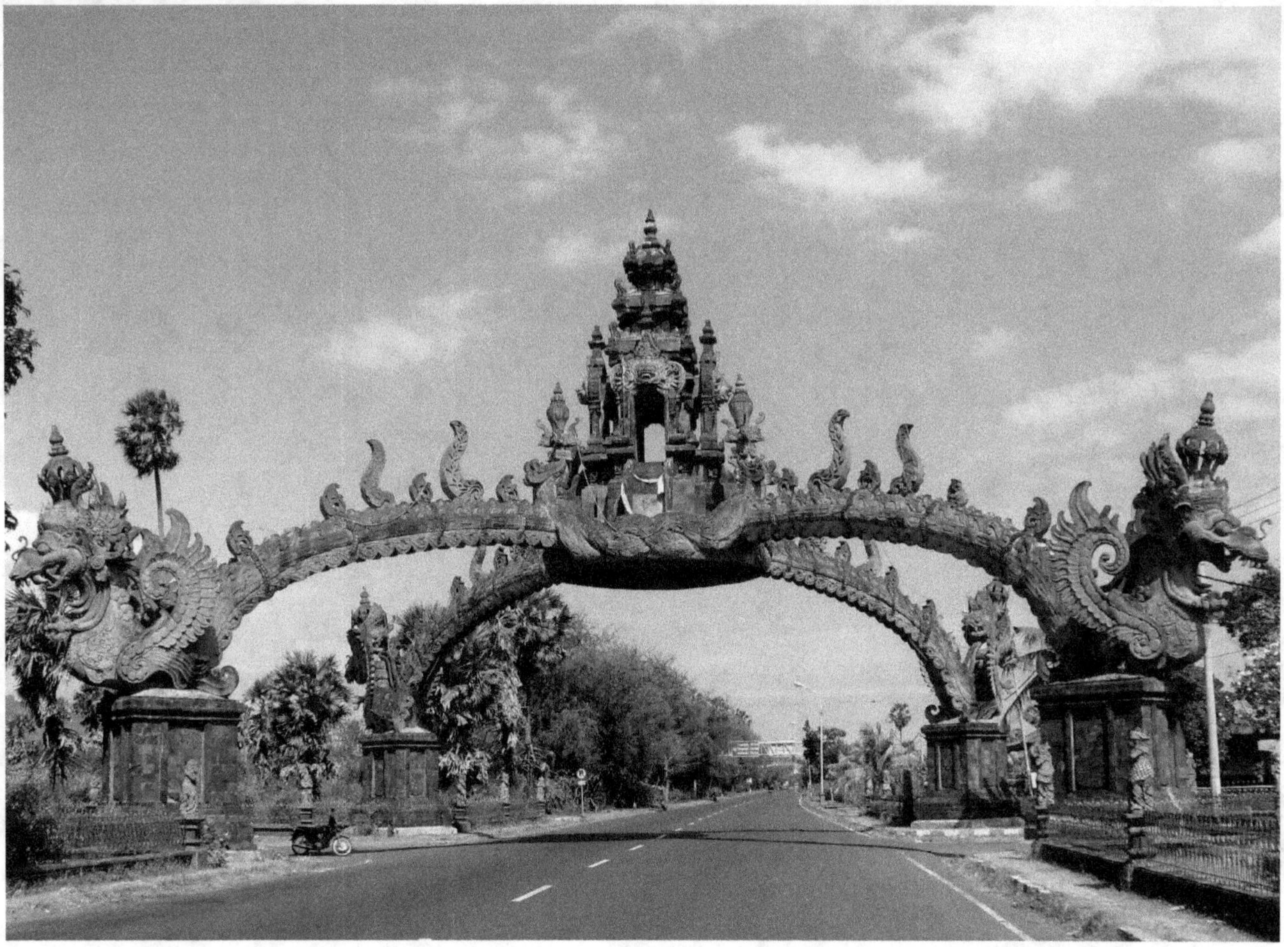

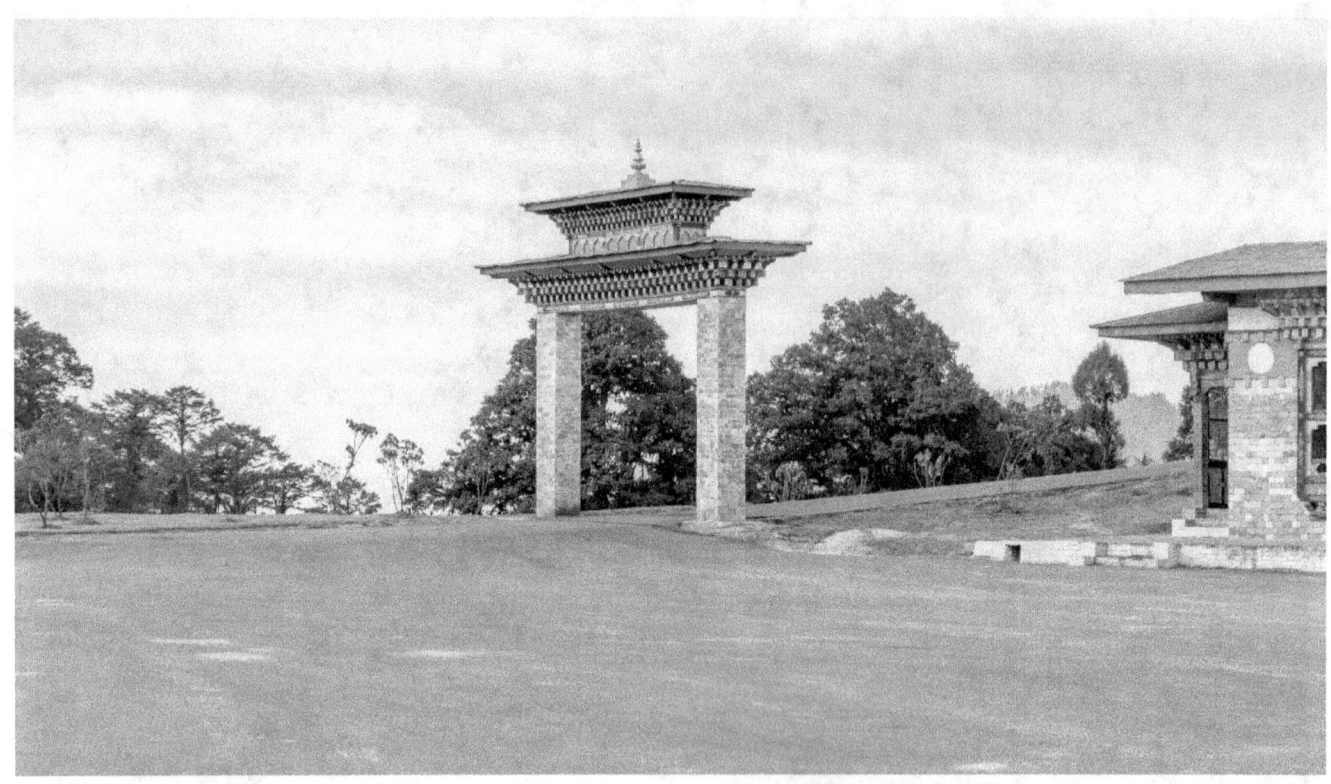

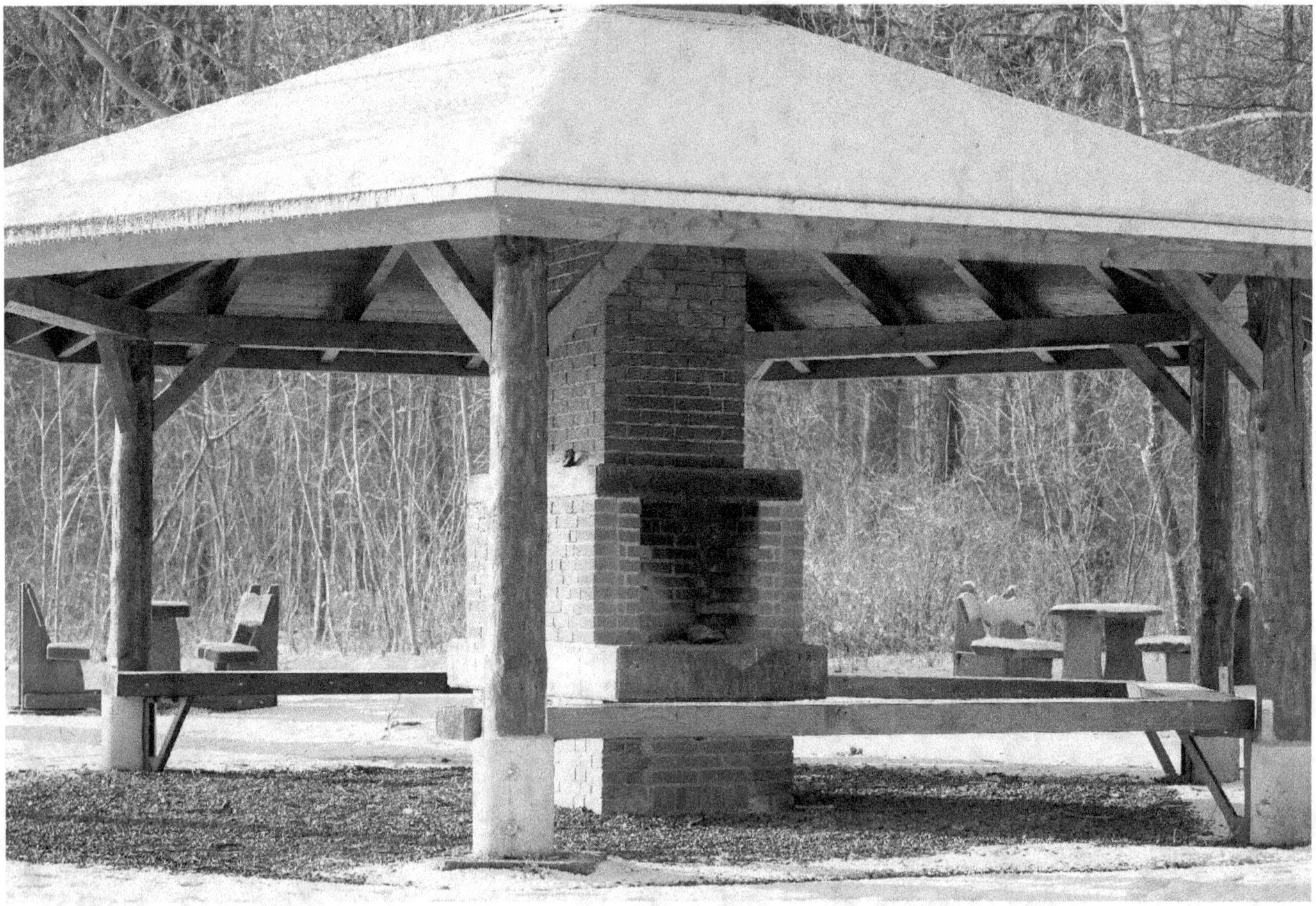

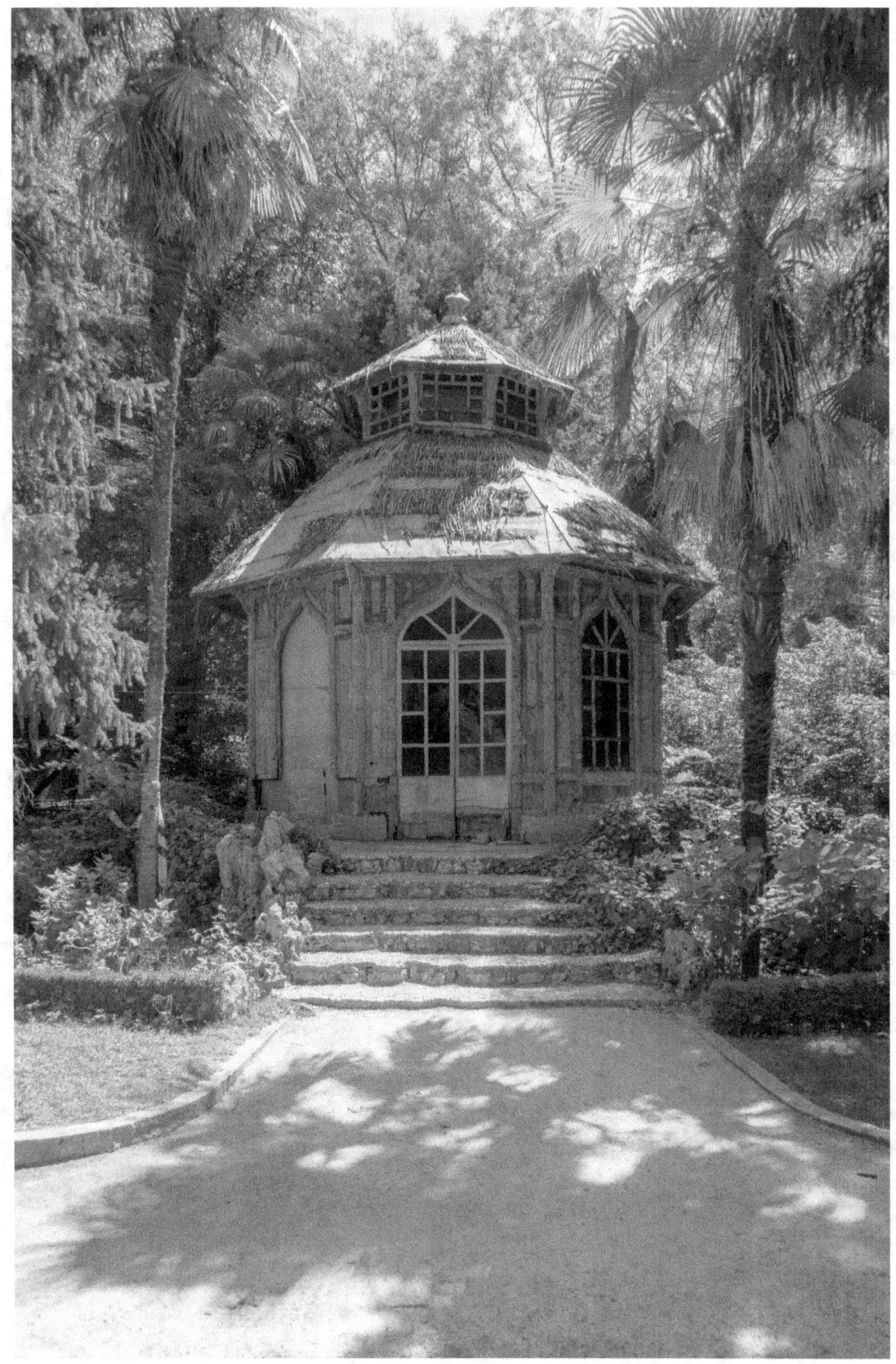

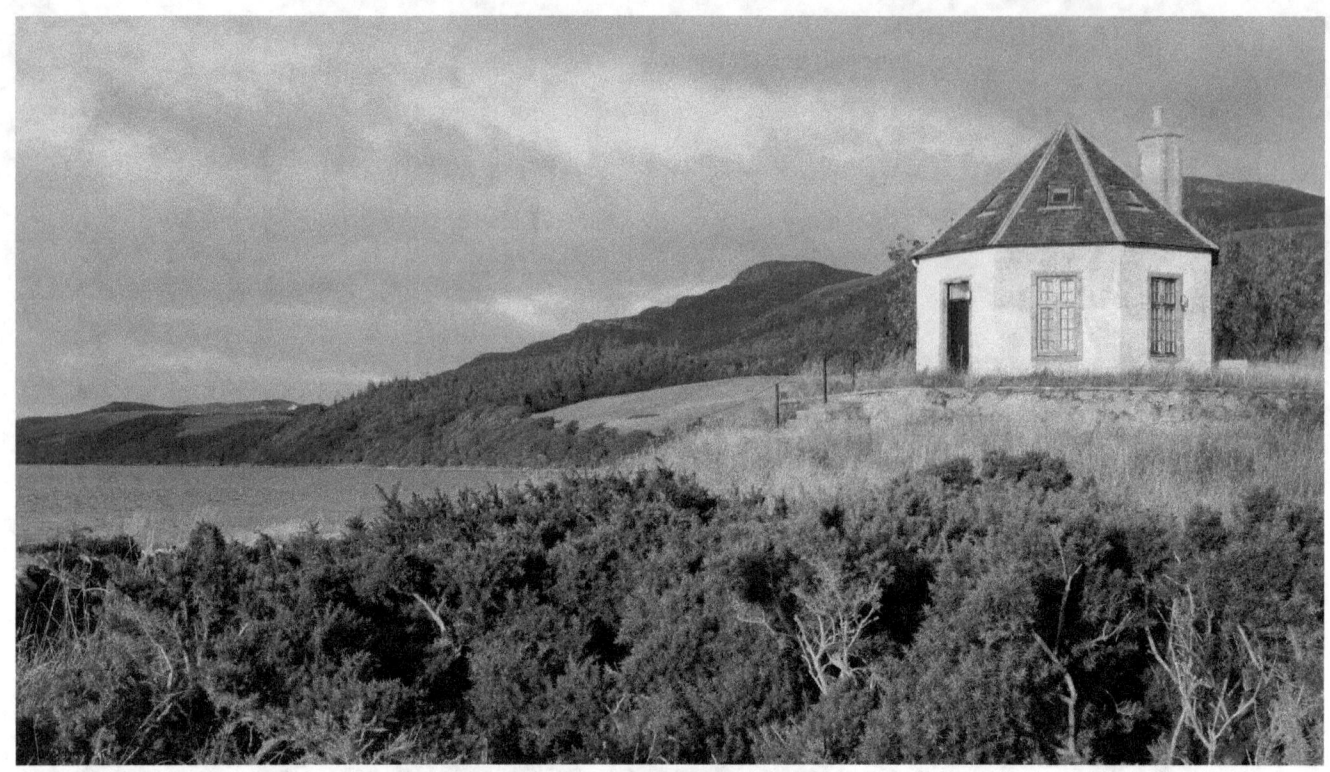

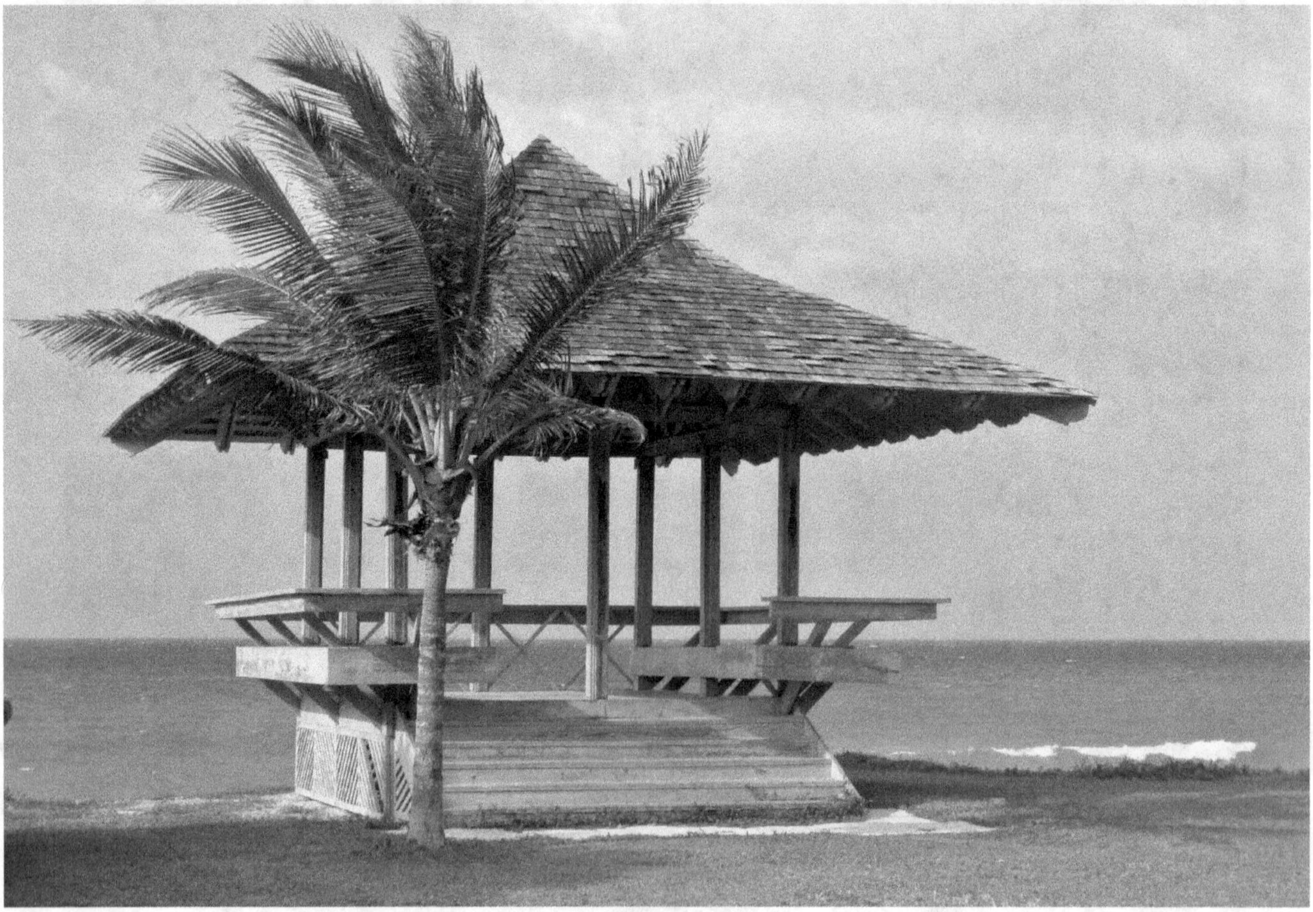

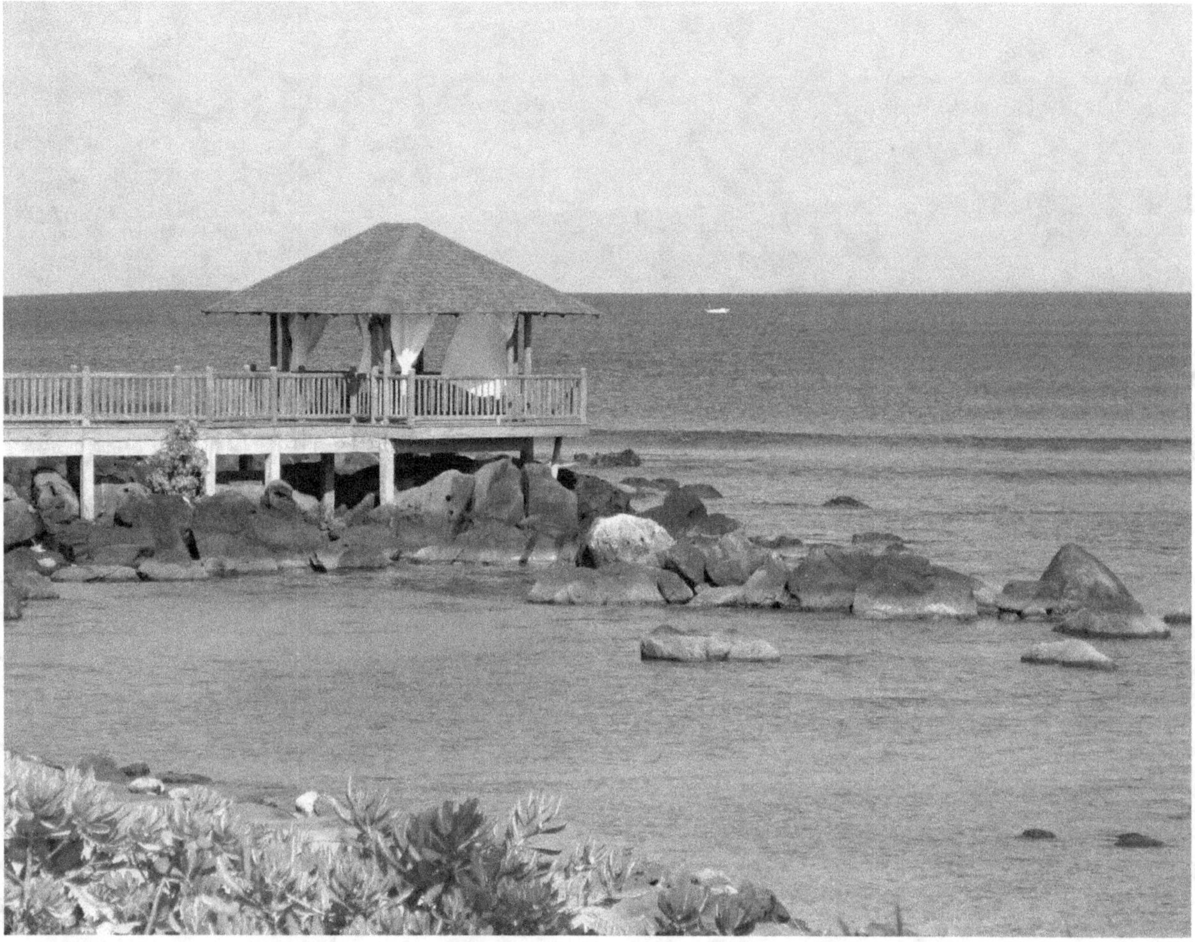

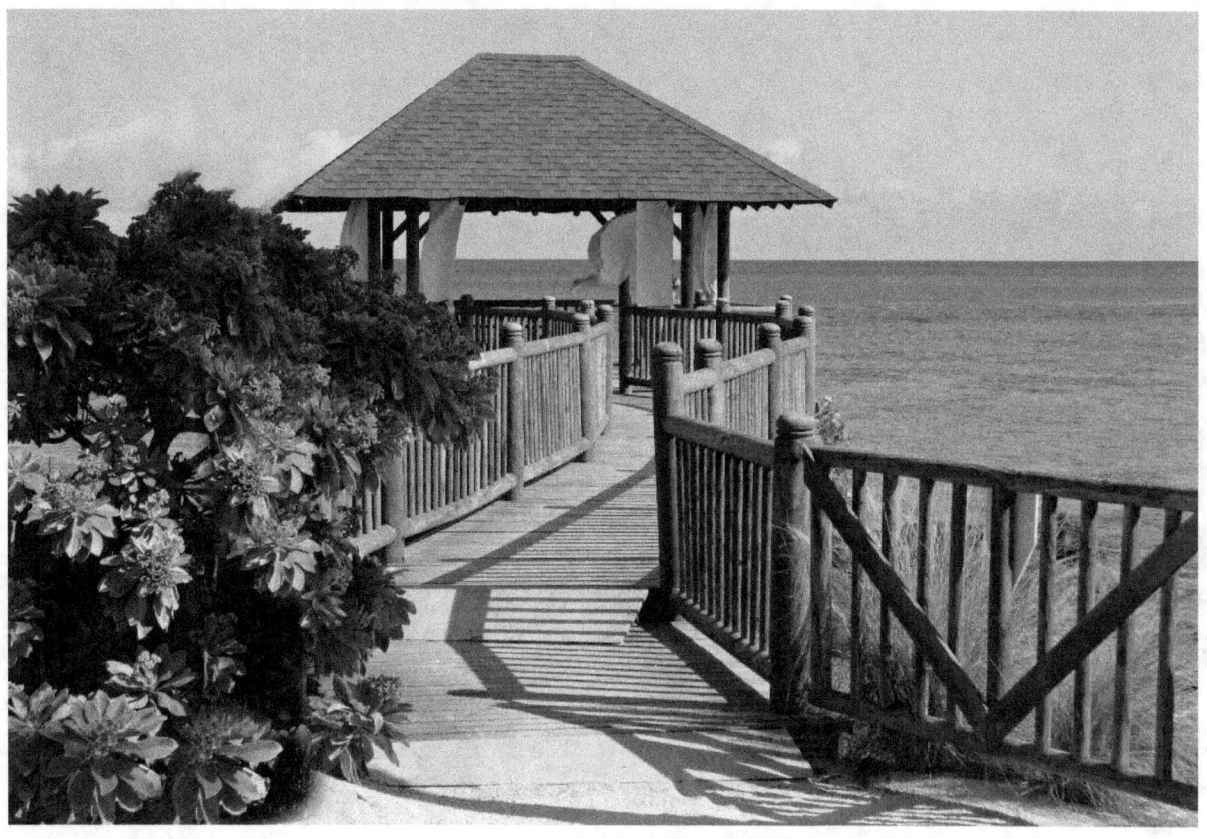

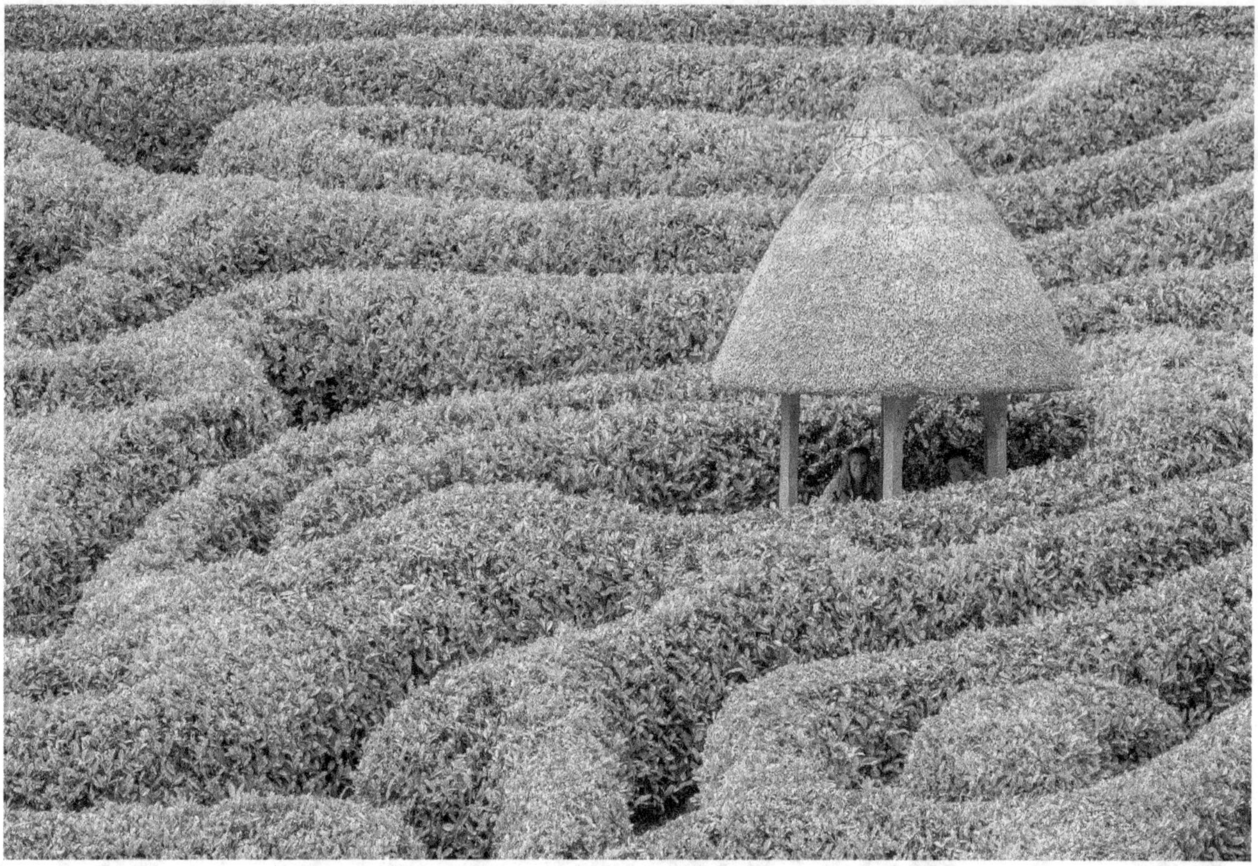

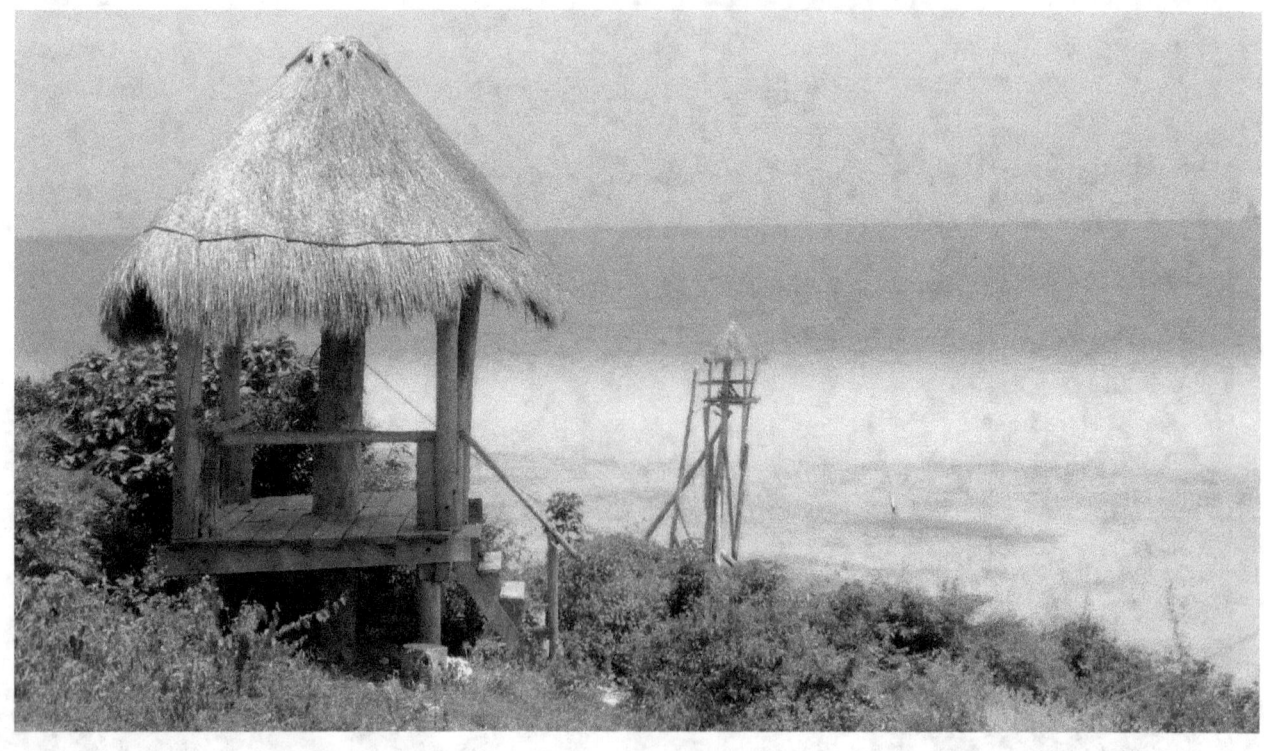

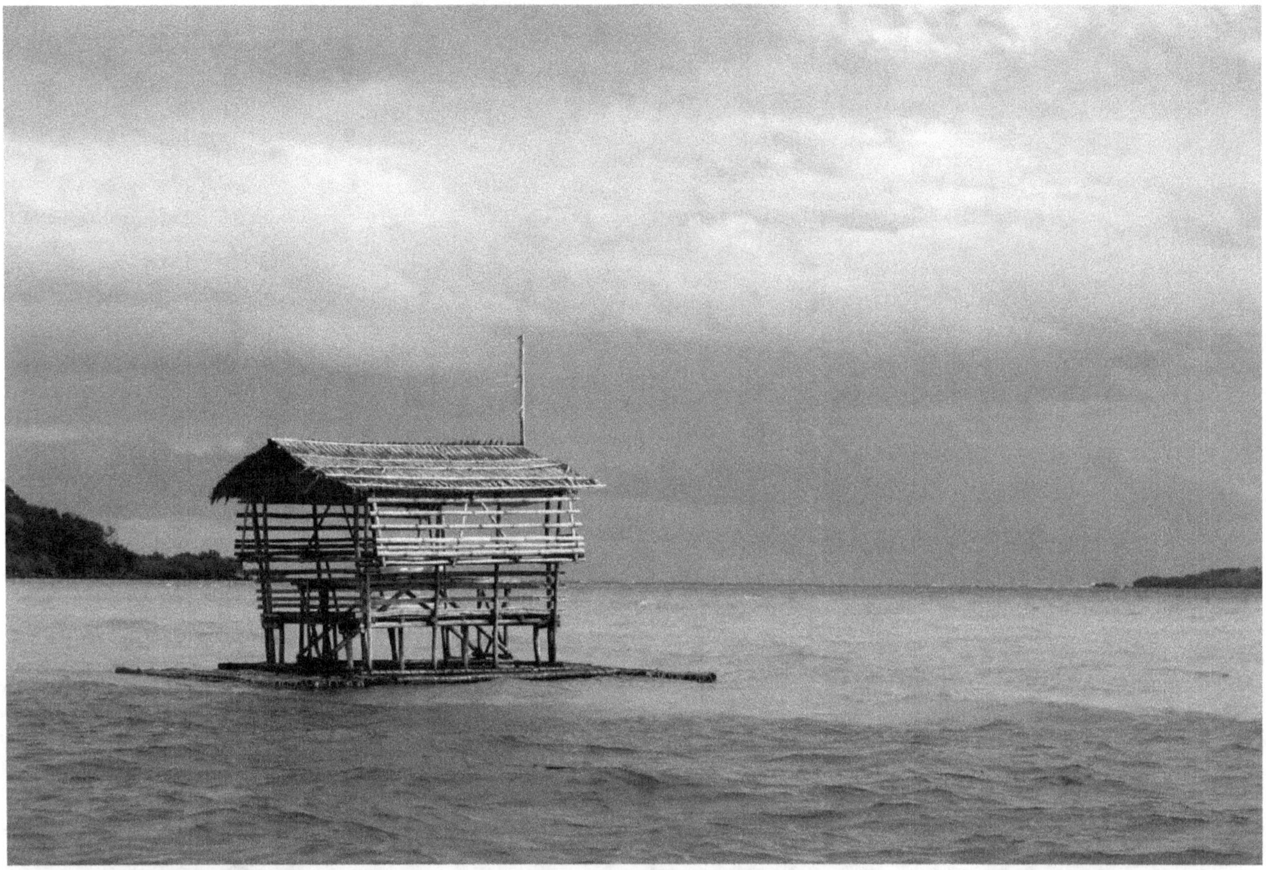

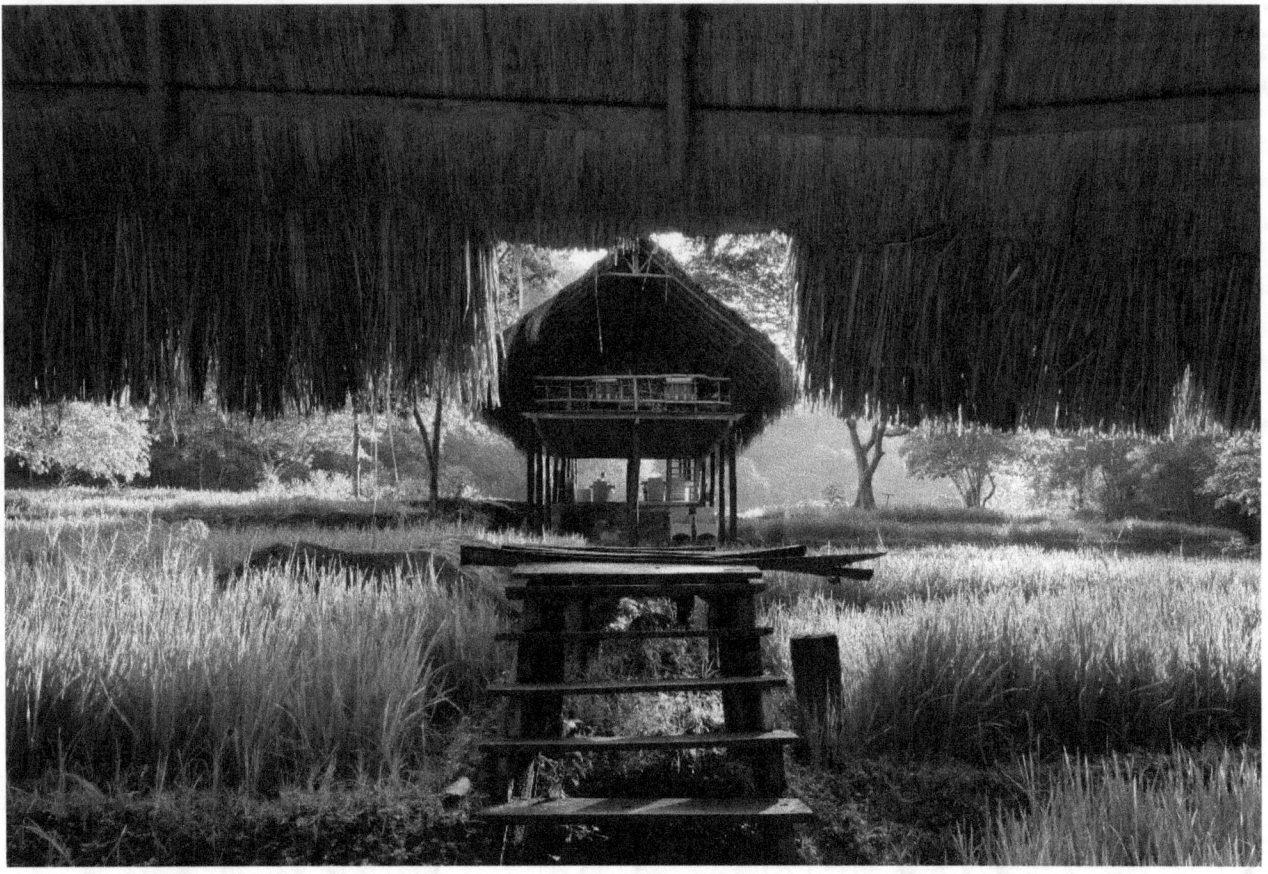

Privies / Outhouses

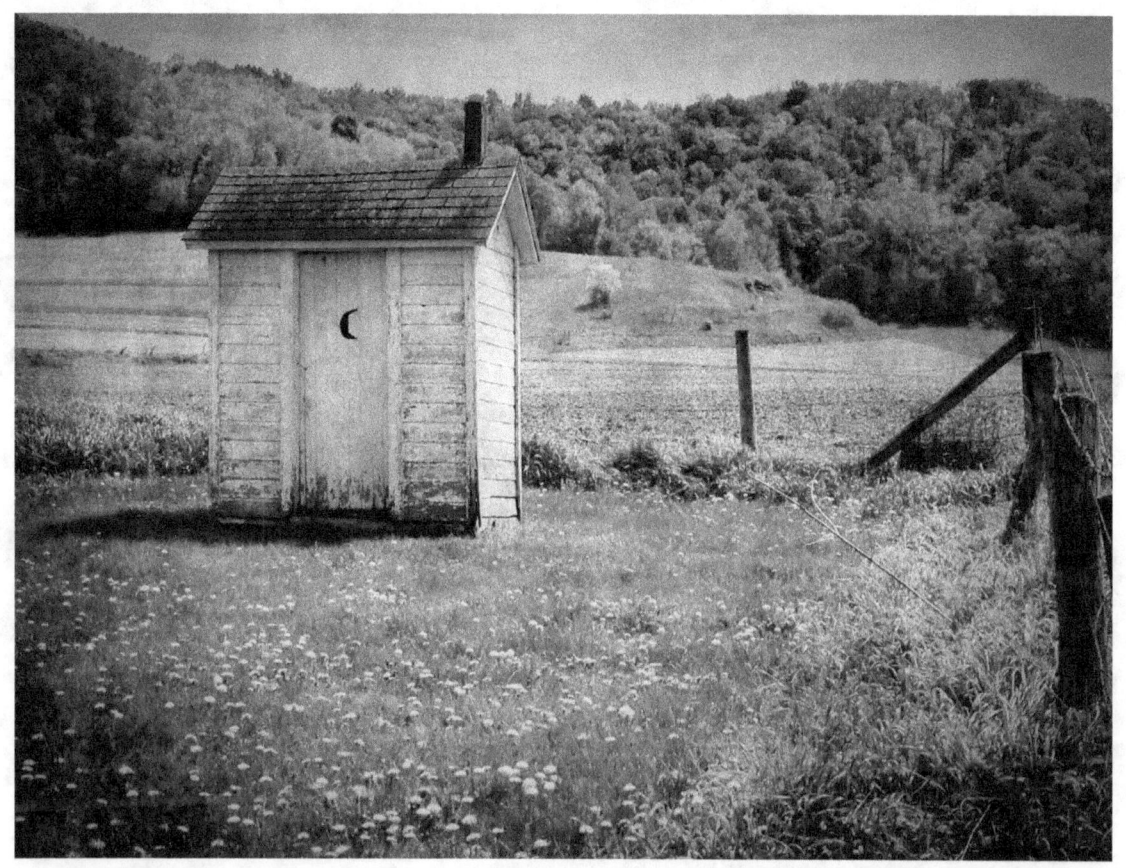

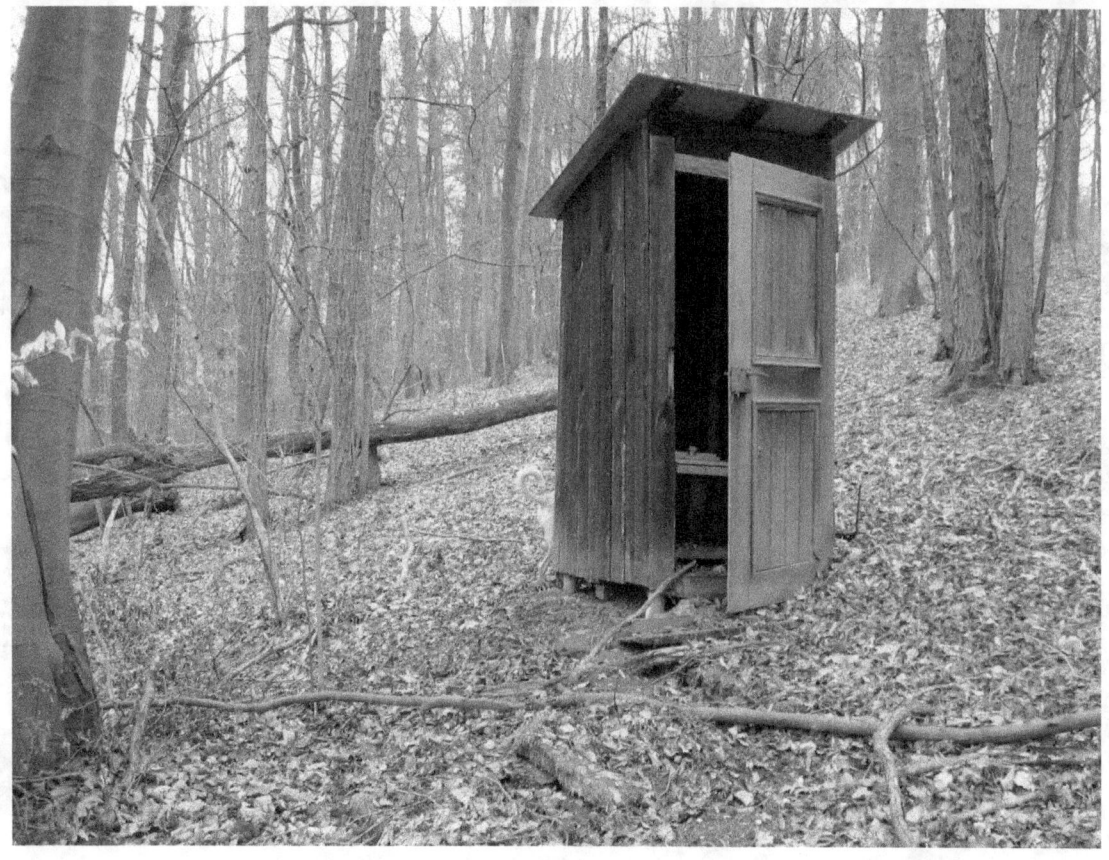

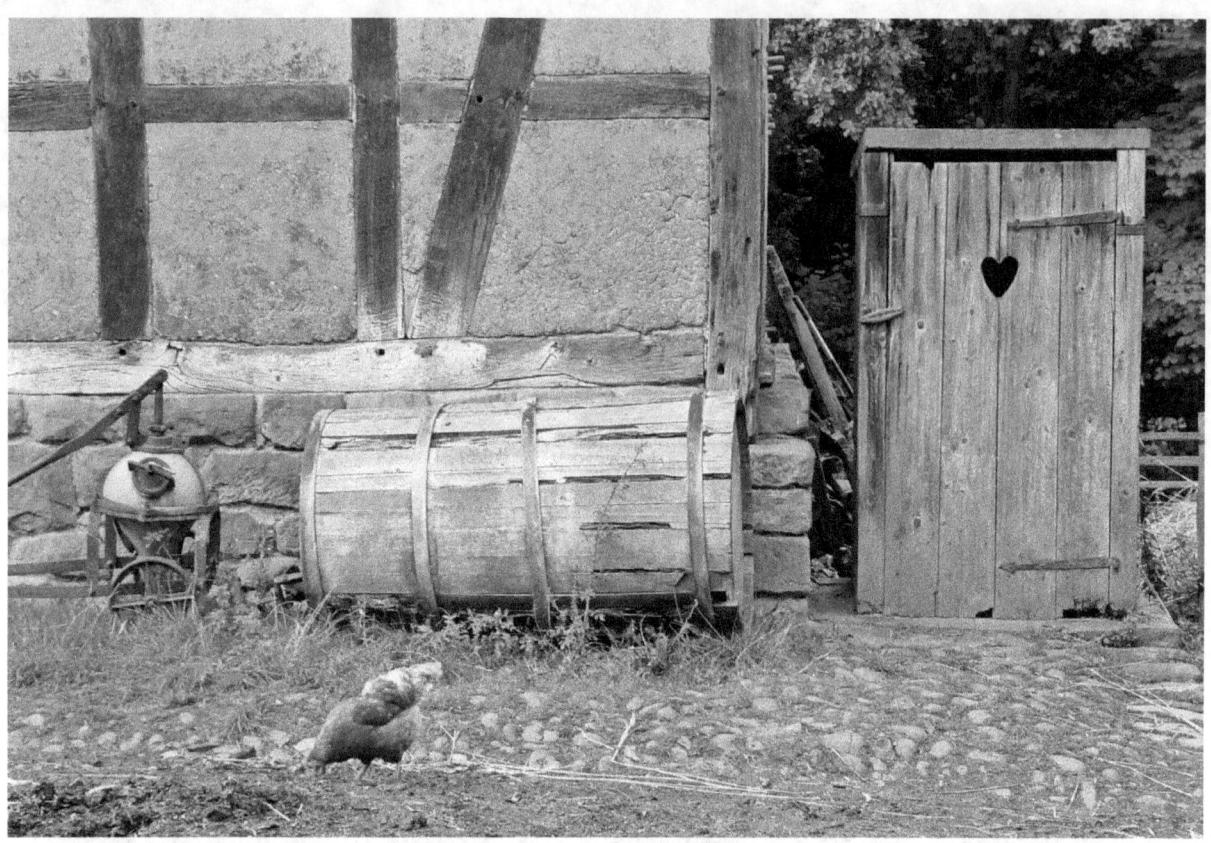

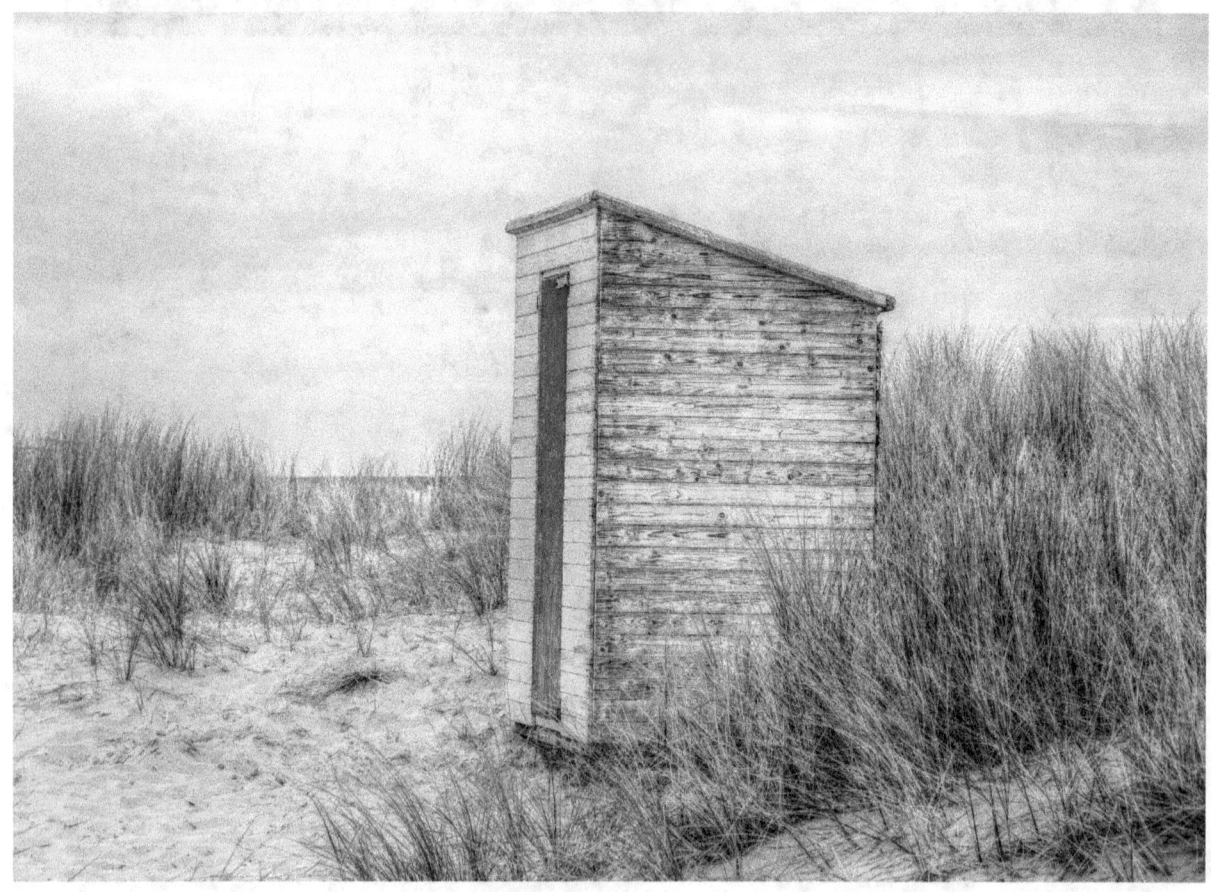

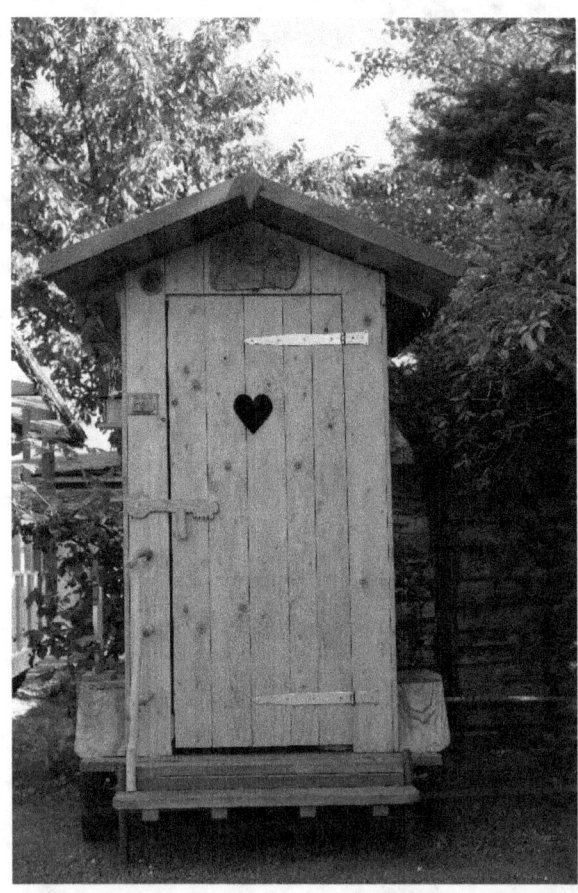

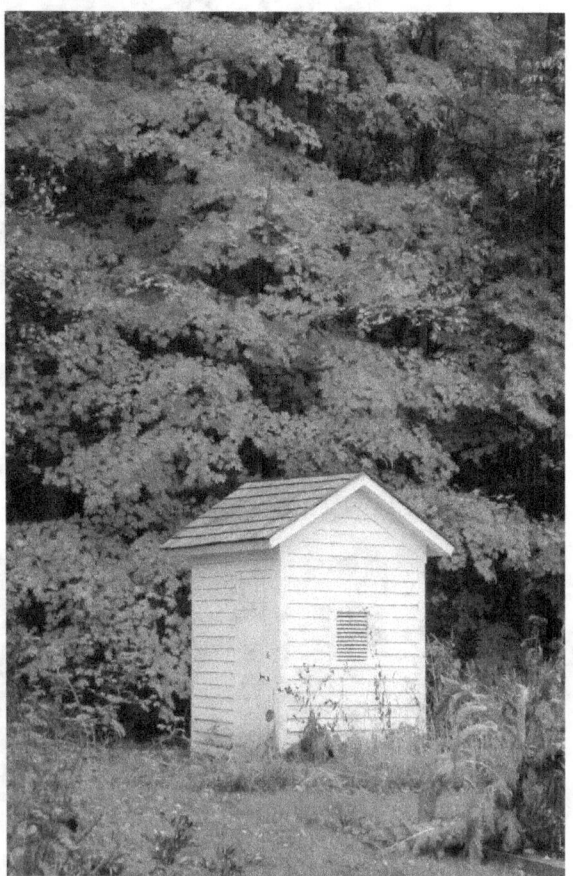

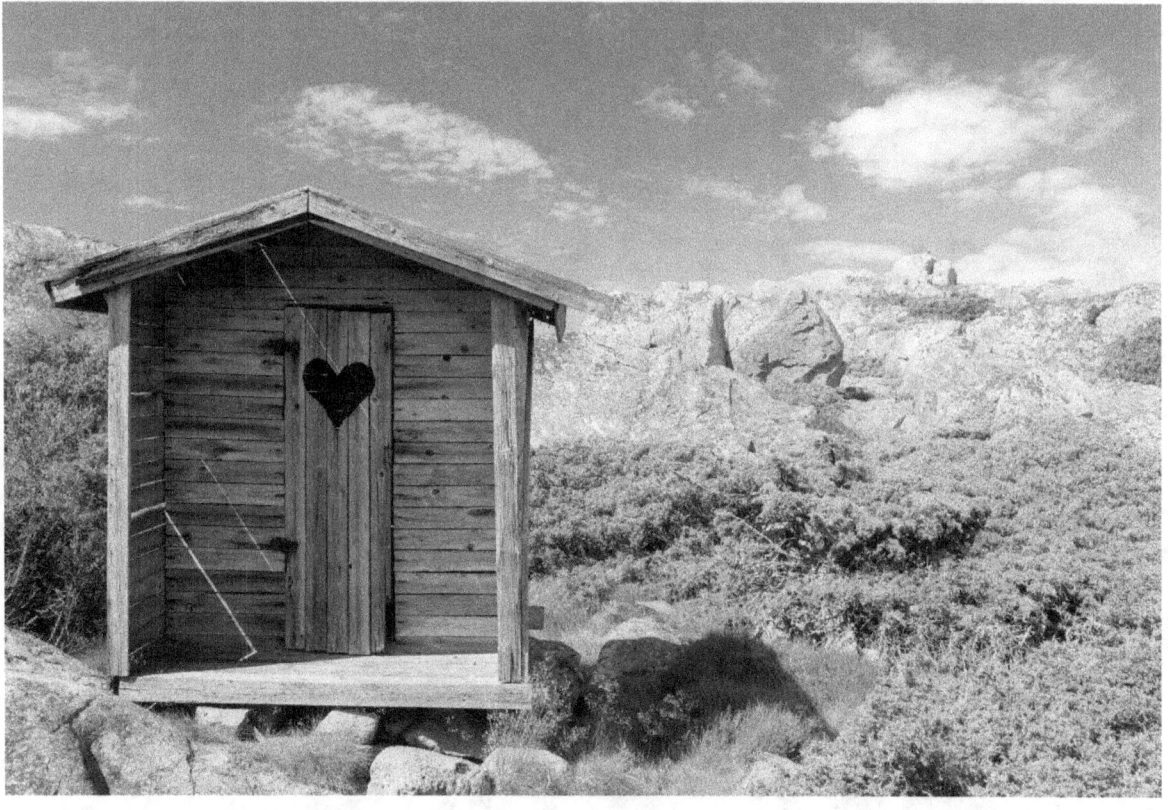

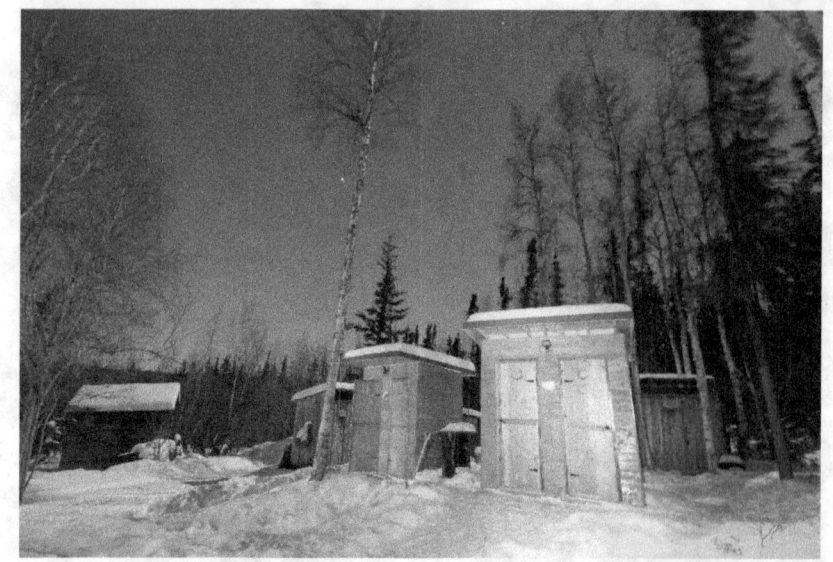

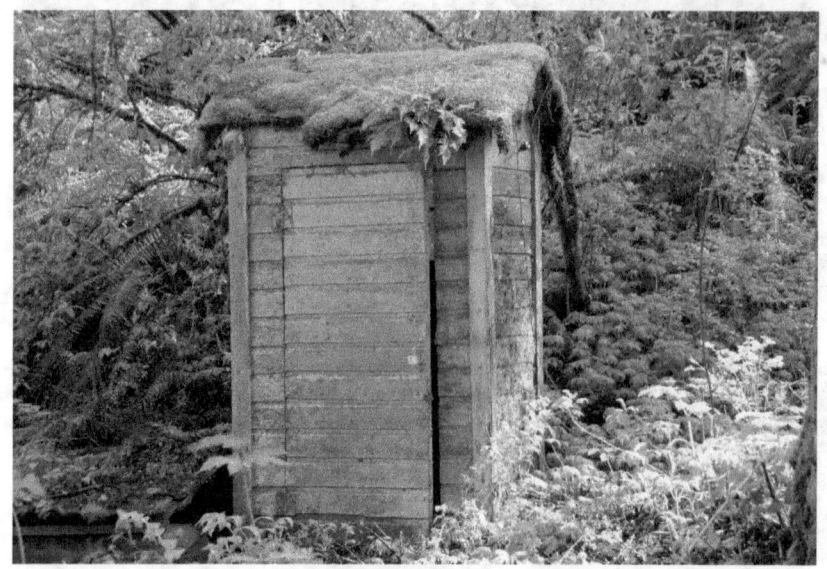

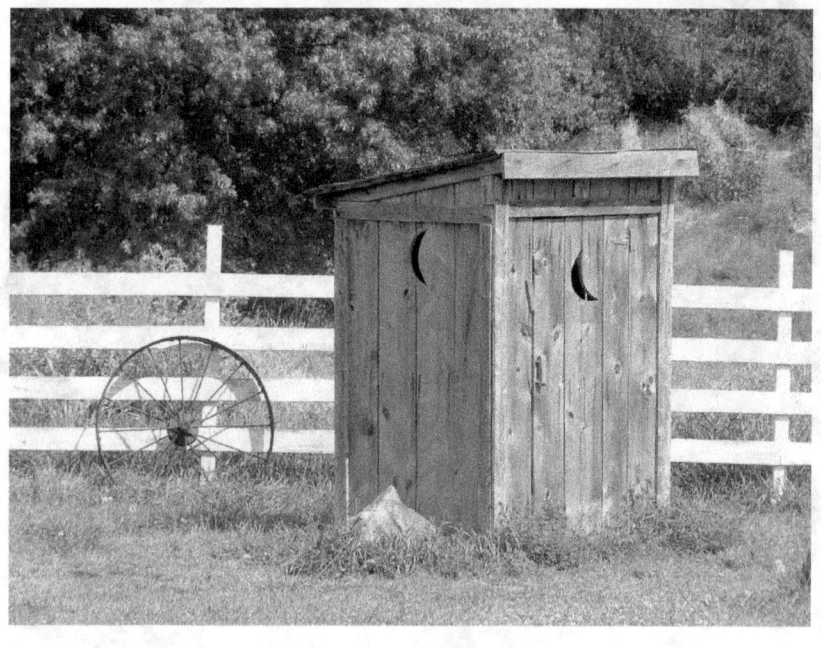

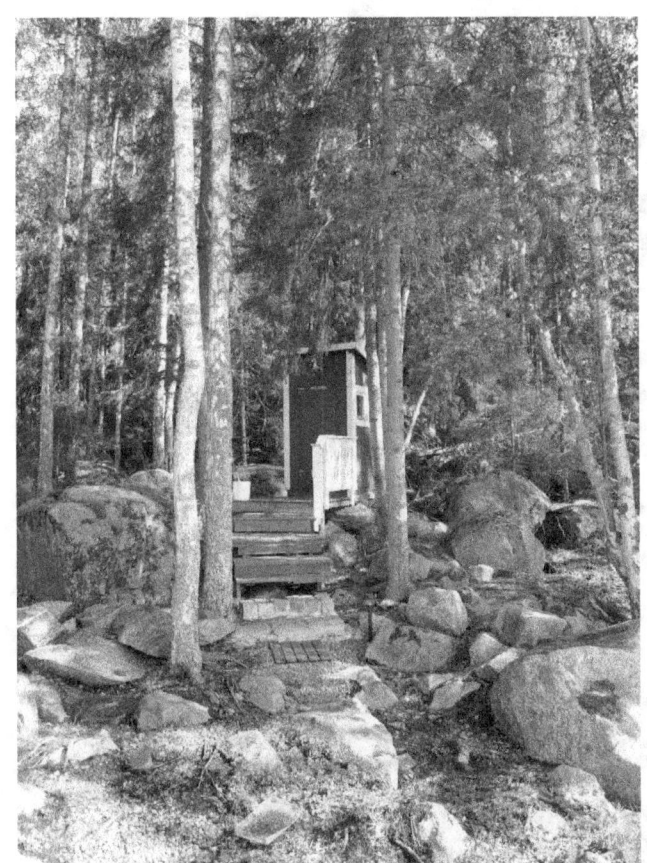
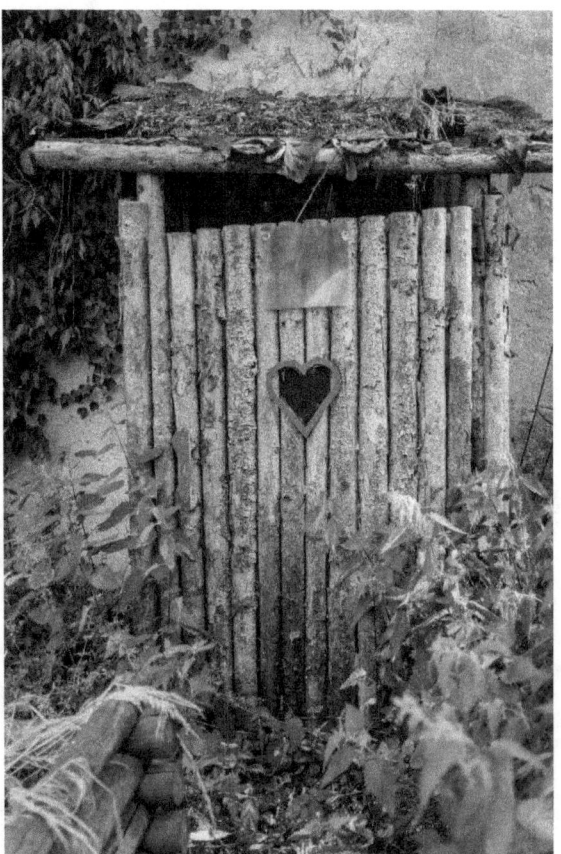
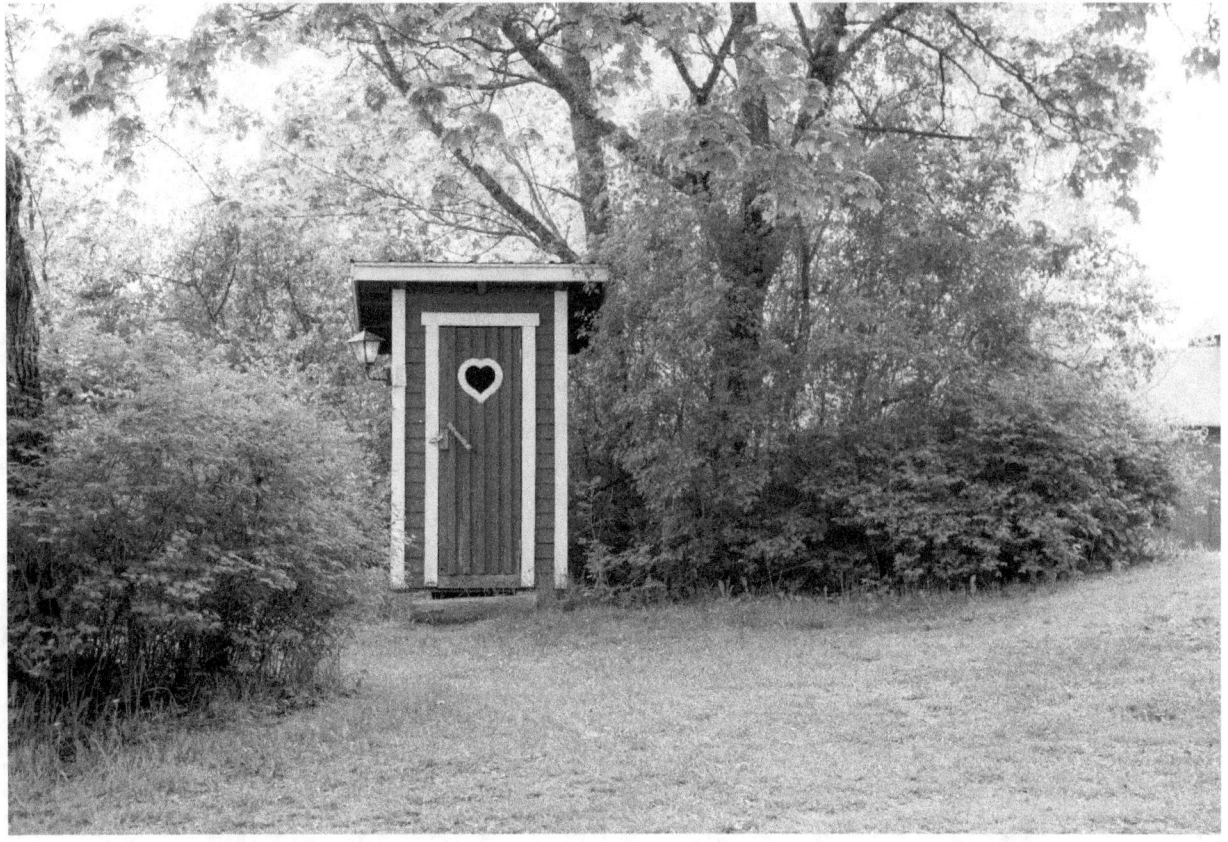

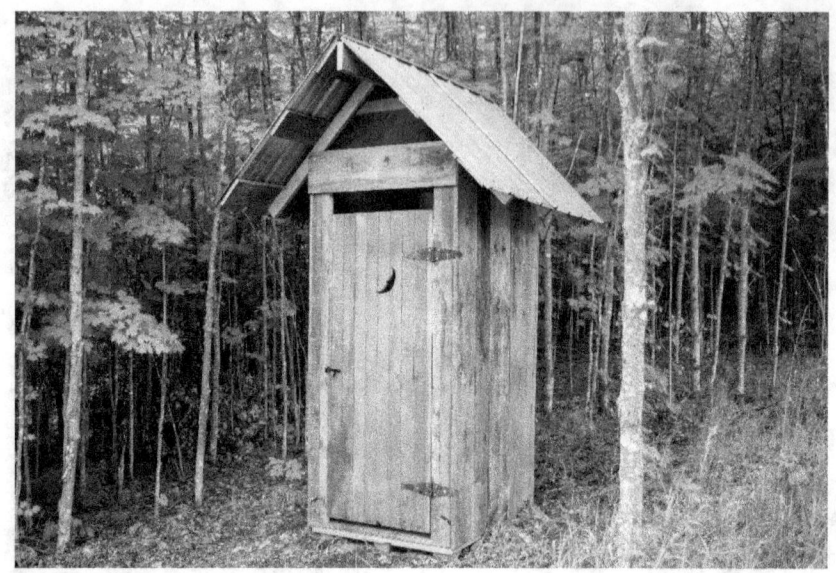

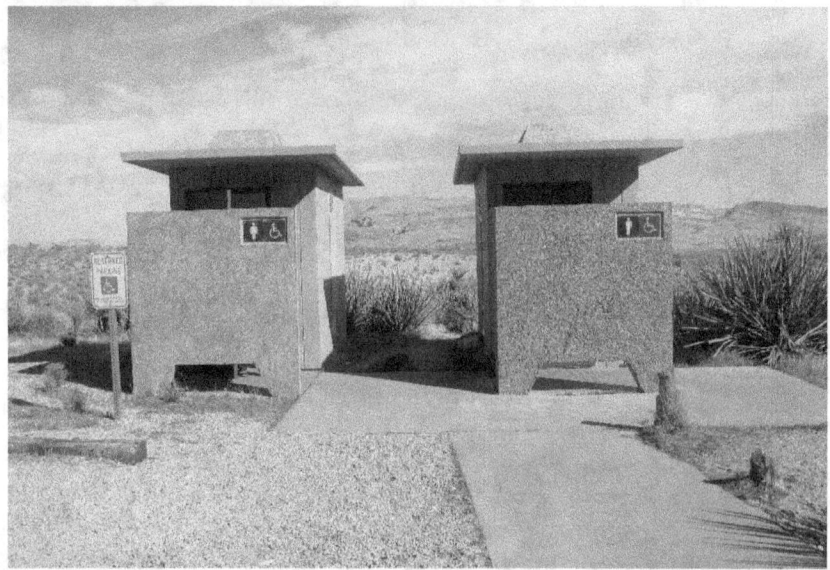

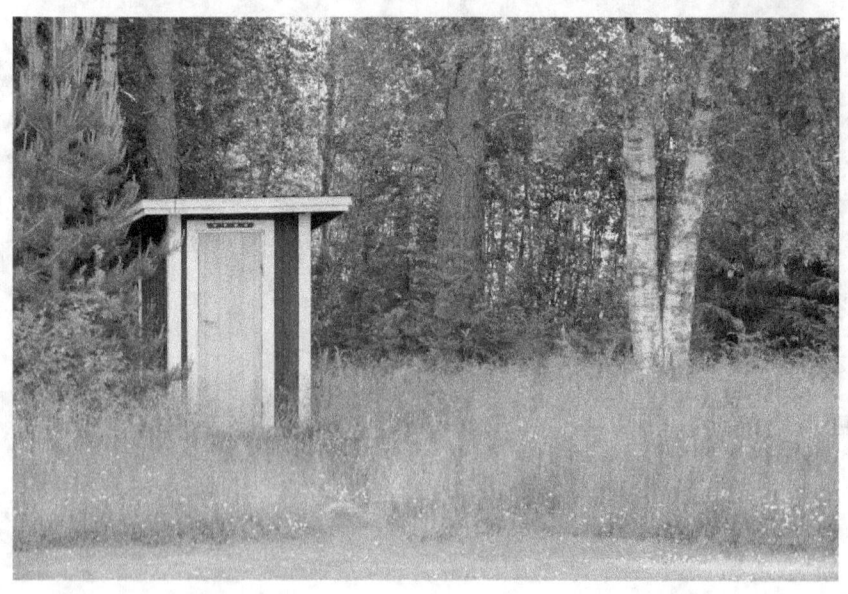

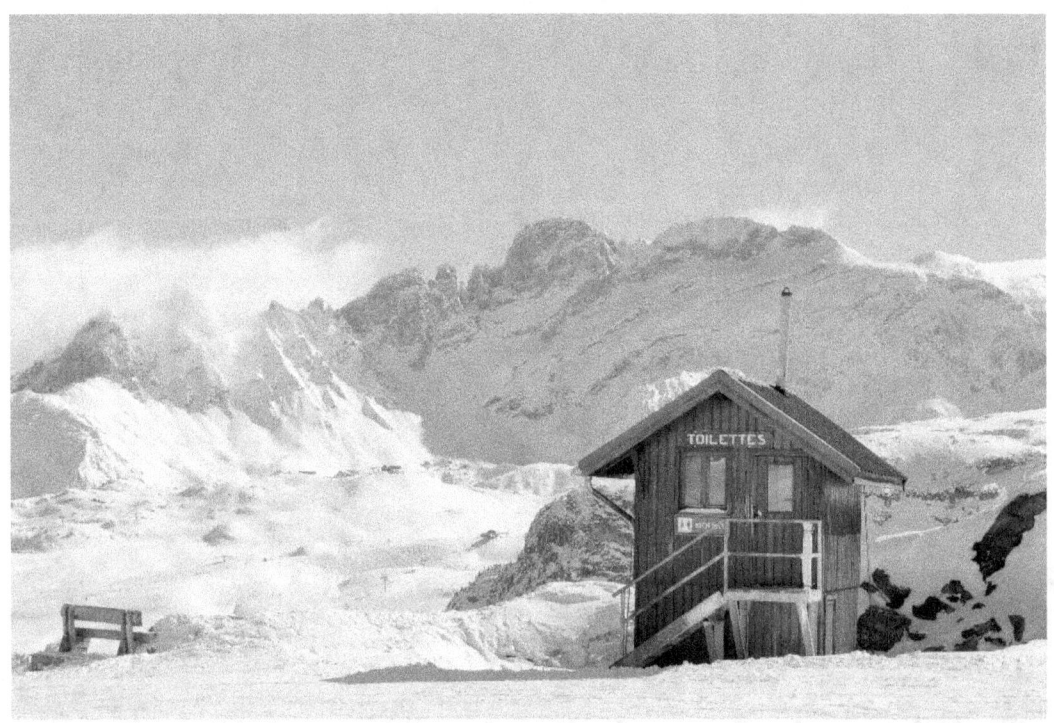

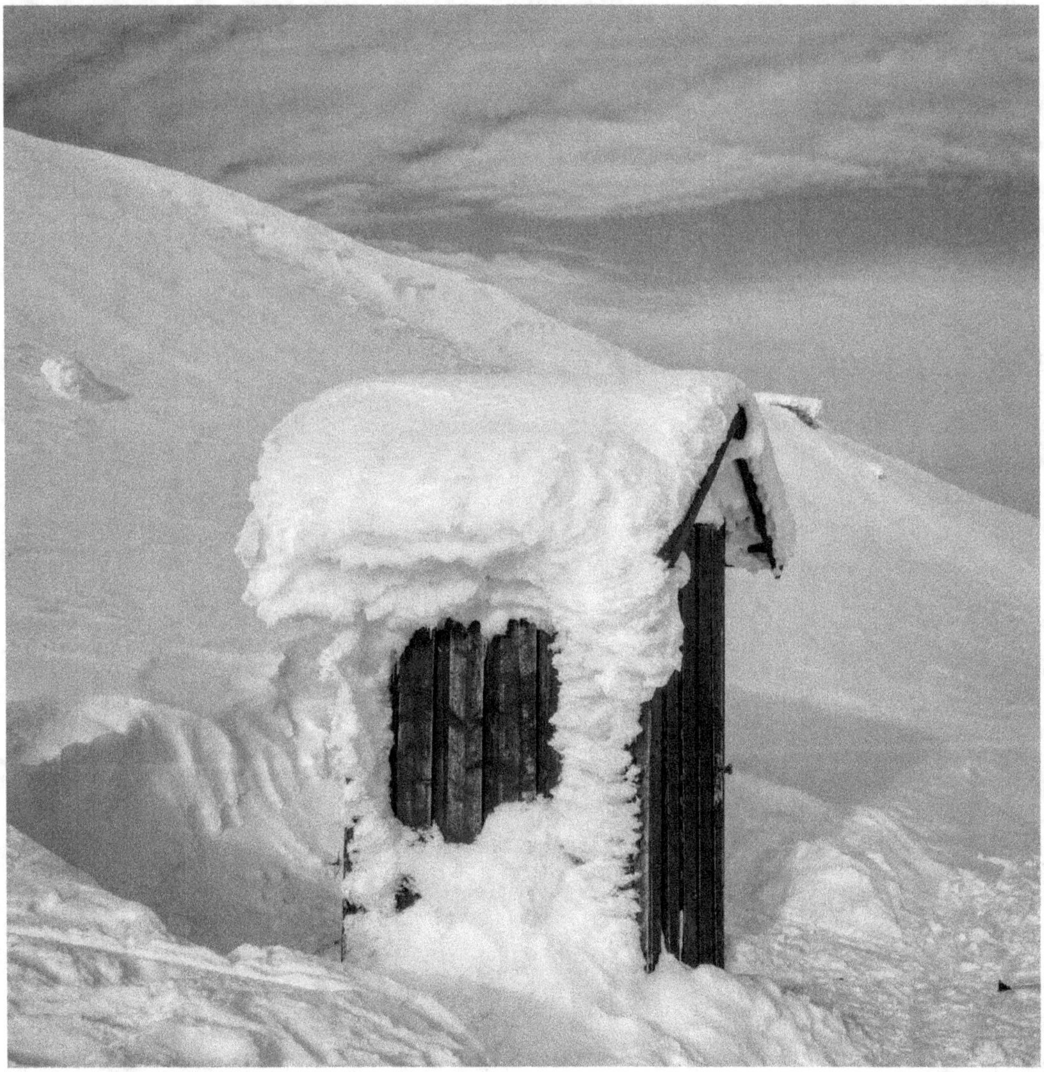

Domes

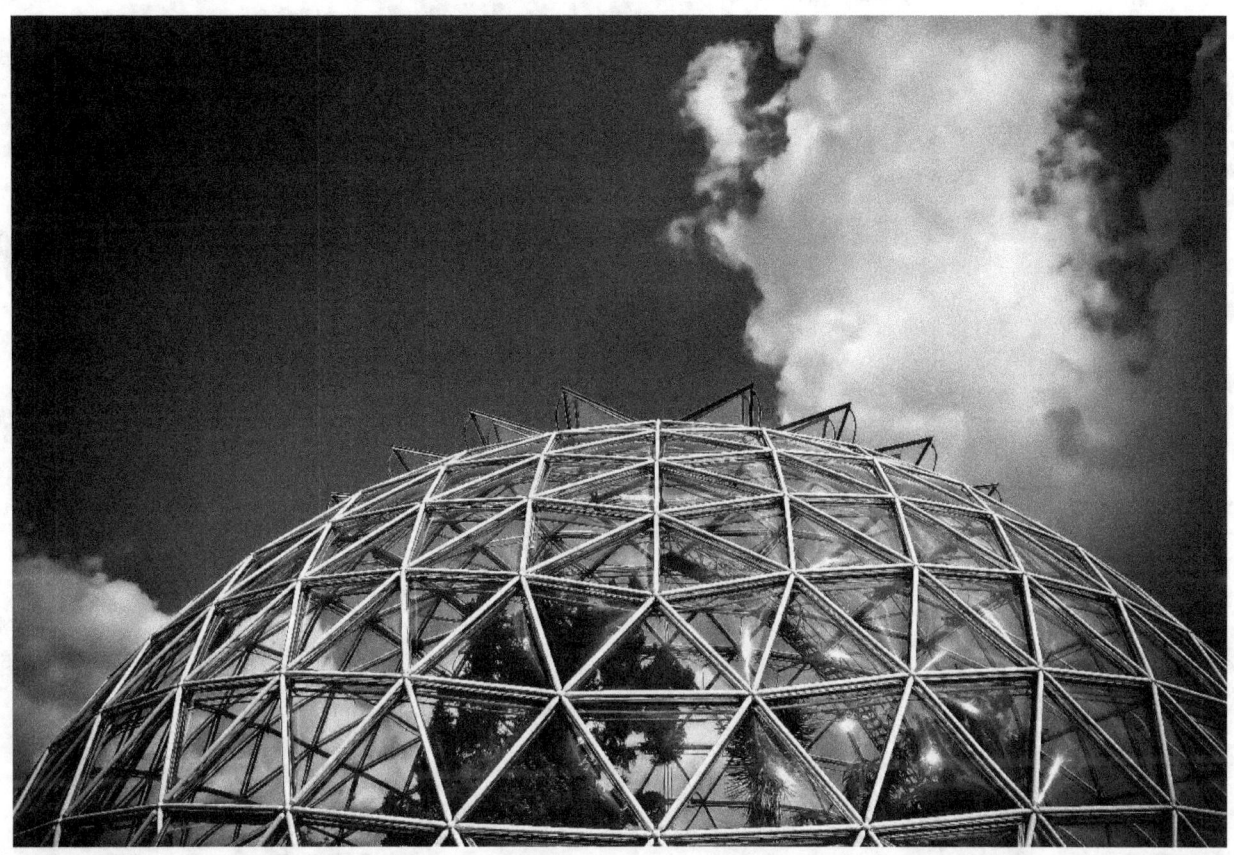

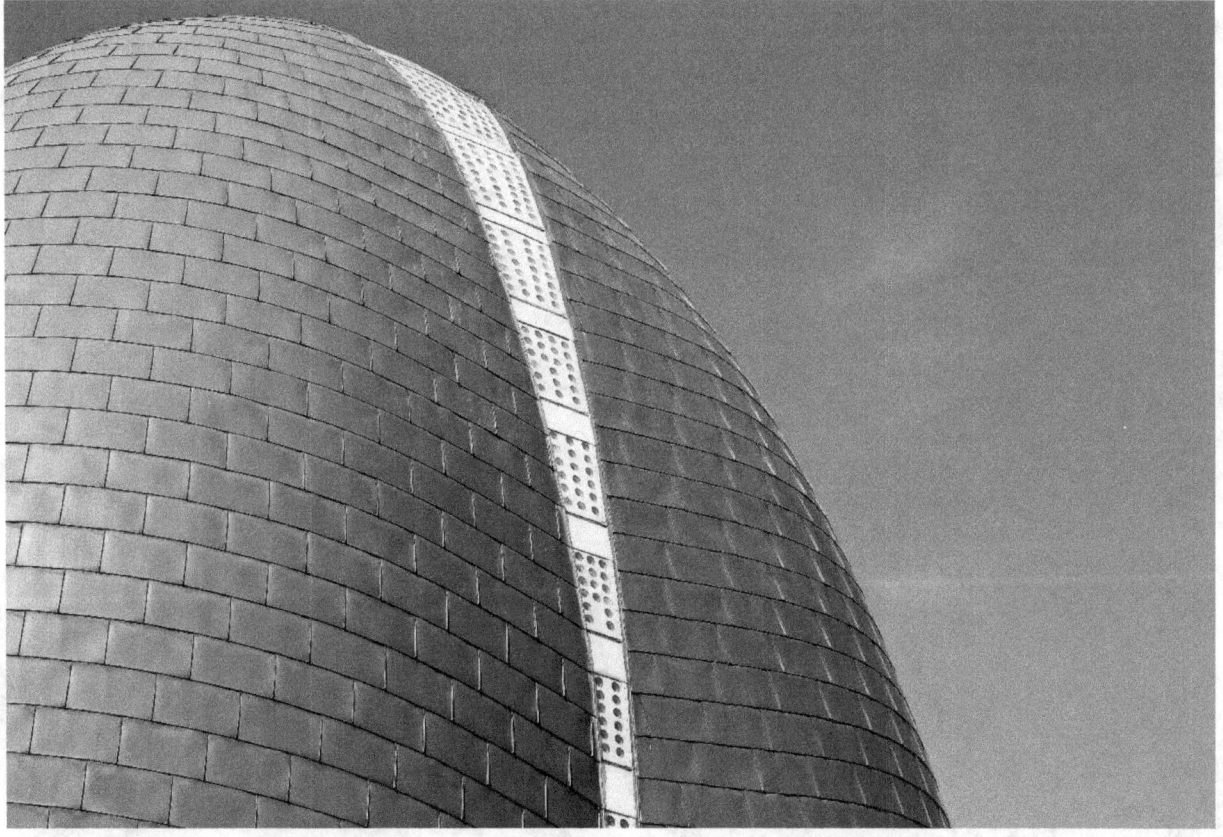

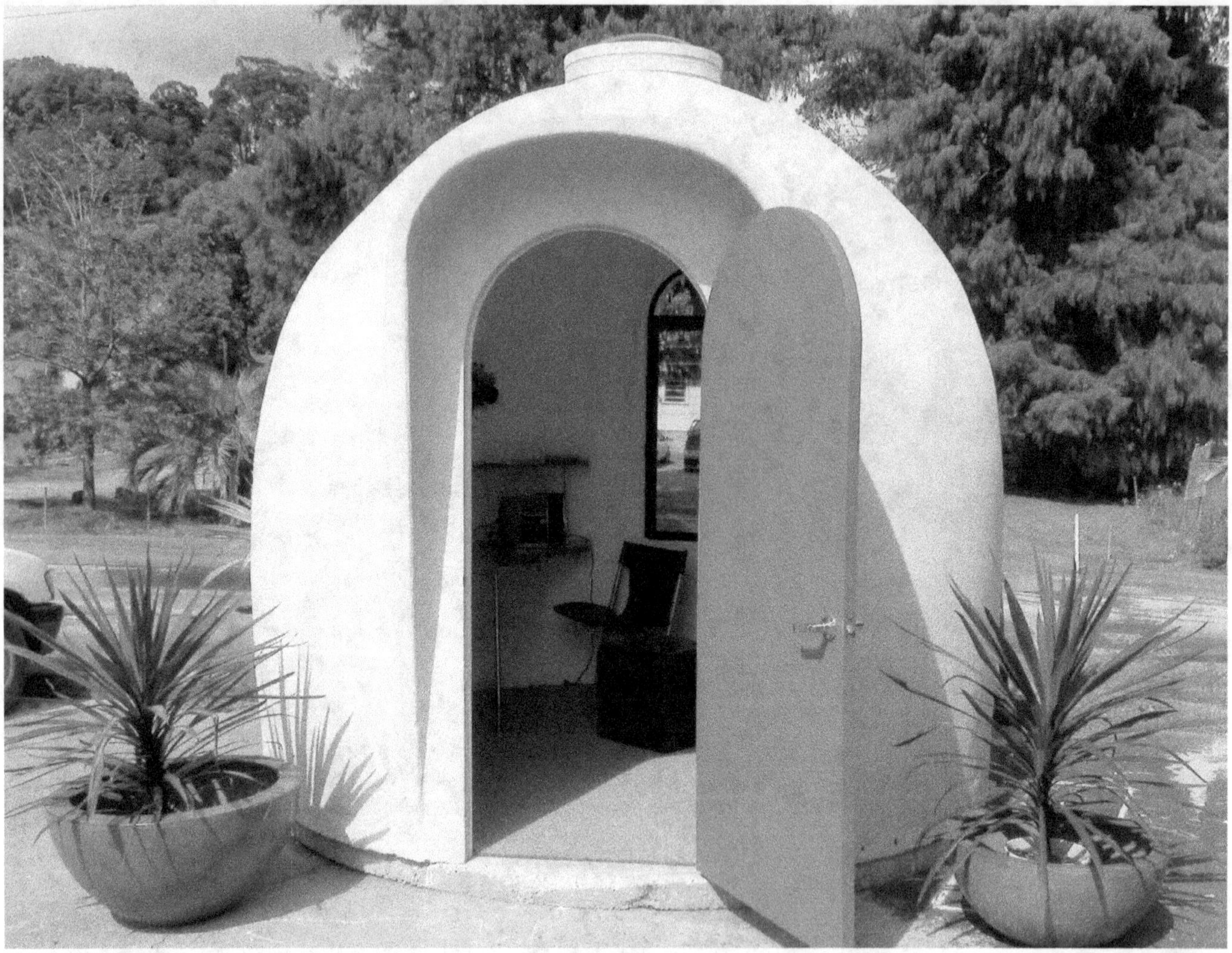

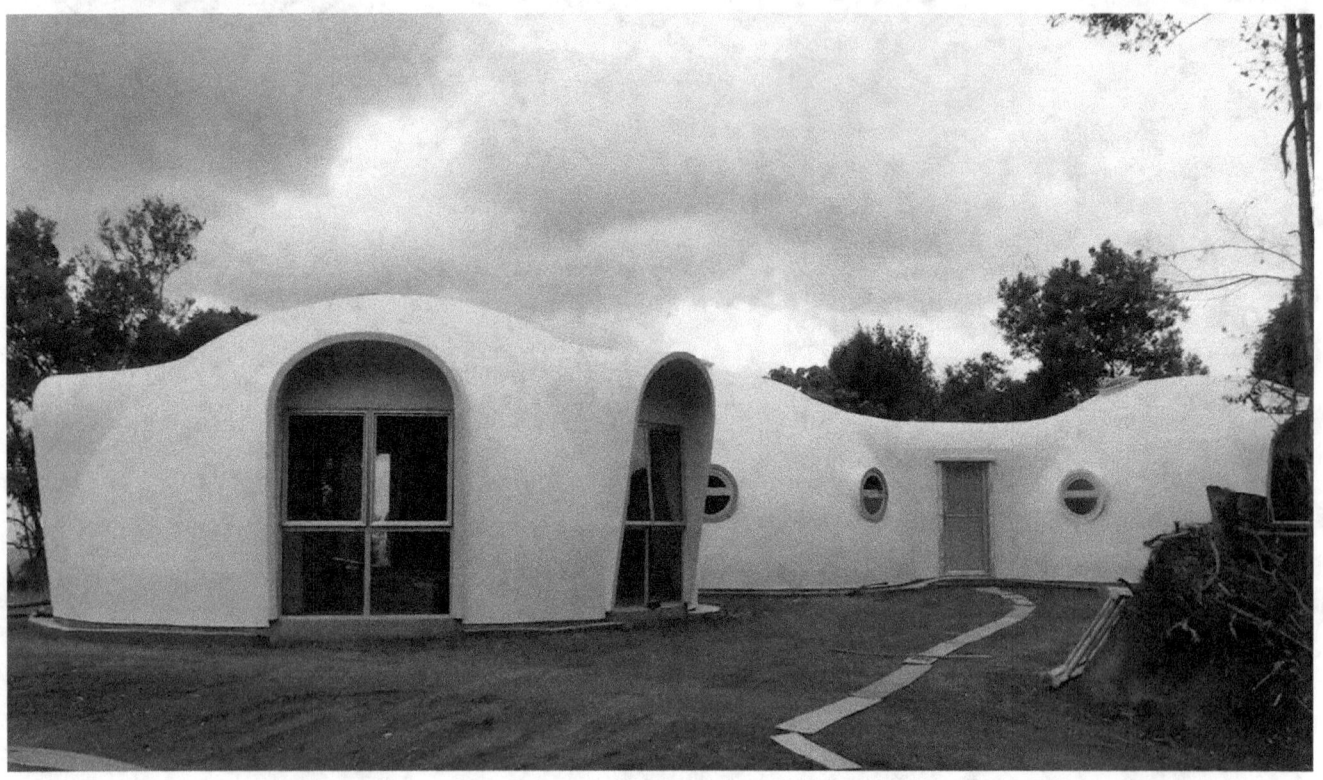

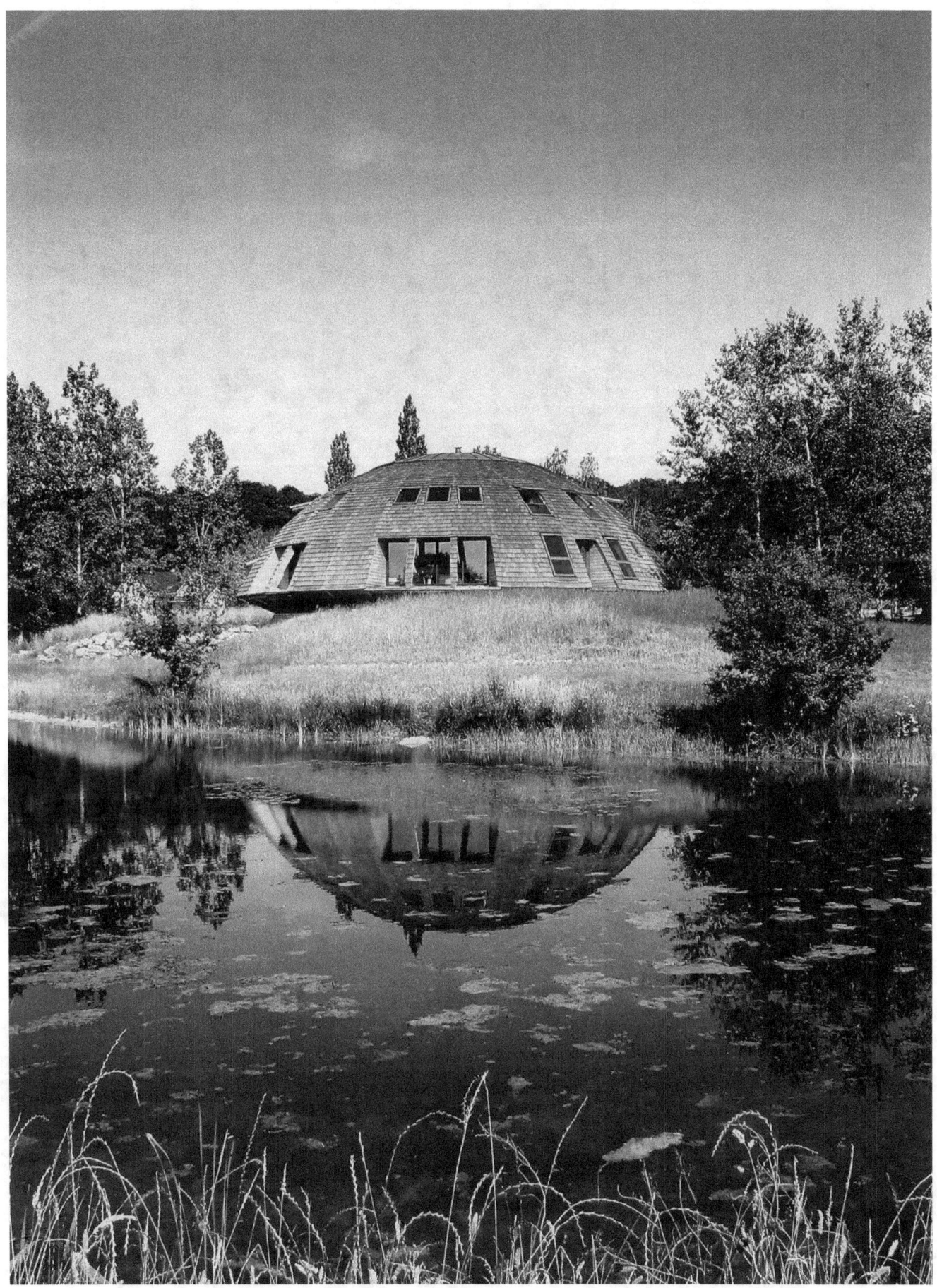

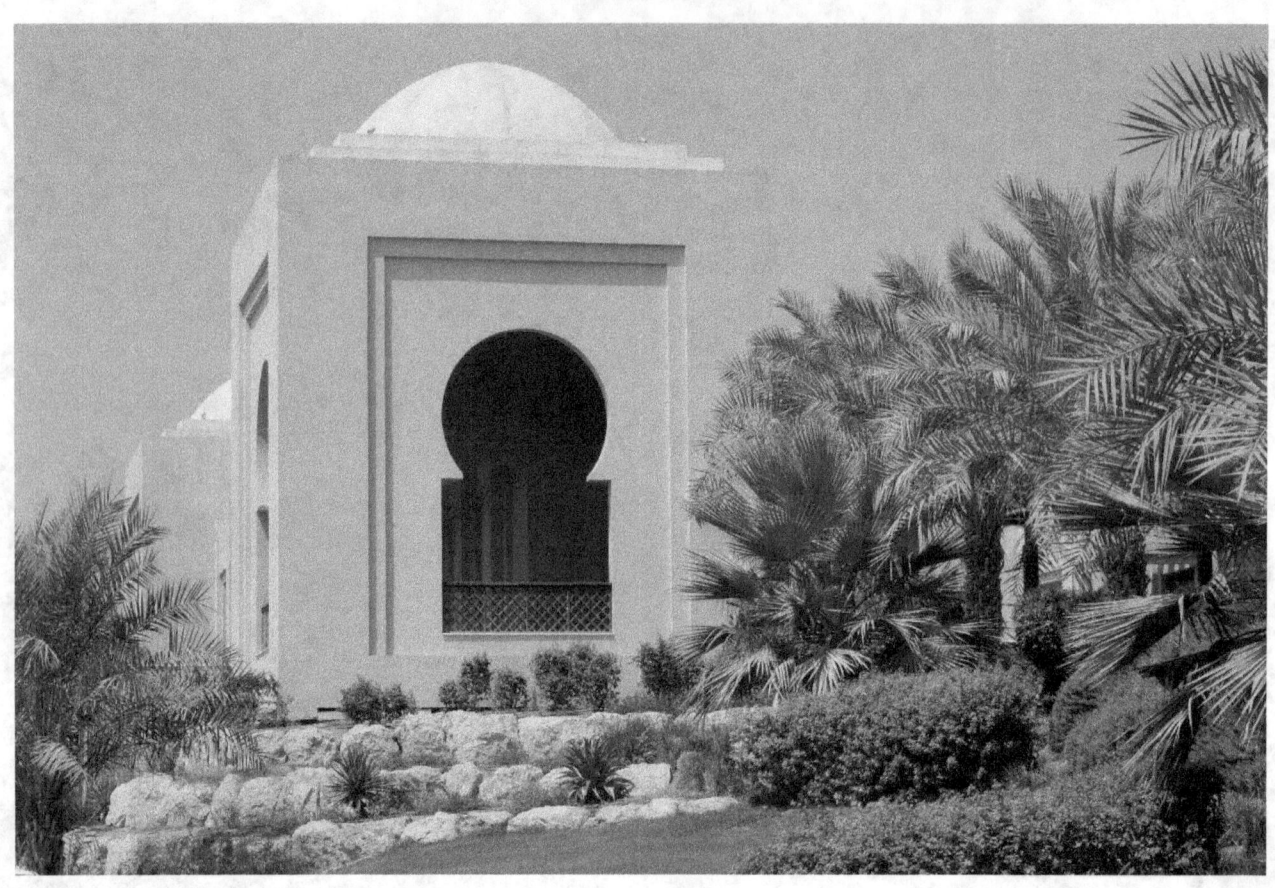

Sheds

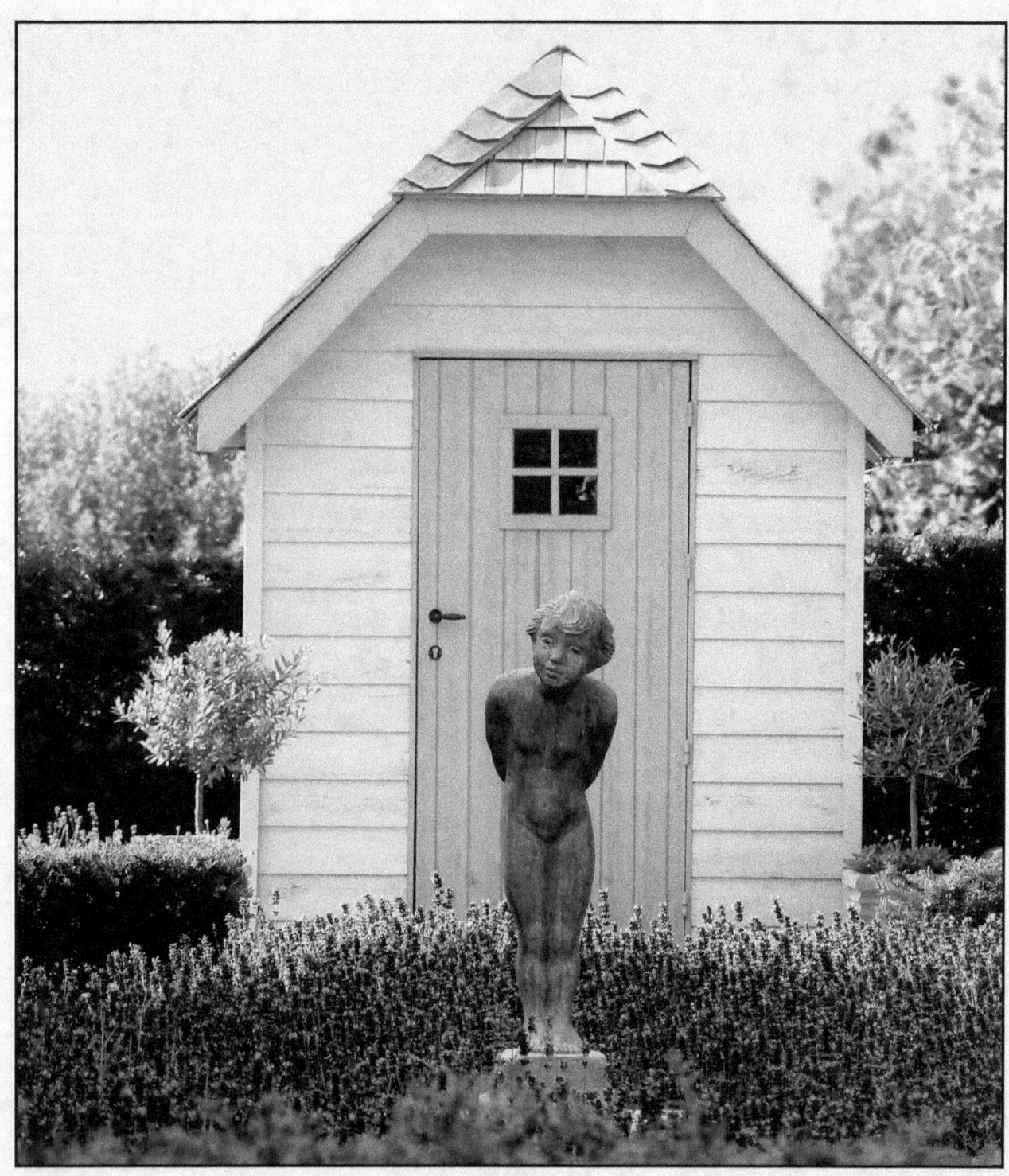

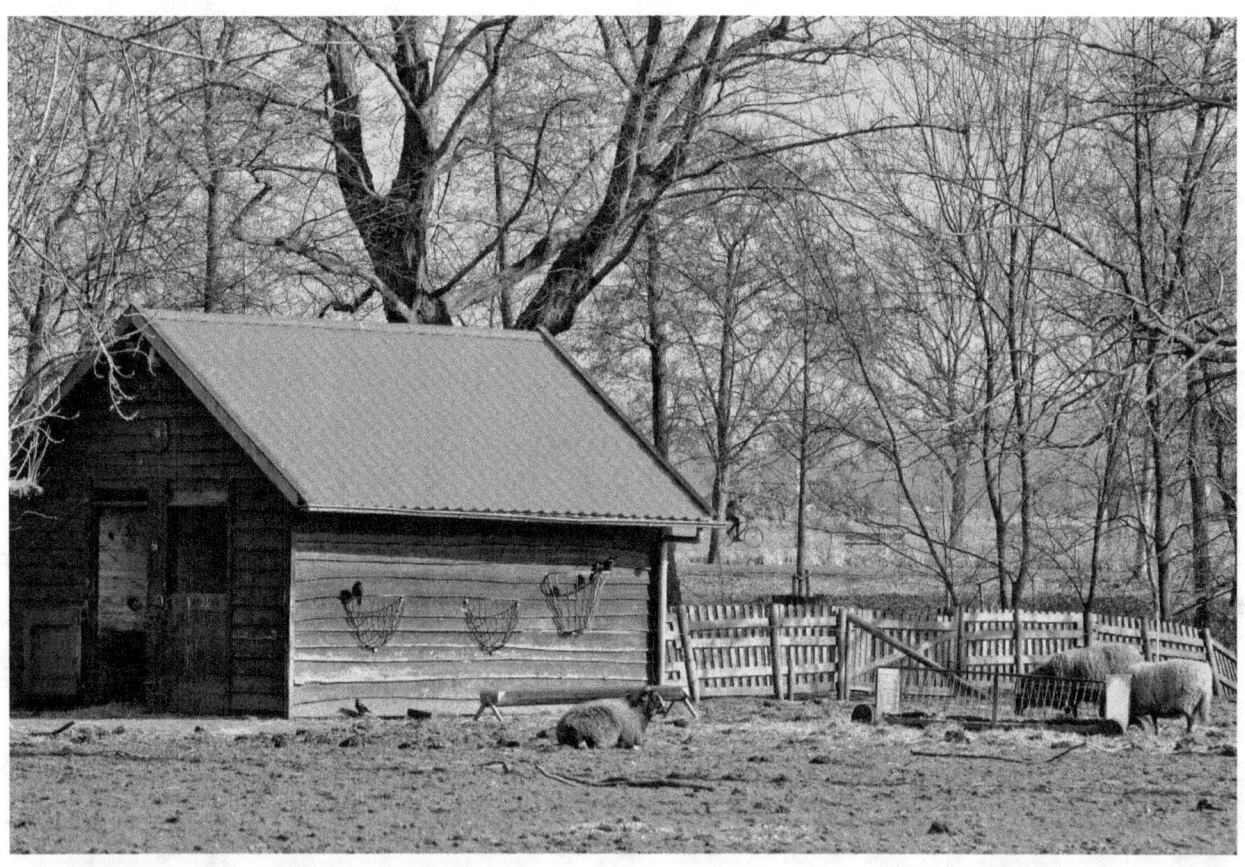

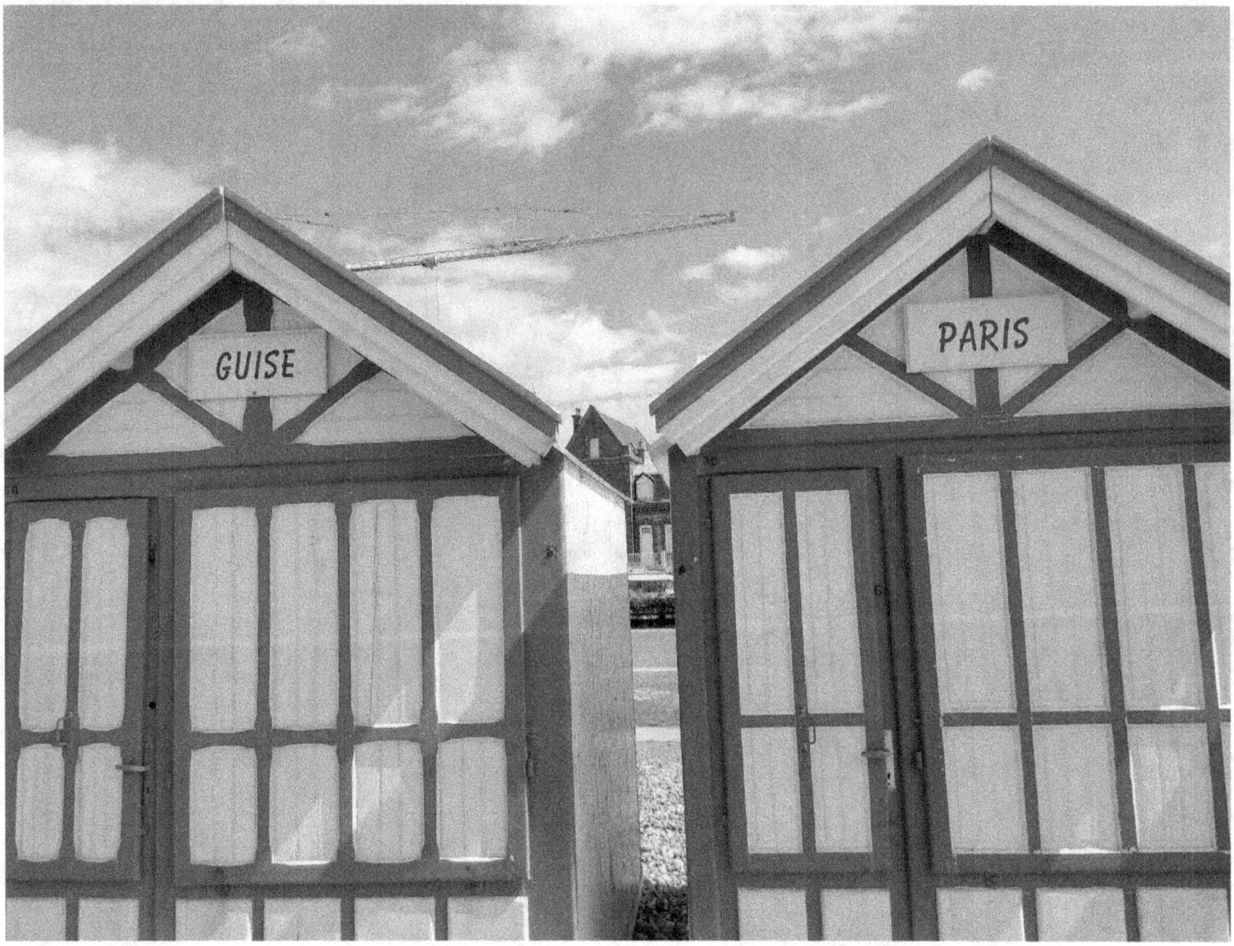

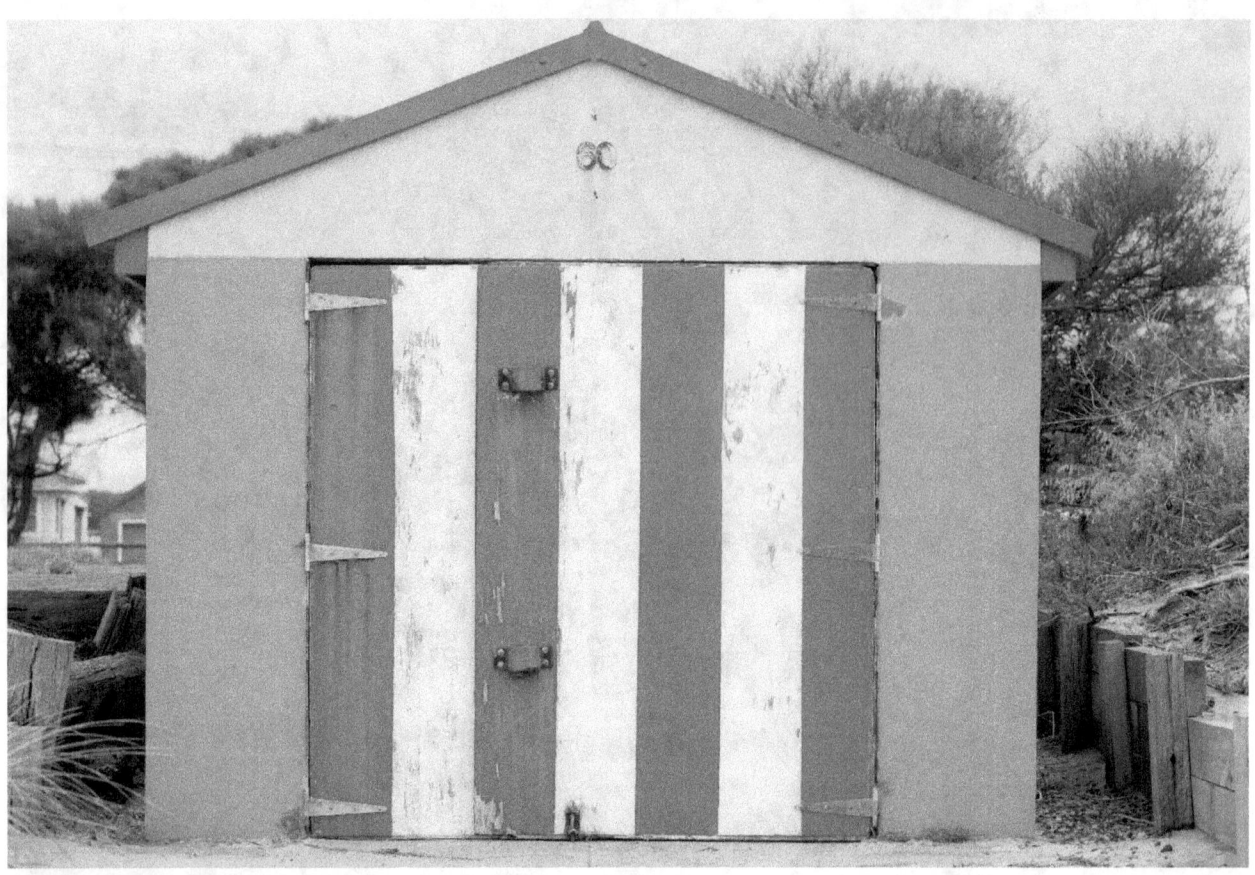

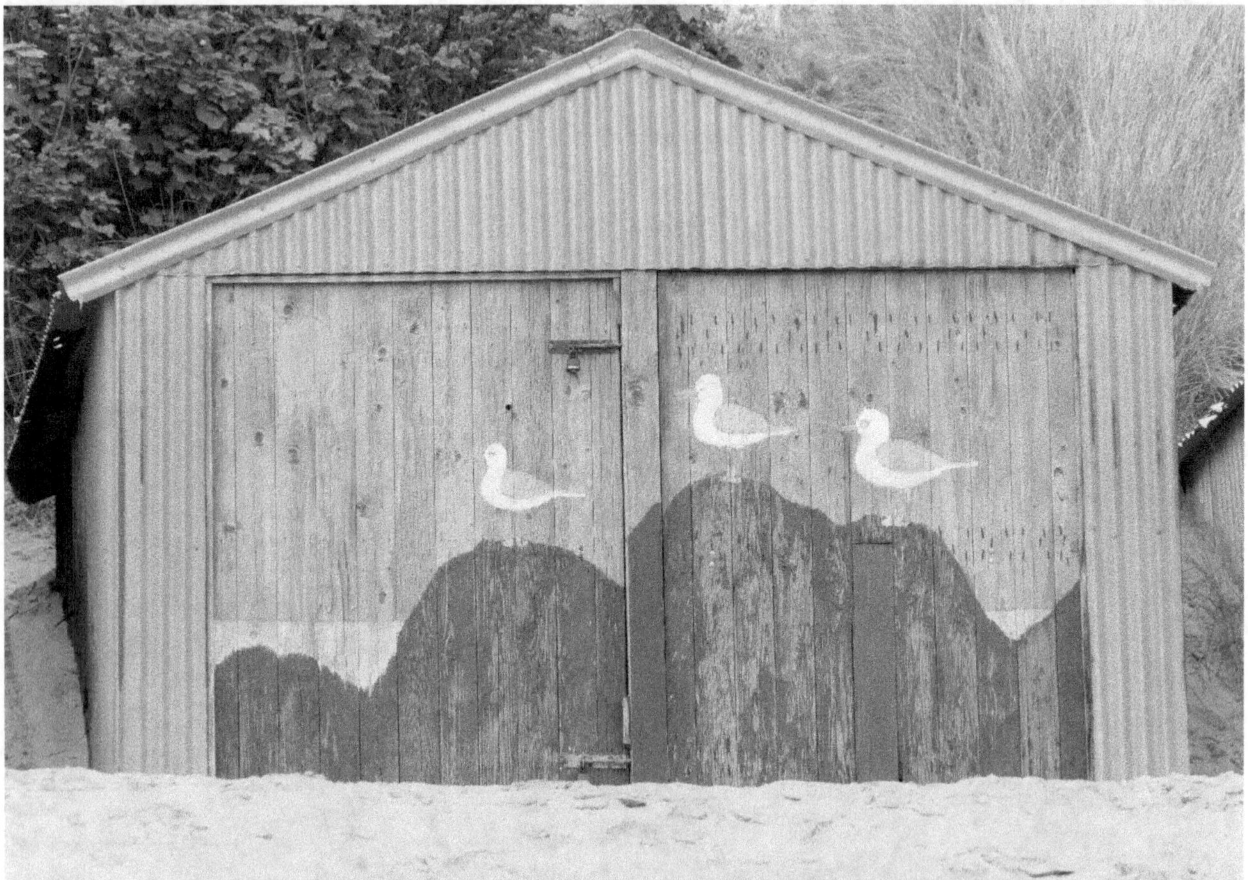

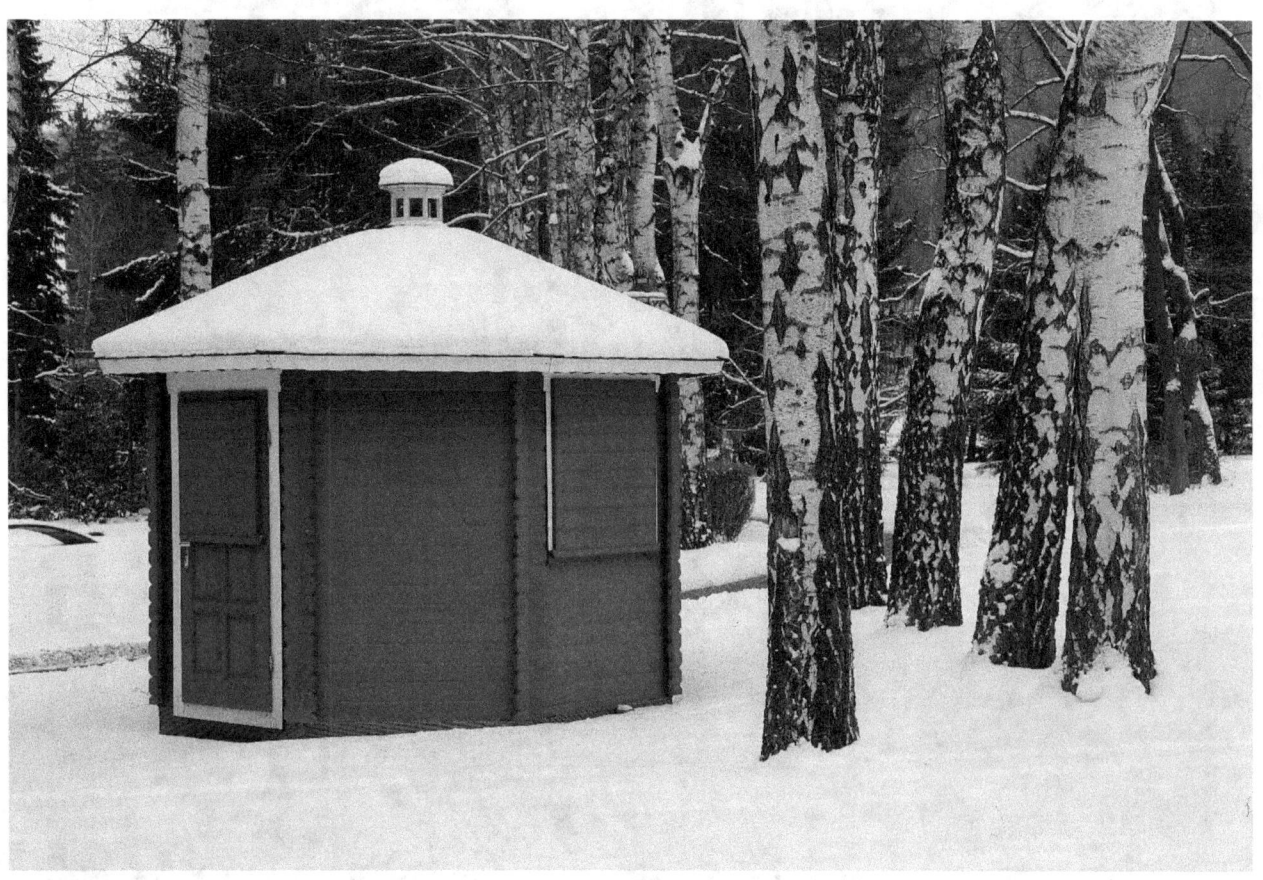

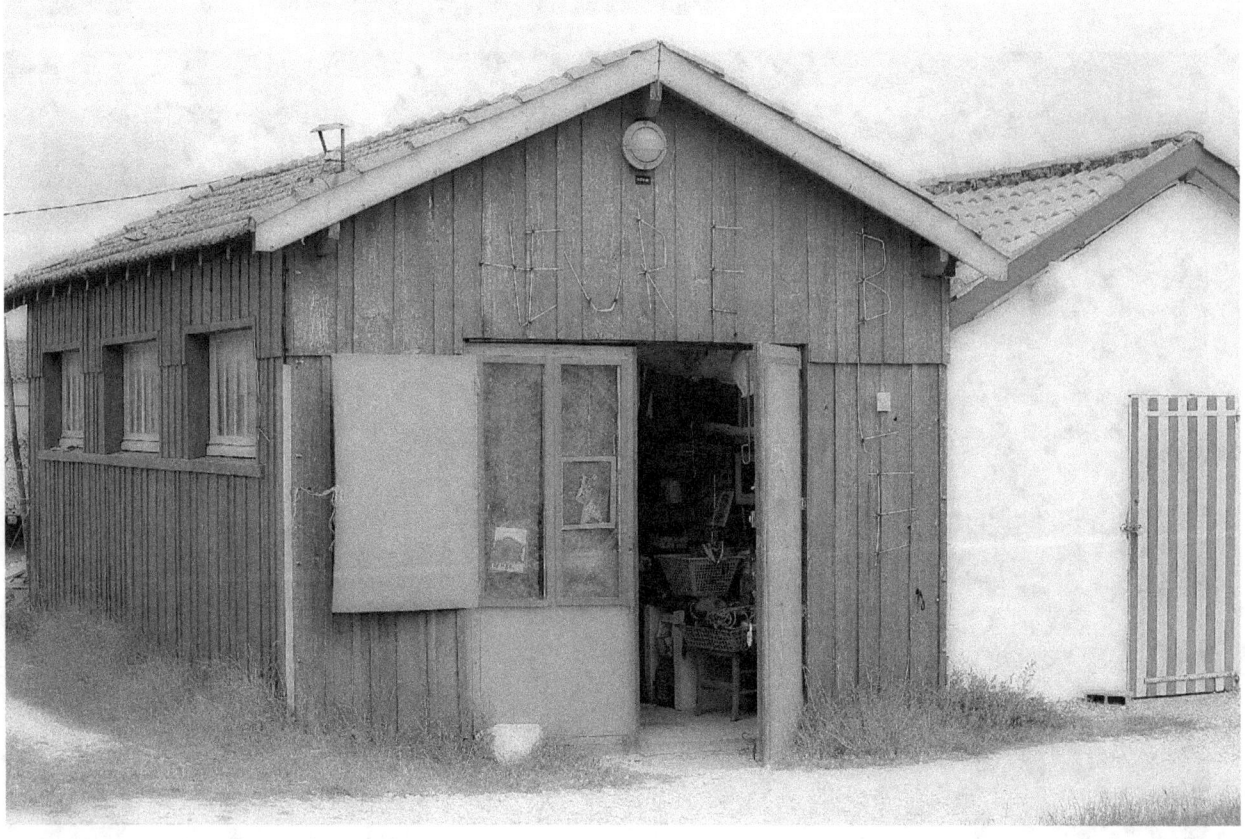

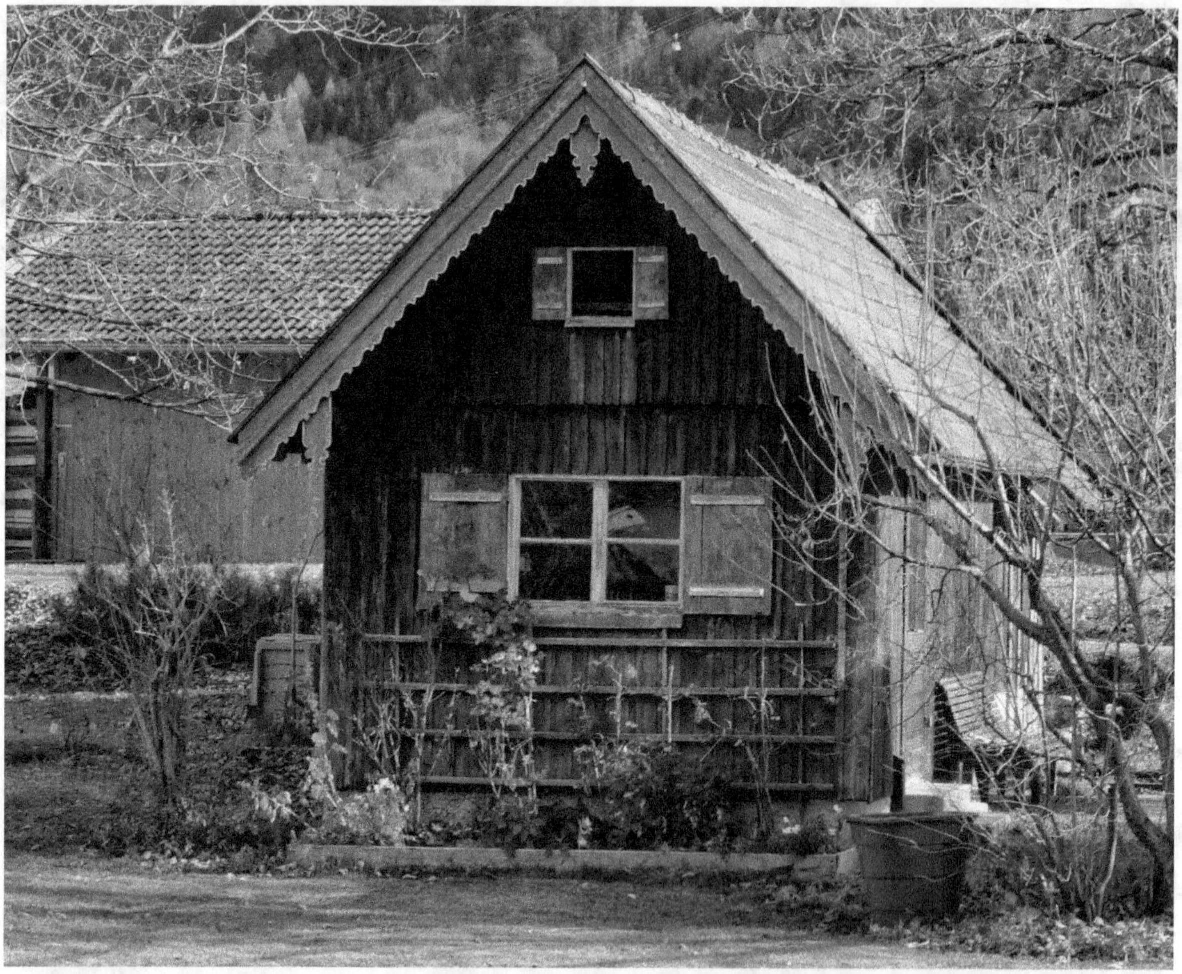

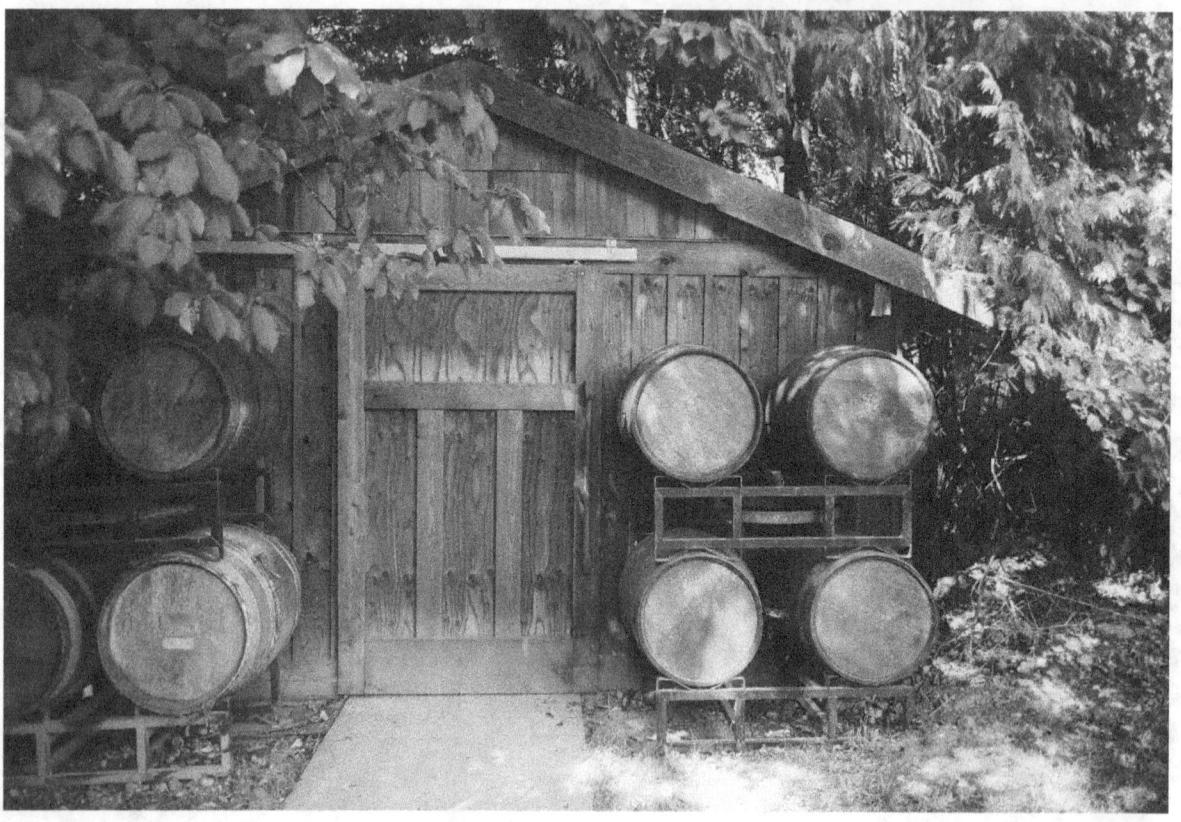

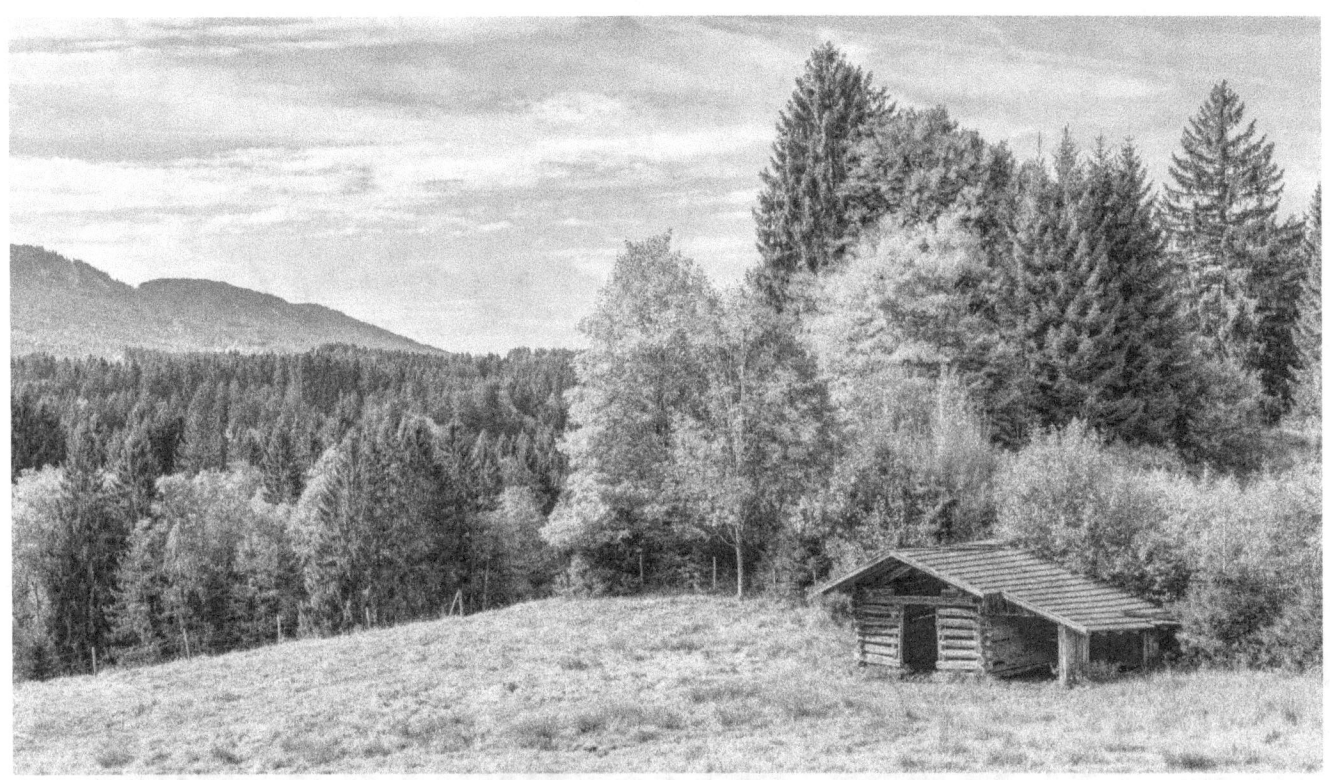

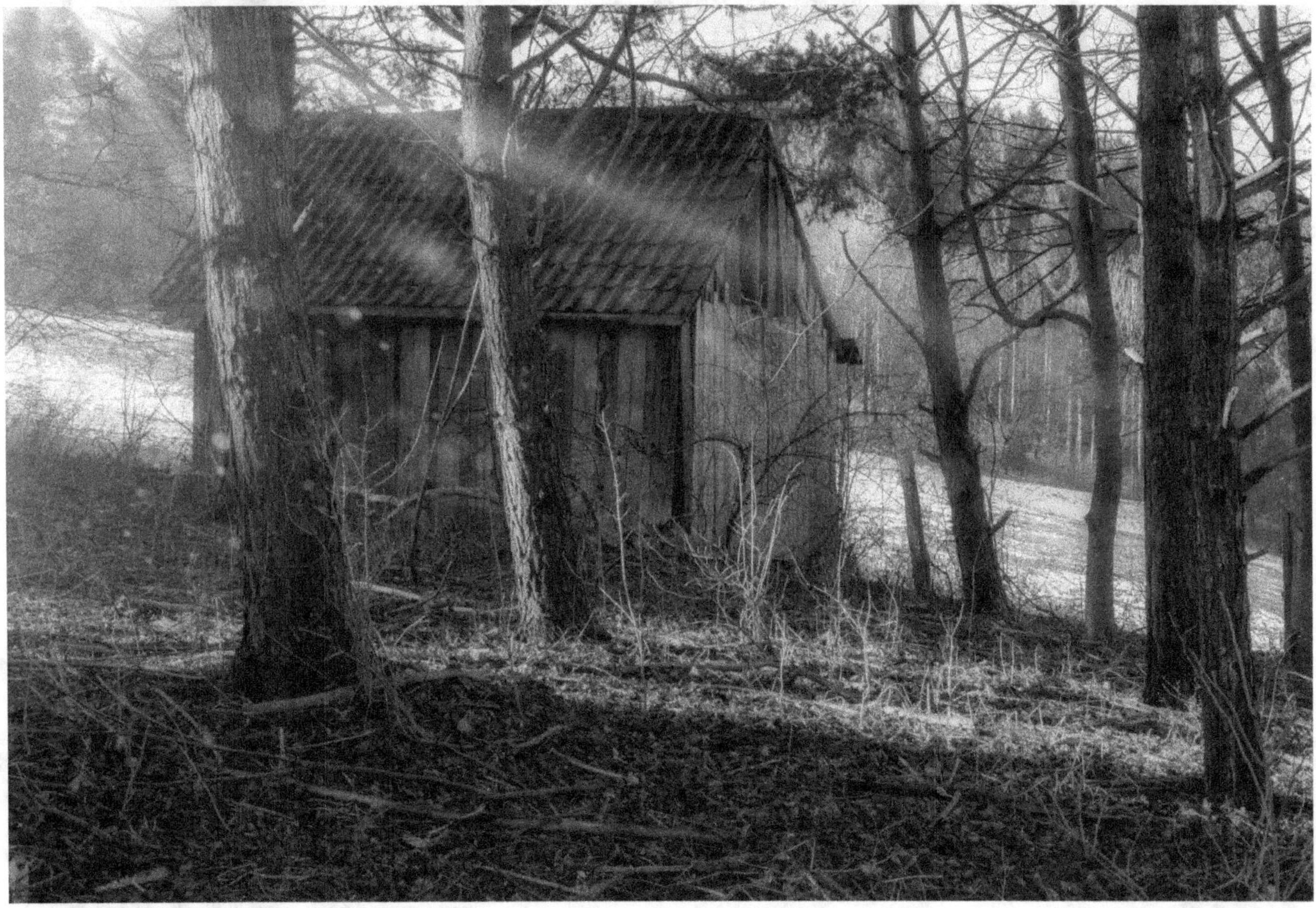

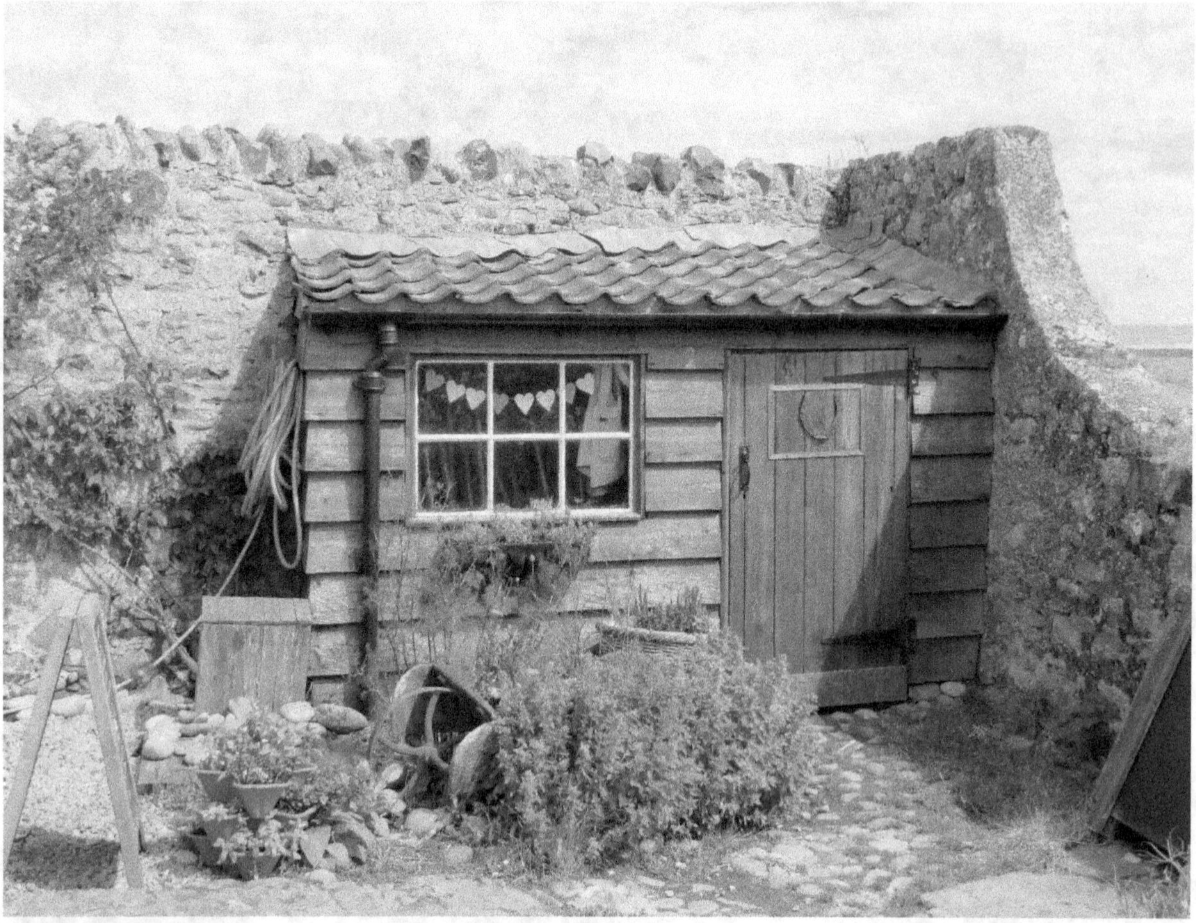

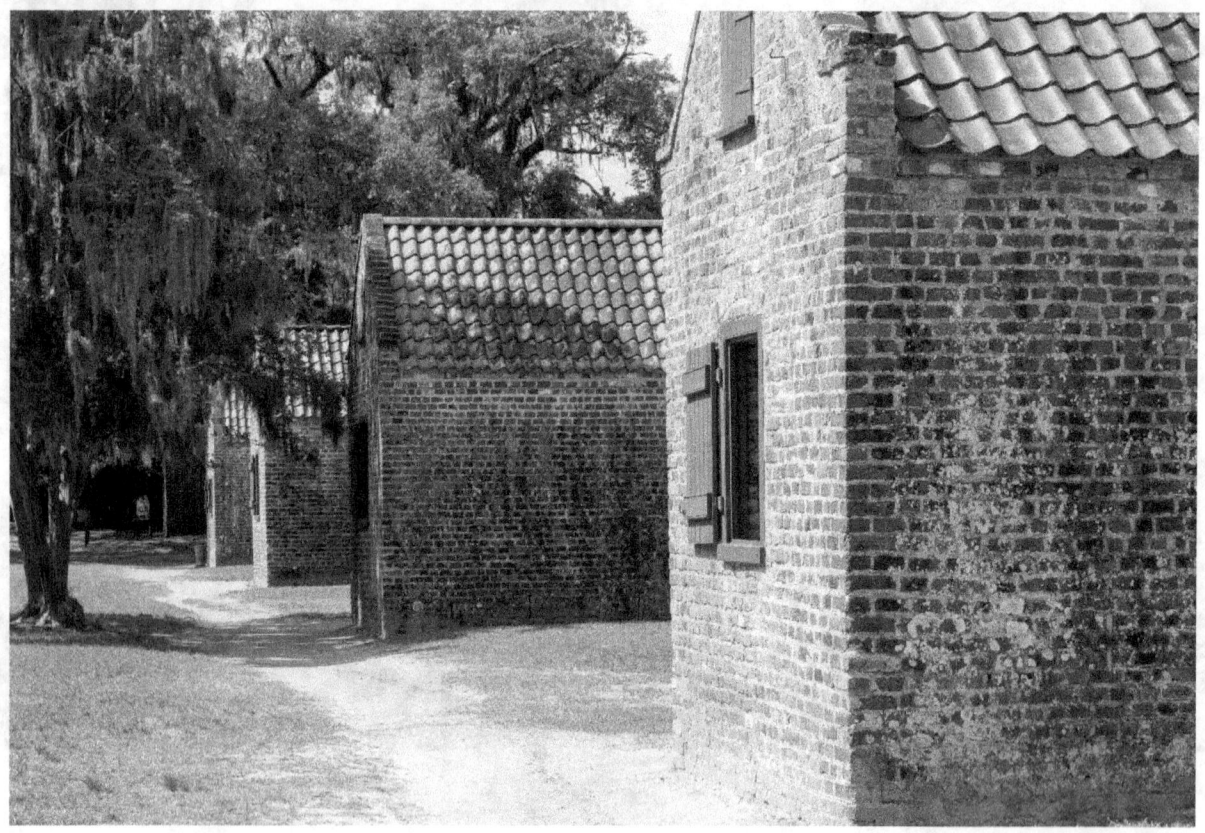

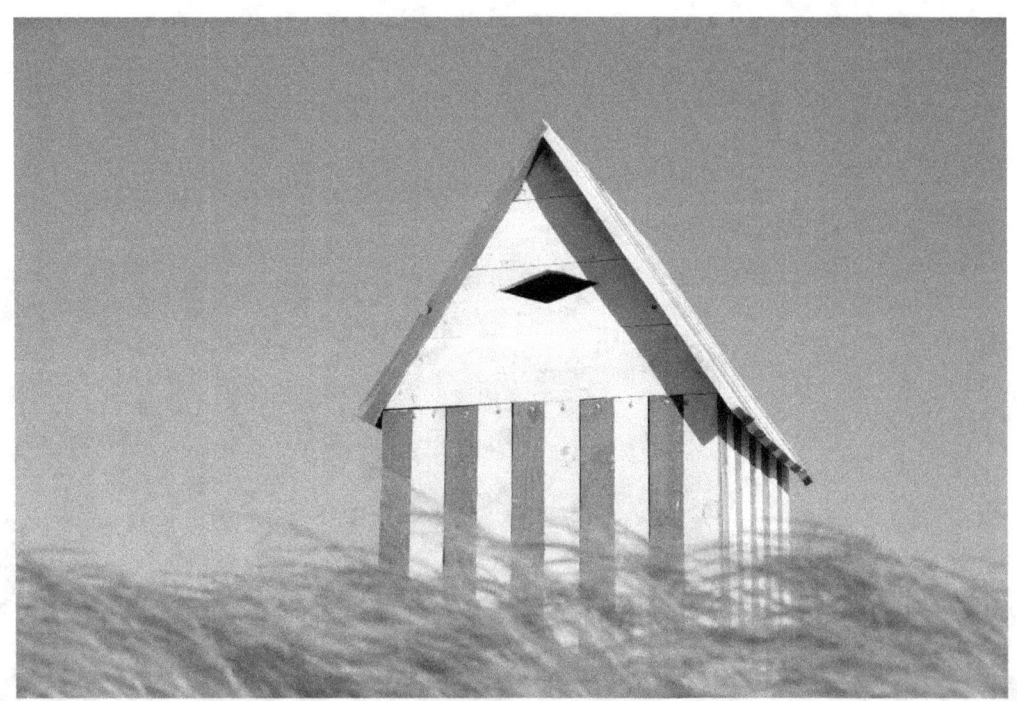

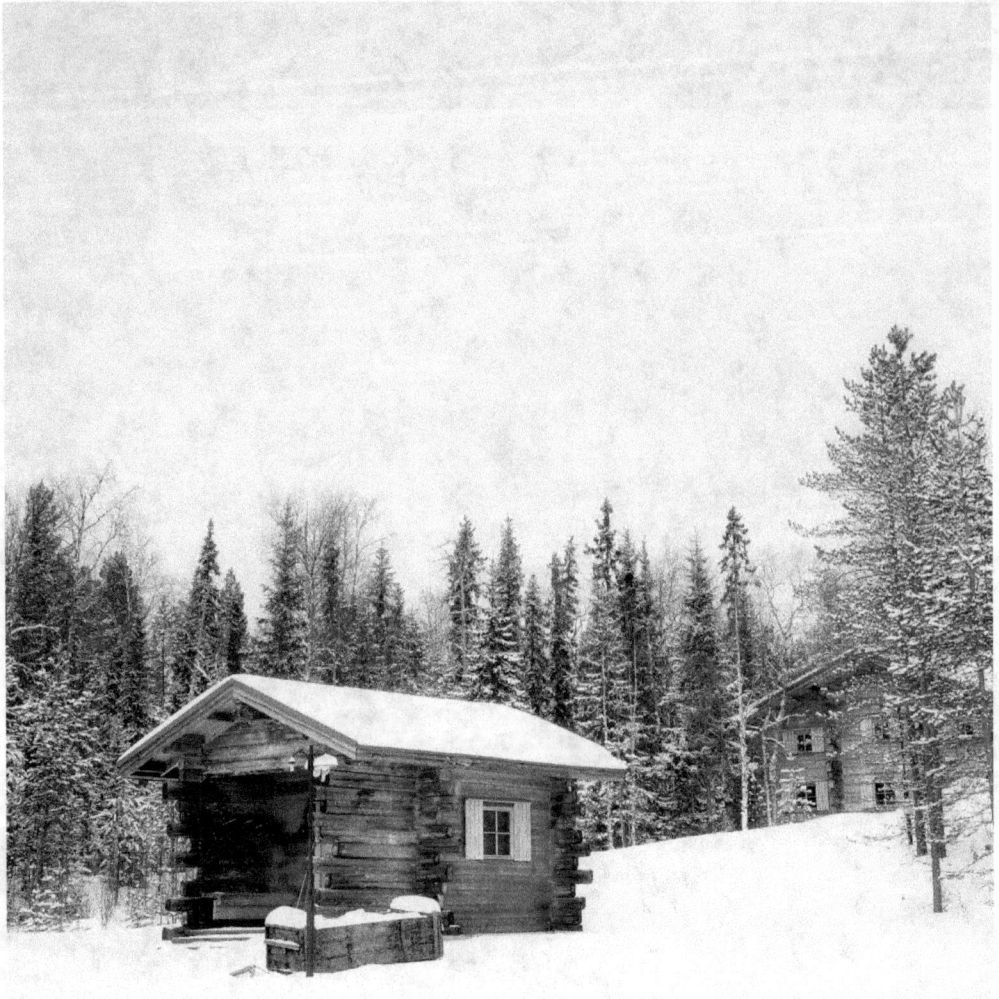

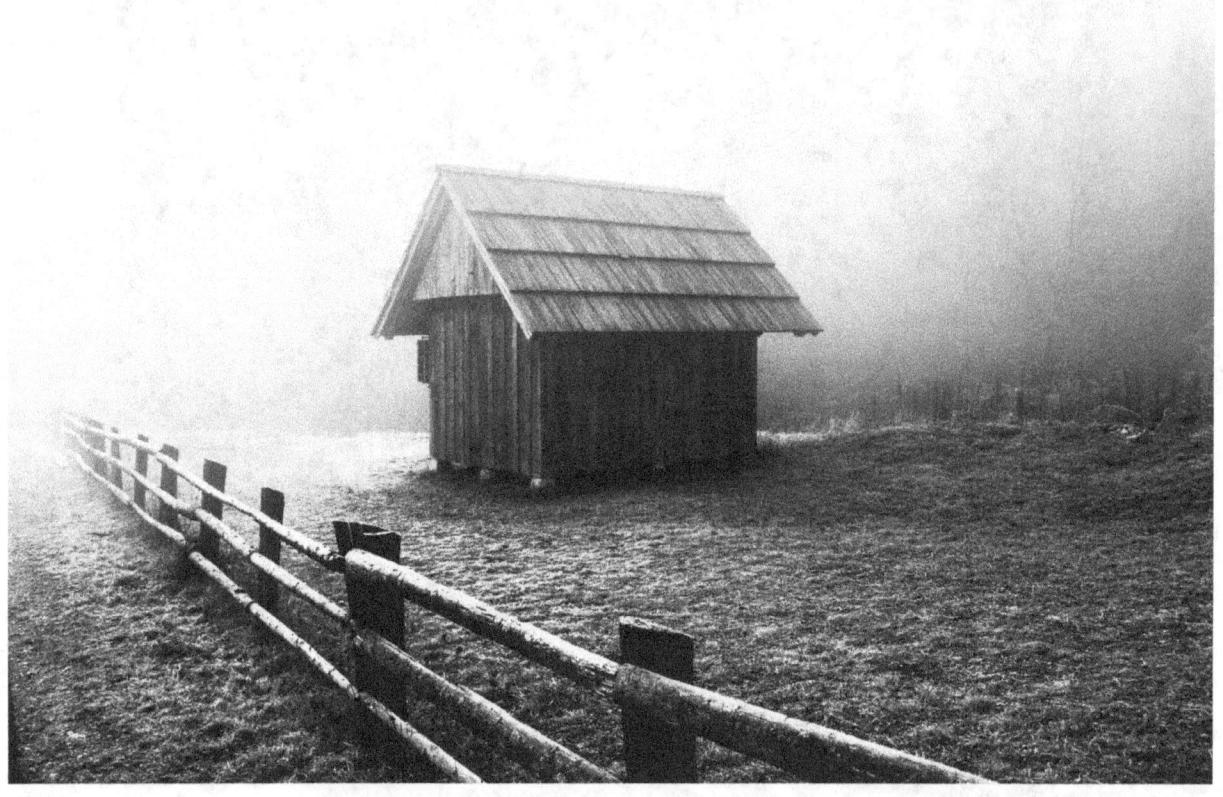

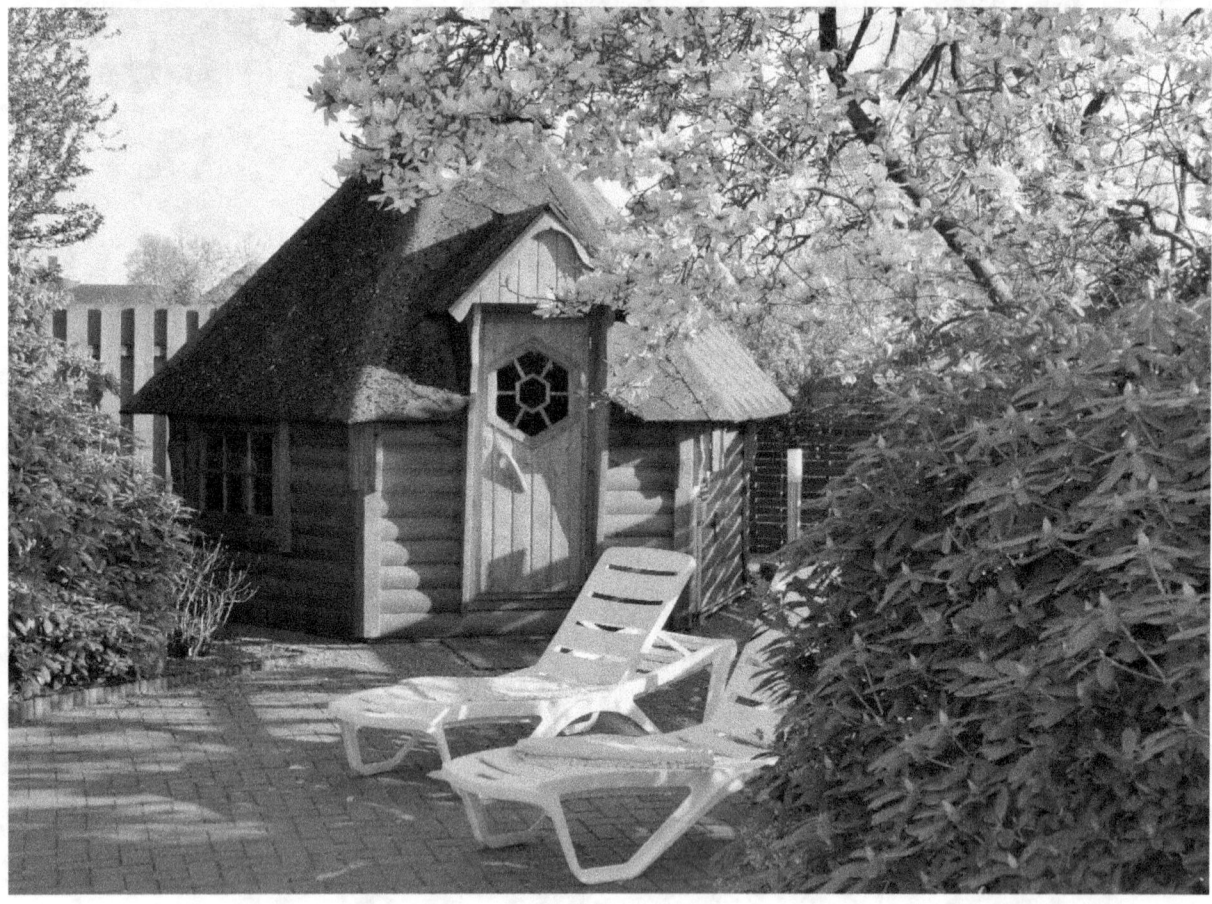

ABOUT THE AUTHOR

Sharon Buydens has written books on tiny houses, passive solar homes,
green (eco-friendly) building and alternative construction, among other topics.
This book is the first in a series of picture books / photobooks that she plans to publish.
Author's website: www.sunstar-solutions.com/wp/

www.ingramcontent.com/pod-product-compliance
Lightning Source LLC
Chambersburg PA
CBHW081507220526
45467CB00010B/2821